Fusion for Profit

How Marketing and Finance Can Work Together to Create Value

Sharan Jagpal

With the assistance of Shireen Jagpal

OXFORD
UNIVERSITY PRESS
2008

OXFORD
UNIVERSITY PRESS

Oxford University Press, Inc., publishes works that further
Oxford University's objective of excellence
in research, scholarship, and education

Oxford   New York
Auckland   Cape Town   Dar es Salaam   Hong Kong   Karachi
Kuala Lumpur   Madrid   Melbourne   Mexico City   Nairobi
New Delhi   Shanghai   Taipei   Toronto

With offices in
Argentina   Austria   Brazil   Chile   Czech Republic   France   Greece
Guatemala   Hungary   Italy   Japan   Poland   Portugal   Singapore
South Korea   Switzerland   Thailand   Turkey   Ukraine   Vietnam

Published by Oxford University Press, Inc.
198 Madison Avenue, New York, New York 10016

www.oup.com

Oxford is a registered trademark of Oxford University Press

Library of Congress Cataloging-in-Publication Data
Jagpal, Sharan, 1947–
Fusion for profit : how marketing and finance can
work together to create value / by Sharan Jagpal;
with the assistance of Shireen Jagpal.
     p. cm.
Includes index.
ISBN 978-0-19-537105-5
1. Marketing—Management.   2. Marketing—Costs.
I. Jagpal, Shireen.   II. Title.
HF5415.J333 2008
658.8´4—dc22   2007049183

9 8 7 6 5 4 3 2 1

Printed in the United States of America
on acid-free paper

Dedicated to
my family and friends

If a man will begin with certainties, he shall end in doubts;
but if he will be content to begin with doubt
he shall end in certainties.
—Francis Bacon (1561–1626)

Fusion for Profit is a one-of-a-kind exposition of how the fusion of marketing skill and financial discipline can drive shareholder value. Sharan Jagpal has written a highly readable book that is buttressed by fascinating examples and easy-to-understand "Maxims." This superb book is a must read for anyone interested in building businesses. Global and domestic markets today are highly competitive and equally complex. Within this environment, firms both large and small are faced with conflicting objectives, blinding uncertainty, and multifaceted challenges, and managers are constantly struggling with confounding questions such as the following:

- Which products should be supported?
- What's the right level of support for existing brands versus new brands?
- What is the right balance between market share growth and profitability?
- How should the firm measure the long-term effects of different marketing strategies?
- What market does the firm really compete in?
- How should one set the optimal price for a new product?
- How does one figure out whether a new product is going to work or not?
- What metrics should the firm use to evaluate consumer behavior?
- What's the right mix of advertising and product promotion?

- How best to compensate a sales force in a single-product situation versus a multiproduct portfolio?
- What is the value of a brand? How best to build further brand equity?
- How does one maximize the return from Internet advertising?

These are just some of the complex questions that managers face in their attempts to build businesses and shareholder value. Sharan Jagpal addresses these complexities with almost surgical precision in this comprehensive, original, well-researched, and thought-provoking book. He takes a multi-disciplinary approach that will appeal to business executives as well as academics; to marketing professionals as well as CFOs; to students as well as seasoned executives.

Many organizations resemble a multihanded Hindu goddess, where one hand is blithely unaware of what the others are doing. It then falls upon the COO or CEO to coordinate and align these disparate activities, causing duplication of work and wasted energy. *Fusion for Profit* is full of insightful observations, detailed examples, and pithy maxims that will be invaluable for managers. It will persuade management to take a more holistic view of business problems and drive streamlined solutions to issues that affect the entire organization. The resulting improvement in efficiency and productivity would be significant.

Sharan Jagpal prefaces his book with a quotation from Francis Bacon (1561–1626): "If a man will begin with certainties, he shall end in doubts; but if he will be content to begin with doubt he shall end in certainties." These words beautifully capture the spirit of *Fusion for Profit*. If you have doubts, go right away into the corridors of this finely written book.

Dinyar S. Devitre
Senior Vice President and Chief Financial Officer,
Altria Group, Inc.

New York
7 January 2008

Business is ideally about serving customers well while delivering good value to shareholders. But like many ideals, when it comes to cases in the real world, the actual service a customer receives is often encumbered by the invisible boundaries that separate different business functions such as marketing and finance.

These impediments to customer service result from confining marketing and finance in "silos" that operate separately and often act independently. In addition to the main divide between them, each of these core business functions also has its own set of internal boundaries. Within marketing, for example, for years there has been a traditional line between brand advertising and direct marketing. Comparable lines within finance divide supply and distribution. However, across both marketing and finance, the rapid and continuous changes in information systems and customer control are quickly making all such boundaries disappear.

More than 30 years ago, strategy guru Peter Drucker recognized that the purpose of business is to create a customer. Based on that goal, he said, "The business enterprise has two—and only two—basic functions: marketing and innovation." Throughout my years in both the manufacturing and services sectors, I have tried to let this profound observation guide me in making resource allocation decisions and developing performance measurements. In my experience, senior executives in every industry and segment are looking for ways to increase measurability of their marketing campaigns, assign more accountability for marketing results, and earn a better return on marketing investment.

Innovation can result from testing new theories and evolving new and improved metrics to quantify and choose the right mix of risk and return to maximize shareholder value. What is the cost of acquiring a new customer? What is the lifetime financial value of a customer? How can we use this information to choose strategies that will maximize shareholder value? Answering these questions will require new empirical methods that cut across silos and boundaries—innovations that can fuse marketing and finance.

In *Fusion for Profit*, Professor Jagpal brilliantly combines these seemingly disparate fields and proposes novel new theories and methods, many of them quite sophisticated. Even so, his ideas and messages are accessible to a wide audience because, in addition to presenting his complex ideas as simply as possible, he has done it without using any math or algebra!

Bringing marketing and finance together is a massive endeavor, making this book unique in its scope and the breadth of the topics it covers. Although not written as a handbook, it is sufficiently comprehensive to be used as one. If you seek overall guidance, you will find an in-depth and holistic look at all the options a business faces in today's world, examining each from multiple perspectives within marketing and finance.

Why is this work so important? I can suggest at least two reasons.

First, if marketing and finance continue to operate in different silos, they will be leaving money on the table. Simply stated, the more marketers understand finance—and vice versa—the stronger their shared competitive capabilities can become. This means they will be better than others at creating a customer, as Drucker puts it, which adds up to shareholder value.

A second, more complex reason embodies all the changes in today's business environment that have put consumers in control of the relationships they will allow business or nonprofit organizations to have with them. Consumers in both their business and personal lives demand communications that are relevant to their individual needs and preferences, and they insist that marketing be done responsibly—respecting their time, attention, and privacy. When marketing and finance can fuse, they can better meet these needs and deliver great results.

Regardless of whether you work in marketing or finance, wherever you stand in your career development, this book will provide you with the theories and methods you need to be successful in taking a holistic approach to your business.

John A. Greco Jr.
President and CEO, Direct Marketing Association

New York
16 November 2007

▲ Why Should You Read This Book?

Most books in business focus on specific subareas such as marketing, finance, and human resources management. Furthermore, the coverage tends to be diffuse. At one end of the academic spectrum, some books focus on developing highly technical "ivory tower" theories that are difficult to use in practice or require information that is not readily available. At the other end of the spectrum, some books provide simplistic box-and-arrow flowcharts ("models") specifying how constructs or business functions relate to one another.

These models have limited value to the manager or executive because they do not specify metrics for measuring key constructs. Nor do they pay sufficient attention to the quantitative effects of real-world complications introduced by such factors as error in measuring key constructs, uncertainty, and incomplete information.

Practitioner books, in contrast, tend to be anecdotal. Specifically, they provide detailed accounts of strategies that have been used by a "successful" firm or firms in a specific industry and exhort managers or executives to follow these "best practices."

This backward-looking and inductive approach is misleading. As casual empiricism shows, strategies that have been successful in the past are often a recipe for poor performance in the future. Alternatively, some practitioner books exhort the firm or organization to use blanket strategies that are in vogue (e.g., strategies based on cost-cutting or outsourcing). These strategies, however, are easily imitated by competitors. Consequently, by pursuing this approach, the firm or organization will not be able to achieve superior long-run results. The net result is that, despite the voluminous business literature, managers (including owner managers) and executives are left with little guidance on how to choose comprehensive strategies that deliver long-run value.

Fusion for Profit attempts to fill this vacuum by bridging the current gap between the academic and business practitioner literatures. To achieve this goal, Fusion for Profit focuses on developing comprehensive business models that integrate the different functional areas in the firm (e.g., marketing, finance, production, and engineering). In addition, the book develops practical methods for improving business decision making that can be implemented using readily available data.

From a business practitioner's viewpoint, the goal is to unlock the ivory tower and provide managers at *all* levels in the firm or organization with knowledge of state-of-the-art theories and empirical methods that go beyond their functional areas and areas of specialization. Consequently, by using these integrated theories and empirical methods, managers can overcome the barriers posed by functional specialization and work together to develop and implement strategies that maximize the long-run performance of the firm.

From an academic viewpoint, the goal is to provide a comprehensive set of theories and empirical methods that can be used for both strategic and tactical decision making at different levels in the firm or organization. Throughout the book, particular emphasis is given to measurability and the impact of measurement error and incomplete information on decision making.

▲ *What Is* Fusion for Profit?

Fusion for Profit is a new approach to decision making that goes beyond the constraints imposed by "silo" effects in business and academe. The corporate world is typically structured in function-based silos. While this type of structure is convenient and may smooth the daily functioning of an organization, the CEO and senior management are left with the task of integrating all functions within the organization and focusing on the "big picture" (in this case, shareholder value).

The academic world tends to be structured in discipline-based silos (e.g., marketing and finance) or subdiscipline-based silos (e.g., the effect of advertising on long-term memory). Because of this ultraspecialization in academe, insufficient attention is given to developing comprehensive models of the firm that explicitly consider the interface among different functional areas, including marketing and finance.

Although we shall focus heavily on marketing-finance fusion, *Fusion for Profit* has a much broader scope. Many of the concepts and theories in the book can be applied to the interface among marketing, finance, and other functional areas in the firm, including human resources, engineering, and production.

◣ *Who Should Read* Fusion for Profit?

Fusion for Profit provides integrated cross-functional solutions to a wide range of short- and long-run problems facing the firm. Hence it should be of interest to managers at all levels in the organization, academics, and students in different disciplines (e.g., marketing, finance, economics, and strategy).

In order to make the material accessible to diverse audiences, I have not used any mathematics or algebra in the book. Throughout, the attempt is to provide intuition without sacrificing rigor. Wherever necessary, technical references have been added for the interested reader.

As a glance at the table of contents will show, *Fusion for Profit* covers a wide spectrum of topics, many of which are not covered in standard books. The reader should peruse the table of contents to obtain a comprehensive overview of the scope of the book and then decide which topics are directly relevant to his or her position in the organization.

Following is a highly abbreviated sampling of topics that are covered in the book. These topics should be of interest to different audiences (i.e., business executives at all levels in the publicly held firm, owner managers, academics in different functional areas, and students in different disciplines, including marketing, economics, finance, and organizational management).

◣ *Managers*

The Chief Executive Officer (CEO)
- How should the firm measure the productivities of divisional managers, and how should these managers be compensated?
- Should the firm set up manufacturing operations immediately, or should it wait until demand or technological uncertainty is resolved?
- How should the firm set up its global operations? How should the firm measure the performances of the relevant global managers, and what compensation plans should the firm use to maximize long-run performance?

The Chief Marketing Officer (CMO)
- How should the firm choose a product positioning and advertising strategy that maximizes its long-run performance?
- How should the firm coordinate the marketing, engineering, and finance functions to determine the optimal mix of products and product designs?

- How should the firm measure the risks and returns from using a multi-channel distribution strategy?

The Chief Financial Officer (CFO)

- What financial criteria should be used to allocate resources across products and markets to achieve the best combination of risk and return for shareholders?
- How will the marketing policy of a given product affect the distribution of cash flows that the product generates now and in the future?
- How will the marketing policy of a given product affect the distribution of cash flows for other products in the firm?

The Chief Operating Officer (COO)

- How should the firm develop and design product bundles based on its market opportunities?
- What metrics should the multiproduct firm or organization use to measure performance?
- How should the firm distinguish between efficiency and effectiveness?

The Chief Technology Officer (CTO)

- How should the firm integrate the R & D and marketing functions in order to translate technology into real customer advantages?
- How should the firm determine the risks and returns from choosing different product portfolios based on a particular technology?
- How can the firm determine the value of the technical synergies from acquiring a target company and rank that company against its competitors?

The Chief Information Officer (CIO)

- How should the firm measure the performance of multichannel distribution strategies (e.g., bricks-and-mortar stores and the Internet)?
- How should the firm measure the performance of its advertising strategy across conventional media and the Internet?
- How should the firm measure the short- and long-run productivities of its call centers?

The Product Manager

- Prior to the launch of a new product, how can the firm use self-stated intentions data (which are inherently imprecise) to forecast demand for that product?
- How can the firm measure the likely effects of new product introductions on cannibalization and the market shares of competitors?
- How should the firm coordinate its marketing policies when it introduces new products sequentially into the marketplace?

The Advertising Manager

- How should the advertising budget be allocated over time and across media (e.g., conventional media and the Internet)?
- What metrics should be used to measure advertising productivity for conventional media? What metrics should the firm use to measure advertising productivity for the Internet? And, how should these decisions factor in measurement error and joint effects across media?
- How should the firm determine whether to prepurchase advertising space in the future? And, what proportion of the advertising budget should be spent on prepurchasing advertising in different media?

The Sales Manager

- How should the multiproduct firm determine the optimal compensation plans for its sales force?
- How should compensation plans be adjusted when the salesperson's effort has an effect on future sales and profits?
- Under what conditions should sales revenue be used as a proxy of a salesperson's productivity?

The Pricing Manager

- How should the firm determine what prices to charge for individual products and product bundles?
- How should the firm price a new product it is planning on adding to its existing product line?
- How should the firm price a product when some consumers or consumer segments have incomplete information?

The Mergers and Acquisition (M & A) Manager

- How should the firm determine the brand equity of a target brand or company that it plans to acquire?
- Under what conditions is it desirable for one firm to acquire another firm with low brand equity?
- How should the firm determine whether an international acquisition or merger will increase the long-run value of the firm?

The Owner of a Privately Held Firm

- What is the appropriate measure of risk and return to the owner from pursuing different marketing strategies?
- Should the privately held firm modify its strategy differently from a publicly held firm when market conditions change?
- Under what conditions will product-line and/or geographical diversification (domestic or international) help the privately held firm?

The Social Marketer

- Under what conditions does advertising make society better off?
- Under what conditions will consumers and society be better off in the long run when firms distribute free samples?
- Are consumers and society better off when firms introduce product upgrades of durable products?

◣ Academics

As noted earlier, *Fusion for Profit* covers a wide range of topics that are not addressed in conventional books. Furthermore, the treatment of standard topics (e.g., pricing) is nontraditional. Since *Fusion for Profit* focuses on providing integrated solutions to a wide class of business problems, it should be of interest to academics in a number of fields, including marketing, finance, economics, human resource management, and strategy.

◣ Students

Over the last 35 years, I have taught a large number of graduate students in the United States and abroad. During this period, I have heard the frequent refrain from many MBA and executive MBA students that standard business courses provide limited guidance in solving the real-world problems that they face (e.g., the decision-making problems posed by measurement error and incomplete information). *Fusion for Profit* addresses this gap by focusing on how to develop actionable strategies that are comprehensive, allow for incomplete and imperfect information, and integrate different functional areas in the firm. To make the ideas in *Fusion for Profit* readily accessible to students, all topics are discussed using a question-and-answer format.

◣ How Should You Read Fusion for Profit?

Fusion for Profit can be read in different ways. As the table of contents shows, the material in the book has been partitioned so that each chapter focuses on a particular managerial topic (e.g., the use of the market share metric for choosing marketing strategies or how to allocate resources across different product lines or market segments). Consequently, it is not necessary to read the chapters in sequence.

Alternatively, if your goal is to obtain a quick overview of the book, you should focus on the "Fusion for Profit Maxims" and the key points at the end of any chapter of interest. Should you decide to study a particular topic in depth, read the sections of interest in the relevant chapters.

Each chapter uses a question-and-answer format and is structured in the same way for readability:

1. When and why the information in the chapter will be useful,
2. The key terms that will be introduced in the chapter,
3. The body of the chapter, including tangible, real-world examples to illustrate key theoretical concepts and the subject matter in question, and
4. Key points summarizing the chapter.

Because of the wide scope of the topics covered in *Fusion for Profit* and its strong multidisciplinary focus, I have added an extensive glossary, which includes definitions of terms from a number of fields, including economics, finance, marketing, strategy, psychometrics, and statistics. Since some of the topics covered in *Fusion for Profit* are highly specialized (e.g., the role of private equity firms in mergers and acquisitions and the pricing of Internet advertising), the glossary also includes a number of terms that are not easily accessible to most readers.

Finally, *Fusion for Profit* provides an in-depth analysis of, and solutions to, a wide range of key problems facing managers in different functional areas and senior management. Importantly, throughout the book we emphasize the critical relationships among the different functional areas in the firm, including marketing and finance. Consequently, you may find it convenient to keep *Fusion for Profit* as a handbook.

◣ Acknowledgments

In alphabetical order, I would like to thank Dinyar Devitre (Senior Vice President and CFO, Altria Group, Inc.); John A. Greco Jr. (President and CEO, Direct Marketing Association); David Luenberger (cofounder of the Department of Engineering-Economic Systems at Stanford University); Harry Markowitz (Nobel laureate in economics and inventor of modern portfolio theory in finance); Edward J. Mishan (emeritus professor, London School of Economics), and Don Morrison (founding editor of *Marketing Science*, the leading marketing journal internationally, and Leonhard Professor of Management, UCLA) for encouraging me to write a book on the marketing-finance interface that helps to bridge the gap between practice and academe, is rigorous but intuitive, and supplements the theory and concepts with real-world examples.

I also thank my family for their critical reading of the manuscript and for forcing me to write more clearly. In alphabetical order I thank Mohini (my wife), Ruby (my sister), and Shireen (my daughter). Shireen, in particular, has provided valuable insight as a corporate executive, suggested a number of topics to be included in the book, provided incisive substantive comments, and made numerous editorial improvements.

Finally, I thank Linda Donnelly and Susan Ecklund (production editor and copyeditor, respectively) for their help.

I hope you enjoy reading *Fusion for Profit* and find it useful for decision making. The usual disclaimer is in order: I am solely responsible for all errors.

Contents

I

Financial Tools Necessary for Understanding the Marketing-Finance Interface

Choosing Marketing Policy in the Short Run

This chapter and the next will introduce you to some financial tools that are essential for understanding *Fusion for Profit*. For simplicity, we will assume that marketing policies (e.g., price and advertising) have *short-term effects*. In the next chapter, we will consider the more general case where the firm's marketing policies have *long-term effects*.

The information covered in this chapter will be useful when you are faced with the following types of decisions:

- How should my firm measure profitability under uncertainty?
- How should my firm use the *return on investment* criterion (ROI) for marketing decision making?
- How should my firm choose marketing policy if my firm is privately held?
- How should my firm choose marketing policy if my firm is publicly held?
- How should my firm use the ROI criterion if my firm sells multiple products or has multiple divisions?

The following terms will be introduced in this chapter (see glossary for definitions):

accounting cost	cost of capital	hedge fund
cash flows	cyclicality	hurdle rate of return
certainty-equivalent profit	economic cost	inventory holding cost
	financial cost	long-term effects

market segmentation	profit	risk-neutral
market value	profitability	risk premium
net profit	rate of return	short-term effects
nonaccounting costs	return on investment (ROI)	uncertainty
privately held firm	risk-adjusted ROI	volatility

1.1 Should the Firm Use Profits to Choose Marketing Policies?

Before we address this issue, it is necessary to define profits. *Profit* is defined as:

$$\text{profit} = \text{revenue} - \text{costs}$$

in any given time period.

Is profit a well-defined quantity? How should profit be computed?

On the surface, profit appears to be a well-defined quantity. However, it is easy to mismeasure profit. The primary danger is omitting hidden, *nonaccounting costs.*

Example 1: Consider an entrepreneur who has invested his or her own money in a business. Since the firm does not have any financial obligations to outsiders, the *accounting cost* of this investment is zero. However, the *financial cost* of this investment is clearly nonzero, since the entrepreneur could have invested the money elsewhere. Similarly, instead of running his or her own business, the entrepreneur could have taken a job elsewhere. The income that the entrepreneur forgoes by running his or her own business is a hidden cost that should be deducted from the firm's gross revenues in order to compute profits.

Example 2: Consider an electronic retailer who has to decide how many DVD players to order. Suppose the retailer orders 50 units and sells 49. Then, the retailer faces an *inventory holding cost* for the one unit that is unsold. However, suppose the retailer orders 50 units, but the demand is 51 units. Since the retailer never purchased the 51st unit, the accounting cost of the 51st unit that *could* have been sold if it were in inventory is zero.

The *economic cost,* however, of the shortage can be considerable. It is the profit that the retailer could have earned on the 51st unit plus the future profits it could have earned via repeat purchases by that customer. In many cases, the economic cost of a shortage can exceed the cost of having unsold inventory.

Fusion for Profit Maxim

Profit should be computed after considering all relevant costs. Standard accounting measures of profit may be misleading.

▶ *Why is the "given time period" important?*

Profit has two dimensions: *money and time* (e.g., profit per month or profit per year). Unless one specifies the time period, the profit maximization criterion is ambiguous.

   Example: If a high-tech firm such as Microsoft seeks to maximize profit over a short time period (say three months), the optimal level of R & D will be zero. Such a policy is likely to lead to poor long-run performance.

Fusion for Profit Maxim

For profit maximization to be a meaningful criterion, it is necessary to specify the appropriate time horizon.

▶ 1.2 Should the Firm Use the Return on Investment Criterion for Marketing Decision Making?

The firm's return on investment for a given product is defined as follows:

$$\text{ROI} = \frac{\text{profit in a given time period}}{\text{investment}}$$

   The ROI criterion explicitly recognizes that the goal of the firm is *profitability* and not profit. For example, suppose a retailer can make a profit of $1 million per year by investing $10 million in one store. Then, the retailer's ROI from the store is 10% (annual profit/investment).

   Now suppose the retailer establishes two identical stores by investing a total of $20 million. As one would expect, the retailer's profit will increase. Let's say that the retailer's annual profit increases from $1 million to $1.5 million per year. Then, the retailer's ROI from opening two stores is 7.5% (1.5/20 × 100%). Note that when the retailer expands its operations, profits increase from $1 million to $1.5 million. However, profitability (ROI) decreases from 10% to 7.5%. Hence the optimal strategy for the retailer may be to open one store only.

   As this example shows, the ROI criterion is appealing because it focuses on profitability and not on profits per se. However, in spite of the intuitive appeal of the ROI criterion, one needs to be careful in measuring ROI.

Valuation and the Single-Product Firm

The metric for investment should reflect market valuations. Consider the following example. Suppose Samsung produces semiconductors using an old plant. Let's say that Samsung purchased the plant several years ago. Suppose Samsung has taken tax write-offs on the plant and that the plant has a book value of $1 million (purchase price of $10 million – accumulated depreciation charges of $9 million).

Suppose Samsung expects to make an annual profit of $1 million by producing and selling semiconductors made at this plant. Then, the ROI based on accounting valuations is 100% (annual profit/book value of the plant). Now suppose that, because of robust demand for semiconductors, there is a shortage of plant capacity. Hence Samsung can sell its old plant in the marketplace for $5 million (> $1 million). Then, Samsung's "true" investment in the old plant is $5 million. Hence, based on market valuations, Samsung's annual ROI from the old plant is only 20% (annual profit/*market value* of the plant). Note that the ROI that is based on accounting data (100%) is seriously overstated.

Fusion for Profit Maxim

ROI should be measured based on the market value of an investment and not on its book value.

Point to consider. What are the policy implications of using historical valuations to measure ROI?

In general, book values and market values will differ. Suppose that the book values of old plants are lower than the corresponding market values. Then, the firm will overstate the ROIs of old plants. Consequently, it will allocate too many resources to old plants and too few to new plants. In addition, the firm will use the wrong performance metrics to measure and reward managerial performance. Thus, for purely fortuitous reasons, the firm will reward managers of old plants for "superior" performance and penalize managers of new plants for performing poorly.

Multiple Products. The standard ROI metric should be adjusted if the firm's product lines are related either on the demand side or on the cost side.

Example 1: AOL generates revenue from selling Internet subscriptions and from advertising revenue generated from AOL's Web site. Since AOL's advertising revenue is based on the number of AOL's paid subscribers, the standard single-product measure of ROI will understate the effect of AOL's Internet subscriptions on the company's overall profitability. In particular, the optimal policy for AOL is to give up some profits on paid subscriptions (i.e., earn a lower ROI on that product) in order to increase profits from paid advertising on the AOL Web site (i.e., earn a higher ROI on that product).

Example 2: When Pfizer bought Pharmacia Upjohn, it integrated the two sales forces, since the two product lines were related on the cost and demand sides. After the merger, it would have been incorrect for Pfizer to attempt to maximize the separate ROIs for each product line.

Fusion for Profit Maxim

The multiproduct firm should use a product-line-based measure of ROI if its product lines are related on the cost or demand sides.

Time Frame

The time frames used to compute ROI should differ across products.

Example: Suppose PepsiCo introduces a new line of soft drinks. Then, PepsiCo may have to advertise the new product line of soft drinks heavily to build demand. Hence the new product line will produce a lower ROI in the short run than PepsiCo's existing products.

Suppose PepsiCo uses the same time frame to evaluate the ROIs of all its products. Then, PepsiCo will *underinvest* in the new product line.

Fusion for Profit Maxim

The ROI criterion is likely to lead to underinvestment in new products unless different time frames are used for established and new products.

Uncertainty

Another critical issue is that *the standard measure of ROI does not allow for uncertainty.* As will be discussed shortly, the standard measure of ROI will lead to poor resource allocation decisions and suboptimal marketing policies.

▶ *Can the firm choose marketing policy to maximize profits when demand and costs are uncertain? Assume that investment is fixed and that the firm produces one product only.*

Example: Suppose a privately owned shoe retailer needs to price a new line of designer fashion shoes it purchases from Nine West. The problem is that demand is uncertain. If the retailer charges a price of $100 per pair, the demand could be either 5,000 or 10,000 pairs of shoes. If the retailer charges a lower price of $90 per pair, the demand could be either 8,000 or 12,000 pairs.

▶ *Assume that the retailer can purchase the shoes from Nine West at a price of $60 per pair. Furthermore, there is no time delay between the time an order is placed and the time that the order is fulfilled. Which price strategy ($100 or $90 per pair) will maximize the retailer's profits?*

Consider the price of $100 per pair. Depending on the number of pairs sold, the retailer will make a profit of either $200,000 or $400,000. If the retailer

Table 1.1
Nine West Example: Comparison of Low- and High-Price Strategies

	Demand 1 5,000 pairs	Demand 2 10,000 pairs	Demand 3 8,000 pairs	Demand 4 12,000 pairs
Revenue scenarios				
Price A ($100)	$500,000	$1,000,000		
Price B ($90)			$720,000	$1,080,000
Cost scenarios				
Cost per pair ($60)	$300,000	$600,000	$480,000	$720,000
Profit scenarios				
Price A ($100)	$200,000	$400,000		
Price B ($90)			$240,000	$360,000

charges a lower price of $90 per pair, it will make a profit of either $240,000 or $360,000 (table 1.1).

Comparing the profits across both pricing plans, we see that the price of $100 per pair could lead to the *highest* profit ($400,000). However, if demand is weak, this pricing strategy could lead to the *lowest* profit ($200,000).

Fusion for Profit Maxim

One cannot choose marketing policies to maximize profits under uncertainty.

▶ *If the firm cannot maximize profits under uncertainty, how should the firm choose its marketing policy?*

The firm should simultaneously consider several factors: the uncertainty in *cash flows*, its risk attitude, and its ownership structure (i.e., whether the firm is privately owned or owned by stockholders). Furthermore, the firm needs to choose an appropriate metric for measuring profitability.

▶ **1.3 How Does the Ownership Structure of the Firm Affect How Marketing Policies Should Be Chosen?**

The Privately Owned Firm

▶ *What criterion should the* privately owned firm *use in choosing its marketing policy?*

Some marketing strategies are more aggressive than others. Hence it is necessary for the firm to determine the trade-off between risk and return for each strategy.

Example: Consider the case of Google prior to the time it went public. Suppose Google had to choose between two marketing strategies. Assume that each strategy required the same level of investment.

Under the first strategy (Strategy A), Google could have allocated resources to obtain new customers in a fast-growing but volatile market segment. Under the second strategy (Strategy B), Google could have attempted to increase the retention rate of its current customers.

▶ *Which strategy should Google have chosen?*

Strategy A is more aggressive and could have produced a higher average profit than Strategy B. However, it is much riskier. Hence, without quantifying the risks and returns from the two marketing strategies, one cannot determine which strategy Google should have chosen.

▶ *What is the simplest way for the privately held firm to compare the risks and returns for any given marketing strategies?*

The simplest approach for the privately held firm is to ignore *volatility* completely and to choose the marketing strategy for which the expected profit is the highest. If the firm uses this expected profit criterion, we say that the firm is *risk-neutral*.

In the Nine West shoe example discussed earlier, suppose that each of the demand levels for the two pricing policies has an equal chance (50%) of occurring. Then, the expected profits for both pricing strategies are equal ($300,000) (table 1.2). Hence risk neutrality implies that the retailer will be indifferent between the two pricing plans.

▶ *Should the firm choose marketing policies to maximize its expected profits?*

In the Nine West shoe example above, suppose the privately owned retailer has incurred debt and will need to pay $210,000 in interest charges. Then, if the retailer chooses the high-price plan ($100 per pair), there is a 50% chance that the retailer's gross profit ($200,000) will be insufficient to meet its interest charge ($210,000). However, if the retailer chooses the low-price

Table 1.2
Nine West Example: Effect of Demand Uncertainty on Profits

	Demand 1 5,000 pairs	Demand 2 10,000 pairs	Demand 3 8,000 pairs	Demand 4 12,000 pairs	Expected Profit
Price A ($100)	$200,000	$400,000			$300,000
Price B ($90)			$240,000	$360,000	$300,000

Note: Each demand scenario's probability is 50%.

plan ($90 per pair), the corresponding probability of failing to meet its interest obligations is zero (since the minimum gross profit is $240,000). Thus, the low-price plan is safer, even though both the low- and high-price strategies provide the same expected profits (see table 1.2).

Fusion for Profit Maxim

In general, the firm should choose its marketing policy only after comparing the risks and returns from different policies.

▶ **How can the privately held firm choose the optimal marketing policy by balancing risk and return?**

Suppose the Yam Company is a small electronic goods manufacturer and has developed a new gadget. Let's say that Yam plans to introduce the product in the marketplace at a price of $100 per unit. Suppose there is a 50% chance of making a *net profit* of $2 million and a 50% chance of making a net profit of $6 million. Then, Yam's expected profit is $4 million ({2 + 6} × 0.5). For simplicity, assume that the gadget will become obsolete after one period.

▶ **Suppose a large manufacturer of electronic goods is willing to purchase all rights to Yam's new gadget. What floor price should Yam be willing to accept?**

If Yam is risk-neutral, the volatility of cash flows does not matter. Hence the floor price that Yam should be willing to accept is $4 million (the expected profit). However, if Yam is risk-averse, the value of the project is reduced because of the uncertainty in profit. Hence Yam's floor price will be less than $4 million.

Suppose Yam's floor price is $3.5 million. Then, we say that Yam's *certainty-equivalent profits* from the electronic gadget are $3.5 million. Equivalently, we can say that Yam's *risk premium* is $0.5 million ($4 million − $3.5 million). Thus, we have the following definition:

$$\text{certainty-equivalent profits} = \text{expected profits} - \text{risk premium}$$

Fusion for Profit Maxim

In general, the firm's marketing policies affect both risk and return. Hence marketing policies should be chosen based on the certainty-equivalent profits that they generate.

▶ *How should marketing policies be chosen under uncertainty?*
Assume that the firm sells one product and that the level of
investment is fixed.

Suppose that Yam has invested $10 million to manufacture the new electronic gadget. In particular, Yam can choose two marketing strategies:

1. If Yam uses the conservative strategy, it will spend less money to promote the new product. For this scenario, Yam's expected profit is $4 million and its certainty-equivalent profit is $3.5 million. Hence, Yam's average ROI is 40% (expected profit/investment) and its *risk-adjusted ROI* is 35% (certainty-equivalent profit/investment).
2. If Yam uses an aggressive marketing strategy, it will promote the product aggressively via its sales force. Suppose the average profit is $5 million. However, because this strategy is risky, the certainty-equivalent profit is only $3 million. Then, the average ROI for this strategy is 50% ($5M/$10M × 100). However, the risk-adjusted ROI is only 30% ($3M/$10M × 100), which is lower than the corresponding risk-adjusted ROI (35%) for the conservative strategy. Consequently, Yam should choose the more conservative strategy *even though it provides a lower expected rate of return.*

Fusion for Profit Maxim

Suppose the owner of the privately held firm is risk-averse. Then, the firm should evaluate marketing policies based on their risk-adjusted ROIs.

The Publicly Held Firm

▶ *Should marketing policies be chosen to maximize the return on*
investment to shareholders?

As discussed above, the effect of marketing policies on profit is uncertain. Hence *the publicly held firm cannot maximize profits.* Since ROI is based on profits (an uncertain quantity), the ROI corresponding to any marketing policy and investment decision is also uncertain. Consequently, *the publicly held firm cannot maximize ROI for a product or product line.*

▶ *How should the publicly held firm allocate resources across prod-*
ucts under uncertainty?

The publicly held firm should allocate resources across products and choose marketing policies using the appropriate risk-adjusted ROI for that product.

▶ *What is the risk-adjusted ROI from a given marketing policy for any given product? Assume a fixed level of investment for that product.*

Example: Suppose Apple expects that it can make a profit of $200 million next year by investing $100 million in the iPhone. However, because of demand and cost uncertainty, the iPhone's profits could be lower or higher than $200 million.

▶ *What is the guaranteed sum of money for which Apple will be willing to give up its title to the uncertain profits from the iPhone?*

Since Apple's stockholders are risk-averse, the certainty-equivalent profit from the iPhone will be less than $200 million. Suppose the certainty-equivalent profit is $150 million. Then, iPhone's risk-adjusted ROI is 150% (certainty-equivalent profit/investment = $150M/$100M × 100).

Fusion for Profit Maxim

The risk-adjusted ROI from a given marketing plan is the return on the certainty-equivalent profit generated by that plan.

▶ *How do the firm's marketing policies affect the risk-adjusted ROIs? Assume that the firm sells one product and that the level of investment is fixed.*

The firm's expected cash flows and the volatilities of those cash flows depend on the firm's *market segmentation* strategies, its production processes, and the competition in the marketplace.

Example 1: Suppose Hewlett-Packard targets the business segment whereas Dell focuses primarily on the individual consumer market. Assume that the revenues from the business segment are more sensitive to the business cycle than those from the individual consumer market. Then, for any given distribution of cash flows, it is riskier for investors to hold Hewlett-Packard stock than to hold Dell stock. Hence Hewlett-Packard's risk-adjusted ROI will be lower than Dell's.

Fusion for Profit Maxim

The risk-adjusted ROI depends on the *cyclicality* of demand in the market segment that the firm targets.

Example 2: Consider two automobile manufacturers, say Toyota and Rolls-Royce. Toyota uses capital-intensive methods to produce cars for the mass market, and Rolls-Royce uses labor-intensive methods to produce customized cars.

Suppose Rolls-Royce's costs are more cyclical than Toyota's. Then stockholders will face greater risk if they hold Rolls-Royce stock. Hence, other factors being the same, Rolls-Royce will earn a lower risk-adjusted ROI than Toyota.

Fusion for Profit Maxim

The risk-adjusted ROI depends on the firm's market segmentation policy and the production technology it uses. Hence the firm should not use an industry-based benchmark ROI for marketing decision making or for evaluating marketing performance.

Comparing Privately Held and Publicly Held Firms

▶ *Suppose two firms face the same market conditions. One is privately held and the other is publicly held. Should both firms choose the same marketing policies?*

In general, the answer is no. Suppose a firm's cash flows are highly uncertain. To compensate for the high degree of uncertainty, the owners of the firm will demand a high risk premium, regardless of whether the firm is privately or publicly held. However, there is an additional factor that affects the risk premium for the firm that is owned by shareholders.

In contrast to private owners, stockholders can diversify. Hence they are only concerned with the residual risk after they have diversified their holdings to achieve their preferred combinations of risk and return.

Consider two extreme scenarios for the publicly held firm:

1. Suppose the profits from a particular stock are perfectly correlated to the performance of the economy. In this case, the firm is a "clone" of the market. Hence an investor cannot reduce his or her risk at all by diversifying.
2. Suppose the firm's profits are uncorrelated to the performance of the economy. In this case, the investor can eliminate his or her risk completely by diversifying.

In most real-life applications, the truth will be somewhere between these two extreme scenarios. Hence, the more highly correlated the firm's profits are to the economy, the higher the risk premium.

Fusion for Profit Maxim

In general, privately and publicly held firms should choose different marketing policies under uncertainty. For the privately held firm, the risk premium depends on the volatility of the firm's cash flows but not on how cyclical the firm's cash flows are. For the publicly held firm, the risk premium depends on both the volatility and the cyclicality of the firm's cash flows.

Example: Suppose two firms introduce two identical food products in the marketplace. One firm is publicly held (e.g., General Foods), and the other, Omega Foods, is privately held. Since both products are new to the marketplace, the cash flows for both firms are volatile. Assume that the volatilities of cash flows for both firms are equal (A). Furthermore, suppose the demand for the new food product is not strongly related to the condition of the economy. Hence the cash flows for both firms have a low correlation to the market (B).

▶ Which firm has the higher risk premium?

Since the owners of Omega Foods (the privately held firm) cannot diversify, the correlation coefficient B is irrelevant. Hence the risk premium for Omega is proportional to the volatility of cash flows, A. In contrast, the shareholders of General Foods can diversify. Hence the risk premium for General Foods depends on *both* A and B. Specifically, the risk premium for General Foods is proportional to the product AB.[1]

Note that the risk premiums for both firms are fundamentally different even though both firms anticipate the same cash flows for their products. In our example, the cash flows from the products are not highly correlated to the economy (i.e., B is small). Hence, other factors remaining the same, the risk premium for General Foods is likely to be smaller than the risk premium for Omega.[2]

Fusion for Profit Maxim

The firm needs to explicitly consider the trade-off between risk and return (equivalently, the risk premium) when choosing marketing policy. This tradeoff depends critically on the ownership structure of the firm.

Point to consider.   Suppose a privately held firm and a publicly held firm face the same market conditions. Which firm will choose a more aggressive marketing strategy?

In many cases, the risk premium for the publicly held firm will be lower than that for the privately held firm. Hence the publicly held firm should choose a more aggressive marketing strategy. For example, it should spend more money on advertising to increase future demand.[3]

Point to consider.   Are there any market conditions under which the publicly held firm should choose marketing policies to maximize expected profits?

As discussed above,

• Regardless of ownership structure, all firms should choose marketing policies to maximize the certainty-equivalent profit = expected profits – risk premium, and

• The risk premium for the publicly held firm varies with the product of two terms: the volatility of the firm's cash flows (*A*) and the correlation of the firm's cash flows with the market (*B*).

Note that, *regardless of how volatile the firm's cash flows (A) are*, the risk premium for the publicly held firm disappears when $B = 0$. In this case, the publicly held firm should choose its marketing strategy to maximize expected profits.

◤ 1.4 What Does the Risk-Adjusted ROI Criterion Imply for Multiproduct and Multidivisional Firms?

In order to maximize performance, the firm should allocate its resources across products and market segments such that the risk-adjusted ROIs are equalized. However, risk premiums vary across products. Hence the multiproduct or multidivisional firm should use different *hurdle rates of return* to measure the profitabilities of different products and divisions.

Furthermore, as discussed earlier, different marketing strategies for the same product involve different combinations of risk and return (e.g., some strategies are more aggressive than others). Hence the risk-adjusted ROI for a given product is segment-specific.

Example 1: Consider a large diversified company such as General Electric. Suppose one division manufactures refrigerators and the other manufactures lightbulbs. In general, the cash flows from the refrigerator division will be more cyclical than the cash flows from the lightbulbs division. Thus, other factors being equal, the expected ROI from the refrigerator division should be higher than the expected ROI from the lightbulbs division to compensate for the additional risk involved by investing in the refrigerator division.

Suppose General Electric uses the same required *rate of return* (e.g., its *cost of capital*) to allocate resources across both divisions. Then General Electric will *overinvest* in the refrigerator division and *underinvest* in the lightbulbs division.

Example 2: Lenovo sells computers to individuals and to corporations. Suppose the demand from the corporate sector is more cyclical than that from the individual consumer segment. Then, other factors being equal, Lenovo's expected ROI from the corporate sector should be higher than the expected ROI from the individual consumer market. If Lenovo uses the same required rate of return to allocate resources across both user segments, it will overallocate marketing resources to the corporate segment and underallocate resources to the consumer segment.

Fusion for Profit Maxim

The risk-adjusted ROI varies across products and market segments. Hence the firm should not allocate resources across product lines or divisions using a common hurdle rate of return.

Chapter 1 Key Points

- In the real world (i.e., a world of uncertainty), profit maximization is an ambiguous concept. Consequently, one cannot choose marketing policies to maximize profits under uncertainty.
- All costs, especially hidden costs, should be included when the firm computes the profitability from a given marketing strategy.
- The ownership structure of the firm has a major impact on the metric used to quantify uncertainty. However, regardless of whether the firm is privately owned or owned by shareholders, marketing policies should be chosen based on the certainty-equivalent profits that they generate.
- In general, privately and publicly held firms should choose different marketing policies under uncertainty. For the privately held firm, the risk premium depends on the volatility of the firm's cash flows but not on how cyclical the firm's cash flows are. For the publicly held firm, the risk premium depends on both the volatility and the cyclicality of the firm's cash flows.
- The firm should evaluate its marketing policies based on their risk-adjusted ROIs (certainty- equivalent profits/investment).
- The risk-adjusted ROIs depend on the firm's marketing strategy, the segments the firm targets, and the production processes the firm uses. Hence the firm should not use industry-based benchmark ROIs for marketing decision making.
- The firm should use risk-adjusted ROIs to allocate resources across multiple product lines, market segments, and divisions. In addition, the firm should use risk-adjusted ROIs to measure and evaluate performance at different levels (e.g., the divisional or product manager levels).

2

Choosing Marketing Policy in the Long Run

This chapter focuses on financial tools that are necessary to determine the *long-run value* of the firm's marketing decisions. In addition, we briefly discuss how to choose managerial incentive plans that are aligned with the firm's long-run goals (e.g., maximizing long-run stock value). Compensation policy will be discussed in detail in chapters 15, 16, and 17.

The information covered in this chapter will be useful when you are faced with the following types of decisions:

- What financial tools should my firm use to determine the long-run effect of marketing policies under certainty?
- What financial tools should my firm use to determine the long-run effect of marketing policies under *uncertainty?*
- Should my firm use different financial metrics if it is privately held or is owned by shareholders?
- What financial tools should my firm use to measure the effect of marketing policies if it sells multiple products?
- What financial criteria should my firm use if it can revise its marketing strategies when new information arrives in the marketplace?
- How should my firm measure and reward managers so that they choose and adjust their marketing strategies over time to maximize my firm's long-run performance?

The following terms will be introduced in this chapter (see glossary for definitions):

annual compound return	uncertainty to be	profit-based contract
annual discount rate	resolved	real options theory
capital asset pricing	first-mover advantage	risk-neutral
model	hurdle rate	salvage value
cash flows	long-run value	stock-option-based
conditional net present	long-term debt	managerial
value (NPV)	market price of risk	contract
cost of capital	net present value (NPV)	strategic flexibility
economic value	outsourcing	synergies
economic value of	planning horizon	test market
waiting for	privately held firm	uncertainty

▶ 2.1 How Should the Firm Choose Long-Run Marketing Policies under Certainty?

In general, marketing policies affect both the magnitudes of profits and their timings. For instance, the firm's pricing policies affect current sales and current profits; *in addition, they also affect future profits by generating repeat business*. For simplicity, we begin with the case where there is no *uncertainty*.

▶ How should the firm value the future profits resulting from a particular marketing policy?

Example: Consider a manufacturer such as AMD that has just developed a new computer chip. Suppose AMD expects this computer chip to become obsolete at the end of two years. Let's say that AMD is evaluating a marketing strategy for the new computer chip that will yield a profit of $11 million at the end of the first year and a profit of $36.3 million at the end of the second year.

▶ How will this marketing strategy affect AMD's stock price?

The critical question in determining the financial impact of AMD's marketing strategy is: What alternative investment opportunities are available to AMD's stockholders? Suppose AMD's stockholders can earn an *annual compound return* of 10% by investing elsewhere in a "similar" product. We say that AMD has an *annual discount rate* of 10%.

1. Then, by investing $10 million elsewhere, AMD's stockholders could obtain a total of $11 million at the end of the first year ($10 million × 1.10).

Table 2.1
AMD Example: Measuring the Long-Run Effects of Marketing Policies

Investment amount	Annual compound interest	Value of investment after year 1	Value of investment after year 2
$40,000,000	10%	$44,000,000	
$10,000,000	10%	$11,000,000	
$30,000,000	10%	$33,000,000	
$30,000,000[a]	10%		$36,300,000
$33,000,000[b]	10%	$36,300,000	

[a]At beginning of year 1.
[b]At beginning of year 2.

2. Similarly, by investing an additional $30 million now, AMD's stockholders could obtain a total of $36.3 million at the end of the second year ($30 million × 1.10 × 1.10) (table 2.1).

Thus, by investing $40 million elsewhere now at an annual compound return of 10%, AMD's stockholders can match the *cash flows* that will be produced by the new product. Specifically, at the end of the first year, AMD's shareholders would have available $44 million ($40 million × 1.10). If AMD's stockholders pay themselves the cash flows generated by the new product at the end of the first year ($11 million), they will have a balance of $33 million at that time. Since AMD's stockholders can invest this amount at an annual return of 10%, the amount available to them at the end of the second year will be $36.3 million ($33 million × 1.1). *This amount is exactly equal to the cash flows generated by the new product at the end of the second year* (see table 2.1).

We say that the *net present value (NPV)* of the new product is $40 million. *Note that the future stream of cash flows generated by the new computer chip is equivalent to an addition of $40 million to the current wealth of AMD's shareholders.* Hence, the new chip will increase AMD's stock price by $40 million.

In general,

$$NPV = \{\text{cash flow in the first period}/(1 + r)\} + \{\text{cash flow in the second period}/(1 + r)^2\} + \{\text{cash flow in the third period}/(1 + r)^3\} + \ldots + \{\text{cash flow in the } n^{th} \text{ period}/(1 + r)^n\},$$

where r denotes the required rate of return and n denotes the firm's planning period.

Fusion for Profit Maxim

Marketing policies typically affect both the firm's current and future cash flows. The NPV criterion can be used to determine how these cash flows affect the firm's current stock price.

▶ *How can the firm compare different marketing policies using the NPV criterion?*

Example: Suppose General Foods has developed a new low-calorie pizza and needs to choose between two pricing plans for the new product: charging a "low" price and charging a "high" price.

Consider two scenarios:

1. Suppose that by charging a low introductory price, General Foods will make less profit in the first year. However, it will sell a higher volume in the first year and generate more repeat business in the future.
2. Alternatively, suppose that by charging a high introductory price, General Foods will make more profit in the first year. However, since it will sell a lower volume in the first year, repeat business in the future will be reduced.

Let's say that by charging a low price in the first year, General Foods will make less profit in the first year ($4.4 million), but it will make more profit in the second ($7.26 million). In contrast, by charging a high introductory price, General Foods will make a higher profit of $5.5 million in the first year and a lower profit of $4.84 million in the second.

▶ *Which pricing strategy will maximize General Foods' stock price? Assume that investors have a two-year planning horizon.*

To address this problem, we compute the NPVs of these cash flows for the two pricing plans. Suppose the annual discount rate is 10%. Then, the NPVs are as follows: $10 million (low-price strategy) and $9 million (high-price strategy) (table 2.2).

Hence the low-price strategy is superior, *even though it yields lower profits in the short run.* Assuming that the stock market and the management of General Foods share the same expectations, General Foods' stock

Table 2.2
General Foods Pizza Example: Comparing the Long-Run Effects of Marketing Policies

| | Expected cash flow | | | | |
	Period 1	Period 2	Discount rate	NPV calculation	NPV
Low-price strategy	$4.4M	$7.26M	10%	$(4.4)/(1 + 0.10) +$ $(7.26)/(1 + 0.10)^2$	$10M
High-price strategy	$5.5M	$4.84M	10%	$(5.5)/(1 + 0.10) +$ $(4.84)/(1 + 0.10)^2$	$9M

price will increase by $10 million if the company chooses the low-price strategy.

Fusion for Profit Maxim

Often, marketing policies have dynamic effects over time. Hence marketing policies that maximize short-run profits can lead to suboptimal results.

▶ 2.2 How Should the Firm Choose Long-Run Marketing Policies under Uncertainty?

In the pizza example, we used the same discount rates to determine the NPVs of two different marketing strategies under certainty. Should the firm use the same discount rates in evaluating different marketing strategies for a given product under uncertainty?

At first glance, this valuation method appears to be fair, since we are comparing different marketing policies for the same product. However, as we discuss below, this method may not be appropriate.

In the pizza example, we assumed that the cash flows generated by both pricing policies were known with certainty. Hence, it was appropriate to use the same discount rates to evaluate both marketing policies.

In real life, the cash flows from both marketing policies are likely to be uncertain. Thus, regardless of which pricing plan General Foods chooses, the demand for the new pizza product cannot be predicted with precision. Furthermore, the prices of raw materials (e.g., cheese) used to make the pizza will fluctuate over the two-year period. Since both demand and cost are uncertain, each marketing policy will have a different effect on the risk that General Foods faces.

To illustrate, let's focus on the cost of one raw material for making pizza: cheese. Given the two scenarios above, the low-price strategy in the first year will lead, on average, to a higher repeat sales volume in the second year than the high-price strategy. Let's say that General Foods chooses the low-price strategy. Since cheese prices are uncertain in the second year and the average sales volume is higher, General Foods' expenditure on cheese in the second year will fluctuate more than if it chooses the high-price strategy. Thus, other factors being held constant, the discount rate for the low-price strategy should be higher than the discount rate for the high-price strategy.

Fusion for Profit Maxim

In general, the firm's marketing policies for any given product are likely to have different effects on the risks and returns that the firm will face in the future. Hence the firm should not use a common discount rate to determine the NPVs from different marketing policies.

▶ *Does the ownership structure of the firm affect the firm's optimal marketing strategy?*

Let's continue with the pizza example and compare the optimal strategies for General Foods (a publicly held firm) and a hypothetical *privately held firm*, Supremo's Pizza.

Suppose that if either firm chooses a high-price policy to launch the new product, none of its competitors will follow. In contrast, if either firm chooses a low-price policy, some competitors will follow. However, it is not clear which competitors will follow and what the magnitudes of their price cuts will be. Thus, for both General Foods and Supremo's, the cash flows from the low-price strategy are less predictable than the corresponding cash flows from the high-price strategy.

▶ *How should the privately held firm, Supremo's Pizza, value future profits?*

The low-price strategy leads to more uncertain cash flows for Supremo's in the second year than the high-price strategy. Since the low-price strategy is more risky, Supremo's Pizza *should use a higher discount rate to evaluate the future profits from the low-price strategy.*

▶ *How should the publicly held firm, General Foods, value future profits?*

In contrast to the owner of Supremo's Pizza, the owners of General Foods (shareholders) can reduce their risk by diversifying. Hence their risk is based on an additional factor: the degree to which the cash flows from the new pizza product are correlated to the return on the market.

In our example, General Foods needs to compare different pricing policies for targeting the *same* set of consumers. Hence the correlations of General Foods' cash flows with the return on the market will be identical for *both* the low- and high-price strategies.

From chapter 1 we know that the risk to a publicly held firm is proportional to AB, where A denotes the volatility of the firm's cash flows and B denotes the correlation between the firm's cash flows and the return on the market. However, the quantity B is the same for both pricing policies. Furthermore, in our example, the volatility of cash flows (B) is higher for the low-price strategy. Since the quantity AB is higher for the low-price strategy, the low-price strategy is more risky. Hence General Foods should use a higher discount rate for the low-price strategy.

Note that, like Supremo's Pizza, General Foods should also use a higher discount rate for the low-price strategy.

Point to consider.   Suppose General Foods and Supremo's Pizza share the same beliefs about the cash flows generated by the low-price strategy for the new pizza product. Should both firms use the same discount rate to evaluate this marketing policy?

The risk to the owner of Supremo's is proportional to the volatility of cash flows generated by the low-price strategy (*A*). Hence the discount rate for Supremo's depends on two quantities:

1. The owner's attitude to risk, and
2. The magnitude of the uncertainty in cash flows (*A*).

In contrast to Supremo's owner, the shareholders of General Foods can diversify[1] and are only concerned with the risk that remains after they have diversified. Hence the discount rate for General Foods will depend on three quantities[2]:

1. The market's attitude to risk (known as the *market price of risk*),
2. The magnitude of the uncertainty in cash flows (*A*), and
3. The correlation between the firm's cash flows and the return on the market (*B*).

Thus, there is no reason why General Foods and Supremo's Pizza should choose the same discount rate for any given marketing policy, *even though* they share the same beliefs about the cash flows that will be generated.

Fusion for Profit Maxim

In general, privately held and publicly held firms should choose different marketing policies, even if they share the same beliefs about how their marketing policies affect cash flows.

▲ 2.3 How Should the Firm Measure the Long-Run Effects of Different Marketing Policies?

We continue with the pizza example. Suppose the cash flows for each price/time period combination represent the average (expected) cash flows. For example, the average cash flow in the first year from the high-price strategy is $5.5 million. As discussed, for the scenarios given, the discount rate for the low-price strategy should be higher than that for the high-price strategy.

Since the effects of uncertainty are qualitatively similar for both the publicly held firm (General Foods) and the privately held firm (Supremo's), it is sufficient to consider one case.

Suppose the annual discount rates for General Foods are as follows: 15% (low-price strategy) and 5% (high-price strategy). Then, the NPVs are as follows: $9.32 million for the low-price strategy and $9.63 million for the high-priced strategy (table 2.3). Thus, the high-price strategy is superior.

Table 2.3

General Foods Pizza Example: How Risk Affects the Long-Run Effects of Different Marketing Policies

| | Expected cash flow | | | | |
	Period 1	Period 2	Discount rate	NPV calculation	NPV
Low-price strategy	$4.4M	$7.26M	15%	$(4.4)/(1 + 0.15) +$ $(7.26)/(1 + 0.15)^2$	$9.32M
High-price strategy	$5.5M	$4.84M	5%	$(5.5)/(1 + 0.05) +$ $(4.84)/(1 + 0.05)^2$	$9.63M

Fusion for Profit Maxim

For any given product or brand, the required rate of return depends on the firm's marketing policies.

Point to consider.   Should the finance department of a company be involved in marketing decision making?

As illustrated in the pizza example above, the discount rate for any product depends on the marketing policy that the firm chooses for that product. Hence the firm should choose the discount rate for a product (market segment) *after analyzing the risks and returns from different marketing policies.* For instance, some pricing strategies are riskier than others. Similarly, the demand from some customer segments is more unpredictable than the demand from other segments.

Consequently, without evaluating the risks and returns from different marketing policies, the firm will make suboptimal resource allocation decisions. One implication is that the finance and marketing functions in the firm should be coordinated. For example, the firm should not use a sequential approach in which the finance department first sets discount rates and the marketing department then chooses marketing policies based on this discount rate.

Fusion for Profit Maxim

The firm should coordinate its finance and marketing functions in order to choose marketing policies and make optimal resource allocation decisions.

Point to consider.   Wall Street typically puts pressure on corporations to meet the earnings forecast for the next quarter. What effect will this have on the firm's choice of marketing strategies?

Given this scenario, management will implicitly use an excessively high discount rate to value future profits. Hence management will pursue short-run profits and choose strategies that could jeopardize the firm's long-run performance (i.e., long-run share value).

▲ 2.4 How Should the Multiproduct Firm Choose Long-Run Marketing Policies under Uncertainty?

In this section, we focus on the publicly held firm that sells multiple products. Consider a multiproduct firm that has issued shares and *long-term debt*. Let's say that the market value of the long-term debt is $400 million and that investors expect to earn 8% per annum on the debt. In addition, suppose the market value of the firm's shares is $600 million. Since shareholders bear more risk than bondholders, shareholders expect to earn a higher rate of return than bondholders, say 20% (>8%) per annum. Suppose an investor owns the entire company (shares + long-term debt). Then, the expected annual rate of return to the investor is 15.2% ($0.4 \times 8 + 0.6 \times 20$). We say that the firm's *cost of capital* is 15.2%.

▲ Should the firm use its cost of capital as the discount rate in computing the NPV from different marketing policies?

Suppose the firm has only one product. Then, it is reasonable to use the firm's cost of capital to compute the NPV from different marketing polices for that product.[3] However, in a multiproduct firm each product offers a different combination of risk and return. Hence, *the discount rate should vary across products*. In addition, as we have discussed, even for a given product, *the discount rate depends on the marketing policy, the target market segment, and the production process chosen*.

Example 1: Consider a large diversified company such as GE whose products range from aircraft to refrigerators to small appliances. Clearly, investment in aircraft is more risky than investment in small appliances.

Hence, if GE uses its cost of capital to make investment decisions across product lines, the discount rate for the small appliance division will be too high, and the discount rate for the aircraft division will be too low. Consequently, *by using the cost of capital as a hurdle rate, GE will overinvest in aircraft and underinvest in small appliances*.

Example 2: Consider a consumer goods company such as Procter & Gamble (P&G), which markets several brands of toothpaste.

Suppose P&G introduces a new brand of toothpaste into the market. Since the cash flows from the new brand are more risky than those from P&G's current brands of toothpaste, *the discount rates for the new brand should be higher* than the discount rate for P&G's extant brands of toothpaste.

Example 3: Consider a company such as Dell, which sells a given line of computers to two groups of consumers: individuals and corporations.

Suppose the demand from the individual-buyer segment is more cyclical than the corresponding demand from the corporate sector. Then, the discount rate for marketing investments in the individual-buyer segment should be higher than that for marketing investments in the corporate sector. If Dell were to use the same discount rate for both segments, it would *overinvest in marketing to the individual-buyer segment and underinvest in marketing to the corporate segment.*

Fusion for Profit Maxim

The multiproduct firm should not use the firm's cost of capital for marketing decision making. The discount rates used to value the profits from different marketing activities should differ across products. In addition, for any given product it may be necessary to use a segment-specific discount rate that is based on how risky the marketing policy is.

▲ 2.5 How Should the Firm Make Long-Run Strategic Marketing Decisions under Uncertainty When It Has Strategic Flexibility?

As we have discussed, the NPV metric can be used to determine the value of future cash flows resulting from the firm's marketing policies.

▲ Is the standard NPV criterion appropriate for strategic marketing decisions when the firm can revise its decisions over time?

The NPV criterion is appealing because it provides an objective metric for comparing profits over different time periods. However, the standard NPV computation implicitly assumes that the future cash flows of the firm cannot be changed. In reality, the firm often has the opportunity to revise its marketing decisions depending on the arrival of new information.

The standard NPV criterion does not recognize the economic value of this strategic flexibility. Consequently, as will be shown shortly, the standard NPV criterion can lead the firm to make suboptimal resource allocation and marketing decisions.

Example: Suppose Nestlé is planning to introduce a new low-calorie soup product. Suppose the demand for the new product in the first period can be either "low" or "high." If the demand is low, Nestlé will withdraw the soup from the market in the second period. If the demand is high, Nestlé will introduce additional product variants (e.g., flavors) or line extensions in the second period. Thus, Nestlé's marketing decisions in the second period are conditional on the outcome in the first period. We say that Nestlé has strategic flexibility. As discussed below, the standard NPV methodology *should not* be used to analyze this type of strategic decision.

Fusion for Profit Maxim

The standard NPV method can lead to poor marketing decisions because it does not consider the economic benefit to the firm of revising its decisions in the future when new information becomes available.

▶ *What financial criterion should the firm use to evaluate marketing strategies when it has strategic flexibility?*

The firm should use a metric for long-run performance that quantifies the benefits of strategic flexibility. One way to proceed is to use *real options theory*.

▶ *How can real options theory be used to evaluate marketing strategies?*

We continue with the Nestlé example. Suppose Nestlé can choose one of two strategies for the new soup:

1. It can go national immediately (Alternative 1) or
2. It can introduce the soup in a limited *test market* to estimate demand. If demand is high, introduce the product nationally. If demand is low, drop the product (Alternative 2).

For simplicity, assume that Nestlé is *risk-neutral* and that the planning horizon is infinite. Suppose Nestlé will need to invest $110 million to launch the new product. Furthermore, assume that there is a fifty-fifty chance that the new soup will succeed in the marketplace. Specifically, if the new product is introduced nationally, Nestlé will make a profit of $100 million every year provided demand is high; however, it will lose $50 million every year if demand is low. Hence the expected annual profit from the new product introduction is $25 million ($0.5 \times \$100M - 0.5 \times \$50M$). (Note: For simplicity, we assume that there is no market growth.)

Suppose the annual discount rate is 10%. Then, according to the standard *NPV* formula, the *economic value* to Nestlé of introducing the new soup nationally now is $140 million (expected annual profit/discount rate – upfront investment = $25M/0.1 – $110M).

▶ *Since the NPV is positive, Nestlé will gain if it launches the new soup nationally now. However, is this strategy optimal?*

The standard NPV formula does not allow for a critical factor: Regardless of whether Nestlé launches the new product immediately or conducts a test market first, *Nestlé has the opportunity to revise its decision when demand uncertainty is resolved at the end of the first year.* Note that Nestlé has the "option" to change its marketing strategy in the future. To distinguish this type of option from financial options, we say that Nestlé has a "real option."

▶ How should Nestlé evaluate the economic value of its real options?

As noted earlier, both strategies (Alternatives 1 and 2) provide Nestlé with the opportunity to revise its decisions in the future. Below, we evaluate the economic values of these strategies.

Immediate National Launch (Alternative 1)

For simplicity, assume that, if Nestlé withdraws the new product from the national market at the end of the first year, the *salvage value* of its investment will be zero. Then, as discussed earlier, the expected profit in the first year is $25 million. However, since demand uncertainty will have been resolved at the end of the first year, future cash flows from the second year on will be conditional.

If the demand for the new product in the first year is low, Nestlé will revise its strategy and withdraw the product from the market at the end of the first year. Since all profits from the second year on will be zeros, the *conditional net present value (NPV)* of these profits will be zero.

If, however, the demand for the new product in the first year is high, Nestlé will continue to sell the new product. Hence Nestlé will make annual profits of $100 million from the second year on. Since these profits will occur *only* if demand is high, the conditional NPV of these profits is $909.09 million (annual cash flow from second year on / discount rate (1 + discount rate) = 100/(10% × [1 + 10%])).

As discussed earlier, there is a fifty-fifty chance that the demand for the new product will be low or high. Consequently, the conditional NPV to Nestlé *after allowing for strategic flexibility* is $367.27 million ([expected profit in the first year/(1 + discount rate)] + (probability of withdrawing the product from the market at the end of the first year × conditional NPV of cash flows from the second year on) + (probability of staying in the market at the end of the first year × conditional NPV of cash flows from the second year on) – up-front investment) = 25/1.1 + (0.5 × 0) + (0.5 × 909.09) – 110. Note that, because the standard NPV formula does not consider the economic value of strategic flexibility, it *seriously understates* the economic value of the new product launch.

Test Market Strategy (Alternative 2)

Suppose Nestlé can introduce the new product in a test market prior to introducing the product nationally. Now, as in the previous case where Nestlé immediately launches the new product nationally, Nestlé also has the opportunity to revise its decisions when the demand uncertainty is resolved at the end of the first year. However, *it now has the opportunity to delay its investment decision until the demand uncertainty is resolved in the test market.*

Assume that the test market represents 10% of the national market, the test market is run for one year, and the cost of running the test market is $15 million. (For simplicity, assume that all test market costs are incurred at the beginning of the first year.)

To focus on essentials, assume that the investment at the end of the first year to launch the new product remains unchanged ($110 million). If the test market results show that demand in the first year is low, Nestlé will not introduce the new soup nationally. If the test market results show that demand is high, Nestlé will invest $110 million and introduce the soup nationally at the beginning of the second year. Hence Nestlé will make a guaranteed annual profit of $100 million from the second year onward. (For simplicity, assume that the test market results are accurate.)

▶ *What is the economic value to Nestlé if it runs a test market?*

During the first year, Nestlé cannot revise its decisions. Since the test market represents 10% of the total market, the expected incremental profit from test-market operations at the end of the first year is $2.5 million ($25 million × 10%). But the up-front cost of the test market is $15 million. Hence, the NPV of the test market is a loss of $12.73 million (expected profit at the end of the year/ (1+ discount rate) − up-front investment = 2.5M/1.1 − 15M). Consequently, on a stand-alone basis, the test market is a losing proposition for Nestlé.

This analysis, however, does not consider a key factor: by running the test market, Nestlé will obtain valuable information for future decision making. Specifically, in our example, demand uncertainty is resolved at the end of the first year. Thus, Nestlé will know with certainty whether demand is low or high (table 2.4).

If demand in the first year is low, Nestlé will not introduce the soup nationally, since this action will lead to losses in all future time periods. Hence the cash flows from the second year onward will be zero. This pattern of cash flows occurs with a probability of 50%.

If demand in the first year is high, Nestlé will invest $110 million at the end of the first year and introduce the soup nationally at the beginning of the second year. Given this scenario, Nestlé will make a guaranteed annual profit of $100 million from the end of the second year onward. This pattern of cash flows occurs with a probability of 50%.

Hence, *after allowing for strategic flexibility,* the incremental value of expected cash flows from the test market strategy is as follows. (Nestlé incurs an up-front cost of $15 million at the beginning of the first year to run the test market, and the annual discount rate is 10%.) As shown in table 2.4, the long-run economic value of the test market strategy is a gain of $391.8 million—*not a loss* of $12.73 million as the stand-alone valuation

Table 2.4
Nestlé Example: Measuring the Economic Value of the Test Market Strategy Using the Real Options Approach

Expected incremental profit from test market / (1 + discount rate)	$2.5M/(1 + 0.10)
+	+
Probability of low demand × (cash flow from year #2 on / discount rate)	0.50* ($0M/0.10)
×	×
1 / (1 + discount rate)	1/(1 + 0.10)
+	+
Probability of high demand × (cash flow from year #2 on / discount rate)	0.50* ($100M/0.10)
×	×
1 / (1 + discount rate)	1/(1 + 0.10)
−	−
(Probability of introducing new product × investment) / (1 + discount rate)	(0.50*$110M)/(1 + 0.10)
−	−
Upfront cost for setting up test market	$15M
=	=
Total incremental value of expected cash flows from test market strategy	$391.8M

of the test market implies. Furthermore, *because of strategic flexibility*, the long-run economic value (conditional NPV) of the test market strategy is higher than the long-run economic value (conditional NPV) from the strategy of going national immediately. In particular, the *economic value of waiting for uncertainty to be resolved* in the test market is $24.53 million ($391.8 million − $367.27 million).

Fusion for Profit Maxim

The firm should use the real options method to determine the economic value of sequential marketing decisions. In such cases, the standard NPV method should not be used.

▶ *Are there any caveats to the real options method described above?*

There is one important caveat: in our analysis, we did not consider the impact of competition. Thus, suppose Nestlé chooses the test market strategy. However, a competitor (say Kraft) introduces a competitive soup product nationally during the test market period. If Kraft's product is successful,

Kraft may have a *"first-mover"* advantage, since it entered the market first. Hence Nestlé will obtain lower expected profits in the future if it launches its new soup product at the end of the first year. In this case, we need to modify the real options method to allow for the effect of competitive behavior.[4]

Fusion for Profit Maxim

The real options method should be modified to determine the economic value to the firm of making sequential marketing decisions after allowing for the effect of potential competitive reaction.

▶ *When else would it be appropriate to use real options theory?*

The firm should use the real options methodology whenever it has the opportunity to revise its decisions in the future based on new information.

Example 1: Suppose a U.S.-based manufacturer of industrial products is evaluating two supply options:

1. Purchasing raw materials from a domestic supplier, or
2. *Outsourcing* to a foreign country (e.g., China).

Suppose demand is uncertain. Then, the U.S.-based manufacturer can purchase all its raw material requirements in the United States (at a high cost) or purchase some raw materials from China (at a low cost) and, depending on the realization of market demand, purchase the additional raw materials domestically.

Example 2: Suppose a major multinational bank is planning to launch its credit cards in different countries. Then, the bank can:

1. Enter one country initially and, if demand is strong, enter more countries, or
2. Enter several countries simultaneously.

As in example 1 above, the bank should use the real options approach to determine which strategy is superior.

▶ **2.6 How Should the Firm Measure and Reward Managers When It Has Strategic Flexibility in Choosing Marketing Policies?**

As one would expect, the real options method has significant implications for how managers should be evaluated and rewarded.

▶ *What are the implications of real options theory for measuring and rewarding managerial performance?*

Consider the Nestlé example again. For simplicity, assume that the stock market and Nestlé's management have the same information; furthermore, the stock market is risk-neutral. Then, Nestlé's stock value will increase by $140 million immediately if the new soup is introduced nationally without conducting a test market. Clearly, this is not a bad investment for Nestlé's shareholders. But, as shown above, it is better for Nestlé's shareholders in the long run if Nestlé runs a test market and launches the new soup only if demand is high.

Consider the manager who is responsible for introducing the new product. For simplicity, assume that there are no demand or cost *synergies* across Nestlé's product lines and that the manager is also risk-neutral. Suppose the manager's compensation is based on a profit-sharing contract.

▶ *Which strategy will the manager choose?*

Suppose the manager chooses to introduce the new product nationally. Then, Nestlé's expected profit in the first year will be $25 million.

▶ *What will happen if the manager chooses the test market strategy?*

Then, the firm's expected loss in the first year is $12.5 million (the difference between the fixed cost of $15 million for running the test market and the expected profit of $2.5 million from the test market in that year). Hence, the manager will *always* choose to introduce the new product nationally, *even though this strategy is suboptimal for Nestlé's shareholders.*

▶ *What can the firm do to encourage the manager of the new product to use the real options method?*

One approach for Nestlé is to absorb the expense of running the test market ($15 million). Now, the expected profits from the test market in the first year will be positive ($2.5 million). Hence Nestlé can pay the manager in two parts:

1. A share of the first-year profits, and
2. A share of the second-year profits.

Note that the second-year profits will be positive only if demand is high and the product is launched nationally in the second period. Alternatively, Nestlé can give the manager stock options that the manager can exercise in the second period. Clearly, these stock options will have value only if the demand for the new soup is high and the product is launched nationally in the second period.

One complicating factor is that Nestlé's stock price is based on the performance of *all* of Nestlé's products and not simply on the performance of the new soup product for which the manager is responsible. Hence a *stock-option-based managerial contract* may be suboptimal. *A profit-based contract based on multiperiod performance for the product in question may be better.*[5]

Fusion for Profit Maxim

Standard managerial compensation plans should be modified if the firm wants managers to use the real option approach to make optimal sequential decisions that maximize the firm's long-run performance.

Chapter 2 Key Points

- In general, marketing policies affect the firm's current and future cash flows. Hence marketing policies that maximize current performance may lead to poor long-run results.
- The firm can use the NPV method to determine the long-term effects of its marketing policies.
- The firm's marketing policies for any given product have different effects on the risks and returns that the firm will face in the future. Hence the firm should not use the same discount rates to determine the NPVs from different marketing policies.
- In general, privately and publicly held firms should choose different marketing policies, *even if* they share the same beliefs about how their marketing policies affect long-run cash flows.
- Managers must understand the *marketing-finance interface* in order to choose discount rates and make optimal resource allocation decisions across products and market segments.
- The multiproduct firm should not use the firm's cost of capital for marketing decision making and resource allocation. The discount rates used to value the cash flows from different marketing activities should vary across products. In addition, for any given product it may be necessary to use a segment-specific discount rate that is based on how risky the marketing policy is.
- The standard NPV method can lead to poor marketing decisions because it does not consider the economic benefit to the firm of revising its decisions in the future when new information becomes available.
- The firm should use the real options method to determine the economic value of sequential marketing decisions, after allowing for the effects of competitive reaction.
- Standard managerial compensation plans should be modified if the firm wants managers to use the real options approach to choose and adjust marketing decisions over time to maximize the firm's long-run performance.

II

Defining the Market

3

What is the Impact on Strategy?

Before we can meaningfully discuss marketing decision making, it is necessary to answer a fundamental question: What market is the firm in? Although the question may appear trivial at first glance, the answer is not. Furthermore, the answer has major implications for measuring performance, designing managerial incentive plans, choosing organizational structure, and optimizing resource allocation.

The information covered in this chapter will be useful when you are faced with the following types of decisions:

- How should my firm define the market in which its product competes?
- Who are the firm's competitors?
- Should my firm define its market based on the physical characteristics of its product or on the basis of the product's benefits?
- What does the definition of the market imply about the optimal organizational structure of my firm?
- How should the definition of the market affect the choice of managerial incentive schemes?

The following terms will be introduced in this chapter (see glossary for definitions):

addressable market   game the system   product positioning
definition of market   positioning   served market

▶ 3.1 In What Market Does the Firm Compete?

For any marketing strategy to be effective, the firm needs to correctly *define the market* or industry in which it operates. One common approach is to define the market as consisting of all products with similar physical attributes. This approach, although intuitive, can lead to strategic errors. On the other hand, if the firm defines the market correctly, it can achieve superior results

Example 1: In the early twentieth century, railroad firms in the United States were convinced that they competed in the railroad industry. *They did not realize that they were in the transportation business.* Consequently, they failed to recognize the growing competition from alternative modes of transport, including trucks, airlines, and water transport. This myopic and narrow definition of the market by railroad firms led them to make strategic errors and precipitated a secular decline in the railroad business.

Example 2: Until fairly recently, Coca-Cola defined its market based on the physical characteristics of its beverage products. This led to a strategic error: Coca-Cola concluded that it was in the cola business and failed to recognize the growing competition from such products as bottled water, mineral water, and juices. To address this problem, Coca-Cola has recently diversified its product line by acquiring a number of brands in these product markets.

Example 3: PepsiCo has also committed a similar error in defining its market. When PepsiCo introduced a new clear cola, Crystal Pepsi, it thought it was competing against other cola products. However, it found that it was competing with noncola, clear sodas such as Sprite and 7-Up. Crystal Pepsi failed in the marketplace.

Example 4: When Southwest Airlines was first established, it focused on the intercity travel needs of customers in three cities in Texas: Dallas, San Antonio, and Houston. Prior to the arrival of Southwest Airlines, customers who planned to travel between any two of the aforementioned cities (say, Dallas and Houston) had the option of using several alternative modes of transportation, including driving, rail, bus, and other airlines.

Southwest Airlines realized that it was incorrect to take a product-centric approach and assume that it was in the airline business. Instead, *it recognized that it was in the transportation business (i.e., its competitors were other airlines, road, bus, and rail transportation).* This broad definition of the market led Southwest Airlines to develop a unique marketing strategy (including pricing) that has been extremely successful. To further differentiate itself from the competition, Southwest positioned itself as the "fun" airline by offering entertainment on board.

The results have been dramatic, and Southwest Airlines has grown from a small, unknown regional airline to become one of the largest and most successful airlines in the United States.

Example 5: In the computer chip industry, product quality was defined for many years by one physical attribute: the speed of the chip. Until recently, Intel dominated the computer chip market because its chips were faster than those made by its competitors. However, during the last few years other product characteristics such as multifunctionality and low power consumption have become increasingly important to industries (e.g., the cell phone industry) that use computer chips as components in their products.

AMD recognized that the market definition of product quality had changed and designed its computer chips accordingly. Intel, in contrast, was slow to recognize that the market had changed and continued to define the quality of a computer chip primarily based on speed.

The result was that Intel lost market share to AMD. In addition, because of the structural change in the computer chip industry (product quality was now defined in terms of multiple attributes such as speed, low power consumption, and multifunctionality), Intel had no alternative but to reorganize itself along customer segment lines. Specifically, Intel had to adapt its product line and develop a portfolio of computer chips that were designed to meet the specific needs of different groups of end users. The organizational restructuring costs for Intel in time and money have been very high.

Example 6: Motorola was immensely successful when it introduced the Razr cell phone in 2004. However, since then Motorola was slow to recognize that cell phones were increasingly being used for a nontraditional purpose: to deliver high-speed data. Since Motorola did not recognize that the boundaries of the cell phone industry had changed, it paid insufficient attention to adapting its product line. In July 2007, Motorola announced that sales would be considerably short of earlier projections and forecast a quarterly loss.[1]

Example 7: For many years, Dell successfully used a business model that focused on directly selling desktop PCs to the business segment. Recently, however, the consumer segment and, in particular, the segment that buys notebook computers has grown rapidly.

Because of these major structural changes in the computer market, Dell has had to make significant changes in its organization structure and business model. Thus, in November 2006, Dell set up a dedicated consumer unit that includes marketing, engineering, and industrial design. This is a fundamental shift in Dell's organizational structure, since previously the company's design teams were organized around *product and not customer* segments. In addition, Dell is making fundamental changes to its business model. Specifically, because consumers who buy notebooks often wish to examine notebooks before making a purchase, Dell is now de-emphasizing direct sales and focusing more heavily on retail sales.[2]

> **Fusion for Profit Maxim**
>
> In general, the firm should define its market (industry) based on the similarity of the functions or benefits provided by different products—and not on the basis of their physical attributes. When the market changes, the firm should redefine its market in a timely manner and adjust its marketing policies and strategies accordingly. In particular, the firm may even need to change its organizational structure when the market's definition of product quality changes.

▶ How can the firm define its market in terms of product benefits and functionalities?

In many cases, a firm's competitors can easily or inexpensively imitate the physical attributes that its products contain. However, it is much more difficult for competitors to steal the brand's *positioning*. (We will discuss branding and *product positioning* strategies in depth in chapter 12.)

Example 1: In the automobile market, Volvo successfully positioned itself as the car for safety. Thus, some consumers perceive the Volvo as superior to other brands—*even though the other brands may have similar objective attributes* (e.g., safety features such as an air bag for the driver).

Example 2: In the snack market, perceptions are likely to be very important. For example, consumers may rate Herr's potato chips (a branded product) as superior to those sold under the Acme name (a private label), even though the chips may be made in the same factory, by the same company, and are indistinguishable in every way other than that they are simply sold under different brand names in different packaging.

Example 3: In the aspirin market, many consumers rate the market leader (Bayer) much more highly than generic brands, even though all brands may have identical physical and functional attributes.

> **Fusion for Profit Maxim**
>
> In general, the firm's long-run marketing strategy should focus on *both* physical attributes and product positioning in the minds of consumers.

▶ How can the firm position itself in its defined market in terms of product benefits?

To define markets in terms of product benefits, one has to simultaneously allow for two factors:

1. Product benefits are often unobservable, and
2. Customers have different perceptions about the benefits of any given product.

Depending on the industry, it is also necessary to understand how consumers translate product attribute information into perceived benefits. Sophisticated analysis is necessary to accomplish these objectives.[3] We will discuss empirical methods in chapters 8 and 12.

▲ 3.2 How Does the Definition of the Market Affect the Firm's Marketing Strategy?

The firm's definition of the market has fundamental implications for marketing strategy and resource allocation. For example, many firms use market share as a metric to define their performance and to allocate marketing resources.[4] Suppose the firm defines the industry incorrectly (i.e., either too broadly or too narrowly). Then, the measures of market share will be meaningless. Consequently, the firm will make poor strategic and resource allocation decisions.

Example 1: As discussed earlier, until fairly recently Coca-Cola used a product-centric approach and defined its market too narrowly. Hence, it is quite possible that Coca-Cola may have used inflated measures of market share for strategic decision making and resource allocation.

Example 2: Suppose Lenovo defines the market for its PCs as the market for all PCs. This definition of the market is too broad and will lead to meaningless market shares and poor marketing decision making. A better approach for Lenovo is to first define which segment of the PC market it is targeting (e.g., PCs that are targeted to individual purchasers and that are priced between $500 and $1,000 per unit) and then compute its market shares based on the size of this target segment. The segment that the firm is targeting is known as the *served market* or the *addressable market.*

Fusion for Profit Maxim

When choosing marketing strategy, the firm should define the market (and hence the market share) for its product using the served or addressable market. In general, the firm should not use the overall market to define market share.

▲ Should the firm measure market size in terms of revenue or in terms of volume?

For present purposes, it is sufficient to note that the metric used to measure market size (i.e., revenue or volume) has major strategic implications. Since firms do not charge identical prices for their products, revenue- and volume-based market shares are likely to differ. In addition, they can move in different directions over time. As we discuss in chapter 4, both measures of market share can be useful.

▶ 3.3 How Does the Firm's Definition of the Market Affect Managerial Incentive Schemes?

Many firms use an incentive scheme in which market share is used as *the* key metric for measuring and rewarding performance for managers. If this is the case, managers are likely to *game the system*. Specifically, by defining their markets narrowly, managers can inflate the market shares of the products for which they are responsible. Consequently, by using an incorrect metric, the firm is likely to make suboptimal resource allocation decisions.

Example: In his letter to shareholders in General Electric's annual report for 2000, Jack Welch noted that General Electric's much-vaunted "Be number one or number two in a market" strategy was being undermined by internal constituencies. Managers were defining their markets narrowly to inflate the market shares of their businesses. To address this problem, Welch mandated that his executives define their markets so that their businesses would have 10% or less market share.[5]

Fusion for Profit Maxim

The firm's definition of the market can have a major effect on how managerial performance is measured and rewarded.

We will discuss managerial incentive schemes in detail in chapter 15. In particular, we will discuss the conditions under which market share is a useful metric for long-run performance.

Chapter 3 Key Points

- The firm should define the industry in which it operates in terms of physical attributes and product benefits rather than in terms of either one or the other.
- The *definition of market* has a critical effect on a popular metric used to measure and reward performance: market share. In general, market share should be defined based on the size of the served or addressable market.
- Since the boundaries of an industry change over time, the firm should continuously monitor how demand is changing in the marketplace. This has major implications for strategic decision making, resource allocation, and organizational structure, and for measuring and rewarding managerial performance.
- Sophisticated analysis is necessary to measure the links among product attributes (which are observable) and product benefits (which are unobservable). The results from such analyses are essential for determining which market the firm is in and who its competitors are.
- The firm's definition of the market has a major effect on how managerial performance is measured and rewarded.

Understanding Market Shares

4

Should the Firm Pursue Market Share?

In chapter 3 we discussed the problem of defining the market. In addition, we briefly noted how the particular definition of a market affects the measure of market share. In this chapter, we analyze the conditions under which the firm should pursue market share as a goal. For simplicity, we focus on the single-product firm. Chapter 5 will focus on the multiproduct firm.

In our analysis we shall focus on the determinants of market share and analyze how these factors affect the firm's marketing policy. In particular, we show that it is critical to distinguish between volume-based and revenue-based market share. As in previous chapters, we shall emphasize how to coordinate marketing and financial decision making (i.e., *Fusion for Profit*).

The information covered in this chapter will be useful when you are faced with the following decisions:

- How should my firm measure the market share of its product?
- Is it better to measure market share in terms of revenue or volume?
- Under what conditions does it make sense to pursue market share as an objective?
- Is there a conflict between pursuing market share and maximizing long-run performance?
- How do *cost* and *demand dynamics* affect market share?
- Under what conditions should my firm attempt to be a pioneer in its industry?

• Are there any conditions under which a low market share will lead to an increase in long-run profits?

The following terms will be introduced in this chapter (see glossary for definitions):

asymmetric information
certainty equivalent
channel of distribution
churn rate
Coase paradox
consumer surplus
cost dynamics
demand dynamics
diffusion
discount rate
dynamic pricing policy
exemplar brand
experience curve effect
first-mover advantage theory
fixed costs
grim-trigger pricing strategy

gross revenue
incremental costs
industry standard
installed-base effect
learning curve effect
limit pricing
marginal cost
marginal profit
marginal revenue
optimal profit
perfect price discrimination
pioneering advantage theory
predatory pricing
present value
price skimming
process innovations— major
process innovations— minor

process innovations— moderate
profitability
repeat purchase behavior
reservation price
reservation price effect
reverse engineering
risk-neutral
sample selectivity bias
spillover effects
strategic flexibility
strategic pricing
switching costs
symmetric information
total costs
variable costs
word of mouth

▲ *4.1 Why Do Firms Pursue Market Share?*

Before we begin our analysis, it is necessary to distinguish between volume-based and revenue-based market share. In general, these two measures of market share are not equivalent.

Example 1: Suppose a computer chip manufacturer sells 100,000 chips per month, and the number of chips sold per month by all firms in the industry (including our firm) is 1 million. We say that the firm's volume-based market share is 10% (number of units sold by the firm/number of units sold by the industry as a whole, expressed as a percentage). Suppose all firms in the industry charge the same prices for the computer chip in question. Then, the firm's revenue-based market share will also be 10%. Hence the concept of market share is unambiguous.

Example 2: Suppose General Motors sells 500 Corvette sports cars per month at an average price of $40,000 per car. Let's say that, in aggregate, the Corvette's competitors sell 2,000 sports cars per month at an average price of $35,000 per unit. Then, the Corvette will have a volume-based market share of 20% (number of Corvettes sold/total number of similar sports cars sold by the industry as a whole, including General Motors = 500/2,500). However, since the average price of the Corvette is higher than the average price charged by its competitors, the Corvette's revenue-based market share is higher. Specifically, the Corvette's revenue-based market share is 22.2% (sales revenue from the Corvette/industry sales revenue = [40,000 × 500] / [(40,000 × 500) + (35,000 × 2,000)]).

Fusion for Profit Maxim

When competitors charge different prices for similar products, the concept of market share is ambiguous. Hence it is necessary to distinguish between volume-based and revenue-based market share.

> ◣ *Why do so many firms use revenue-based market share as a performance metric?*

The reason is that many empirical studies have consistently found that *profitability* and revenue-based market share are positively correlated. This consistent set of findings appears to provide strong evidence supporting the use of revenue-based market share to measure performance. However, as we discuss below, this inference may not be correct.

The proportion of new products that fail in the marketplace is high. According to some studies, this proportion can be as high as 80%. Consequently, many empirical studies are biased because they are based on unrepresentative data. That is, the samples overrepresent successful firms and underrepresent firms that have not done well or have gone out of business.

Because of this *sample selectivity bias*, empirical studies find a consistent but spurious positive correlation between revenue-based market share and profitability. When one corrects for sample selectivity bias, the correlation between revenue-based market share and profitability is sharply reduced.

Fusion for Profit Maxim

The strong and consistent positive relationship between revenue-based market share and profitability is spurious.

> ◣ **4.2 Does an Increase in Market Share Lead to Higher Short-Run Profits?**

The answer to this question depends on the firm's cost and demand structures and on whether the firm uses revenue or volume to measure market share. We begin with the case where the firm's current marketing policies do not have any effect on future cost or demand. Furthermore, assume that both demand and cost are predictable. These assumptions will be relaxed later in the chapter.

▶ *Suppose the* incremental costs *of the product are zero (e.g., the product is computer software). Will an improvement in revenue-based market share increase profits?*

By assumption, the firm's *total costs* do not increase when the number of units sold increases. For example, the product sold is software that the consumer can download from the Internet. Since the firm's incremental costs are zero, profits equal revenue less *fixed costs*. Note that the firm's marketing policy affects revenue but not fixed cost. Consequently, any marketing policy that improves revenue (and hence revenue-based market share) will always increase profits.

Fusion for Profit Maxim

If the incremental costs of a product are zero, maximizing profit is equivalent to maximizing revenue-based market share.

▶ *Suppose the incremental costs of the product are positive (e.g., the product is computer hardware). Will an improvement in revenue-based market share lead to an improvement in profit?*

The firm's profits are defined by *gross revenue* less *variable costs* (which are nonzero) less fixed costs. Now, in contrast to the computer software case, the firm's marketing policies affect *both* revenues and total costs. Hence an improvement in market share based on either revenue or volume does not necessarily imply an increase in profits.

Example: Suppose Lenovo's variable cost for manufacturing a basic PC is $100 per unit and the marketing decision variable is price. Let's say that Lenovo can sell 1 million PCs at a price of $300 per unit (Price 1) and 1.6 million units (> 1 million) if it reduces its price to $200 per unit (Price 2). Then, if Lenovo lowers the price from $300 to $200 per PC, its revenue will increase from $300 million to $320 million. This implies that Lenovo's revenue-based market share will increase (table 4.1).

Table 4.1
Lenovo Example: The Effect of Price on Revenue

	Units Sold	Revenue
Price 1 ($300)	1M units	$300,000,000
Price 2 ($200)	1.6M units	$320,000,000

Note that, for this scenario, *both* revenue-based and volume-based market share will increase when Lenovo reduces the price of the PC from $300 to $200 per unit.

▶ **What is the effect of the price decrease on Lenovo's profits?**

When Lenovo decreases the price of its PC from $300 (Price 1) to $200 per unit (Price 2), its revenue increases by $20 million (table 4.2). We say that the *marginal revenue* is $20 million. Since Lenovo sells more units when it reduces the price of its PC, Lenovo's total cost increases by $60 million (number of additional units sold × additional cost per unit). We say that the *marginal cost* is $60 million. Since the increase in cost (marginal cost) is greater than the increase in revenue (marginal revenue), the *marginal profit* is negative (−$40 million). Hence Lenovo's price cut will decrease profits.

Note that Lenovo's profits will fall *even though both its revenue-based and volume-based market shares have increased.*

Fusion for Profit Maxim

Suppose incremental costs are nonzero. Then, an increase in volume-based or revenue-based market share does not necessarily imply an increase in profits.

▶ **What does profit maximization imply about pricing?**

In the Lenovo example, the price cut from $300 to $200 per PC reduced profits because the marginal profit was negative. We now illustrate the following principle: *profit maximization implies that the firm should choose marketing policy such that the marginal profit is zero.*

Table 4.2
Lenovo Example: The Effect of a Price Cut on Profit

	Units sold	Revenue	
Price 1	1,000,000	$300,000,000	
Price 2	1,600,000	$320,000,000	
Additional units sold	600,000		
Marginal revenue			$20,000,000
Additional cost per unit	$100		
Marginal cost			−$60,000,000
Marginal profit			−$40,000,000

Suppose Lenovo is presently charging a price of $300 per PC and is planning a small decrease in price to $297 per unit (a 1% reduction) (table 4.3). Assume that, as a result of the price reduction, the number of Lenovo PCs sold will increase from 1,000,000 units to 1,060,000 (a 2% increase). Then, Lenovo's revenue will increase from $300,000,000 to $314,820,000 after the price reduction.

Note that costs increase by a smaller amount ($6 million) than revenue does ($14,820,000) when the price is reduced (table 4.4). Thus, the marginal profit is $8,820,000 (marginal revenue – marginal cost).
Since the marginal profit is positive, the price cut will increase profits.

▲ **Should Lenovo reduce the price further below $297 per unit?**

Let's say that Lenovo lowers the price of its PC further from $297 to $290 per unit. Suppose the marginal profit from this price reduction is also positive. Then, by reducing the price of its PC from $297 to $290, Lenovo will increase its profits even more.

▲ **Should the price be lowered below $290 per unit?**

Lenovo should continue to lower the price of the PC until the point where the marginal profit becomes zero. At this point, further price cuts will reduce profits (i.e., marginal profits will be negative).

Table 4.3
Lenovo Example: The Effect of a Small Price Cut on Revenue

	Units Sold	Revenue
Price 1 ($300)	1M	$300,000,000
Price 3 ($297)	1.06M	$314,820,000

Table 4.4
Lenovo Example: The Effect of a Small Price Cut on Profit

	Units sold	Revenue	
Price 1	1,000,000	$300,000,000	
Price 3	1,060,000	$314,820,000	
Additional units sold	60,000		
Marginal revenue			$14,820,000
Additional Cost per Unit	$100		
Marginal cost			−$6,000,000
Marginal profit			$8,820,000

> **Fusion for Profit Maxim**
>
> To maximize short-run profits, the firm should set the price of its product such that the marginal profit is zero.

▶ What does profit maximization imply about market share?

As discussed, profit maximization implies that marginal profit (marginal revenue—marginal cost) is zero. But *marginal cost is generally positive.*[1] Hence marginal revenue must be positive. This implies that, when the firm chooses the optimal pricing policy, further price reductions will increase revenue (and hence revenue-based market share). *Thus, except for the special case where marginal costs are zero, the price that maximizes short-run profits cannot maximize revenue-based market share.*

> **Fusion for Profit Maxim**
>
> Maximizing short-run profits is incompatible with maximizing revenue-based market share. The price that maximizes the firm's current profits is *always* higher than the price that maximizes the firm's revenue-based market share.

▶ 4.3 When Does an Increase in Market Share Lead to Higher Long-Run Profits?

The previous analysis assumed that the firm's marketing policies do not have any long-run effects. As we have shown, this scenario implies that the firm should focus on maximizing short-run profits and not even consider market share as a metric. However, in many cases, the firm's current marketing policies are likely to affect its future cost and demand. We distinguish two scenarios:

1. Suppose the firm's marketing policies affect future demand. For example, some of the firm's current customers will purchase the firm's product again in the future. In this case, we say that demand dynamics are present.
2. Suppose the firm's current marketing policies affect the firm's future costs. Then, we say that cost dynamics are present.

For example, by producing more units in the short run, the firm will become more efficient in the future (i.e., future production costs will decline). Note that cost dynamics (often known as the *experience curve effect* or the *learning curve effect*) do not pertain only to manufacturing. There are many other sources of cost dynamics (e.g., information management, advertising, and channels of distribution).

As we discuss below, if either cost or demand dynamics are strong, it may be desirable for the firm to forgo some current profits by pursuing current volume-based market share in order to make higher profits in the future.[2]

Example: A key component of Amazon's strategy was the anticipated benefit from cost dynamics in information management. Specifically, Amazon's strategy was to build volume-based market share and sacrifice short-run profits. Thus, Amazon's business model was based on the premise that, by leveraging cost dynamics, Amazon would be able to reduce its future costs and hence increase its future profits. Initially, the stock market reacted very positively, and Amazon's stock price soared. However, when the anticipated increases in future profits were not forthcoming, Amazon's stock price fell.

Fusion for Profit Maxim

Building volume-based market share in the presence of cost dynamics does not guarantee an increase in long-run profits.

Point to consider.   "Our fixed costs are very high. Since average costs decrease with volume, we should attempt to maximize volume-based market share."

By assumption, the firm's marketing policies do not affect either future cost or future revenue. *Since there are no cost or demand dynamics, the firm should maximize short-run profits.* This implies that the firm should not pursue volume-based market share—even though current unit costs fall sharply with current volume.

Point to consider.   Suppose raw materials account for a significant proportion of a firm's costs. Should the firm pursue market share if it can obtain quantity discounts on raw material purchases? Assume that there are no demand dynamics.

A quantity-discount schedule only implies that the firm's *current* cost structure is affected by the firm's *current* volume. However, this does not imply that cost dynamics are present. Since neither cost nor demand dynamics are present, the firm should focus on maximizing short-run profits and not pursue either revenue-based or volume-based market share.

Example: Suppose there are two firms facing identical demand conditions: one firm (Inside-Line Inc.) can obtain quantity discounts on raw material purchases, and the other (Looking-In Co.) cannot.

Suppose Looking-In has a constant marginal cost of $10 per unit and maximizes profits by charging a price of $20 per unit. Then, at the profit-maximizing price (and volume), Looking-In's marginal profit will be zero. Hence Looking-In's marginal revenue must equal marginal cost ($10 per unit).

Suppose Inside-Line charges the same price as Looking-In ($20 per unit). Then, it will also obtain a marginal revenue of $10 per unit. *However,* *its marginal costs are less than $10 per unit because it can obtain quantity discounts.* This implies that, at a price of $20 per unit, Inside-Line's marginal profits are positive. Hence Inside-Line should reduce prices below $20 per unit and sell a larger volume.

As this example shows:

- The firm that can obtain quantity discounts will obtain a higher volume-based market share, and
- The firm that can obtain quantity discounts will obtain a higher revenue-based market share.

Fusion for Profit Maxim

If the firm can obtain quantity discounts on the purchase of raw materials, it will obtain a higher volume-based *and* a higher revenue-based market share than a firm that faces the same market conditions and pays fixed prices for its raw materials. However, the higher market shares are *outcomes* of profit maximization and *not objectives*.

▶ 4.4 Should the Firm Enter High-Growth Markets?

Many firms believe that it is a good idea to enter high-growth markets. Although this strategy is intuitively appealing, it may not be optimal.

Example: In the 1990s, Dell entered the retail sector for PCs because this segment was growing rapidly. However, this distribution channel was inconsistent with Dell's business model. In the past, Dell's successful strategy had been based on building customized PCs according to customer specifications and holding minimum inventory of finished products. In contrast, the retail segment sold standardized PCs primarily on the basis of price; in addition, retailers had to invest fairly heavily in inventory. *Since the retail channel was incompatible with Dell's business model, Dell's profits fell even though its market share (based on revenue and volume) increased.* Dell recognized this strategic error and withdrew from the retail channel in a matter of months.

Point to consider. The Chinese packaged goods industry is growing rapidly. Is China an attractive market for foreign multinationals in the packaged goods sector?

The Chinese market is growing rapidly, but the market is highly uncertain. For example, many foreign multinationals are unfamiliar with the channels of distribution in China and have a limited understanding of consumer behavior in that country. Thus, it does not follow that investing in the packaged goods sector in China will lead to high profitability—even though the market is growing rapidly.

Fusion for Profit Maxim

Before entering a high-growth market, the firm should evaluate how demand and cost uncertainty will affect its cash flows. In addition, the firm should enter only high-growth markets that are compatible with its business model and strategy.

▲ 4.5 Should the Firm Pursue Market Share in a High-Growth Market?

The answer to this question depends on whether and in what way the firm's marketing policies affect the growth rate of the market.

Example 1: Suppose the market growth rate for a product depends on factors outside the firm's control (e.g., the influx of population to a given geographical area). Then, other factors being the same, since the firm cannot influence the market growth rate, it should maximize short-run profits and not focus on market share (either revenue-based or volume-based). Note that the firm will need to revise its marketing policies from period to period based on the size of the market at that time. Hence the market growth rate is extremely relevant for marketing decision making. However, *the optimal marketing strategy for the firm is to focus on maximizing current profits period by period.*[3]

Fusion for Profit Maxim

If the firm's marketing policies do not affect the growth rate of the market, the firm should focus on short-run profits and not on market share (revenue-based or volume-based).

Example 2: Suppose the market growth rate depends on the firm's marketing policies such as price and advertising. For example, suppose Samsung introduces a new type of cell phone with increased capacity to download music and video from the Internet. Then, one strategy for Samsung is to increase its volume-based market share in the short run by charging a low introductory price and advertising heavily. This strategy will stimulate *word-of-mouth* activity and hence can increase future demand for Samsung's cell phone. By pursuing this low-price/high-advertising strategy, Samsung will sacrifice some current profits in exchange for higher future profits. This is an example of demand dynamics. Given our assumptions, it is reasonable for Samsung to focus on volume-based market share in the short run.

> **Fusion for Profit Maxim**
>
> If the firm's marketing policies affect future demand, current volume-based market share can be a useful proxy of future profits.

Example 3: A consortium of companies that makes radio-based identification tags, scanners, and related software recently announced that its members planned to pool their patents in order to provide one-stop licensing and royalty management. The goal was to stimulate the growth of the radio frequency identification (RFID) industry. A similar strategy has been used in the past by firms in the DVD industry and in the development of products that use the MPEG-2 standard for encoding audio and video programming.[4]

In this case, the optimal strategy for each firm in the industry is to stimulate the market growth rate (hence increasing its future profitability) rather than to focus on market share. The intuition is straightforward: it is generally more profitable to obtain a small share of a large market than to obtain the lion's share of a much smaller market.

> **Fusion for Profit Maxim**
>
> Under certain conditions, firms should cooperate with each other to increase the market growth rate instead of attempting to gain market share.

▲ 4.6 Should the Firm Attempt to Increase Its Volume-Based Market Share in the Short Run When Cost Dynamics Are Present?

As discussed below, a number of conditions must be satisfied for a volume-based market share strategy based on cost dynamics to maximize long-run performance. We will use the following definition in our analysis: the firm uses *strategic pricing* if it pursues a volume-based market share strategy that forgoes some current profits in order to obtain higher profits in the future.

The Discount Rate

When the firm leverages cost dynamics, it trades off current profits for an increase in future profits based on future cost reductions. Hence the *discount rate* is critical. Suppose the discount rate is very high. Then, the *present value* of the anticipated gain from future cost reductions via cost dynamics will be *smaller* than the loss in current profits. Hence the firm should maximize current profits and not pursue volume-based market share.

Fusion for Profit Maxim

The firm's long-term gain from leveraging cost dynamics depends on the discount rate. If the discount rate is sufficiently high, the firm should focus on short-run profits and not on volume-based market share.

Uncertainty of Learning Effects

A volume-based market share strategy implicitly assumes that the firm has a good idea about how current volume will affect future costs and hence future profits. That is, the learning curve is predictable.

Example: Suppose an auto manufacturer has developed a new car engine that is based on a refinement of existing methods for making gasoline-powered cars.

▶ *Should the auto manufacturer pursue a volume-based market share strategy?*

In this case, the learning curve is likely to be fairly predictable. Since the uncertainty of the future benefits from the learning curve is low, it may be optimal for the manufacturer to pursue volume-based market share in order to improve future production efficiency and to increase future profits.

Point to consider.   What if the learning curve is not predictable?

Example 1: Suppose an auto manufacturer has developed a new car engine that is based on a radically new technology: the car can run on hydrogen. Since the technology is radical, the future cost reductions that the firm can achieve via the learning curve are likely to be highly uncertain. If this uncertainty is sufficiently high, the firm should focus on maximizing current profits rather than on pursuing market share, *even if the firm is risk-neutral* (i.e., the firm is not concerned about the volatility of profits).[5]

Example 2: During the 1990s, many firms flocked to the Internet as a *channel of distribution*. Specifically, they priced strategically, hoping to benefit from anticipated future cost reductions via the experience curve. However, since the Internet industry was new, the experience curve was highly uncertain. Hence, for many firms, the anticipated gains in future profits (from increased volume by using the Internet as the channel of distribution) did not materialize. Many Internet firms failed because they attempted to build volume-based market share instead of focusing on short-run profits.

> **Fusion for Profit Maxim**
>
> The benefits from a strategy that is based on leveraging cost dynamics will be reduced when the learning curve is uncertain. If the learning curve is sufficiently uncertain, the firm should focus on short-run profits instead of on volume-based market share.

Spillover Effects

The volume-based market-share strategy implicitly assumes that all knowledge is proprietary to the firm. This may not be the case. Suppose the firm prices strategically to benefit from the experience curve. However, its trained employees leave to join other firms. We say that there are *spillover effects*.

Since the firm's knowledge is no longer proprietary, it will not have a cost advantage over competitors in the future. Consequently, the anticipated long-run strategic benefits to the firm via cost reductions will not occur. Hence it is suboptimal for the firm to pursue volume-based market share.

Technology Shifts

The volume-based market-share strategy implicitly assumes that technology is static. This may not be the case. Suppose the manufacturing technology improves in the future. Then, firms that play the volume-based market share game may find that they have invested heavily in technology that becomes obsolete in the future. In contrast, firms that enter later will have access to the superior technology and will be more cost-efficient. Under these conditions, it is a poor strategy for the firm to invest heavily in the extant production technology and pursue volume-based market share.

> **Fusion for Profit Maxim**
>
> If demand and cost or technological uncertainty are high or spillover effects are significant, the firm should not pursue a volume-based market share strategy.

Point to consider.   Suppose the firm has developed a superior technological process for making its product and there is a learning curve in manufacturing. What is the effect on the firm's volume-based and revenue-based market shares? Assume that the old production process does not involve any learning.

Since the new technological process involves a learning curve, in general the firm should forgo some current profits in order to achieve future cost reductions. This implies that the firm will reduce the price of its product when it introduces the new process. Consequently, the firm's volume (and hence volume-based market share) will always increase (figure 4.1). However, the effect on the firm's revenue-based market share is more interesting.

Since the old technology does not involve any learning, the firm currently prices its product such that the marginal profit (marginal revenue – marginal cost) is zero. In figure 4.1, the current volume is given by OD.[6] We now distinguish three scenarios: minor, major, and moderate *process innovations*.

1. If the process innovation is *minor*, the benefits from future cost reductions by expanding current volume will be low. Hence the firm will not increase its current volume significantly. As shown in figure 4.1, the firm will increase its production by a small amount, say from OD

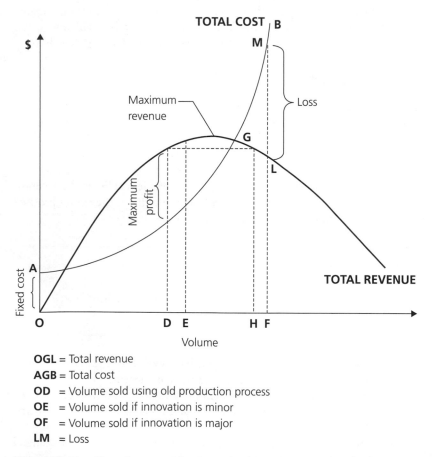

OGL = Total revenue
AGB = Total cost
OD = Volume sold using old production process
OE = Volume sold if innovation is minor
OF = Volume sold if innovation is major
LM = Loss

Figure 4.1 The effect of a new production technology on current-period volume, revenue, and cost.

to OE. Thus, the firm's revenue (and hence its revenue-based market share) will increase.

2. If the process innovation is *major*, the incremental benefits from future cost reductions by expanding current volume will be large. Hence the firm will increase its current volume sharply from OD to OF, say. Note that the firm will need to charge extremely low prices in order to achieve this increase in volume. Consequently, the firm's revenue (and hence its revenue-based market share) will fall. Note that the firm is actually willing to make a loss in the current period (ML in figure 4.1) in order to increase future profits.

3. If the process innovation is *moderate*, volume will increase as in the cases where the process innovation is minor or major. However, the effects on revenue (and hence on revenue-based market share) are ambiguous. In figure 4.1, if the new volume is less than OH, the revenue-based market share will increase. However, if the new volume is greater than OH, the revenue-based market share will fall.

Fusion for Profit Maxim

If the firm introduces a new production process involving a learning curve, it should always increase its current volume-based market share. However, the effect on the firm's current revenue-based market share depends on whether the innovation is minor, major, or moderate.

▲ 4.7 Should the Firm Pursue Volume-Based Market Share When Demand Dynamics Are Present?

Suppose the firm's current pricing policy affects future demand. We say that there are demand dynamics. As discussed below, there are different sources of demand dynamics, and each has a different effect on the firm's current volume-based market share.

Installed Base Effect

If the willingness to pay of future consumers for the firm's product depends on the number of consumers who already have that product, we say that there is an *installed base effect*. In this case, the firm should build short-run volume (and hence increase its volume-based market share) to increase future demand and profits.

Example: Suppose Nokia introduces a new type of cell phone with a variety of new features. Then, future consumers may be willing to pay higher prices if the number of current users (the "installed base") is large. Consequently, by increasing current volume (and necessarily compromising current profits to some degree), Nokia will increase future demand. Hence, in this case, *volume-based market share is a good proxy for future profitability.*

Repeat Purchase Behavior

Suppose a firm sells a frequently purchased product, say soap. Then, the firm should choose its current pricing policy after considering the effects of demand dynamics.

Example: Suppose Crest introduces a new flavor of toothpaste into the marketplace. Since consumers purchase toothpaste regularly, it may be optimal for Crest to build volume-based market share in order to generate repeat business (and profits) in the future.

Switching Costs

The firm should choose its current policy after considering consumers' *switching costs* in shifting their purchases to another firm. These costs may be financial or psychological.

Example 1: SAP is one of the major software suppliers to industry. Consider any SAP customer whose IT department is presently using SAP's software. Since the customer will incur considerable time and expense in retraining its IT employees to use different software (say Oracle's competing software), it will incur considerable switching costs if it changes its vendors. Consequently, SAP should focus on building volume-based market share in order to increase its long-run profits.

Example 2: Many consumers who purchase low-involvement products such as shampoo may not wish to switch brands because of inertia. In other words, the psychological cost of switching is high. In such cases, the firm should focus on building volume-based market share to increase future profits.

Example 3: During the 1990s, many large telephone companies such as AT&T attempted to build their volume-based market shares by issuing checks that consumers could redeem only when they switched to their service. However, this strategy was flawed, since consumers' switching costs were low. In AT&T's case, consumers simply switched back to other carriers when the other carriers replicated AT&T's strategy. The result was that, although AT&T increased its volume-based market share in the short run, its long-run profits fell.

Fusion for Profit Maxim

If switching costs are high, the firm should focus on increasing volume-based market share. However, if switching costs are low, the firm should focus on current profits.

Churn Rate

The *churn rate* measures the rate at which current subscribers (users) to a service defect to other suppliers. Thus, *if the churn rate is high, the firm should focus more heavily on current profits than on long-run profits and volume-based market share.*[7] Of course, a better long-run approach for the firm is to determine what factors determine the churn rate, develop marketing strategies to lower the churn rate (e.g., by providing better service), and focus on long-run profits.

Example: XM Satellite Radio Holdings more than doubled the number of its subscribers during the 2004–2005 period. However, the churn rate was constant at 1.4%.[8] Since the churn rate was almost zero, roughly speaking, long-term profits would have approximately doubled as a result of market growth. Suppose, however, that the churn rate (subscribers defecting from XM Satellite Radio Holdings to competitors) had increased as a result of market growth. Let's say that the churn rate had increased to 5% over the period. Then, the gain in future profits to XM Satellite Radio Holdings by pricing low to build current volume would have been reduced. Hence the optimal policy for the firm would have been to focus more heavily on current profits than on volume-based market share.

Word of Mouth and Diffusion

Suppose word-of-mouth effects are significant. Then, it is worthwhile for the firm to price low in order to stimulate future demand via *diffusion*. Hence the firm should build volume-based market share in order to increase future profits.

Fusion for Profit Maxim

If demand dynamics are strong, the firm should focus on building volume-based market share in the short run.

▶ *4.8 Should the Firm Pursue Market Share If Neither Cost Nor Demand Dynamics Are Present?*

Suppose the firm does not have either cost or demand dynamics. Are there any conditions under which the firm should pursue market share?

In general, firms should not pursue market share unless cost and/or demand dynamics are present. However, there are two important exceptions: *limit pricing* and *predatory pricing.*

Limit Pricing

Suppose potential competitors are not well informed about the industry cost and demand structures. For example, suppose they use the price charged by the first mover as a proxy of the profit potential of the emerging industry.

For this scenario, the prudent strategy for the first mover may be to charge a price that is *lower* than the price that maximizes short-run profits. Since this price is "low," potential competitors will conclude that the industry is not highly profitable. Hence they will not enter the industry. This entry deterrence strategy is known as limit pricing.

Note that, since neither cost nor demand dynamics are present (by assumption), limit pricing implies that the first mover's volume-based market share will always be *higher* than the volume-based market share that the first mover would have obtained if it had maximized profits period by period. In addition, limit pricing will always *increase* the first mover's revenue-based market share.

▶ *Are there any conditions under which limit pricing will not be successful?*

Limit pricing implicitly assumes that there is *asymmetric information* across firms. That is, the first mover has superior information about the industry cost and demand structures than potential competitors. Furthermore, it is expensive for potential entrants to obtain cost and demand information. As we discuss below, limit pricing will not succeed if these conditions do not hold.

Asymmetric Information

Suppose potential competitors are well informed and have the same information as the first mover does about cost and demand structures in the emerging industry. Given this scenario of *symmetric information*, the first mover's current policy (e.g., whether to pursue current market share or to maximize current profits) will have no effect on competitors' decisions on whether to enter the industry. Consequently, since there are no cost or demand dynamics (by assumption), the optimal strategy for the first mover is to focus on short-run profits and to maximize profits (after adjusting for risk) period by period.

Reverse Engineering and Market Research

In many cases, potential competitors may be able to estimate the first mover's cost structure fairly accurately by using a tactic known as *reverse engineering*. That is, competitors can disassemble the firm's product and hence estimate the first mover's production costs (e.g., the costs of the individual components contained in the product and other assembly and manufacturing costs). In addition, competitors may be able to conduct market research studies to estimate the demand structure of the industry (e.g., the willingness to pay of customers).

Given this cost and demand information, potential competitors will not need to use proxies (e.g., the first mover's price) to estimate the future profitability of the industry. Hence limit pricing will be ineffective in deterring competitive entry.

Predatory Pricing

Consider an industry in which there are a few firms that produce highly similar products. Suppose one firm (the "cost-efficient" firm) has a lower cost structure than the others. Then, one strategy for the cost-efficient firm is to charge a price that is lower than the variable cost(s) of its competitors—a strategy known as predatory pricing.

Given this predatory pricing strategy, competitors will be unable to cover their variable costs. Hence they will be forced to leave the industry. Consequently, the net result is that the predator will become a monopolist in the future and earn high long-run profits.

Note that *both* limit pricing and predatory pricing imply that high current market share (volume-based) will lead to high future profits, *even though there are no cost or demand dynamics.*

▶ **Are there any conditions under which predatory pricing will not be successful?**

Predatory pricing does not guarantee that the predator's long-run profits will increase. Thus, the predator may face antitrust litigation by the government for restricting competition.

Firms that are more efficient than the predator could acquire the inefficient firms that are forced to leave the industry; in addition, the acquiring firms may have more financial resources than the predator. If the acquiring firms are able to produce at lower cost than the predator (e.g., those firms are likely to invest in R&D that will allow them to produce more efficiently), the predator may be forced to leave the industry in the future.

Suppose the less-efficient firms are market leaders in other product categories or geographical markets that the predator plans to enter. Then, predatory pricing could reduce the predator's performance overall. Specifically, those competitors are likely to retaliate sharply when the predator attempts to enter the markets in which they are strong. Hence, the firm will win in the current market by using predatory pricing but lose heavily in new markets.

▶ **Suppose predatory pricing is not feasible. What alternative strategies can the firm use to increase long-run profits?**

Suppose the cost-efficient firm does not wish to pursue a predatory pricing, perhaps because of potential antitrust litigation in the future. Then, the firm can use the following strategy to increase its long-run profits: act as a price leader and set price high enough so that an inefficient (high-cost) firm *can* survive in the industry.

Suppose a competitor attempts to increase its profits by underpricing the leader ("cheating"). Then, the cost-efficient firm can impose a heavy penalty on the cheater by lowering its price below the cheater's variable cost per unit. When this happens, the cheater will be forced to leave the industry. Not surprisingly, this price-leadership policy by the cost-efficient firm is known as a *grim-trigger pricing strategy.*

Note that a number of conditions must hold for grim-trigger pricing strategy to work. The leader should be able to detect whether a competitor has failed to cooperate and lowered its price below the leader's price ("cheated"). This is difficult to do when the industry demand is uncertain (e.g., demand is cyclical). In addition, it is necessary that the managers of competing firms have a sufficiently long horizon. This condition may not hold.

For example, suppose the manager of a competing firm is rewarded based on short-term metrics (e.g., bonus payments that depend on the extent to which short-run profits exceed some target level for profits). If this is the case, the firm's competitors will have a strong incentive to charge low prices ("cheat") in order to increase their short-term profits. Hence the leader's grim-trigger pricing strategy will not be successful.

Fusion for Profit Maxim

Limit pricing and predatory pricing can be effective strategic tools even if there are no cost or demand dynamics.

▶ 4.9 Should the Firm Pursue Market Share by Being the Pioneer in Its Industry?

Many firms seek to be the pioneers in their industry. This strategy is based on the *first-mover/pioneering advantage theory*—a theory that argues that, *in general, firms will be successful in the long run if they are the first entrants in an industry.* One implication of this theory is that firms should pursue market share when they introduce new products into the marketplace. We will discuss both the empirical and the theoretical rationales for this theory.

Empirical Arguments Supporting the First-Mover Advantage Theory

Researchers have found that, in many industries, first movers are more profitable in the long run than late entrants.

▶ *Does this finding imply that all firms should be first movers?*

This conclusion does not follow. *We do not know the history of first movers that were unsuccessful and were forced to leave the industry.* Because of this sample selectivity bias, the observed positive correlation between first movers and profitability in any given industry is inflated.

Theoretical Arguments Supporting the First-Mover Advantage Theory

A number of theoretical arguments have been offered in support of the pioneering advantage theory. We first present these arguments and then discuss the conditions under which they are valid.

Cost and Demand Dynamics

Suppose there are strong cost or demand dynamics. For example, by increasing volume early on, the firm can accumulate experience and become more efficient in the future (cost dynamics). Alternatively, by generating higher volume for a new product early on, the firm will stimulate future sales and increase future profits via *repeat purchase behavior* and word-of-mouth activity (demand dynamics). According to this argument, if these cost and demand dynamics effects are significant, the first mover will have an advantage over late entrants.

Exemplar Brand

Suppose the first mover's product becomes the *industry standard*. We say that the first mover's product is an *exemplar brand*. Then, the first mover will have an advantage because late entrants will be forced to compare their products to the pioneer's product on an attribute-by-attribute basis or on the basis of the benefits provided by the pioneer's product.

Strategic Flexibility

The pioneering firm has *strategic flexibility* and can adjust its policy over time as new information becomes available. (You may wish to review the discussion on real options in chapter 2 for more details.) For instance, if the pioneering product succeeds, the firm can launch a whole new product line based on the initial product that was marketed.

Example: Apple introduced the iPod and, based on the success of this product, introduced new product-line extensions based on the iPod.

The theoretical arguments discussed above suggest that it may be optimal for the firm to be a first mover. However, *these conditions do not always hold.*

Demand and Product Improvements

Suppose demand is highly uncertain (e.g., the industry standard for the product is fluid) or consumers' switching costs are low. Alternatively, suppose late entrants are able to benefit from future improvements in technology or by learning from the mistakes of early entrants. Under any of these conditions, the optimal strategy for the firm may be to exercise strategic flexibility by waiting until the uncertainty is resolved before it enters a given market.

Example: Toyota and Acura have done well in the SUV market even though they were late entrants.

Cost and Technological Uncertainty

Suppose any combination of the following conditions holds: the learning curve is uncertain, learning is not proprietary, technology is changing rapidly, and investment in the pioneering product is highly specific (e.g., the salvage value of a plant to manufacture the new product is close to zero if the product fails). Then, the late entrant may have an advantage over the pioneer.

Fusion for Profit Maxim

The firm should attempt to be the first mover in an industry *only* if certain cost and demand conditions are satisfied. The empirical correlation between being a first mover and profitability is inflated because the data sets analyzed do not include many first movers that have attempted to be pioneers and have failed.

▲ 4.10 Is It Ever Optimal for the Firm to Keep Its Volume-Based Market Share Low?

The previous discussion has focused on cases where the optimal strategy for the firm is to build its volume-based market share in the short run. However, under certain conditions, the optimal policy for the firm may be to keep its volume-based market share low.

Example: Suppose IBM has developed and patented a new handheld computer that can perform multiple functions. For simplicity, suppose there are three consumer segments of equal size (1 million). Let's say that the maximum amounts (*reservation prices*) that these consumers are willing to pay for IBM's new handheld computer are as follows:

1. Segment A's reservation price (RP) for the new handheld computer is $1,000 per consumer,

2. Segment B's reservation price for the new handheld computer is $600 per consumer, and
3. Segment C's reservation price for the new handheld computer is $500 per consumer.

Assume that IBM's marginal cost of producing each handheld computer is constant and equals $200 per unit. Furthermore, each consumer will either buy one unit or not make a purchase (table 4.5).

Suppose IBM charges all consumers the same prices. Then, IBM will charge a price of $500 per handheld computer, sell to all three segments, and make a profit of $900 million (see table 4.5).

Is this pricing strategy optimal?

To answer this question, we need to introduce a new concept: *consumer surplus*. This quantity measures the net gain to a consumer from purchase and is defined as the difference between that consumer's reservation price (RP) and the price paid. If IBM charges all customers a price of $500 per unit, the consumer surplus amounts for consumers in each segment are as shown in table 4.6.

Note that, if IBM charges $500 per unit, consumers, in aggregate, obtain a net benefit (consumer surplus) of $600 million. Thus, the total dollar value of the money "on the table" is $600 million.

Table 4.5
IBM Example: Comparison of Different Pricing Strategies

Segment	RP	Units sold	Marginal revenue	Marginal cost	Marginal profit
Price = $1,000					
A	$1,000	1,000,000	$1,000,000,000	$200,000,000	$800,000,000
B	$600	0	$0	$0	$0
C	$500	0	$0	$0	$0
Total		1,000,000	$1,000,000,000	$200,000,000	$800,000,000
Price = $600					
A	$1,000	1,000,000	$600,000,000	$200,000,000	$400,000,000
B	$600	1,000,000	$600,000,000	$200,000,000	$400,000,000
C	$500	0	$0	$0	$0
Total		2,000,000	$1,200,000,000	$400,000,000	$800,000,000
Price = $500					
A	$1,000	1,000,000	$500,000,000	$200,000,000	$300,000,000
B	$600	1,000,000	$500,000,000	$200,000,000	$300,000,000
C	$500	1,000,000	$500,000,000	$200,000,000	$300,000,000
Total		3,000,000	$1,500,000,000	$600,000,000	$900,000,000

Note: RP, reservation price.

Table 4.6
IBM Example: The Effect of Uniform Pricing

Segment	RP	Price paid	Consumer surplus per customer	Total consumer surplus
A	$1,000	$500	$500	$500,000,000
B	$600	$500	$100	$100,000,000
C	$500	$500	$0	$0
Total				$600,000,000

Note: Each segment consists of 1M customers. RP, reservation price per customer. Consumer surplus per customer = RP − price paid.

Table 4.7
IBM Example: The Effect of Perfect Price Discrimination

Segment	RP	Units sold	Revenue	Marginal cost	Marginal profit
A	$1,000	1,000,000	$1,000,000,000	$200,000,000	$800,000,000
B	$600	1,000,000	$600,000,000	$200,000,000	$400,000,000
C	$500	1,000,000	$500,000,000	$200,000,000	$300,000,000
Total		3,000,000	$2,100,000,000	$600,000,000	$1,500,000,000

Note: RP, reservation price.

▲ *What pricing strategy should IBM use to increase its profits?*

Suppose *perfect price discrimination* is feasible. Then, IBM can set prices so that each segment pays its reservation price (i.e., all consumer surpluses will be zeros (table 4.7).

Note that IBM's *optimal profit* is $1,500 million—the sum of the profits from the "myopic" policy that maximizes short-run profits ($900 million) and the total consumer surplus if IBM uses the myopic policy ($600 million).

Fusion for Profit Maxim

Perfect price discrimination allows the firm to maximize its profits by eliminating the consumer surpluses from each market segment.

▲ *Suppose that, for legal or other reasons, IBM cannot use the price discrimination strategy described above. Can IBM achieve the same results by using an alternative pricing strategy?*

Assume for simplicity that the discount rate is zero (i.e., the long-run profit is the sum of the profits in different time periods). As before, consumers will either purchase one unit or purchase nothing (table 4.8).

Table 4.8
IBM Example: The Effect of Price Discrimination over Time

Segment	RP	Units purchased	Revenue	Cost	Profit
Period 1					
A	$1,000	1,000,000	$1,000,000,000	$200,000,000	$800,000,000
B	$600	0	$0	$0	$0
C	$500	0	$0	$0	$0
Total		1,000,000	$1,000,000,000	$200,000,000	$800,000,000
Period 2					
A	$1,000	0	$0	$0	$0
B	$600	1,000,000	$600,000,000	$200,000,000	$400,000,000
C	$500	0	$0	$0	$0
Total		1,000,000	$600,000,000	$200,000,000	$400,000,000
Period 3					
A	$1,000	0	$0	$0	$0
B	$600	0	$0	$0	$0
C	$500	1,000,000	$500,000,000	$200,000,000	$300,000,000
Total		1,000,000	$500,000,000	$200,000,000	$300,000,000
Total profit					$1,500,000,000

Note: RP, reservation price.

Consider the following *dynamic pricing policy*:

1. In the first period, IBM charges a price of $1,000 per unit,
2. In the second period, IBM reduces the price to $600 per unit, and
3. In the third period, IBM reduces the price to $500 per unit.

Note that IBM's long-run profit under this strategy ($1,500 million) is the same as the profit that it could have obtained via a price discrimination strategy. This pricing policy is known as *price skimming*.

Fusion for Profit Maxim

Price skimming is price discrimination over time. Given this strategy, the firm forgoes short-run volume- and revenue-based market share in order to obtain increased profits in the long run.

Point to consider.   In the IBM example, suppose IBM's future costs are uncertain. Should IBM use a price-skimming approach? For simplicity, assume that the reservation prices are known with certainty.

Suppose IBM's expected marginal cost of making handheld computers in the second period is $200 per unit. That is, the marginal cost per unit could be lower or higher than $200 per unit. Since IBM's stockholders are risk-averse, the *certainty equivalent* of this marginal cost will be greater than $200 per unit.

Suppose this certainty equivalent is $250. This implies that, for any pricing policy in the second period, the certainty-equivalent profit margin will be reduced. In other words, the benefits from price skimming will be reduced. Indeed, if the cost uncertainty is sufficiently large, the optimal policy for IBM may be to focus on short-run profits.

Fusion for Profit Maxim

If future costs are uncertain, the gain from price skimming is reduced.

The Discount Rate

Other conditions being equal, price skimming leads to higher *total* profits than alternative pricing strategies. However, a price-skimming strategy may not maximize long-run performance because it changes the timings of the firm's profits (i.e., the firm reduces its short-term profits in exchange for higher long-run profits). *If the discount rate is sufficiently high, the present value of the gains from higher profits in the future will be less than the loss in current profits.* Under these conditions, short-run profit maximization can be superior to price skimming.

Point to consider.   The demand for many high-tech products is highly uncertain. Hence firms in these industries face high discount rates. Since high discount rates mean that future profits are less valuable, why do firms in high-tech industries use price-skimming strategies?

As discussed above, other conditions being the same, high discount rates will reduce the gain to the firm from price skimming (the *discount rate effect*). On the other hand, the reservation prices for high-tech products tend to vary considerably across consumers (the *reservation price effect*). Hence, other conditions being the same, the reservation price effect will increase the gain to the high-tech firm from using a price-skimming strategy.

Note that the discount rate effect and the reservation price effect act in opposite directions. In general, since consumers' reservation prices for a high-tech product (e.g., the iPhone) vary considerably in the population, the reservation price effect is likely to be stronger than the discount rate effect. The net result is that firms in high-tech industries will often gain by using price-skimming strategies.

Competitive Entry

We return to the IBM example. Suppose IBM uses a skimming approach and charges a price of $1,000 per unit in the first period. Then, Segment A

Table 4.9
IBM Example: The Effect of Competitive Entry (Period 1)

Segment	RP	No. of units purchased	Revenue	Cost	Profit
A	$1,000	1,000,000	$1,000,000,000	$200,000,000	$800,000,000
B	$600	0	$0	$0	$0
C	$500	0	$0	$0	$0
Total		1,000,000	$1,000,000,000	$200,000,000	$800,000,000

Note: RP, reservation price.

will buy the product, and Segments B and C will remain in the market in the second period. Thus, IBM will make a profit of $800 million in the first period (table 4.9).

Suppose a new entrant is able to clone IBM's product (e.g., by using reverse engineering) and enters the market in the second period. *To highlight the effect of competitive entry, assume that the new entrant is much less efficient than IBM.* Specifically, the new entrant's marginal cost of production ($400 per unit) is double that of the corresponding cost for IBM ($200 per unit).

▶ *What will happen in the second period?*

Consumers in Segment B (RP = $600) and in Segment C (RP = $500) are still in the market in the second period. Hence, the new entrant will underprice IBM in the second period *even though the competitor has a higher cost structure than IBM.* Specifically, by charging a price just below $500 per unit, the new entrant will be able to sell to *both* Segments B and C. Thus, IBM's profits in the second and subsequent periods will be zero.

Note that, because of competitive entry in the second period, the only profit that IBM makes is $800 million in the first period. Thus, IBM is worse off than it would have been if it had maximized current profits by charging a price of $500 per unit in the first period.

Fusion for Profit Maxim

The gains from a price-skimming strategy may disappear if the discount rate is sufficiently high or if competitors enter the market in the future.

New Products

We continue with the IBM example. Suppose a more efficient production process becomes available for manufacturing the handheld computer in the second period because of innovation. Then, competitors who enter in the second period will be able to undercut IBM's prices. Alternatively, suppose competitors are able to develop a better handheld computer in the second period. Then, they may be able to provide consumers with better value (i.e., higher consumer surpluses) than IBM. Consequently, IBM's price-skimming strategy will not work.

Example 1: Nokia used a price-skimming approach to introduce cell phones in China in the 1990s. This pricing strategy had been successful in Europe, but it was a strategic error in China because Chinese firms were able to develop and market copycat products quickly.

Example 2: During the first half of 2006, firms in the flat-panel TV industry pursued a skimming policy and charged high prices. However, in the second half of 2006, the supply of flat-panel TVs increased dramatically as a large number of major manufacturers such as Samsung, Sony, and Panasonic added substantial capacity and flooded the market with new flat-panel TVs. This led to a drastic 40% to 50% price cut and an even sharper reduction in profit margins in the second half of 2006.

In hindsight, one can argue that early entrants in the flat-panel TV industry should have focused on immediate profits rather than on skimming.[9]

Consumer Behavior

The IBM example assumed a very simple model of consumer choice: consumers are myopic and will purchase IBM's handheld computer immediately if they obtain a positive consumer surplus. However, consumers know from experience that, in the high-tech field, all firms will lower the prices of their durable products over time. Thus, all three segments (A, B, and C) expect that IBM will lower the price of the handheld computer in the future. *Hence it may be optimal for consumers to behave strategically.* That is, even if current purchase provides a positive consumer surplus, postponing purchase may be a preferred strategy because it leads to an even larger surplus.

We now show that, if consumers choose to postpone purchase, IBM's price-skimming policy may not work. To focus on essentials, assume that the consumer's implicit discount rate is zero. (By postponing purchase, the consumer loses the benefit of owning the product now but gains in the future because of the price reduction. Hence the consumer uses an implicit discount rate to compare these gains and losses.)

Suppose IBM introduces the computer in the first period at a price of $1,000 per unit. If Segment A purchases the computer in the first period, it will obtain zero consumer surplus, since its reservation price equals the price paid. Suppose Segment A expects IBM to lower the price of the handheld computer to $600 in the second period. Then, by postponing purchase, Segment A will be able to obtain a consumer surplus of $400 in the second period. Thus, Segment A will not purchase the computer in the first period.

▶ However, will Segment A purchase the IBM computer in the second period?

Following the same logic as before, we see that, if Segment A expects IBM to reduce the price to $500 in the third period, it should postpone purchase to the third period. Similarly, the other segments (Segments B and C) will also postpone purchase to the third period. Since no consumers will purchase the product in the first two periods, *IBM's skimming strategy will collapse—even if no new competitors enter the market in the future.* This problem is known as the *Coase paradox.*

In reality, consumers are likely to have different expectations about future prices. Furthermore, they are likely to have different implicit discount rates. Hence some consumers will purchase immediately; others will postpone purchase to take advantage of the anticipated price reductions in the future. Consequently, *price skimming can, and does, work in practice.*

Fusion for Profit Maxim

If consumers behave strategically, the firm may not gain from using a price-skimming strategy.

Installed Base or Diffusion Effect

The previous analyses assumed that the number of potential buyers is fixed. In reality, new customers are likely to enter the market in the future. Suppose the reservation prices of consumers who enter the market in the future increase with the number of units sold in the first period (the installed base effect). Alternatively, suppose the market growth rate increases with the number of current customers because of word-of-mouth activity (the diffusion effect).

Since price skimming requires the firm to set a high introductory price for its new product, the installed base and diffusion effects will be low if the firm chooses this strategy. Hence future demand will be lower than it could have been. Consequently, for this scenario, *price skimming will not lead to optimal long-run performance.*

Example: In contrast to cell phone manufacturers in the United States and in Europe, cell phone manufacturers in India did not use a price-skimming strategy. Instead, they kept the price of cell phones low in order to grow the market via the installed base and diffusion effects. This strategy has been extremely successful.

Fusion for Profit Maxim

Price skimming leads to low short-run market share both in terms of volume and in terms of revenue. Under certain conditions, price skimming can lead to optimal long-run profits.

Point to consider. Is a privately held firm more likely to choose a price-skimming policy than a publicly held firm? Assume that both firms face identical cost and demand conditions.

Wall Street typically puts pressure on the publicly held firm to focus on short-run profits. Hence managers of publicly held firms will implicitly use a high discount rate to value future profits. Thus, other conditions being equal, a publicly held firm is less likely to use price skimming than a privately held firm.

Point to consider. What marketing and sales strategies should a firm follow to implement a price-skimming approach?

Since the firm is using a price-skimming strategy, it should charge a high introductory price for the product and lower the price over time. Then, consumers will sort themselves into segments and purchase accordingly. For simplicity assume that there are two segments:

1. Those who will purchase in the first period at a high price (Segment 1), and
2. Those who will postpone purchase to the second period and pay a lower price (Segment 2).

In practice, this self-selection strategy is likely to be inefficient. A better strategy for the firm is to proceed in three steps:

1. Group consumers into the two segments,
2. Find a set of observable characteristics for the buyer (e.g., household income or target end-user industry) that are related to segment membership, and
3. Use a sequential strategy to target buyers in different segments over time.

Thus, in the first period the firm should focus its resources (e.g., sales effort) on consumers with high reservation prices (Segment 1). In the next period, the firm should focus its resources on consumers with lower reservation prices (Segment 2), and so on.[10]

Fusion for Profit Maxim

In order to implement a successful price-skimming strategy, the firm should use a strategy in which it targets segments sequentially over time, based on their reservation prices for the new product.

Chapter 4 Key Points

- When competitors charge different prices for similar products, the concept of market share is ambiguous. Hence it is necessary to distinguish between volume-based and revenue-based market share.
- The observed correlation between revenue-based market share and profitability is spurious.
- Market share and short-run profitability are mutually inconsistent objectives except in the special case where marginal costs are zero.
- In general, the price that maximizes the firm's current profits is always higher than the price that maximizes the firm's revenue-based market share.
- The firm may find it desirable to pursue volume-based market share in the short run if cost or demand dynamics are present in the marketplace.
- If the firm's marketing polices do not affect the growth rate of the market, the firm should focus on short-run profits and not on market share (revenue-based or volume-based).
- The potential future gains to the firm from pursuing short-term market share depend on a number of factors, including the discount rate, the likelihood of competitive entry in the future, the degree of cost and demand uncertainty, and the likelihood of technological innovation or obsolescence in the future. If the firm's discount rate is sufficiently high, the firm should focus on short-run profits and not on volume-based market share.
- Limit pricing and predatory pricing can be effective strategic tools even if there are no cost or demand dynamics.
- The first-mover (pioneering) advantage will not occur unless certain market conditions hold. The empirical correlation between being a first mover and profitability is inflated because the data sets analyzed do not include many first movers that have attempted to be pioneers and have failed.
- Under certain conditions, the firm should choose marketing policies that lead to low volume-based and revenue-based market shares.
- Under certain conditions, a price-skimming policy may lead to superior long-run profits. However, this strategy is not always optimal, especially in a world of cost, demand, and technological uncertainty.

5

Should the Multiproduct Firm Use the Market Share Metric?

In the previous chapter we showed that, under certain conditions, the firm should use market share (revenue-based or volume-based) as a metric to measure performance. However, for simplicity, we focused on the single-product firm. In practice, most firms produce or sell multiple products.

This chapter extends the analysis to the multiproduct firm. Specifically, we focus on the following fundamental questions. Under what conditions should the multiproduct firm focus on the short-run market shares of the individual products in its product line? And, should the multiproduct firm use market share metrics to allocate resources across different product lines?

The information covered in this chapter will be useful when you are faced with the following types of decisions:

- What performance metrics should my firm use if it is a manufacturer that sells equipment and also sells spare parts for that equipment?
- What performance metrics should my firm use if it sells products and also sells after-sales contracts for maintaining those products?
- In a world of uncertainty, how should my firm choose its marketing policies and performance metrics if it sells proprietary spare parts or after-sales contracts?
- What performance metrics should my firm use if it introduces product upgrades over time?
- How should my firm change the marketing policies of its product line when competitors introduce new products?

- How should my firm coordinate the marketing policies for products that must be used together?
- Should my firm allocate resources across products or product lines on the basis of their respective market shares?

The following terms will be introduced in this chapter (see glossary for definitions):

BCG portfolio model	joint costs	problem children
cash cows	marginal buyer	product life cycle
common customers	marginal consumer	retention rate
cost structure	marginal profitability	secondhand market
cyclical industry	market segmentation	shareholder wealth
diffusion rate	net present value	stars
discount rate	(NPV)	targeted market
dogs	price war	segment
economies of scope	price-cutting strategy	volatility

▶ 5.1 Market Share and Pricing for the Durable Goods Manufacturer That Sells Spare Parts

We begin with the case of a firm that sells durable equipment and also sells proprietary spare parts for maintaining the equipment.

Example: Consider a firm in the aircraft industry (e.g., Boeing). Boeing sells aircraft to airlines and will also sell proprietary spare parts to those airlines in the future.

▶ How should Boeing set the price of its aircraft?

Suppose that by charging $400 million per aircraft, Boeing can sell 1,000 aircraft and maximize its profits from aircraft sales. By definition, at this price, the *marginal profit* on the sale of the 1,000th aircraft is zero. (If the marginal profit is positive, the firm can increase its profits by reducing price. If the marginal profit is negative, the firm can increase its profits by increasing price.) However, the buyer of the 1,000th aircraft will purchase spare parts from Boeing in the future. Hence, at a volume of 1,000 aircraft, the marginal profit (*including* the value of the future profit on the sales of proprietary spare parts) is positive. *This implies that by increasing the number of aircraft sold (i.e., by reducing the price of aircraft below $400 million), Boeing will increase profits.*

Fusion for Profit Maxim

Volume-based market share can be a proxy for long-run profits for durable goods manufacturers that sell proprietary spare parts.

Point to consider.   Suppose generic spare parts for Boeing aircraft become available. How should Boeing change the price of its aircraft?

Suppose the optimal policy for Boeing is to charge a price of $390 million (<$400 million) for its aircraft when it sells proprietary spare parts for its aircraft. By definition, at this price, the incremental *net present value (NPV)* of profits generated by the *marginal buyer* from the purchase of aircraft *and* proprietary spares must be zero.

Suppose cheaper generic spare parts become available. Then, if Boeing charges a price of $390 million per aircraft, the incremental net present value of profits generated by the marginal buyer will become negative. *Hence Boeing should increase the price of its aircraft following the availability of generic spare parts.* That is, Boeing should sell fewer aircraft than before.

▶ **As discussed, Boeing's volume-based market share will fall when generic spare parts become available. What will happen to Boeing's revenue-based market share?**

This effect depends on the profits from the sales of the aircraft, the profits from the sales of spare parts, and Boeing's *discount rate*. Depending on the magnitudes of these joint effects, Boeing's revenue-based market share could decrease or increase. (We will discuss these effects in detail shortly.)

Fusion for Profit Maxim

If cheaper generic spare parts are introduced by a competitor, the durable goods manufacturer should increase the price of its product. This will decrease the firm's volume-based market share for the durable; however, the effect on the firm's revenue-based market share is ambiguous.

▶ **5.2 Market Share and Pricing for the Firm That Sells After-Sales Contracts**

We now consider the case of a firm that sells products and, in addition, also sells after-sales contracts. The analysis is unaffected by whether the products are physical (e.g., computers) or intangible (e.g., after-sales service contracts for a company that manufactures elevators).

Example: IBM sells computers and associated consulting services to the business sector. How should IBM change the price of its computers if the market for consulting services becomes more competitive?

Since the relevant market for consulting services is now more competitive, IBM's profitability from obtaining a *marginal consumer* will be reduced. Hence, at the old price for IBM computers, the marginal profit (i.e., the sum of the profits from the sale of computers to the marginal consumer and the additional profits generated via associated consulting services) will become negative. *Thus, IBM should increase the price of its computers. Hence IBM's volume-based market share in the computer market will fall.*

▶ **What will happen to IBM's revenue-based market share in the computer market?**

The effect on IBM's revenue-based market share will depend on the magnitudes of IBM's profits from the sale of computers and associated consulting services and on IBM's discount rate. Hence, as in the Boeing example, the effect of increased competition in the computer consulting market on IBM's revenue-based market share is ambiguous.

This leads to an interesting possibility. Since the consulting market for computers has become more competitive, IBM's stock price (which measures IBM's long-run profits from the sale of computers and consulting services) will fall. *Note that it is possible that IBM's revenue-based market share for computers will increase when the market for IBM's consulting services becomes more competitive.*

Fusion for Profit Maxim

An increase in the multiproduct firm's revenue-based market share does not imply that the firm's stock price will be higher than before.

▶ **5.3 How Does Uncertainty Affect Pricing Policy and Market Share for the Firm That Sells Proprietary Spare Parts or After-Sales Contracts?**

As noted above, the firm's future profit from spare parts or after-sales contracts depends on the discount rate (i.e., the uncertainty in future cash flows resulting from those sales). Hence the firm's trade-off between current and future profits will vary from industry to industry.

Example: Suppose generic spare parts become available in two industries: one is highly *cyclical* (e.g., the aircraft industry), and the other is less cyclical (e.g., the razor blade industry). Assuming that other factors are held constant, in which industry will the effect on marketing policy be stronger?

Since the aircraft industry is more cyclical than the razor blade industry, the discount rate for the aircraft industry will be higher. Thus, the impact of reduced future profits resulting from the availability of generic spare parts in the aircraft industry will be dampened. Hence, other factors being held constant, the introduction of generic spare parts in the aircraft industry will have a weaker effect on prices, volumes, and market shares than the corresponding effects for the razor blade industry.

Fusion for Profit Maxim

If the firm's discount rate is high, the introduction of generic spare parts will have a smaller effect on the firm's marketing policy and on the firm's volume-based and revenue-based market shares.

▶ 5.4 Should the Firm That Introduces Product Upgrades over Time Pursue Market Share or Current Profits?

When the firm introduces product upgrades over time, it needs to distinguish among several segments. Consider a two-period model in which the firm's profits come from three segments:

1. Consumers who buy in the first period only,
2. Consumers who buy in the second period only, and
3. Consumers who buy in the first period and upgrade to the new product in the second.

Given this scenario, the firm's optimal product-line policy depends on the cost structures for the different product qualities, the percentage of buyers that upgrades to the new product, whether the firm's current marketing policy affects the growth rate of the market (the *diffusion rate*), and the firm's discount rate.[1]

Example: Suppose Hewlett-Packard plans to sell a basic notebook computer now and introduce a more sophisticated model one year later. (For simplicity, assume that no new buyers enter the market after one year, and nonbuyers in the current period leave the market.)

▶ What product-line pricing policy should Hewlett-Packard use?

Suppose Hewlett-Packard can maximize its current profits from the basic notebook computer by charging a price of $500 per unit. Let's say that Hewlett-Packard will be able to sell 100,000 units at this price and will make a current profit of $20 million.

▶ What will happen if Hewlett-Packard charges a lower price for the basic notebook computer, say $450?

Since the current price of the basic computer is now less than $500 per unit, Hewlett-Packard will sell more than 100,000 units, say 130,000 units.

In addition, Hewlett-Packard's profit will be less than $20 million, say $15 million.

▶ Should Hewlett-Packard accept a profit reduction in current profits of $5 million on the basic notebook computer?

To focus on essentials, assume that Hewlett-Packard is risk-neutral (i.e., it seeks to maximize expected profits) and that the discount rate is zero. The critical question is the following: How many customers who purchase the basic Hewlett-Packard computer will upgrade to the more sophisticated model next year?

As discussed, the number of current buyers for the low-price strategy (130,000) is larger than the number of customers if Hewlett-Packard maximizes its profits from the basic computer (100,000). Suppose that, on average, 50% of first-time buyers will upgrade and that the profit margin on the sophisticated computer is $400 per unit (table 5.1).

Then, if Hewlett-Packard charges a lower current price for the basic computer, its profits from the basic computer will fall by $5 million. However, it will make an additional profit of $6 million from customers who upgrade next year (see table 5.1). Hence Hewlett-Packard will increase its long-run product-line profit by $1 million.

Note that the optimal multiproduct strategy for Hewlett-Packard is to forgo some current profits by increasing its volume-based market share for the basic computer. Furthermore, this policy could reduce the revenue-based market share of the basic notebook model. For example, if the profit margin on the sophisticated notebook model sold one year later is very high, it may be optimal for Hewlett-Packard to charge a very low price for the basic computer in order to increase its profits from upgrades. This low-price policy for the basic notebook model could decrease Hewlett-Packard's current revenue-based market share.

Table 5.1
Hewlett-Packard Example: Dynamic Effect of New Product Introduction

	Initial units sold	Percent who upgrade	Upgraded units sold	Profit margin per unit for upgrade units	Profit on upgraded units
High price ($500)	100,000	50%	50,000	$400	$20,000,000
Low price ($450)	130,000	50%	65,000	$400	$26,000,000
Additional profit at lower price					$6,000,000

Fusion for Profit Maxim

If a firm introduces product upgrades over time, it may be optimal to compromise current profits to some degree by building volume-based market share in order to increase future profits.

Point to consider.   What additional factors should Hewlett-Packard consider when determining its product-line pricing strategy?

Hewlett-Packard should recognize that, when current buyers upgrade, they can sell their used notebook computers on the *secondhand market*. These used Hewlett-Packard computers on the secondhand market will compete with Hewlett-Packard's new notebook model when they are introduced next year. In addition, when pricing its new notebook model, Hewlett-Packard should recognize that the market contains three segments:

1. Customers who buy the basic model and upgrade (Segment 1),
2. Customers who buy the basic model and do not upgrade (Segment 2), and
3. Customers who buy the sophisticated model (Segment 3).

As one would expect, Hewlett-Packard's optimal product-line policy will depend on a number of factors, including the discount rate, the cost structures for the basic and new computers, and the degree of improvement in product quality. Different scenarios can be constructed.[2]

Fusion for Profit Maxim

When a firm introduces product upgrades over time, it needs to coordinate its marketing policies after considering the combined effect of secondhand markets, its discount rate, the cost structures of the different products, and the improvement in the quality of its products over time.

▶ 5.5 How Should the Firm Change Its Market Share and Long-Run Pricing Policy When Competitors Introduce New Products?

The previous examples focused on new product introductions by the firm. However, they did not consider competitive behavior in the marketplace. How should the firm choose its pricing policy after allowing for competition?[3]

Example: Consider the wireless industry. How should a major player like Verizon Wireless set the price of its cell phone service? One strategy is to sell consumers long-term service contracts (e.g., for two years) with punitive clauses for switching before the contract expires. In this case, volume-based market share is a good proxy for Verizon's long-run profits.

Fusion for Profit Maxim

Volume-based market share can be a good proxy for long-run profits if the firm sells its products with long-term contracts that include punitive clauses for consumers who switch to a competitor before the contract expires.

▲ 5.6 Should the Firm Focus on Market Share If It Sells Products That Must Be Used Together?

The firm's products can be related in a number of ways. Some products can only be used in conjunction with others. For example, razor blades can only be used with compatible razors. Similarly, the volume of one product (e.g., the number of newspaper subscriptions) can affect the revenue from another product (e.g., advertising revenue to the newspaper).

Should the firm use market share as a metric in such cases? Consider the following examples.

Example 1: Suppose Gillette has developed a new patented razor that can only use proprietary Gillette blades. This problem is similar to the Boeing example involving the sale of proprietary spare parts. Hence volume-based market share is a good proxy for future profits from the sale of the proprietary Gillette blades.

Note that, in contrast to the Boeing example, the profit from the sale of "spare parts" (razor blades) is likely to be much higher than the profit from the sale of the original "equipment" (razors). Since Gillette's razor blades are proprietary, it may even be optimal for Gillette to give free samples of the razors.

Example 2: Yahoo does not charge consumers for using its basic Internet services. It makes profits based on advertising revenues from firms that advertise on its Web site. In addition, Yahoo makes profits from users who purchase some of its "add-on" Internet services. (Note: This is a special case of the razor blade model in which the basic product, Internet service, is given free of charge.)

In contrast, until recently AOL used a paid subscription model in which the strategy was to focus on profits from the subscriptions division. In hindsight, AOL's pricing approach of focusing on single-product profits was suboptimal. The Yahoo model of focusing on building volume-based market share has produced superior long-run results for Yahoo's product portfolio.

Fusion for Profit Maxim

In a multiproduct firm with *economies of scope*, it is suboptimal to attempt to maximize the performances of each product separately. In some cases, volume-based market share can be a good proxy for long-run profit for the firm's product portfolio.

▶ *Are there any conditions under which a multiproduct firm should attempt to maximize the profits from each product line separately? How likely is it that these conditions will be satisfied in real life?*

The firm can choose the optimal marketing policies separately for each product if the products are independent. That is, there are no *joint costs* or *common customers* across product lines. In other words:

1. Each product is manufactured using a separate production process or sold using a separate sales force, and
2. Each product is sold to different and nonoverlapping market segments.

These conditions will not be satisfied in most cases. Thus, in general it is suboptimal for the multiproduct firm to attempt to maximize the profits from each product line separately.

Fusion for Profit Maxim

In general, the multiproduct firm needs to coordinate its marketing policies across products.

▶ **5.7 Should the Multiproduct Firm Allocate Resources across Products on the Basis of Their Respective Market Shares?**

This resource allocation method makes a fundamental assumption: *the current market share of a product is a good proxy for that product's future profitability.* Before choosing this resource allocation method, however, the firm should address the following issues:

Definition of the market: How is the market for each product defined? Is the measure of market share based on revenue or on volume? If these quantities are not carefully defined, the firm will make suboptimal resource allocation decisions.

Market segmentation: For each product, the firm should first determine the profitabilities of different market segments. Often, one or more segments of a given product produce low profits, or even produce losses. In such cases, the prudent strategy may be to remove resources from low-profit segments and transfer them elsewhere.

Example: Several years ago, a large multinational brokerage firm performed a segment-based profitability analysis of its customers. The analysis showed that the firm's revenue-based market share in certain market segments (e.g., small investors) was high, but the profitabilities of those segments were low. The brokerage firm used these results to reallocate its advertising and sales budgets based on the *marginal profitability* of each market segment. Overall, the firm's revenue-based market share fell. However, profits increased.

Investment: In many cases, the firm can increase the market share of a product by investing more resources in that product. However, current market share is a poor measure of the effectiveness of incremental investments. Thus, the firm may have a dominant market share for a given product. Alternatively, the product may be in the maturity phase of the *product life cycle*. In such cases, the incremental return from further investment in the product is likely to be poor. A better strategy for the firm may be to invest marketing resources in a product in a growing market in which the firm's current market share may not be very high.

Uncertainty: The firm's marketing policy can affect the *volatility* of market share and profits. For instance, suppose the firm pursues an aggressive *price-cutting strategy* to increase its volume-based market share. This price policy is likely to destabilize the industry and lead to a *price war*. Hence price-cutting can be a risky strategy, *even if it produces a higher expected profit or expected market share.*

An alternative strategy may be to use a focused sales force strategy that increases the *retention rate* of a *targeted market segment*. This strategy may lead to a lower expected profit than the price-cutting strategy; however, it could result in lower volatility in long-run profits. Hence the focused marketing strategy may be superior to the aggressive price-cutting strategy even though it leads to a lower expected volume-based market share.

Interrelated products: As discussed, products in the multiproduct firm are often interrelated. Some products may be purchased by a *common set of customers*; alternatively, other products may share common production or other resources (e.g., these products may be sold through a common sales force). In such cases, it is inappropriate to analyze each product separately and to allocate resources based on that product's market share or some other simplistic proxy to measure profitability.

▲ *Suppose a firm allocates resources across product lines on the basis of market share. Will this policy maximize shareholder wealth?*

Shareholder wealth is the present value of current and anticipated future profits. As discussed, in many cases, allocating resources across product lines on the basis of current market shares will not maximize shareholder wealth.

Point to consider.   According to the *Boston Consulting Group (BCG) portfolio model*, the multiproduct firm should allocate resources across products as follows. First, classify each product based on relative market share (low or high) and market growth rate (low or high). Thus, each product belongs to one of four groups:

1. *Cash cows*: high market share, low growth rate
2. *Stars*: high market share, high growth rate

3. *Dogs*: low market share, low growth rate
4. *Problem children*: low market share, high growth rate

Once this classification has been done, hold a balanced product portfolio by eliminating the dogs and use the cash flow from the cash cows to finance the stars and, if necessary, the problem children.

▶ How useful is this market-share-based resource allocation model?

The Boston Consulting Group resource allocation model does not specify whether the appropriate market share metric is volume-based or revenue-based. More fundamentally, the BCG model implies that the current market share of a product and the market growth rate are good proxies for long-run profits. This conclusion is based on a number of implicit assumptions:

The experience curve is strong and predictable,
The firm's learning is proprietary,
Technology is static,
The discount rate is sufficiently low (i.e., the firm is willing to forgo current profits in exchange for higher future profits),
The market growth rate is predictable,
The firm's products or brands are independent (i.e., there are no cost or demand interdependencies across the firm's product lines), and
All resources are internally generated.

However, these assumptions may not hold.

For example, the BCG model assumes that all cash flows are internally generated in the firm. In many cases, though, it may be optimal for a firm with profitable opportunities to augment its internal cash flows by floating additional shares to obtain resources from the capital market. In addition, the model implicitly assumes that the number of products and the designs of all products in the product line are fixed. However, these are key strategic decisions that are directly under the firm's control (i.e., which products to make and what attributes to include in each product). Hence the firm should explicitly consider these strategic decisions when allocating resources across products.

Furthermore, the model implicitly assumes that it is appropriate for the firm to classify its brands or products one at a time. This classification method can lead to serious errors if the firm's products (brands) are interrelated on the demand or cost sides.

Thus, in many cases, the multiproduct firm should not use the BCG model for making resource allocation decisions.

Example: Gillette markets razors and deodorants. In particular, some consumers buy both Gillette products. Since both the razor and deodorant brands have common customers, Gillette should allocate resources to the razor and deodorant brands *after* allowing for this demand interdependence.

From a decision-making viewpoint, the danger is that, by using the BCG model in a mechanistic manner, the firm is likely to make poor resource allocation decisions. To illustrate, suppose the firm automatically eliminates all products with low market shares in low-growth markets (dogs). This strategy could be suboptimal. For example, it may be possible for the firm to make a dog profitable if the firm targets a different market segment or uses different marketing policies. Similarly, by dropping all products that are classified as dogs, the firm will forgo the opportunity to serve niche markets that could be highly profitable.

Fusion for Profit Maxim

In general, the multiproduct firm should not allocate resources across products or brands on the basis of their market shares.

Chapter 5 Key Points

- Volume-based market share can be a useful proxy for long-run profits for durable goods manufacturers that sell proprietary spare parts.
- If a firm sells a durable product and related products or services, an increase in the firm's revenue-based market share for the durable product does not imply that the firm's stock price will be higher than before.
- The multiproduct firm that has *economies of scope* cannot maximize the long-run performances of each product in its product portfolio separately.
- A firm that introduces product upgrades over time should coordinate its pricing policies after analyzing a number of factors, including the *cost structures* of the different models, the fraction of buyers who upgrade, whether the firm's current marketing policy affects the growth rate of the market, secondhand markets, the diffusion rate, and the discount rate.
- Under certain market conditions, the optimal strategy for the multiproduct firm may be to focus on volume-based market share by selling a product for a loss or even by giving the product away for free.
- In general, it is suboptimal for the multiproduct firm to allocate resources across products based on the market shares of individual products in its portfolio.

IV

Strategies and Pricing Policies for New Products and Product Bundles

6

Pricing New Products: Strategies and Caveats

This chapter discusses some basic concepts on how to price new products under uncertainty. In particular, we focus on the *Fusion for Profit* aspects of pricing. Chapters 7 and 8 discuss new product pricing for more general scenarios when the firm sells multiple products and needs to consider multiple time periods. For simplicity, this chapter assumes that the firm sells only one product and has a single-period planning horizon.

The information covered in this chapter will be useful when you are faced with the following types of decisions:

- How should my firm price new products to maximize *profitability*?
- What is the effect of my firm's financing decisions on new product pricing?
- How should my firm price new products under uncertainty?
- Under what conditions should my firm use cost-based methods to price a new product?
- Should privately and publicly owned firms use the same approach to set new product prices?
- What is the effect of *fixed costs* and product development costs on new product pricing?
- How does the *risk attitude* of my firm affect the price my firm should charge for a new product?
- Under what conditions should my firm *preannounce* its new products in the marketplace?

The following terms will be introduced in this chapter (see glossary for definitions):

asymmetric cash flows	fixed costs	product
break-even pricing	gross margins	preannouncements
break-even sales	hedge fund	profitability
volume	information release	reservation prices
cannibalization	events (IREs)	risk adjustment
certainty case	long-term debt	risk attitude
certainty equivalent (CE)	markup pricing	risk-averse
closing wealth	mutual fund	risk-neutral
conjoint analysis	opportunity cost	risk seeking
constant absolute risk	planning horizon	signaling effect
aversion	preannouncements	sunk costs
cost-plus pricing	price sensitivity	supply chain
downside risk	privately held firm	uncertainty case
economic fixed costs	product	upside gain potential
financial leverage	announcements	utility function

▰ 6.1 Can the Firm Price a New Product to Maximize Its Profitability?

Intuitively, one could argue that the firm should set the price of a new product to maximize its profitability over a given planning horizon. However, this answer is ambiguous. In contrast to established products, the demand for new products is likely to be highly uncertain, especially for radically new products. Furthermore, costs are also likely to be highly uncertain. For example, the firm may need to use a new production process or new channels of distribution to market the new product. Since both demand and cost are uncertain, the firm's profits are also uncertain. However, as we know, one cannot maximize an uncertain quantity (see chapter 1). Hence it is necessary for the firm to choose a different criterion for pricing new products.

Fusion for Profit Maxim

The firm cannot price a new product to maximize profitability when demand and cost are uncertain.

▰ What criterion should the firm use when demand and cost are uncertain?

We begin with the simplest case where the privately or publicly owned firm is *risk-neutral* and has a short planning horizon (one period). That is, the firm sets the price of the new product to maximize its expected profits in the period.

▶ *Suppose the firm seeks to maximize expected profits. Should the firm set the price of the new product based on the profits corresponding to the average numbers of units sold at different prices?*

At first glance, this approach seems to be reasonable. However, as the following example shows, the method is flawed.

Example: Suppose the Attach-It Company has developed a new staple gun for industrial use. Let's say that, if Attach-It charges a price of $100 per staple gun, the demand will be as shown in table 6.1.

Assume that each demand level is equally likely. Then, if Attach-It charges a price of $100, on average it will sell 600 units.

Suppose Attach-It uses a production process where the average cost of producing the new staple gun decreases with the number of units produced. Specifically, the average costs are as shown in table 6.2.

Then, Attach-It's expected (average) profit is $27,000. However, the profit corresponding to the average demand (600 units) is lower ($24,000).

Fusion for Profit Maxim

The firm should not use average demand to set the price of its new product.

Point to consider.   Are there any cases where the risk-neutral firm should use average demand to set the price of its new product?

Table 6.1
Attach-It Company: Scenario for Uncertain Demand

	Demand (units)			
Price	Low	Moderate	High	Average
$100	500	600	700	600

Table 6.2
Attach-It Company: Computation of Expected Profit

Average cost per unit	Number of units sold	Gross margin per unit	Gross margin
$70	500	$30	$15,000
$60	600	$40	$24,000
$40	700	$60	$42,000
			$81,000
Expected (average) profit			$27,000

This approach is correct under certain conditions. Suppose the cost per unit does not change with volume. For example, suppose Attach-It's unit cost is $40 regardless of the number of staple guns manufactured, and the price charged is $100 per unit as before. Then, the unit profit margin is $60 (price – unit cost). Hence the profit corresponding to the average demand is $36,000 (average demand × unit profit margin). Note that this value is the same as the expected profit ($36,000).

▲ 6.2 How Should the Firm Price a New Product under Uncertainty?

In the previous section, we assumed that the firm seeks to maximize its expected profits. In reality, most decision makers are concerned about both expected profits and fluctuations in profits. We say that the firm is *risk-averse*. A more precise definition is given later in the chapter.

▲ How should the risk-averse firm price a new product?

For simplicity, we focus on the case where costs are predictable but the demand for the new product is uncertain. One approach for setting prices is *break-even pricing*.

Example: Suppose a publicly owned firm, Canon, has developed a new camera with Internet capabilities. Suppose the fixed cost of producing the new camera is $10 million per year, the variable cost per camera is $60, and the camera will become obsolete after one year (table 6.3).

If Canon charges a price of $100 per camera, the gross margin per camera is $40. Thus, unless Canon can sell at least 250,000 cameras it will make a loss. We say that the *break-even sales volume* at a price of $100 per camera is 250,000 units.

Canon can now use the break-even approach to make heuristic comparisons for different prices (table 6.4). For example, if Canon increases the price to $160 per camera, the break-even volume will be reduced to 100,000 cameras.

Table 6.3
Attach-It Company: Break-Even Analysis for a Price of $100 per Unit

Price per unit	$100	
Variable cost per unit	$60	
Gross margin per unit	$40	
Fixed cost per year		$10,000,000
Fixed cost/gross margin per unit = break-even volume (units)		250,000

Table 6.4
Attach-It Company: Break-Even Analysis for a Price of $160 per Unit

Price per unit	$160	
Variable cost per unit	$60	
Gross margin per unit	$100	
Fixed cost per year		$10,000,000
Fixed cost/gross margin per unit = break-even volume (units)		100,000

Table 6.5
Attach-It Company: Comparison of Break-Even Volumes

	Scenario#1	Scenario#2	Change
Unit price	$160	$100	−37.5%
Break-even volume (units)	100	250	150%

Note that the relationship between break-even volumes and prices is nonlinear even though the variable cost per camera is constant.

In our example, when the price is reduced by 37.5%, the break-even volume increases by 150%—a considerably higher percentage (table 6.5). Thus, *break-even pricing tends to lead to high prices for a new product.*

Fusion for Profit Maxim

The firm can use break-even pricing to price new products under uncertainty. In general, firms that use this pricing method will charge high prices for new products.

▶ *What are the potential pitfalls in using break-even pricing for new products?*

The firm should be careful to include all relevant economic costs.

Example: Suppose an inventor (Jane Smith) has developed a new navigation guide system and established a privately owned firm to produce and sell the new product (table 6.6). Suppose the annual fixed costs are $100,000. Let's say that if Jane Smith runs the firm herself, she has to forgo an opportunity to earn $70,000 per year by working for General Motors. Suppose, in addition, that Jane Smith has invested $200,000 of her own money in the firm. This money could have been invested elsewhere.

Table 6.6
Calculating Economic Fixed Cost

Fixed cost	$100,000	
Opportunity cost of labor	$70,000	
Subtotal		$170,000
Personal investment in firm	$200,000	
Expected return	10%	
Implicit interest cost		$20,000
Economic fixed cost		$190,000

Suppose that, if this new product opportunity were not available, Jane Smith would have invested in a *mutual fund* that is expected to yield an annual return of 8%. (Recall that Jane Smith has given up diversification opportunities by investing in her own firm.) Hence, the expected return that is necessary on the new product opportunity should exceed 8% per annum. Suppose the expected return on the investment in the firm is 10%, after allowing for the additional risk involved. Then Jane Smith should charge herself an implicit interest cost of $20,000 per year (see table 6.6).

Note that the economic fixed costs per year ($190,000) are considerably larger than the accounting fixed costs ($100,000) because the latter fail to allow for the opportunity costs of Jane Smith's labor and personal capital that are invested in the firm.

Fusion for Profit Maxim

Break-even pricing for new products should be based on a correct measure of fixed costs. These include hidden costs such as the opportunity cost of the owner's labor and personal capital that are invested in the firm.

▶ **Is break-even pricing a good method for pricing new products under uncertainty?**

Break-even pricing focuses on the minimum volume that the firm must achieve before it begins to earn a profit. Hence break-even pricing focuses exclusively on *downside risk* and ignores *upside gain potential*. However, the *cash flows for new products are typically asymmetric.* Specifically, if the product succeeds, the upside gain potential can be substantial.

Thus, in the Canon example, it is possible that the low-price strategy ($100 per camera) could lead to substantially higher profits than the high-price strategy ($160 per camera). Hence *break-even pricing tends to lead to conservative decision making.*

> **Fusion for Profit Maxim**
>
> Break-even pricing for new products focuses exclusively on downside risk and ignores upside gains. Hence the firm is likely to charge a high price for the new product.

▲ *Many firms use* markup *or* cost-plus pricing. *Is this pricing policy a good method for pricing new products under uncertainty?*

Markup/cost-plus pricing means that the firm sets the price of a new product by adding a fixed percentage to unit cost. This markup or cost-plus pricing method is simple but flawed.

Example: Suppose Black & Decker has developed a new cordless drill. Suppose the average cost for a volume of 100,000 units is $10 per unit, and the corresponding average cost for a volume of 130,000 units is reduced to $8 per unit. Then, the unit cost—and hence the markup price—is ambiguous. Furthermore, the number of drills sold (and hence the average cost per drill) depends on price. Hence markup or cost-plus pricing is based on circular reasoning.

▲ *Why do firms use markup or cost-plus pricing?*

The price charged for the new product should reflect the *price sensitivity* in the market. Thus, the more price-sensitive the market is, the lower price should be. In practice, firms often have a much better idea about cost than they do about demand. Hence they use markup/cost-plus pricing as a heuristic method for pricing under demand uncertainty.

Point to consider.   The marginal cost of manufacturing a compact disc is very low (less than $.50). Should a music company use the same percentage markups for an album by the Beatles as it does for an album by an unknown new artist?

The demand for a Beatles album is less price-sensitive than the demand for an album by the unknown new artist. Hence, the percentage markup on a Beatles album should be considerably higher than the percentage markup on the album by the new artist.

▲ *6.3 How Does the Firm's Ownership Structure Affect New Product Pricing?*

Consider a firm in which the owner has invested a substantial fraction of his or her own resources. Given this scenario, it is prudent for the owner to be conservative and to focus on the downside risk of any new product pricing strategy.

In contrast, consider a large multiproduct firm that is owned by many stockholders. In this case, the optimal strategy for the firm is to price the new product after evaluating *both* downside risk and upside gain potential.

Thus, *given the same market conditions (e.g., demand uncertainty), the privately owned firm is likely to charge a higher price for the new product than the publicly held company.*[1]

Fusion for Profit Maxim

In general, a privately held firm should focus on downside risk whereas a publicly owned firm should consider both downside risk and upside gains. Hence, if both firms face the same market conditions, the privately held firm should charge a higher price when it introduces a new product into the marketplace.

▶ *Should privately owned and publicly held firms have the same* planning horizons *for pricing new products?*

The firm's planning horizon, and hence its pricing policy, will depend on the ownership structure of the firm and the frequency with which the product is purchased by consumers.

Example: Suppose two firms have developed identical new toothpastes that combine a gel with a mouthwash. One firm, Shine-E, is small and privately owned. The other is large and is owned by stockholders (e.g., Procter & Gamble). Assume that demand and cost uncertainty are the same for both firms.

Since toothpaste is a nondurable product that is purchased frequently, the firm's introductory price for the new product will affect future cash flows. Because Shine-E is small and is privately owned, it should focus on short-run performance to control downside risk. Hence it is reasonable for Shine-E to ignore the upside gain potential and to set a high introductory price using break-even pricing. This conservative pricing strategy will lead to a low sales volume (on average) and low repeat sales (on average). *However, the cash flows are likely to be relatively stable.*

In contrast, Procter & Gamble is large and is owned by many shareholders who can reduce risk by diversifying. Hence it is reasonable for P&G to focus more heavily on the upside gain potential and to use a more aggressive low-price strategy. Note that P&G's low-price strategy will lead to a higher sales volume (on average) and higher repeat sales (on average) than Shine-E's high-price strategy. However, P&G's cash flows will be more uncertain than Shine-E's.

> **Fusion for Profit Maxim**
>
> In general, privately and publicly held firms should use different planning horizons when pricing new products.

▶ 6.4 Are Fixed Costs Relevant for Pricing New Products When the Firm Is Privately Owned?

The Certainty Case

We first consider the effect of *fixed costs* on new product pricing under certainty. We will examine the more realistic case of *uncertainty* in the next section. Since the firm's cash flows are predictable, the firm does not face risk. Hence it is not necessary to distinguish whether the firm is privately or publicly held.

For any pricing plan, the firm's profit equals the difference between the firm's gross profit margin and its fixed costs. However, the firm's marketing policies (pricing in this case) only affect *gross margins*. Hence any pricing plan that maximizes gross margins will also maximize the firm's profit.

▶ Does this imply that fixed costs are irrelevant for new product pricing?

Although fixed costs are irrelevant for pricing the new product, they do affect the firm's profit. Thus, suppose the firm's fixed costs (say $100,000 per year) exceed the maximum gross profit that the new product can earn (say $90,000 per year). Then, the firm should not launch the new product.

> **Fusion for Profit Maxim**
>
> Regardless of the ownership structure of the firm, fixed costs are irrelevant for new product pricing *under certainty*. The exception is that, if fixed costs are too high, the firm should not introduce the new product.

The Uncertainty Case

We begin with the case where the firm is privately owned. Since the firm's cash flows are now uncertain, the effect of uncertainty on new product pricing depends on how the firm values expected returns and risk.

Risk and Return.   To address the problem of new product pricing under uncertainty, we introduce the concept of a *utility function*. Basically, the utility function measures the value that the owner of the firm places on a certain level of wealth. Naturally, more wealth is preferred to less wealth (i.e., *the utility function slopes upward*).[2] However, to analyze how the owner trades off risk and return, we need more specific information about the shape of the owner's utility function. We need to distinguish three types of risk-return trade-off:

1. Risk neutrality,
2. Risk aversion, and
3. Risk-seeking behavior.

Risk Neutrality.   If the owner of the firm cares only about expected wealth and is indifferent to fluctuations in wealth, we say that the owner is risk-neutral. In this case, *the utility function is linear* (figure 6.1).

Since the risk-neutral owner seeks to maximize expected wealth (initial wealth + expected profits), he or she does not care about how marketing

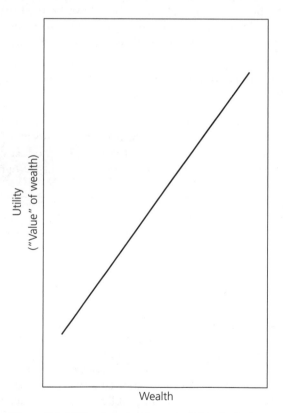

Figure 6.1 Utility function for an individual who is risk-neutral.

policies affect fluctuations in profits. Hence the owner will price the new product to maximize expected profits (expected gross margin – fixed costs). Note that price affects gross margins but not fixed costs. That is, maximizing expected profits is equivalent to maximizing expected gross margin. *Hence fixed costs are irrelevant for pricing the new product—regardless of the degree of uncertainty.*

Fusion for Profit Maxim

Regardless of the magnitude of uncertainty, fixed costs do not affect new product pricing for the risk-neutral owner.

Risk Aversion.   If successive additions to wealth become less and less valuable, we say that the owner is risk-averse (figure 6.2). In this case, *the utility function becomes flatter as wealth increases.*

In contrast to the risk-neutral owner, the risk-averse owner is concerned about both expected profits *and* fluctuations in profits. Since fixed costs

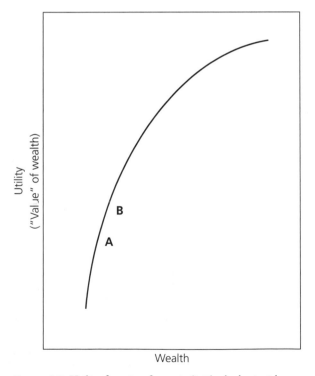

Figure 6.2 Utility function for an individual who is risk-averse.

reduce the owner's wealth, the firm's pricing policy will affect the combination of risk and return that the owner can obtain. Hence *the effect of fixed costs on pricing depends on the magnitude of the profit uncertainty* (e.g., whether the product is a new brand in an established product category or the new product is a radical innovation).

Case 1: Small Uncertainty. Let's begin with the case where the profit uncertainty is small. That is, the firm's profits or losses from the new product are small compared with the firm's existing wealth level. Now, since the profit uncertainty is small, the utility function is approximately linear over the appropriate wealth levels (compare Points A and B in figure 6.2). Thus, the risk-averse firm will behave like a risk-neutral firm and seek to maximize the expected profits from the new product. But this implies that the firm will seek to maximize expected gross margins. *Since fixed costs do not affect gross margins, we get the same result as in the case where the firm is risk-neutral.*

Fusion for Profit Maxim

If the risk-averse firm is privately held and uncertainty is small, fixed costs are irrelevant for pricing new products.

Case 2: Large Uncertainty. Suppose the profit uncertainty is large. That is, the firm's profits or losses from the new product are large compared with the firm's existing wealth level. For instance, the new product is radical and involves significant investment in plant and machinery, and its benefits are unfamiliar to consumers (e.g., the product is a new car radio with Internet capabilities).

Alternatively, the production process for the new product uses raw materials whose prices fluctuate considerably over time (e.g., semiconductors). Then, the firm's wealth level can vary considerably depending on fluctuations in the prices of raw materials. In these cases, the effect of fixed costs on pricing depends critically on how risk-averse the owner is at different wealth levels.

Let's begin with the simple case where the owner's willingness to take risk is constant for the range of wealth levels that can be realized.[3] Then, since marketing policies do not affect the owner's willingness to take risk, intuition would suggest that the owner should focus only on expected profits. Hence fixed costs should have no effect on the firm's marketing policies. This result is, indeed, correct.

In many cases, however, the owner will be more willing to take risks when the owner's wealth is greater. Hence, when fixed costs *increase,* the owner will be *less willing* to take risks. Consequently, other conditions being the same, when fixed costs increase, the owner should charge a higher price than before.

Fusion for Profit Maxim

When uncertainty is high, fixed costs will, in general, affect the firm's new product pricing policy. In the special case where the owner's risk aversion is constant over the likely wealth levels resulting from a particular marketing policy, fixed costs are irrelevant for new product pricing.

Point to consider. Suppose a privately held pharmaceutical firm has just paid $50 million to settle a lawsuit for one of its established products. The CEO of the firm asserts that the firm needs to charge a high price for its new products in order to recoup the loss quickly. Is this argument correct?

We first consider the *certainty case.* Since the firm has lost $50 million, its initial wealth is reduced by $50 million. By definition, the firm's *closing wealth* equals the firm's initial wealth plus profit. Since the firm's pricing policy for the new product does not affect either profit or initial wealth, the loss of $50 million is irrelevant for decision making, including pricing.

In the *uncertainty case,* the answer depends on the firm's risk aversion. If the loss of $50 million is large compared with the firm's assets, the firm's wealth will be sharply reduced. Hence, the firm is likely to be more risk-averse than before. Consequently, it should charge a higher price for the new product.

Note that the rationale for charging a higher price for the new product is not to recoup losses quickly: it is to provide the firm with a better combination of risk and return based on the reduction in its wealth level following the lawsuit.

If the loss of $50 million is small compared with the firm's assets, it is possible that the firm's risk aversion will remain unchanged. In this case, the loss of $50 million should have no effect on the firm's pricing policy.

Fusion for Profit Maxim

Suppose a privately held firm is risk-averse. Then, any changes in the firm's wealth level (e.g., payments to settle a lawsuit or *sunk product development costs*) are relevant for pricing new products under uncertainty.

Risk Seeking. If successive additions to wealth become more and more valuable, we say that the owner is *risk seeking.* In this case, *the utility function becomes steeper as wealth increases* (figure 6.3).

Suppose the risk-seeking owner can choose one of two pricing plans for the new product: high price or low price. Let's say that both pricing strategies will produce the same expected profits. However, the low-price strategy will lead to more uncertain cash flows than the high-price strategy.

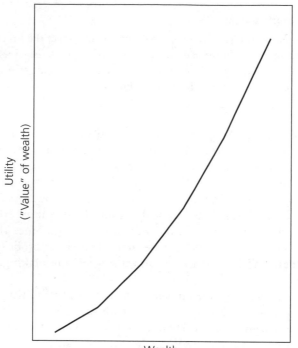

Figure 6.3 Utility function for an individual who is
risk-seeking.

Now, in contrast to the risk-averse owner, the risk-seeking owner enjoys
volatility. Hence he or she will choose the low-price strategy *because* it provides more risky cash flows.

▲ 6.5 Are Fixed Costs Relevant for Pricing New Products When the Firm Is Publicly Owned?

We now discuss new product pricing when the firm is owned by shareholders. As we discuss, the answer depends critically on whether the firm has
issued *long-term debt*.

▲ *Suppose the firm is 100% owned by a large number of stockholders
(i.e., there is no long-term debt). Will new product pricing depend
on the firm's fixed costs?*

As discussed below, the answer is surprising: *fixed costs do not have any effect
on new product pricing, even though investors are risk-averse in aggregate.*

Example: Microsoft introduced a new product, Zune, to compete with Apple's iPod. Suppose Zune will become obsolete one year after it is introduced into the marketplace. For simplicity, assume that Zune is a standalone product (e.g., there are no *joint costs* with other products in Microsoft's product portfolio) and that Microsoft has no long-run debt (this assumption will be relaxed).

Then, for any given marketing policy for Zune, *Microsoft's stock value will increase by an amount that is equal to the present value of Zune's future profits*. This quantity is known as the *certainty equivalent (CE)* of Zune's future profits and is defined by:

$$CE = \frac{[(\text{expected gross profit} - \text{risk adjustment}) - \text{fixed costs}]}{1 + \text{risk-free interest rate}}$$

Note that Zune's fixed costs will affect CE and hence Microsoft's stock price. However, Zune's pricing policy only affects the term (expected gross profits – *risk adjustment*). Hence, Zune's fixed costs will have *no* effect on Microsoft's pricing policy.

► *Suppose the firm is owned by stockholders and has issued some long-term debt. Is this financial structure relevant for new product pricing?*

When the firm uses long-term debt, we say that it is using *financial leverage*. Since long-term debt increases the firm's fixed costs, this will increase the probability that the firm will default on its interest payments to bondholders. Consequently, bondholders will demand a higher rate of return on their investment. Since shareholders are entitled only to the residual income left *after* paying bondholders, long-run debt will have a direct impact on the net return and risk to shareholders from using a particular pricing (marketing) policy for the new product and hence affect stock price.

Fusion for Profit Maxim

In general, the financial structure of the publicly held firm is relevant for new product pricing.

► *Suppose the publicly owned firm has issued long-term debt. How will this affect new product pricing?*

The firm should choose more conservative pricing strategies for the new product because financial leverage increases the firm's fixed costs and hence increases the risk borne by shareholders.

> **Fusion for Profit Maxim**
>
> In general, firms with financial leverage should choose more conservative new product pricing policies than firms that have not issued long-term debt.

Point to consider.   Continental Airlines recently retired some long-term debt. What is the likely effect on pricing in the airline industry?

By retiring some long-term debt, Continental will reduce its fixed costs. Hence Continental Airlines can be more aggressive in its marketing efforts. For example, Continental may decide to reduce prices. If this happens, other airlines will be forced to reduce their prices, since airline seats sold by competing airlines are close substitutes for each other.

◣ 6.6 Should Firms Preannounce Their New Products?

The previous analysis focused on how to price new products under uncertainty. In practice, however, the manager of the firm needs to make an additional decision: Should the firm preannounce new products? If so, what information should it provide? In this section, we consider theoretical arguments for and against the preannouncement of new products by privately and publicly held firms. In addition, we discuss empirical evidence.

Theoretical Arguments

As discussed below, *preannouncements* are a mixed blessing for firms that introduce new products into the marketplace.

The Supply Chain.   Preannouncing a new product may encourage other firms in the *supply chain* (e.g., those who provide inputs to the preannouncing firm or distribute its products) to commit resources to the new product, especially if these firms perceive that the new product will be substantially superior to existing products in the market. For example, to encourage other firms in the supply chain to commit resources to its new Vista operating system, Microsoft preannounced Vista long before it was released in the market.

Competition.   Preannouncing a new product conveys information to the firm's competitors. Hence a necessary condition for a preannouncing strategy to work is that the preannouncing firm has strong patent protection for the new product. Alternatively, it should be difficult for competitors to copy the new product (e.g., the new product is a durable that involves a long or complex manufacturing process).

The Effect of Market Share.   Suppose the preannouncing firm has a low market share. Then, other factors being the same, the loss from *cannibalization* will be smaller than it is for a firm with high market share. Consequently, firms with low market shares are likely to gain more from preannouncing new products than firms with high market shares.

Consumers.   As we discuss below, preannouncements are likely to have industry- and product-specific effects. If a firm preannounces a new product, consumers (including those who might otherwise buy a competitor's product) may decide to postpone purchase, especially if they perceive the preannounced product to be of substantially higher quality than existing products. Hence the preannouncing firm will cannibalize its existing products. However, at the same time, it will *increase* the size of the market in the future.[4]

Suppose consumers' *reservation prices* for the preannounced product are significantly higher than they are for the currently available products in the market because the preannounced product is a significant improvement over the existing products in the market. Furthermore, suppose the marginal cost to the firm of providing this improved product quality is small. Then, the profit margin on the preannounced product will be higher than the corresponding profit margin on the firm's existing products. Hence, other factors being the same, cannibalization should *increase* the preannouncing firm's profits.

Since consumers perceive the preannounced product to be of high quality, a large fraction of potential customers who are in the market are likely to postpone purchase and will purchase the preannounced product when it becomes available in the future. Consequently, the preannouncing firm will gain more new customers in the future.

The net result of the effects listed above is that, other factors being the same, the preannouncing firm's product-line profits (increased profits from cannibalization + increased profits from new customers in the future) should increase.

On the other hand, future consumers could be disappointed if the firm "overpromises" product performance. Hence the planned increase in sales and profits may not materialize. This implies that the preannouncing firm should carefully evaluate its message strategy and the type of product-specific information it provides.

Preannouncements and the Ownership Structure of the Firm

The Privately Held Firm.   In general, the potential gains from preannouncing new products are likely to be uncertain. Furthermore, small privately held firms are likely to be more risk-averse than large privately held firms. Hence, other factors being the same, small privately held firms will be less likely to preannounce new products than large privately held firms.

The Publicly Held Firm.   Preannouncements can have an important *signaling effect* on the stock market. When the publicly held firm preannounces new products, several results could take place:

- The stock market could increase its estimates of the firm's future cash flows. This effect will tend to increase the preannouncing firm's stock value.
- Suppose the new product is targeted at a market segment whose demand is more uncertain than the demand for the firm's current products. This effect will tend to lower the preannouncing firm's stock value.
- The information in a preannouncement is public and is therefore available to both the stock market and the firm's competitors. Consequently, the firm's competitors could use the preannouncement information to revise the marketing plans for their current products or to change their new product introduction policies.

How these multiple *signaling effects* change the stock market's beliefs about the preannouncing firm's future cash flows is not clear. Hence, on balance, the effect of product preannouncements on the firm's stock price is ambiguous.

Empirical Evidence on the Effects of Preannouncements.   We distinguish product announcements and product preannouncements. *Product announcements* are *information release events (IREs)* close to the time when the new product is introduced. *Product preannouncements* are IREs made significantly before the time of new product introduction.

Empirical evidence shows that product announcements and preannouncements have different effects on stock prices.[5] In particular, *on average, product announcements do not increase the firm's stock price.* However, on average, *product preannouncements produce a small but statistically significant increase in stock value for the preannouncing firm.*

Importantly, the effect of product preannouncements on stock value is industry-specific. Thus, in aggregate, preannouncements have significantly below-average effects on abnormal stock returns in the following industries: computers (Standard Industrial Code [SIC] 350), the pharmaceutical/chemical industry (SIC 280), and the photographic instruments/equipment industry (SIC 380).

Interestingly, preannouncements in the manufacturing industry (SIC 390) lead to a significantly above-average increase in the preannouncing firm's stock price.[6]

Fusion for Profit Maxim

Preannouncing new products is a mixed blessing for the firm, regardless of its ownership structure. The empirical evidence suggests that, on average, the gains to publicly held firms are small. However, for particular industries (e.g., manufacturing), preannouncing new products can lead to a significant increase in the firm's stock price.

Chapter 6 Key Points

- In a world of uncertainty, the firm should not use average demand to set the prices of its new products.
- The optimality of break-even pricing for new products depends on the ownership structure of the firm, the relative magnitudes of downside risk and upside gain, and the firm's planning horizon.
- Break-even pricing for new products focuses exclusively on downside risk and ignores upside gains. Hence the firm is likely to charge a high price for its new products.
- Markup or cost-plus pricing is not a useful method for pricing new products.
- In a world of uncertainty, fixed costs are relevant to the pricing policy of the privately held firm, especially when these costs are large with respect to the owner's wealth level. In contrast, regardless of their magnitude, fixed costs are irrelevant to the pricing policy of the publicly held firm that has no long-term debt.
- Preannouncing new products, including preannouncing new product prices, is a mixed blessing for the firm, regardless of its ownership structure. In general, the gains from preannouncing new products appear to be small and industry-specific. In certain industries (e.g., manufacturing), preannouncing new products can lead to a significant increase in the firm's stock price.

7

Choosing Strategies for New Products Using Market-Level Data

This chapter examines methods that the firm can use for choosing new product strategy when only market-level data are available. In the next chapter, we will examine methods for choosing new product strategy when the firm can collect primary data (e.g., by running controlled experiments).

Suppose only market-level data are available. The information covered in this chapter will be useful when you are faced with the following types of decisions:

- Which industry or industries should my firm enter?
- What new product design and manufacturing process should my firm choose if it enters a competitive industry?
- How should my firm price a new product when consumers are fully informed?
- How should my firm price a new product when consumers have imperfect information?
- Under what conditions should my firm use market *signals* in its *marketing plan* for a new product?

The following terms will be introduced in this chapter (see glossary for definitions):

barriers to entry	breakdown rate	dependent variable
barriers to exit	cost structure	dummy variables

external cues	marginal cost	product life cycle
hedonic pricing	marketing plan	profitability
incremental costs	mature product	regression model
law of one price	perceptual product benefits	signals

▶ 7.1 Which Product Qualities Should the Firm Produce?

We will assume that the firm has already determined that it has the technical, marketing, and other competencies to compete in the industry or industries it is planning to enter. To focus on essentials, we will begin with the case where the firm has already determined which industry or industries to enter. (This assumption will be relaxed later.) The next step is to determine what product quality or qualities to produce.

Some argue that the firm should produce high-quality products. They support this conclusion based on the empirical finding that, in many industries, product quality and *profitability* are positively correlated. As discussed below, this conclusion may be incorrect.

Competition

The observed correlation between product quality and profitability may not be causal. For example, suppose that, because of *barriers to entry*, only large firms in an industry currently produce high-quality products. Then, a small firm should not mimic large firms in the industry by marketing high-quality products in the hope of achieving high profitability.

Market Size

The size of the market segment that is willing to buy high-quality products in an industry may not be sufficiently large. Furthermore, it may be uneconomical to reach this segment. Since the market size is small, even though unit gross profit margins for high-quality products may be high, profitability could be low.

Measurement of Product Quality

The concept of high quality is likely to be ambiguous when quality has multiple dimensions.

Example 1: In the 1970s, Polaroid introduced a new camera that was much easier to use than the Instamatic cameras that were available at the time. However, the new Polaroid camera provided a lower picture quality than the Instamatics.

Since amateurs valued ease of use more highly than picture quality, the amateur photographer segment would have concluded that the new Polaroid was of *higher* quality than the Instamatics. However, since more serious photographers valued picture quality more highly than ease of use, the more serious photographer segment would have concluded that the Polaroid was of *lower* quality than the Instamatics.

Note that, since neither camera (Instamatic or Polaroid) was superior on all dimensions, product quality was an ambiguous concept. As this example illustrates, when preferences differ across consumers, it may be necessary to define product quality on a segment-by-segment basis.

Example 2: The iPhone is superior to currently available cell phones in terms of ease of Internet accessibility on the go. However, the iPhone currently relies upon a slower wireless data network than competing cell phones. Since the iPhone does not dominate its competitors on all key dimensions of performance, the concept of product quality is ambiguous. For example, cell phone users who exchange large data sets via the Internet will conclude that the iPhone is of lower quality than one of the available cell phones that is faster. Alternatively, cell phone users who value ease of access to the Internet more highly than speed will conclude that the iPhone is superior.[1]

Example 3: Consider the market for subcompact cars. Suppose two brands are available, Toyota and Honda. Furthermore, suppose consumers choose subcompact cars based on only two attributes: miles per gallon and horsepower.

Let's say that the Toyota provides better gas mileage and horsepower than the Honda. Since all consumers prefer more horsepower and better gas mileage to less, the Toyota is unambiguously a higher-quality product. However, suppose the Toyota delivers more horsepower but lower gas mileage than the Honda. Then, the concept of high quality is ambiguous. For example, consumers who value horsepower more highly than gas mileage are likely to conclude that the Toyota has higher quality. In contrast, consumers who value gas mileage more highly than horsepower are likely to conclude that the Honda has higher quality.

Point to consider.   What do these examples imply about the observed positive correlation between product quality and profitability?

Since quality is often multidimensional and consumers' preferences vary across those dimensions, quality should not be measured using one number. Consequently, the observed positive correlations between product quality (measured using one number only) and profitability are likely to be biased.

Fusion for Profit Maxim

The observed positive relationship in many industries between quality and profitability is not causal. One implication is that firms that enter an industry with high-quality products may not achieve high profitability.

▶ 7.2 Choosing New Product Strategy: The Case Where Consumers Are Fully Informed

Our earlier discussion assumed that the firm had already determined which industry or industries to enter. We now relax this assumption.

When deciding which industry to enter and which marketing policies to use, the firm should consider how well-informed consumers in the industry are. We begin with the case where all consumers are well-informed and then discuss the case where information varies across consumers.

▶ Suppose consumers are well-informed and firms can freely enter or exit an industry. What is the relationship between price and product quality?

Example: Let's say that two automobile manufacturers, Honda and Toyota, produce identical automobiles with the same combinations of horsepower and gas mileage ("quality"). For simplicity, assume that consumers make decisions based on only these two product attributes. By assumption, all consumers are fully informed.

Suppose Honda charges a higher price than Toyota. Since consumers are fully informed and know that both Honda and Toyota provide the same quality, no one will buy a Honda. Similarly, if Toyota charges a higher price than Honda, no one will buy a Toyota. Thus, Honda and Toyota have no choice but to charge the same prices for their automobiles. We say that the *law of one price* holds. That is, for any combination of product attributes (i.e., horsepower and gas mileage in our example), there is only one market price. Note that, if the law of one price holds, once either Honda or Toyota chooses a given product design, it has no control over the price of the product.

Fusion for Profit Maxim

If the industry is competitive, the law of one price holds for all competing products of identical design.

▶ Suppose consumers are well-informed. How can the firm determine the relationship between market prices and the different dimensions of product quality?

We continue with the automobile example. Suppose the market currently contains 15 brands of automobile, each of which offers a different combination of horsepower and gas mileage. Since all consumers are fully informed, the law of one price holds. That is, there is only one price for each product design configuration (quality) in the marketplace. Now we can estimate the relationship between the price of a brand (the *dependent variable*) and the different dimensions of quality for that brand (the explanatory variables) using the *hedonic pricing* model.

Note that the hedonic pricing model is essentially a *regression model* in which one uses brand-level data to estimate the relationship between price and the different objective dimensions of quality.[2] In our example, suppose that the estimated hedonic pricing model is as follows:

$$Price = 0.1 \text{ (horsepower)} + 0.4 \text{ (gas mileage)},$$

where price is measured in thousands of dollars and gas mileage is measured in miles per gallon.[3]

Let's say that an automobile manufacturer chooses a new design such that the new automobile delivers 200 horsepower and 30 miles per gallon. Then, the market price for this design configuration is $32,000 ([0.1 × 200 + 0.4 × 30] × 1,000)—*regardless of which manufacturer makes the new automobile*. Note that, once the firm chooses a particular design configuration, it has no control over the market price.

Fusion for Profit Maxim

The hedonic pricing model gives the market prices for products with different design configurations (qualities) in a competitive industry.

▶ *Suppose a new firm is planning to enter the automobile industry. What product design should the firm choose, and what price should it charge?*

When choosing a product design, the firm should take the following steps:

1. Estimate a hedonic pricing model using market-level data to determine the market price for each feasible product design,
2. Determine the costs of using different production processes to produce each feasible new product design, and
3. Choose that combination of product design and production process that maximizes profits.

Note that the firm cannot simultaneously choose product design and price. Once the firm chooses the product design configuration, the market determines price.

We illustrate the methodology by returning to the automobile example where the hedonic pricing model was: price = 0.1 (horse power) + 0.4 (gas mileage). Let's say that a new firm is considering entering the automobile industry with the following product design: 200 horsepower and 30 miles per gallon. As previously discussed, the market price for an automobile with this design configuration is $32,000.

Suppose the firm can use two different production processes to manufacture a new automobile with this design configuration: Process A and Process B. Process A involves higher fixed costs but lower variable costs per unit for any given volume than Process B (table 7.1). Since the firm seeks to maximize its profits and the price for the new car ($32,000) is fixed by the market, the firm will choose a production volume such that the *marginal cost* is $32,000.[4]

Suppose the profit-maximizing volumes for the new car design are as follows:

1. 10,000 units per year (Process A), and
2. 9,000 units per year (Process B).

Then, the optimal strategy for the firm is to use the high fixed-cost technology (Process A) to manufacture a car with the specified design configuration. As shown in table 7.1, if the firm chooses this combination product design and manufacturing strategy, it will make an annual profit of $80 million.

Similarly, the firm can determine the optimal production process for other feasible product designs. Once these results are available, the firm can choose the optimal combination of product design and production process that maximizes profits.

Point to consider.   Can the firm use the hedonic pricing model to choose a multiproduct strategy for entering a given industry?

For simplicity, suppose the firm is planning to introduce two product designs only. Continuing with the automobile example, let's say that the firm has chosen two models of automobile:

1. The first model delivers 200 horsepower and 30 miles per gallon (Model 1), and
2. The second model delivers 250 horsepower and 26 miles per gallon (Model 2).

Now, the hedonic pricing model in our example implies the following market prices: $32,000 (Model 1) and $35,400 (Model 2). Since the prices of the models are determined by the market, the only decision for the firm is to choose the optimal production plan conditional on its product design

Table 7.1
How Different Production Processes Affect Profits

Process	Units sold	Revenue	Fixed cost	Variable cost	Total cost	Profits
A	10,000	$320M	$100M	$140M	$240M	$80M
B	9,000	$288M	$80M	$135M	$215M	$73M

Note: A denotes the optimal production process.

strategy, that is, to determine how many units of each model it should make to maximize its profits. This analysis is straightforward, since the firm knows its *cost structure* and the market prices for the two new models it is planning to introduce, $32,000 for Model 1 and $35,400 for Model 2.[5]

 Are there any conditions under which the firm will be unable to use the hedonic pricing model?

The hedonic pricing model is based on a number of assumptions.

New Attributes

The hedonic pricing model assumes that the product attributes are fixed. Only the levels of attributes vary across different products in the industry. This assumption is reasonable for many industries. However, it does not hold for innovative products that introduce new product features into the marketplace.

Example: Suppose Nissan plans to introduce the first commercially available hydrogen-powered automobile into the market. As discussed above, the hedonic pricing model measures only the historical relationship between market prices and *currently available* product attributes. Since Nissan is introducing a new product attribute into the marketplace, it cannot use the hedonic pricing model.

Number of Brands in the Marketplace

The hedonic pricing model can be estimated only if the number of brands is significantly larger than the number of relevant product attributes. This condition may not be satisfied. For example, one cannot use the hedonic pricing model to analyze an industry in which there are only a few brands and quality is multidimensional.

Barriers to Entry and Exit

The hedonic pricing model assumes that all firms can freely enter or exit an industry. This assumption may not hold. For example, a firm could have patent protection for its production technology (a barrier to entry); alternatively, the firm may need to make product-specific investments with a low salvage value (a *barrier to exit*).

Fusion for Profit Maxim

The hedonic pricing model cannot be used if the new product introduces new attributes into the marketplace or if the number of brands is small compared with the number of dimensions of product quality.

▶ *7.3 Choosing New Product Strategy: The Case Where Consumers Are Not Fully Informed*

In the previous section, we considered the case where consumers are fully informed. In many cases, however, consumers may not be fully informed about product attributes or product performance. We now examine how the firm can choose its new product strategy when consumers do not have full information, and only market-level data are available. More general scenarios will be examined in chapter 8.

▶ *How should the firm price its new product? (Assume that the product design is fixed.)*

In the case where all consumers are uninformed and cannot judge the quality of the new product, consumers are likely to use *external cues* or signals (e.g., high prices) to determine how much they are willing to pay for the new product. Under these conditions, one strategy for the firm is to "overprice" in order to increase the consumer's willingness to pay (reservation price) and hence stimulate demand.

Fusion for Profit Maxim

If consumers are not fully informed, the firm can use signals when introducing a new product.

▶ *What other signals besides price can the firm use to appeal to uninformed consumers?*

Suppose the manufacturer knows its product quality (e.g., the *breakdown rate* for a durable product), but the consumer does not. Then, it may be desirable for the manufacturer to offer the consumer a strong warranty program in which it promises to replace a defective product free of charge for a specified time period. In this case, the warranty program is a signal of quality.

Example: Several years ago, Hyundai was not doing well in the U.S. market. When Hyundai introduced its ten-year, 100,000-mile warranty program, its sales and profits from its U.S. operations increased sharply.

Note that for a product warranty program to succeed as a signal of quality, the signal has to be credible. Thus, consumers will trust a warranty program offered by an established firm with a reputation to protect. However, they will be reticent to trust a warranty program offered by a new and unknown firm with no reputation.

Fusion for Profit Maxim

The firm can use a variety of signals to reach uninformed consumers. These signals include pricing and warranty policies.

▶ 7.4 Choosing New Product Strategy: The Case Where Some Consumers Are Well Informed but Others Are Not

If some consumers are fully informed but others are not, signaling can be a mixed blessing for the firm.

Example: Consider price as a signal. On the one hand, by overpricing, the firm gains by appealing to uninformed consumers who interpret high prices as a signal of high quality. On the other hand, if the firm overprices, it loses customers who are well informed. Whether or not the firm gains by price signaling depends on the relative sizes of the informed and uninformed segments.

▶ Under what conditions should the firm use market signals for a new product?

Signaling should be used depending on the firm's strategy for the new product. For example, if the firm targets the informed consumer segment, it should not use any signals (including price), since external cues do not affect the reservation prices of the consumers in the target segment. Similarly, if the firm seeks to appeal to the uninformed consumer segment, it should use a signal (e.g., a high price) to convince this segment that its product is of high quality.

In practice, it may be difficult for the firm to selectively target either the informed or the uninformed segments. Hence, if the firm uses a price signaling strategy, it will lose profits from the informed consumer group. However, it will increase its profits from the uninformed segment. Thus, the firm has to carefully balance the *incremental costs* and benefits from using signaling.

Fusion for Profit Maxim

When the firm uses a signaling strategy, it needs to balance the gain in profit from the uninformed segment with the corresponding loss in profits from the informed segment.

▶ *What is the effect of price signaling over the* product life cycle?

Suppose a firm introduces a new product into an industry that is in the early phase of its *product life cycle*. Then, a significant proportion of consumers is likely to be uninformed. Hence the firm may find it profitable to use a high price to signal high quality in the introductory phase.

In general, the proportion of uninformed consumers will decrease over time as consumers become more familiar with the product. Hence price signaling will become less attractive as the product enters the *maturity phase* of its life cycle. In the extreme case, when all consumers are fully informed, firms should not use price signals.

Point to consider.   Consider a product that is in the maturity phase of its life cycle. Are there any conditions under which the firm should use price signaling?

Suppose the *product benefits are perceptual*. Alternatively, suppose that consumers cannot verify the product's performance after using the product. Then, even if a product is in the maturity stage, the proportion of uninformed consumers could be high. Hence price signaling can be effective even though the product is in the maturity phase of the product life cycle.

Example: Bayer is able to command a significant price premium in the aspirin market, even though the aspirin market is mature and Bayer's competitors offer aspirin brands that have identical chemical compositions.

Fusion for Profit Maxim

In general, the firm's gains from signaling will diminish as a product becomes mature. However, in a perception-driven market, signaling can be effective even though the product is in the maturity phase.

▶ *How can the firm use market-level data to choose a price-signaling policy when it introduces a new product into the marketplace?*

One approach is to use market-level data to test a price-signaling model that includes the standard hedonic pricing model as a special case. Kalita, Jagpal, and Lehmann analyzed brand-level data across a number of durable and nondurable products. Their results show that price signaling is common.[6] Furthermore, the intensity of price signaling varies across industries. In particular, the markets for nondurable products are generally less informed than those for durables. Hence, in general, the intensity of price signaling is stronger for nondurable goods (e.g., tissue paper, laundry detergents, and paper towels) than for durables.

Fusion for Profit Maxim

If consumers in an industry are not well informed, the firm can use a price-signaling model to determine how it should set the price of its new product.

▶ *Should the firm use more than one signal for its new product? If so, which signals should the firm use, and how strong should each signal be?*

This is an interesting theoretical and managerial problem. For example, suppose the firm is considering two signals: price and a product warranty program.

▶ *Should the firm use only price or a product warranty as a signal, or should the firm use both price and a product warranty? In addition, how strong should these signals be?*

These problems are difficult to address using market-level data alone. One practical approach for the firm is to conduct a suitable choice experiment to determine how different signals (used alone or together) and signal strengths affect consumers' reservation prices; then, use these results to choose the optimal signaling strategy. We will discuss the choice experiment methodology in the next chapter.

Fusion for Profit Maxim

Under certain conditions, the optimal policy for the firm may be to use a combination of signals. In such cases, the firm should not rely on market-level data alone to choose its signaling strategy.

Chapter 7 Key Points
- The observed positive correlation in many industries between quality and profitability is not causal.
- If an industry is competitive, the law of one price will hold for all competing products of identical design.
- If an industry is competitive and consumers are fully informed, the firm can use the hedonic pricing model to determine which new product design and production process to use if it enters the industry.
- The hedonic pricing model cannot be used if the new product introduces new product attributes into the marketplace of if the number of brands in the industry is small compared with the number of dimensions of product quality.

- If consumers are not fully informed, the optimal strategy for the firm may be to use market signals such as high prices and/or product warranty programs to appeal to uninformed consumers in the marketplace.
- In general, market signaling will become less important as products progress through their life cycles. However, this conclusion does not hold for industries that are perception-driven or those in which consumers cannot accurately determine product quality even after using the product.
- Under certain conditions, the optimal policy for the firm may be to use a combination of signals. In such cases, the firm should not rely on market-level data alone to choose its signaling strategy.

8

Choosing Strategies for New Products Using Primary Data

In many cases, the firm cannot choose strategies for new products using market-level data. For example, the new product may include product attributes that are new to the market. The market may not be perfectly competitive (e.g., there may be *barriers to entry*). Consumers may not be well informed. The number of brands in the marketplace may be small, especially if the product category is new. Hence the firm may have no alternative but to estimate demand by collecting and analyzing primary data (e.g., by conducting *controlled purchase experiments*). In this chapter we discuss theoretical concepts and empirical methods for choosing marketing strategies for new products using primary data.

The information covered in this chapter will be useful when you are faced with the following types of decisions:

- How should my firm price a new product if the product design has already been determined?
- How useful are purchase intentions studies in estimating:
  - The demand for my firm's new products?
  - How my firm's new product will *cannibalize* the existing product line?
  - How my firm's new product will affect competitors' market shares?
  - How my firm should choose the optimal combination of product design *and* price for a new product?
- Should my firm price new products using studies that measure consumers' willingness to pay?

- Should my firm use *choice experiments* to estimate the demand for a new product?
- Should my firm use *auctions* to determine consumers' willingness to buy?
- How should my firm change its product-line policy when it introduces a new product into the marketplace?
- What are *simulated test markets* (STMs), and when should my firm use them to forecast new product demand?
- Should my firm conduct a *test market* before it launches a new product, and how should it analyze the test market results?

The following terms will be introduced in this chapter (see glossary for definitions):

auction	equilibrium repeat	panel data
barriers to entry	purchase rate	part worths
brand equity	incentive compatible	point-of-purchase
cannibalization	incentive money	advertising
choice experiment	intention studies	preference study
competition-based	intention-purchase	price skimming
pricing	relationship	product profile
competitive set	intentions data	random sampling
conjoint analysis	law of one price	reservation price
consumer	marginal cost	self-stated intentions
surplus	marketing mix	simulated test market
control	matched samples	(STM)
controlled purchase	MCT methodology	test market
experiments	net economic benefit	top-box
cost structure	no-purchase option	top-two box
cumulative trial	normal distribution	trial rate
rate equilibrium	panel	

▲ 8.1 Controlled Purchase Experiments

One simple method for forecasting the demand for a new product is to use a controlled purchase experiment.

▲ How can the firm measure demand using a controlled purchase experiment?

We begin with the case where the firm has already chosen the product design.

Example: Consider a packaged goods firm, Slick, that has developed a new shampoo product, VeriClean. Let's say that Slick has chosen the exact combination and levels of ingredients to use. In addition, it has chosen the package form and package size for the new product (e.g., a 6-ounce tube).

Suppose Slick is considering two prices for VeriClean: $3.00 and $2.50 per tube. Then, Slick could run two separate experiments with *matched samples* of consumers. (Two samples are matched if *random sampling* has been used to select each sample from the same target segment of consumers.)

In the first experiment, consumers are offered the opportunity to buy VeriClean at a price of $3.00 per tube. In the second experiment, consumers can purchase VeriClean at a price of $2.50 per tube. Suppose 25% of consumers in the first sample and 35% of those in the second sample purchase VeriClean. Then, depending on its objective (e.g., short-run profits or market share), Slick can use these demand estimates along with the appropriate production cost data for VeriClean to determine which price policy is superior.

▶ How useful are such controlled purchase experiments for pricing new products?

Controlled purchase experiments of the type discussed above are not always feasible. For example, in contrast to a shampoo manufacturer like Slick, General Motors cannot use controlled purchase experiments to estimate the demand for a new model of automobile.

Regardless of whether the product is a durable or not, it is expensive to run controlled purchase experiments of the type discussed above using a large number of potential prices. The experimental method described above assumes that the product design is fixed a priori. Thus, the method implicitly assumes that the firm should use a sequential approach in which it first determines the product design and then chooses price. This approach does not allow the firm to coordinate all elements of its *marketing mix* policy (e.g., product design and pricing). Finally, the forecasts from the purchase experiment may not be valid in the marketplace, since the experiment does not allow consumers to purchase other brands.

Point to consider.   Can the firm use controlled purchase experiments to simultaneously determine the optimal combination of product features and price?

In principle, the firm can use controlled purchase experiments to simultaneously choose the optimal product design and price for the new product. However, the method will not work in most practical applications.

Consider the Slick example discussed above. Suppose Slick's new shampoo product, VeriClean, contains three design attributes: color, package type, and water content. Then, Slick has to choose the optimal product design and price for VeriClean before launching it into the marketplace. Let's say that Slick is considering three colors, two packaging types, four levels of water content, and five prices. Then, to use the controlled experiment approach described above, it will be necessary for Slick to run 120 experiments ($3 \times 2 \times 4 \times 5$) to determine the optimal combination of product design and price for VeriClean. And, this is a small problem with only four product design attributes.

Fusion for Profit Maxim

In most cases, it is not practical for firms to use controlled purchase experiments to simultaneously choose the optimal product design and price for a new product.

We now discuss alternative methods for estimating the demand for new products. In contrast to controlled purchase experiments, these methods can be used to simultaneously determine the optimal combination of product features and prices. In addition, they can allow for competitive effects.

▲ 8.2 Intentions Studies

One approach for estimating the demand for a new product is to obtain estimates of how likely consumers are to purchase the new product. Thus, instead of directly collecting purchase data in an experiment, the firm can use a two-step method:

1. Ask consumers to state their intentions to purchase the new product, and
2. Use this information to estimate demand.

▲ How can the firm use intentions studies to predict the demand for a new product?

We begin with the case where the product design has already been determined. Hence the only issue is to forecast demand. In the Slick example, suppose Slick has already chosen the following features for VeriClean: blue color, 50% water content, 6-ounce tube, and a price of $4.50 for the tube. Now, instead of conducting a purchase experiment, Slick can ask consumers to state their intentions to buy VeriClean. This information can be collected in two ways.

First, suppose Slick has already developed a prototype of VeriClean with the features mentioned above. Then, Slick can show consumers a tube of VeriClean and ask them the following question: "On a scale of 1 to 5, how likely is it that you will purchase this tube of VeriClean at a price of $4.50?" (Responses to intentions questions are often coded on 5- or 7-point scales. For example, on a 5-point scale, 1 = will not purchase and 5 = will definitely purchase.) Second, if Slick has not made the new shampoo, it can provide consumers with a description of VeriClean and ask consumers the same intentions question as above.

Suppose Slick conducts an intentions study using 100 respondents from the target segment for VeriClean. Let's say that 15% of the respondents assign VeriClean a score of 5 on a 5-point scale. Then, according to the *top-box* method, VeriClean will obtain a market share of 15%. Suppose an additional 12% of respondents assign VeriClean a score of 4 on a 5-point scale. Then the *top-two box* method will predict that VeriClean will obtain a market share of 27% (the sum of the percentages in the top two boxes).

▶ *How useful are top-box intentions scores for predicting the demand for a new product?*

As discussed above, the top-box methods are easy to use. However, they may not give accurate demand estimates for new products.

The Intention-Purchase Relationship

The relationship between *self-stated intentions* (e.g., top-box methods) and purchase is not simple. Furthermore, the strength of the *intention-purchase relationship* as measured by top-box scores varies across industries.

Example: A large study was conducted to measure the relationship between self-stated intentions to purchase a new telecommunication product and actual purchase behavior.[1] Self-stated intentions were measured on a 10-point intention scale (1 = lowest score, 10 = highest score). See table 8.1 for some of the results.

Note that, even though the product (a telecommunication product) was important to consumers, less than half (45%) of those who said that they would definitely purchase the product actually purchased it. Furthermore, the relationship between self-stated intentions and actual purchase behavior is not well defined. Thus, the purchase rate (20%) for those consumers whose self-stated intentions scores were low (2s) was *higher* than the corresponding purchase rate (17%) for those consumers whose self-stated intentions score were

Table 8.1
Telecommunications Example: The Relationship between Self-Stated Intentions and Purchase Behavior

Self-stated intention score	Proportion who bought the product
10	45%
5	17%
3	5%
2	20%
1	5%

much higher (5s). In addition, the purchase rate (20%) for consumers whose self-stated intentions scores were 2s is much higher than the corresponding purchase rate (5%) for those whose self-stated intentions scores were 3s.

Another problem is that the types and magnitudes of measurement error can vary across new products, depending on whether the new product is made by a market leader or a new entrant in the product category.

Thus, in the Slick example, consumers may overstate their intentions to purchase VeriClean if Slick is a market leader in the shampoo category. If this is the case, the top-box methods will lead to overly optimistic estimates of demand for VeriClean. Alternatively, consumers may understate their intentions to purchase VeriClean if Slick is an unknown firm in the shampoo category. If this is the case, the top-box methods will lead to excessively pessimistic demand estimates for VeriClean.

Multiproduct Firms

Standard *intention studies* measure only the intentions to purchase the new product. Hence it is not possible to estimate the effect of the new product on the firm's competitors. Nor can the firm measure how the new product will cannibalize or augment sales of the other products in its product portfolio. *This information is necessary, since the multiproduct firm seeks to maximize product-line performance—not only the profits from the new product.* Furthermore, it is necessary for the firm to determine which competitors are most likely to react when it introduces the new product and choose its policy accordingly *before launching the product.*

Segmentation

Standard intentions studies provide aggregate results only for the new product. Of course, if the firm has sufficient prior knowledge, it can segment consumers a priori, measure the intentions of different segments, and forecast the demand for the new product at the segment level. However, in many cases, especially when the firm introduces radically new products, such a priori segmentation may not be feasible.

▶ *Can more sophisticated intentions-based methodologies be used to address these limitations?*

As noted above, the key issues are to develop a multibrand intentions-based methodology that:

1. Allows for measurement error (self-stated intentions are not likely to be accurate, especially for new products),
2. Allows for different types of bias across brands in an industry (e.g., those made by market leader and those made by firms with no prior reputation in the industry),

3. Captures *cannibalization* and competitive effects, and
4. Allows for unobservable segments.

Jagpal, Jedidi, and Jamil developed a Multibrand Concept Testing methodology (MCT) for simultaneously addressing these problems.[2] The authors tested the *MCT methodology* using self-stated *intentions data* from a large pharmaceutical study involving physicians in a multibillion-dollar product category. In particular, they showed that the MCT methodology can be used to remove the biases in self-stated intentions data across different brands in the industry (e.g., those made by the market leader and by a new entrant), identify physician segments, and develop customized marketing plans on a segment-by-segment basis.[3] Importantly, the market-level validation studies conducted one year after the experiment showed that the MCT model accurately forecasted the market shares of the new brand and the incumbent brands in the marketplace.

Fusion for Profit Maxim

Self-stated intentions data are likely to be biased, especially for new products. These biases are likely to vary across brands, segments, and product categories. By using the MCT multibrand intentions methodology, the firm can remove these biases. Specifically, the firm can obtain meaningful demand forecasts for new products and measure both cannibalization and competitive effects at the segment level, even if the segments are unobservable.

▶ *In general, the industry will contain a large number of brands. Hence intentions studies cannot include all brands in the marketplace. Will this omission affect the results from the MCT methodology?*

Omitting other brands will not affect the accuracy of the MCT demand estimates provided one of the alternatives that consumers are asked to evaluate is the *no-purchase option*. However, this strategy will limit the usefulness of the results.

Managerially speaking, if the MCT intentions study excludes a particular competitor, the firm will be unable to determine how its new product policy will affect that competitor's sales or market share. Nor will the firm be able to determine the effect of competitive retaliation by that competitor following its new product introduction. Hence, from a practical viewpoint, *the intentions study should include the new product, key competitive brands, and the no-purchase option*. Note that the set of key competitive brands should include the firm's existing products so that the multiproduct firm can estimate how the new product will affect cannibalization and hence product-line profits.

Fusion for Profit Maxim

Multibrand intentions studies should include key brands in the market and explicitly include the no-purchase option.

▶ 8.3 Preference and Choice Studies

The multibrand intentions-based methodology (MCT) for estimating new product sales requires the consumer to *simultaneously* evaluate different brand profiles for each scenario. As discussed, the firm can use this method to determine the segment-specific effects of different new product introduction strategies and measure the effects of competitive retaliation.

An alternative method for evaluating new products is to conduct a *preference study* in which the consumer is asked to *separately* evaluate different *product profiles*. One popular preference methodology is *conjoint analysis*.

▶ What is conjoint analysis?

Briefly, the conjoint analysis methodology is as follows. First, choose the relevant set of product attributes. Then, determine a set of product profiles that consumers will be asked to evaluate. To illustrate what a product profile means, we return to the Slick example, where the new shampoo possesses four attributes: color, percentage of water, size of tube, and price.

Consider the following combination of attributes: blue color, 50% water content, 6.5-ounce tube, and a price of $5 per tube. A shampoo product with this combination of attributes is known as a product profile. Note that product profiles can pertain to existing or hypothetical products.

Once a group of product profiles has been chosen for analysis, each consumer is shown a smaller number of product profiles from this group, one at a time. Note that, to avoid respondent fatigue, each consumer is asked to evaluate a limited number of profiles. In the experiment, each consumer is asked to assign a preference score (say, on a 7-point scale ranging from 1 to 7, where 1 denotes the least preferred score and 7 denotes the most preferred score) to *each* product profile that he or she is asked to evaluate. Note that, in contrast to the MCT intentions-based methodology, consumers do *not* evaluate multiple product profiles simultaneously.

Given these results, the conjoint analysis methodology proceeds as follows:

1. Use the evaluation scores for different profiles by consumers to estimate the values (*part worths*) of each attribute.[4] This analysis can be done at different levels of aggregation (e.g., the individual consumer or segment levels),

2. Use these part worths to predict the consumer's preference scores for different product profiles. This analysis is generally performed by assuming that the consumer will always choose the product alternative that maximizes his or her preference score,[5] and

3. Combine these results across consumers (segments) to estimate the demand for different product profiles, including the new product.[6]

▶ *Should the firm use intentions or preference studies to predict the demand for new products?*

In our analysis, we will focus on the MCT intentions-based method and conjoint analysis because both methods are based on multibrand data. In deciding which method to use, the firm should consider the following factors.

Missing Brands

As noted earlier, if the MCT method includes the no-purchase option in the experiment, omitting competing brands from the experiment will not bias the demand estimates. As previously discussed, the reason is that the no-purchase option implicitly includes the purchase of other brands. This is *not* the case for preference studies.

For example, the conjoint model implies that the consumer will always choose that alternative for which the predicted preference score is the highest. Hence conjoint analysis could provide misleading demand estimates for the new product unless all relevant competing products are included in the experiment.

Example: Suppose Black & Decker has conducted a conjoint experiment to predict the demand for a new power drill that it has designed. Consider a particular consumer (Pete). Suppose the conjoint model predicts that Pete's preference for the new Black & Decker power drill is a 5 on a 7-point scale, where 7 denotes the highest possible score. In addition, suppose the model predicts that Pete's highest preference score for any of the other brands included in the experiment is a 4. Then, the conjoint model will predict that Pete will always buy the new Black & Decker drill.

However, this conclusion could be wrong. For example, it is possible that Pete's preference for a brand that was not included in the conjoint study (e.g., a Stanley power drill) is a 6. Hence Pete will buy the Stanley drill—not the Black & Decker drill as predicted by the model. Furthermore, it is also possible that, if Pete had been offered the no-purchase option, he would have preferred not to purchase a power drill instead of picking the profile to which he assigned the highest score in the conjoint experiment.

Missing Attributes

Consider the Black & Decker example. Suppose the power drill is battery-powered, and the experiment does not include battery life as an attribute.

Then, regardless of whether one uses an intentions-based or a preference-based method, the demand estimates will be biased.

Fusion for Profit Maxim

Regardless of whether the firm uses conjoint analysis or the MCT intentions-based methodology to forecast the demand for a new product, it is essential to include key brands and attributes in the study.

Data Accuracy

The consumer's task in a conjoint experiment is relatively easy because the consumer is required to evaluate only one profile at a time. In contrast, in multibrand intentions-based experiments such as MCT, the consumer is required to *simultaneously* evaluate all profiles in a given scenario. Thus, it is possible that conjoint experiments may give "cleaner" data than intentions-based experiments.

Competition and Cannibalization

Both conjoint analysis and the MCT method provide multibrand data. Hence both methods allow the firm to measure how the new product will affect competitors' market shares. In addition, both methods allow the multiproduct firm to determine how the new product will cannibalize its existing products. However, as discussed above, the conjoint estimates are sensitive to the set of brands that are included in the study. In addition, typical conjoint studies do not allow for uncertain choice behavior (i.e., they assume that the consumer always picks the alternative that he or she ranks the highest).

Consequently, other factors being the same, the MCT methodology should provide more accurate estimates of competitive and cannibalization effects than conjoint analysis.

Market Expansion

The conjoint method implicitly assumes that all respondents will make a purchase. Hence conjoint analysis implicitly assumes that the market size is fixed. In contrast, the MCT method explicitly includes the no-purchase alternative. Hence the MCT method allows the new product to increase the size of the market for the product category in question.

Fusion for Profit Maxim

The MCT methodology is general because it allows the firm to measure how its new product will affect the sales of its own product line, the sales of competitive brands, *and* the market growth rate.

▶ 8.4 Estimating Demand Using Reservation Prices

The previous methods for estimating demand were based on measuring consumers' intentions to buy or their preferences for different products. An alternative and more direct approach is to estimate the demand for a new product based on consumers' *reservation prices* (RPs). We will use the following definition: a consumer's reservation price for a brand with a given set of attributes is the maximum price that the consumer is willing to pay for a brand with these attributes.[7]

In this section, we focus on the theoretical relationship between reservation prices and demand. That is, we assume that the firm knows consumers' reservation prices. In the next section, we discuss empirical methods for measuring reservation prices and using these results to forecast new product demand.

▶ *Suppose Sony has developed a new DVD player with features that are new to the market. What price should Sony charge for the new DVD player?*

Suppose there are three segments of equal size. For simplicity, assume that each segment is of equal size, say 100,000. By assumption, Sony knows consumers' reservation prices for its new DVD player. Suppose each consumer in Segment A is willing to pay up to $200 for the new Sony DVD player. We say that Segment A's reservation price for the new DVD player is $200. Similarly, suppose the reservation prices for consumers in Segments B and C are $160 and $120, respectively.

Now, a consumer will buy the new Sony DVD player only if he or she obtains a *net economic benefit* or *consumer surplus* (reservation price – price paid). Thus, if Sony charges $200 per unit, only Segment A will buy the new Sony DVD player. Similarly, if Sony charges $160 per unit, Segments A and B will buy the new player. Hence, Sony can sell 100,000 units of the new DVD player at a price of $200; 200,000 units at a price of $160; and 300,000 units at a price of $120.

Fusion for Profit Maxim

The firm can forecast the demand for a new product if it knows the reservation prices of different consumers for this product.

▶ *Suppose Sony knows the reservation prices of consumers for the new DVD player. What price should Sony charge?*

The answer depends on Sony's objective and its *cost structure* for manufacturing the new DVD player. Suppose the *marginal cost* of the new player

Table 8.2
Sony DVD Player Example: Effect of Different Pricing Strategies on Profits

Price	Units sold	Revenue	Variable cost	Gross profit margin
$200	100,000	$20,000,000	$8,000,000	$12,000,000
$160*	200,000	$32,000,000	$16,000,000	$16,000,000
$120	300,000	$36,000,000	$24,000,000	$12,000,000

Note: Variable cost = marginal cost × units sold.
*The price that maximizes Sony's short-run profits.

is $80 per unit, regardless of volume. Let's say that Sony expects competitors to introduce a similar product in the near future. Then, it may decide to maximize the short-run profit from selling the new DVD player. Given this strategy, Sony should charge a price of $160 per unit and make a profit of $16 million (table 8.2).

Alternatively, suppose Sony does not expect competitors to introduce a similar product in the near future. Then, Sony may decide to use a *price-skimming* approach. That is, it will introduce the DVD player at a price of $200 per unit to capture Segment A, the segment with the highest reservation price ($200). Subsequently, Sony will reduce the price of the new DVD player over time to capture the remaining segments, B and C, whose reservation prices are lower ($160 and $120, respectively).

> **Fusion for Profit Maxim**
> Suppose the firm knows the reservation prices of consumers for its new product and its cost structure for producing that product. Then, the firm can choose the optimal price for the new product given its objectives.

► How general is the previous method for new product pricing?

The pricing methodology discussed above implicitly assumes that the firm's product is unique (i.e., there are no close substitutes). Thus, a consumer will buy the new product provided the net benefit or surplus from purchase (consumer's reservation price for the new product – price charged) is zero or positive.

As we discuss below, this conclusion does not hold if similar competitive products are available. Now, since consumers have different purchase options, they will buy the new product only if they obtain a *higher* surplus than by purchasing the product(s) already available in the marketplace.

In the Sony DVD player example above, the simple reservation price model discussed above implies that Sony can sell 100,000 units of the new

DVD player at a price of $200 per unit. However, this may not be the case if competing DVD players are available in the marketplace—*even if they are of lower quality*. Thus, suppose a lower-quality Toshiba DVD player is presently available in the marketplace at a price of $130 per unit, and consumers are well-informed about product quality. Then, Segment A knows that the Toshiba DVD player has lower quality than the Sony. Consequently, Segment A's reservation price for the Toshiba is lower than its reservation price for the Sony ($200).

Suppose Segment A's reservation price for the Toshiba DVD player is $150. Now, by purchasing the Toshiba at a price of $130, each consumer in Segment A will obtain a net economic benefit of $20 (Segment A's reservation price for the Toshiba – price of the Toshiba) (table 8.3). Since consumers maximize their net economic benefits, a consumer in Segment A will buy the new Sony DVD player only if he or she obtains a higher surplus than $20. However, if Sony charges $200 per unit for the new DVD player, consumers in Segment A will obtain zero surplus from purchasing the Sony. Hence Sony will not be able to sell any of the new DVD players if it charges a price of $200 per unit. *Note that, by failing to analyze consumers' reservation prices for competing brands (Toshiba in our example), Sony will obtain biased demand estimates for its new DVD player.*

Fusion for Profit Maxim

If competitive products are available, the firm can choose the optimal price of the new product only if it knows consumers' reservation prices for the new product *and* competing products.

Point to consider.   Many marketing studies assume that the reservation prices for a brand are *normally distributed* across consumers. Is this a reasonable assumption?

The normality assumption implies that the fraction of consumers with high reservation prices for the new product is very small. Suppose the market contains a niche segment of reasonable size with high reservation prices.

Table 8.3
Sony-Toshiba DVD Player Example: How Reservation Prices (RP) Affect Consumer Choice

DVD player brand	Segment A's RP	DVD player price	Surplus to Segment A
New Sony model	$200	$200	Zero
Toshiba	$150	$130	$20*

*Segment A's choice.

Then, this niche segment offers the potential for high profits. Since the *normal distribution* implies that the fraction of consumers with high reservation prices for the new product is small, the firm will not be able to identify this potentially lucrative niche segment.

▶ *Should a firm use* competition-based pricing *for its new product?*

Competition-based pricing implies that the firm has no *control* over price once it has chosen a particular product design. Hence competition-based pricing is necessary when the firm's new product is a clone of existing products and consumers are well informed. We say that the *law of one price* holds. (See chapter 7 for a discussion.)

However, suppose the new product is differentiated from products that are already available in the marketplace. Then, as discussed below, competition-based pricing will lead to suboptimal results.

We continue with the Sony-Toshiba DVD player example. For simplicity, assume as before that there are two competitors: Toshiba and Sony. In particular, Toshiba is the only brand in the market prior to Sony's introduction of its new DVD player. Suppose, as before, that there are three consumer segments (A, B, and C) each of size 100,000. Let's say that the reservation prices for consumers in Segments A, B, and C for the Toshiba DVD player are $180, $150, and $130, respectively (table 8.4). As before, the corresponding reservation prices for consumers in Segments A, B, and C for the new Sony DVD player are $200, $160, and $120, respectively.

For simplicity, assume that each consumer will purchase at most 1 unit. Since the Toshiba DVD player is of lower quality than the new Sony DVD player, assume that the marginal cost of the Toshiba DVD player ($60 per unit) is lower than the marginal cost of the Sony DVD player ($80 per unit). Assume also that both Toshiba and Sony seek to maximize their respective short-run profits. Then, before Sony's new DVD player is introduced, Toshiba will charge a price of $130 for its DVD player and make a profit of $21 million.

Table 8.4
Sony-Toshiba DVD Player Example: Toshiba's Optimal Pricing Policy before Sony Introduces Its New DVD Player

Price	Units sold	Revenue	Variable cost	Gross profit margin
$180	100,000	$18,000,000	$6,000,000	$12,000,000
$150	200,000	$30,000,000	$12,000,000	$18,000,000
$130*	300,000	$39,000,000	$18,000,000	$21,000,000

Note. Variable cost = marginal cost × units sold.
*Toshiba's optimal price prior to the introduction of Sony's new DVD player.

Table 8.5

Sony-Toshiba DVD Player Example: Effect of Competition-Based Pricing by Sony after It Introduces Its New DVD Player

Segment	Toshiba DVD player			Sony DVD player		
	RP	Price	Surplus	RP	Price	Surplus
A	$180	$130	$50	$200	$130	$70*
B	$150	$130	$20	$160	$130	$30*
C	$130	$130	$0*	$120	$130	−$10

Note. RP, reservation price.

*The choices made by each segment.

Note that Toshiba's price ($130 per DVD player) is *less* than the reservation prices of consumers in Segments A and B ($180 and $150, respectively). Hence each consumer in Segments A and B will obtain a positive net economic benefit by purchasing the Toshiba ($50 and $20, respectively). Consumers in Segment C will pay their reservation prices and obtain zero economic benefit.

If Sony uses competition-based pricing, it will match Toshiba's price and charge a price of $130 per unit for its new DVD player (table 8.5). Given this scenario, the consumer's net economic benefits (surpluses) from different purchase decisions are as shown in table 8.5.

Now consumers in each segment seek to maximize their net economic benefits. Given these choices, consumers in Segments A and B will purchase the new Sony DVD player, and consumers in Segment C will purchase the Toshiba.

Since Sony will sell 200,000 units at the competition-based price of $130 per unit, Sony will make a gross profit margin of $10 million (gross margin per unit × number of units sold = [$130 − $80] × 200,000).

▶ *However, is this the optimal price for Sony to charge?*

Suppose Sony charges a price of $139 per unit for its new DVD player. Then, the consumers' net economic benefits (surpluses) from different purchase decisions will be as shown in table 8.6.

Given these prices, Segments A and B will buy the new Sony DVD player, and Segment C will buy the Toshiba as before. However, there is one key difference: *Segments A and B will pay higher prices than under competition-based pricing.* Since Sony will obtain a higher margin per unit sold ($139 − $80 = $59) and the number of units sold is unchanged, Sony's gross profit margin will increase from $10 million to $11.8 million ($59 × 200,000).[8]

Table 8.6
Sony-Toshiba DVD Player Example: Optimal Pricing Policy for Sony after It Introduces Its New DVD Player

Segment	Toshiba DVD player			Sony DVD player		
	RP	Price	Surplus	RP	Price	Surplus
A	$180	$130	$50	$200	$139	$61*
B	$150	$130	$20	$160	$139	$21*
C	$130	$130	$0*	$120	$139	−$19

Note. RP, reservation price.
*The choices made by each segment.

Fusion for Profit Maxim

Suppose a firm produces a new product that is differentiated from competitive offerings. Then, the firm should set prices only after analyzing consumers' reservation prices for its new product *and* competitive brands in the marketplace. Competition-based pricing is likely to lead to suboptimal results.

▶ 8.5 Estimating the Demand for New Products Using Self-Stated Reservation Prices

In the previous section, we showed how the firm can use knowledge of consumers' reservation prices to determine the price of its new product and estimate demand. In practice, the firm does not know consumers' reservation prices. Hence it is necessary to choose an empirical method for accurately estimating reservation prices.

The simplest and most intuitive method for measuring reservation prices is to ask consumers how much they are willing to pay for particular brands (the self-stated method). As discussed below, this method is likely to give biased results—*even in the best-case scenario.* We first discuss the self-stated method for eliciting reservation prices and then discuss alternative methods.

▶ *Suppose the firm conducts an experiment in which consumers are asked to state their reservation prices for different products. If consumers provide correct responses on average, will demand be correctly estimated?*

At first glance, the answer would appear to be yes. But this conclusion is incorrect.

Example: Let's say that the Fixit company is planning to introduce a new type of glue gun, Gloo-Glock, into the market. Suppose there are two segments, A and B, respectively, whose true (and unobserved) reservation prices for Gloo-Glock are $10 and $20 per unit. Suppose consumers' self-stated reservation prices are, on average, correct. Then, the self-stated reservation prices for Gloo-Glock will correctly measure the *average* reservation prices for both segments in the population.

In practice, it is very unlikely that consumers can accurately state their reservation prices—especially for new products such as Gloo-Glock. Thus, some consumers in Segment A will state that their reservation prices for Gloo-Glock are lower than $10 (say $7), and some consumers in Segment B will state that their reservation prices for Gloo-Glock are higher than $20 (say $25). Consequently, even though the average reservation price is correctly measured, the measured range of reservation prices in the population will be overstated.

As discussed below, this implies that Fixit will obtain biased estimates of demand for Gloo-Glock. For example, Fixit will incorrectly conclude that there will be positive demand for Gloo-Glock if it is priced at $25. In reality, the market demand for Gloo-Glock at this price will be zero, since the maximum reservation price in the market is only $20. Similarly, Fixit will conclude that it will sell more units of Gloo-Glock if it reduces the price of Gloo-Glock below $10. In reality, the number of units of Gloo-Glock that can be sold will not change if the price is reduced from $10 to $7 per unit.

Fusion for Profit Maxim

Suppose the firm asks consumers to state their reservation prices for different products. Then the demand estimates for different pricing strategies will be biased—even for the most optimistic scenario where, on average, consumers correctly state their reservation prices.

▶ **What will happen if consumers tend to overstate or understate their reservation prices for the new product?**

We distinguish three scenarios. On average, consumers correctly state their reservation prices (Scenario 1), overstate them (Scenario 2), or understate them (Scenario 3).

Scenario 1: We continue with the Fixit example. As before, suppose there are two segments, A and B, whose true reservation prices for Gloo-Glock are, respectively, $10 and $20. Suppose that, on average, consumers correctly state their reservation prices for Gloo-Glock. As discussed above, for this scenario the range of reservation prices will be overstated. Hence Fixit will incorrectly conclude that some consumers will be willing to pay more than $20 for Gloo-Glock. If this proportion of consumers is sufficiently high, Fixit will significantly overestimate the demand for Gloo-Glock at high prices. Consequently, Fixit is likely to overprice Gloo-Glock.

Scenario 2: Suppose Fixit is a well-known national brand. Then, it is possible that, because of a *brand-equity* effect, consumers will tend to *overstate* their reservation prices for Gloo-Glock. Now, two effects will occur. On average, the self-stated reservation prices for both segments (A and B) will be too high. Furthermore, the *range* of measured reservation prices will be larger than in Scenario 1 above.[9] One implication is that Fixit will significantly overstate the demand for Gloo-Glock at high prices. Consequently, Fixit will overprice more than in the case where consumers' reservation prices for Gloo-Glock are correct on average (Scenario 1).

Scenario 3: Suppose Fixit is not a well-known company. Then, it is possible that consumers will, on average, *understate* their reservation prices for Gloo-Glock. However, *the effect on the estimated range of reservation prices for Gloo-Glock in the population is ambiguous.* Thus, suppose the measurement error in the self-stated reservation prices is large (e.g., consumers are unfamiliar with glue guns). Then, the estimated range of reservation prices in the population will be too high. Hence Fixit will incorrectly conclude that there will be a significant demand for Gloo-Glock at high prices. In this case, Fixit is likely to overprice. Suppose instead that the measurement error in the self-stated reservation prices for Gloo-Glock is small (e.g., consumers are reasonably familiar with glue guns). Then, it is possible that the estimated range of reservation prices in the population will be too low.[10] If this is the case, Fixit is likely to underprice Gloo-Glock.

Fusion for Profit Maxim

Suppose the firm prices a new product based on consumers' self-stated reservation prices. Then, the firm is likely to choose the wrong price for its new product—even in the best-case scenario where, on average, consumers can correctly state their reservation prices. If consumers tend to overstate their reservation prices, the firm is likely to overprice. However, if consumers tend to understate their reservation prices, the effect on the firm's pricing policy for the new product is ambiguous.

▲ 8.6 Estimating the Demand for New Products by Inferring Reservation Prices

As discussed above, the firm is likely to obtain biased estimates of demand for a new product if it uses self-stated reservation prices. This raises a fundamental question:

▲ Is there a way in which the firm can more accurately measure consumers' reservation prices for new products?

One approach for the firm is to conduct a choice experiment in which consumers are asked to make choices rather than to state their intentions to buy or to state their preferences for particular products.

► *How can the firm use a choice experiment to determine what price it should charge for the new product?*

The purpose of the choice experiment is to measure consumers' choice behavior in a controlled setting and to use this information to *infer* consumers' reservation prices. Once the firm has determined consumers' reservation prices for different brands, it can choose the optimal price for its new product.

► *To understand how the results from a choice experiment can be used to estimate new product demand, we first analyze a simpler problem: How do reservation prices affect consumers' choices?*

Example: Suppose Sony has developed a new DVD player and that a competing DVD player made by Toshiba is already available in the market. Suppose there are two consumer segments (Segments D and E) with the reservation prices (RPs) as shown in table 8.7.

Suppose consumers are given the following choice scenario: buy the Sony DVD player for $140, buy the Toshiba DVD player for $120, or make no purchase.

► *What choices will Segments D and E make?*

To answer this question, we compute the net economic benefits to consumers from different purchase strategies, including nonpurchase, under the given scenario (table 8.8).

Since consumers seek to maximize their net economic benefits, Segment D will purchase the Sony DVD player. In contrast, Segment E will choose the no-purchase option because each of the purchase alternatives gives a *negative* net economic benefit.

Suppose consumers are asked to make choices for different price scenarios (i.e., price combinations for the Sony and Toshiba DVD players and the no-purchase option). Then, we can combine the results from the choice

Table 8.7
**Sony-Toshiba DVD Player Example:
Reservation Prices (RP) for Sony
and Toshiba DVD Players**

Segment	RP for Sony DVD player	RP for Toshiba DVD player
D	$150	$125
E	$135	$115

Table 8.8
Sony-Toshiba DVD Player Example: How Reservation Prices (RP) Affect Choice for a Given Pricing Scenario

Segment	Sony DVD player			Toshiba DVD player			Surplus from nonpurchase
	RP	Price	Surplus	RP	Price	Surplus	
D	$150	$140	$10*	$125	$120	$5	$0
E	$135	$140	−$5	$115	$120	−$5	$0*

*The choices made by each segment.

experiment across consumers and forecast the market demand for the new product for different sets of market prices for Sony and Toshiba.

As the example shows, it is easy to forecast new product demand if we know consumers' reservation prices for different products. The problem, of course, is that *we do not know consumers' reservation prices.*

▶ *Hence the critical question is: How can one use the self-stated choices from a choice experiment to determine consumers' reservation prices?*

Jedidi, Jagpal, and Manchanda developed and tested a methodology for addressing this question.[11] Their method is based on the following intuitive model of consumer behavior. For any purchase scenario, the consumer will choose the alternative that maximizes his or her net economic benefit (reservation price – price). If none of the available alternatives provides a positive net economic benefit, the consumer will choose the no-purchase option.

Jedidi et al. used their choice-based methodology to estimate consumers' reservation prices for different brands in a number of product categories ranging from expensive (e.g., television sets) to inexpensive (e.g., magazine subscriptions). Their results and validation studies suggest that choice-based experiments provide unbiased estimates of demand. In addition, the authors showed how the firm can combine the estimated reservation price data for different products and cost information for those products to determine the optimal product-line pricing policy.

▶ *Is it necessary to include the no-purchase option alternative in the choice experiment?*

Including the no-purchase option is critical. Unless the no-purchase option is included, one cannot obtain unique dollar values for the reservation prices of different products.[12] These values are necessary to estimate the demand for the new product at different prices.

▶ *No choice experiment can include all available brands in the marketplace. Will this omission affect the results and the firm's pricing policy for the new product?*

The no-purchase alternative implicitly refers to either nonpurchase *or the purchase of another brand that was not included in the experiment*. As we have discussed, the choice methodology assumes that the consumer will always choose the option that provides the largest net economic benefit. Hence omitting brands from the choice experiment will not bias the estimates of reservation prices for the brands or products that are included in the study, *provided the no-purchase option is included*.

However, as in the MCT multibrand intentions model, omitting brands from a choice experiment can have important policy implications. Specifically, the firm will not be able to determine from which of its competitors its new product will steal sales and market share. Hence the firm may not be able to analyze competitive retaliation in detail. Furthermore, if the choice experiment does not include the firm's existing brands, the firm will not be able to determine cannibalization or other product-line effects. Consequently, the firm will not be able to optimize its product-line pricing policy following the new product introduction.

Fusion for Profit Maxim

If the choice experiment omits certain brands, the estimates of the reservation prices for the brands that are included in the study will be unbiased provided the choice experiment includes the no-purchase alternative.

Point to consider.   Will the results of the choice experiment be affected if consumers have different price expectations for other brands in the market and consider different sets of brands for purchase?

The no-purchase alternative implicitly allows consumers to consider different sets of brands. In addition, the no-purchase alternative implicitly allows consumers to have different price expectations for those brands. Hence the estimated reservation prices for the brands that are included in the study (including the new product) will not be affected by these omissions.

▶ *Are there any conditions under which the firm can use self-stated reservation prices to estimate the demand for a new product?*

Jedidi, Jagpal, and Manchanda examined this issue for a number of product categories, ranging from expensive (e.g., television sets) to inexpensive (e.g., magazine subscriptions). Their results showed that, regardless of the type of product category, the choice method for eliciting reservation prices led to much more accurate demand predictions than the self-stated method.

In fact, self-stated reservation prices performed *no better than chance* in predicting the choice of product bundles.[13]

Fusion for Profit Maxim

Firms should use the choice-based method for inferring reservation prices. In general, self-stated reservation prices will lead to biased demand estimates, regardless of product category.

▶ *Can the firm use the results from a choice experiment to analyze the effects of competitive retaliation following the introduction of a new product?*

The firm can analyze how competitive behavior will affect the demand for the new product, provided those competing brands (the *competitive set*) are included as purchase alternatives in the choice experiment.[14]

▶ *Can the choice-based method for estimating reservation prices be used to forecast the demand for new products in the service sector?*

The choice-based methodology can be used to estimate reservation prices, regardless of whether the product is a physical product or a service.

▶ *Can the firm use choice experiments to simultaneously choose the optimal product design and price for the new product?*

The choice-based method can be extended to allow the firm to simultaneously choose the optimal product design and price for a new product.[15]

▶ *Consumers sometimes use brand as a proxy of product quality. Can the choice-based methodology for measuring reservation prices capture these brand-equity effects?*

Brand equity can have a significant effect on consumers' reservation prices for a new product. These brand-equity effects can be positive or negative.

Example: Suppose an industrial firm such as Union Carbide plans to enter the food business. Specifically, let's say that Union Carbide plans to introduce a new food product line under its corporate name. Then, it is essential for Union Carbide to know if this new product launch policy will place it at a disadvantage with respect to major competitors who have strong brand names in the food industry (e.g., Nestlé and Kraft). If the brand-equity effect for Union Carbide is negative, it may be necessary for Union Carbide to launch its new food product line under a different name.

The choice experiment method can be extended to capture such brand-equity effects.[16]

Fusion for Profit Maxim

Choice-based experiments can capture the effect of brand equity on consumers' reservation prices for a new product.

▶ *Consumers will learn over time as they use new products. In addition, consumers' reservation prices can change when consumers obtain new information. Can the choice methodology capture these effects?*

The choice-based method can allow for reservation prices to change over time; in addition, it can be used to determine the impact of product information (e.g., different advertising message strategies) on reservation prices, choices, market shares, and profits.[17]

Point to consider. How general is the proposed choice methodology for choosing new product policy?

The firm's new product decisions include (but are not limited to) product design, price, advertising message, advertising expenditure, and channels of distribution. As discussed, the firm can use the results from a choice experiment to determine the optimal combination of product design, price, and advertising message strategy.

However, choice experiments are not a panacea for optimizing all parts of the marketing mix for new products. For example, the firm cannot use choice experiments to choose the optimal level of advertising expenditure or optimal channel strategy. Furthermore, for some new products (e.g., prescription drugs), the firm cannot use choice experiments to estimate demand. In such cases, the firm can use the MCT multibrand intentions methodology discussed earlier to forecast new product demand.

▶ 8.7 Measuring Reservation Prices Using Auctions

The previous methods for measuring reservation prices (e.g., the MCT multibrand intentions model, conjoint analysis, and choice experiments) have one feature in common: they are all based on self-stated information provided by the consumer in an experimental setting. Hence it is necessary for the firm to extrapolate how this self-stated information will translate into actual purchase behavior in the marketplace.

▶ *This raises an interesting question: Can the firm estimate reservation prices more accurately by conducting experiments in which consumers are required to make actual purchases?*

One such method is to conduct an auction.

▶ *What are the advantages of the auction methodology for estimating reservation prices?*

There are many types of auctions.[18] The primary theoretical advantage of the auction methodology in general is that consumers have an incentive to truthfully reveal their reservation prices. If this condition is satisfied, we say that the auction is *incentive compatible*. Note that, if the incentive-compatibility condition is satisfied, the auction will provide the firm with unbiased estimates of demand for its new product.

Fusion for Profit Maxim

The main theoretical advantage of the auction method is that consumers have an incentive to truthfully reveal their reservation prices for products.

▶ *What are the disadvantages of the auction methodology for estimating reservation prices?*

Interestingly, notwithstanding the theoretical arguments that have been proposed in the auction literature, there is no guarantee that real-life auctions will satisfy the incentive-compatibility condition. For example, if an auction is conducted repeatedly with the same set of bidders, bidders are likely to use sophisticated bidding strategies in which they may not truthfully reveal their reservation prices for a product in the auctions. If this is the case, the incentive-compatibility condition will not hold. Consequently, the firm will obtain incorrect demand estimates for its new product.

However, there is an even more basic problem. Unlike the other methods we have discussed (i.e., the multibrand MCT intentions model, conjoint analysis, and choice experiments), *the auction method does not allow the firm to simultaneously choose the optimal product design and price for new products.*

We return to the Slick example. Suppose Slick is considering which combination of features to include in its new shampoo product, VeriClean: color, water content, type of package, package size, and price. Suppose Slick is considering five colors, four levels of water content, three types of package, and three different package sizes. Then, Slick can choose 180 different design configurations for VeriClean (5 × 4 × 3 × 3). Suppose Slick plans to simultaneously choose the optimal product design and price for VeriClean. Then, Slick would have to conduct 180 separate auctions (one for each product configuration). For each auction, Slick would have to determine consumers' reservation prices. Using this information and cost data for different product configurations, Slick would be able to choose the optimal price for each of the 180 possible product designs. Clearly, this strategy is not practical.

Furthermore, from a practical viewpoint, it is only feasible to conduct auctions for low-priced products with a low number of design configurations. Hence firms that sell durables cannot use the auction methodology to estimate demand. In addition, for some products, *point-of-purchase advertising* can be an important determinant of demand. Standard auction methods cannot capture these effects.[19]

Fusion for Profit Maxim

In practical applications, there is no guarantee that consumers will truthfully reveal their reservation prices in auctions. In general, the auction method for measuring reservation prices is feasible only for low-priced products and cannot be used to simultaneously determine the optimal product configuration and price for a new product.

▲ 8.8 When Should Firms Use Auctions?

Suppose the firm seeks to estimate the demand for a new low-priced nondurable product. Then, a pragmatic approach for the firm is to use a hybrid approach. In the first step, conduct multibrand intentions or choice-based experiments in which product design features and prices are varied, and use these results to determine a candidate marketing strategy or several candidate strategies. In the second step, conduct an auction to determine consumers' reservation prices for the marketing policy (policies) in question for the new product, and use these results to estimate demand for the new product.

Suppose the firm sells expensive durables. Then, it has no alternative but to choose its marketing policy based on the first step discussed above.

Fusion for Profit Maxim

Firms may find it efficient to use a hybrid approach to forecast new product demand in which they first conduct multibrand or choice-based experiments and then supplement these studies with auctions.

▲ 8.9 Perceptions and New Product Demand

The new product forecasting methods discussed above focused on objective attributes of new product design, including price and brand name. However, in many industries, perceptions can also have an important effect on demand for the new product.

▲ What methods should the firm use to estimate the demand for new products when consumers' perceptions differ?

The previous methods are based on a simple model of consumer behavior: objective product design attributes and prices (explanatory variables) affect consumers' intentions to buy, preferences, or choices (outcomes). As discussed, these methods are flexible and can allow the links among the explanatory variables and the outcomes to vary across consumers and segments. Consequently, the firm can use these methods to indirectly capture differences in perceptions across consumers.[20]

However, although information from such studies is useful in estimating the demand for a new product, it is incomplete. For example, the firm cannot use these studies to answer the following questions regarding its new product strategy:

- What product benefits are most important to different consumer segments?
- How will a particular advertising message strategy affect consumers' perceptions of the firm's new product and of other brands in the marketplace?
- How will these perceptions affect the demand for the new product, competitors' products, and the other products in the firm's existing product line?
- What combination of advertising message, product design, and price should the firm use to launch the new product?

These issues can be addressed by extending the basic multibrand intentions (MCT) and choice-based models. Essentially, one needs to use a two-step methodology:[21]

1. Estimate the relationships among the product design attributes and price (explanatory variables) and consumers' perceptions (which are unobservable).
2. Estimate the relationships among consumers' perceptions and consumers' responses (i.e., self-stated intentions, preferences, and choices).

Fusion for Profit Maxim

The multibrand intentions-based MCT model and the choice methodology can be extended to simultaneously measure how the firm's advertising message, product design, and price affect perceptions and the demand for the new product.

▲ 8.10 How Useful Are Experiments for Measuring New Product Demand?

▲ *Should the firm introduce a new product into the marketplace on the basis of the results from experiments that measure consumers' preferences, intentions, or choices?*

As discussed above, experimental methods (including auctions) can be useful in new product design and forecasting. But how useful are these methods in practice? Should the firm perform additional analyses before launching a new product in the marketplace? We discuss these issues below.

Experimental methods for new product design and forecasting provide an important advantage. They allow the firm to measure the effects of changes in marketing policies (e.g., changes in product design) in a carefully controlled setting where a number of factors are held constant. *However—precisely because of the tight controls used in standard experiments—they cannot fully capture real-life market conditions.* For example, consumers may behave differently in the marketplace than they do in experimental settings. In addition, for practical reasons, no experiment can accurately capture all key aspects of the marketplace (e.g., the marketing policies of major competitors).

Given the enormous risks involved in new product introduction, the firm should, wherever possible, proceed sequentially. Specifically, the firm should:

1. Choose a candidate marketing strategy or marketing strategies based on experiments measuring preferences, intentions, or reservation prices. This analysis should allow for segment-specific, cannibalization, and competitive effects, and
2. Implement the candidate strategy or strategies on a limited scale in simulated test markets (STMs) or actual test markets before launching the product nationally. These studies will provide the firm with additional information to refine its marketing policies and reduce the risk of product failure.

Fusion for Profit Maxim

By using simulated test markets and test markets, the firm can refine the demand estimates for its new product and reduce the risk that the new product will fail in the marketplace.

Note that the STM and test market methods are not always feasible (e.g., determining the optimal marketing policy for a new automobile). In these cases, the firm may have no alternative but to choose its marketing policy using the results from preference, intentions, or choice experiments.

▚ 8.11 Simulated Test Markets

Both the simulated test market and test market methods can be used to estimate the demand for low-priced nondurable products. In this section, we focus on the STM methodology. In the next section, we shall discuss the use of test markets.

▶ *What is an STM? How can the firm use STM results to estimate the demand for a new product?*

Suppose the firm has already conducted a series of experiments and determined the candidate marketing policy or policies for the new product. The next step is to estimate the potential demand for the new product before launching the product nationally.

One approach for estimating the demand for the new product conditional on any given marketing policy is to set up an STM. That is, the firm sets up a simulated store in a shopping mall, where the firm sets the prices of different products in the STM experiment, including the new product and competing brands.[22] Potential customers from the target segment are recruited and given *incentive money* that they are free to spend in the STM or take home. Some time after consumers have made their purchase decisions, those consumers who bought the new product are asked to provide self-stated intentions data about the likelihood that they will repurchase the new product. These purchase and intentions data are then combined to estimate market demand.

We return to the Slick example in which Slick is planning to introduce its new shampoo product, VeriClean, into the market. Suppose Slick has conducted experiments and used the results to choose the following marketing policy for VeriClean: the shampoo will be green, have a 60% water content, be packaged in a 12-ounce tube, and be priced at $5.50 per tube.

Slick now conducts an STM experiment in which it gives consumers the option of buying different toiletries and different brands of shampoo, including VeriClean. In the STM, Slick sets the price of VeriClean at $5.50 per 12-ounce tube and also sets the prices of the remaining products that are available for sale. Each consumer is given incentive money that he or she is free to spend as they wish or take home.

Suppose 20% of the consumers in the STM purchase VeriClean at a price of $5.50 per tube. We say that the *trial rate* for VeriClean is 20%. Subsequently, say a week later, the consumers who purchased VeriClean in the STM are asked to provide self-stated probabilities that they will repurchase VeriClean. Suppose the self-stated repurchase rate is 40%. (For simplicity, assume that the average quantities of VeriClean that are purchased are the same as the average quantities of shampoo purchased for other brands in the industry.) Then, the best estimate of long-run, volume-based market share for VeriClean given the marketing policy tested is 8% (trial rate × repurchase rate = 20% × 40%).

This estimate of long-run market share can be refined. For example, the trial and repeat purchase rates can be measured at the segment level and aggregated to estimate market-level demand. Furthermore, the estimates can be adjusted to allow for different consumption rates across consumers and segments.[23]

▶ *What are the advantages and disadvantages of the STM methodology for estimating the demand for new packaged goods products?*

The STM methodology provides several managerial advantages. First, STM studies can be conducted quickly. This feature is important for firms in industries that are changing rapidly. Second, STM studies are inexpensive to conduct. Hence the firm can conduct several STM experiments inexpensively to estimate the demand it can expect if it uses different marketing strategies to launch the new product. And the firm can experimentally manipulate the prices of competitors' products in the STM experiment. Consequently, it can obtain demand estimates for the new product after allowing for the effects of likely competitive price reactions.

However, the STM methodology also has several disadvantages. Since only two measurements are taken (the trial rate and the repeat rate), the STM method does not allow the firm to determine how the trial and repeat purchase rates will change over time after the new product is introduced. Hence the firm cannot determine how sales for the new product will change over time before reaching their *equilibrium* levels, or how long this process will take. These problems will be compounded if the demand for the new product is seasonal (e.g., the new product is an allergy medication). Another disadvantage is that the firm cannot test the effectiveness of the entire marketing mix for the new product. For example, the firm cannot determine the effectiveness of its distribution strategies.

One method for addressing these problems is to conduct a test market prior to launching the new product. We discuss this methodology next.

Fusion for Profit Maxim

The simulated test market methodology can be used to estimate the demand for nondurables by combining information about trial and repeat rates.

▶ **8.12 Test Markets**

As discussed, the STM method can be useful in estimating the demand for nondurable products. An alternative method for estimating the demand for nondurable products is to conduct a test market.

▶ *What is a test market? How can the firm use test market results to forecast the demand for a new product?*

We return to the Slick example. The first step for Slick is to choose a test city (test market) or test cities that are reasonably representative. For each test city, Slick will need to implement a given marketing mix (e.g., price, advertising budget, advertising message, and product design) for VeriClean and track retail sales for VeriClean over time. In addition, Slick will need to examine the purchase behavior of a fixed group of consumers in each test city (a *panel*) over time.

In contrast to the STM methodology, Slick can examine in detail how the trial and repeat rates in the consumer panel change over time. Typically, those consumers who are most interested in the product category will be the first to purchase VeriClean. Hence the trial rate will be the highest in the period immediately following the introduction of VeriClean into the market. Over time, the trial rate for VeriClean will go down. For the same reason, the repeat rate among early triers will be high. Since consumers who are less interested in the product will enter the market over time, the average repeat rate across all buyers will decrease over time.

The critical issue is to estimate the long-run demand for VeriClean. This demand estimate depends on three quantities, each of which can be estimated from the consumer *panel data*:

1. The *cumulative trial rate* (T),
2. The *equilibrium repeat purchase rate* (R), and
3. The average number of units purchased (U).

The cumulative trial rate is the maximum percentage of consumers who will *ever* try VeriClean. Suppose this value is 25%. The equilibrium repeat purchase rate is the fraction of consumers who will purchase VeriClean in the future, after they have had the chance to experiment and determine their long-run purchase behaviors. Suppose the equilibrium repeat rate for VeriClean is 40%. Finally, suppose that the panel data show that, on average, consumers will purchase 4 tubes of VeriClean every year. Then, the estimated annual demand for each consumer in the target segment for VeriClean will be 0.4 units (cumulative trial rate × equilibrium repeat rate × average number of units purchased = 25% × 40% × 4).

▶ *Why is it important to measure both the trial and repeat rates in a test market?*

The firm can use the test market results for both prediction and control.

We return to the Slick example. If Slick's sole objective is to predict the long-run demand for VeriClean, it could, in principle, simply examine the pattern of retail sales for VeriClean over time in the test market and forecast its long-run demand. But, Slick has an additional goal—to use the test market as a diagnostic tool to refine the marketing policies for VeriClean before launching it nationally.

Consider two scenarios, both of which generate the same sales results. The trial rate for VeriClean could be high and the repeat rate low. Alternatively, the trial rate could be low and the repeat rate high. As we discuss below, the policy implications for the two scenarios are very different.

High Trial/Low Repeat Rate

Suppose the trial rate for VeriClean is high but the repeat purchase rate is low. Since the trial rate is high, this implies that Slick's price and advertising policy for VeriClean are reasonable. However, the low repeat rate for VeriClean implies that its product quality (real or perceived) is low. Hence it may be necessary for Slick to change the product design of VeriClean before launching VeriClean nationally.

Low Trial/High Repeat Rate

Suppose the trial rate for VeriClean is low but the repeat purchase rate is high. In this case, the high repeat rate implies that the product quality is satisfactory. Hence there is no need for Slick to modify the product design before launching VeriClean nationally.

However, the policy implications of the low trial rate are less clear. Thus, the low trial rate could imply that there is a problem with VeriClean's pricing, advertising strategy, or both. Alternatively, the low trial rate could simply mean that VeriClean appeals to a niche market.[24]

Note that if Slick does not obtain trial and repeat purchase data in the test market, it will be unable to distinguish the two scenarios (low trial/high repeat and high trial/low repeat) and therefore unable to modify marketing policy accordingly.

> ***Fusion for Profit Maxim***
>
> By measuring both the trial and repeat rates in a test market, the firm can obtain important diagnostic information for refining its marketing policy for its new product.

How accurate are test market results?

The test market should be run for a sufficiently long period so that seasonal fluctuations in demand can be captured and consumer purchase behavior has stabilized.[25] As discussed, the cumulative trial rate will level off over time. In addition, the average repeat rate will fall over time and eventually stabilize. The combined effect is that short-run sales will provide an overly optimistic picture of long-run demand for the new product.

Example: Suppose Halls has introduced a new cough drop, Silentia, in a test market. Suppose also that, because of seasonality and other factors, it will take the market 18 months to stabilize. For simplicity, assume that when the market for Silentia stabilizes, the average consumption rate per consumer will be 1 unit per year, the cumulative trial rate will be 25%, and the repeat purchase rate will be 40%. Then, the average long-run annual consumption rate per consumer in the target segment for Silentia will be 0.1 units (average annual consumption rate × cumulative trial rate × equilibrium repeat purchase rate = 1 × 25% × 40%).

Suppose the test market shows the following results at the end of 12 months: the average consumption rate is 1 unit per year, the cumulative trial rate is 24% (<25%), and the average repeat rate is 50% (>40%). Thus, consumer behavior has not stabilized. If Halls uses these results, it will incorrectly conclude that the average long-run annual consumption rate per consumer in the target segment is 0.12 units (1 × 24% × 50%). Note that this sales estimate is 20% higher than the true long-run demand.

Fusion for Profit Maxim

Test markets should be run for a sufficiently long period so that the firm can obtain accurate estimates of the cumulative trial rate and the repeat purchase rate for the new product. Short-term sales results are likely to be too optimistic.

▲ *What are the limitations of test markets?*

Test markets require time, especially if the purchase cycle (i.e., time between successive purchases) is long. Hence the firm cannot use this strategy when markets are changing rapidly or competitive entry is imminent. In addition, competitors can disrupt the test market. For example, suppose Johnson & Johnson test markets a new type of diaper in Buffalo. Then, a competitor in Buffalo can change its short-run marketing policy drastically so that Johnson & Johnson's controls in the test market do not hold. For example, the competitor can deeply discount the prices of its brand in Buffalo, flood the market with coupons, increase its short-run advertising spending sharply, or use a combination of these marketing policies. Consequently, the test market results will be biased.

Chapter 8 Key Points
- Controlled purchase experiments to estimate the demand for new products are of limited use.
- Standard intentions studies are likely to lead to biased estimates of new product demand. In addition, they do not allow the firm to measure cannibalization effects or to determine which competitors the new product will steal sales from.
- The firm can use the MCT multibrand intentions model to estimate the demand for its new product. This methodology allows the firm to identify segments, determine cannibalization and competitive effects, estimate how the new product affects the market growth rate for the

product category, and choose customized or segment-specific marketing policies.

- The firm can use preference models such as conjoint analysis to estimate the demand for new products. However, the results from these studies are sensitive to the set of brands included in the experiment. Furthermore, these studies cannot allow for market expansion by the new product.
- Competition-based pricing should not be used when the firm's product is differentiated.
- The firm can estimate the demand for a new product if it knows the reservation prices for the new product and competitive brands. However, the firm should not use consumers' self-stated reservation prices to estimate the demand for its new product—even for the most optimistic scenario where consumers, on average, correctly state their reservation prices.
- The firm can use a choice-based methodology to estimate the reservation prices for a new product. This method allows the firm to simultaneously determine product design and price after allowing for competitive effects. In addition, the methodology allows the firm to measure brand-equity effects and estimate the effects of competitive retaliation following the new product introduction.
- In general, the auction method for measuring reservation prices is feasible only for low-priced products and cannot be used to simultaneously determine the optimal product configuration and price for a new product.
- Firms may find it efficient to use a hybrid approach to forecast new product demand in which they first conduct multibrand or choice-based experiments and then supplement these studies with auctions.
- The multibrand intentions-based MCT model and the choice methodology can be extended to simultaneously measure how the firm's advertising message, product design, and price affect perceptions and the demand for the new product.
- Intentions and choice-based studies should be augmented by simulated test market and test market studies wherever possible.

9

Bundling

Most firms sell more than one product. In addition, many firms enter into *strategic alliances* with other firms to co-market their products. Hence firms need to choose marketing policies that maximize product-line performance. This chapter focuses on how the multiproduct firm should make and implement these key marketing decisions.

The information covered in this chapter will be useful when you are faced with the following types of decisions:

- When should my firm use a *bundling* strategy for its product line?
- Should my firm use a *pure* or a *mixed-bundling strategy*?
- How should my firm price product bundles if my firm has a strategic marketing alliance with another firm?
- If my firm uses a bundling policy, does it make sense to discontinue selling some products on a stand-alone basis in the marketplace?
- If my firm uses a *one-stop shopping* business model, under what conditions will my firm have a strategic advantage over its competitors?
- When should my firm use a *cross-couponing strategy*?
- What does cross-couponing imply about the metrics my firm should use to measure and reward managerial performance?
- How many models of a product should my firm sell, and how should it price them?
- If my firm makes a unique product, does it make sense to bundle this product with a *commodity*?

- How can my firm choose the right bundling policy when there are capacity constraints?
- Why do so many bundling strategies fail in the marketplace?
- What steps can my firm take to increase the chances that its bundling strategy will succeed?
- How do bundling and cross-couponing strategies affect consumer well-being and *social welfare*?

The following terms will be introduced in this chapter (see glossary for definitions):

bundling	economies of scope	one-stop shopping
choice experiment	joint costs	positively correlated
commodity	joint distribution of	reservation prices
complementary products	reservation prices	pure bundling strategy
conditional reservation	joint profits	reservation price
prices	marginal cost	social welfare
consumer surplus	mixed bundling	strategic alliance
coupons	strategy	synergies
cross-couponing	negatively correlated	
strategy	reservation prices	

▲ 9.1 What Is a Bundling Strategy?

Bundling refers to the practice of selling two or more products together as a package.

▲ What types of bundling strategies can the firm use?

The firm can use either pure or mixed bundling. Under a pure bundling strategy, the firm does not sell individual products separately. It only offers a package of products.

Example 1: Lexus sells fully loaded automobiles with air-conditioning and leather seats. Consumers do not have the option of buying Lexus cars without these features.

Under a mixed bundling strategy, the firm sells individual products separately. In addition, the firm offers consumers the option of buying packages of products.

Example 2: Verizon sells cable, cell phone, and hard-line phone services separately. In addition, it offers various combinations of these services.

In the instances discussed above, all products and bundles are made by the same firm. As illustrated below, this is not necessary for a bundling strategy.

Example 3: An airline company (e.g., United Airlines) offers customers a one-day free car rental if they rent from a strategic partner with which the airline has a marketing alliance (e.g., Hertz).

◣ 9.2 When Should Firms Use a Bundling Strategy?

The answer depends on the demand and cost structures for the products and bundles in question. As one would expect, the firm will always gain from bundling if it is able to realize cost savings by producing bundles of products (i.e., there are *economies of scope* in production). Similarly, the firm will always gain by using a bundling strategy if consumers' *reservation prices* for a bundle are greater than the sum of the reservation prices for the separate products (i.e., the products are *complementary*).

To exclude these trivial cases (although they are perhaps realistic for certain industries), we shall make the following assumptions about demand and cost:

1. On the demand side, the products are independent. That is, a consumer's reservation price for a bundle is the sum of the consumer's reservation prices for the individual products in the bundle.
2. On the cost side, each product is produced by a separate process. Hence there are no *joint costs*. For simplicity, we shall also assume that the *marginal cost* of each product does not change with volume.

In addition, all consumer segments contain the same numbers of consumers. (These assumptions can be easily relaxed.)

◣ When should the firm use a pure bundling strategy?

Example: Consider two firms in the telecommunication business: one firm markets a cable TV service, and the other markets an Internet service. Suppose the market consists of three segments, each of which contains 1 million customers. The reservation prices (RPs) for the monthly cable TV and Internet services are shown in table 9.1.

Suppose the marginal costs for both the cable TV and the Internet firms are zeros. (This assumption is reasonable for these industries because total costs do not change much with volume in the short run.) We begin with the case where each firm acts independently and maximizes its own profits. Then, each firm can choose from the alternatives shown in table 9.2.

Table 9.1
Telecommunications Example: Reservation Prices for Cable TV, Internet, and the Bundle

Segment	Cable TV	Internet	Bundle
A	$30	$10	$40
B	$20	$20	$40
C	$10	$30	$40

Table 9.2
Telecommunications Example: Pricing Policy
When Each Firm Acts Independently

Price per month	Units sold per month	Gross margin per month
$30	1 million	$30 million
$20*	2 million	$40 million
$10	3 million	$30 million

*The optimal price.

Thus, each firm will charge a monthly price of $20 for its service and earn a monthly gross margin of $40 million. Hence, the combined monthly profit for the two firms acting independently is $80 million.

Now, suppose both firms form a strategic alliance and sell a cable TV–Internet bundle for a monthly price of $40. Since each segment is willing to pay $40 per month for the bundle, all three segments (3 million consumers) will buy the bundle (see table 9.1). Hence the *joint profits* for both firms will increase from $80 million per month to $120 million per month (a 50% improvement).

Note that after the strategic alliance is formed, the firms will not offer consumers the opportunity to purchase either the cable TV service or the Internet service separately. The only product that will be offered is a pure bundle. We say that the firms are using a pure bundling strategy.

▶ *Why was a pure bundling strategy optimal in the cable TV–Internet example?*

Consumers have different reservation prices for the cable TV and Internet services. However, they have identical reservation prices for the bundle.

▶ *What strategy should firms use if consumers have different reservation prices for the bundle?*

The key issue is how similar consumers' reservation prices are for each individual product and for the bundle. In the cable TV–Internet example, suppose the reservation prices for each product can have one of the following values: high, medium, or low.

Consider the following two cases.

Case 1. Suppose consumers with *high* reservation prices for cable TV have *low* reservation prices for the Internet service and vice versa (table 9.3). Then, we say that the reservation prices for the two products are *negatively correlated.* If this scenario occurs, consumers' reservation prices for the bundle will be more similar than the corresponding reservation prices for cable

Table 9.3
Telecommunications Example: Negatively Correlated Reservation Prices

Segment	Cable TV	Internet
A	High	Low
B	Medium	Medium
C	Low	High

Table 9.4
Telecommunications Example: Reservation Prices Are Negatively Correlated

Segment	Cable TV	Internet	Bundle
A	$45	$5	$50
B	$30	$35	$65
C	$5	$40	$45

Table 9.5
Telecommunications Example: Pricing Policies When Firms Act Independently

Cable TV			Internet		
Subscription price	Subscriptions sold	Gross margin	Subscription price	Subscriptions sold	Gross margin
$45	1 million	$45 million	$40	1 million	$40 million
$30*	2 million	$60 million	$35*	2 million	$70 million
$5	3 million	$15 million	$5	3 million	$15 million

*The prices chosen.

TV and the Internet service. In such cases, the optimal policy for the firms may be to use the following mixed bundling strategy: sell the cable TV at a high price, sell the Internet service at a high price, and sell the bundle at a medium price.

To illustrate, consider the following example. The market consists of three consumer segments, each of size 1 million. The segments' reservation prices are shown in table 9.4.

Suppose the cable TV and Internet firms act independently. Then, the firms can choose from the alternatives shown in table 9.5.

Given these alternatives, the cable TV firm should charge a price of $30 per month and make a monthly gross profit of $60 million. The Internet firm should charge $35 per month and make a monthly gross profit of $70 million. Hence both firms will make a joint gross profit of $130 million per month.

► *Can the firms increase their joint profits?*

One possibility is to use a pure bundling strategy and charge a price of $45 per month for the bundle. If this strategy is used, joint profits will increase from $130 million to $135 million (price of bundle × number of customers = $45 × 3 million).

Now suppose the firms use the following mixed bundling strategy. Charge a high price of $45 per month for cable TV, a high price of $40 per month for the Internet service, and a moderate price of $65 per month (< price of cable TV + price of Internet service) for the bundle. Then, based on their reservation prices (see table 9.4.), Segment A will buy the cable TV service, Segment B will buy the bundle, and Segment C will buy the Internet service. Hence joint profits will increase from $130 million per month to $150 million (sum of profits from all three segments = $45M + $40M + $65M). *Note that this mixed bundling strategy leads to higher joint profits than the pure bundling strategy.*

Case 2. Suppose consumers with high reservation prices for cable TV also have high reservation prices for the Internet service. In addition, consumers with low reservation prices for cable TV have low reservation prices for the Internet service (table 9.6). We say that the reservation prices are *positively correlated.*

In this case, the reservation prices for the bundle will be less similar than the corresponding reservation prices for the bundle in Case 1. Hence the potential gains from bundling will be reduced. Although different scenarios can be constructed, in many cases the firms will be able to increase their joint profits if they use a mixed bundling strategy.

Fusion for Profit Maxim

The optimal bundling strategy depends on whether the reservation prices of the individual products are positively or negatively correlated. In general, the increase in profits from bundling will be higher when the reservation prices are negatively correlated.

Table 9.6
Telecommunications Example: Positively Correlated Reservation Prices

Segment	Cable TV	Internet
A	High	High
B	Medium	Medium
C	Low	Low

▶ *Suppose a multiproduct firm uses a mixed bundling strategy. Is it ever optimal to drop one or more individual products from the marketplace?*

Example: Suppose Quicken sells two software programs: TurboTax and RealEstate. Let's say that there are three segments, each of which contains 10,000 consumers. The segments' reservation prices are shown in table 9.7.

Since both TurboTax and RealEstate are software programs, the marginal costs for both products are approximately zero.

Suppose Quicken has two brand managers: one is responsible for TurboTax and the other for RealEstate. Then, following the previous approach, we can show that the TurboTax manager will charge a price of $80 per unit and produce a gross profit of $1.60 million (price per unit × units sold = $80 × [10,000 + 10,000]). The RealEstate manager will charge a price of $50 per unit and produce a gross profit of $1 million ($50 × [10,000 + 10,000]). Hence, if both managers act independently, Quicken's gross profit across product lines will be $2.60 million.

Suppose the two brand managers coordinate their policies to maximize product-line profits. Then, they should use the following mixed bundling strategy:

1. Sell the TurboTax-RealEstate software bundle for $130,
2. Sell the TurboTax program for $50, and
3. Do not sell the RealEstate program on its own.

Given this pricing plan, Segments A and B will buy the bundle and provide a gross profit of $2.6 million (price of bundle × number of customers in Segments A and B combined = $130 × [10,000 + 10,000]). Segment C will buy the TurboTax program and provide a gross profit of $500,000 (price of TurboTax × number of consumers in Segment C = $50 × 10,000).

Hence, if both managers coordinate their pricing policies, Quicken's product-line profits will increase from $2.6 million to $3.1 million.

Fusion for Profit Maxim

Depending on the structure of the reservation prices for individual products and the bundle, the firm may choose a mixed bundling strategy in which certain products are withdrawn from the marketplace.

Table 9.7
Quicken Example: Reservation Prices for Different Software Programs and the Bundle

Segment	TurboTax	RealEstate	Bundle
A	$100	$60	$160
B	$80	$50	$130
C	$50	$30	$80

▲ *What does bundling theory imply about the one-stop shopping model used by such Internet firms as Amazon?*

In many cases, as the firm increases the number of products that it sells, the reservation prices of consumers for product assortments (e.g., bundles) will become more similar. Hence multiproduct Internet firms, such as Amazon, that offer a large assortment of products can use a mixed bundling strategy to outperform specialized firms with limited product lines.

   Note that this result is based purely on the condition that consumers' reservation prices for product assortments are likely to become more similar as the number of products increases. In particular, the result is not based on the fact that it is more convenient for consumers to shop at one store rather than at many. Obviously, the added convenience to consumers from one-stop shopping will provide additional gains to multiproduct Internet retailers such as Amazon.

Fusion for Profit Maxim

Multiproduct retailers are likely to have a strategic advantage over specialized firms because they can use mixed bundling strategies.

▲ **9.3 Bundling and Cross-Couponing Strategies**

Multiproduct firms sometimes give consumers who purchase one of their products a *coupon* good toward the purchase of one of their other products. We say that the firm is using a cross-couponing strategy.

▲ *When should the firm use a cross-couponing strategy?*

Example: Suppose Procter & Gamble (P&G) seeks to optimize its product-line profits for two brands: Crest toothpaste and Head & Shoulders shampoo. Suppose the marginal costs per unit for Crest and Head & Shoulders, respectively, are $1.00 and $2.00. Assume that the market consists of two segments, each containing 1 million consumers. Furthermore, each consumer will purchase at most one unit of each product. Suppose the reservation prices for Crest and Head & Shoulders are shown in table 9.8.

Table 9.8
Procter & Gamble Example: Reservation Prices
for Crest, Head & Shoulders, and the Bundle

Segment	Crest	Head & Shoulders	Bundle
A	$3.00	$4.50	$7.50
B	$1.50	$5.00	$6.50

Table 9.9
Procter & Gamble Example: Product Managers Choose Policies Independently

		Crest				Head & Shoulders	
		Gross				Gross	
		Margin	Gross			Margin	Gross
Price	Units Sold	per Unit	Profit	Price	Units Sold	per Unit	Profit
$3.00*	1 million	$2.00	$2M*	$5.00	1 million	$3.00	$3M
$1.50	2 million	$0.50	$1M	$4.50*	2 million	$2.50	$5M*

*Policies chosen.

Suppose the brand managers for Crest and Head & Shoulders act independently and maximize their respective gross profits. Then, the pricing alternatives available are as shown in table 9.9.

Given these alternatives, the Crest brand manager will charge $3.00 per unit of Crest, and Crest will provide a gross profit of $2 million. The Head & Shoulders brand manager will charge $4.50 per unit, and Head &Shoulders will provide a gross profit of $5 million. Hence, if the Crest and Head & Shoulders managers act independently, P&G's product-line profits will be $7 million.

Now, suppose the brand managers for Crest and Head & Shoulders coordinate their pricing policies. However, they consider only pure bundling strategies. Then, the "optimal" strategy is to charge a bundle price of $6.50 per unit. Since each consumer has a bundle reservation price of $6.50 or more, all consumers will buy the bundle. Since the gross margin per bundle is $3.50 (bundle price – marginal cost of one unit of Crest – marginal cost of one unit of Head & Shoulders = $6.50 – $1.00 – $2.00), product-line profits under this pure bundling policy will be $7 million (number of consumers × gross margin per bundle = 2 million × $3.50). Thus, P&G will not gain if it uses a pure bundling strategy.

Now consider the following cross-couponing strategy. Suppose the price of Crest is kept at $3 per unit, but the price of Head & Shoulders is increased from $4.50 to $5.00 per unit. In addition, any consumer who buys one unit of Crest now receives a coupon for $0.50 that is only good toward the purchase of one unit of Head & Shoulders.

▶ *Given this cross-couponing pricing policy, what will consumers in Segments A and B do?*

Segment A: Since Segment A's reservation price for the bundle is $7.50, consumers in this segment will purchase one unit of Crest at the regular price ($3.00 per unit) and use the $0.50 coupon to purchase one unit of Head & Shoulders. Since the regular price of Head & Shoulders is $5.00 per unit, consumers in Segment A will pay a net price of $4.50 per unit (regular price of Head & Shoulders – coupon value = $5.00 – $0.50).

Note that each consumer in Segment A will pay his or her reservation price for the bundle ($7.50). Hence consumers in Segment A will obtain zero *consumer surpluses*. Since the marginal cost per unit of the bundle is $3 (marginal cost of one unit of Crest + marginal cost of one unit of Head & Shoulders = $1.00 + $2.00), P&G will make a gross profit of $4.5 million from Segment A.

Segment B: Consumers in Segment B will purchase Head & Shoulders at the price of $5.00 per unit. Note that each consumer in Segment B will pay his or her reservation price for Head & Shoulders.[1] Hence consumers in Segment B will obtain zero consumer surpluses. Since the gross margin per unit of Head & Shoulders is $3.00 (price of Head & Shoulders – marginal cost per unit of Head & Shoulders = $5.00 – $2.00), P&G will make a gross profit of $3 million from Segment B.

Hence, by using a cross-couponing strategy, P&G will make a higher product-line profit ($7.5 million) than if it uses a pure bundling policy or the brand managers for Crest and Head & Shoulders act independently ($7 million) (table 9.10).

Fusion for Profit Maxim

Under certain conditions, a multiproduct firm can increase its product-line profits by using a cross-couponing strategy.

▶ *What does cross-couponing imply about measuring and rewarding the performances of brand managers in multiproduct firms?*

To answer this question, it is necessary to examine the multiproduct firm's profits for two scenarios. Continuing with the P&G example, we need to compare the gross profits generated by Crest and by Head & Shoulders for two scenarios: when the brand managers choose policy independently (table 9.11) and when they use a cross-couponing strategy (table 9.12).

Table 9.10
Procter & Gamble Example: Effect of a Cross-Couponing Strategy

Segment	Purchase decision	Number of consumers	Revenue	Variable cost	Gross profit	Consumer surplus
A	Buy bundle using coupon	1 million	$7.5M	$3.0M	$4.5M	$0
B	Buy Head & Shoulders	1 million	$5.0M	$2.0M	$3.0M	$0
Total			$12.5M	$5.0M	$7.5M	$0

Table 9.11
Procter & Gamble Example: Profits When Brand Managers Act Independently

Brand	Price per unit	Units sold	Gross revenue	Variable costs	Gross profits
Crest	$3.00	1 million	$3.00M	$1.00M	$2.00M
Head & Shoulders	$4.50	2 million	$9.00M	$4.00M	$5.00M
Product-line gross profits					$7.00M

Table 9.12
Procter & Gamble Example: Profits When Brand Managers Cooperate Using Cross-Couponing

Brand	Segment	Price per unit	Units sold	Gross revenue	Gross profits
Crest	A	$3.00	1 million	$3.00M	$2.00M
	B	$3.00	0	$0	$0
	Total		1 million	$3.00M	$2.00M
Head & Shoulders	A	$4.50*	1 million	$4.50M	$2.50M
	B	$5.00	1 million	$5.00M	$3.00M
	Total		2 million	$9.50M	$5.50M
Product-line gross revenue				$12.5M	
Product-line gross profits					$7.50M

*After coupon.

Note that when P&G uses a cross-couponing strategy, Crest's volume, revenue, and profits will remain the same as when the Crest manager acts independently. In contrast, Head & Shoulders' volume remains unchanged; however, its revenue and gross profits will increase. Hence, Head & Shoulders will increase its revenue-based market share even though its volume-based market share will remain unchanged.

▶ *What does this imply about measuring and rewarding managerial performance?*

Suppose the same manager is responsible for coordinating the policies for Crest and Head & Shoulders. Then, P&G should simply delegate pricing authority (i.e., setting prices for both brands and choosing an appropriate cross-coupon plan) to the manager. In addition, P&G should pay the manager using a compensation plan that consists of a base salary and a profit-sharing plan based on gross product-line profits. (This organizational structure is not always feasible, especially in large multiproduct firms such as

P&G that sell major brands such as Crest and Head & Shoulders in different product categories. *In such cases, as discussed below, the market share (volume-based or revenue-based) of any given product is a poor metric for measuring and rewarding the brand manager for that product. In addition, the gross profit of any given product is also a poor metric.*)

Thus, in the P&G example, when Crest and Head & Shoulders choose the optimal product-line pricing policy, the market shares of Crest (volume-based and revenue-based) remain unchanged. In contrast, the volume-based market share of Head & Shoulders remains unchanged, but its revenue-based market share increases. When Crest and Head & Shoulders use the optimal cross-couponing strategy, Crest does not increase its profits. However, Head & Shoulders does.

Since one brand manager's decisions affect the performance of another brand manager, the firm should proceed as follows. Each brand manager's compensation should depend, to some degree, on the profits from other brands for which he or she is not directly responsible.

In the P&G example, the Crest brand manager's compensation should consist of three parts:

1. A fixed salary,
2. A part that is based on Crest's gross profits, and
3. A part that is based on Head & Shoulders' gross profits (net of coupons).

Similarly, the Head & Shoulders' brand manager's compensation should also consist of three parts:

1. A fixed salary,
2. A part that is based on Crest's gross profits, and
3. A part that is based on Head & Shoulders' gross profits (net of coupons).

In general, the optimal profit-sharing plans will depend on the structure of consumers' reservation prices for Crest, Head & Shoulders, and the bundle. In addition, the optimal profit-sharing plan will also depend on the marginal costs of Crest and Head & Shoulders. Consequently, the profit-sharing rate for the Crest manager based on Head & Shoulders' profitability need not be the same as the profit-sharing rate for the Head & Shoulders' brand manager based on Crest's profitability.

Fusion for Profit Maxim

If the firm's product lines are interdependent, the market shares and profits from individual products are poor metrics of performance. In such cases, the compensation of any brand manager should be based in part on the profits from related products.

Point to consider. How does cross-couponing affect consumer well-being and social welfare?

We know that social welfare = profits + consumer surplus.[2] Hence we need to determine the joint effect of cross-couponing on P&G's product-line profits and on the total consumer surplus across both products (Crest and Head & Shoulders). Below we illustrate the methodology using the P&G example.

As discussed above, by using a cross-couponing strategy, P&G will obtain a product-line profit of $7.5 million. In addition, all consumers will pay their reservation prices for the products/bundles that they purchase. Hence the total consumer surplus will be zero. This implies that social welfare under the cross-couponing strategy will be $7.5 million (product-line profits + total consumer surplus across product lines).

In the P&G example, the firm will obtain a product-line profit of $7 million if the Crest and Head & Shoulders brand managers act independently to maximize their respective profits. The consumer surpluses corresponding to these strategies are shown in table 9.13.

Hence social welfare when the brand managers of Crest and Head & Shoulders act independently will be $7.5 million (product-line profits + total consumer surplus = $7.0M + $0.5M).

Note that when P&G uses a cross-couponing strategy, consumers are worse off, since the total consumer surplus across product lines is reduced from $0.5 million to zero. However, this loss to consumers ($0.5 million) is exactly equal to the increase in P&G's profits. Hence social welfare remains unchanged at $7.5 million. We say that P&G's cross-couponing policy is socially neutral.

Fusion for Profit Maxim

The effect of cross-couponing on social welfare depends on how consumers' surpluses and the firm's product-line profits are affected. These effects depend on the structure of consumers' reservation prices for the products in question and the relevant costs to the firm.

Table 9.13
Procter & Gamble Example: Effect of Cross-Couponing on Consumer and Social Welfare

Segment	Number of customers	CREST			Head & Shoulders			Total surplus
		RP	Price	Surplus	RP	Price	Surplus	
A	1 million	$3.00	$3.00	$0	$4.50	$4.50	$0	$0
B	1 million	$2.50	$3.00	$0	$5.00	$4.50	$0.5M	$0.5M
Total								$0.5M

Note: RP, reservation price.

For a detailed discussion of how marketing policies in general affect social welfare, see chapter 20.

► 9.4 Applications of Bundling Theory

In this section, we discuss some extensions of the basic bundling theory. First, how should a firm price its products that are related in the sense that the value to the consumer of one product depends on use of the other but not vice versa? For example, leather seats that are custom-made for a Toyota Corolla will have no value to a consumer unless the consumer purchases the basic automobile. However, the basic Toyota Corolla model will have value to the consumer even if this automobile does not have leather seats. Hence Toyota needs to decide whether to offer two models (i.e., a base model and a loaded model with leather seats) or only one loaded model.

Second, is it ever profitable for a firm that produces a differentiated product to bundle its product with a commoditized product (on which the return is typically low)?

Third, what bundling strategy should the firm use when it has capacity constraints?

We begin with the case of related products.

Example: Suppose Canon has developed a new camera with a special telephoto lens. Which models should Canon sell, and what prices should it charge?

This is a bundling problem in which the products are related. Thus, the telephoto lens has no value to the consumer unless the consumer has the base camera. We say that the *reservation price for the telephoto lens is conditional* on the purchase of the base camera.

To determine its product mix and pricing policies, Canon should proceed as follows:

1. Determine the reservation prices for the base camera and the telephoto lens.
2. Use this information along with cost data for manufacturing the camera and the telephoto lens to determine the optimal policy.

We illustrate this methodology below.

Suppose Canon's marginal costs of producing base cameras and the telephoto lens are $50 and $30 per unit, respectively. Let's say that the market contains three segments each of size 100,000. Assume that each consumer will purchase at most one camera unit (with or without the telephoto lens) and that the reservation prices for the three segments are shown in table 9.14.

Suppose Canon sells only the "loaded" model (base camera + telephoto lens). Given this pure bundling strategy, Canon has the pricing options shown in table 9.15.

Table 9.14
Canon Example: Reservation Prices (RP) for Camera,
Telephoto Lens, and the Bundle

Segment	Base camera	Telephoto lens	Bundle
A	$200	$150	$350
B	$170	$40	$210
C	$150	$50	$200

Table 9.15
Canon Example: Comparison of Pure Bundling Strategies

Bundle price	Units sold	Marginal cost per bundle	Gross profit per bundle	Gross profit
$350	100,000	$80	$270	$27M
$210	200,000	$80	$130	$26M
$200*	300,000	$80	$120	$36M

*Policy chosen.

Hence Canon should sell the loaded model for $200 per unit and make a gross profit of $36 million. Note that, if Canon uses this strategy, it will leave a considerable amount of money "on the table." For example, consumers in Segment A are willing to pay up to $350 for the loaded model. However, they can purchase the loaded model for only $200. Thus, each consumer in Segment A obtains a surplus of $150 (reservation price – price of bundle = $350 – $200).

▲ How can Canon improve its performance?

Suppose Canon sells the base camera and the telephoto lens separately. *Note that this strategy is equivalent to a mixed bundle strategy.* For example, suppose Canon charges $150 per unit for the base camera and $40 per unit for the telephoto lens. This is equivalent to selling two models: a base model ($140 per unit) and a loaded model containing both the base camera and the telephoto lens ($190 per unit). Then Canon can obtain the product-line profits shown in table 9.16.

To see how these profit numbers are obtained, consider the following pricing plan. Suppose Canon charges a price of $170 for the base camera and a price of $50 for the telephoto lens. Since the telephoto lens has no value on its own, consumers will purchase either the base camera for $170 or the bundle (base camera + telephoto lens = $170 + $50) for $220 (table 9.17).

Table 9.16

Canon Example: Optimal Product-Line Pricing Policy

Base camera price	Telephoto lens price		
	$40	$50	$150*
$150*	$33M	$34M	$42M
$170	$26M	$26M	$36M
$200	$16M	$17M	$27M

Note: Values in table are profits.
*Policy chosen.

Table 9.17

Canon Example: How Different Segments Choose Their Purchase Strategies for a Given Product-Line Pricing Scenario

Segment	Base camera			Bundle		
	RP	Price	Surplus	RP	Price	Surplus
A	$200	$170	$30	$350	$220	$130*
B	$170	$170	0*	$210	$220	Negative
C	$150	$170	Negative	$200	$220	Negative

Note: RP, reservation price.
*Segment decisions.

Given this pricing structure, each segment will maximize its consumer surplus if the surpluses are positive. If the maximum surplus from purchase is negative, consumers will make no purchase.

Thus, Segment A will purchase the bundle for $220. Since the marginal cost of the bundle is $80 (marginal cost of the base model + marginal cost of the telephoto lens = $50 + $30), the gross profit margin per bundle sold is $140 (price – marginal cost of bundle = $220 – $80). Hence Segment A will provide Canon a gross profit of $14 million (gross profit margin per bundle × number of consumers in Segment A = $140 × 100,000).

Segment B will purchase the base camera for $170. Hence Segment B will provide Canon a gross profit of $12 million (gross profit margin per base camera × number of consumers in Segment B = $120 × 100,000).

Segment C will make no purchase, since all purchase strategies result in negative surpluses.

Thus, Canon's gross profit across all three segments is $26 million ($14M + $12M + $0M). Similarly, one can obtain the other gross product-line profit values shown in table 9.16.

Since Canon maximizes its product-line profits, it will sell the base camera for $150 and the telephoto lens for $150. Given this strategy, Canon will increase its profits from $36 million (pure bundling strategy) to $42 million (pricing the base camera and the telephoto lens separately). Note that the optimal two-part pricing strategy is equivalent to selling two models of camera: a base unit for $150 and a loaded unit for $300 (price of base camera + price of telephoto lens).

Fusion for Profit Maxim

Selling related products is a special case of bundling where the value to the consumer of one product depends on use of the other but not vice versa.

Point to consider.   In the Canon example, the optimal strategy was to sell two camera models. Is it ever optimal for the firm to sell only one model?

The answer depends on the reservation prices of the different consumer segments. In the Canon example, suppose Segment A's reservation price for the telephoto lens is only $50. Following the previous approach, we can show that the best pure bundling strategy is the same as before. That is, Canon can charge a price of $200 per unit and make a profit of $36 million. However, the maximum profit from a two-part pricing strategy is only $34 million. Hence the optimal strategy for Canon is to sell only one model (base camera + telephoto lens) for $200 per unit.

This example illustrates why luxury auto manufacturers such as Lexus sell only loaded automobiles. In contrast, manufacturers of economy automobiles often sell base automobiles with add-on options.

▶ *Suppose a firm has developed a unique product. Does it make sense for the firm to sell a bundle of this product and a commoditized product?*

At first glance, this bundling strategy does not make sense. After all, why should a firm that has developed a unique product (on which margins are high) also sell a commoditized product (on which profit margins are generally low)? However, this conclusion is too hasty.

Example: Let's say that Microsoft has developed a unique new software program, XCLusv. Suppose there are three segments (A, B, and C) of equal size (10 million each) that are potential buyers of this unique program. Let's say that a commoditized software program, LCDenom, is also available in the market at a price of $10 per unit. In particular, although XCLusv and LCDenom perform different functions, both software programs are compatible with one other. Assume that all three segments will purchase the LCDenom at the market price for that product ($10 per unit).

Suppose the marginal costs of XCLusv and LCDenom are zeros (a reasonable assumption for software) and that the reservation prices for the new XCLusv software program for Segments A, B, and C, respectively, are $100, $90, and $80. See table 9.18.

Table 9.18
Microsoft Example: Reservation Prices (RPs) for Different Software Programs and the Bundle

Segment	XCLusv	LCDenom	Bundle
A	$100	$10	$110
B	$90	$10	$100
C	$80	$10	$90

Table 9.19
Microsoft Example: Microsoft Sells Only the XCLusv Software Program

Price	Units sold	Gross profits
$100	10 million	$1,000 million
$90	20 million	$1,800 million
$80*	30 million	$2,400 million

*Policy chosen.

Suppose Microsoft sells only the XCLusv program. Then, Microsoft has the pricing options shown in table 9.19.

Since Microsoft seeks to maximize its profits, it should charge $80 per unit of XCLusv and make a profit of $2,400 million. Note that all three segments will purchase XCLusv; in addition, all three segments will purchase the commoditized product, LCDenom, at a price of $10 per unit.

▶ *Is there any gain to Microsoft if it sells a bundle of XCLusv and a clone of the commoditized product, LCDenom?*

Suppose Microsoft sells the bundle at a price just below $90, say $89.90 (discount = $0.10). Now, since Microsoft is implicitly selling the clone of LCDenom at a (small) discount, all three segments will purchase the bundle from Microsoft. *Note that none of the consumers will purchase the commoditized product, LCDenom, from other vendors.* Thus, Microsoft's gross profits will increase from $2,400 million to $2,697 million (gross margin per unit of the bundle × number of bundles sold = $89.90 × 30 million).

Fusion for Profit Maxim

A firm that makes a differentiated product may be able to increase its profits by bundling this product with a commoditized product that is already available in the marketplace.

Point to consider.   In the Microsoft example, how will Microsoft's bundling policy affect consumer and social welfare?

If Microsoft uses a bundling strategy, the effects on profits, consumer surpluses, and social welfare (profits across industries + consumer surpluses across industries) will be as shown in table 9.20.

Note that when Microsoft uses a bundling strategy, the profits of the commoditized industry will fall by $300 million (gross profit per unit of LCDenom × number of consumers who buy Microsoft's clone of LCDenom = $10 × 30 million).

Since Microsoft offers consumers a small discount for buying its clone of LCDenom, consumers will obtain a marginal gain of $3 million (discount on clone × number of consumers who buy the clone = $0.10 × 30 million). However, the increase in Microsoft's gross profits ($297 million) is exactly equal to the sum of the loss in profits to the commoditized industry ($300 million) and the gain to consumers ($3 million). Hence social welfare is unchanged.

Fusion for Profit Maxim

When two industries share a common customer base, a monopolist may find it profitable to sell a pure bundle that includes a commoditized product. This bundling policy can have a strong negative impact on the profitability of the commoditized industry. However, this bundling strategy does not necessarily imply that society is worse off.

So far, we have considered bundling examples where the firm does not face capacity constraints. However, some bundling problems inherently involve capacity constraints.

Example: Suppose an airline (e.g., British Airways) flies from New York to New Delhi via London.

Table 9.20
Microsoft Example: Effect of Bundling Strategy by Microsoft on Profits in Different Industries, Net Consumer Welfare, and Social Welfare

	Microsoft sells XCLusv only	Microsoft sells bundle	Gain or loss when Microsoft uses bundling
Microsoft profits	$2,400M	$2,697M	Gain of $297M
Commoditized industry profits	$Z + $300M	$Z	Loss of $300M
Consumer surplus across industries	$Q	$Q + $3M	Gain of $3M
Social welfare	$2,700M + $Z + $Q	$2,700M + $Z + $Q	$0

► *How should British Airways price its tickets?*

This is a bundle pricing problem where the firm faces a capacity constraint (the number of available seats on each flight sector). Assume that British Airways offers only economy class. (This assumption will be relaxed.) Then, the market consists of three segments:

1. Customers who plan to travel from New York to London (Segment A),
2. Customers who plan to travel from London to New Delhi (Segment B), and
3. Customers who plan to travel from New York to New Delhi (Segment C).

Define the New York–London trip as Product 1, the London–New Delhi trip as Product 2, and the New York–New Delhi trip as the bundle, Product 3. Consider any consumer in Segment A. Suppose this consumer's reservation price for the New York–London trip is $200. Then, this consumer's reservation prices for the London–New Delhi trip will be zeros, and the corresponding reservation price for the bundle (i.e., the New York–New Delhi trip) will be $200. Similarly, one can define the reservation prices for each product for consumers in Segments B and C.

Then, British Airways should proceed as follows. Determine the *joint distribution of reservation prices* across all consumer segments for all products (the New York–London trip, the London–New Delhi trip, and the bundled New York–New Delhi trip). Then, choose the product-line pricing policy that maximizes the total revenue from both flights. (For simplicity, we assume that the cost of each flight is fixed. This assumption is easily relaxed.) Note that British Airways needs to perform this analysis using the following capacity constraints:

- New York–London trip: Product 1 seats + Product 3 seats ≤ seat capacity of aircraft used for this sector.
- London–New Delhi trip: Product 2 seats + Product 3 seats ≤ seat capacity of aircraft used for this sector.

Note that the seat capacities for the New York–London and the London–New Delhi sectors need not be the same. In fact, depending on the demands (i.e., the distributions of reservation prices for each sector) and the costs of flying different aircraft, British Airways may decide to use aircraft with different seat capacities for the two sectors.

► *Suppose British Airways sells both economy and business class tickets. How should British Airways price these tickets on the New York–London, London–New Delhi, and New York–New Delhi routes?*

Since British Airways sells both economy and business class seats, it will offer three additional products—a business class ticket from New York to London (Product 4), a business class ticket from London to New Delhi

(Product 5), and a bundled business class ticket from New York to New Delhi (Product 6).

Now, British Airways can solve this multiproduct problem using the previous approach. The first step is to determine the joint distribution of reservation prices across all consumer segments for all six products (economy and business class). Using this information, British Airways can choose the optimal pricing structure that maximizes its total revenue, subject to the appropriate seating capacity constraints for each class.

Fusion for Profit Maxim

The firm can use bundling theory to price individual products and bundles that are sold subject to capacity constraints. The key information that is necessary is the joint distribution of reservation prices for different segments for each of the products and bundles in question.

▶ 9.5 Why Do So Many Bundling Strategies Fail?

As discussed, in many cases bundling provides the firm with the potential to increase its profits. However, it is often the case that the anticipated increase in profits does not occur. There are three major reasons why bundling strategies fail:

1. Incorrect measurements of reservation prices,
2. Consumer confusion, and
3. Overestimation of cost savings to the firm by pursuing a bundling strategy.

Measuring Reservation Prices

Reservation prices are unobservable and must be inferred. Asking consumers to state their willingness to pay often leads to biased results. (See chapter 8 for a detailed discussion.) For example, consumers may overstate their willingness to pay for a branded soft drink but understate the corresponding value for a generic brand. Furthermore, consumers may be uncertain about their reservation prices, especially for products with which they are not familiar or products they have not used. Hence self-stated reservation prices may be misleading.

Example: Suppose a telecommunications firm is evaluating a bundle containing the following products: a hard-line telephone connection, a cell phone, an Internet connection, and a cable TV connection. Since this bundle is complex and has not previously been sold in the marketplace, consumers may be unable to accurately state their reservation prices for the bundle. The result is that the firm is likely to mismeasure the distribution of reservation prices for different products, especially for those that are new to the marketplace.[3] Because reservation prices are likely to be incorrectly measured, bundling may actually lead to reduced performance.

Consumer Confusion

Consumers may be confused if the firm sells too many bundles. Consequently, the anticipated gains in profit from a bundling strategy may not materialize.

Example: In the 1990s, AT&T offered consumers a wide range of telephone services, communication services, and bundle options. For example, consumers could choose from a wide array of pricing plans based on usage; in addition, they could choose different combinations of add-on features such as call waiting and teleconferencing services. Given the plethora of pricing and bundling plans that were available, consumers were confused. Consequently, AT&T's bundling policy did not increase performance as had been anticipated.

Cost Synergies *and Coordination Costs*

Firms sometimes sell bundles to take advantages of economies of scope. In many cases, firms overestimate the cost savings that are likely to result from bundling. In addition, the firm may have underestimated the coordination costs of administering a bundling policy. Hence bundling strategies may not lead to the anticipated improvement in product-line performance.

▲ 9.6 How Can the Firm Improve the Chances That a Bundling Strategy Will Succeed?

The key issues are twofold. First, the firm needs to obtain accurate estimates of the costs of the individual products and of the bundle. In addition, the firm needs to know the costs of administering a bundling policy. Second, the firm needs to obtain accurate estimates of consumers' reservation prices for individual products and bundles. In general, the latter is more difficult.

▲ How can the firm measure consumers' reservation prices for individual products and bundles?

An intuitive approach is to ask consumers to state their reservation prices for the individual products and the bundle. As discussed below, this approach is problematic—*even in the best-case scenario where, on average, consumers are able to correctly state their reservation prices.* (See chapter 8 for a full discussion.)

In general, the joint distribution of reservation prices for the individual products and bundles depends on the following information:

- The average reservation prices for the individual products and the bundle,
- The correlations among these reservation prices, and
- The extent to which the reservation prices for the individual products and the bundle vary in the population.

Suppose consumers are able to correctly state their reservation prices on average. Then the means and correlations will be correctly measured. *However, in all cases, the range of reservation prices will be overstated.*[4] In other words, consumers' reservation prices for *all* products and bundles will appear to be more different than they are. Consequently, the firm is likely to choose the wrong pricing policies for the individual products and the bundle.

To address this problem, the firm can proceed as follows. Run a *choice experiment* and use consumers' self-stated choices to infer the joint distribution of reservation prices among consumers.[5] (See chapter 8 for a detailed discussion.)

Fusion for Profit Maxim

Where possible, the firm should use a choice-based methodology to infer consumers' reservation prices for individual products and the bundle. Even under the best of conditions, using self-stated reservation prices will lead to suboptimal bundling strategies.

Chapter 9 Key Points
- A firm's decision to use a bundling strategy depends on the cost structures of the different products, whether there are economies of scope in production, and on the joint distribution of consumers' reservation prices for the individual products and the bundles.
- The decision to use a pure or a mixed bundling strategy depends on whether the reservation prices for the individual products are positively or negatively correlated. In general, the gain in profits from using a bundling strategy is higher when the reservation prices for the individual products are negatively correlated.
- Depending on the structure of consumers' reservation prices, it may be optimal for the firm to discontinue selling certain products when it uses a bundling strategy.
- Firms that use cross-couponing strategies should not use the market shares (volume-based or revenue-based) or profits of individual products to measure and reward managerial performance. In addition, these firms should compensate brand managers using multipart

compensation plans. In general, the profit-sharing rates for individual products will not be symmetric across brand managers.
- Firms can use bundling theory to decide how many models of a product to sell and how to set their prices.
- A multiproduct firm can use bundling theory to choose the optimal pricing strategy for its product line when it has capacity constraints.
- A firm that makes a unique product can increase its profits by bundling its product with a commodity. This bundling strategy can have a strong negative impact on the profitability of the commoditized industry.
- Bundling strategies often fail because firms mismeasure reservation prices, consumers are confused by the firm's policy, or firms overestimate the benefits from economies of scope in production.
- The firm is likely to choose poor bundling strategies if it relies on self-stated consumers' reservation prices—even in the best-case scenario where this information is correct, on average. Hence, where possible, the firm should use choice-based experiments to estimate the joint distribution of reservation prices for individual products and bundles. The firm can use this information along with cost data to choose the optimal bundling strategy.
- When the firm uses a bundling or cross-couponing strategy, social welfare can increase even though consumers may be worse off.

Part V

*Integrating Marketing Strategy
and the Supply Chain*

10

Channels of Distribution

In many cases, it is not efficient for the firm to sell its products or services directly to the consumer. Instead, it is better for the firm to sell its products through third parties such as wholesalers, distributors, and retailers. Often, these third parties also sell products made by the firm's competitors. In some cases, firms use a hybrid approach. That is, they sell their products directly to the consumer (e.g., via the Internet or their own dedicated sales forces) and also through third parties. In this chapter we discuss how the firm should coordinate its marketing policies across these different channels to maximize its performance.

The information covered in this chapter will be useful when you are faced with the following types of decisions:

- What pricing strategy should my firm use when it sells its product through an *exclusive distributor*?
- What pricing strategy should a powerful manufacturer use vis-à-vis a distributor?
- What pricing strategy should a powerful retailer use vis-à-vis a manufacturer?
- What pricing strategy should a manufacturer use vis-à-vis a distributor if the manufacturer also sells its product on the Internet?
- Under what conditions should manufacturers and distributors share advertising costs? How should these costs be shared?
- Should branded and generic products use different channel pricing strategies?

- What pricing strategies should my firm use when it has distributors in different geographical areas and countries?
- What pricing strategy should my firm choose when it uses *nonexclusive distributors*?
- Under what conditions should my firm *vertically integrate* its operations?
- How should different firms in a *supply chain* coordinate their marketing activities?

The following terms will be introduced in this chapter (see glossary for definitions):

arbitrage	multilevel channels	social welfare
asymmetric information	net of cannibalization	strategic
channel of distribution	nonexclusive	interdependence
channel stability	distributor	supply chain
consumer surplus	price sensitivity	tapered vertical
economic power	product differentiation	integration
economic profit	quantity discounts	transaction costs
exclusive distributor	reservation price	vertical integration
gross channel profit	risk-adjusted economic	backward or
joint profits	profit	upstream
marginal cost	sharing rule	vertical integration
mixed channel strategy	slotting fee	forward or downstream

▶ 10.1 Choosing a Channel Strategy

In some cases, firms sell directly to consumers or end users. For example, a manufacturer may use its own sales force to directly sell equipment to industrial firms. However, in most cases, it is more efficient for the manufacturer to use intermediaries such as wholesalers and retailers to sell its products. As discussed below, this raises interesting questions regarding marketing strategy.

▶ What is a channel of distribution?

Suppose a manufacturer sells its products to retailers who in turn sell the product to consumers. This supply chain network is known as a channel of distribution. In practice, manufacturers can choose among a wide range of channels of distribution. For example, an electronics firm such as Sony may sell its products directly to consumers over the Internet. In addition, Sony may also sell its products through bricks-and-mortar retail stores. We say that Sony is using a *mixed channel strategy*.

Furthermore, manufacturers often use *multilevel channels* to sell their products. Thus, many industrial firms use a supply chain with three or more levels. For instance, at the first level, the manufacturer sells its products to wholesalers. At the second level, wholesalers sell the product to retailers. At the third level, retailers sell the product to consumers.

If the distributor sells only the firm's product, we say that the distributor is exclusive. If the distributor sells a number of competing products including the firm's product, we say that the distributor is nonexclusive.

For simplicity we shall focus on two-level channels where the product flows from the manufacturer to distributors who, in turn, sell the product to consumers. However, the concepts that we discuss can be used to analyze more complicated multilevel channels.

Fusion for Profit Maxim

In many cases, it is inefficient for the firm to sell its products directly to consumers or end users. The optimal policy for the firm may be to use mixed channels or a multilevel channel of distribution.

▶ *Is pricing in a channel different from pricing a product directly for sale to the consumer?*

There is a fundamental difference between pricing in a channel and pricing directly for sale to the consumer. Specifically, the price that a manufacturer charges a distributor is a cost to the distributor. Since the manufacturer's price to the distributor affects the distributor's cost, this price will affect the price that the distributor charges the consumer.

The manufacturer should recognize this *strategic interdependence* between itself and the distributor. The manufacturer should also recognize that the distributor may carry products made by several competing manufacturers. Hence there is a potential conflict of interest between the manufacturer and the distributor. Specifically, the manufacturer seeks to maximize the profits of its own product line. However, the distributor is interested in maximizing its profits across all product lines it sells, including the manufacturer's products *and* competing products made by the manufacturer's competitors.

Fusion for Profit Maxim

A manufacturer should choose its marketing policy after recognizing the strategic interdependence between itself and its distributors.

▶ *10.2 Choosing a Channel Strategy Using an Exclusive Distributor: The Case Where the Manufacturer Has Economic Power*

We begin with the simplest case where a firm produces only one product and sells it to consumers or end users through an exclusive distributor. As discussed below, the channel strategy depends on whether the manufacturer or the distributor has *economic power*. Both supply chain scenarios occur in real life. For example, large consumer goods companies such as Procter & Gamble often have economic power over supermarkets that sell their products. In contrast, large retailers such as Wal-Mart often have economic power over their suppliers.

▶ *How should a manufacturer price its product if it uses an exclusive distributor for its product? Assume that the manufacturer has all the economic power in the channel.*

Example: Consider the following two-level channel example. At the first level, the Coca-Cola Company sells Coke concentrate to an exclusive bottler. At the second level, the bottler uses the concentrate to produce and sell cans of Coke to consumers. By assumption, Coca-Cola has all the economic power in the channel.

Suppose the *marginal cost* of manufacturing Coke concentrate is constant ($1 per unit); in addition, the marginal costs for the bottler are also constant ($2 per unit). Then, the combined marginal cost to the channel is $3 per unit. Suppose that, given the requisite investment in plant and machinery, the bottler needs to earn a minimum gross profit of $10,000 per month to remain in business.

▶ *How should Coca-Cola price its concentrate to the bottler in order to maximize its own profits?*

Suppose Coca-Cola knows the retail demand for Coke and the bottler's cost structure. Specifically, Coca-Cola knows that the monthly demand for Coke will be as follows: 8,000 units if the retail price is $6 per unit, 15,000 units if the retail price is $5 per unit, and 17,000 units if the retail price is $4 per unit. Then, Coca-Cola can determine the net monthly gross profits in the channel for different demand scenarios (table 10.1).

Table 10.1
Coca-Cola Example: Effect of Retail Prices on Total Channel Profits

Retail price per unit	Marginal cost of channel per unit	Gross channel profit margin per unit	Units sold	Gross profit of channel	Minimum gross profit for bottler to stay in business	Economic profit of channel
$6	$3	$3	8,000	$24,000	$10,000	$14,000
$5*	$3	$2	15,000	$30,000	$10,000	$20,000
$4	$3	$1	17,000	$17,000	$10,000	$7,000

*The policy that maximizes the economic profit of the channel.

Suppose the retail price is $6 per unit. Then, the *gross channel profit per unit* is $3 (retail price − marginal cost per unit of channel = $6 − $3). Hence the *gross channel profit* will be $24,000 per month (gross margin per unit × volume sold = $3 × 8,000). Since the bottler needs to make a gross profit of at least $10,000 per month to stay in business, the *economic profit* of the channel is $14,000 per month (gross channel profit − minimum profit required by the bottler = $24,000 − $10,000). Similarly, we can compute the economic profits for the other two pricing scenarios. As shown in table 10.1, the maximum economic profit from the channel is $20,000 per month.

▶ *Since Coca-Cola has all the power in the channel, it should price its concentrate to the bottler such that Coca-Cola obtains all the economic profit in the channel ($20,000 per month). How can Coca-Cola achieve this result?*

Both Coca-Cola and the bottler seek to maximize their respective profits. Since Coca-Cola has economic power, it should price its concentrate such that, given this pricing schedule, the maximum profit that the bottler can earn is $10,000 per month (table 10.2).

As discussed, Coca-Cola wants the bottler to buy 15,000 units of concentrate and to charge a retail price of $5 per unit of Coke. If the bottler uses this strategy, it will obtain a monthly revenue of $75,000 and incur variable costs of $30,000 per month (marginal cost of bottler × units sold = $2 × 15,000 units). Hence the bottler will earn a gross margin of $45,000 per month *before paying Coca-Cola for the concentrate.*

Since the bottler needs to make a gross profit of at least $10,000 per month to stay in business, the *maximum amount* that it will be willing to pay Coca-Cola to purchase 15,000 units per month of concentrate is $35,000 (gross margin − minimum profit to stay in business = $45,000 − $10,000). Similarly, the maximum amount that the bottler is willing to pay Coca-Cola

Table 10.2
Coca-Cola Example: Optimal Pricing Policy for Coca-Cola

Retail price	Units sold	Gross retail revenue	Bottler's variable cost	Bottler's gross margin before paying for concentrate	Minimum gross profit for bottler to stay in business	Bottler's gross economic margin before paying for concentrate
$6	8,000	$48,000	$16,000	$32,000	$10,000	$22,000
$5*	15,000	$75,000	$30,000	$45,000	$10,000	$35,000
$4	17,000	$68,000	$34,000	$34,000	$10,000	$24,000

*The retail price that Coca-Cola wants the bottler to choose.

Table 10.3

Coca-Cola Example: Optimal Quantity-Discount Policy for Coca-Cola

Units of concentrate sold	Total price of concentrate	Price per unit of concentrate	Bottler's profit	Bottler's economic profit
8,000	> $22,000	> $2.75	< $10,000	negative
15,000	$35,000	$2.33*	$10,000	0*
17,000	> $24,000	> $1.41	< $10,000	negative

*The bottler's optimal decision given Coca-Cola's quantity-discount policy.

for 8,000 units of concentrate is $22,000. Correspondingly, the maximum amount that the bottler is willing to pay for 17,000 units of concentrate is $24,000 (see table 10.2).

Given this information, Coca-Cola can choose a pricing schedule such that the bottler's optimal strategy is to order 15,000 units of concentrate and make a gross profit of $10,000 per month (i.e., zero economic profit). To achieve this result, Coca-Cola can use any of the following *quantity-discount* policies shown in table 10.3.

Faced with this quantity-discount pricing schedule, the best decision for the bottler is to purchase 15,000 units of concentrate at a price of $2.33 per unit ($35,000/15,000 units) and make a monthly gross profit of $10,000. If the bottler chooses any other order policy (e.g., purchasing 17,000 units of concentrate at a unit price exceeding $1.41 per unit), it will earn a monthly gross profit of less than $10,000 (see table 10.3). Hence the bottler will be put out of business. Note that, when the bottler orders 15,000 units of concentrate, Coca-Cola's monthly gross profits will be $20,000 (gross channel profits – minimum monthly profit for the bottler = $30,000 – $10,000).[1]

As this example shows, by using a quantity-discount policy, Coca-Cola can obtain all the economic profit in the channel ($20,000). Note that it is optimal for Coca-Cola to use a quantity-discount schedule *even though Coca-Cola's marginal costs do not decrease with volume.*

Fusion for Profit Maxim

Suppose a manufacturer uses an exclusive distributor. Then, by choosing an appropriate quantity-discount schedule, the manufacturer can obtain all the economic profits in the channel.

▶ *Are there other ways in which Coca-Cola can obtain the economic profits in the channel?*

Instead of using a quantity-discount schedule, Coca-Cola can use the following equivalent policy. Sell the concentrate to the bottler at cost. That is, charge the bottler a fixed price of $1 per unit (Coca-Cola's marginal cost per unit of concentrate). In addition, charge the bottler a lump-sum franchise fee of $20,000 per month. Given this two-part contract, the bottler will sell 15,000 units at a price of $5 per unit and make a monthly gross profit of $10,000. Coca-Cola will obtain a gross monthly profit of $20,000 as before.

Fusion for Profit Maxim

The manufacturer can charge the distributor a lump-sum franchise fee to achieve the same results as it would by using a quantity-discount schedule.

Point to consider. Consider two companies. Suppose one sells a branded product and the other a generic version. Each brand is sold by an exclusive distributor. Suppose the marginal costs to the distributors are constant and equal for both brands. Which brand should offer the distributor a steeper quantity-discount schedule?

To answer this question, we modify the Coca-Cola example. Suppose consumers are less *price-sensitive* than before. Specifically, the bottler can charge consumers $.50 more per unit (i.e., a price of $6.50 per unit) if it sells 8,000 units. Following the same approach as before, we can show that the maximum economic profit in the channel remains unchanged at $20,000. Hence Coca-Cola would like the bottler to sell 15,000 units per month at a price of $5 per unit.

Now, suppose Coca-Cola uses the same quantity-discount schedule as before; in particular, Coca-Cola charges the bottler a price of $2.80 (>$2.75) per unit if it purchases 8,000 units. Given this quantity-discount schedule, the bottler will choose the "wrong" order policy. Specifically, the bottler will order 8,000 units and make a gross profit of approximately $14,000 (>minimum profit to stay in business). To make sure that the bottler makes the "right" decision, Coca-Cola should offer the bottler a steeper quantity-discount schedule than before. Specifically, Coca-Cola will need to charge a minimum price of $3.25 ($2.75 + $0.50) per unit if the bottler orders 8,000 units of concentrate.

As the Coca-Cola example illustrates, *the steepness of the optimal quantity-discount schedule for the manufacturer reflects how sharply the unit gross margins of the distributor (price paid by the consumer − marginal cost of the distributor) decrease with volume.*

We now use this result to analyze the question above. Since a branded product is differentiated from competitive brands, the demand for a branded product will be less price-sensitive than the corresponding demand for a generic. Hence the retailer who sells a branded product can obtain a higher profit margin at low volumes than a retailer who sells a generic. This implies that, other factors being the same, the manufacturer who sells a branded product should use a steeper quantity-discount schedule than the manufacturer of the generic.

Fusion for Profit Maxim

In general, a firm that makes a branded product should offer its distributor a steeper quantity-discount schedule than a firm that makes a generic version of that product.

Point to consider. In the Coca-Cola example, suppose Coca-Cola charges the bottler a fixed price per unit of concentrate. What are the implications for Coca-Cola, the bottler, consumers, and *social welfare*?[2]

Suppose Coca-Cola charges the bottler a fixed price per unit of concentrate regardless of volume. It is sufficient to consider the case where Coca-Cola charges the bottler a fixed price of $2.33 per unit of concentrate. Given this pricing policy, the bottler will buy the "wrong" quantity (from Coca-Cola's point of view). Specifically, the bottler will buy only 8,000 units of concentrate and charge a retail price of $6 per unit of Coke.

Consequently, compared with the case where Coca-Cola uses a quantity-discount policy, the following results will occur. Since the bottler will order the "wrong" quantity (8,000 ≠ 15,000), channel profits will decrease. However, the bottler's profits will *increase*. Specifically, the bottler's marginal cost (including the cost of concentrate) is now $4.33 per unit ($2.00 + $2.33) regardless of the number of units sold. Hence the bottler will sell 8,000 units at a retail price of $6 per unit, make a gross profit margin of $1.67 per unit ($6.00 − $4.33), and make a gross profit of $13,333 (unit gross profit margin × volume). Note that, in contrast to the quantity-discount case, when Coca-Cola charges the bottler a fixed price per unit for its concentrate, the bottler will make an economic profit ($13,333 > $10,000).

Since the bottler's profits have increased and total channel profits have decreased, Coca-Cola's profits will fall. Since the retail price paid by consumers is too high ($6 > $5), the volume sold will be too low. Hence consumers will be worse off (i.e., *consumer surplus* will fall). Furthermore, as discussed earlier, total channel profits will decrease when Coca-Cola charges a fixed price per unit of concentrate. Hence, compared with the case where Coca-Cola uses a quantity-discount policy, social welfare will decrease (social welfare = consumer surplus + channel profits).

Fusion for Profit Maxim

If the manufacturer charges the distributor a fixed price per unit, the only party who gains is the distributor. The manufacturer and consumers lose; in addition, social welfare is reduced.

▶ 10.3 Choosing a Channel Strategy Using an Exclusive Distributor: The Case Where the Distributor Has Economic Power

In general, economic power can vary across the supply chain. Thus, the previous analysis assumed that the manufacturer has all the economic power. However, major retailers (e.g., Wal-Mart and hypermarkets) often have economic power over the manufacturers whose products they sell. What pricing strategy should such retailers use vis-à-vis their suppliers?

There are several possibilities. The retailer can obtain all the economic profit in the channel by charging the manufacturer a flat fee for stocking its product(s). This type of charge is known as a *slotting fee*. Supermarkets often charge manufacturers a slotting fee to place their products in preferred locations in the store. For instance, supermarkets charge manufacturers fees to have their products displayed at the end of aisles where store traffic is high. Similarly, supermarkets charge manufacturers a fee for the privilege of having their products placed in locations that are generally occupied by top-selling items in the store.[3]

Alternatively, the retailer can offer the manufacturer an appropriately chosen quantity-discount schedule that allows the retailer to obtain all the economic profit in the channel. To illustrate, consider the Coca-Cola example above. Suppose the demand and cost data now pertain to Wal-Mart (the distributor) and the LittleGuy Corporation, a small manufacturing firm. In addition, the minimum profit that LittleGuy needs to make to stay in business is $10,000 per month. Now, in contrast to the Coca-Cola example, the distributor (Wal-Mart) has the economic power in the channel.

▶ Given these cost and demand data, the maximum economic profit in the channel is $20,000 per month as before. What pricing schedule should Wal-Mart use to obtain this profit?

First, Wal-Mart should determine the minimum revenues that LittleGuy will accept for different order quantities (table 10.4). Then, Wal-Mart should

Table 10.4
Wal-Mart Example: Optimal Retail Quantity for Wal-Mart

Units sold	LittleGuy's marginal cost per unit	LittleGuy's variable cost	LittleGuy's minimum profit	Minimum revenue LittleGuy will accept
8,000	$1	$8,000	$10,000	$18,000
15,000*	$1	$15,000	$10,000	$25,000
17,000	$1	$17,000	$10,000	$27,000

*The number of units that Wal-Mart plans to purchase.

choose a pricing policy that allows it to obtain the maximum economic profit that the channel can generate.

From the Coca-Cola example, we know that the economic profits in the channel will be maximized if 15,000 units are sold. So, the first step for Wal-Mart is to determine the minimum revenue that LittleGuy will accept for this order quantity. As shown in table 10.4, LittleGuy's variable cost for this order quantity is $15,000 (LittleGuy's marginal cost per unit × volume = 1 × 15,000). Furthermore, LittleGuy needs to make a gross profit of at least $10,000 per month to stay in business. Hence the minimum revenue that LittleGuy will accept for an order of 15,000 units is $25,000. Similarly, the minimum revenue that LittleGuy will accept for an order of 8,000 units is $18,000. Correspondingly, the minimum revenue that LittleGuy will accept for an order of 17,000 units is $27,000.

In the second step, Wal-Mart should choose a pricing schedule such that the best policy for LittleGuy is to sell 15,000 units and make $10,000 per month (zero economic profit). As shown in table 10.5, Wal-Mart can achieve this result by using any of the following quantity-discount schedules.

Note that Wal-Mart can use many quantity-discount schedules. The only feature that these discount schedules have in common is that Wal-Mart should offer LittleGuy a unit price of $1.67 ($25,000/15,000 units) for a purchase quantity of 15,000 units.

Fusion for Profit Maxim

Suppose the distributor has the economic power in the supply chain. Then, the distributor can obtain all the economic profit in the channel by using an appropriately chosen quantity-discount policy. Equivalently, the distributor can charge the supplier a fixed slotting fee for stocking its product.

Table 10.5
Wal-Mart Example: Optimal Quantity-Discount Policy for Wal-Mart

Units purchased from LittleGuy	Revenue offered to LittleGuy	Price per unit to LittleGuy	LittleGuy's profit	LittleGuy's economic profit
8,000	< $18,000	< $2.25	< $10,000	negative
15,000*	$25,000	$1.67	$10,000	$0
17,000	< $27,000	< $1.59	< $10,000	negative

*The number of units that LittleGuy will sell.

▶ *10.4 Coordinating Price and Advertising Decisions in the Channel*

In our discussion so far, we have focused on one marketing decision variable: price. We now discuss how both price and advertising decisions should be coordinated in the channel. In our analysis, we shall assume that the manufacturer has economic power. The analysis can be easily extended to the case where the distributor has economic power over the manufacturer.

▶ *Suppose a manufacturer has one exclusive distributor and advertises directly to consumers to increase the demand for its product. Should the manufacturer share the advertising costs with the distributor? What pricing strategy should the manufacturer use? Assume that the manufacturer has economic power and demand is predictable.*

The manufacturer should proceed as follows. First, determine the retail price-advertising policy that maximizes gross channel profits. Given this price-advertising strategy, choose an appropriate quantity-discount schedule. Note that the manufacturer's quantity-discount schedule must satisfy two conditions:

1. The retailer will choose the retail price that maximizes gross channel profits, and
2. At this retail price, the retailer's economic profit is zero.

By assumption, the effect of advertising on demand is predictable. (This assumption will be relaxed later.) Since no risk is involved, the manufacturer should pay all the advertising costs.

To illustrate, we return to the Coca-Cola example. Suppose Coca-Cola has determined that channel profits can be maximized by spending $15,000 per month to advertise Coke. As before, suppose the marginal cost per unit of the channel (marginal cost per unit for Coca-Cola + marginal cost per unit for the bottler) is $3. Let's say that Coke's advertising message focuses on *product differentiation*. Hence advertising increases consumers' *reservation prices*. In particular, advertising at the rate of $15,000 per month increases the demand for Coke at different prices as shown in table 10.6.

Note that advertising can be used to increase the gross economic profit in the channel from $20,000[4] (no advertising scenario) to $40,000 (gross channel margin − minimum profit for the bottler = $50,000 − $10,000) per month (optimal advertising spending). Since advertising costs $15,000 per month, the maximum net economic profit that can be generated by the channel is $25,000 per month ($40,000 − $15,000)—an improvement of $5,000 per month over the case where no advertising is done. Hence, advertising is worthwhile for Coca-Cola. To achieve this improvement in channel profits, however, the retail price needs to be increased from $5 to $8 per unit.

Coca-Cola should therefore choose the following advertising-pricing strategy. Spend $15,000 per month on advertising. In addition, choose a

Table 10.6
Coca-Cola Example: Optimal Retail Price-Advertising
Strategy for Coca-Cola

| Retail price per unit | Marginal costs per unit for channel | Gross channel profit margin per unit | Units sold | Net economic profit in channel | |
				Before paying advertising costs	After paying advertising costs
$8*	$3	$5	10,000	$40,000	$25,000
$6	$3	$3	16,000	$38,000	$23,000
$5	$3	$2	20,000	$30,000	$15,000

*The policy that maximizes the net economic profit in the channel after paying advertising costs.

Table 10.7
Coca-Cola Example: Optimal Quantity-Discount
Policy for Coca-Cola When It Advertises

Units of concentrate sold	Price per unit
10,000	$5.00
16,000	> $3.375
20,000	> $2.50

quantity-discount schedule for the Coke concentrate such that the best policy for the distributor is to buy 10,000 units, charge a retail price of $8 per unit, and make a monthly profit of $10,000 as in the no-advertising case.

Following the approach in the case where no advertising is done,[5] we can show that Coca-Cola can achieve this result by using any of the quantity-discount schedules for its concentrate shown in table 10.7.

If Coca-Cola uses any of these quantity-discount schedules, it can obtain all the economic profit generated by the channel ($25,000 per month). Note that when Coca-Cola advertises, the bottler will continue to earn the competitive return of $10,000 per month (zero economic profits).

Fusion for Profit Maxim

In a world of certainty, the manufacturer does not need to share advertising costs with the distributor. The manufacturer should first determine the advertising policy that maximizes channel profits. Given this policy, the manufacturer should choose a quantity-discount policy that allows it to obtain all the economic profit in the channel.

Point to consider. Suppose the effect of advertising on demand is uncertain. Should the manufacturer pay the advertising costs as in the certainty case? Assume that the manufacturer has all the economic power.

Demand uncertainty implies that channel profits are also uncertain. Hence the manufacturer should choose some type of risk-sharing contract with the distributor. (For a detailed discussion of optimal risk sharing, see chapters 15 through 17.) This implies that advertising costs should be shared between the manufacturer and the distributor.

Suppose the manufacturer chooses both the retail price and the advertising budget. By assumption, the manufacturer has all the economic power. Then, the manufacturer should choose a risk-sharing contract such that the distributor's *risk-adjusted economic profit* is zero.

In general, the *sharing rule* can be nonlinear and will depend on the risk attitudes of the manufacturer and the distributor.[6] (For a detailed discussion, see chapters 15 through 17.)

For simplicity, suppose the optimal risk-sharing contract is the following linear contract: the manufacturer charges the retailer a fixed fee and gives the retailer 20% of net channel profits. This implies that the manufacturer and the distributor should share advertising costs in the ratio 80:20. Note that, because of uncertainty, the distributor's expected profit will be greater than $10,000 per month when the risk-adjusted economic profit is zero.

▶ *How do the risk attitudes of the manufacturer and the distributor affect the ratio in which advertising costs should be shared by both parties?*

Suppose the distributor is small relative to the manufacturer. Then, the distributor is likely to be much more risk-averse than the manufacturer. Hence the manufacturer should "insure" the distributor more fully than otherwise. That is, the manufacturer should charge the distributor a lower fixed fee. However, the manufacturer should also pay the distributor a lower share of gross channel profits. This implies that the manufacturer should pay a higher proportion of the advertising costs.

Fusion for Profit Maxim

When demand is uncertain, the manufacturer and the distributor should share advertising costs. In general, the cost-sharing formula will depend on the risk attitudes of the manufacturer and the distributor.

▶ *10.5 Channel Strategy in the Multiproduct Case*

In our discussion so far, we have implicitly assumed that the manufacturer sells only one product. Furthermore, the manufacturer uses an exclusive distributor who sells only that product. In reality, most manufacturers sell multiple products. In addition, distributors also sell multiple products, including those made by the manufacturer's competitors. In this section, we examine channel strategies for these multiproduct scenarios.

▶ *Suppose the manufacturer sells multiple products, and the exclusive distributor sells all these products. How should the manufacturer price its product line to the distributor?*

We continue with the Coca-Cola example. Suppose the exclusive bottler buys several types of concentrate (e.g., Coke and Sprite) from Coca-Cola. Then, Coca-Cola should proceed as follows:

1. Determine the set of prices and volumes for its product portfolio that maximizes the net economic profit from the channel, and
2. Establish appropriate quantity-discount schedules for the product portfolio such that the bottler's economic profits across the product line are zero.

▶ *Suppose a manufacturing firm has been using an exclusive distributor in the past to sell its product. The manufacturer now decides to sell its product using an additional channel: the Internet. How should the manufacturer revise the pricing schedule it offers the distributor?*

As illustrated below, this problem is conceptually similar to the case where the manufacturer sells through an exclusive distributor and advertises directly to consumers. When the manufacturer uses the new mixed channel strategy (distributor + Internet), it should proceed as follows:

1. Choose the optimal set of prices (the retail price at the bricks-and-mortar store and the Internet price) to maximize the *joint profits* from the mixed channel strategy, and
2. Revise the quantity-discount schedule it offers the distributor so that the distributor charges the optimal retail price (from the manufacturer's viewpoint) and the distributor makes zero economic profits.

Example: Suppose the Stanley Company initially sells power drills using an exclusive distributor. Assume that the marginal manufacturing cost per unit is $20, the marginal cost per unit for the distributor is $5, and the distributor needs to make a gross monthly profit of at least $50,000 to stay in business.

Suppose the demand for the Stanley power drills before Stanley uses the Internet as an additional channel is as shown in table 10.8.

Then, following the approach in the Coca-Cola example, we can show that Stanley can obtain all the economic profit in the channel by using any of the quantity-discount schedules shown in table 10.9.

Table 10.8
Stanley Example: Optimal Retail Price for Stanley before Stanley Sells via the Internet

Retail price	Units sold per month
$50*	10,000
$40	15,000
$30	20,000

*The price that maximizes channel profits before Stanley sells via the Internet.

Table 10.9
Stanley Example: Optimal Quantity-Discount Policy for Stanley before Stanley Sells via the Internet

Volume	Price per unit to distributor	Distributor's gross profits per month
10,000*	$40	$50,000
15,000	> $31.67	< $50,000
20,000	> $25	< $50,000

*Policy chosen by distributor.

Given this pricing schedule, the distributor will purchase 10,000 power drills every month from Stanley at a unit price of $40, charge a retail price of $50 per unit, and make a gross monthly profit of $50,000 (zero economic profits).

► *What will happen to the retail demand for the distributor when Stanley uses the Internet as an additional channel?*

Since some consumers will now purchase the Stanley power drill on the Internet, the retail demand for the distributor will fall. That is, at any given retail price, the distributor will sell fewer Stanley power drills than before. Suppose gross channel profits are maximized if the Internet price is $25 per unit and the price charged by the distributor is $30.[7] Then, for this strategy to be effective, Stanley should choose a pricing policy for the distributor such that the distributor earns a gross profit of $50,000 per month (zero economic profit) as before.

Given Stanley's Internet price ($25 per unit), suppose the new demand for Stanley power drills sold by the distributor is as shown in table 10.10.

Then, Stanley can maximize its profits by using any of the quantity-discount schedules for the distributor listed in table 10.11.

Given this price schedule and Stanley's Internet price ($25 per unit), the distributor will purchase 12,000 power drills every month from Stanley, sell

Table 10.10
Stanley Example: Optimal Retail Demand for
Stanley after Stanley Sells via the Internet

Retail price	Units sold per month
$40	10,000
$30	12,000*

*Optimal demand.

Table 10.11
Stanley Example: Optimal Quantity-Discount Policy for
Stanley after Stanley Sells via the Internet

Volume	Price per unit to distributor	Distributor's gross profits per month
10,000	> $30	< $50,000
12,000	$20.83	$50,000

them at $30 per unit, and make a gross profit of $50,000 (zero economic profit) as before.

Fusion for Profit Maxim

Suppose a manufacturer changes from an exclusive distributor strategy to a mixed channel strategy using an exclusive distributor and the Internet. Then, the manufacturer should offer a revised quantity-discount schedule to the distributor in order to maximize its own combined profits across both channels.

▶ **10.6 Choosing Channel Strategy Using Multiple Exclusive Distributors**

In the previous section, we focused on the case where the manufacturer sells its product(s) using only one exclusive dealer. We now extend the analysis to the case where the firm uses multiple distributors, each of whom sells only its products. In the next section, we will consider the case where the firm uses nonexclusive distributors.

▶ *Suppose the manufacturer has several exclusive distributors, each of whom is assigned a separate geographical area. What price schedule(s) should the manufacturer use for its distributors?*

Suppose the manufacturer assigns separate geographical areas to its exclusive distributors. In addition, suppose the transshipment of products from one exclusive distributor to another is expensive. For example, the distributors are in different countries or are geographically far apart. Then, the manufacturer can obtain all the channel profits by using a separate quantity-discount schedule for each distributor. As previously discussed, *the less price-sensitive the demand for the product is in any given geographical area, the steeper the quantity-discount schedule should be for the distributor in that area.*

Example 1: Suppose a multinational firm faces strong competition for its products abroad but not at home. Since the domestic market is less competitive than the foreign market, the multinational firm should offer its distributors in the home country a steeper discount schedule than its distributors in foreign countries.

Example 2: Suppose Procter & Gamble faces stronger competition for its diapers in urban areas than in rural areas. Then, other factors being the same, Procter & Gamble should offer its distributors in rural areas bigger discounts than those in urban areas.

Point to consider.   Suppose distributors can *arbitrage*. Can the manufacturer absorb all the channel profits?

Suppose the manufacturer uses different quantity-discount schedules for its distributors in different territories or countries. For example, suppose a multinational firm uses a steep quantity-discount schedule in its home country (where demand is less price-sensitive) and a flatter quantity-discount schedule in its foreign markets (where demand is more price-sensitive). Then, if transshipment costs are not too high, it will be profitable for the firm's distributors in the foreign market to arbitrage. Thus, distributors in the foreign market have an incentive to proceed as follows. They will buy more than they can sell in the foreign market and export the remainder at a profit to distributors in the firm's home market. This arbitrage strategy will undermine the manufacturing firm's efforts to absorb all the channel profits generated in both its domestic and foreign markets.

▰ How can the manufacturer address this arbitrage problem?

If demand is predictable, the manufacturer knows with certainty how many units each distributor "should" buy in a given period. Thus, the manufacturer will be able to unambiguously detect any arbitrage activity and take punitive action. For example, the manufacturer can discontinue doing business with any distributors who have participated in arbitrage activities, either as resellers or as purchasers of resold products. Since the manufacturer can impose a significant long-run penalty on distributors, they will not arbitrage. Hence the manufacturer will be able to obtain all the channel profits.

If demand is uncertain, however, the manufacturer will not be able to detect arbitrage activity with certainty. Hence some distributors (especially those in markets where demand is highly uncertain and transshipment costs are low) can gain from arbitrage. This reduces the manufacturer's ability to obtain all the channel profits across different geographical markets.

> **Fusion for Profit Maxim**
>
> If the firm uses different quantity-discount schedules on a regional basis, its distributors will have an incentive to arbitrage—provided transshipment costs are not too high and demand is uncertain.

▲ 10.7 Choosing Channel Strategy Using Nonexclusive Distributors

Our previous analyses focused on the cases in which the manufacturer sells using exclusive distributors only. We now discuss the more general case where the firm uses distributors who sell other products also, including those made by its competitors.

▲ *Manufacturers often have to use distributors who also sell products made by other manufacturers. How should the manufacturer price its products to such nonexclusive distributors?*

Suppose a manufacturer seeks to introduce a new product into the marketplace. Then, the manufacturer needs to choose a channel policy such that, when it introduces a new product into the marketplace, the distributor's product-line profits, *net of cannibalization*, increase.

Example: A number of years ago, Rohm and Haas introduced a superior new biocide product, Kathon MWX, into the marketplace.[8] Kathon MWX's primary benefit was that it kept metalworking fluids in tanks clean for a longer period of time than competing alternatives. Consequently, Kathon MWX users would need to replace the metalworking fluid in their tanks less often.

An inferior biocide product, Tris Nitro, was available at the time when Kathon MWX was introduced into the marketplace. Rohm and Haas chose a pricing policy such that the distributor's margins on both Kathon MWX and Tris Nitro were approximately equal at $1 per unit. However, because of the product design, Tris Nitro users needed to repurchase Tris Nitro every 3 days on average. In contrast, Kathon MWX users needed to repurchase Kathon MWX less frequently (approximately every 21 days).

Since both Tris Nitro and Kathon MWX gave the distributor the same margins per application ($1) and users needed to purchase Tris Nitro 7 times more often (21/3), in any given time period the distributor would have made 7 times more profit by selling Tris Nitro rather than by selling Kathon MWX.

An additional factor was that, because Kathon MWX kept tanks clean for a longer period, sales of Kathon MWX cannibalized the distributor's sales of metalworking fluid. Since Kathon MWX led to reduced product-line profits for distributors, Kathon MWX failed in the marketplace, even though it was a superior product.

Point to consider.   How could Kathon MWX have succeeded in the market?

The root causes of the problem were twofold: the low distributor margins for Kathon MWX, and the degree to which Kathon MWX cannibalized the distributor's existing product line.

To address these problems, Rohm and Haas could have proceeded as follows. It could have developed a strong advertising campaign and advertised heavily to educate users about the cost savings from using Kathon MWX. This would have increased users' reservation prices. Consequently, Rohm and Haas would have been able to charge higher retail prices for Kathon MWX, increase the distributor's margin per unit sold, and make sure that the distributor's net profit from selling Kathon MWX (after allowing for cannibalization and reduced frequency of use vis-à-vis the main competitor, Tris Nitro) exceeded the corresponding net profit from selling Tris Nitro.[9]

Fusion for Profit Maxim

When the firm uses nonexclusive distributors, it should price its product after analyzing how this pricing policy affects the distributors' product-line profits. This requires an explicit analysis of cannibalization, the margins on competing products, and how the firm's product affects the frequency of purchase by consumers.

▲ 10.8 Should the Firm Use a Vertical Integration Strategy?

Our analysis so far has assumed that all the firms in the supply chain (e.g., raw materials suppliers, the manufacturing firm, and its distributors) are separately owned. We now ask a basic question.

▲ Under what conditions should a manufacturer set up its own distribution channel or produce its own raw materials?

To address this question, we need to introduce some definitions. Suppose a manufacturer produces its own raw materials instead of purchasing them from an outside supplier. We say that the manufacturer has *vertically integrated backward or upstream.* Suppose a manufacturer sets up its own distribution outlets. We say that the manufacturer has *vertically integrated forward or downstream.*

▶ *Under what conditions should the manufacturer vertically integrate backward or forward?*

The answer depends on the following factors:

1. The competitive structure of the market,
2. The quality and supply of inputs, and
3. The firm's information about the supply chain.

Competitive Structure

Consider a manufacturer that has vertically integrated forward.

Example: Suppose Pepsico sets up its own bottling plants and that the bottling industry is competitive (i.e., bottlers have limited economic power). Then Pepsico can obtain all the economic profit in the channel by using an appropriate quantity-discount schedule. Consequently, Pepsico should not vertically integrate forward.

Similarly, there is no reason for a firm to vertically integrate backward if the market from which it purchases inputs or raw materials is competitive.

Quality and Supply of Inputs

Suppose input quality has a major effect on the performance of the manufacturer's product. Then, it may be optimal for the manufacturer to vertically integrate backward to maintain quality control of its product. Alternatively, suppose there are few suppliers of an important input. Then, by vertically integrating backward, the firm can reduce its dependence on suppliers and the ability of those suppliers to make economic profits.

Information about the Supply Chain

In the Pepsico example, suppose Pepsico does not know the cost structure of its distributors in different geographical areas. Then, Pepsico should set up a limited number of its own bottling plants in different geographical areas so that it can determine the cost structure of the bottling industry. This strategy—known as *tapered vertical integration*—will allow Pepsico to optimize its performance by developing the optimal quantity-discount schedules for pricing its concentrate in different regions.

Similarly, suppose Pepsico does not know the retail demand for Pepsi with certainty. Then, by partially integrating forward into the bottling industry, Pepsico can obtain timely and superior information about the demand for Pepsi. Most important, Pepsico can obtain current information about changes in the demand structure for the industry. Hence Pepsico will be able to improve its long-run performance by using this information to adapt its pricing strategy to changing market conditions. In addition, Pepsico will be in a stronger position vis-à-vis its bottlers in the future when it renegotiates contracts with them.

Point to consider.   Should firms in the oil industry (e.g., Exxon) own and operate their own tankers?

By using this tapered vertical integration strategy, firms in the oil industry can obtain more accurate information about the cost structure of the oil tanker industry. This improved knowledge of costs will allow firms in the oil industry (e.g., Exxon) to bargain more effectively with tanker companies when they negotiate shipping contracts. Hence, by using a tapered vertical integration strategy, oil companies will be able to increase their profits.

Fusion for Profit Maxim

Forward or backward vertical integration can add value if the relevant part of the channel is not competitive, the firm needs to control the supply and quality of inputs, or there is *asymmetric information* in the supply chain.

▲ 10.9 Long-Term Channel and Supply Chain Strategy

In our previous analyses, we assumed that the relationships among the manufacturer, its suppliers, and its distributors are rivalrous. Specifically, the manufacturer's goal is to choose strategies and contracts under which its suppliers and distributors earn zero economic profits.

▲ Is it optimal for the manufacturer to choose contracts such that its distributors and suppliers earn zero economic profits? Assume that the manufacturer has the economic power.

This strategy can be optimal if all parties in the supply chain have symmetric information about the marketplace. Furthermore, all parties incur minimal *transaction costs* in renegotiating contracts or finding new partners.

In practice, however, these conditions may not be met. Thus, the various contracting parties in the supply chain (e.g., raw material suppliers, the manufacturing firm, and its distributors) often have different degrees of knowledge about the market. Furthermore, it is expensive and destabilizing, in terms of both money and time, for the manufacturing firm to continually renegotiate contracts and find new suppliers and distributors for its products.

Hence it may be better for the manufacturing firm to collaborate with its suppliers and distributors and allow them to earn some economic profit.

Example 1: Japanese automobile manufacturers typically use a long-run collaborative approach when they negotiate contracts with their suppliers and distributors. In contrast, U.S. automobile manufacturers have historically chosen short-run channel strategies in which they have attempted to force their suppliers and distributors to earn zero economic profits. Many would argue that the Japanese channel strategy of collaboration is superior because it leads to *channel stability* and to improved long-run performance for all parties in the supply chain (a "win-win" outcome).

Example 2: Coca-Cola has recently increased the extent to which it collaborates with its bottlers. Thus, on a monthly basis, Coca-Cola and its bottlers will now exchange ideas on how to sell more Coke Zero (a new soft drink made by Coca-Cola). In addition, they will jointly analyze consumer feedback. This collaborative strategy should help Coca-Cola to adapt its strategy nimbly when market conditions change.[10] Hence channel profits should increase.

Chapter 10 Key Points

- A powerful manufacturer can use a quantity-discount schedule or a lump-sum franchise fee to obtain the economic profit in a channel of distribution.
- A powerful distributor can use a quantity-discount schedule or charge a fixed slotting fee to obtain the economic profits in a channel of distribution.
- If a manufacturer charges a distributor a fixed price per unit, the distributor will gain, consumers will pay higher prices, and social welfare will be reduced.
- In a world of certainty, the manufacturer should pay all the advertising costs for the product and use a quantity-discount schedule when selling to the distributor. In a world of uncertainty, the manufacturer and the distributor should share advertising costs. The precise formula for cost sharing will depend on their respective risk attitudes.
- If the manufacturer uses a mixed channel strategy (e.g., it sells its product via an exclusive distributor and via the Internet), the manufacturer should coordinate prices across channels and revise the quantity-discount schedule it offers the distributor.
- In general, firms that sell branded products should offer their distributors steeper quantity-discount schedules than firms that sell generic versions of the branded product.
- If a manufacturer's distributors can arbitrage, the manufacturer's ability to obtain the economic profits from the channels will be reduced.
- Forward or backward vertical integration can add value if the relevant part of the channel is not competitive, the firm needs to control the supply and quality of inputs, or there is asymmetric information in the supply chain.

Part VI

Marketing Policy and Consumer Behavior

- How should the *customer relationship management* (CRM) group in my firm use these theories of consumer behavior to improve its performance?
- What do these theories of consumer behavior imply about the behavior of investors in the financial market?
- What do these theories of consumer behavior imply about my firm's target profits and dividend policy?
- What types of research should my firm conduct to use these models of consumer behavior for marketing decision making?

The following terms will be introduced in this chapter (see glossary for definitions):

acquisition utility (AU)	discount rate	reference price
assimilation-contrast theory	dividends	repeat purchase rate
	external reference price	reservation price
cash rebate	income shortfall	standard economic theory
consumer surplus	incremental loss of value	
cost dynamics		sticker shock
cost structure	internal reference price	strategic pricing
coupons	just noticeable differences (JNDs)	threshold effect
customer relationship management (CRM)		transaction utility
	prospect theory	willingness to pay (WTP)
demand dynamics	quota system	
demand structure	reference point	windfall gain

▶ 11.1 What Is the Standard Economic Model of Consumer Choice?

The *standard economic theory* is based on a simple and intuitive idea: all individuals seek to maximize their well-being. To understand how consumers make purchase decisions, we need to briefly discuss the concept of a *reservation price*.

▶ What is the consumer's reservation price for a given purchase alternative?

Consider a consumer who is planning to purchase a car. Suppose the consumer is willing to pay a maximum price of $24,000 for a Toyota Camry with certain features (e.g., leather seats, a CD player, and air-conditioning). We say that the consumer's reservation price for the Camry is $24,000.[1]

Note that the consumer's reservation price for the Camry (a particular model of car) is *not* the same as the maximum price that the consumer is willing to pay to purchase a car (e.g., the amount that the consumer has budgeted for this purpose).

Fusion for Profit Maxim

The consumer's reservation price is alternative-specific and not product-specific. Thus, the reservation price for a given purchase alternative (or brand) depends on the attributes provided by that alternative (or brand).

▶ *How do reservation prices affect the consumer's purchase decision?*

Suppose a consumer is considering buying one of two cars: a Toyota Camry (with certain options) priced at $20,000 or a Honda Accord (with certain options) priced at $22,000. Suppose the consumer's reservation prices for the Toyota Camry and the Honda Accord are $24,000 and $27,000, respectively.

Then, by purchasing the Toyota Camry, this consumer will obtain a net benefit of $4,000 (reservation price – price). We say that the consumer obtains a *consumer surplus* of $4,000. Similarly, by purchasing the Honda Accord, the consumer will obtain a consumer surplus of $5,000 (table 11.1).

Since the consumer seeks to maximize his or her well-being, he or she will choose the car that provides the largest consumer surplus. Thus, the consumer will purchase the Honda Accord.

▶ *What happens if both consumer surpluses are negative?*

Then the consumer will not purchase either the Toyota Camry or the Honda Accord.

Fusion for Profit Maxim

The consumer will choose the alternative that maximizes his or her consumer surplus. If all the consumer surpluses are negative, the consumer will not make any purchase.

Table 11.1
Honda-Toyota Example: How Reservation Prices Affect Consumer Choice

	Toyota Camry	Honda Accord
Reservation price	$24,000	$27,000
Price	$20,000	$22,000
Consumer surplus	$4,000	$5,000*

*Consumer's decision

▶ *What information does the firm need to estimate the demand for its product?*

To determine the demand for its product, the firm needs to determine consumers' reservation prices for its own products *and the products marketed by its competitors*. We illustrate the methodology below.

For simplicity, suppose as before that the price of the Toyota Camry is $20,000 and the price of the Honda Accord is $22,000. Let's say that there are three segments each of equal size (100,000) with reservation prices as shown in table 11.2.

Given these prices, each segment will choose the alternative that maximizes its surplus. Thus, Segments A and B will purchase the Honda Accord, and Segment C will purchase the Toyota Camry. Hence, Honda will sell 200,000 Accords, and Toyota will sell 100,000 Camrys.

Now, consider what would happen if Honda (say) measures only consumers' reservation prices for the Accord and fails to consider consumers' reservation prices for its competitor (the Toyota Camry). Then, Honda will incorrectly conclude that Segment C will purchase the Accord because consumers in that segment obtain a positive consumer surplus ($1,000) from purchasing the Accord. In reality, Segment C will purchase the Camry instead, since it will obtain a higher consumer surplus from buying the Camry ($6,000 > $1,000). Hence, Honda will overestimate the demand for the Accord.

Fusion for Profit Maxim

In order to estimate the demand for its product, the firm needs to estimate consumers' reservation prices for its product *and* competing products.

▶ *How can the firm determine its profits if it chooses a particular pricing policy?*

The firm needs to know both its *demand* and *cost structures*.

Table 11.2
Honda-Toyota Example: How Incorrect Reservation Prices Affect Consumer Choice Across Different Segments

	Segment A		Segment B		Segment C	
	Toyota Camry	Honda Accord	Toyota Camry	Honda Accord	Toyota Camry	Honda Accord
Reservation price	$24,000	$27,000	$18,000	$25,000	$26,000	$23,000
Price	$20,000	$22,000	$20,000	$22,000	$20,000	$22,000
Consumer surplus	$4,000	$5,000*	–$2,000	$3,000*	$6,000*	$1,000

*Policies chosen.

We continue with the Honda-Toyota example, where Toyota charges a price of $20,000 for the Camry and Honda charges a price of $22,000 for the Accord. Suppose the marginal cost of a Camry is $14,000, and the marginal cost of an Accord is $15,000. Then, Toyota will obtain a gross profit margin of $6,000 per Camry (price of Camry − marginal cost of Camry) and make a gross profit of $600 million (unit profit margin of Camry × number of Camrys sold = $6,000 × 100,000). Similarly, Honda will obtain a gross profit margin of $7,000 per Accord and make a gross profit of $1.4 billion ($7,000 × 200,000).[2]

Fusion for Profit Maxim

The firm can determine how its pricing policy will affect its profits by estimating the demand for its product based on knowledge of consumers' reservation prices for its own product and competitive products and by combining this information with cost data for its product.

▶ 11.2 Is the Standard Economic Model of Consumer Choice Good Enough for Marketing Managers?

As illustrated above, the standard economic model of consumer choice is a useful tool for managerial decision making. However, in many cases, the manager will need to adapt the model for marketing decision making. The key additional factors to include are consumers' expectations, how consumers value gains and losses, how consumers react to price changes, and how consumers adjust their behavior based on new information.

The Role of Consumer Expectations

Standard economic theory assumes that consumers *derive economic value only from using a product or service.* Thus, the reservation price for a given product equals this dollar value, known as *acquisition utility.*

However, this conventional measure of reservation price (i.e., acquisition utility) *fails to consider the gain or loss to the consumer from the transaction itself.* This effect is known as *transaction utility* and can be either positive or negative. As we discuss below, these transaction utility effects can influence consumers' purchase decisions and hence the firm's sales and profits.

Example: Consider a consumer who goes to the supermarket to buy a jar of Folger's instant coffee. Let's say the consumer expects to pay a price of $4 per jar. However, when the consumer visits the store, the consumer finds that the price of Folger's is higher (say $6). Since the expected price ($4) is lower than the actual price ($6), the consumer experiences *sticker shock*. We say that the transaction utility (expected price − actual price = $4 − $6 = −$2) is negative. Similarly, suppose the consumer discovers that the store is running an unannounced sale on Folger's instant coffee for $2.50 a jar. Since the actual price ($2.50) is lower than the expected price ($4), the consumer's transaction utility is positive ($4 − $2.50 = $1.50).

 ### How should the manager incorporate these price expectation effects into decision making?

One approach is to redefine the consumer's *willingness to pay* as the sum of the acquisition utility (which is always positive) and the transaction utility (which can be either positive *or negative*).

Fusion for Profit Maxim

Consumers' price expectations are likely to affect their willingness to pay for a particular brand or product. Hence the firm should choose its marketing policy after evaluating *both* acquisition utility and transaction utility.

The Effects of Gains and Losses

Standard economic theory argues that consumers aggregate gains and losses and evaluate only the net effect of these changes. However, empirical evidence suggests that consumers may evaluate gains and losses separately.

Example: Suppose Debbie finds a $100 bill and takes it home (a gain of $100). When she goes home, she finds that the $100 bill is missing (a loss of $100). Thus, the net dollar gain to Debbie is zero. According to standard economic theory, Debbie will be unaffected by this sequence of events.

However, according to *prospect theory* (a theory that we will examine shortly), Debbie will value the gain of $100 separately from the loss of $100. Furthermore, Debbie will value gains and losses of the same dollar amount differently.

Not surprisingly, as we discuss below, prospect theory will often lead to very different marketing policy implications than standard economic theory.

Fusion for Profit Maxim

Consumers may value gains and losses separately. As will be discussed shortly, this has major managerial implications.

The Effect of Price Changes

The magnitude of a price change can have a major effect on the consumer's behavior both in the short run and in the long run. We distinguish three scenarios: small, moderate, and large price changes. To focus on essentials, assume that there are no *cost dynamics* or *demand dynamics*.

Small Price Changes

If a price change is too small, it will have no effect on the demand for the firm's product. We say that there is a *threshold effect*. Importantly, *the threshold effect does not depend on the absolute magnitude of the price but on the relative magnitude.* This theory, known as the theory of *just noticeable differences* (JND) is not surprising. Thus, a price cut of $1 for a tube of shampoo that normally costs $2 will exceed the threshold effect. However, a price cut of $1 on a Mercedes Benz that normally costs $80,000 will not.

Example: When sugar prices went up several years ago, candy manufacturers had a choice of either increasing prices or reducing the sizes of candy bars. They chose the latter strategy. Specifically, they held prices constant but reduced the sizes of the candy bars such that the changes in size were just below the threshold levels.

Fusion for Profit Maxim

Unless the change in a stimulus (e.g., price) is sufficiently large, it will have no effect on consumers' purchasing behavior.

Moderate Price Changes

Suppose the price change (either a price decrease or a price increase) is moderately large vis-à-vis the initial price.[3] Since the price change exceeds the threshold value, the price change will affect current demand. For example, a price reduction in the current period will lead to a higher sales volume in that period. However, the more interesting question is: What is the effect on future demand?

According to *assimilation-contrast theory,* when the price change is moderate, consumers will change their price expectations in the future. For example, if the firm reduces its price in the first period, consumers will expect future prices to be low. Hence, other factors remaining the same, the moderate price change in the first period will lead to lower (and possibly negative) transaction utility for consumers in the future. Consequently, for any given price that the firm charges in the future, the demand in that period will be lower.

Fusion for Profit Maxim

When the firm introduces a moderate price change, both current and future demand will be affected. Hence the firm needs to consider both short-run and long-run effects.

Large Price Changes

Suppose the firm introduces a large price change. Then, as in the case where the price change is moderate, current demand will change. For example, the firm will sell a larger volume in the current period if it reduces current prices.

▶ *What will happen in the second period?*

According to assimilation-contrast theory, since the price change is large, consumers will *contrast* this information. That is, they will not adjust their price expectations (and hence their transaction utilities) for the second period. Hence the price change in the first period will have no effect on consumers' purchase behavior in the second. Consequently, other factors being the same, the firm does not need to consider the long-run effects of a price change.

Fusion for Profit Maxim

If the firm introduces a large price change in the current period, other factors being held constant, the price change will not have any long-run effects.

Point to consider.   Suppose the marketing manager for Dove soap introduces a moderate price cut for Dove. Suppose Dove's short-run profits increase by $500,000. Can one conclude that the price cut was a good marketing decision?

Not necessarily. According to assimilation-contrast theory, the moderate price reduction will be assimilated by consumers. Since consumers will revise their price expectations downward, future demand for Dove will decrease. Hence the short-run increase in profits "borrows" some profits from the future and overstates the gain from the price reduction.

The Role of Information

Consider an extreme scenario where each consumer is well informed about prices (i.e., the expected price for any product equals its market price). Then, the transaction utility for each consumer will be zero. Hence the standard economic model will apply (willingness to pay = acquisition utility).

Alternatively, suppose consumers have imperfect information about prices. Specifically, some consumers expect the price of the product to be higher than it is. However, others expect the price of the product to be lower than the market price.

Consider the most optimistic scenario where, on average, consumers are unbiased (i.e., the average of the expected prices of the product across consumers equals the market price of the product). Then, the average transaction utility across consumers for that product will be zero. Consequently, since willingness to pay = acquisition utility + transaction utility, one might expect that the standard economic model (willingness to pay = acquisition utility) should be a good approximation of reality. However, as we discuss below, this is not the case—*even for the scenario described above where consumers have unbiased price expectations.*

We continue with the Honda-Toyota example. Let us begin with the limiting case where all consumers are perfectly informed about the price of the Honda Accord. Then, for all consumers the transaction utilities for the Honda Accord will be zeros. Hence the standard economic theory and the behavioral extension will lead to the same estimates of each consumer's willingness to pay for the Honda Accord. Consequently, both theories will lead to the same estimates of market demand for the Honda Accord.

Now consider the more realistic case where consumers are not perfectly informed about prices. As before, we consider the most optimistic scenario where consumers are, on average, unbiased. Then, the average transaction utilities across consumers for the Honda Accord will be zero. However, as illustrated below, *this does not mean that transaction utilities are irrelevant in estimating the demand for the Honda Accord.*

Consider the following illustration. Suppose the highest acquisition utility value in the marketplace for the Honda Accord is $30,000. Then, standard economic theory implies that no one will buy the car if it is priced above $30,000. Suppose the market consists of two consumers (John and Jane), each of whom has an acquisition utility of $30,000 for the Honda Accord. Furthermore, the market price of the Honda Accord is $30,000. Let's say that John expects the price of the Honda Accord to be $31,000; however, Jane expects the price to be $29,000. Hence, on average, consumers are unbiased in their price expectations for the Honda Accord (i.e., the average expected price across both consumers is $30,000). Given these price expectations, John will obtain a positive transaction utility of $1,000 from purchasing the Accord (expected price – actual price of the car). This implies that John's willingness to pay for the Accord is $31,000 (acquisition utility + transaction utility)—not $30,000 (acquisition utility). Hence, contrary to standard economic theory, Honda can charge as much as $31,000 for the Accord.[4]

Fusion for Profit Maxim

If consumers' price expectations affect consumers' willingness to pay, standard economic theory can lead to incorrect demand estimates for a product, even if consumers' price expectations are correct, on average. Hence the firm is likely to make incorrect pricing decisions.

▶ 11.3 Do Marketing Managers Use These Theories of Consumer Behavior in Practice?

At least implicitly, marketing managers in many industries set prices based on their assumptions about consumers' price expectations in general, and about consumers' transaction utilities in particular. Following are a few examples.

Automobile Industry

Recently, the U.S. automobile industry faced the problem of accumulating inventories of unsold cars. One strategy for automobile manufacturers would have been to get rid of the excess inventory by reducing the prices of their cars. However, this would have led consumers to expect lower prices in the future (i.e., their *reference prices* would have been reduced). Consequently, it would have become difficult for automobile manufacturers to raise prices in the future to their "normal" levels.

To prevent future reference prices from falling, U.S. automobile manufacturers used the following price reduction strategy: they reduced prices but described the price reductions as "employee discount pricing," implying that the price cuts were temporary.[5]

Point to consider. Suppose a U.S. automobile manufacturer (say General Motors) had introduced major price reductions for its cars without describing them as "employee discount pricing." Would it have been necessary for General Motors to consider long-run effects?

According to assimilation-contrast theory, consumers' reference prices for General Motors cars in the future would not have been affected, since the price changes would have been large. Hence, other factors being held constant, it would not have been necessary for General Motors to consider long-run transaction utility effects.

Airline Industry

Recently, world oil prices have risen sharply. To address this problem of rising fuel costs, airlines could have simply increased prices. Instead, to avoid a negative transaction utility effect on future demand, many international airlines have simply added a variable fuel surcharge to ticket prices, where the fuel surcharge depends on the fluctuating prices of jet fuel.[6]

The Packaged Goods Industry

Firms in the packaged goods industry always have the option of using price reductions to stimulate sales. Instead, they often prefer to use such pricing strategies as "30% Bonus. Get 13 ounces of Noxema for the regular price of 10 ounces." In this way, a de facto current price reduction will not have a negative effect on consumers' transaction utilities (and hence demand) in the future.

11.4 Some Applications of Prospect Theory

As discussed previously, standard economic theory implies that a consumer's willingness to pay for a product equals the value to the consumer from using that product (acquisition utility). However, prospect theory argues that a consumer's willingness to pay for a product is also based on the difference between the actual price paid and a reference price. In this section, we present some examples showing how prospect theory can lead to significantly different managerial implications than standard economic theory.

Example: Consider an industrial firm (FunCo) that sells a plastic component for toys. Suppose FunCo is presently charging a price of $10 per unit and selling 500,000 units every month. For simplicity, assume that the reference price is also $10 per unit and is common across consumers. Furthermore, suppose that consumers do not anticipate the price reduction.

Suppose standard economic theory predicts that volume will increase from 500,000 to 550,000 units if FunCo reduces its price from $10 to $9 per unit.

What does prospect theory suggest for the same pricing scenario?

When FunCo reduces the price of the component from $10 to $9 per unit, consumers will obtain a positive transaction utility because of the unforeseen price reduction. Hence any given consumer's willingness to pay (acquisition utility + transaction utility) will exceed that consumer's acquisition utility. Consequently, the increase in demand will be larger than the increase predicted by standard economic theory. In other words, according to prospect theory, standard economic theory will understate the price sensitivity of the market to unanticipated price reductions.

> **Fusion for Profit Maxim**
>
> Suppose the firm introduces an unanticipated price cut in the market. Then, prospect theory implies that standard economic theory will understate the quantity that the firm can sell at the lower price.

Point to consider.   What will happen if FunCo increases the price of the component from $10 to $11 per unit? As before, suppose consumers do not anticipate the price increase.

Let's say that standard economic theory predicts that FunCo will sell 460,000 units (<500,000 units) if it increases the price of its component from \$10 to \$11 per unit. Since consumers do not anticipate the price increase, prospect theory implies that consumers will obtain a negative transaction utility (sticker shock). Hence any consumer's willingness to pay will be less than his or her acquisition utility. Consequently, demand will be less than the volume predicted by standard economic theory (460,000 units).

Fusion for Profit Maxim

Suppose the firm introduces an unanticipated price increase in the market. Then, prospect theory implies that standard economic theory will overstate the quantity of the product that the firm can sell at the higher price.

▶ *Firms, particularly those in the service sector, often have flexibility with respect to how frequently they bill their customers. What does prospect theory suggest about the frequency with which firms should bill customers? Assume that the discount rates for the firm and customers are zeros.*

According to standard economic theory, consumers consider only *net* gains and losses. In contrast, prospect theory implies that

1. Consumers value each gain and loss separately, and
2. Each successive dollar that is gained or lost has a lower value than the previous dollar.

Example: Suppose a telecommunication firm (e.g., Verizon) is considering two billing plans: send the consumer two monthly bills of \$50 each, or send the consumer one large bill of \$100 every two months. Since the discount rates for the firm and its customers are zeros (by assumption), standard economic theory implies that all parties should be indifferent to which billing plan Verizon uses.

▶ *However, what does prospect theory imply?*

Suppose Verizon sends a customer (Mary) two separate bills of \$50 each. Let's say that Mary will obtain a loss in "value" of −6 when she pays a bill of \$50. According to prospect theory, Mary will evaluate the losses from both bills separately. Hence Mary will obtain a net value of −12 (negative value from paying the first bill + negative value from paying the second bill) (table 11.3).

Suppose, in contrast, that Verizon sends Mary one combined bill for \$100 (\$50 + \$50). As discussed above, the value to Mary from the first \$50 she owes Verizon is −6. However, according to prospect theory, the absolute value of the loss in value to Mary from paying the first \$50 she owes to Verizon will be higher than the absolute value of the loss in value to Mary from paying the additional \$50 that she owes Verizon. Let's say that the

Table 11.3
Verizon Example: A Comparison of Optimal Billing Cycles Using Standard Economic Theory and Prospect Theory

Type of billing cycle	Cost to consumer (standard theory)	Value to consumer (prospect theory)
Monthly		
Payment for first month	$50	–6
Payment for second month	$50	–6
Total	$100	–12
Bimonthly		
Money owed for first month's service	$50	–6
Money owed for second month's service	$50	–4
Total	$100	–10

latter loss in value is –4. This implies that Mary will obtain a loss of –10 if she has to pay Verizon one bill for $100.

Note that Mary prefers a negative net value of –10 (by paying one bill of $100) to a negative net value of –12 (by paying two bills of $50 each). Hence, other factors remaining the same, prospect theory implies that Verizon should bill customers less frequently.

Point to consider. Suppose a health spa charges customers an annual membership fee of $1,200. Should the spa use a monthly billing cycle and charge customers $100 every month, or should it charge them a lump-sum fee of $1,200? (To focus on essentials, assume that the discount rate is zero and that the spa does not incur any additional costs as a result of changing the billing cycle.)

By assumption, both plans cost the same ($1,200 per year), and all parties have discount rates of zero. Hence, according to standard economic theory, both the spa and the consumer will be indifferent to the length of the billing cycle. However, according to prospect theory, the customer will prefer to pay the lump-sum fee. The reasoning is the same as that in the Verizon example above.

Fusion for Profit Maxim

Other factors being the same, the firm should choose marketing plans where consumers are required to pay less frequently.

▶ *Many firms use cash rebate plans when they sell their products. What do standard economic theory and prospect theory suggest about this practice?*

As discussed below, standard economic theory and prospect theory lead to different predictions about how cash rebates affect market behavior.

Example: Suppose Ford is considering two pricing plans for the Ford Explorer. Under the first plan, Ford plans to charge a price of $40,000 for the Explorer. Under the second plan, Ford plans to charge a slightly higher price of $41,000 and give the consumer a cash rebate of $1,000 at some point after purchase. To focus on essentials, assume that the discount rates for both Ford and the consumer are zeros. In addition, assume that Ford's incremental cost of administering a rebate plan is zero.

Now, the net cost to the consumer ($40,000) is the same for both pricing plans. Similarly, Ford receives the same net revenue ($40,000) regardless of which pricing plan it chooses. Thus, conventional economic theory suggests that both Ford and the consumer will be indifferent to whether a cash rebate plan is used.

▲ What does prospect theory suggest?

Suppose the negative value to the consumer of paying $40,000 for the Ford Explorer is –30 (say), and the negative value to the consumer of paying a higher price for the Ford Explorer ($41,000) is –31. Then, the incremental loss of value to the consumer by paying $1,000 more for the Explorer is –1 (table 11.4).

Suppose the positive value to the consumer of a cash rebate of $1,000 is 3. Since prospect theory implies that consumers evaluate gains and losses separately, this implies that the value of the rebate plan to the consumer is –28 (negative value of paying $41,000 to purchase the Explorer + positive value of the cash rebate = –31 + 3).

Note that, contrary to standard economic theory, prospect theory implies that the consumer will prefer the cash rebate plan even though the net price paid is the same as the price the consumer would have paid for an outright cash purchase.

Table 11.4
Ford Example: Comparing a Rebate Policy Using Standard Economic Theory and Prospect Theory

Pricing plan	Dollar amounts (standard theory)	Value (prospect theory)
Cash sale	–$40,000	–30
Rebate plan		
Cash paid	–$41,000	–31
Cash rebate	$1,000	3
Total	–$40,000	–28

Fusion for Profit Maxim

Consumers may prefer a pricing plan that provides them with a cash rebate, even though the net price they pay is the same as the price under an outright cash purchase plan.

Point to consider.   Suppose consumers behave according to prospect theory. Is it possible that the firm's profits will fall if the firm uses a cash rebate plan?

The critical issue is how large the cash rebate is with respect to the purchase price. In the Ford Explorer example, the cash rebate ($1,000) was small compared with the purchase price ($40,000). What is likely to happen if the cash rebate is large compared with the purchase price of the product?

Example: Suppose Duracell sells a battery for $2 and offers consumers a mail-in cash rebate of $1. The alternative strategy is to charge a price of $1 per battery. As in the Ford Explorer example, assume that the discount rates for both Duracell and the consumer are zeros. Suppose Duracell and the consumer behave according to standard economic theory. Since both pricing plans lead to the same net prices, Duracell and the consumer will be indifferent to whichever pricing policy Duracell chooses. However, suppose the consumer behaves according to prospect theory and values gains and losses as shown in table 11.5.

Note that, consistent with prospect theory, a small monetary gain ($1) has a larger effect on value to the consumer than an equivalent monetary loss (–$1). Furthermore, the negative effect of paying a price of $2 is less than double the negative effect on value of paying a price of $1.

Table 11.5
Duracell Example: Comparing a Rebate Policy Using Standard Economic Theory and Prospect Theory

	$ Value (standard theory)	Value (prospect theory)
Duracell rebate plan		
Cost to consumer	–$2	–23
Cash rebate	$1	10
Net value	–$1	–13
Duracell direct purchase		
Cost to consumer	–$1	–12
Net value	–$1	–12

If Duracell charges a cash price of $1, the consumer's value is −12. If Duracell charges a price of $2 and offers the consumer a cash rebate of $1, the consumer will value the loss of $2 and the gain of $1 separately. Hence, the net value of the rebate plan to the consumer will be −13 (−23 + 10).

Note that the consumer will prefer to pay a price of $1 instead of paying $2 and obtaining a cash rebate of $1. Consequently, Duracell should not use the cash rebate plan.

Fusion for Profit Maxim

According to prospect theory, the effectiveness of a cash rebate plan depends on how large the rebate is with respect to the purchase price of the product.

▶ 11.5 Multiperiod Applications of Prospect Theory

So far, we have focused on the case where the firm has a short-run horizon; alternatively, there are no cost or demand dynamics. We now contrast the policy implications of standard economic theory and prospect theory when the firm's marketing policies have long-run effects. Specifically, we present examples involving new-product pricing, customer relationship management, and the use of *coupons*.

Example 1: Consider the following new-product pricing problem. Suppose Procter & Gamble (P&G) has developed a new brand of toothpaste. Assume that P&G has a two-period planning horizon and plans to use a *strategic pricing* approach. That is, it will charge a low introductory price to increase the trial rate for the product and then raise prices in the second period once consumers have had the opportunity to try the new toothpaste.

Suppose P&G uses standard economic theory and chooses the following strategic pricing policy to maximize long-run profits: charge an introductory price of $2.00 per tube of toothpaste in the first period, then increase the price in the second period to $2.50.

▶ Will this strategic pricing policy lead to the anticipated gains in long-run profits for P&G?

According to prospect theory, consumers in the second period will use the first-period price of $2.00 per tube as a *reference point*. Consequently, when P&G increases the price per tube of the new toothpaste from $2.00 in the first period to $2.50 in the second, consumers in the second period will experience a negative transaction utility of −$0.50 (reference price − price charged in the second period). As discussed, prospect theory implies that a consumer's willingness to pay is the sum of acquisition utility and transaction utility (which is negative in the second period). *Hence prospect theory implies that the second-period demand for the new toothpaste will be less than the demand predicted by standard economic theory.* Consequently, P&G will obtain lower profits than it expects in the second period.

▶ How can P&G address this problem?

Suppose P&G sets a "regular" price of $2.50 for the new toothpaste and offers a temporary $.50 discount per tube in the first period. Since consumers know that the $.50 discount in the first period is a one-shot deal, their reference price in the second period will be the regular price of $2.50. Hence, when P&G charges a price of $2.50 in the second period, the transaction utility will be zero (i.e., for each consumer the willingness to pay will equal the acquisition utility from using the product). Consequently, the results from the standard economic model will hold.

Fusion for Profit Maxim

Firms should recognize the impact of consumers' price expectations on consumers' willingness to pay, especially when pricing new products. One approach is to use a "list" or "regular" price and to encourage consumers to use this price as a reference point.

Example 2: Consider the following marketing decision involving customer relationship management. A critical strategic decision in CRM is what level of product or service performance the firm should promise to consumers.

Suppose an airline (e.g., Continental Airlines) is planning to choose one of the following strategies:

1. Promise a very high level of product performance ("overpromise"), or
2. Promise a moderate level of product performance ("underpromise").

For simplicity, consider a two-period model.[7] In addition, assume that the unit profit margins are fixed.

Overpromising Strategy

Because the overpromising strategy claims a high level of product performance, it will lead to high sales and profits for Continental in the first period.

▶ But what will happen in the second period?

Since Continental has promised a very high level of product performance, it is possible that some first-period consumers will conclude that Continental's performance is below the level that was promised (the reference point). Since, according to these consumers, Continental has "underperformed," the transaction utilities to these first-period consumers from purchase in the second period will be negative. This will reduce these customers' willingness to pay in the second period and hence reduce the *repeat purchase rate* for Continental. Thus, the increase in first-period sales will "borrow" sales from the second period, hence reducing Continental's second-period profits.

Underpromising Strategy

If Continental underpromises in the first period, its first-period sales and profits will be lower than they would have been if Continental had promised a higher level of performance. Hence, it is likely that some first-period buyers will conclude that Continental's performance is above the level that was promised (the reference point). This implies that the repeat purchase rate in the second period (and hence the associated profits to Continental) will be higher, since the product has exceeded expectations for these consumers.

◤ Is it better to overpromise or to underpromise?

According to prospect theory, the effects of overpromising and underpromising performance will be asymmetric. In particular, the incremental positive effect of overperformance on the repeat purchase rate will be less than the corresponding incremental negative effect of underperforming by the same amount. Consequently, from a long-run perspective, it may be more prudent for Continental to underpromise product performance, even though this strategy delivers lower first-period profits than the strategy of overpromising.

Fusion for Profit Maxim

From a long-run perspective, it may be better for the firm to underpromise performance and exceed consumers' expectations.

Point to consider.   How will the firm's discount rate affect its customer relationship management policy?

The firm's discount rate is critical because overpromising performance produces higher profits in the first period, but underpromising generates higher profits in the second period.

In the Continental example, if the discount rate is sufficiently high, the optimal policy for Continental may be to focus on first-period profits and forgo future profits. If this is the case, the optimal CRM strategy is to overpromise product performance. An extreme example of this is a fly-by-night company (i.e., the implicit discount rate is infinitely high).

> **Fusion for Profit Maxim**
>
> The firm's CRM policy can involve a trade-off between current and future profits. If the discount rate is sufficiently high, the optimal policy for the firm may be to overpromise product performance.

Example 3: According to prospect theory, one of the key factors that affects a consumer's willingness to pay is the consumer's reference point. Suppose a firm (e.g., Nestlé) plans to issue coupons in the first and second periods for a new coffee product (Alert). However, it does not plan to issue any coupons in the third period.

▶ What will happen if Nestlé issues coupons in the first two periods?

Then, consumers will expect coupons for Alert in the third period. However, since Nestlé will not issue coupons in the third period, consumers will experience negative transaction utilities in that period. Hence, other factors being held constant, consumers' willingness to pay (acquisition utility + transaction utility) for Alert in the third period will be reduced. Consequently, by using coupons in the first and second periods, Nestlé will reduce the demand for Alert in the third period.

▶ How can Nestlé address this problem?

Nestlé can issue coupons for Alert in the first and second periods, making it clear that the coupons are strictly "limited-time" offers. Then, by not issuing coupons in the third period, Nestlé will avoid a negative reference point effect on the demand for Alert in the third period.

Point to consider.   What coupon policy should Nestlé use for its products over time?

Suppose Nestlé plans to use coupons as a marketing tactic for its products (new or established). Then, the key issue for Nestlé is to make sure that consumers do not come to expect coupons to be a routine event for any given product. If this happens, consumers will experience a negative transaction utility in any period in which Nestlé does not offer a coupon for the product in question.

To address this potential reference point problem, Nestlé should randomize its use of coupons over time for any given product. Given this randomization strategy, consumers will not know when to expect a coupon. Hence their reference points for the product will not change over time. The result is that, other factors being held constant, Nestlé's coupon policy in any given period will not have a negative effect on consumers' willingness to pay for the product in question in the future.

> **Fusion for Profit Maxim**
>
> According to prospect theory, a firm's coupon policy can have an effect on consumers' willingness to pay in the future. To minimize this dynamic effect, the firm should randomize its use of coupons over time.

▲ 11.6 How Should the Firm Change Its Prices over the Business Cycle?

Many firms reduce the prices of their products during an economic downturn.[8] However, is this strategy optimal?

To focus on essentials, assume that there are no *demand* or *cost dynamics*. As discussed previously, according to prospect theory, a consumer's reservation price is the sum of two quantities: acquisition utility and transaction utility, where the former quantity measures the benefit from using the product, and the latter quantity can be negative or positive depending on whether the price paid is higher or lower than the consumer's reference price.

▲ Suppose the firm reduces the price of its product during an economic downturn. What will happen to consumers' willingness to pay after the downturn is over and the firm increases prices?

When the firm increases the price of its product after the downturn is over, the transaction utilities for consumers will become negative. Hence by charging a low price during the economic downturn, the firm will reduce consumers' willingness to pay for its product in the future.[9] Consequently, other factors being the same, future demand and future profits will decrease. In other words, to some degree, a price decrease in the economic downturn will "borrow" sales from the future.

> **Fusion for Profit Maxim**
>
> Prospect theory implies that the price decrease in an economic downturn should be less than that implied by conventional economic theory.

Point to consider. What does prospect theory imply about price increases when the economy is in an upswing?

Suppose the firm increases the price of its product when the economy is in an upswing and subsequently reduces the price when the economy is back to "normal." Then, when prices are reduced after the upswing is over, consumers will obtain a positive transaction utility.

Hence, other factors being the same, prospect theory implies that consumers' willingness to pay for the product (acquisition utility + transaction utility) will increase in the normal period. That is, for any price charged in the normal period, prospect theory implies that the demand will be higher than that implied by conventional economic theory.[10] Hence prospect theory implies that the firm should increase price more sharply during an economic upswing than conventional economic theory does.

Fusion for Profit Maxim

Prospect theory implies that the price increase in an economic upswing should be higher than that implied by conventional economic theory.

Point to consider.   Will prices fluctuate more over the business cycle if consumers behave according to prospect theory?

As discussed earlier, when the economy is in an upswing, prospect theory implies that firms should charge higher prices than standard economic theory suggests. Furthermore, prospect theory implies that, when the economy is in a downturn, firms should reduce prices by less than standard economic theory predicts. Hence, one cannot conclude on a priori grounds whether prospect theory implies that price fluctuations over the business cycle will be greater or less than standard economic theory implies.

▶ 11.7 Implications of Prospect Theory for the Human Resources Manager

Prospect theory has important implications for human resource management. We consider two examples: bonus plans and sales force compensation plans.

Bonus Plans

One important issue for the human resources manager is what type of bonus plan to use for employees. For example, should the firm give its employees bonuses in one lump sum, or should it stagger bonus payouts?

Example: Suppose IBM plans to give the manager (Joe) of its new fourth-generation computer chip an annual bonus of $120,000 in addition to his salary. Should IBM pay Joe a lump-sum bonus of $120,000 at the end of the year, or should it pay him two smaller bonuses of $60,000 each every six months? Assume that the discount rates for the firm (IBM) and its employees (e.g., Joe) are zeros.

According to standard economic theory, both IBM and Joe will be indifferent between the two bonus plans, since the total amounts ($120,000) for both bonus plans are equal and the discount rates are zeros (i.e., a dollar today is worth the same as a dollar tomorrow for both IBM and Joe). However,

Table 11.6
IBM Example: Comparing Bonus Plans Using Standard Economic Theory and Prospect Theory

Type of Bonus Plan	$ Value (standard theory)	Value (prospect theory)
Payment made once every 6 months		
Payment after 6 months	$60,000	10
Payment at end of 12 months	$60,000	10
Total	$120,000	20
Payment made at the end of 12 months		
Bonus amount for months 1–6	$60,000	10
Bonus amount for months 7–12	$60,000	< 10
Total	$120,000	< 20

according to prospect theory, Joe will prefer to be paid according to the six-monthly bonus plan.[11] The reasoning is as follows.

Prospect theory implies that individuals evaluate each gain separately (table 11.6). Thus, suppose Joe attaches a value of 10 (say) to a monetary gain of $60,000. Then, if IBM pays Joe two bonuses of $60,000 each, the total value to Joe is 20 (value of first bonus of $60,000 + value of second bonus of $60,000).

▶ *What is the value of Joe obtaining one lump-sum bonus of $120,000?*

As discussed above, Joe attaches a value of 10 to a monetary gain of $60,000. However, prospect theory implies that each successive dollar adds less and less value to Joe. Hence the value to Joe of a lump-sum payment of $120,000 ($2 \times \$60,000$) will be less than 20 ($2 \times 10$).

Fusion for Profit Maxim

Other factors being the same, the firm should reward managers (consumers) using a staggered reward plan instead of paying them one lump sum.

Sales Force Compensation Plans

Suppose General Foods has hired a salesperson (Bill). Let's say that General Foods allows Bill to choose his sales call policy (i.e., Bill decides how to allocate his time across clients and product lines); furthermore, Bill has a target income (say $150,000 per year). Suppose Bill can sell to two segments: one is mature, and the other is growing.

▶ *What compensation plan should General Foods use?*

Growth markets provide more potential for long-run profits than mature markets; however, they are typically more uncertain. According to prospect theory, Bill will value a *windfall gain* (i.e., income in excess of Bill's target income of $150,000 per year) less highly than an *income shortfall* of the same magnitude (i.e., income that is below Bill's target income). Consequently, other factors remaining the same, Bill will choose an overly conservative *sales call policy* from General Foods' viewpoint. Specifically, Bill will spend too little time on selling to the growth segment where the uncertainty in demand is higher than in the mature segment.

▶ *How can General Foods address this incentive problem when it has delegated the sales call policy to Bill?*

One method is for General Foods to use a *quota system*. Specifically, to induce Bill to allocate enough effort to the growth segment, General Foods should set the sales quota for the growth segment at a high level. In addition, General Foods should choose a compensation plan for Bill where he is given asymmetric rewards (penalties) for exceeding (falling short of) the quotas for the mature and growth segments.[12] For a detailed discussion of compensation plans, see chapters 15 through 17.

Fusion for Profit Maxim

Prospect theory has significant implications for human resources management, including the choice of bonus and compensation plans.

▶ *11.8 Implications of Prospect Theory for Financial Markets*

Prospect theory has significant implications for how investors are likely to react to gains and losses in the financial market. In addition, the theory has major implications for how the firm should set profit expectations for Wall Street and for how the firm should determine its dividend policies.

Effects of Gains and Losses in the Stock Market

Suppose an individual (Laura) has a current wealth level of $100,000 that she has invested in the stock market. Let's say that the following events occur. On the first day after Laura invests in the stock market, her investment appreciates by $5,000. On the second day, this gain is wiped out. Thus, at the end of the second day, Laura's net wealth is unchanged.

Conventional economic theory argues that, since Laura's wealth is unchanged at the end of the second day, Laura's well-being at the end of the second day is the same as it was before she invested in the stock market. Prospect theory, in contrast, implies that Laura is worse off. Specifically, Laura values gains and losses separately; furthermore, the positive value to Laura from a gain of $5,000 (say 12) is smaller than the negative value to Laura from a loss of the same amount of $5,000 (say –15). Since the net change in value is negative (–3), Laura will be worse off at the end of the second day.[13] Note that, in contrast to standard economic theory, prospect theory suggests that it is very likely that Laura will readjust her investment decisions at the end of the second day.

Fusion for Profit Maxim

Standard economic theory and prospect theory lead to different predictions of investor behavior in financial markets.

Dividend Policy

According to prospect theory, individuals value gains and losses with respect to a reference point. Furthermore, a gain of $100 (say) is valued less than a loss of $100. Hence the prudent strategy for the firm may be to set a low reference point for future *dividends* by underpromising future dividends. Since the actual dividend paid out by the firm in the future will exceed the anticipated dividend, investors will experience a positive transaction utility at that time. Consequently, the firm's stock price should increase after the firm pays the dividend in the future.

Point to consider. Suppose the CEO of a firm has the opportunity to exercise stock options in the near future. What dividend policy is the CEO likely to use?

Let's suppose that the stock market is likely to react positively to current news about the firm's anticipated future dividends. This implies that, since the CEO has the opportunity to exercise his or her stock options in the near future, the CEO will have an incentive to overpromise dividends.

Profit Targets

Consider a publicly held firm that sets a profit target of $0.50 per share for the next quarter. Suppose the actual profit generated exceeds this target by $0.02 per share (say). Given this scenario, suppose the firm's share price will appreciate by 5%.

▶ *What will happen if there is a profit shortfall of an equivalent amount ($0.02 per share)?*

According to prospect theory, the negative impact on investors of a loss ($0.02 per share, say) will be stronger than the positive impact of a gain of the same magnitude ($0.02 per share). Hence, if there is a shortfall of profits, the firm's stock price will fall by more than 5%. Thus, it may be better for the firm to "understate" profit targets rather than to overstate them.

Fusion for Profit Maxim

According to prospect theory, other factors being held constant, firms should understate profit targets and likely future dividend payouts.

▶ *11.9 What Metrics Should the Firm Use to Evaluate Consumer Behavior?*

Depending on which theory of consumer behavior the manager uses, the manager may need to measure one or more of the following quantities:

- Acquisition utility,
- Transaction utility, and
- Reference points.

This task is complicated by the following factors:

- All three quantities (acquisition utility, transaction utility, and reference points) are unobservable. Hence it is necessary to use proxies that are reliable and valid.
- All three quantities can vary across consumers at any point in time.
- Because of a consumer's experience, the arrival of new information, and the firm's marketing policies, each of these quantities for any given consumer can change over time.

Measuring Acquisition Utility

Regardless of whether the manager uses standard economic theory or a behavioral extension of this theory (e.g., prospect theory), it is necessary to obtain accurate estimates of acquisition utility. A variety of methods can be used, ranging from asking consumers to self-state their reservation prices (a process that is prone to considerable measurement error) to conjoint analysis to choice-based methods to auctions. For a detailed discussion, see chapter 8.[14]

Measuring Transaction Utility

Despite the simplicity of the concept of transaction utility (= reference price – actual price), this construct is not easy to measure. The key issue is how to measure the reference price. We address this issue below.

Measuring the Reference Point

Consider the simplest case where the reference point is based on only one criterion or dimension. Which metric should the firm use to measure the reference point for any given consumer: the expected price of the product, the last price paid, a "fair" price, an *external reference price* (e.g., the published price or the list price of the product), an *internal reference price*, or some combination of these metrics?

In general, it is likely that reference points are based on multiple criteria or dimensions. For example, consider an industrial buyer who has purchased a new tractor. Then, the buyer will have different expectations for each of the following dimensions: the performance of the tractor, the quality of after-sales service, and the reliability of the tractor. Hence the buyer's willingness to pay for the tractor will depend on reference values for *each* of the three criteria.[15]

In addition, the firm needs to know how its policies and those of its competitors affect acquisition utility, transaction utility, and reference points. Consider the following examples:

- The sales force of an industrial firm informs buyers of the cost savings that they can achieve by purchasing the firm's product.
- A cell phone manufacturer uses an advertising message in which it informs consumers how they can use its cell phone to download data rapidly from the Internet.
- A perfume company charges a high price to convince consumers that its product is of high quality.

These questions can be answered only if the firm has accurate measures of acquisition utility, transaction utility, and reference price or the appropriate dimensions of reference prices.[16]

Fusion for Profit Maxim

The key factors that determine a consumer's willingness to pay are acquisition utility, transaction utility, and reference points. Sophisticated methods are necessary to measure willingness to pay and to determine how the marketing policies of the firm and its competitors affect the willingness to pay for different brands in the market.

Chapter 11 Key Points

- The consumer's reservation prices are alternative-specific and not product-specific. Thus, the reservation price for a given purchase alternative (or brand) depends on the attributes provided by that alternative (or brand).
- In order to estimate the demand for its product, the firm needs to estimate reservation prices for its own product *and* competing products.
- According to conventional economic theory, consumers' willingness to pay is equivalent to acquisition utility. However, according to prospect theory, willingness to pay depends on acquisition utility *and* on transaction utility.
- Prospect theory implies that, in order to measure a customer's willingness to pay, the manager needs to estimate acquisition utilities, transaction utilities, and reference points.
- If consumers' price expectations affect their willingness to pay, standard economic theory can lead to incorrect demand estimates for a product, even if consumers' price expectations are correct, on average. Hence the firm is likely to make incorrect pricing decisions.
- If the firm unexpectedly reduces the price of its product, prospect theory implies that standard economic theory will understate the quantity of the product that the firm can sell at this lower price. On the other hand, if the firm unexpectedly increases the price of its product, prospect theory implies that standard economic theory will overstate the quantity of the product that the firm can sell at this higher price.
- Prospect theory implies that a firm's coupon policy can have an effect on consumers' willingness to pay for the firm's product in the future. To minimize this dynamic effect, the firm should randomize its use of coupons over time.
- Prospect theory implies that the price decrease in an economic downturn should be less than implied by conventional economic theory. However, the price increase in an economic upswing should be higher.
- Prospect theory implies that, other factors being the same, the firm should charge consumers a lump-sum fee for a product or service instead of requiring them to make multiple payments of smaller amounts. In addition, the firm should use a cash rebate plan when the rebate is small compared with the purchase price of the product.
- Prospect theory has important implications for human resource management (e.g., bonus plans) and customer relationship management. For example, the firm's customer relationship management policy often involves a trade-off between current and future profits. If the firm's discount rate is sufficiently high, the optimal policy for the firm may be to overpromise performance.

- Prospect theory has different implications from standard economic theory for investor behavior, setting profit targets for Wall Street, and dividend policy. For example, prospect theory implies that, other factors being held constant, firms should understate profit targets and likely future dividend payouts.

Part VII

How to Choose Advertising and Promotion Strategies

12

Coordinating Advertising Strategy, Branding, and Positioning

This part focuses on advertising and promotion. In this chapter, we discuss how the firm should coordinate its advertising message, *branding*, and *product positioning* strategies. In our discussion we will distinguish between the short and long run, single-product and multiproduct firms, and established and new products. We will also examine which strategies are appropriate for market leaders and for brands with low market shares. Finally, the concepts in this chapter provide the background that is necessary to understand how the marketing-finance interface can be used to measure the value of the firm's *brand equity* (chapter 19).

In the next chapter (chapter 13) we will focus on how the firm should determine its advertising budget. In chapter 14 we will examine how the firm should choose a media plan and how it should measure advertising productivity.

The information covered in this chapter will be useful when you are faced with the following types of decisions:

- What is product positioning?
- Should my firm's advertising message focus on product features or on product benefits?
- Should my firm use different message strategies across different media?
- What message strategy should my firm use if it is a market leader or a small player in the market?

- How should my firm measure the effectiveness of its advertising message?
- What message strategies should my firm use for its existing products? And how can my firm coordinate the advertising message and product positioning strategies for its existing products?
- What advertising message policy should my firm use if it introduces a rebranding strategy?
- What advertising message strategy should my firm use if it introduces new products?
- What message strategy should my firm use if it sells multiple products?
- How can my firm determine how the message and product positioning strategies for a new product cannibalize its existing products and affect the sales of competing brands?
- How should my firm coordinate its product positioning and message strategies for new products in the short and long runs?
- How should my firm coordinate its advertising message strategy with other marketing decision variables?

The following terms will be introduced in this chapter (see glossary for definitions):

aided recall	customized segment-	matched samples
asymmetric	specific message	"me-too" product
information	strategies	peripheral information-
audience duplication	demographic	processing
benefit-based message	segmentation	planning horizon
brand equity	discount rate	product positioning
branding	dual advertising	psychographic
cannibalization	message strategy	segmentation
central information-	halo effect	sequential message
processing	latent class	strategy
choice criteria	methodology	target segment
commoditization	law of one price	unaided recall
commodity market	lexicographic choice	value proposition
consideration set	model	word of mouth

▶ 12.1 What Is Product Positioning?

Before choosing an advertising message strategy, the firm needs to determine how to position its product. Although product positioning is defined in a number of ways, we will use the following definition: product positioning is the space occupied by a specific brand in the consumer's mind. This "space" is defined by the benefits provided by the brand in question.

◣ 12.2 Choosing Advertising Message Strategy

In this section, we discuss broad principles the firm should consider in choosing its advertising message strategy. In particular, we emphasize the linkages among branding, product positioning, and advertising message strategy.

◣ How should the firm choose its advertising message strategy?

The firm's advertising message strategy should be based on the following:

- The *target segment* (market),
- The product positioning,
- Selling messages that support the chosen positioning,
- An appropriate matching of specific selling messages to the selected media vehicles chosen (e.g., television, newspapers, or the Internet), and
- A comparison of different message strategies and execution formats using a controlled experiment.

◣ What criteria should the firm use in defining its target segment?

Defining the target segment is critical. The target segment is defined as the specific group of customers that will purchase the firm's product. One approach for firms that make consumer products is to define the target segment in terms of its demographic characteristics (e.g., income, age, ethnic group, and gender).[1] However, this approach is not always feasible.

Example: Consider the target segment for Harley Davidson motorcycles. Since the product is likely to appeal to consumers with different demographic profiles, it may be difficult to define the target segment using only demographic data. In such cases, a better approach may be to define the target segment in terms of its psychographic profile (e.g., consumers who are fun-loving and enjoy being unconventional). Note that these psychographic characteristics do not translate to any specific demographic profile. For example, men and women alike can be unconventional.

Fusion for Profit Maxim

The firm should integrate its advertising message and market segmentation strategies. Wherever possible, the firm should use *demographic segmentation*. However, in some cases, *psychographic segmentation* may be necessary.

◣ Should the firm's advertising message strategy focus on product features or on product benefits?

Both methods can be useful.

Example 1: Suppose Honda is planning to launch a new hydrogen-powered car in the market and is targeting a technically sophisticated market segment. Then, Honda's advertising message strategy should focus on product features and provide technical details. In contrast, suppose Honda plans to target a broad segment of the market, including nontechnical buyers. Then, the optimal message strategy may be to focus on the product benefits of the new hydrogen-powered car rather than on its product features or technical specifications.

Example 2: Suppose Merck is planning to launch a new headache remedy. In general, consumers are not interested in technical details or information about the chemical composition of the new drug. However, they are interested in the benefits of the new drug (e.g., how effective the new drug is vis-à-vis existing products in the headache remedy market). Consequently, Merck's advertising message should focus on product benefits.

Example 3: Suppose Chanel is planning to launch a new perfume in the market. As in the Merck example, suppose that consumers are interested in the product benefits of the new perfume and not in its product attributes per se. Hence Chanel's advertising should focus on the benefits provided by its new product.

Note that message strategies based on product attributes or on product benefits can be used in a complementary manner. Thus, in the Honda example, it may be optimal for Honda to target the broad market using a dual message strategy in which it provides information about product features *and* product benefits. For example, the message can provide both attribute-based information (e.g., details about horsepower and acceleration) and benefit-based information (e.g., details about how the hydrogen-powered car will reduce environmental pollution vis-à-vis conventional cars).

Fusion for Profit Maxim

The firm's advertising message strategy should be chosen based on how consumers in the target segment process information. In some cases, it may be optimal for the firm to use a dual message strategy that provides information about both product features and product benefits.

Point to consider.   Suppose a luxury car manufacturer such as BMW plans to launch an expensive new model. Should BMW choose an advertising message that focuses on secondary product features (e.g., the fact that the new model includes a retractable coffee cup holder for the driver as a standard feature)? Assume that BMW is the only luxury car manufacturer that offers this feature.

On the surface, the strategy of focusing on secondary product features appears to be suboptimal. However, consider the following scenario. Suppose consumers in the target segment already believe that all competing luxury cars such as the new BMW model provide high performance (e.g., quick acceleration and short stopping distances when brakes are applied). Now, since consumers believe that these performance characteristics are similar across competing models, and BMW is the only manufacturer that offers a retractable coffee cup holder (a luxury feature), consumers will be more likely to buy the new BMW model instead of a competing brand. (This assumes that consumers who purchase luxury cars follow a *lexicographic choice model*.)[2]

Note that BMW will gain even more if there is a *halo effect*. This will happen if consumers conclude that, since the new BMW model offers more luxury in one dimension (the first retractable coffee cup holder), it also offers more luxury in other dimensions. If this is the case, consumers will be even more likely to buy the new BMW model.

Fusion for Profit Maxim

If competing products have similar attributes, it may be optimal for the firm to choose an advertising message strategy that focuses on secondary attributes or features. If there is a halo effect, the gain to the firm from using this strategy will increase.

▶ *Should the firm vary its advertising message strategies across different media such as television, newspapers, and the Internet?*

Television ads tend to be short, typically 15 or 30 seconds. Hence TV advertising messages can provide only limited information to the consumer. Consequently, TV advertising is most useful when the firm's goal is limited (e.g., to create awareness for the firm's product). Newspaper advertisements, in contrast, allow the firm to provide much more detailed information. Hence newspaper advertising is likely to be more effective for selling products where the consumer is highly involved with the purchase task.

Internet advertising, on the other hand, is fundamentally different from television, newspapers, and other conventional media. Specifically, Internet advertising allows the firm to vary the order in which information is presented and to customize the advertising message to the consumer. Consequently, Internet advertising allows the firm to use a more focused advertising message strategy.[3] For a detailed discussion of Internet marketing, see chapter 21.

Note that, if the firm uses multiple media, it is necessary to coordinate message strategies across media. For example, many firms (e.g., Dell) use conventional media such as TV and newspapers to provide information about how consumers can access their Web sites to obtain more detailed product-related information. In such cases, each medium will provide different types of information and levels of detail.

Fusion for Profit Maxim

The firm should coordinate its media message and media planning decisions. These decisions are likely to vary depending on the product and the firm's segmentation strategy.

▶ Should the firm's advertising message include price information?

Suppose the firm is selling a highly differentiated product or seeks to position its product as exclusive. Then, the firm's goal is to reduce price sensitivity for its product. Consequently, the firm's advertising message should exclude price information. In contrast, suppose the firm is selling a *"me-too" product* or a generic version of a branded product. Now, the firm's goal is to increase the price sensitivity of demand in the market by convincing consumers that the available products in the marketplace are very similar to each other. One way to accomplish this is to choose an advertising message strategy that focuses heavily on price.

Fusion for Profit Maxim

The firm's decision on whether to include price information in its advertising message depends on the firm's product positioning strategy.

Point to consider.   How important is the firm's advertising message strategy in a world that is becoming increasingly commoditized?
Strictly speaking, a *commodity market* implies that the *law of one price* holds in the marketplace. That is, there is only one market price for products with a given configuration of product attributes (see chapter 7).

Given this scenario, one might be tempted to conclude that the firm's advertising message strategy will be irrelevant. However, this conclusion is too hasty: we need to distinguish *commoditization* from a "commodity." Specifically, by commoditization in an industry we mean that many firms offer products with *similar* configurations of attributes. Given this distinction, one might conclude that, as commoditization increases, the firm's advertising message strategy will become less and less relevant. However, this conclusion is not necessarily correct.

Even in a market that is becoming increasingly commoditized, the firm may be able to develop a unique product positioning for its product in terms of consumer benefits—*not in terms of the physical attributes of the brand*. For instance, Johnson & Johnson has, over the years, developed a corporate image for itself as a "caring" company. Thus, although competitors may be able to clone Johnson & Johnson's products, a significant segment of consumers is still willing to pay a premium price for products made by Johnson & Johnson.

In general, *benefit-based message* strategies will be more successful in industries where consumers process information in terms of product benefits rather than in terms of product attributes/features. Furthermore, these benefit-based message strategies are likely to be more successful in perception-driven industries such as the cold medication market. An additional factor is that, even within an industry that is becoming more commoditized, some consumers may process information by product attributes whereas other consumers process information by product benefits.

Example: Consider the HDTV industry, which is becoming increasingly commoditized. For simplicity, assume that some consumers are "experts" and others are "novices." Suppose each segment uses a different information-processing strategy. Specifically, suppose experts tend to process information by product attributes (e.g., the technical specifications of an HDTV) whereas novices tend to process information by product benefits (e.g., the prestige of owning the HDTV brand in question). In this case, the HDTV manufacturer should use a *dual advertising message strategy*. The experts should be given attribute-based information, and the novices should be given a message that focuses on the HDTV's benefits.

Note that, in general, it is more difficult for a competitor to clone the firm's product positioning strategy (which is based on product benefits that are subjective) than it is to clone the firm's product design, features, and attributes (which can be objectively measured). For example, a Sony HDTV may connote a greater status than an HDTV made by Acme, regardless of each HDTV's product specifications. Hence, even in an increasingly commoditized world, the firm's message strategy can have a significant effect on the firm's long-run performance.

Fusion for Profit Maxim

The firm's product positioning and advertising message strategies can have a significant effect on the firm's performance even if industries become increasingly commoditized.

▶ How relevant is the name or logo of the company or its products?

Consumers often associate names with product categories. Hence the name of a product or company can have a major influence on how effective the firm's advertising message is.

Example 1: Apple Computers, Inc., recently expanded its product portfolio significantly. On the day that the company introduced its new products, the iPhone and Apple TV, the company renamed itself Apple Inc. The new name is meant to signal to consumers that Apple has expanded its product portfolio well beyond its existing product line. Consequently, Apple's new products such as the iPhone should have a better chance of entering consumers' *consideration sets* than they would have had if the company had continued with the old name, Apple Computers, Inc.

Example 2: Several years ago Citigroup purchased the Travelers Insurance Company. Following this purchase, Citigroup changed its logo to incorporate the red umbrella that had been the hallmark of Travelers' logo prior to the acquisition. Recently, based on market research, Citigroup concluded that the red umbrella logo was restrictive because consumers associated it with the insurance business only; however, Citigroup has a vast, diversified product portfolio that goes well beyond the insurance industry. Consequently, Citigroup decided to sell the red umbrella logo. This decision is based on the assumption that, once the red umbrella is removed from the Citigroup logo, Citibank's noninsurance products will have a better chance of entering consumers' consideration sets for the corresponding categories.

Fusion for Profit Maxim

Company and product logos are likely to influence consumers' consideration sets and hence the effectiveness of the company's advertising message strategy, especially in the multiproduct firm.

◆ *Should the firm's advertising message focus on the brand name or on the corporate name?*

The brand name–based or corporate name–based message strategy can be useful, especially for firms that sell differentiated products or products where consumers face considerable uncertainty in evaluating product quality.

Example: Over the years, Volvo has established a strong reputation for safety in the automobile market. Similarly, Johnson & Johnson has established a strong reputation among consumers for the purity of the ingredients that it uses in its toiletry products. We say that the names Volvo and Johnson & Johnson have brand equity.[4] For a detailed discussion of brand equity, see chapter 19.

We return to the HDTV example. In this example, consumers associate Sony with high quality and trust the brand. Hence, by focusing on the brand name, Sony can increase its likelihood that its brand will enter the consumer's consideration set. Consequently, this message strategy should increase the likelihood that the consumer will purchase the Sony brand.

Fusion for Profit Maxim

Firms can gain by using advertising message strategies that focus on brand or corporate name, especially when they sell differentiated products or products that consumers have difficulty in evaluating.

In general, multiproduct firms have the potential to gain more than firms with narrow product lines if they choose advertising message strategies that focus on brand name. However, as we discuss below, they also face a higher potential downside risk.

▶ Are large or small firms more likely to use advertising message strategies that focus on brand or corporate name?

Example 1: Suppose Nestlé introduces a new coffee flavor in the marketplace and uses an advertising message that prominently features the name Nestlé. For example, Nestlé runs a TV commercial for the new coffee flavor and prominently shows the name Nestlé several times in a 30-second spot. If the new coffee flavor succeeds, the sales of other Nestlé products are likely to increase because of a halo effect. However, if the new product fails in the marketplace, this could have a negative impact on the sales of Nestlé's other product lines.

Example 2: Consider two risk-averse firms that make toothpaste, Colgate-Palmolive and a small, privately owned firm, Smiley. Let's say that Colgate-Palmolive presently sells ten different flavors of toothpaste whereas Smiley sells only one. Suppose each firm plans to add a new flavor of toothpaste to its product line. Furthermore, each firm is considering using its corporate name to advertise the new product. Then, the downside risk to Smiley from using this advertising message strategy is likely to be higher than it is to Colgate-Palmolive because Smiley is a small firm and sells only one product whereas Colgate-Palmolive sells ten. Consequently, other factors being the same, Colgate-Palmolive is more likely than Smiley to advertise using its corporate name.

> **Fusion for Profit Maxim**
>
> In general, other factors being the same, large multiproduct firms will gain more from using advertising message strategies that focus on brand or corporate name than will small firms with specialized product lines.

Point to consider.   Suppose a firm has brand equity in a particular product category. Which products will the brand equity be transferable to?

The answer depends on how consumers categorize products.

Example: Breyer's is a major player in the ice cream market. Hence Breyer's brand equity in the ice cream market is likely to be readily transferable to other dairy products. Suppose two firms, Breyer's and KingMilk (an unknown company) introduce identical yogurt drinks in the marketplace. Let's say that, prior to the new product introductions, neither Breyer's nor KingMilk sells any yogurt drinks. Then, other factors being the same, Breyer's new product is more likely to enter the consumer's consideration set than KingMilk's product because Breyer's has brand equity and KingMilk does not. Hence Breyer's new yogurt drink is more likely to succeed than KingMilk's, even though both firms are new to the yogurt drink market.

In contrast, suppose Breyer's enters the frozen vegetable market. Then, it is likely that Breyer's brand equity in the ice cream market will not help the company in the frozen vegetable market.

▶ How can the firm determine which product categories its brand equity can be transferred to?

From a practical standpoint, the firm can use two methods to determine which product categories its brand equity can be transferred to. One method is to find product categories where consumers obtain *similar* benefits to those provided by its current product line. Then, these product categories provide the potential for the firm to leverage its brand equity.[5]

Example 1: Let's say that Johnson & Johnson's current product line provides its current customers with two key benefits: personal hygiene and safety. Furthermore, Johnson & Johnson has brand equity in these markets. Suppose Johnson & Johnson adds the following hypothetical product to its existing product line: a new type of toothpaste for dogs. Since the new product provides the same benefits as Johnson & Johnson's current product line, it is very likely that Johnson & Johnson's brand equity will be transferable to the new product.

A second method for the firm is to find products that are complementary to its existing products. Note that, in contrast to the first approach, the firm's goal is to find products that provide *dissimilar* benefits to its existing products.[6]

Example 2: Nike's running shoes and Apple's iPods are independent product lines that provide different types of consumer benefits. Recently, both firms introduced the following bundle: an iPod and a new type of Nike running shoe whose sole contains a device that the consumer can use to remotely operate the iPod. This combination device substantially reduces (eliminates) the impact of vibration on the sound quality of the iPod. Since the products in the bundle are complementary, brand equity is transferable across the two product categories (running shoes and portable music devices).

Fusion for Profit Maxim

The firm's brand equity can be transferred to other product categories if those product categories provide similar benefits to its existing product line or if they are complementary. The firm can choose a multiproduct advertising message strategy to leverage these effects.

▶ 12.3 Measuring the Effectiveness of an Advertising Message

In the previous section, we discussed general principles that the firm should consider when choosing its advertising message strategy. In particular, we emphasized the linkages among branding, product positioning, and advertising message strategy. In this section, we focus on measurement issues.

▶ How should the firm determine the effectiveness of an advertising message?

There are many ways in which to measure the effectiveness of an advertising message. The simplest method is to choose the message-execution combination that leads to maximum awareness in the target segment. We will discuss additional metrics for measuring advertising effectiveness shortly.

▶ How should awareness be measured?

Awareness can be measured using *unaided* or *aided recall*. When unaided recall is used, the researcher does not give the subject any cues or prompts. When aided recall is used, the researcher gives the subject cues before measuring awareness.

Example: Let's say that Garnier is testing a new TV commercial for its Fructis brand of shampoo. Specifically, subjects are shown a series of commercials, including the commercial being tested. Suppose the researcher asks respondents the following question: "You saw a number of commercials yesterday. Which commercials do you remember seeing?" Then the researcher is measuring awareness using unaided recall.

Suppose the researcher asks the following question instead: "You saw a number of commercials yesterday about toiletry products. Which of these commercials do you remember seeing?" Alternatively, the researcher could ask a more pointed question such as, "Do you remember seeing an ad for Fructis shampoo yesterday?" In both cases, since the researcher is giving the subject cues and prompts, awareness is measured using aided recall.

▶ Should the firm use aided or unaided recall to measure awareness?

Both aided and unaided recall are proxies for whether the consumer will consider purchasing the firm's product. Unaided recall is a more stringent measure than aided recall because the consumer is not given any cues or prompts. In general, unaided recall will be more useful for firms that sell high-involvement products such as automobiles or for firms that seek to change consumers' cognitive structures. Aided recall will be more useful for firms that sell low-involvement products such as shampoo and for firms that are not attempting to change consumers' cognitive structures.

Example: Vicks introduced a new multicondition medication called Vicks Versus 3 (VV3) into a test market in 1979. One year after the test market was begun, the unaided recall for VV3 was only 2% whereas the aided recall was considerably higher (36%). The low unaided recall score suggests that Vicks's advertising had not succeeded in changing consumers' cognitive structures. That is, consumers were still categorizing medications into three groups: those that were suitable for treating colds, sinus problems, and allergies, respectively. Consequently, it became clear that Vicks's message and product positioning strategies were not working. The result was that VV3 failed to meet its sales and market share objectives.[7]

Fusion for Profit Maxim

The firm can measure awareness using either aided or unaided recall. In general, unaided recall should be used to measure advertising message effectiveness for high-involvement products and for product positioning strategies that seek to change consumers' cognitive structures. Aided recall is a less stringent criterion and may be more useful for low-involvement products.

▶ *Suppose a firm has tested two advertising messages in a consumer experiment. Is the message with the higher recall value superior?*

We return to the Garnier example. Suppose Garnier seeks to determine which of two advertising messages it should use for Fructis shampoo. Let's say that Garnier proceeds as follows. It chooses two *matched samples* from the target market segment and conducts the following experiment. One sample is shown a set of commercials that includes the first advertising message (Message 1), and the other sample is shown a set of commercials that includes the second advertising message (Message 2). For each sample, aided recall is measured one day after subjects have been exposed to the advertising messages.

Suppose the aided recall percentages are as follows: 35% (Message 1) and 42% (Message 2). Furthermore, let's say that the difference between these aided recall rates is statistically significant. These "day-after" recall results suggest that Message 2 is superior.

▶ *Is this a reasonable conclusion?*

For any group of consumers, the percentage of consumers who recall seeing any given ad will decline over time because subjects forget advertising messages over time. Suppose Message 1 is more distinctive than Message 2. Then, it is quite possible that, at a later point in time (e.g., two weeks after respondents see the ad), the aided recall percentage for Message 1 will be *higher* than the corresponding percentage for Message 2. Hence Message

1 could be superior in the long run, even though it has a lower "day-after" recall score.

One way to address this issue is to supplement the "one-day-after" recall score with other information obtained at the same time (e.g., metrics to measure product-specific information that is recalled, message credibility, and attitude change).

▶ *Many commercial firms (e.g., Burke) measure recall one day after subjects are exposed to a commercial. Is it better to measure recall after a longer period of time?*

Commercial firms typically measure recall soon after advertising exposure. This allows them to obtain "clean" recall measurements subject to tight experimental controls.

Alternatively, suppose recall is measured two weeks after a subject is exposed to an advertising message. Then, during this two-week period, the subject could have been exposed to many other factors (e.g., advertising by competitors) that cannot be controlled in the advertising experiment. Thus, the longer one waits before measuring recall, the more likely it is that the measured recall results will be biased.

Fusion for Profit Maxim

Standard commercial metrics rank advertising messages based on short-run measures of awareness. These metrics should be supplemented with additional information that is collected at a later point in time regarding the effectiveness of the advertising message.

▶ *How useful is awareness as a criterion to measure the effectiveness of an advertising message?*

The answer depends on a number of factors, including the firm's strategy and whether the firm sells one or multiple products.

Firm's Strategy

Suppose the primary goal of the advertising message is to let consumers know that the firm's brand is available for purchase. Then, it may be reasonable for the firm to choose the advertising message that maximizes awareness. In general, however, the advertising message will include additional information about the attributes and/or benefits provided by the firm's brand. In such cases, it may be incorrect to rank advertising messages by using awareness scores alone.

Example 1: Suppose that a firm has conducted an experiment and obtained the following awareness scores using matched samples: 40%

(Message 1) and 50% (Message 2). Suppose, however, that 15% of the respondents who are exposed to Message 1 experience positive attitude change toward the firm's product whereas only 10% of the respondents who are exposed to Message 2 experience positive attitude change. Then, Message 1 leads to positive attitude change for 6% of the subjects (awareness score × percentage of those who are aware and experience positive attitude change = 40% × 15%) whereas Message 2 leads to positive attitude change for only 5% of the subjects. Hence Message 1 will increase sales and profits more than Message 2 will, *even though Message 2 has a higher awareness score.*

When evaluating advertising messages, another factor to consider is *word-of-mouth* activity. As discussed below, an advertising message that generates high awareness scores may not lead to optimal long-run results.

Example 2: Let's say that the firm has conducted two experiments and obtained the following awareness scores using matched samples: 30% (Message 1) and 45% (Message 2). However, Message 1 leads to higher word-of-mouth activity than Message 2. Then, Message 1 could lead to superior long-run results than Message 2.[8]

Fusion for Profit Maxim

Awareness is a necessary but not sufficient condition for advertising effectiveness.

Multiple Products

When choosing the advertising message and positioning strategy for any given brand, the multiproduct firm should measure the net effect on product-line profits. As we discuss below, the message strategy that maximizes brand awareness for a given product may not be optimal.

We return to the Garnier example. Suppose Garnier is considering two advertising messages for Fructis shampoo. Let's say that the aided recall scores are as follows: 35% (Message 1) and 42% (Message 2).

▶ *Do these results mean that Message 2 will lead to superior financial results than Message 1?*

Consider the following scenario. Suppose Message 1 increases the net profits from Fructis shampoo by $1.5 million per month, whereas Message 2 increases the corresponding monthly net profit from Fructis shampoo by $2.0 million. However, *Message 2 leads to cannibalization of one of Garnier's other shampoo brands*; in particular, the lost profits from cannibalization are $700,000 per month. Then, the net increases in Garnier's monthly product-line profits are as follows: $1.5 million (Message 1) and $1.3 million (Message 2). Hence Message 1 is superior *even though it leads to lower awareness scores.*

▶ *What additional factors should the firm consider in measuring the effectiveness of an advertising message?*

Two conditions must be satisfied for a consumer to purchase the advertised brand:

1. The brand must be included in the set of brands from which the consumer will make a choice. We say that the brand must be included in the consumer's consideration set. If this is the case, awareness (e.g., recall) will increase the probability that the brand will be included.
2. Once the brand is included in the consideration set, it must be valued highly by the consumer.

We return to the Vicks example. Vicks conducted a product name test before introducing its multicondition VV3 product into the marketplace in 1979. In consumer tests, the name Vicks Versus 3 scored high on the "multicondition" dimension. (As previously discussed, Vicks's strategy was to change the traditional boundaries of the industry by combining the cold, sinus, and allergy markets.)

This result by itself suggests that the advertising message would have supported Vicks's product positioning strategy in the marketplace. However, Vicks Versus 3 scored poorly on a number of key product benefits, including "appropriateness," "effectiveness," and "strength." Since consumer preference for VV3 was low, consumers had low probabilities of buying VV3, *even if VV3 was included in their consideration sets.* Subsequent test market results confirmed that the name Vicks Versus 3 was not a good choice.[9]

▶ *What other criteria should the firm use to determine which advertising message to use for a particular brand?*

As discussed, awareness is a necessary but not sufficient condition for the firm's advertising message to succeed. Hence the firm should use additional criteria to evaluate its message strategy.

Since the firm's goal is to maximize its product-line profits, the firm should supplement awareness scores with measurements of attitude change and/or consumers' perceptions about different brands, including the firm's own brands and competitive brands.[10] The firm can then combine this information to determine the effect of its advertising message on consumer choice, sales of the brand that is advertised, cannibalization of the firm's own brands, and sales of competitive brands. The firm can then use these results to choose the advertising message that maximizes its product-line profits.[11]

Fusion for Profit Maxim

In general, the firm should supplement recall scores for an advertising message with measurements of attitude change and changes in perception for consumers following exposure to an advertising message. This information is necessary to determine how the advertising message for the firm's product affects competitors' sales and the cannibalization of the firm's other products.

▶ 12.4 Managerial Implications for Branding and Positioning Existing Products

We now discuss in more detail how the firm should coordinate its advertising message, branding, and product positioning strategies to maximize long-run performance. In particular, we focus on the firm's existing product line. The next section will discuss how the firm should coordinate its advertising message, branding, and positioning strategies when it introduces new products.

▶ Should the firm's advertising message attempt to change the consumer's choice criteria?

In general, this is a risky strategy. Furthermore, it is likely that multiple advertising exposures will be necessary to induce consumers to change their *choice criteria* (i.e., the importance that they place on particular product features or product benefits). Hence this advertising message strategy is likely to be expensive as well.

Point to consider.   How useful are standard metrics of advertising message effectiveness when a firm is seeking to change the choice criteria?

Example: Many medications in the cold, sinus, and allergy markets contain the same or highly similar ingredients. Suppose the firm's goal is to change the way in which consumers categorize different products. Then, unaided recall is a better measure than aided recall. Furthermore, since these medications are low-involvement products for many consumers, several advertising exposures may be necessary in order to change consumers' cognitive structures. Hence standard metrics such as "day-after" recall after one exposure may lead to suboptimal decisions.

Consequently, it may be desirable for the firm to conduct experiments in which it measures unaided recall after consumers have been exposed to the ad several times. In addition, it may be necessary for the firm to use more stringent measures of advertising message effectiveness than recall. For example, the firm can measure attitude change. Alternatively, the firm can examine how the advertising message affects consumers' consideration sets after consumers have been exposed to an ad message several times.

Note that, by using this experimental approach, the firm can determine which advertising message it should choose and how often it should run the ad. For example, if consumers are exposed to an ad too many times, there may be no gains from additional advertising. Hence the firm can use the results from the experiment to determine the optimal combination of advertising message and frequency.

Fusion for Profit Maxim

If the firm seeks to change consumers' choice criteria, it may need to use nonstandard experiments to choose the optimal advertising message.

▶ *Suppose the firm uses television commercials. Is it better to use 15-second or 30-second spots?*

The answer to this question depends on the firm's message strategy and on whether consumers' perceptions are correlated. Suppose the firm's primary goal is to create brand awareness. Alternatively, suppose the advertising message focuses on one primary benefit. For instance, an automobile manufacturer such as Volvo seeks to emphasize one product benefit only: the safety of its cars. Then, it may be optimal for the firm to use a short, 15-second TV message.

In contrast, suppose the firm seeks to emphasize more than one benefit. Now, the firm's message strategy and the optimal length of the message depend on whether the product benefits are correlated.

Example 1: Suppose consumers perceive that drugs with higher dosage strengths are more effective. That is, dosage strength and effectiveness are positively correlated. If this is the case, we say that there is a positive halo effect. Then, it may be optimal for the firm's message to focus on one benefit only (say, dosage strength). Since dosage strength and effectiveness are positively correlated, by focusing on dosage strength only, the firm will be successful in convincing consumers that its drug is also more effective.

Example 2: In contrast to Example 1, suppose an automobile manufacturer seeks to emphasize two key benefits: economy and safety. However, consumers believe that an economical car must be less safe (i.e., economy and safety are negatively correlated). Now, the firm will need to advertise *both* benefits simultaneously.

This implies that the firm may need to use a longer TV commercial. Furthermore, since the product benefits are negatively correlated in the consumer's mind, it may also be necessary for the automobile manufacturer to advertise more frequently to convince consumers that its car is more economical than those made by other manufacturers *and* is safer.

Fusion for Profit Maxim

Short TV commercials may be sufficient if there is a positive halo effect. The firm may need to use longer TV commercials and run them more frequently if the product benefits are negatively correlated in the minds of consumers.

Point to consider. Some consumers *process information centrally* whereas others *process information peripherally.* How do these information-processing strategies affect the firm's message strategy?

Suppose a consumer processes information centrally. That is, the consumer analyzes product-based information in depth. For example, the consumer uses the information to revise his or her perceptions of the benefits provided by the firm's brand. Then, it may be necessary for the firm to use a longer TV message strategy. As discussed above, the optimal message strategy will depend on the precise correlation structure of the consumer's perceptions.

In contrast, suppose a consumer processes information peripherally. That is, the consumer does not analyze the information in a commercial in depth, and his or her behavior is driven by cues that may not directly pertain to product benefits. Then, a short TV message that creates awareness may be sufficient.

Point to consider. Suppose the firm is considering two advertising message strategies. One strategy leads to *central-information processing* by the consumer while the other message strategy leads to *peripheral information-processing.* Suppose both message strategies lead to the same average increases in preference for (i.e., attitude toward) the product. Which message strategy is better?

In general, the advertising message that leads to central information-processing will result in more stable attitudes than the message strategy that leads to peripheral information-processing. By assumption, both message strategies lead to the same average increases in preference across consumers. Hence, if other factors are the same, the firm should choose the message strategy that leads to more stable attitude change (i.e., the message that encourages central information-processing). Such a choice will make the consumer less vulnerable to competitive advertising.

Fusion for Profit Maxim

The stability of attitude change can vary depending on how consumers process information. An advertising message strategy that produces high attitude change, on average, may be suboptimal if the attitude change is unstable.

Point to consider. Should the firm's advertising message focus on humor or on product features/benefits?

In view of the glut of advertising in today's world, a humorous ad may be more successful in cutting through the clutter and creating awareness than an advertising message strategy that is based on product features/benefits. As previously discussed, for the consumer to purchase the advertised brands, two conditions must hold:

1. The firm's product must enter the consumer's consideration set. Humorous ads may be more successful than attribute-based message strategies in achieving this goal.
2. The brand should be valued highly once it has entered the consumer's consideration set. In this case, an attribute-based message strategy may be more effective than a humorous ad. This is because attribute-based ads provide information that allows the consumer to differentiate among brands in the consideration set. Hence attribute-based messages have the potential to increase consumers' preferences and lead to sales.

Note that humorous ads are likely to be superior in the first step, but attribute-based ads are likely to be superior in the second. Hence one cannot generalize a priori which type of ad is superior overall. Thus, it may be appropriate to use a hybrid approach that combines humor and product-benefit information.

Example: For many consumers, automobile insurance is a "boring" product. Geico has been very successful by using humorous TV ads that feature a cartoon character (the "gecko") who announces that consumers can save money by buying insurance from Geico. One reason for the success of Geico's hybrid advertising message strategy is that the cartoon format is very different. Hence the ad does well in the first step. The second is the fact that the product benefit is simple (the price of buying insurance) and is an integral part of the ad message. Hence the ad also does well in the second step.

Fusion for Profit Maxim

Humorous ads may be more effective than attribute-based message strategies in getting the firm's product into consumers' consideration sets. However, attribute-based message strategies are likely to be more effective in strengthening the link between consideration sets and actual purchase. Hybrid advertising strategies may be superior to ads that are based purely on humor or those that focus exclusively on product benefits.

▶ *Is it desirable for the firm to use different advertising messages to target different segments?*

For any given product, a firm can use different advertising messages to target different segments. Recent changes in technology (e.g., the Internet) have made *customized segment-specific message strategies* and even *individual-specific message strategies* economically feasible. However, this strategy is not likely to succeed in all cases.

Example 1: Consider a pharmaceutical company such as Pfizer that uses a sales force to target doctors of different specialties (e.g., general practitioners, internists, and cardiologists). If the target segments do not overlap, it may be efficient for Pfizer to use a customized message strategy to target each physician segment.

Example 2: Consider a hypothetical new movie that attempts to appeal to two segments: young adults and families. Suppose the movie distributor can identify media or messages that appeal to either young adults or families, but not to both. Then, the distributor can use different advertising media or messages to target the two segments.

▶ *What will happen if the media audiences overlap significantly?*

Consider the movie example above. If the audiences across media overlap significantly, the distributor's customized advertising message strategy may perform poorly. Suppose one medium (e.g., HBO) portrays the film as a family film, and a second medium (an Internet Web site) portrays the film as being meant for young adults. Then, if young adults are exposed to both these media (HBO and the Internet Web site), the distributor's customized message strategy will lead to inconsistent product positioning. The resulting consumer confusion could lead to poor financial results.

Fusion for Profit Maxim

Advertising message strategies can be customized across different media provided *audience duplication* is small. If audience duplication is significant, consumer confusion regarding a product's positioning can lead to poor financial results.

Point to consider.   Should the firm vary its advertising messages across different media?

This strategy can be effective, especially if respondents are exposed sequentially to different media.

Example: Suppose AIG has developed a new financial instrument and advertises the new product on national TV using a 30-second spot. Specifically, suppose the ad focuses on creating awareness for the new product and recommends that viewers go to a special AIG Web site for additional information regarding that product. Then, the AIG Web site should focus on providing additional information regarding the new product rather than on repeating information from the TV ad.

Note that, by using a dual advertising message strategy, AIG can measure the effectiveness of its TV and Web site advertising. Specifically, AIG will be able to accurately measure how many viewers of the TV ad visit its Web site. In addition, it will be able to track the behaviors of each of these visitors to the Web site, including their repeat visits to the site and subsequent purchasing behavior. Hence AIG will be able to measure the productivities of its advertising strategies for each medium.

Fusion for Profit Maxim

Under certain circumstances, the optimal policy for the firm is to use different message strategies across media.

▶ Should the firm's advertising message target competitive brands?

The answer depends on whether the firm is a market leader or not.

Market leader. A rule of thumb is that the market leader should not target its competitors by name. This strategy can harm the leader in two ways. First, it will provide free awareness for its competitors. This will reduce the demand for the leader's brand by increasing the chance that competitors' brands enter consumers' consideration sets. Second, this comparative advertising strategy will enhance the credibility of competitive brands.

▶ Does this mean that the market leader should not compare itself to other brands?

As discussed, the market leader should not compare its brand to a specific brand or brands. However, this does not imply that all comparative advertising is bad for the leader. To illustrate, one reasonable strategy for the market leader may be to compare its attributes/benefits to those of a "well-known brand" or "well-known brands" without naming those brands.

Firms that are not market leaders. Such firms (including new entrants) may find it desirable to choose an advertising message strategy that targets the market leader's brand by name. At the very least, this strategy will increase the chance that the firm's brand enters consumers' consideration sets. Hence there is no downside risk to the advertiser.

Example: In the late 1970s, Bristol-Myers (now Bristol Myers Squibb) introduced a new brand, Comtrex, into a crowded market for cold medications. Since Comtrex was a new entrant in the cold market, Comtrex's advertising message focused directly on the leaders in the cold market, Dristan and Contac, and on the leader in the aspirin market, Bayer. Specifically, the TV message emphasized that Comtrex was "the new multisymptom cold reliever [which] all by itself...gives more kinds of relief than Dristan or Contac or Bayer [the dominant brand in the aspirin market] because none has a cough suppressant."

Comtrex's product launch was extremely successful, in part because of the clear product positioning strategy and the advertising message that was chosen to emphasize the new brand's *value proposition*. Note the use of the phrase "because none [of the market leaders named] has a cough suppressant" to increase Comtrex's message credibility.[12]

Fusion for Profit Maxim

In general, only firms with low market shares should use comparative advertising. Firms with high market shares may also gain from using comparative advertising provided the ads do not specify the names of the competing brand or brands.

▰ When and how should the firm change its advertising message strategy?

Consumers are likely to get bored if they see the same advertising message too often. One approach for the firm is to introduce different ad executions while focusing on the same theme (benefits) as before. This is particularly important for low-involvement products.

We return to the Geico example. As noted earlier, for most consumers, automobile insurance is a "boring" product. To address this problem, Geico uses a cartoon format featuring an amiable gecko, which continually reminds consumers that they can save money if they purchase car insurance from Geico. Furthermore, to address potential consumer boredom with its advertising, Geico uses different cartoon executions, each of which features the gecko in different situations but presents the same product-based message.

Fusion for Profit Maxim

The firm should vary the ad execution for its product periodically, even if the advertising message is unchanged.

▰ 12.5 Managerial Implications for Positioning New Products and Rebranding Existing Products

We now discuss how the firm should coordinate its advertising and positioning strategies when it rebrands itself or introduces new products.

▶ *Suppose a firm plans to change its branding strategy. How should it change its advertising message strategy?*

Changing branding strategy is potentially risky, especially if the firm does not change the name of the brand. The main hurdle for the firm is to enter the consideration set of the new target segment without confusing its existing customer base.

To achieve this, the firm will need to develop a new advertising message that is matched to the new segment. In addition, the firm will need to choose a new media plan that is compatible with the demographic or other characteristics of the new segment. The firm may also need to advertise more frequently to change the cognitive structures of the new segment.

Example: Historically, Wal-Mart has had a reputation of selling low-priced, mass-merchandized products. Since growth in this market segment has slowed down, Wal-Mart is attempting to rebrand itself as an upscale store that sells high-quality products and expensive durables such as plasma TVs. In order to successfully implement this rebranding strategy, it is necessary for Wal-Mart to choose an advertising message strategy that allows Wal-Mart to enter the consideration set of the new target segment (i.e., affluent consumers).

This type of cognitive change is not easy to achieve. Specifically, Wal-Mart will have to choose a new media plan that is matched to the new target segment and also advertise more frequently. In addition, Wal-Mart will have to adjust its advertising message and move away from focusing on price as its main theme.

▶ *How should the firm choose its advertising message strategy for a new product?*

Since the firm's product is new, consumers are likely to be imperfectly informed about the product's benefits and/or attributes. Suppose one segment of consumers ("experts") is well informed, and a second segment of consumers ("novices") is highly uncertain about the benefits provided by the firm's product. Then, it is critical for the firm to distinguish between the two segments. Specifically, the firm should choose an advertising message strategy that targets the novice segment and focuses on reducing that segment's uncertainty.

Note that the firm's advertising strategy has two goals vis-à-vis the novice segment:

1. To increase the perceived benefits from the firm's new product, and
2. To simultaneously reduce uncertainty.

In some cases, especially for radically new products, the firm may not have sufficient knowledge to form these segments a priori. Hence it will be necessary to use a more sophisticated methodology that allows one to classify consumers into segments.[13]

> **Fusion for Profit Maxim**
>
> The firm's advertising message can focus on increasing the levels of the perceived benefits from the new product. An additional goal may be to reduce the uncertainty in the perceived benefits provided by the new product. If the firm can segment the market, it can use a customized advertising message strategy.

▶ *Suppose a firm launches a new product in a market in which it does not have a reputation. What advertising message strategy should the firm use? Assume that the firm's product is of high quality.*

This is a case where consumers and the firm do not have the same information. We say that there is *asymmetric information*. Given these conditions, one strategy for the firm that manufactures durables is to send a signal to consumers that its product is of high quality.

For example, the firm could offer an extended warranty on its product and prominently feature this information in its advertising message. Similarly, a firm that sells nondurables can offer consumers a money-back guarantee if the product does not meet their expectations and can prominently feature this in its advertising message strategy. Note that, regardless of whether the product is a durable, firms whose products are of low quality will not be able to mimic these policies because they will lose heavily by doing so.[14] Consequently, the firm's advertising message will be credible to consumers.

Example: Several years ago, Hyundai had a poor reputation for quality in the U.S. automobile market. To address this problem, Hyundai introduced an extended ten-year/100,000-mile warranty on its cars in the United States that was far superior to those offered by its competitors. In addition, Hyundai featured this information prominently in its advertising campaigns. The strategy was extremely successful for Hyundai.

> **Fusion for Profit Maxim**
>
> When consumers are uninformed about the firm's product quality, it may be optimal for the firm to use such strategies as product warranties and money-back guarantees. To make these strategies successful, the firm should use an appropriate advertising message strategy that emphasizes these benefits.

▶ *Suppose the firm has developed a new product. Should the advertising message focus on product attributes or on product benefits?*

The answer depends on a number of factors, including how consumers process information, the difficulty that competitors will face in developing and launching similar products, the firm's planning horizon, and the firm's *discount rate*.

Information-Processing

Suppose consumers process information in terms of product benefits rather than in terms of product attributes. Then, it may be optimal for the firm to choose a message strategy that emphasizes the benefits provided by its new product rather than the new product's features. An additional advantage provided by this strategy is that it expands the boundaries of the industry in which the firm's product competes. Consequently, a benefit-based message strategy is likely to increase sales by more than a product attribute–based message strategy.

Example: Many soft drinks provide a common set of benefits to the consumer. For example, all soft drinks purport to be refreshing. Suppose Coca-Cola introduces a new flavor of soda and chooses an advertising message that emphasizes how refreshing the new flavor is. This benefit-based message strategy will allow the new product to compete with all other products that provide the same benefit (e.g., carbonated drinks and fruit juices).

If, instead, Coca-Cola were to choose a product-attribute-based message strategy, the new soda would only be positioned against other products with similar physical attributes (i.e., carbonated drinks). Since a product-attribute-based message strategy defines the industry narrowly, this message strategy could lead to lower sales revenues and profits for Coca-Cola's new soda than a benefit-based message strategy.

Planning Horizon

In the long run, it is often easier for the firm's competitors to imitate the features of the firm's new product rather than to imitate the new product's positioning. In view of this, the firm can use a *sequential message strategy* in which the initial advertising message focuses on product attributes and later advertising messages emphasize product benefits. Alternatively, the firm could choose a benefit-based message strategy from the beginning to achieve a distinctive positioning in the minds of consumers. The firm can also combine these approaches by using a hybrid advertising message strategy that simultaneously provides consumers with information about product attributes and product benefits.

Example: Many over-the-counter cold medications have identical chemical compositions. Hence firms in the cold industry cannot use attribute-based message strategies. Furthermore, consumers cannot determine a brand's quality even after using the brand. Consequently, the cold market is heavily perception-driven.

Because of this, a firm in the cold medication market can successfully differentiate itself from its competitors in the long run by using a carefully chosen benefit-based message strategy, *even though its product may be identical to those made by its competitors.*

Competitive Entry

Suppose the firm's new product has patent protection and contains different product attributes than competitive offerings. Alternatively, for technological or other reasons, suppose it will take the firm's competitors a long time to develop similar products. Since competitive entry is not imminent, the firm will have more flexibility in choosing its advertising message strategy.

Discount Rate

If the firm's *discount rate* is high, it should choose an advertising message that focuses on short-run profits. However, if the firm's discount rate is low, it is better to use a longer planning horizon and focus on long-run profits. As we have discussed earlier, different advertising message strategies have different short- and long-run effects.

Fusion for Profit Maxim

The firm should choose its long-run positioning and advertising message strategies based on how consumers process information for its product, the likelihood of competitive entry into the market, and the firm's discount rate.

▶ **How can the multiproduct firm choose the advertising message for a given brand to maximize its product-line performance?**

One method is to set up a choice experiment in which the multiproduct firm controls a number of key marketing decision variables such as price and advertising message.[15] The results of the choice experiment can then be used to answer a number of key managerial questions, including the following:

- How many unobservable market segments are there?
- Which products in the firm's product line will the new product cannibalize, and to what degree?
- Which customized advertising message strategy should the firm use to target particular segments in order to maximize its product-line profits?
- Which competitors are most likely to be hurt in a particular segment if the firm chooses a customized message strategy for that segment?

For a discussion of the methodology, see chapter 8.

▶ 12.6 How Should the Firm Coordinate Its Advertising Message Strategy with Other Marketing Decision Variables?

As we have discussed, a number of methods are available for measuring the effectiveness of an advertising message. However, these methods typically do not address the vital problem of coordinating the advertising message strategy with the other marketing mix variables (e.g., price and product design). One integrated methodology to address this issue is discussed below.

Example: Recently, the market leader in a multibillion-dollar pharmaceutical category was faced with the following problem. A new branded competitor had announced that it was going to enter the market. The key issue for the market leader was how to change its marketing policy following the new product entry.

To address this problem, the market leader conducted a large commercial study in which it varied key aspects of marketing policy for its brand (price, dosage, and advertising message) and measured physicians' intentions to purchase different brands.

Jagpal, Jedidi, and Jamil analyzed the results of the experiment using a model that they developed based on the approach described above.[16] Their results showed the following:

- That the market contained five unobservable physician segments,
- How the market leader could use a customized message strategy to target each physician segment, and
- How different segment-specific marketing policies (e.g., combinations of price and advertising message strategy) would affect the market shares of the firm's products and those of their competitors in each segment.

The Jagpal et al. model was able to accurately estimate the market shares of all brands in the experiment on a segment-by-segment basis. In addition, it was able to accurately predict the market shares of all brands one year after the experiment was conducted.

Chapter 12 Key Points
- The firm's advertising message strategy depends on how consumers in the target segment process information. In some cases, it may be optimal for the firm to use a dual message strategy that provides information about product features and product benefits.
- The firm should coordinate its media message and media planning decisions. These decisions are likely to vary depending on the product and the firm's market segmentation strategy.
- The firm's product positioning and advertising message strategies can have a significant impact on the firm's performance even when industries become increasingly commoditized.

- The firm's brand equity can be transferred to other product categories if those product categories provide similar benefits to its existing product line or if they are complementary. The firm's multiproduct advertising message strategy can be chosen to leverage these effects.
- Awareness is a necessary but not sufficient condition for an advertising message to be effective.
- When choosing an advertising message, the multiproduct firm should consider the effects of cannibalization.
- It may be incorrect to choose the advertising message for a given brand based on awareness scores for that brand, especially if the advertising messages are based on different product positioning strategies.
- A high recall score does not guarantee that an advertising message will be effective.
- The stability of attitude change can vary depending on how consumers process information. An advertising message strategy that leads to high attitude change, on average, may be suboptimal if the attitude change is unstable.
- Under certain circumstances, the optimal policy for the firm is to use different message strategies across media. Advertising message strategies can be customized across different media provided audience duplication is small.
- In general, only firms with low market shares should use comparative advertising strategies. Firms with high market shares may also gain from using comparative advertising provided the ads do not specify the names of the competing brand or brands.
- When consumers are uninformed about the firm's product quality, it may be optimal for the firm to use such strategies as product warranties and money-back guarantees. To make these strategies successful, the firm should use an appropriate advertising message strategy that emphasizes these benefits.
- The firm should choose its long-run positioning and advertising message strategies based on how consumers process information for the product, the likelihood of competitive entry into the market, and the firm's discount rate.

13

Determining the Advertising Budget

This chapter focuses on the firm's advertising budget decisions. Particular attention will be given to the distinction between the short and long runs and how to set advertising budgets under uncertainty. We also examine how the firm should coordinate its advertising decisions with the other elements of the marketing mix such as price and promotion. In addition, we analyze how the firm should vary its advertising spending over the *product life cycle* (i.e., from the time it introduces a new product into the marketplace until the time the product becomes mature) and the business cycle.

The information covered in this chapter will be useful when you are faced with the following types of decisions.

- Should my firm advertise to obtain new customers or to increase the customer retention rate?
- What advertising strategy should my firm use if its product is differentiated?
- What advertising strategy should my firm use if its product is a *me-too product*?
- How should my firm determine the optimal promotional mix when it uses different marketing strategies over the product life cycle? And, does the answer vary depending on whether the product is a national brand or a generic?

- How should my firm coordinate its price and advertising policies over time when demand is uncertain? And, does the optimal policy depend on whether my firm is privately or publicly held?
- Should my firm choose price and advertising policies based on estimates of average demand?
- How should my firm revise its price and advertising policies in different phases of the business cycle (e.g., economic downturns and economic upswings)?

The following terms will be introduced in this chapter (see glossary for definitions):

advertising elasticity	demand-push strategy	promotion elasticity
advertising goodwill	Dorfman-Steiner	reservation price effect
advertising-sales ratio	theorem	risk-adjusted advertising
cash flows	goodwill	elasticity
certainty-equivalent	informative advertising	risk-adjusted price
demand	me-too brand	elasticity
certainty-equivalent	me-too product	risk-adjusted promotion
revenue	persuasive advertising	elasticity
corporate image	price elasticity	risk-averse
advertising	private equity firm	supply chain
demand-pull strategy	product life cycle	volatility

◣ 13.1 Advertising and Marketing Strategy

Decision makers typically look at advertising as a tool for increasing sales. For example, advertising can induce current customers to purchase larger quantities of the firm's product. In addition, advertising can bring in new customers. However, advertising has an equally important role that is often overlooked: *Advertising may be necessary to prevent sales from decreasing.*

For example, if consumers do not receive reminder advertising about the benefits of the firm's product, they may be more responsive to advertising by competitors. Hence, in the absence of reminder advertising by the firm, the retention rate of current customers can fall. Furthermore, the effects of changes in advertising need not be symmetric. For example, if the firm increases its advertising budget by $100,000 per month, the gain in sales may be less than the corresponding loss in sales if the firm were to reduce its advertising budget by the same amount ($100,000 per month).

Fusion for Profit Maxim

Advertising has two major roles: to increase sales and to prevent a loss of sales. The effects of equivalent increases and decreases in advertising spending need not be symmetric.

◥ *What advertising strategy should the firm use?*

Advertising can affect sales in different ways. Suppose the firm advertises to create awareness of its product or to communicate information about the benefits/features that its product provides. We say that advertising is *informative*. In contrast, if advertising attempts to change the importance that consumers place on particular product benefits/features, we say that advertising is *persuasive*. In general, persuasive advertising is more difficult than informative advertising and requires a larger budget.

Point to consider. Suppose Apple advertises a new model of the iPod on its Web site. Let's say that a competitor, Bosc, introduces a clone of the old iPod model and also advertises on the Internet. What advertising strategies should Apple and Bosc use?

Apple and Bosc should use different advertising strategies. Apple's goal is to differentiate the new iPod from existing products in the marketplace and to downplay the importance of price. Hence the Apple Web site should present information on the new iPod in the following order: product benefits/features first, and then price information.

Bosc, on the other hand, seeks to convince potential buyers that its clone is as good as the old iPod. The primary difference is that Bosc's price is lower. Hence Bosc's goal is to encourage consumers to focus on price. Thus, Bosc should use the following advertising strategy on its Web site: present price information first, and then present other product-related information.

Fusion for Profit Maxim

The firm's advertising strategy depends on whether its product is differentiated from other alternatives or is a "me-too" product.

◥ *Who should determine the advertising budget?*

Both price and advertising affect sales volume. Hence, as we discuss below, the price and advertising decisions should be coordinated.

Example: Consider any price-advertising strategy. Let us refer to this strategy as the status quo. Suppose the firm reduces price without changing its advertising budget. Then, volume will increase, but unit profit margins will fall. Suppose instead that the firm increases advertising without changing price. Then, volume (and hence gross profits) will increase. However, the firm will incur the incremental cost of advertising. Thus, it is not immediately obvious which strategy is better (table 13.1). Nor is it obvious whether the firm will gain by changing the status quo marketing policy.

Example 1: Suppose the firm produces a highly differentiated product. Let's say that Honda is a pioneer and is the first auto manufacturer to introduce a new hydrogen-powered car into the market. Then, it is reasonable for Honda's advertising message for the new car to focus on its unique features. *Since Honda's advertising increases the degree of product differentiation, the price sensitivity of demand for the new hydrogen-powered car will fall when Honda's advertising is increased.*

Example 2: Suppose the firm markets a *"me-too" brand* that attempts to clone the market leader's product. For example, suppose Kia introduces a new hybrid car that is very similar to the hybrid currently being sold by the market leader. Then, Kia's advertising should focus on the fact that the new Kia hybrid is cheaper than the market leader's brand but offers the same performance (features). Hence an increase in Kia's advertising will make the demand for Kia's new hybrid more price-sensitive.

Fusion for Profit Maxim

Depending on the firm's strategy, higher advertising can either reduce or increase the price sensitivity of demand for the firm's product.

▶ What additional factors should the firm consider?

The firm should consider how price and advertising affect the uncertainties in the firm's *cash flows*, the ownership structure of the firm (e.g., whether the firm is privately owned or owned by shareholders), and the firm's planning horizon.

In order to analyze how these conditions affect the firm's price and advertising policies, we need to define several terms: *price elasticity, advertising elasticity, certainty-equivalent demand, risk-adjusted price elasticity*, and *risk-adjusted advertising elasticity.*

Price Elasticity

We return to the GM example. Suppose GM is presently charging a price of $50,000 per Seville and spending $600,000 per month on advertising. Now suppose GM reduces the price of the Seville by 1% but keeps advertising spending unchanged at $600,000 per month.

▶ What is the percentage increase in the number of Sevilles sold?

Suppose the answer is 3. Then, we say that the price elasticity of demand for the Seville is 3. *Note that the price elasticity is not fixed*; in particular, the price elasticity can vary depending on the initial marketing strategy that GM has chosen (i.e., the price *and* the level of advertising for the Seville).

> **Fusion for Profit Maxim**
>
> The price elasticity of demand measures how responsive sales volume is to a change in price. In general, the answer depends on the initial marketing strategy chosen.

Advertising Elasticity

Suppose GM's current strategy is as before. That is, the price of the Seville is $50,000, and GM is spending $600,000 per month on advertising. Suppose GM increases its advertising for the Seville by 1% but keeps price unchanged at $50,000. We now ask the following question:

▶ *What is the percentage increase in the number of Sevilles sold?*

Suppose the answer is 2. Then, we say that the advertising elasticity of demand for the Seville is 2. *Note that the advertising elasticity, like the price elasticity, is not fixed and can also vary depending on the initial marketing strategy GM has chosen for the Seville.*

> **Fusion for Profit Maxim**
>
> The advertising elasticity of demand measures how responsive sales volume is to a change in advertising expenditure. In general, the answer depends on the initial marketing strategy chosen.

Certainty-Equivalent Demand

Demand is often uncertain. For example, GM does not know its competitors' policies. Nor can GM accurately predict consumers' responses to its marketing efforts. Hence we need a metric for valuing the uncertain cash flows generated by any marketing policy (e.g., a given price-advertising combination).

Suppose GM is presently charging a price of $55,000 for the Seville and spending $750,000 per month on advertising. Let's say that, because demand is uncertain, management believes that the following outcomes are possible: monthly demand can be low (3,000 units), medium (4,500 units), or high (6,000 units). Suppose each level of demand is equally likely. Then, on average GM expects that it will be able to sell 4,500 Sevilles every month if it charges a price of $55,000 and spends $750,000 per month on advertising.

▶ *Given GM's current marketing strategy, what guaranteed level of demand will the company's owners be willing to accept in exchange for the cash flows from the uncertain demand described above?*

We shall consider two cases: GM is owned by stockholders, and GM is owned by a *private equity firm*.

Stockholders.   Let's begin with the current scenario where GM is owned by stockholders. We now ask the following hypothetical question: From the viewpoint of GM's stockholders, what guaranteed sales volume for the Seville is equivalent to selling 4,500 Sevilles every month, on average?

Since the stock market is *risk-averse*, GM's stockholders will be willing to pay a premium to avoid risk. This implies that *the guaranteed level of demand must be less than the average demand of 4,500 units under GM's strategy.*

Assume that GM's stockholders are indifferent to the following scenarios for the company's current marketing policy: obtaining a guaranteed monthly sales volume of 3,800 (<4,500) units or facing demand uncertainty as described. We say that the certainty-equivalent demand for the Seville is 3,800 (<average demand) when GM prices the Seville at $55,000 and spends $750,000 per month on advertising.

Private Ownership.   To see how private ownership affects valuation, consider a hypothetical situation where GM is taken over by a private equity firm. Let's say that these private investors are less risk-averse than the stock market as a whole.

Since the new private owners are more willing to take risk than the stock market, the certainty-equivalent demand for the private equity firm will be higher (say 4,100 units) than it was when GM was owned by stockholders. Note that, *regardless of the ownership structure of the firm, as long as the owners are risk-averse, the certainty-equivalent demand will always be lower than the expected demand (4,500 units in our example).* Furthermore, the concept of certainty-equivalent demand can be applied to all firms, regardless of their ownership structure (e.g., whether they are privately or publicly held).

Fusion for Profit Maxim

If the owners of a firm are risk-averse, the certainty-equivalent demand from any marketing strategy is always lower than the expected demand from that strategy. The more risk-averse the owners are, the lower the certainty-equivalent demand is. This result holds regardless of whether the firm is privately or publicly held.

Point to consider.   Will privately held firms choose the same marketing (advertising) policies as publicly held firms?

It is very unlikely that privately and publicly owned firms have the same risk attitudes. Hence the certainty-equivalent demands from any given marketing policy will differ across firms, depending on ownership structure. Thus, privately and publicly owned firms that face identical market conditions are likely to choose different marketing (including advertising) policies.

Risk-Adjusted Elasticities

We can now use the concept of certainty-equivalent demand to define two additional concepts: risk-adjusted price elasticity and risk-adjusted advertising elasticity. As discussed below, these concepts are very useful in analyzing how the firm should make price and advertising decisions under uncertainty.

We continue with the GM example. Since the concepts do not change depending on the ownership structure of the firm, it is sufficient to consider the scenario where GM is owned by stockholders. In our example, we assumed that the certainty-equivalent demand for the Seville was 3,800 units (<average demand) if GM chooses a price of $55,000 and spends $750,000 per month on advertising.

Using a similar approach, GM can determine the certainty-equivalent demands for the Seville for other marketing policies (i.e., price-advertising combinations). We can now measure how sensitive the certainty-equivalent demands are to changes in marketing policy.[1]

Suppose GM is presently using the following marketing policy: price the Seville at $55,000 and spend $750,000 per month on advertising. Then, the certainty-equivalent demand is 3,800 units. Suppose GM reduces the Seville's price by 1% but keeps advertising unchanged at $750,000 per month. Let's say that the certainty-equivalent demand increases by 2%. Then, we say that the risk-adjusted price elasticity of demand for the Seville is 2. Note that, as in the certainty case, the risk-adjusted price elasticity of demand depends on the initial marketing strategy chosen by GM.

The concept of risk-adjusted advertising elasticity is defined similarly. Thus, suppose the risk-adjusted advertising elasticity of demand is 3. This means that if GM were to increase its advertising spending by 1% from its initial value of $750,000 per month while keeping the price of the Seville unchanged ($55,000), the certainty-equivalent demand would increase by 3%.

Fusion for Profit Maxim

The risk-adjusted price elasticity of demand measures how sensitive the firm's certainty-equivalent demand is to a change in price, holding advertising spending constant. The risk-adjusted advertising elasticity of demand measures how sensitive the firm's certainty-equivalent demand is to a change in advertising, holding price constant.

We can now use these definitions and concepts to analyze how the firm should choose its short- and long-run price-advertising policies under different scenarios.

▲ 13.3 How Should the Firm Coordinate Its Price and Advertising Policy to Maximize Short-Run Performance under Certainty?

In the simplest case, advertising and pricing strategy affect only short-term results. Furthermore, there is no uncertainty. Hence the optimal strategy for the firm is to maximize short-run profits. Intuitively, one would expect the optimal marketing strategy to depend on how sensitive the market is to price changes (price elasticity) and changes in advertising (advertising elasticity). This is indeed the case.[2] As Dorfman and Steiner showed, short-run profit maximization implies that the firm should coordinate its price-advertising policy such that the following relationship holds:

$$\frac{\text{advertising expenditure}}{\text{sales revenue}} = \frac{\text{advertising elasticity}}{\text{price elasticity}}$$

This result is known as the *Dorfman-Steiner theorem*.

▲ What is the intuition behind the Dorfman-Steiner result on price and advertising policy?

Suppose demand is highly responsive to advertising. For example, consider a firm that has developed a new product. Then, it is necessary for the firm to educate consumers about the attributes/benefits of the new product and to create awareness about the availability of the new product. Since demand is responsive to advertising, the firm should advertise heavily. Hence, other factors remaining the same, the *advertising-sales ratio* should be high.

The effect of price elasticity on the advertising-sales ratio is more interesting.

▲ Why is the advertising-sales ratio high when sales volume is not sensitive to price changes?

As we have discussed, advertising elasticity measures how responsive volume is to an increase in advertising. However, this measure of advertising effectiveness is insufficient because *the firm is interested in the incremental revenue from additional advertising and not in the incremental volume generated.*

Example: Consider two firms, Novo and Copycat, that compete in the digital camera market. For simplicity, assume that both firms have similar cost structures. Suppose one firm, Novo, has developed a highly differentiated digital camera, and the other firm, Copycat, is selling a "me-too" product that is similar to other digital cameras in the marketplace. Since Novo's digital camera is highly differentiated from competitive models and Copycat's is not, Novo should charge a higher price than Copycat and earn a higher unit profit margin than Copycat.

▶ *Which firm gains more from a given increase in volume?*

Since Novo has a higher unit profit margin than Copycat, Novo will gain more from a given increase in volume than Copycat (incremental gross profits = unit profit margin × increase in volume). Consequently, other factors remaining the same, Novo should have a higher advertising-sales ratio than Copycat. Hence the *less* responsive sales volume is to a price cut, the *higher* the advertising-sales ratio.

Fusion for Profit Maxim

To maximize short-run profits under certainty, the firm should coordinate its price and advertising policies such that the following condition holds:

$$\frac{\text{advertising}}{\text{sales revenue}} = \frac{\text{advertising elasticity}}{\text{price elasticity}}$$

Point to consider.   Advertising is generally a highly effective medium for large manufacturers of packaged goods (e.g., Procter & Gamble). However, some automobile manufacturers (e.g., Toyota) spend more money on advertising than these packaged goods firms. Does this contradict the Dorfman-Steiner theorem?

The Dorfman-Steiner theorem pertains to the *ratio* of advertising to sales revenue and *not* to the size of the total advertising budget. Hence the observation that Toyota spends more on advertising than Procter & Gamble does not contradict the Dorfman-Steiner theorem.

▶ **13.4 Implications for Choosing Advertising Policy over the Product Life Cycle**

In this section, we analyze how the firm should vary its price and advertising policies over the product life cycle. In particular, we distinguish among store brands and national brands.

▲ *Should national brands advertise more heavily than store brands in a given phase of the product life cycle?*

In general, we expect that national brands will be more differentiated than store brands. Hence, other factors remaining the same, the demand for national brands should be less price-elastic than the demand for store brands. However, as discussed above, the Dorfman-Steiner theorem implies that each brand should coordinate its price-advertising policy such that:

$$\frac{\text{advertising}}{\text{sales revenue}} = \frac{\text{advertising elasticity}}{\text{price elasticity}}$$

Hence, assuming that advertising is equally effective for both national and store brands, it follows that national brands should spend more heavily on advertising. That is, they should have higher advertising-sales ratios than store brands.

▲ *How should the firm vary its price and advertising policies over the product life cycle? Will the results differ for branded products and generics?*

Consider the introductory phase of the product life cycle.

Example: Suppose Glad launches a new type of plastic wrap, Fool-Proof, that is a highly differentiated, branded product. At the time of the launch, the product is unique. Hence sales volume will not be very sensitive to price (i.e., the price elasticity will be low). Since consumers are likely to be unaware of the new product at this stage, sales volume will be highly responsive to advertising (i.e., the advertising elasticity is high). Hence, per the Dorfman-Steiner theorem, the advertising-sales ratio for Fool-Proof should be high.

As Fool-Proof progresses through its life cycle, competing brands will enter the market. This will make the market more price-sensitive than before (i.e., the price elasticity will increase). In addition, the market will become less responsive to advertising, since Fool-Proof has already created awareness (i.e., the advertising elasticity will decrease). These effects imply that the advertising-sales ratio for Fool-Proof should decrease over time.

Now consider a store brand (or a generic product) that is introduced into the market some time after Fool-Proof. *Since the store brand is similar to Fool-Proof, the price elasticity of demand for the store brand will be high even in the introductory period of its life cycle.* Thus, other factors remaining the same, during the introductory phase, the store brand should choose a lower advertising-sales ratio than the corresponding ratio for Fool-Proof when Fool-Proof was launched. Following the same argument as in the previous paragraph, we can show that the advertising-sales ratio for the store brand should also decline over time.

Fusion for Profit Maxim

In general, firms should reduce the advertising-sales ratio for their products over time, regardless of whether the products are branded or generics.

▶ *The previous analysis considered only one promotional tool: advertising. However, firms often use several promotional tools. How should the firm choose its price and promotional mix to optimize performance?*

We continue with the Fool-Proof example. Let's say that Glad simultaneously uses two sales-enhancing tools: advertising and consumer promotions. To analyze Glad's decision, we need to measure how responsive Fool-Proof's sales volume is to consumer promotions. We now introduce a new concept, *promotion elasticity*, which is defined analogously to advertising elasticity.

Suppose Glad is presently charging a price of $1 per unit for Fool-Proof, spending $500,000 per month on advertising, and spending $300,000 per month on consumer promotions. Suppose consumer promotion expenditure is now increased by 1%, holding price and advertising constant. Let's say that the sales volume increases by 2%. Then we say that, given Glad's current marketing policy for Fool-Proof, Fool-Proof's promotion elasticity is 2.

As in the simpler case where Glad uses only one promotional tool (advertising), *the key factor is how responsive Fool-Proof's revenues and profits are to changes in* each *of its marketing decision variables*: price, advertising, and consumer promotion (i.e., the relevant elasticities).

Interestingly, the Dorfman-Steiner theorem still holds, though in a slightly modified form. Specifically, Glad will maximize its short-run profits when the following conditions hold simultaneously:

$$\frac{\text{advertising expenditure}}{\text{sales revenue}} = \frac{\text{advertising elasticity}}{\text{price elasticity}}$$

and

$$\frac{\text{promotion expenditure}}{\text{sales revenue}} = \frac{\text{promotion elasticity}}{\text{price elasticity}}$$

This result can be generalized to the case where Glad uses multiple promotional tools (e.g., TV, newspapers, the Internet, and consumer promotions) and price to maximize its short-run profits for Fool-Proof.[3]

▶ *What do these results imply about promotion and advertising expenditures over the product life cycle?*

We continue with the Fool-Proof example. Combining the Dorfman-Steiner results above, we see that Glad should choose its promotion and advertising budgets so that the following condition is satisfied:

$$\frac{\text{advertising expenditure}}{\text{promotion expenditure}} = \frac{\text{advertising elasticity}}{\text{promotion elasticity}}$$

Note that both advertising and promotion elasticity vary over the product life cycle. Hence the ratio of advertising and promotion outlays should also vary over the life cycle.

In general, we expect that the advertising elasticity for Fool-Proof will decrease over time as more consumers become informed about the product. Furthermore, the promotion elasticity for Fool-Proof is likely to increase over time because of competitive entry. *Hence the ratio of advertising to promotion outlays for Fool-Proof should decrease over time as Fool-Proof becomes mature.*

▶ *Suppose the firm uses retailers to sell its product. Specifically, the firm uses retailer promotions (a demand-push strategy), as well as consumer promotions and direct advertising to consumers (a demand-pull strategy). How should the firm coordinate its marketing policies over the product life cycle?*

As discussed below, demand-push and demand-pull strategies are likely to have opposite effects on key decision variables such as the price set by the retailer.

We continue with the Fool-Proof example. Suppose Glad uses the following combination strategy. It offers quantity discounts to retailers (a demand-push strategy). In addition, it advertises to consumers and directly sends consumers promotional offers (a demand-pull strategy). Because of Glad's quantity discount policy, the retailer has an incentive to order larger quantities of Fool-Proof and to *lower* its retail price. However, because consumer demand for Fool-Proof has simultaneously increased, the retailer has an incentive to *increase* Fool-Proof's retail price (especially if the *reservation price effect* is strong). An additional complicating factor is that Glad needs to choose its dynamic promotional policy *after* recognizing the various leads and lags involved in the *supply chain* (e.g., the time between order placement by a retailer and the fulfillment of the order). Hence the net effect of Glad's combination demand-push and demand-pull strategies on marketing decisions over Fool-Proof's life cycle is likely to be conditional.

> **Fusion for Profit Maxim**
>
> When the firm uses a combination demand-pull/demand-push strategy, the ratio in which promotional funds should be allocated across consumers and the retail channel is conditional and varies over the product life cycle.

▲ 13.5 How Should the Firm Vary Its Price and Advertising Policies over the Business Cycle?

Firms need to adjust their marketing policies over time in response to changes in macroeconomic conditions.

▲ How should the firm revise its price and advertising decisions over the business cycle?

Suppose the economy is in a downturn. Then, intuition might suggest that the firm should always reduce both price and advertising. However, as we discuss below, this strategy may not always be optimal.

Case 1: Price Sensitivity Increases When the Economy Is in a Downturn. Suppose the market for the firm's brand or product becomes more price-sensitive when demand falls during the economic downturn. Then, the firm should reduce price. However, should the firm increase or decrease its advertising? The answer depends on the competitive structure of the market.

Example: Suppose the Lumen Company produces LCD screens for PCs; in particular, Lumen's LCD screens are similar to those made by its competitors. Now, because of the economic downturn, there is substantial excess capacity in the LCD screen industry. Consequently, all firms in the LCD screen industry are reducing prices sharply.

▲ How should Lumen revise its advertising budget?

Suppose Lumen has a similar cost structure to its competitors. Then, Lumen should cut back on its advertising spending in the downturn. If, however, Lumen has a lower cost structure than its competitors, Lumen should reduce its price sharply and simultaneously advertise heavily to steal customers from its competitors.

Case 2: Price Sensitivity Decreases When the Economy Is in a Downturn. We continue with the Lumen example. Suppose that during the economic downturn only loyal customers will purchase Lumen's LCD screens. Now, since price sensitivity has decreased, Lumen should increase its price. The remaining question is: How should Lumen revise its advertising budget?

Assume that loyal customers do not need reminder advertising. Then, advertising should be reduced. Suppose, however, that reminder advertising is necessary to convince loyal customers to continue purchasing Lumen's LCD screens. Then, Lumen should increase its advertising.

In summary, the effect of an economic downturn (economic upswing) on price and advertising is likely to vary across industries. Furthermore, even within an industry, the optimal price-advertising strategy is likely to vary depending on the firm's market segmentation policies. One implication is that branded and generic products in a given industry may need to adjust their price and advertising policies in different directions during any given phase of the business cycle (e.g., an economic downturn).

Fusion for Profit Maxim

The firm should vary its price and advertising policies over the business cycle. Depending on the cost structures and the price and advertising elasticities for their products, firms in the same industry may need to adjust their price and advertising policies in different directions when the economy is in a downturn (upswing).

▲ 13.6 How Should the Firm Coordinate Its Price and Advertising Policy in the Short Run When Demand Is Uncertain?

We first discuss the simple case where advertising is the only marketing decision variable and then extend the analysis to the case where the firm needs to coordinate both its price and advertising decisions under uncertainty.

So far we have assumed that the primary goal of advertising is to increase sales. This is often the case. However, as mentioned earlier, advertising has another equally important role. *Advertising can be used to stabilize sales rather than to increase expected sales.*

Example: Consider the telephone service industry. Should AT&T advertise to increase the number of new customers? Or, should AT&T advertise to reduce the rate at which its existing customers switch to other companies? The answer depends on AT&T's trade-off between expected profits and risk. Specifically, AT&T should choose the advertising strategy (i.e., segmentation strategy and associated advertising budget) that maximizes its *certainty-equivalent profits.*

Fusion for Profit Maxim

The firm should always evaluate its price and advertising policies based on risk and return. A strategy that promises higher average profits may be inferior to a strategy that promises lower average profits but is less risky.

We now discuss how the firm should coordinate its price *and* advertising policies in the short run when demand is uncertain. Our analysis is based heavily on the concept of certainty-equivalent demand. As discussed above, the certainty-equivalent demand from a given marketing policy is the *lowest* guaranteed demand that the firm is willing to accept in exchange for the uncertain demand it faces in the market when it chooses a particular marketing policy. Furthermore, the risk-adjusted price (advertising) elasticity measures how sensitive the certainty-equivalent demand is to changes in price (advertising).

Intuition suggests that the firm's decisions under uncertainty should depend on how the certainty-equivalent demand responds to changes in price and advertising (i.e., on the risk-adjusted price and risk-adjusted advertising elasticities). This is indeed the case.

The Dorfman-Steiner theorem holds, but in a slightly modified form.[4] Specifically, when demand is uncertain, the firm should choose its price and advertising policies such that:

$$\frac{\text{advertising}}{\text{certainty–equivalent revenue}} = \frac{\text{risk–adjusted advertising elasticity}}{\text{risk–adjusted price elasticity}}$$

where the *certainty-equivalent revenue* = certainty-equivalent demand $\times$ price per unit.

As previously discussed, if the owners of the privately or publicly held firm are risk-averse, the certainty-equivalent demand from any marketing policy will always be less than the corresponding average demand from using that marketing policy. Hence, for any price-advertising policy, the certainty-equivalent revenue is always lower than the expected sales revenue generated.

Fusion for Profit Maxim

When demand is uncertain, the risk-averse firm should coordinate its price and advertising policies based on how these policies affect the certainty-equivalent demand. These effects depend on the firm's market segmentation strategy and on how uncertain the demand is for the product.

▶ *What are the managerial implications for price-advertising policy?*

The primary implication is that managers should choose their price and advertising policies based on the certainty-equivalent demands corresponding to those strategies, *not the average demand levels*.

Example: Suppose the Colgate brand manager is comparing two price-advertising policies, each of which involves the same prices ($3 per tube of toothpaste) and advertising budgets ($1 million per month). Let's say that the manager plans to choose one of two advertising targeting strategies:

1. The first is to focus on obtaining new customers. Suppose the manager expects that this strategy will lead to an average sales volume of 300,000 tubes per month. However, this strategy is risky.
2. The second advertising strategy is to focus on increasing the customer retention rate. Suppose this strategy will lead to a lower average sales volume of 280,000 tubes per month. However, it leads to more stable sales than the more aggressive strategy of focusing on obtaining new customers.

▲ Which strategy is better?

To answer this question, the brand manager must determine the certainty-equivalent demands for both strategies. Since stockholders are risk-averse, the certainty-equivalent demands for both strategies will be lower than their corresponding expected demands.

Let's say that the certainty-equivalent demands are as follows: 250,000 tubes (risky new customer acquisition strategy) and 260,000 tubes (less risky customer retention strategy). Then the brand manager should choose the customer retention strategy *even though the average demand for this strategy (280,000) is lower than the average demand from the new customer acquisition strategy (300,000).*[5]

Fusion for Profit Maxim

The manager should choose marketing policies based on the certainty-equivalent demands from those policies. Since marketing policies have different effects on the certainty-equivalent demands, managers should not choose policies based on the average demand levels from using those strategies.

▲ 13.7 How Should the Firm Coordinate Its Price and Advertising in the Long Run When Demand Is Certain?

So far, we have focused on the short-run effects of advertising. However, in many cases advertising is likely to have significant long-run effects. Thus, advertising can increase the firm's current customer base. Some of these customers will repurchase the firm's products in the future. In addition, by increasing the number of current customers, advertising will increase word-of-mouth activity (e.g., blogging). This, in turn, will increase future sales.

As these market scenarios illustrate, advertising is similar to an investment in an unobservable asset, *goodwill*, which leads to future sales. Specifically, in the absence of reminders (advertising), consumers will forget about the firm's product. Hence goodwill depreciates over time, just like the value of physical assets such as plant and machinery. This raises two important marketing questions:

Is there an optimal level of goodwill that the firm should strive to attain?

In particular, how should the firm coordinate its price-advertising policy to choose the optimal level of goodwill and maximize long-run performance (net present value)?

We begin with the certainty case. This problem was first analyzed by Nerlove and Arrow.[6] From a marketing manager's viewpoint, their main results are twofold:

1. A Dorfman-Steiner-type result holds even when the firm maximizes long-run profits (net present value). Thus, the optimal advertising-sales ratio depends on how sensitive demand is to changes in price and advertising.
2. There is an optimal level of goodwill that the firm should attempt to maintain in order to maximize the net present value of profits.[7] If the current goodwill level is too low, the firm should advertise heavily so that it reaches the optimal goodwill level as rapidly as possible. If the current level of goodwill is too high, the firm should not advertise at all. Instead, the firm should allow goodwill to depreciate until the optimal level is reached. Once the optimal level of goodwill is reached, the firm should advertise only enough to offset the reduction in goodwill over time because of consumers forgetting.[8]

Point to consider.   Suppose the firm has introduced a new product into the marketplace. How should the firm vary its advertising expenditure over the life cycle of the product? Does the answer depend on whether the firm has a reputation in the industry?

Begin with the case where the firm has zero goodwill. For example, suppose the firm is unknown in the marketplace. Then, the firm will need to advertise heavily initially to reach the optimal level of goodwill as soon as possible. Subsequently, the firm should reduce advertising, since it is necessary only to maintain goodwill at the optimal level, after allowing for the fact that goodwill will depreciate over time.

Alternatively, suppose the firm is well known in the marketplace (e.g., the firm has brand equity). Since the initial goodwill is positive, the required level of advertising to reach the optimal level of goodwill will be lower than for the unknown firm. Hence the firm with a reputation should advertise less heavily initially. Once the optimal level of goodwill is reached, the firm should advertise just enough to keep goodwill at the optimal level.

These results suggest that advertising can be a significant barrier to entry in industries where goodwill has a major effect on sales. Specifically, established firms may have an advantage over new entrants who introduce new products in that industry.

Fusion for Profit Maxim

Advertising can be a significant barrier to entry in industries where demand is sensitive to *advertising goodwill.*

▲ 13.8 Coordinating Price and Advertising in the Long Run When Demand Is Uncertain

We now consider the general case where the firm's price and advertising policies have long-run effects that are uncertain. Since the cash flows that accrue from any marketing policy are uncertain, it is necessary to consider two factors: the ownership structure of the firm and how price and advertising affect demand uncertainty in the short and long runs.

Generally speaking, the optimal long-run policy will depend on how the firm's marketing policies affect the *volatilities* in cash flows over time and on the precise way in which goodwill affects sales volume. Different scenarios are possible, depending on what phase of the product life cycle the product is in and on the firm's segmentation policies.[9]

To illustrate, suppose the product is in the growth phase of the product life cycle. Furthermore, both the privately held firm and the publicly held firm target the same segments and use the same marketing policies (e.g., both firms use an aggressive pricing policy to increase the number of new customers). Then, as discussed earlier, stockholders can reduce their risk by diversifying; however, private owners cannot (see chapters 1 and 2). Hence it is very likely that the privately and publicly held firms will choose different price and advertising policies in the long run, even if they face the same market conditions.[10]

Fusion for Profit Maxim

If price and advertising have significant and uncertain long-run effects, the firm's optimal long-run marketing policy will depend on its ownership structure and on how its policies affect demand uncertainty and goodwill over time.

▲ 13.9 Corporate Image Advertising

So far, we have focused on the case where advertising by the firm is brand- or product-specific. In practice, many firms supplement these types of advertising expenditure with non-product-specific advertising to improve their corporate images or to boost their sales revenues across product lines. For example, General Electric advertises using the tag line "We bring good things to life."

▶ *How should the firm measure the productivity of corporate image advertising?*

If historical sales data are available, the firm can measure the productivities of its brand (product) advertising expenditures and corporate image advertising. Briefly, in contrast to the previous methods, it is now necessary to specify a causal path through which each type of advertising (brand or corporate image) affects sales. Thus, corporate image advertising affects the sales of the firm's products indirectly through an unobservable construct, goodwill. In contrast, brand- or product-level advertising can affect the sales of a given product *both* indirectly (via goodwill) and directly. These effects, including dynamic carryover effects, can be statistically estimated.[11]

Fusion for Profit Maxim

The firm can measure the joint effects of brand-specific and corporate image advertising by analyzing historical sales data.

Chapter 13 Key Points

- Advertising has two major roles: to increase sales and to prevent a loss of sales. The effects of equivalent increases and decreases in advertising spending need not be symmetric.
- In general, the price and advertising budget decisions should not be separated. The firm should not use a sequential "top-down" approach in which price is determined first and advertising budgets are set subsequent to that decision.
- Depending on the firm's strategy, higher advertising can either increase or decrease the price sensitivity of demand for the firm's product.
- The optimal advertising-sales ratio increases with advertising elasticity and decreases with price elasticity.
- When the firm uses a combination demand-pull/demand-push strategy, the ratio in which promotional funds should be allocated across retailers and consumers is conditional and should vary over the product life cycle.
- Depending on the cost structures and the price and advertising elasticities for their products, firms in the same industry may need to adjust their price and advertising policies in different directions when the economy is in a downturn or in an upswing.
- When demand is uncertain, the firm should coordinate its price and advertising policies based on its segmentation policy and the associated

risk-adjusted price and advertising elasticities. In general, the firm should not choose its marketing policy based on average demand.

- Advertising can be a significant barrier to entry in industries where demand is sensitive to advertising goodwill.

- If price and advertising have significant and uncertain long-run effects, the firm's optimal long-run marketing policy will depend on its ownership structure and on how its policies affect demand uncertainty and goodwill over time.

- The firm can measure the joint effects of brand-specific and corporate image advertising by analyzing historical sales data.

Measuring Advertising Productivity

The previous chapter focused on the theory of advertising and, in particular, on how the firm should determine its advertising budget. In practice, however, the firm cannot set advertising budgets without being able to measure advertising productivity in the first place. In this chapter, we focus on these measurement issues. Our focus here will be on traditional media such as television and magazines. The measurement of advertising productivity for the Internet and mixed-media plans—Internet and traditional—will be discussed in chapter 21.

We first discuss methods for determining how productive the firm's aggregate advertising spending is, both in the short run and in the long run. Then, we analyze methods for determining the productivities of different media (e.g., television and print) when the firm uses multiple media. Finally, we show how the firm can use these results to simultaneously determine optimal advertising budgets and media allocation plans.

The information covered in this chapter will be useful when you are faced with the following types of decisions:

- Should my firm use experiments or historical data to measure advertising productivity?
- How should my firm analyze historical sales data to measure short-run and long-run productivity?
- How do the data-collection period and accounting methods used by my firm affect the measures of advertising productivity?

- How should my firm use intermediate criteria such as *reach* and *gross rating points* (GRPs) to choose the media plan?
- What other methods should my firm use to choose the optimal media plan?
- How much should my firm be willing to pay to advertise in a given advertising medium based on commercial ratings such as the Nielsen ratings?
- How should my firm determine when to prepurchase advertising space and how much to spend?

The following terms will be introduced in this chapter (see glossary for definitions):

advertising-sales ratio	dynamic carryover	return on the market
anchoring effect	effects	portfolio
audience duplication	frequency	reverse causality
barrier to entry	gross rating points	risk-averse
budgeting rule	(GRPs)	risk-neutral
buzz	GRP model	sales response
cash flows	intermediate quantity	function
certainty-equivalent	lag effect	scatter ads
profits	marginal cost	switching regime
cola wars	market portfolio	regression model
consideration set	media mix	threshold effects
data-intervalling	private equity firm	two-way causality
problem	product life cycle	up-front advertising
diminishing returns to	reach	volatility
advertising	reach model	word of mouth

▲ 14.1 How Can the Firm Measure Advertising Productivity?

In order to choose the optimal advertising budget, the firm needs to measure advertising productivity. Broadly speaking, the firm can use two methods:

1. Conduct an experiment in which the firm varies its advertising expenditure over regions and time periods and measures how advertising affects sales and profits, or
2. Determine advertising productivity by analyzing historical data on advertising and sales or some intermediate measures of productivity (e.g., awareness) that affect sales.

▲ Should the firm use experimental or historical data to measure advertising productivity?

Experimentation provides an important advantage: the firm can control the study by changing the levels of its own advertising spending while holding a number of its own marketing decisions (e.g., price) constant in the experiment. In addition, the experiment can be conducted over a period of time. Hence the firm can measure both the short-run and the long-run effects of advertising on sales and profits.[1]

In many cases, however, experimentation may not be feasible. For example, the industry may be changing rapidly, and there may not be enough time to run a controlled experiment. In addition, experimentation may be too expensive (e.g., the product is a durable such as an automobile). There may be a danger that competition will preempt the firm if it waits too long before choosing its final advertising strategy. Consequently, the firm may have no alternative but to use historical data to measure advertising effectiveness.

In this chapter we will focus on how to measure advertising productivity by analyzing historical data.[2]

▶ 14.2 How Can the Firm Measure Advertising Productivity Using Historical Data?

In this section, we focus on measurement issues where the outcome of advertising is sales. Later, we consider the case where the outcome of advertising is an *intermediate quantity* such as brand awareness.

▶ What factors should the firm consider in measuring advertising productivity using historical data?

When analyzing historical advertising and sales data, the firm should include the key factors that affect sales (e.g., competitive behavior) and use an empirical methodology that has a strong theoretical foundation. In our discussion, we will focus on managerial issues.[3]

Threshold Effects

We begin with a basic question: How do consumers respond to advertising? Suppose a potential consumer sees an advertisement for the firm's product only once. Then, the firm's advertising message may not enter the consumer's long-term memory. Thus, unless the consumer sees the advertisement several times, advertising may be wasted. In such cases, we say that there are *threshold effects*.

These threshold effects for consumers are likely to vary by industry and segment, depending on how involved the consumer is in the task of buying the product in question.

Fusion for Profit Maxim

The firm should choose an empirical method that allows for threshold effects of advertising. This implies that advertising has a nonlinear effect on sales.

Point to consider.   Will the threshold effect be higher for a packaged goods product than for an automobile?

For most consumers, packaged goods products (e.g., soap and tooth-paste) represent a low-involvement purchase.[4] In contrast, purchasing an expensive durable (e.g., an automobile) is a high-involvement activity. Hence the threshold effect for a packaged goods product is likely to be higher than the threshold effect for an automobile. Thus, other factors being the same, a packaged goods firm may need to advertise more frequently than a durable goods manufacturer in order to obtain any benefit from advertising.

Point to consider.   How do threshold effects affect the structure of an industry?

Suppose threshold effects are significant. Then, unless a new entrant advertises beyond a minimum level, all advertising will be a waste. Hence, if the threshold value of advertising (in dollars) in an industry is sufficiently high, advertising will be a *barrier to entry* in that industry.

Other Marketing Mix Decisions by the Firm

Firms often change several marketing variables (e.g., pricing and advertising expenditure) simultaneously. Hence it is necessary to include all relevant marketing variables in the analysis.

Example: Consider an automobile manufacturer (say General Motors) that increases its advertising spending each time it offers a cash rebate on the purchase of its cars. Suppose General Motors (GM) analyzes the historical relationship between advertising and sales without considering the effect of the price rebate. Let's say that GM's sales revenue increases by $4 million when it uses the rebate plan. Then, GM will incorrectly conclude that the entire increase in sales revenue is caused by advertising. Hence the estimated advertising productivity will be too high.

To illustrate, consider the extreme case where advertising has no effect on consumers; in particular, the price rebate is the sole factor that increases sales revenue. Then, by not allowing for the effect of the rebate plan on sales, GM will incorrectly conclude that advertising is very productive. Consequently, GM will waste its resources on advertising.

Fusion for Profit Maxim

When measuring advertising productivity, the firm should include all relevant explanatory factors (e.g., price) in addition to advertising that can affect sales. This is necessary, since firms often simultaneously vary several marketing policy instruments over time, including advertising.

Competitive Behavior

When analyzing historical advertising and sales data, the firm should explicitly allow for the effects of competitors' marketing policies on its sales.

Example: Suppose Coca-Cola estimates the historical relationship between its own advertising and sales without considering the impact of Pepsi's advertising. How will this omission affect the advertising productivity estimates for Coke?

Suppose that historically the cola industry has been involved in the *cola wars*. That is, whenever Coke increased its advertising spending, Pepsi also increased its spending (though not necessarily by the same amount), and vice versa.

▶ *Suppose Coca-Cola increased its advertising spending in a certain month by $1 million. Let's say that Coca-Cola's sales revenue in that month increased by $3 million. Is the increase in sales revenue of $3 million a correct measure of advertising productivity for Coke?*

This net increase in sales revenue for Coca-Cola ($3 million) is the sum of two effects: the *increase* in Coke's sales if Pepsi does not react (A), and the *decrease* in Coke's sales when Pepsi reacts by increasing its own advertising (B).

Since B is a negative quantity, A must be greater than $3 million. Thus, by not allowing for the effects of Pepsi's advertising, Coca-Cola will underestimate its own advertising effectiveness.

Fusion for Profit Maxim

In order to obtain meaningful estimates of advertising productivity, the firm needs to explicitly analyze how competitors' marketing policies affect the sales of its own product.

Nonlinear Effects

As discussed above, advertising will have no effect at all unless the advertising budget is larger than some threshold level. In the Coca-Cola example, suppose the threshold level of advertising spending is $500,000 per month.

▶ *What will happen when Coke's spending exceeds this threshold level ($500,000 per month)?*

More potential consumers will be exposed to Coke's advertising. We say that reach increases. In addition, potential consumers will see Coke's advertising more often when Coke increases its advertising spending. We say that *frequency* has increased.

Now, the net effect of Coke's advertising on Coke's sales will depend on how *both* reach and frequency increase when Coke increases its advertising beyond the threshold level ($500,000 per month). As discussed below, the combined effect of reach and frequency is likely to be highly nonlinear. That is, the incremental effect of additional advertising spending on sales will not be constant. Consider the following scenarios.

First, suppose Coke can segment its consumers by volume into two categories: heavy and light users. Furthermore, suppose Coke knows which media are effective in reaching each segment. Then, Coke should use the following targeted advertising strategy:

- If the advertising budget is small, advertise to the heavy user segment only.
- If the advertising budget is larger, advertise to both the heavy and the light user segments.

If Coke chooses this advertising strategy, its advertising productivity will be high at low levels of spending when Coke targets heavy users (assuming that the advertising spending is greater than the threshold level). In addition, the incremental gains from additional advertising will fall off when Coke targets both heavy and light users. We say that there are *diminishing returns to advertising.*

Second, suppose Coke advertises heavily. Then potential consumers will see Coke's advertising very often (i.e., frequency is high). If this happens, consumers can react in a number of ways, *some of which can lead to a negative effect on sales.* For instance, consumers may become irritated or bored; in addition, they may develop counterarguments to Coke's advertising message. The net result is that, if Coke's advertising increases beyond a certain point, additional advertising may actually lead to lower sales.

Fusion for Profit Maxim

Advertising is likely to have highly nonlinear effects on sales. These effects will vary depending on the type of product, the firm's market segmentation strategy, and the level of advertising spending.

Point to consider.   Empirical studies sometimes find that linear advertising-sales models fit the data reasonably well. Does this evidence imply that it is unnecessary to estimate nonlinear advertising models?

This conclusion is empirically and theoretically flawed. Empirically, there are two problems:

1. Suppose the firm has not varied its advertising spending significantly over the data analysis period. For example, suppose the minimum monthly advertising spending has been $400,000, and the maximum monthly advertising spending has been $500,000. Let's say that a

linear model fits the data well. In addition, suppose the linear model implies that, whenever advertising is increased by $100, sales revenue will increase by $200.

By definition, the empirical results show that this conclusion is supported for the range of advertising values in the sample ($400,000 to $500,000 per month). However, *this does not allow us to conclude that the result will be true for all levels of advertising spending.* For example, it will be incorrect for the firm to conclude that, if it increases its monthly advertising spending significantly, to $3 million (say), advertising productivity will remain as high as before.

2. Suppose the firm has historically used a linear budget rule (e.g., spend 20% of last year's sales revenue on advertising in the current year). Then, the linear fit could simply be picking up this decision rule.

Theoretically, linear advertising-sales models can lead to implausible advertising budgeting policies. In our example, suppose the *marginal cost* of production is zero (e.g., the product is software sold via the Internet). Then, the linear advertising-sales model implies that, regardless of the firm's current level of advertising spending, each time the firm spends an additional $100 on advertising, its net profits will increase by $100 (increase in sales revenue – incremental cost of advertising). This leads to an implausible result: the optimal policy is to spend an infinite amount of money on advertising.

Fusion for Profit Maxim

Linear advertising models should not be used even if they predict sales accurately.

Dynamic Carryover Effects

In many cases, regardless of whether the product is a nondurable or a durable, advertising will affect both current and future sales. If this is true, we say that advertising has *dynamic carryover effects.*

▶ *What will happen if the firm fails to allow for dynamic carryover effects?*

The firm will obtain incorrect estimates of advertising productivity. Consequently, it will make poor advertising budgeting decisions. Consider the following examples.

Nondurable Product.   Suppose Good Humor introduces a new flavor of ice cream into the marketplace. For simplicity, we consider two periods: introduction and future. In the introduction period, some consumers (triers) will purchase the new ice cream flavor because of advertising. Of this group of triers, some will purchase the new flavor again in the future period, provided they are satisfied with the new flavor.

If Good Humor's advertising message in the introductory period is catchy, this will induce *word-of-mouth* activity (*buzz*) in that period. This, in turn, will increase the number of new customers in the future period. Additionally, Good Humor may have to advertise in the future period to reinforce consumers from the introduction period and hence increase their retention rate.

▶ *What will happen if Good Humor does not consider these dynamic carryover effects?*

The measured advertising productivity in the introduction period will be too low. The reason is that this measure does not include the additional profits from repeat purchases in the future by triers in the introduction period. Similarly, the measured advertising productivity in the future period will be too high. Consequently, Good Humor is likely to underadvertise in the introductory period and overadvertise in the future period.

Durable Product.   Suppose Ford advertises a year-end clearance sale on Ford Explorers. Then, some consumers who would otherwise have purchased the new model of Explorer in the future will purchase the old model. If this is the case, Ford's advertising will "borrow" sales from the future.

▶ *What will happen if Ford fails to consider this dynamic carryover effect?*

Ford will spend too much money on advertising the year-end clearance sale.

Fusion for Profit Maxim

In many cases, advertising has long-run effects. Hence the firm should choose an empirical method that explicitly allows for dynamic carryover effects.

Asymmetric Effects.   The effects of advertising increases and decreases may be asymmetric and discontinuous.[5] If this is the case, we say that there is an *anchoring effect*. In figure 14.1, the firm's current level of advertising is OA. If the firm decreases its advertising below OA (the anchor value), its sales will be reduced along the curve BC. However, if the firm increases its advertising above OA, its sales will increase along a *different* curve, BF. Note that the effects of advertising are asymmetric and discontinuous. Furthermore, each time the firm changes its advertising expenditure, the anchor value will change.

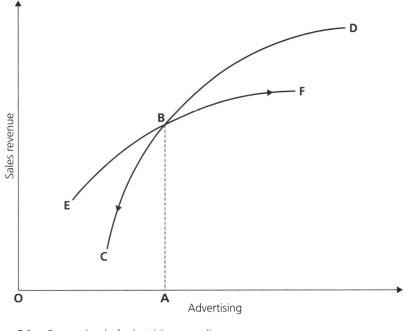

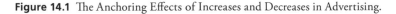

OA = Current level of advertising spending
CB = Sales response curve if advertising is reduced below **OA**
BF = Sales response curve if advertising is increased above **OA**

Figure 14.1 The Anchoring Effects of Increases and Decreases in Advertising.

▶ *What does anchoring imply about measuring advertising productivity and choosing advertising budgets over time?*

The anchoring model of advertising has important managerial implications. For example, when advertising increases, the typical effect is an immediate sharp increase in sales followed by a decline to an equilibrium level somewhere between the peak and the initial level of sales, *even if the increase in advertising is maintained in future periods.* From a managerial viewpoint, it is important to note that standard empirical methods cannot estimate these asymmetric and discontinuous effects of advertising. One approach for capturing anchoring effects is to use a general nonlinear *switching regime regression model.*[6]

Fusion for Profit Maxim

If there is an anchoring effect, increases in advertising spending and equivalent decreases in advertising spending may have different effects on sales. The anchoring effect can be captured statistically.

Reverse Causality.   Suppose advertising has an effect on sales, but, in addition, sales affect advertising through a *budgeting rule.* For example, the firm could have used the following decision rule: reduce advertising when sales are poor or the economy is in a downturn. If this is the case, we say that there is *reverse causality.*

▶ **What will happen if the firm directly estimates the impact of advertising on sales when reverse causality is present?**

In this case, the estimates of advertising productivity will be biased because there is a *two-way causality* between advertising and sales (i.e., advertising causes sales and vice versa). To address this problem, it is necessary to *simultaneously* estimate the impact of advertising on sales and the impact of sales on advertising, after allowing for the appropriate lag structures.

Fusion for Profit Maxim

Reverse causality occurs when advertising affects sales and sales also affect advertising (e.g., the firm uses a sales-based rule to set its advertising budget). If this is the case, the firm should not estimate the advertising-sales relationship alone, even if this method has high predictive accuracy.

Point to consider.   How can the firm avoid the reverse causality problem in measuring advertising productivity?

The firm should use sufficiently short time intervals for collecting advertising and sales data. In this way, there will be no reverse causality from sales to advertising through a budgeting rule. Hence, if the data intervals are sufficiently short, it is appropriate to directly measure the advertising-sales relationship.[7]

Data Matching.   Using unadjusted accounting data can lead to incorrect measures of the impact of advertising.

Example: Consider a manufacturer of electrical parts. Suppose the manufacturer pays for an ad two months before it is run. In addition, the manufacturer records sales when orders are shipped from the factory.

Consider the following scenario. Suppose the manufacturer pays for the ad in February and runs the ad in April. Following the ad in April, retail sales for the manufacturer's product increase immediately in that month. Suppose retailers send in orders to the manufacturer in April to replenish their stocks. Following receipt of these orders in April, the manufacturer ships the orders in June.

If the manufacturer uses accounting data, it will conclude that advertising in February (the month in which it paid for the ad) leads to sales in June (the month in which the electrical parts are shipped to retailers). This implies that advertising has a lagged effect of three to four months. In reality, there is no *lag effect*: advertising that is run in April leads to increased retail sales in the *same* month.

Fusion for Profit Maxim

Since the firm's accounting system may use different conventions to define when advertising and sales occur, by using standard accounting data the firm could obtain spurious estimates of advertising productivity. To address this problem, the accounting information should be adjusted prior to estimating the advertising-sales relationship.

Data-Intervalling Bias. Suppose the firm collects and analyzes quarterly advertising and sales data. However, the effects of advertising are felt within a much shorter period (say a week) after the ad is run. This discrepancy is known as the *data-intervalling problem*.

▶ *How does this mismatch of data affect the estimates of advertising productivity?*

The estimated advertising productivities are likely to be biased.[8]

Point to consider. How can the firm address the data-intervalling problem?

The firm can address the data-intervalling problem by using short enough data periods for tracking *both* advertising and sales. Note that, in view of the ready availability of sophisticated real-time computerized data management systems, the data-intervalling problem can be easily addressed.

Fusion for Profit Maxim

Advertising and sales data should be collected over sufficiently short periods in order to obtain accurate measures of advertising productivity.

▶ *14.3 How Can the Firm Measure the Productivities of Different Advertising Media?*

So far, we have focused on methods for measuring the productivity of aggregate advertising spending. In practice, the firm has to solve a more basic problem: What is the productivity of advertising in different media (e.g., national TV)?

At this level of disaggregation, most firms do not analyze the advertising-sales relationship. Instead, they examine the impact of advertising on intermediate criteria such as awareness or the total number of advertising exposures that, in turn, have an effect on sales. We will follow this approach initially. Later, we will show how to develop a *media mix* model of advertising that uses sales as the criterion of advertising effectiveness.

For simplicity, we begin with the case where the advertising budget is fixed. This assumption will be relaxed later.

▲ 14.4 Measuring Media Productivity Using Reach Models

We begin with the case where the firm uses awareness as a metric to measure advertising productivity.

▲ *Consider a firm that has developed a new product. Suppose the price of the product and the advertising budget have been determined by management. How should the firm allocate the advertising budget across media?*

One intuitive approach is to choose the media plan that maximizes awareness of the new product. The rationale is straightforward: the more consumers that are aware of the firm's product, the higher sales (and profits) will be.

▲ *How can the firm measure awareness?*

One method is to use the reach of a medium as a proxy for awareness. The reach of an advertisement is defined as the number of individuals who have been exposed to that advertisement in a given period.

▲ *Should the firm choose a media plan that maximizes the reach that is attainable from a given advertising budget?*

At first glance, this method appears to be reasonable. However, using reach to measure advertising effectiveness can lead to theoretical and empirical difficulties.

▲ *What are the theoretical difficulties in using reach to measure advertising productivity?*

Theoretically, the reach criterion implies that repeat exposures to advertising have no value at all. This assumption may not hold, especially for low-involvement products. In such cases, reminder advertisements are necessary so that consumers store the advertised information in their long-term memory. Indeed, as we have discussed, there may be threshold effects. If this is the case, it is possible that a single advertising exposure will have *no* effect at all on the consumer.

The reach criterion implicitly assumes that the effectiveness of advertising exposures is equal across media. This assumption may not hold. For example, an advertising exposure to a one-page ad in *Time* magazine could have a higher impact than an advertising exposure to a 15-second national television ad.

To address this problem, the manager can assign differential subjective weights to the reaches in different media before computing the combined reach of a given media plan. Thus, in our example, the manager could assign a higher weight to reach in *Time*. This approach, however, is ad hoc and difficult to justify. We will discuss methods for addressing this problem later in the chapter.

Fusion for Profit Maxim

The reach criterion assumes that only the first advertising exposure has an effect on the consumer. Furthermore, this criterion also assumes that an advertising exposure has the same effect on the consumer, regardless of the medium or media to which the consumer has been exposed.

▲ *What are the empirical difficulties in measuring the reach from a given media plan?*

On the surface, measuring the reach of a media plan appears to be straightforward. However, as illustrated in the examples below, measuring reach is complicated by *audience duplication*. This problem is likely to be significant for the following reason: the firm uses multiple media to reach the *same* target audience. *Hence the firm's advertising strategy will inevitably lead to audience duplication.*

We begin with the simplest case where the advertising plan uses two media only. Let's say that a firm simultaneously advertises its product in *Newsweek* and *Time*. Suppose *Newsweek* has a reach of 100,000, *Time* has a reach of 50,000, and 15,000 individuals read both *Newsweek* and *Time*. Then, because of audience duplication, the correct value of reach (135,000) is less than the sum of the separate reach values across media (150,000; table 14.1).

Fusion for Profit Maxim

In order to measure the reach of a media plan, it is necessary to correct for audience duplication.

▲ *In the* Newsweek-Time *example, it was only necessary to consider one duplicated audience in computing reach. What will happen if the firm uses several media?*

Suppose the firm uses a third medium (*People* magazine), which has a reach of 60,000. Then, the sum of the separate reach values across the three media is 210,000 (table 14.2).

Table 14.1
***Newsweek-Time* Example: The Effect of Audience Duplication on Reach**

	Time	*Newsweek*	*Time* and *Newsweek*	Total
Number of readers	100,000	50,000	15,000	
Unadjusted reach	100,000 +	50,000		= 150,000
Actual reach	100,000 +	50,000 −	15,000	= 135,000

Table 14.2
***Newsweek-Time* Example: Unadjusted Reach for a Multimedia Plan**

Medium	Reach
Time	100,000
Newsweek	50,000
People	60,000
Unadjusted reach	210,000

▶ *What is the true reach from this media plan?*

To obtain this answer, we need the following additional information: What is the audience duplication for each pair of media (three in this case), and what is the audience duplication for all three media taken together?

Suppose the results are as shown in table 14.3. Then, the reach from the media plan is 171,000 (210,000 − 44,000 + 5,000). Note that the number of duplicate audiences increases much faster than the number of media. Thus, when the number of media in the media plan increases from two to three (a 50% increase), the number of duplicate audiences increases from 1 to 4 (a 300% increase). Similarly, we can show that if the number of media increases from 2 to 4 (a 100% increase), the number of duplicate audiences increases dramatically from 1 to 11 (a 1000% increase).

Fusion for Profit Maxim

Measuring audience duplication and hence reach becomes increasingly complicated when the number of media in the media plan increases.

▶ *Suppose the firm uses multiple media. How can the firm measure the reach of a multimedia plan?*

As discussed above, it is difficult to obtain an exact measure of the reach of a multimedia plan when the number of media is moderate or large. However,

Table 14.3
***Newsweek-Time* Example: Audience Duplication Effects for a Multimedia Plan**

Audience duplication	Number
Newsweek-Time	10,000
Newsweek-People	18,000
Time-People	16,000
Total pairwise duplication	44,000
Newsweek-People-Time (triple duplication)	5,000

approximation formulae are available. Specifically, these formulae require only the following information: the individual reaches for each medium, and the sizes of the pairwise duplicate audiences. Such information is often available in the marketplace.

Fusion for Profit Maxim

If the firm uses a multimedia plan, it can obtain an approximate measure of the combined reach for that plan. This measure depends on the reach of each individual medium and the duplicated audiences for each pair of media in the media plan.

► *The previous analysis assumed that the advertising budget is given. Can the firm simultaneously choose the optimal advertising budget and the optimal media plan? Assume that reach is a reasonable criterion.*

Example: Suppose the price of the product is $30, and the marginal cost per unit is $10. Then, the unit profit margin is $20. Suppose the firm is considering the media plans shown in table 14.4.

Note that there are diminishing returns to both advertising and reach. For example, when advertising is doubled from $100,000 to $200,000 (a 100% increase), reach increases by a smaller proportion from 100 to 140 (a 40% increase). Similarly, when reach increases from 100 to 130 (a 30% increase), the sales volume increases by a smaller proportion, from 20,000 to 24,000 (a 20% increase).

Suppose the advertising budget is increased from $100,000 to $150,000 (an increase of $50,000). Then, sales will increase by 4,000 units, and gross profits (before paying for the additional advertising) will increase by $80,000 (4,000 units x $20 profit margin per unit). Hence the firm's net profits will increase by $30,000 (increase in gross profits – incremental cost of advertising = $80,000 – $50,000). Thus, an advertising budget of $150,000 is superior to an advertising budget of $100,000.

Table 14.4
An Example of the Relationships among Advertising Budgets, Reach, and Volume Sold

Advertising budget	Maximum reach across media	Units sold
$100,000	100	20,000
$150,000	130	24,000
$200,000	140	25,000

► *What will happen if the advertising budget is increased further from $150,000 to $200,000?*

Now the number of units sold will increase by an additional 1,000 units, and gross profits (before paying for the additional advertising) will increase by $20,000 (1,000 units × $20 profit margin per unit). Since the increase in sales revenue is not large enough, the firm's net profits will fall by $30,000 ($20,000 − [$200,000 − $150,000]).

Hence the optimal advertising budget is $150,000.

Fusion for Profit Maxim

The firm can simultaneously choose the optimal advertising budget and the optimal media plan if the relationships between advertising and reach and between reach and sales are known.

► *14.5 Measuring Media Productivity Using Gross Rating Point Models*

In the previous section, we focused on reach models that implicitly assume that only the first advertising exposure affects the consumer; that is, all repetition is a waste of resources for the firm. *If repetition matters, the firm should not use the reach criterion.*

Suppose repetition makes a difference; in addition, the firm uses several media. How should the firm choose its media plan?

One approach is to use gross rating points (GRPs). The GRP for a given medium is defined as the total number of exposures (reach × frequency) for that medium. Thus, suppose the firm advertises using two media: TV and magazines. Suppose the GRPs for the TV and magazine schedules are, respectively, 100 and 50. Then, the GRP for the media plan is the sum of the GRPs generated across media (150).

▶ *Can the firm use the GRP criterion for simultaneously choosing the advertising budget and the media plan?*

The firm can do this provided it knows the relationship between GRP and sales.

▶ *How useful is the GRP criterion for choosing a media plan? Assume that the advertising budget is fixed.*

We distinguish two scenarios: the one-medium and the multimedia cases.

Single-Medium Case.   Suppose the firm uses one medium, TV, and can choose three different TV schedules for the same advertising expenditure. Each TV schedule provides 600 GRPs but offers a different combination of reach and frequency. Suppose the reach-frequency combinations for the three TV schedules are as shown in table 14.5.

▶ *Is it reasonable to conclude that all three media plans are equivalent because each plan generates the same GRP (600) and all three media plans cost the same?*

Suppose there are threshold effects. Then, one advertising exposure may be insufficient to get the product into the consumer's long-term memory. Thus, Plan 1 may have no effect at all on sales. Suppose excessive frequency leads consumers to counterargue (e.g., to focus on making price comparisons across brands), hence reducing the likelihood that they purchase the firm's product. Then, Plan 2 could be inferior to Plan 3 *even though both plans provide the same GRPs.*

Fusion for Profit Maxim

The GRP criterion assumes that only the total number of advertising exposures in a medium matter. This measure does not allow for threshold effects in a medium; in addition, it implies that high reach/low frequency schedules can be equivalent to low reach/high frequency schedules.

Table 14.5
A Comparison of Media Plans That Provide the Same Gross Ratings Points (GRPs)

Plan	Reach	Frequency	GRP
1	600	1	600
2	150	4	600
3	200	3	600

Multimedia Case.   Suppose the firm uses a multimedia plan (e.g., TV, newspapers, and magazines). *Summing GRPs across media implicitly assumes that advertising exposures are equivalent across media. The GRP criterion also assumes that the firm always gains from repeated exposures across media. These assumptions may not hold.* For instance, one should not add GRPs across media if some media are more credible than others.

Similarly, repetition may have different effects for new and mature products. Thus, for a new product, the firm may gain from repetition across media because repetition increases the probability that a consumer will buy the firm's product. In contrast, for an established brand, repetition across media could be redundant and could lead to counterargumentation. In such cases, an *increase* in GRPs could result in *lower* sales.

Fusion for Profit Maxim

The GRP criterion assumes that only the total number of advertising exposures across media matters. In addition, it assumes that the firm always gains from additional advertising exposures, both within a medium and across media.

▶ 14.6 How Much Should the Firm Be Willing to Pay for Advertising in a Given Medium Based on Standard Commercial Rating Scores?

So far, we have not considered the effect of measurement error on such intermediate measures of advertising productivity as reach and GRP. In practice, these measures are based on samples of consumers. Hence these measures are likely to be imprecise and may even be biased.

For example, suppose the firm uses awareness as the criterion for measuring advertising productivity. These awareness scores are often based on self-reported data and are therefore subject to error. Similarly, other measures such as reach, frequency, and gross rating points are also imprecise and can be biased.

We now ask the following question: How does measurement error in intermediate scores such as awareness affect the estimates of advertising productivity? And, how much should the firm be willing to pay to advertise in a given medium based on commercial rating scores such as the Nielsen ratings?

In this chapter we will focus on commercial ratings for conventional media. Chapter 21 discusses the case where the firm uses the Internet as an advertising medium or uses a combination media plan (Internet + conventional media).

▚ *Suppose the firm uses one medium only. How will measurement error affect the estimates of advertising productivity? Assume that the firm estimates advertising productivity based on the measured relationship between a standard commercial rating score for that medium and sales.*

Consider a hypothetical firm that manufactures a detergent, Klean. Suppose the firm uses a conventional medium (national TV advertising) and advertises Klean during a particular episode of *The Cosby Show* (say). Let's say that the Nielsen rating score for this episode is 15%.

Under ideal conditions, this Nielsen rating score will be correct on average (unbiased). Hence, intuitively one might expect that the firm will obtain unbiased estimates of advertising productivity by examining the relationship between the Nielsen rating score and Klean's sales. Interestingly, this will not be the case. *Even if* the Nielsen score is unbiased, the firm will underestimate the effect of advertising on the sales of Klean.[9] In fact, we can show the following results summarized in table 14.6.

Fusion for Profit Maxim

If the firm uses intermediate measures, the measures of advertising productivity will be biased, even in the best-case scenario where the intermediate measures are unbiased.

▚ *Suppose the firm uses multiple media. How will measurement error affect the estimates of advertising productivity? Assume that the firm estimates advertising productivity based on the measured relationship between the commercial rating scores for the different media and sales.*

In this case, as in the single-medium case, the estimated advertising productivities of the different media will be biased.

However, in contrast to the single-medium case, the directions and magnitudes of these biases cannot be determined a priori.[10]

Table 14.6
How Commercial Rating Scores Affect Estimates of Advertising Productivity

Commercial rating score	Effect on advertising productivity
Unbiased	Biased downward
Biased upward	Biased downward
Biased downward	Conditional

▶ *How can the firm address this measurement error problem?*

We will discuss this issue in the next section.

Point to consider.   Nielsen Media Research recently announced that it will soon introduce a new measure of advertising exposures that will allow ad buyers to know how many persons are watching commercials and not just programs.[11] How will this affect the demand for TV advertising spots?

Prior to the introduction of Nielsen's new measure of advertising exposures, advertisers had no alternative but to subjectively adjust the old Nielsen rating scores. This was necessary because ratings were based on programs, not on commercials. Hence, the advertiser's estimates of advertising exposure for its commercial in a given medium could have been unbiased, biased upward, or biased downward. We refer to these scenarios as Cases 1, 2, and 3.

To focus on essentials, we begin with the case where the advertiser uses a single advertising medium both before and after the new technology is introduced. Our analysis will draw heavily on the results shown in table 14.6.

Case 1.   Suppose that, prior to the introduction of the new technology, the advertiser's estimates of audience exposure to its commercial were correct on average (i.e., unbiased).[12] Since the new technology provides more precise rating scores, the firm's estimates of advertising productivity will increase. Hence the firm should be willing to pay more to advertise during the program than in the past.

Case 2.   Suppose that, prior to the introduction of the new technology, the advertiser's estimates of audience exposure were biased upward. Then, the advertiser would have underestimated advertising productivity more than the advertiser in Case 1. Hence, after the introduction of the new technology, the advertiser will make a bigger upward adjustment in its estimate of advertising productivity than the advertiser in Case 1. Thus, the advertiser should be willing to spend substantially more to advertise during the program than in the past.

Case 3.   For this scenario, prior to the introduction of the new technology, the advertiser's estimates of advertising exposure were biased downward. As previously discussed, the impact on the estimated advertising productivity is ambiguous. Hence, after the new technology is introduced, the impact on the firm's willingness to pay to advertise on the program will also be ambiguous.

Now suppose the advertiser uses a multiple-media advertising plan. Then, regardless of which of the three cases occurs, the impact of the old Nielsen metric on the firm's estimates of advertising productivity for any medium is ambiguous. Consequently, it is unclear how the new Nielsen metric will affect the advertiser's willingness to pay for TV spots.

Fusion for Profit Maxim

The effect of the new Nielsen metric on the demand for commercials depends critically on the magnitudes and directions of the past biases in advertisers' estimates of advertising exposures.

▶ 14.7 How Should the Firm Determine When to Purchase Advertising Space and How Much to Spend on It?

This is an important decision, especially for firms for which advertising represents a significant outlay. Consider the following decision facing an advertiser.

Every May or June the TV industry presells a significant proportion of advertising space (roughly 75%) of its prime-time ad inventory for the coming fall season that year.[13] Hence, advertisers have a choice of purchasing prime-time advertising space early in May or June (buying *up-front advertising*) or waiting until the fall season to purchase the advertising slots (*scatter ads*) that have not been presold in May or June.

Which advertising purchase strategy should the firm choose? To focus on essentials, we will assume that the firm's discount rate is zero; in addition, we will examine how the firm's risk attitude affects its advertising decision.

▶ How will a risk-neutral *firm decide whether to purchase advertising on the up-front market or on the scatter market?*

We begin with the case of a risk-neutral advertiser. Suppose that the advertiser is uncertain about the demand for its product. Specifically, suppose that in May the firm believes that, by advertising in a particular slot on NBC TV (say) in the fall, it will obtain the uncertain gross margins (before paying for advertising) listed in table 14.7.

Suppose that in May the up-front advertising cost for the NBC fall TV slot is $100,000. Then, by purchasing the fall TV slot in advance, the advertiser will obtain an expected net profit of $50,000 (expected gross margin – up-front advertising cost).

An alternative strategy for the advertiser is to wait until the fall and, if necessary, purchase the ad slot in the fall at the prevailing scatter advertising rate. For simplicity, suppose the demand uncertainty is resolved in the fall prior to the purchase of the ad slot.

We begin with the case where the advertiser believes that the average price of the scatter ad in the fall will be the same as the up-front rate in May/June ($100,000). Then, the advertiser will reason as follows. Suppose it

Table 14.7
Gross Margins under Different Market Conditions

Market condition	Gross margin	Probability
Bad	$100,000	50%
Good	$200,000	50%
Expected gross margin	$150,000	

Table 14.8
Net Profits under Different Market Conditions

Market condition	Net profit	Probability
Bad	$0	50%
Good	$100,000	50%
Expected net profit	$50,000	

purchases an ad in the scatter market in the fall. If the market condition at that time is bad, the net profit margin after paying the expected advertising cost will be zero. Hence the optimal policy will be not to purchase advertising space on the scatter market. However, if the market condition at that time is good, the net profit margin after paying advertising costs will be positive. Hence the firm will purchase a scatter ad at that time.

Thus, by waiting for the demand uncertainty to be resolved in the fall, the advertiser anticipates the following net *cash flows* in the fall (after paying advertising costs) at that time as shown in table 14.8.

Since both advertising purchase strategies provide the same expected net profit ($50,000), the risk-neutral firm will be indifferent to purchasing the advertising slot in May/June or waiting until the demand uncertainty is resolved in the fall.

Suppose the risk-neutral firm anticipates that the expected price on the market for scatter ads in the fall will be lower than the up-front advertising cost ($100,000). Then, the firm's expected net profit from using a waiting strategy will be greater than $50,000. Hence the firm will not purchase ad slots on the up-front market.

Similarly, if the risk-neutral firm anticipates that the expected price on the market for scatter ads in the fall will be greater than $100,000, it will purchase ad space on the up-front market. Note that, since the advertiser is risk-neutral, the future *volatility* of prices on the scatter market is irrelevant—only the expected price for scatter ads in the future matters.

Fusion for Profit Maxim

The risk-neutral firm will decide whether to purchase up-front advertising or scatter ads based on the average scatter ad rate that it expects in the future. If the average scatter ad rate is lower than the up-front advertising rate, the firm should postpone its advertising decision and purchase a scatter ad in the future.

▶ *How will a* risk-averse *firm decide whether to purchase advertising on the up-front market or on the scatter market?*

To focus on essentials, consider the case where the up-front advertising cost is $100,000 and the expected advertising cost on the scatter market is also

$100,000. For this scenario, as in the risk-neutral case, both advertising purchase strategies will lead to the same expected profits for the advertiser ($50,000). However, the advertiser is risk-averse. Hence the advertiser is concerned about *both* expected profit and risk. Consequently, the advertiser will compare the advertising purchase strategies based on their *certainty-equivalent profits* (expected net profits – risk adjustment) and *not* on the basis of their expected net profits alone.

Suppose the advertiser buys advertising on the up-front market. Then, the advertiser faces demand uncertainty; however, it faces no uncertainty in advertising costs. Since future revenues and hence profits are uncertain, the certainty-equivalent profit by purchasing up-front advertising will be lower than the expected net profits ($50,000) from this strategy. Furthermore, the more uncertain demand is, the lower the certainty-equivalent profit will be. This implies that, other factors remaining the same, the more uncertain demand is, the greater the gain from waiting until demand uncertainty is resolved. Thus, the risk-averse advertiser is less likely to purchase advertising on the up-front market.

Suppose the risk-averse firm chooses a waiting strategy and buys advertising in the future on the scatter market. Then, the firm will face both demand uncertainty and uncertainty in advertising costs.

Consider any given level of demand uncertainty. Then, the greater the uncertainty in advertising rates in the scatter market, the more risky it is to wait and purchase advertising in the future. That is, the certainty-equivalent profit from waiting is lower.

Hence we have the following results. If demand is highly uncertain, other factors being the same, the risk-averse firm is more likely to purchase advertising on the scatter market. If advertising costs are highly uncertain, other factors being the same, the risk-averse firm is more likely to purchase up-front advertising.

Fusion for Profit Maxim

The risk-averse firm's decision whether to purchase up-front advertising depends on how demand uncertainty and advertising-rate uncertainty affect the variability of the firm's cash flows.

▶ *What other factors should the advertiser consider when deciding whether to purchase up-front advertising or to buy ad spots later on the scatter market?*

When deciding when to purchase advertising, the firm should consider several factors in addition to its risk-return trade-off.

Interindustry Effects

Demand uncertainty varies considerably across industries. Hence there will be significant industry-specific differences in the demand for up-front advertising. Other factors being the same, firms in industries with highly uncertain demand should wait until demand uncertainty is resolved. Hence they should purchase advertising on the scatter market.

Intra-industry Effects

Even within an industry, demand uncertainty is likely to vary across firms. Thus, demand uncertainty will vary depending on whether the firm's product is branded or generic, new or established, and whether the firm is pursuing conservative or aggressive marketing policies (e.g., retaining existing customers or obtaining new customers). Hence different scenarios are possible. In general, other factors being the same, the higher the demand uncertainty facing the firm, the more likely it is that the firm should purchase advertising on the scatter market.

Advertising Policies

A firm's choice of advertising purchase strategy will vary depending on the role of advertising in its marketing mix. For example, suppose the firm is in an advertising-intensive industry. Alternatively, suppose the firm has a higher *advertising-sales ratio* than its competitors (e.g., the firm sells to a less price-sensitive segment than its competitors). These scenarios imply that the firm will face high profit uncertainty if it purchases advertising in the future at uncertain scatter ad prices. Consequently, other factors remaining the same, the firm should choose the lower-risk strategy of purchasing advertising on the up-front market.

Generics and Branded Products

In many industries, generics have lower advertising-sales ratios than firms that sell branded products. This implies that demand uncertainty has a larger effect on profit fluctuations for generics than does advertising-rate uncertainty. Consequently, other factors being the same, generics will be more likely than branded products to purchase ad space in the scatter ad market.

Firm Size

The effect of firm size on the firm's advertising decision depends on the risk aversion of the firm, the magnitudes of demand and advertising-rate uncertainty, and the advertising intensiveness of the industry (e.g., the firm's advertising-sales ratio). Hence different scenarios are possible.

Suppose large firms face greater demand uncertainty than small firms. For example, suppose small firms target stable niche segments whereas large firms focus on market growth. Then, other factors being the same, large firms will gain more by waiting for the demand uncertainty to be resolved. This effect suggests that large firms should wait and purchase advertising on the scatter ad market in the future.

However, suppose large firms also have higher advertising-sales ratios than small firms. Then, other factors being the same, large firms have an incentive to use the safer strategy of purchasing advertising on the up-front market. Note that both factors have opposite effects on the firm's strategy. As this example illustrates, it is difficult to generalize how firm size will affect the firm's decision to participate in the up-front or scatter ad market.

Fusion for Profit Maxim

The firm's decision to purchase up-front or scatter ads will depend on the firm's marketing strategy, the target segment, whether the firm's product is branded or generic, where the *product* or brand is in its *life cycle*, whether the firm is pursuing a conservative or aggressive policy, and the size of the firm.

▲ *How does competitive reaction affect the firm's decision whether to purchase up-front advertising or scatter advertising?*

Consider two advertisers that are in an industry with uncertain demand and in which firms advertise heavily (e.g., Procter & Gamble and Colgate-Palmolive). Since advertising expenditures are significant, each firm has an incentive to purchase advertising in the scatter ad market after the demand uncertainty is resolved. However, this strategy is unlikely to be optimal.

Specifically, by purchasing an ad on the up-front advertising market, each firm can preempt its competitor (e.g., by purchasing a preferred ad spot). Consequently, in the face of competitive reaction, the optimal strategy for each firm may be to purchase advertising on the up-front market—*even if demand is highly uncertain and the advertising-sales ratio is high.*[14]

Fusion for Profit Maxim

The optimal strategy for the firm may be to preempt its competitors by purchasing up-front advertising. The gain from this preemptive strategy can be large, especially in markets where the advertising-sales ratio is high.

▶ *How does the ownership structure of the firm affect the firm's decision to purchase up-front advertising or scatter advertising?*

The ownership structure of the firm can have a major effect on the firm's advertising purchasing strategy. The key point is that owners of publicly held firms can diversify more fully than owners of privately held firms. Hence, for any given market conditions, the risk-return trade-off will vary depending on the ownership structure of the firm.

For privately held firms, demand uncertainty is based solely on the volatility of revenue. Similarly, advertising uncertainty is based on the volatility of advertising costs. In contrast, for publicly held firms, the corresponding measures of volatility are based on the degree to which revenues and/or advertising costs are correlated with the *return on the market portfolio* (i.e., the return that an investor can obtain by holding a fully diversified portfolio of assets across the economy). As discussed below, this is a critical distinction. In our analysis, we shall distinguish between single-product and multiproduct firms.

Single-Product Firms.   Consider two firms that operate in the same industry. One is privately held (Alpha) and the other is publicly held (Beta). Suppose both firms face the same volatilities in revenue and scatter advertising rates. However, these revenues and advertising costs are uncorrelated to the return on the market portfolio. In addition, suppose the expected price of scatter advertising is the same as the up-front advertising rate ($100,000). By assumption, the owners of both firms are risk-averse.

Let's say that both Alpha and Beta purchase advertising on the up-front market. Suppose the expected net profits for both firms after paying up-front advertising costs are $50,000. Since Alpha is privately held, its owners have limited diversification opportunities and cannot eliminate risk. Hence the certainty-equivalent profits for Alpha is *lower* than the expected net profit ($50,000). In contrast, since Beta is publicly held, its owners can diversify across assets in the economy. Consequently, since revenues are uncorrelated to the return on the market portfolio, Beta's stockholders can eliminate all profit uncertainty. Hence, in contrast to Alpha, the certainty-equivalent profit for Beta if it purchases up-front advertising *equals* the expected profit ($50,000) from this strategy.

Suppose both firms use a waiting strategy and purchase scatter ads in the fall. Let's say that the expected gross profit for both firms before paying advertising costs is $150,000, and the expected scatter advertising rate is the same as the up-front advertising rate ($100,000). Furthermore, the scatter advertising rates are uncorrelated to the return on the market portfolio.

Hence the certainty-equivalent profit to Beta (the publicly held firm) is the same as the corresponding expected profit if it purchases advertising on the up-front market ($50,000). Consequently, Beta will be indifferent to purchasing up-front advertising or waiting and purchasing advertising later in the scatter market.

▶ *Which strategy will the privately held firm Alpha choose?*

As discussed earlier, regardless of which advertising purchase strategy Alpha uses, Alpha's owners cannot eliminate risk by diversifying. Suppose demand is highly volatile compared with scatter advertising rates. Then, the gain to Alpha from waiting until demand uncertainty is resolved will outweigh the additional risk that Alpha will face in the future by paying an uncertain price for scatter advertising. Hence, in contrast to Beta, it is very likely that Alpha will choose to wait and purchase advertising in the scatter market.[15]

Multiproduct Firms

We continue with the Alpha and Beta example. Suppose each firm produces several products. Specifically, the demand for each product and the scatter advertising rates that each firm faces are uncertain. In addition, suppose that the revenues for all products and the scatter advertising rates are uncorrelated to the return on the market portfolio.

Given this scenario, regardless of which advertising purchase strategy Beta uses, its stockholders can eliminate all risk by diversifying. Hence Beta will behave like a risk-neutral firm. Specifically, Beta's stock price will be maximized if Beta chooses that policy which maximizes its expected profits.

In contrast, since Alpha is privately held, its owners cannot eliminate risk by diversification. Hence, regardless of which advertising strategy Alpha uses, its owners are faced with risk. Thus, if Alpha purchases up-front advertising, it faces demand uncertainty for all products. Alternatively, if Alpha purchases scatter advertising in the future, it faces uncertainty resulting from fluctuations in advertising rates. Consequently, in contrast to Beta, Alpha's advertising purchasing decision is based on Alpha's expected product-line profits *and* on the volatility of these product-line profits.

These results imply that, as in the single-product case, Alpha and Beta should choose different advertising purchase strategies.

Fusion for Profit Maxim

In general, privately and publicly held firms should choose different advertising purchase strategies, even if they face the same demand and advertising-rate uncertainties.

▶ *How will the Internet affect the prices of up-front and scatter ads?*

The answer will depend on the combined effect of a number of factors. In general, these factors can have different qualitative effects on the prices of up-front and scatter ad rates. For example, consider the following factors.

Supply Effects

Suppose that, in view of increasing competition from Internet advertising, TV networks reduce the number of up-front ad slots that they sell. This reduction in supply will put upward pressure on advertising rates for up-front TV network slots. On the other hand, by definition, the Internet will increase the pool of scatter advertising space available to advertisers in the future. This will put downward pressure on the price of scatter TV ads.

Demand Effects

Consider a firm in the packaged goods industry. Alternatively, consider a firm in the high-tech industry that is planning to introduce an innovative new product for sale in the mass market. An important goal for both types of firms is for their products to enter consumers' *consideration sets* (e.g., by creating brand or product awareness in the population). To achieve this goal, both firms should allocate a high proportion of their advertising budgets to network TV advertising and a small proportion to Internet advertising. Consequently, the Internet is likely to have a limited effect on the firms' decisions on whether to purchase up-front or scatter ads on television.

Alternatively, consider a firm that targets a specialized market segment. Then, it may be efficient for the firm to reach this segment via the Internet rather than through TV networks. Hence the firm should revise its media plan and allocate a high proportion of its advertising budget to Internet advertising and a lower proportion to TV advertising. Thus, the firm should reduce its demand for TV advertising (up-front or scatter).

Advertising-Rate Uncertainty

The effect of the Internet on advertising-rate uncertainty in the scatter ad market will depend on a number of factors, including how rapidly Internet advertising space increases in the future. For example, suppose Internet advertising space increases rapidly, and this leads to a decrease in advertising-rate uncertainty on the scatter ad market. Then, other factors being the same, advertisers will prefer to advertise on the scatter market. This will reduce the demand for up-front advertising and put downward pressure on up-front advertising rates. Since more firms will advertise on the scatter market, this will put upward pressure on scatter ad rates.

Fusion for Profit Maxim

The effect of the Internet on up-front and scatter advertising rates will depend on the combined effect of changes in supply and demand and advertising-rate uncertainty.

▸ *14.8 Measuring Media Productivity Using Sales Models*

As discussed, intermediate measures such as reach, GRP, and standard rating scores are likely to contain measurement error. Consequently, by using these measures, the firm may not obtain accurate estimates of advertising productivity.

▸ *If reach and GRP models are limited, what alternative method can the firm use in choosing a media plan?*

As discussed, both reach and GRP models make strong assumptions about advertising productivity. The *reach model* implies that multiple exposures both within and across media are irrelevant. The *GRP model* implies that, within a given medium, different combinations of reach and frequency generate equivalent results. Furthermore, audience duplication across media is irrelevant (e.g., GRPs can be summed across media).

We now present a more general method for measuring media productivity. For simplicity, we consider the case where the firm advertises using two media. The method can be generalized to the case where the firm uses multiple-media vehicles.

Example: Suppose a cosmetics manufacturer (say L'Oreal) advertises its hair colorant product, ColorSpa, monthly in two media, *Cosmopolitan* magazine and NBC television. In addition, L'Oreal has historical data on monthly sales and media spending for ColorSpa. Let's say that the average monthly sales for ColorSpa are the sum of three effects: the direct effect of advertising in *Cosmopolitan* (A), the direct effect of advertising on NBC (B), and the joint effect of advertising in *Cosmopolitan* and on NBC (C).[16]

We say that the relationship among the sales of ColorSpa and these three media effects (A, B, and C) is the *sales response function*. To understand the managerial implications of this specification, we begin with the simple case where ColorSpa advertises only in one medium, say *Cosmopolitan* magazine ($B = 0$, $C = 0$). Now, by specifying a flexible relationship between ColorSpa's sales and ColorSpa's advertising expenditure in *Cosmopolitan* (A), we can allow for threshold effects.[17] (As discussed previously, threshold effects are important, since advertising will have no value unless the advertising message gains a foothold in the consumer's long-term memory.) In addition, we can specify that the relationship between advertising expenditure in *Cosmopolitan* and ColorSpa's sales is nonlinear. As previously discussed, this is necessary in order to obtain plausible estimates of advertising productivity.[18]

We now consider the general case where ColorSpa advertises using both media, *Cosmopolitan* magazine and NBC television ($A > 0$ and $B > 0$).

- If $C = 0$, this implies that there is no audience overlap between *Cosmopolitan* magazine and NBC television. Hence advertising in each medium has a separate effect on sales.

- If $C < 0$, this implies that audience overlap across media is a waste (the whole is less than the sum of the parts). This is consistent with reach models, which implicitly assume that multiple exposures across media are redundant.
- If $C > 0$, this implies that repeated exposures across media reinforce the effects of advertising in either medium (e.g., each medium provides different types of information about ColorSpa).

Note that the model is general because it can allow for nonlinear and threshold effects (that can vary across media); in addition, it allows for general audience duplication effects across media.

Fusion for Profit Maxim

If the firm has historical data on sales and media spending, it can measure the productivity of its multimedia plan without using intermediate criteria such as reach and GRP.

Point to consider.   Suppose billboard advertising makes TV advertising more productive. However, billboard advertising alone has no effect on sales. In contrast, suppose TV advertising is effective, even if there is no billboard advertising. Can the model capture such asymmetric media effects?

This is a special case of the general model discussed above. Suppose the direct effects of billboard and TV advertising are A and B, respectively. In addition, the joint effect of advertising on billboards and on TV is C. If advertising on billboards alone has no effect on sales, this implies that $A = 0$. Hence, the model can capture the asymmetric media effects mentioned above.

▲ 14.9 Dynamic Carryover Effects

For simplicity, we have focused on estimating media mix effects for a single period. However, in real-world applications, it is necessary to allow for dynamic carryover effects. To capture these effects, one can allow both the firm's previous sales history and the firm's current media plan to affect current sales.[19] Once the augmented model has been estimated, the firm can simultaneously choose the current advertising budget and the optimal media allocation plan.

Chapter 14 Key Points
- The firm should choose an empirical method for measuring advertising productivity that allows for threshold and nonlinear effects. The threshold and nonlinear effects of advertising will vary according to

the type of product, the firm's segmentation strategy, and the level of advertising spending.

- When estimating advertising productivity, the firm should allow for the effects of other marketing decision variables such as pricing. In addition, the firm should explicitly allow for the effects of competitors' marketing policies on the sales of its products.
- If there is an anchoring effect, increases in advertising spending and equivalent decreases in advertising spending will have different effects on sales.
- Empirical studies should allow for reverse causality and data-intervalling bias. Using unadjusted accounting data may lead to incorrect estimates of how advertising affects sales.
- The firm can simultaneously choose the optimal advertising budget and the optimal media plan if the relationships between advertising and reach and between reach and sales are known.
- Commercial rating scores can lead to poor measures of advertising productivity, even if these scores are unbiased.
- In general, privately and publicly held firms should choose different advertising purchase strategies, even if they face the same demand and advertising-rate uncertainties.
- The effect of the Internet on up-front and scatter advertising rates will depend on the combined effect of changes in supply and demand and advertising-rate uncertainty.
- Standard measures of media mix productivity (such as awareness and gross rating points) may not lead to optimal results. A better approach may be to directly estimate the advertising-sales relationship by choosing a flexible specification that includes standard methods (such as reach and GRP models) as special cases.

VIII

How to Choose Compensation Plans

15

How Should the Firm Compensate Managers to Maximize Performance?

In previous chapters, we have focused on how the firm should choose the optimal marketing policy. Of course, if the firm is privately held and is managed by the owner, the owner will always seek to choose the optimal policy.

If the firm is publicly held, ownership and management will be separated. Hence there is a potential for goal conflict unless the appropriate managerial incentive schemes are in place.

This raises a fundamental question. How should the owners of privately and publicly held firms compensate managers so that they choose marketing policies and strategies that maximize the owners' well-being? This chapter focuses on how compensation plans can be chosen to achieve this goal.

The information covered in this chapter will be useful when you are faced with the following types of decisions:

- How should my firm compensate managers if it has one product and the appropriate time horizon is short (one period)?
- How should my firm compensate managers if it has one product and the appropriate time horizon is long (multiperiod)?
- How should my firm compensate managers if it has multiple products and the appropriate time horizon is short (one period)?
- How should my firm compensate managers if it has multiple products and the appropriate time horizon is long (multiperiod)?
- Should Wall Street's expectations affect my firm's compensation policy?

- What roles should the finance department and senior management play in determining the compensation plans for other managers in the multidivisional or multiproduct firm?

The following terms will be introduced in this chapter (see glossary for definitions):

certainty-equivalent profits	demand structure	net present value
cost dynamics	diffusion	planning horizon
cost of capital	discount rate	profit-sharing plan
cost structure	downside risk	realized future profit
cross-couponing	economies of scope	strategic pricing
cross-product effects	exercise price	top-down approach
cross-product marketing interdependencies	fixed costs	two-part stock option plan
deferred stock options	incremental cost	volume-based market share
demand dynamics	learning curve marginal cost marginal revenue	

◤ 15.1 The Single-Product Firm: Short-Run Horizon

We begin with the case of a firm that sells one product only.

◤ Should the firm compensate the manager based on current profits?

The answer depends on the firm's *cost and demand structures* and on the firm's *planning horizon*.

Suppose the firm's current marketing policies do not affect future demand or cost conditions for the product. Alternatively, suppose the firm is privately owned and the owner has a single-period planning horizon. Then, the firm should compensate the manager based on short-run profits.

Special Cases

Suppose the *incremental cost* of producing higher volume is zero (e.g., the firm sells an information product such as software). Alternatively, suppose incremental costs are small in comparison to *fixed costs* (e.g., the music industry). Then, maximizing revenue-based market share (after adjusting for risk) will lead to maximum short-run profits (see chapter 4).

Point to consider. For most products, incremental costs vary with volume and are not small with respect to fixed costs. Suppose the firm compensates the manager based on revenue-based market share. Will the manager choose the optimal marketing policy?

Short-run profit maximization requires the manager to choose marketing policies so that the marginal profitability (*marginal revenue – marginal cost*) of the product is zero. (This analysis assumes certainty. We will discuss the effects of cost and demand uncertainty later in this chapter.) For the current scenario, marginal cost is positive regardless of volume. Hence profit maximization implies that, when the optimal policy is chosen, marginal revenue should also be positive.

But if the manager's compensation increases with revenue, he or she will set price such that revenue is maximized (i.e., marginal revenue = 0). This implies that, for the price chosen, marginal profit will be negative. That is, profits would have been higher if the manager had charged a higher price. Consequently, *if the manager is rewarded based on revenue-based market share, the manager will always underprice.*

Fusion for Profit Maxim

Suppose the firm's current marketing policies will not affect future cost or demand. Then, regardless of whether the firm is privately owned or publicly held, the firm should compensate the manager on the basis of short-term profits and not on the basis of market share.

▶ 15.2 The Single-Product Firm: Long-Run Horizon

Suppose the firm's current marketing policies will affect future cost or demand conditions. That is, there are *cost dynamics* or *demand dynamics*. For instance, the firm has a *learning curve* (i.e., future costs fall as current volume increases). Alternatively, suppose future demand depends on the firm's current pricing policy (e.g., a higher current volume increases future demand via *diffusion*). In addition, the firm has a multiperiod horizon.

Given these conditions, the optimal strategy for the firm may be to forgo some current profits in order to increase future profits.[1] (See chapters 4 and 5 for a detailed discussion of cost and demand dynamics.)

Fusion for Profit Maxim

Suppose the firm's current marketing policies affect future cost or demand conditions. Then, the firm should not compensate the manager based on short-run profits.

▶ *Suppose there are cost dynamics or demand dynamics. Can the firm use a short-run metric to compensate managers so that they focus on long-run performance? Assume that costs and demand are certain.*

One useful metric for the privately held firm with a long planning horizon and for the publicly held firm that seeks to maximize shareholder value is *volume-based market share.*

Cost Dynamics

Cost dynamics implies that the firm's future costs depend on the firm's current volume. Note that cost dynamics can occur in any industry and not just in manufacturing. For example, cost dynamics can be highly significant in information goods industries and in service industries such as consulting.

Suppose cost dynamics are strong. This implies that the firm should sacrifice some short-run profits in order to increase future profits. Hence current volume-based market share can be a good proxy for future profits.

Example 1: Let's say that Nissan has developed a new manufacturing process to make cars. Suppose there is a predictable learning effect as Nissan's workers become more familiar with the new production technology. Then, the higher Nissan's current production is, the lower Nissan's future costs will be as a result of its experience. Hence Nissan should compensate its managers based on volume-based market share.

Example 2: In the 1960s, the Japanese motorcycle industry was capital-intensive and was characterized by a steep but fairly predictable learning curve in manufacturing. Thus, companies such as Honda set volume-based market share targets for their managers. This compensation strategy helped Honda increase its long-run performance.

In contrast, U.S.-based motorcycle manufacturers (e.g., Harley Davidson) used traditional labor-intensive methods to produce their motorcycles. Furthermore, the learning effects in production had already taken place. Hence, other factors being held constant, U.S.-based motorcycle manufacturers should have compensated their managers on the basis of short-term profits and not on the basis of volume.

Fusion for Profit Maxim

If cost dynamics are predictable, current volume can be a good proxy for long-run profits. Hence it is appropriate for the firm to use volume-based market share (a short-run metric) to compensate its managers. One implication is that, if firms in the industry use different production processes, they should not use industry-based metrics to compensate their managers.

Demand Dynamics

Suppose the current marketing policies for a product affect the product's future demand. Then, volume-based market share can be a proxy for long-run profits.

Example: Suppose Procter & Gamble (P&G) introduces a new type of toothpaste, Smyle, into the marketplace. Then, the introductory price for Smyle will affect the number of first-time triers. This, in turn, will affect the volume of repeat purchases of Smyle in the future—that is, there are demand dynamics.

Hence, as in the cost dynamics case, it may be optimal for P&G to forgo some short-run profits in exchange for higher profits in the future. Thus, it is appropriate for P&G to use volume-based market share as a proxy for long-run profits.

Fusion for Profit Maxim

If demand dynamics are present, current volume can be a good proxy for long-run profits. Hence it is appropriate for the firm to use volume-based market share to compensate its managers.

▶ *Suppose cost and demand dynamics effects are uncertain. How should the firm compensate managers so that they focus on long-run performance?*

In many cases, the effects of cost and demand dynamics will be uncertain. For example, the firm may not be able to predict exactly what the future cost savings from learning will be if it increases its current volume (e.g., the technology involved is new). Similarly, for any given marketing policy, the firm may not be able to predict the repeat purchase rate with a high degree of accuracy (e.g., the product is new to the market).

Suppose the firm is privately held. One strategy to address this problem of uncertainty stemming from cost and demand dynamics is to compensate the manager using a profit-sharing plan in which the manager's future income is based on *realized future profits* and not on current volume-based market share (an imprecise proxy for uncertain future profits).

Note that, under this profit-sharing compensation plan, the privately held firm will share the risk from future profits with the manager. Consequently, the firm will need to pay the manager a higher expected income than if the firm had compensated the manager based on current volume-based market share (an imprecise short-term metric for measuring future profits).

Suppose the firm is publicly held. As discussed below, the publicly held firm can use a *deferred stock options* plan to encourage the manager to focus on long-run performance.

Consider the Nissan example. Suppose the cost and demand dynamics effects for the new car are uncertain; in addition, these effects are likely to occur over a three-year period. Given these cost and demand uncertainties, to encourage the manager to focus on long-run performance, Nissan can proceed as follows. Offer the manager a three-year employment contract based on a *two-part stock option plan* consisting of an annual salary and stock options. For instance, Nissan can offer the manager an annual salary of $200,000 plus the option to purchase up to a specified number of shares (say 10,000 shares) at a fixed *exercise price* (say $40 per share) at any time during the second or third years of the contract.

▶ *Will this two-part compensation plan encourage the manager to focus on long-term performance?*

Suppose Nissan's manager chooses the optimal long-run marketing policy after allowing for the uncertain effects of cost and demand dynamics on future profits. Then, Nissan's profits in the first year will be lower, on average, than the profits that Nissan could have obtained by focusing on short-term profits. However, because of the gains from cost and demand dynamics, Nissan's future profits after adjusting for risk (i.e., the *certainty-equivalent profit*) should increase. As a result, let's say Nissan's stock price should increase to $70 per share during the third year.

▶ *What will the manager do in the third year?*

During the third year, the manager can exercise his or her option of buying 10,000 shares of Nissan's stock at the exercise price of $40. If the manager decides to sell the stock at the prevailing market price, he or she can sell the stock for $70 per share. Hence the manager can make a profit of $300,000 (number of shares purchased × profit per share = 10,000 × ($70 − $40)).

Note that, under the deferred stock option plan, the manager will face more uncertainty than the manager would face if he or she were paid based on a short-run metric (e.g., current volume-based market share). Thus, Nissan's future stock price will depend on the realized future profits. If these future profits are not sufficiently high, Nissan's stock price during the second and third years could be less than $40 per share. If this happens, the stock options will have no value to the manager. Consequently, to compensate the manager for this additional risk, as in the case of the privately held firm, the publicly held firm (Nissan) will need to pay the manager a higher expected income, on average.

> **Fusion for Profit Maxim**
>
> If cost or demand dynamics are uncertain, the privately held firm can offer the manager a profit-sharing plan in the future. The publicly held firm can compensate its manager using a deferred stock option plan to encourage the manager to focus on long-run performance.

Point to consider.   Suppose cost and demand dynamics are uncertain. How should the publicly held firm design a two-part stock option plan?

The answer depends on the length of the managerial contract and the extent to which it is necessary for the firm to "insure" the manager against *downside risk*.

Length of Managerial Contract

As discussed, the benefits from cost and demand dynamics are likely to be uncertain. This implies that the firm will share more risk with the manager if it uses the two-part stock option plan. Hence, other factors being the same, the firm will prefer to pay the manager using a stock option plan. However, for this compensation strategy to work, the firm will need to offer the manager a long-run contract of the appropriate duration (i.e., the time period over which the cost and demand dynamics effects are likely to occur).

Suppose the firm does not plan to give the manager a long-run contract. Then, it may be necessary for the firm to compensate the manager based on a short-run metric such as the volume-based market share.

Base Salary

If the firm uses a two-part stock option plan, the manager's downside risk will be limited. Specifically, except in the extreme case where the firm becomes bankrupt, the manager will be paid a guaranteed minimum amount (i.e., the base salary).

In contrast, shareholders face downside risk, since the share price could fall sharply (possibly to zero in the worst-case scenario) if the firm performs poorly. Since a two-part stock option plan limits the manager's downside risk, the manager has an incentive to take excessive risks (from a shareholder's viewpoint). In fact, unless the manager's base salary is sufficiently low, the manager may even choose projects or marketing policies that have the potential to make shareholders worse off (i.e., projects with negative *net present values*).

▶ *How can the firm address this potential conflict of interest?*

One strategy for the firm is to eliminate the base wage and pay the manager exclusively on the basis of deferred stock options.[2]

Example: Steve Jobs of Apple was paid an annual salary of $1. However, he was given the option to buy a large number of Apple shares. Since Jobs's future income was directly related to Apple's future stock price, there was no potential conflict of interest between Jobs and Apple's shareholders.

▶ *15.3 The Multiproduct Firm: Short-Run Horizon*

In most cases, the firm sells multiple products; furthermore, these products are likely to be related. For instance, the firm may use a common sales force to sell its products. Alternatively, some customers may buy more than one product from the firm. In addition, the marketing decisions of one manager may affect the performance of another manager but not vice versa. We say that there are *cross-product marketing interdependencies*. In such cases, the firm (privately or publicly held) should use a three-part formula to compensate the manager of each product: a fixed salary, a component that is based on the short-run profits from that product, and a component that is based on the short-run profits from related products.[3]

▲ 15.4 The Multiproduct Firm: Long-Run Horizon

We now discuss how the multiproduct firm should compensate its managers when the marketing policy of one product affects the performances of other products in the firm's product line. In addition, the current marketing policy for any product affects the future performance of that product (i.e., cost or demand dynamics are present). In our discussion, we shall assume that all costs and demands are uncertain.

▲ How should the multiproduct firm compensate its managers so that they maximize the long-run performance of the firm?

Suppose the firm produces many product lines; in particular, each manager is responsible for a given product line. For simplicity, we begin with a publicly held firm that produces two products for which there are no *economies of scope* (e.g., the customer groups for both products are distinct, and there are no joint costs). In our analysis, we shall assume that all costs and demand levels are uncertain.

Example: Let's say that Intel has developed a new generation of Pentium chips. Suppose the price of the new Pentium chip will affect the future growth rate of the market for that chip (i.e., demand dynamics are present). In addition, suppose there is a strong learning curve effect for the new chip (i.e., Intel's future costs will decline if current volume is increased). In contrast, there are no demand dynamics for the "old" Pentium chip. Furthermore, all gains from learning have already taken place for manufacturing the old chip.

In this case, Intel should give stock options to the manager of the new generation of Pentium chips so that the manager will focus on long-run profits. In contrast, Intel should compensate the manager of the old generation of Pentium chip based on current profits.

Now, suppose there are demand dynamics for *both* the old and the new Pentium chips. Alternatively, suppose both the old and the new Pentium chips are sold to common customers or that they share costs (e.g., both types of Pentium chip are sold by a common sales force). Now, the performance of each chip (old or new) will depend on the marketing policies chosen by *both* managers.

▲ What should Intel do to encourage the managers of the old and new Pentium chips to focus on long-run performance?

Intel should use a three-part compensation plan for the managers of *both* Pentium chips: a salary (A), a stock option plan (B), and a share of future profits from the chip for which the manager is responsible (C).

Note that, in general, the demand dynamics effects are likely to vary for the old and the new Pentium chips because each product is in a different phase of the product life cycle. Furthermore, the *cross-product effects* of marketing policies for the old and new chips are likely to be asymmetric. For instance, the marketing policy of the new Pentium chip may have a stronger effect on the sales of the old Pentium chip than vice versa. *Hence the relative importance of each of the three components of compensation (A, B, and C) should be different for the managers of the old and the new generations of Pentium chips.*

Point to consider.   Suppose AOL has two products lines. One product is paid subscriptions to AOL's Internet service, and the other is advertising revenue generated from ad placements on AOL's Web site. How should AOL compensate the managers of both product lines?

The marketing policy for one product line (paid subscriptions) affects the profitability of the other product line (ad placements) but *not vice versa.* Hence the relative importance of each of the components of compensation (A, B, and C) should be different for both AOL product managers.

Fusion for Profit Maxim

In general, the publicly held, multiproduct firm with related products should use a three-part compensation plan to reward the manager of each product.

Point to consider.   Suppose an Internet firm uses the Yahoo model of not charging consumers a fee for basic Internet service. What compensation plans should the firm use for the manager of the subscription unit?

This business model implies that the subscription division will not make any profits. However, advertising revenue increases with the number of subscribers. Hence it is reasonable for the Internet firm to compensate the manager of the subscription division on the basis of the number of subscribers (i.e., volume-based market share is a useful performance metric).

► Should privately held, multiproduct firms use the same compensation formula as publicly held multiproduct firms?

To encourage managers to focus on long-run performance, the privately held, multiproduct firm should also compensate its managers using a three-part formula. However, since the privately held firm is not traded in the marketplace, the firm cannot use a stock option plan.

Consequently, the three-part compensation formula for the manager of a particular product should include a fixed salary, a share of future profits from that product, and a share of future product-line profits. As in the case of the publicly held multiproduct firm, the profit-sharing rates need not be symmetric across product lines. For example, the profit-sharing rates should not be symmetric if the marketing policies of one product (division) affect the cash flows of another product (division) but not vice versa.

▲ 15.5 How Do Wall Street's Expectations Affect the Firm's Compensation Policy?

Wall Street puts pressure on publicly held firms to meet short-run performance metrics (e.g., quarterly profits). *Because of this pressure, managers implicitly use a high discount rate to value long-run profits.* Thus, managers are likely to place insufficient emphasis on the firm's future gains from cost and demand dynamics.

▲ Given Wall Street's focus on short-term profits, what incentive schemes should the firm use to encourage its managers to focus on long-run performance?

The firm should not use *profit-sharing/bonus plans* that are based on short-performance metrics (e.g., those used by Wall Street). Instead, to increase long-run performance, the firm should compensate managers by using one or more metrics that are proxies for long-run profits.

For example, since senior management is responsible for resource allocation decisions at the corporate level, the firm can use a deferred stock option plan to compensate these managers. Since other managers (e.g., product managers) have a limited effect on corporate performance, these managers should be compensated using a mixed plan where the performance component of income is based on revenue-based market share (as a proxy for future revenues when demand dynamics are present), volume (as a proxy for future costs when cost dynamics are present), or a combination of these metrics. These mixed plans can be refined using appropriate industry benchmarks if necessary.

▲ 15.6 What Roles Should the Finance Department and Senior Management Play in Determining the Firm's Compensation Plans?

Firms sometimes use a sequential approach to set market share or profit targets for managers. For example:

- The finance department or senior management determines what rate of return a given product or product line should produce.
- The finance department or senior management sets market share or profit targets for individual products or product lines.
- The marketing department chooses its marketing policy (e.g., pricing) based on the predetermined rates of return (discount rates).

As we have discussed, marketing policies (e.g., *strategic pricing*) often involve a trade-off between short-run and long-run profits. Different marketing policies imply different risk-return trade-offs. For instance, a market growth strategy may promise higher expected profits than a customer retention strategy but is likely to be much riskier. This implies that the discount rate for the market growth strategy should be higher than the corresponding rate for the customer retention strategy. Thus, *the firm should not proceed sequentially by first determining discount rates and then setting market share goals or profit targets for different products.*

An additional problem is that firms sometimes use a common discount rate (e.g., the firm's *cost of capital*) across products in order to be "fair." The danger with this method is that low-risk products will subsidize high-risk products. To address this problem, the firm should use different discount rates across products and market segments, since different marketing policies provide different combinations of risk and return.

Finally, as we have discussed, the firm's products are often interrelated either on the cost side or on the demand side. Consequently, *the firm should only set targets and choose managerial compensation plans after explicitly analyzing these interdependencies.*

Fusion for Profit Maxim

Firms should not use a *top-down*, sequential approach for determining compensation plans and setting market share or profit targets. The multiproduct firm should choose the compensation plans for its managers only after analyzing cost and demand dynamics for a given product, and cost or demand interdependencies across product lines.

Chapter 15 Key Points

- If cost or demand dynamics effects are significant and can be measured reasonably accurately, the firm should choose a managerial incentive plan that encourages managers to focus on building volume-based market share.
- If cost or demand dynamics effects are uncertain, volume-based market share will be an imprecise proxy of future profits. To address this problem, the privately held firm can compensate the manager based on the realized level of future profits. The publicly held firm can compensate the manager using a deferred stock option plan.
- In multidivisional firms, the marketing policies of one division may affect the performance of another division but not vice versa. In such cases, it may be optimal for the firm to pay divisional managers using a three-part compensation plan consisting of a fixed salary, a component that is tied to the division's performance, and a component that is tied to overall company performance.

- Given Wall Street's focus on short-run profits, the publicly held firm should use multipart incentive plans that tie the manager's compensation to long-run performance.
- Firms should not use a top-down sequential approach for setting goals and targets and determining the compensation plans for their managers. Optimal results can only be achieved by jointly analyzing cost and demand dynamics, the risks and returns from different market segments, and cross-product marketing interdependencies.

16

How Should the Firm Compensate Its Sales Force? The Basic Model

The previous chapter focused on the design of managerial compensation plans. In this chapter and the next, we analyze how the firm should compensate its sales force.

This chapter discusses sales force compensation strategies for the simple scenario where the firm produces one product and employs one sales agent. Chapter 17 focuses on the general case where the firm sells multiple products and/or employs many sales agents. In addition, it discusses what metrics the multiproduct firm should use to measure the performances of sales agents and to infer a sales agent's ability.

To focus on essentials, we will consider the case where the firm is privately owned. The analysis can be easily extended to the case where the firm is owned by shareholders.[1]

The information covered in this chapter will be useful when you are faced with the following types of decisions.

- How should my firm choose the optimal sales force compensation plan when the sales agent's effort can be observed?
- Should my firm pay the sales agent using a *draw* system?
- Should my firm pay the sales agent based on sales revenue or gross profits?
- How does my firm's *cost structure* affect the optimal sales force compensation plan?

- How should my firm compensate the sales agent if the sales agent has some control over the price of the product he or she sells?
- How should my firm revise its sales force compensation plan if it advertises on the Internet?
- How should my firm compensate the sales agent if it has hired the sales agent using a multiperiod contract?
- How does my firm's market segmentation policy affect the optimal sales force compensation plan?
- How should my firm choose the optimal sales force compensation plan when marketing policies have long-run (multiperiod) effects?

The following terms will be introduced in this chapter (see glossary for definitions):

capacity	hybrid sales-based	progressive slab system
certainty-equivalent	contract	pure commission plan
profit	income volatility	recoverable draw
competitive labor market	irrecoverable draw	regressive commission
constant absolute risk	learning curve	plan
aversion	linear cost structure	reservation income
cost of capital	linear profit-sharing plan	risk-adjusted equivalent
cost structure	market condition	risk-averse
discount rate	mixed wage-bonus plan	risk-neutral
downside risk	mixed wage-commission	sales call policy
draw	plan	sales revenue–based
economies of scale	net present value	contract
fixed wage contract	piece rate	time-additive utility
forcing contract	progressive commission	function
franchising	structure	volatility

◣ 16.1 Reservation Income

We begin with the case where the firm chooses the agent's *sales call policy* (i.e., the firm decides how the sales agent will allocate his or her time across customers) and the sales agent has no control over the price of the product. To address this issue, we need to introduce the concept of *reservation income*. In our discussion, we shall use the terms "sales agent" and "salesperson" interchangeably.

◣ What is the sales agent's reservation income?

Consider a sales agent with a given level of ability/productivity. Suppose the firm knows the sales agent's ability and can hire sales agents of this ability for $600 per day. We say that the sales agent has a reservation income of $600 per day. Then, if the firm pays less than $600 per day (or its equivalent), the sales agent will not work for the firm. If the firm pays the sales agent more than $600 per day, the firm is wasting its money.

► **How does the sales agent's reservation income affect the firm's compensation policy?**

We begin with the certainty case. That is, the relationship between sales effort and productivity is predictable. Suppose the sales agent has no control over the price of the product. (These assumptions will be relaxed later.)

Example: Suppose the gross profit margin is $50 per unit; furthermore, the sales agent can sell 100 units per day, assuming that he or she does not shirk. Hence the maximum gross profit the sales agent can produce per day is $5,000 (gross profit margin × number of units sold = 50 × 100). Assume that the sales agent's reservation income is $600 per day.

Given this scenario, the firm can pay the sales agent in many equivalent ways. One strategy is to pay the sales agent a *piece rate* (commission) of $6 per unit. Given this *pure commission plan*, the sales agent will not shirk. If the sales agent shirks, he or she will earn less than his or her reservation income ($600 per day).

Note that the firm can achieve the same result by paying the sales agent 12% of gross profits (5,000 × 12% = 600). Equivalently, the firm can assign the sales agent a daily quota of 100 units. If the sales agent sells 100 units, the agent gets paid $600. However, if fewer than 100 units are sold, the sales agent gets paid nothing. This compensation formula is known as a *forcing contract*. Yet another possibility is to use a *mixed wage-commission plan* (e.g., a base wage of $300 per day plus $3 per unit sold (300 + 3 × 100)).

Note that regardless of which contract the firm chooses, if the sales agent shirks, the agent will obtain less than his or her reservation income. Hence the firm will not need to monitor the sales agent's effort.

Fusion for Profit Maxim

If the sales agent has no control over price and the sales agent's productivity is predictable, the firm can pay the agent using a number of equivalent compensation plans (e.g., a forcing contract, a pure commission plan, and a mixed wage-commission plan). Furthermore, the firm does not need to monitor the sales agent's effort.

► **16.2 How Should the Firm Compensate Its Sales Agent if the Sales Agent's Effort Is Observable?**

In most cases, sales depend on many factors in addition to the sales agent's effort. For example, regardless of which industry the firm is in, the firm cannot predict exactly what prices its competitors will charge. Similarly, a durable goods manufacturer cannot predict what interest rates will be and exactly how these rates will affect the demand for its product. Consequently, regardless of the sales agent's effort, sales are uncertain.

▶ *Suppose the sales agent's productivity is uncertain. How should the firm pay the sales agent? Assume that the firm chooses the sales agent's sales call policy (i.e., the firm assigns the sales agent particular customers and can observe the agent's effort). In addition, the agent has no control over price.*

In the previous example, we considered the special case where the agent's productivity could be precisely measured. Specifically, the agent was able to sell 100 units per day with certainty. Now we consider the more realistic case where the sales agent's productivity is uncertain. That is, the agent can sell 100 units per day on average; however, sometimes the agent will sell fewer than 100 units, and at other times the agent will sell more than 100 units.

As we discuss below, when the sales agent's productivity is uncertain, the optimal contract will depend on the risk attitudes of the firm and the sales agent. Note that, by assumption, the sales agent's effort is observable. Hence, the agent will not shirk. (This assumption will be relaxed later.)

As shown in table 16.1, four scenarios are possible.

Scenario 1: Both the Firm and the Sales Agent Are Risk-Neutral

Since both the firm and the sales agent are *risk-neutral*, each party seeks to maximize its expected income. *Thus, neither party needs to insure the other against downside risk.* Because of this, as we discuss below, the firm can use multiple equivalent contracts.

Case 1. Suppose the firm pays the sales agent a guaranteed wage of $600 per day (Contract A). As discussed earlier, the expected gross income generated by the agent is $5,000 per day (unit profit margin × average number of units sold = 50 × 100). Hence the firm will obtain an expected income of $4,400 ($5,000 − $600) per day.

Table 16.1
Different Risk-Attitude Scenarios for the Firm and the Sales Agent

	Firm	Sales agent
Scenario 1	Risk-neutral	Risk-neutral
Scenario 2	Risk-neutral	Risk-averse
Scenario 3	Risk-averse	Risk-neutral
Scenario 4	Risk-averse	Risk-averse

Note that the sales agent is fully insured because the agent gets a guaranteed wage of $600 per day, regardless of whether sales are low or high. *Hence the firm bears all the risk.*

Case 2.   Suppose the firm pays the sales agent a commission of $6 per unit (Contract B). Then, the incomes of both the firm and the sales agent will be uncertain. Since the average (expected) number of units sold per day is 100, the sales agent will obtain an average (expected) income of $600. However, the agent's income will fluctuate, since the number of units sold on a particular day could be either above or below the average level (100 units). Since the expected gross income generated is unchanged ($5,000), the firm will obtain an expected income of $4,400 as in Contract A.

Note that Contracts A and B are equivalent because they generate equally preferred outcomes for both the firm and the sales agent.

Fusion for Profit Maxim

If both the firm and the sales agent are risk-neutral, neither party needs to insure the other. Hence the firm can use multiple equivalent contracts; in particular, it is not necessary for the firm to provide downside risk protection to the sales agent.

Scenario 2: The firm is risk-neutral, and the sales agent *is* risk-averse.

The risk-neutral firm seeks to maximize expected profit, *regardless of the volatility of income.* In contrast, the risk-averse sales agent is concerned about both expected income and *income volatility.* Since the firm does not care about income volatility, we would expect that the optimal strategy for the firm is to provide full downside risk protection to the sales agent by paying the agent a fixed wage that is equivalent to the agent's reservation income. This is indeed the case, as we show below.

One strategy for the firm is to pay the sales agent a fixed wage equal to the agent's reservation income ($600 per day) as in Contract A above. Since the average (expected) number of units sold is 100, the expected gross income generated is $5,000 per day. Hence the firm will earn an expected profit of $4,400 ($5,000 − $600). Note that, *under this fixed-wage plan the agent is fully insured.* That is, the firm bears all the risk.

Alternatively, the firm can share risk with the sales agent. Consider any arbitrary risk-sharing plan (e.g., a pure commission, a mixed wage-commission plan, or a *mixed wage-bonus plan*). Call this Contract C. Since the agent is risk-averse and Contract C requires the agent to assume some risk, the risk-averse sales agent's expected income must increase to $600 + X$, where X is a positive quantity. Since the expected gross profit is constant ($5,000), this implies that the firm's expected income will be reduced to $4,400 − X$.

However, for this scenario, the firm is risk-neutral and seeks to maximize its expected profits, regardless of income volatility. *Hence the firm will prefer the fixed-wage plan (Contract A) because it provides a higher expected profit than the risk-sharing plan (Contract C).*

Fusion for Profit Maxim

If the firm is risk-neutral but the sales agent is risk-averse, the optimal strategy for the firm is to absorb all the risk and pay the sales agent a fixed wage.

Point to consider. How should the risk-neutral firm pay the risk-averse sales agent if the sales agent's effort is not observable?

As discussed above, if the sales agent's effort is observable, the firm would like to provide the sales agent with full downside risk protection by offering a *fixed wage contract*. However, if the firm uses a fixed wage contract in the unobservable effort case, the sales agent will put in zero effort because the agent will get the fixed wage regardless of the outcome. (This analysis assumes that the sales agent has a single-period horizon. That is, the sales agent's future reservation income is unrelated to current performance.) To address this incentive problem, the firm has no alternative but to use some sort of risk-sharing plan (e.g., a pure commission plan or a mixed wage-quota-bonus plan).

▲ Will a risk-sharing plan eliminate shirking?

No matter which risk-sharing plan the firm uses, the sales agent will shirk to some degree, since the marginal value of leisure is always positive. Thus, the "unobservability" of effort leads to two harmful consequences for the firm:

1. Shirking (i.e., a loss in productivity), and
2. Suboptimal risk sharing.

Point to consider. How can the firm reduce the loss from shirking?

One strategy for the firm is to monitor the sales agent. In this case, the firm will need to balance the marginal gain in gross profits via reduced shirking with the increase in costs because of monitoring.

An alternative strategy is to charge the sales agent a large fee up front (negative fixed wage) and give the sales agent a share of the gross profits. Of course, this strategy is not feasible for most sales agents. However, this strategy is often used in *franchising*. In franchising contracts, the franchisee often pays a franchise fee up front and is paid a share of the gross profits/revenues generated.

Scenario 3: The firm is risk-averse, and the sales agent is risk-neutral.

Since the sales agent is risk-neutral, the agent is only concerned about expected income and does not care about fluctuations in income. However, the firm is risk-averse. Hence the firm is concerned about both expected income *and* fluctuations in income. Given this scenario, the agent should provide full downside risk protection to the firm. In our example, the optimal contract is as follows. The firm gets a flat fee of $4,400 ($5,000 – $600), and the sales agent keeps the remainder of the gross profits. Note that, depending upon the actual level of sales achieved, the sales agent will earn more or less than $600. However, on average, the agent's income will be $600.

On the surface this scenario appears to be unrealistic. However, consider the following example. Suppose the "firm" is a risk-averse individual with limited assets who owns a patent for a new product, and the "sales agent" is a large risk-neutral firm. Then, the optimal strategy for the large firm may be to purchase the patent from the patent holder for a fixed fee, market the product, and keep the remainder of the uncertain gross profits.

Fusion for Profit Maxim

If the firm is risk-averse and the sales agent is risk-neutral, the sales agent should absorb all the risk and pay the firm a flat fee regardless of the sales outcome.

Scenario 4: Both the firm and the sales agent are risk-averse.

This scenario is most likely in practice. That is, both the firm and the sales agent seek to balance their returns (expected incomes) and risks (the volatilities of income). In our example, assume for simplicity that for feasible changes in wealth levels, both the firm and the sales agent have constant *but different* risk attitudes. We say that the firm and the sales agent have *constant absolute risk aversions.*[2]

In most cases, the firm has more wealth than the sales agent. Since the firm is less risk-averse than the sales agent, it is more willing to take risk. Hence we would expect the firm to provide the sales agent with some downside risk protection (i.e., the compensation contract should include a fixed wage component). This is indeed the case. Specifically, since each party has constant risk aversion, the optimal contract is a *linear profit-sharing plan.*[3] Thus, the firm should pay the sales agent a fixed wage (less than $600 per day) plus a fixed percentage of gross profits.

▶ *What does this risk-sharing contract imply about each player's expected income?*

Since the sales agent is risk-averse and the contract requires the agent to assume some risk, the sales agent's expected income will be greater than $600 per day. However, the expected gross profit is $5,000 per day. This implies that the firm's expected income will be less than $4,400 ($5,000 – $600) per day.

▶ *Why does the firm choose a risk-sharing contract even though it could earn a larger average profit ($4,400) by paying the sales agent a fixed wage of $600 per day?*

The intuition is that, under the profit-sharing contract, the firm's risk goes down by more than the decline in the firm's average return (expected profit). Hence the firm is better off by using a risk-sharing contract rather than by paying the agent a fixed wage and absorbing all the risk.

▶ *Which contract does the sales agent prefer?*

Since the sales agent is risk-averse, the sales agent's expected income will increase when the firm uses a profit-sharing contract. However, the volatility of the sales agent's income will also increase. Since the *labor market is competitive*, the firm only needs to pays the sales agent the equivalent of the agent's reservation income. Hence *the sales agent does not gain when the firm uses a risk-sharing contract.*

Fusion for Profit Maxim

If both the firm and the sales agent have constant (but different) risk aversions, the firm should use a mixed compensation plan and pay the sales agent a guaranteed wage plus a fixed percentage of gross profits.

Point to consider.   Suppose two firms are in the same industry; one is small and the other large. Which firm should offer the sales agent a higher commission rate?

The larger firm has more wealth than the smaller one. Hence the larger firm will be less risk-averse. This implies that the larger firm should offer the sales agent more downside risk protection than the smaller one. Thus, the larger firm should offer the sales agent a higher base wage *and* a lower profit-sharing rate than the small firm.

Note that the sales agent who works for the larger firm will make a lower *expected* income than the sales agent who works for the smaller firm; however, the agent's income will fluctuate less. In both cases, since the labor market for salespersons is competitive, the agent will be paid the equivalent of his or her reservation income.

◣ 16.3 Should the Firm Pay the Sales Agent Using a Draw System?

Sometimes firms allow sales agents to take a cash advance (a draw) against future sales. Is this a good idea? We distinguish two scenarios.

Recoverable Draw

Under a *recoverable draw*, the sales agent will return some money to the firm if the agent's future earnings are below a certain prespecified level. Suppose the optimal contract for the firm is to pay the sales agent a fixed salary of $400 per day and a commission of $5 per unit. Assume that, on average, the sales agent can sell 100 units per day. This compensation formula is equivalent to the following alternative contract.

Under a recoverable draw, the firm will pay the sales agent a lump sum of $900 (i.e., the fixed salary of $400 plus a cash advance of $500 against the anticipated future profits if 100 units are sold). If sales are *above* the average level of 100 units, the firm will pay the sales agent an additional amount based on the overage. For example, if the agent sells 104 units, the firm will pay the agent an additional sum of $20 (overage × commission per unit = 4 × $5).

Similarly, if sales are *below* the average level of 100 units, the sales agent will return to the firm an amount based on the shortfall. For example, if the agent sells 97 units, the agent will return $15 to the firm (shortfall × commission per unit = 3 × $5) (table 16.2).

Note that *under this contract, the firm will recover money from the sales agent if there is a shortfall in sales and profits.* Consequently, this contract is known as a recoverable draw.

Table 16.2
An Example of a Recoverable Draw

	Daily salary	Commission per unit	Daily sales (units)	Total daily sales calculation	Total daily sales	Money to be exchanged
Sales = average	$400	$5	100	400 + [5 × (100)]	$900	None
Sales > average	$400	$5	104	400 + [5 × (104)]	$920	Firm pays sales agent additional $20
Sales < average	$400	$5	97	400 + [5 × (97)]	$885	Sales agent returns $15 to firm

▶ *If a recoverable draw is equivalent to the optimal contract, why should the firm use a recoverable draw?*

Both contracts are equivalent for the firm. However, the sales agent may prefer a recoverable draw to smooth out his or her income.

▶ *What is an irrecoverable draw?*

Under an *irrecoverable draw*, the firm pays the sales agent a lump sum up front as before. If sales are above a prespecified level ("quota"), the firm pays the sales agent an additional amount based on the sales above the quota. However, in contrast to the recoverable draw, the sales agent does not return money to the firm if sales are below this quota.

▶ *Will the firm prefer a recoverable or an irrecoverable draw?*

A recoverable draw allows for more complete risk sharing than an irrecoverable draw. Hence, other factors being held constant, the firm will prefer a recoverable draw.

▶ *How do recoverable and irrecoverable draws affect the sales agent's income?*

The sales agent bears more risk under a recoverable draw. Hence the sales agent's expected income will be higher under a recoverable draw system.[4]

▶ **16.4 Should the Firm Pay the Sales Agent on the Basis of Sales Revenue or Gross Profits?**

In the previous discussion, we assumed that the firm pays the sales agent on the basis of gross profits. However, in general, the firm does not wish to share profit information with the sales agent.

▶ *Can the firm choose an optimal compensation plan in which it does not provide profit information to the sales agent? Assume that the sales agent's effort is observable.*

Since the firm knows its cost structure, it knows the exact relationship between sales revenue and profit. Consequently, as we discuss below, the firm can transform a profit-sharing contract into an equivalent sales-based contract.

▶ **16.5 How Does the Firm's Cost Structure Affect the Sales Force Compensation Policy?**

The answer depends on whether the firm's current volume affects future costs. Thus, the results will vary across industries. For example, for many frequently purchased products (e.g., soap or toothpaste), the firm's costs in any given period depend only on current volumes. In contrast, for firms in high-technology industries (e.g., computer chips), a high current volume will allow the firm to reduce future costs by becoming more efficient.

▶ *Suppose the firm's current volume does not affect future costs. How will the firm's cost structure affect the sales force compensation policy?*

We distinguish several cost scenarios. For simplicity, assume that the sales agent sells one product, price is fixed, and a linear profit-sharing contract is optimal. Suppose the optimal plan for the firm is to pay the sales agent a fixed wage of $10,000 plus 5% of gross profits.

Linear Costs

Suppose the firm has a *linear cost structure*. Then gross profits are a fixed percentage of sales revenue. Hence the firm can use a linear *sales revenue–based contract* instead of a linear profit-based contract. For example, suppose gross profits are 20% of sales revenue. Then, the firm can use the following sales revenue–based contract instead of a profit-sharing contract. Pay the sales agent a fixed wage of $10,000 and 1% (profit sharing rate $\times$ gross profit margin percentage = 5% $\times$ 20%) of sales revenue.

Economies of Scale

Suppose the firm has economies of scale (e.g., it can purchase raw materials at a discount when volume is high). Since profits increase faster as volume increases and the optimal profit-sharing rate is linear, the firm should use a progressive commission plan based on sales revenue.

For example, pay the sales agent a fixed wage of $10,000 and use a *progressive slab system* such as the following: ½% on the sales revenue from the first 2,000 units sold, ⅔% on the sales revenue from the next 1,000 units sold, and ¾% on the sales revenue from all additional units. Note that if unit costs decrease sharply with volume, the commission rates on additional units sold should increase sharply.

Fusion for Profit Maxim

If the firm's average costs decrease with volume (i.e., there are economies of scale), the commission rate should increase with volume.

Increasing Costs

Suppose the firm is working at *capacity* and is facing increasing costs (e.g., the plant has to be run overtime, and workers have to work extra shifts).

Now, profits increase slower than volume. Hence the firm should use a *regressive commission plan* based on sales revenue. That is, the commission rates on successive slabs of volume are reduced.

For example, use the following formula: pay a fixed wage of $10,000, a commission rate of 2% on the revenue from the first 1,500 units sold, 1% on the revenue from the next 3,000 units sold, and ½% on the revenue from all additional units. Note that *this regressive scheme will not lead to any motivation problems in our example, since the sales agent's effort is observable.*

Fusion for Profit Maxim

If the firm's average costs increase with volume, the commission rate should decrease with volume.

U-Shaped Cost Curve

Suppose the firm faces a U-shaped cost curve in which unit costs are minimized at a volume of 3,000 units. We say that the firm has a capacity of 3,000 units. Now, unit costs fall as volume increases from 0 to 3,000 units. Since gross profits increase faster than volume in this range of output, the firm should use a *progressive commission structure* for sales volumes that are lower than 3,000 units. Similarly, since unit costs increase as volume is expanded beyond 3,000 units, gross profits will increase slower than volume. Hence the firm should use a regressive commission structure for volumes that are higher than 3,000 units. This implies that the firm should use the following *hybrid sales-based contract: a progressive commission structure for sales between 0 and 3,000 units (capacity) and a regressive commission structure thereafter.*

Fusion for Profit Maxim

The firm can convert a profit-based compensation formula into an equivalent sales revenue–based contract. The precise form of this contract depends on how costs vary with volume (e.g., the firm operates under a capacity constraint).

▶ What types of compensation schemes does one observe in the marketplace?

All four types of sales-based commission structures are found in practice (i.e., linear, progressive, regressive, and hybrid). This empirical result is not surprising, since cost structures (constant, decreasing, increasing, or U-shaped) vary across industries.

▶ *Suppose the firm has a* learning curve *(i.e., by increasing its current volume the firm will become more efficient in the future, thereby reducing future costs). How should the firm change its sales force compensation plan?*

The learning curve implies that the firm's future costs will fall if current sales volume increases. However, the current sales volume is uncertain. Hence the firm should revise the compensation plan so that it can share risk and return for both current *and* future profits with the sales agent. Consequently, the firm should increase the commission rate on current volume (a proxy of future cost savings through the learning curve) and lower the base salary.

Fusion for Profit Maxim

If the firm has a learning curve, the optimal policy is to reduce the sales agent's base wage and use a sales revenue–based contract in which the commission rate increases as current sales volume increases.

▶ *Suppose the firm uses a learning curve–based contract to compensate the sales agent. How will this affect the income of the sales agent?*

For simplicity, assume that the *discount rate* is zero. Since the sales agent is risk-averse and bears more risk when there is a learning curve, the sales agent will earn a higher average income than otherwise. However, the agent will face higher risk (income volatility).

▶ *How will the new contract based on the learning curve affect the well-being of the sales agent and the firm?*

Since the labor market is competitive, the sales agent will continue to earn the equivalent of his or her reservation income. Thus, while the agent's average income will increase, the agent's risk will also increase by a commensurate amount. Hence, the sales agent will not gain under the new contract.

How will the learning-curve-based contract affect the firm? As discussed above, the sales agent's average income will go up when the firm uses a learning-curve-based contract. This implies that the firm's average income *must* go down. However, the firm's risk will go down even more sharply (i.e., the firm's *certainty-equivalent profit* will increase). Consequently, the firm will gain by using a learning-curve-based contract.

▶ 16.6 What Compensation Plan Should the Firm Use When It Delegates Decision-Making Authority to the Sales Agent?

In our discussion so far, we have assumed that the sales agent has no control over price. In many cases, however, the firm cannot a priori accurately determine the customer's willingness to pay. However, during a sales call visit, the sales agent has an opportunity to more accurately assess the customer's willingness to pay (*market condition*). Hence it may be optimal for the firm to delegate some price authority to the sales agent.

▶ *Suppose the firm delegates pricing decisions (within limits) to the sales agent. What pricing policy will the sales agent use? Assume that the firm pays the agent a commission that is based on sales revenue.*

Let's say that the sales agent observes a particular market condition (e.g., demand is poor). Given this market condition, suppose the revenues that can be generated at different prices and the associated costs (before the firm pays the sales agent) are as shown in figure 16.1.

Then, regardless of the precise form of the sales revenue–based compensation plan (e.g., linear or progressive), the sales agent will set the price so that the sales revenue is maximized (see PQ in figure 16.1).

Note that this pricing policy compromises gross profits. Specifically, if the sales agent had priced higher (i.e., sold a lower volume OD), the gross profits available for sharing between the sales agent and the firm would have been higher (ST > PR). In addition, this pricing policy produces a revenue-based market share that is too high (PQ > SD) and a volume-based market share that is also too high (OQ > OD).

▶ *How can the firm address this incentive problem when the sales agent has some pricing authority?*

The firm can address this incentive problem by tying the sales agent's commission earnings to gross profits and not to sales revenue. The precise form of the profit-based commission structure will depend on the risk aversions of the firm and the sales agent; in addition, it will depend on the firm's cost structure.

Fusion for Profit Maxim

The firm should use a profit-based compensation contract if it delegates price authority. If the firm uses a revenue-based compensation contract, the sales agent will always compromise profits. Specifically, the sales agent will underprice, and the firm's volume-based and revenue-based market shares will be too high.

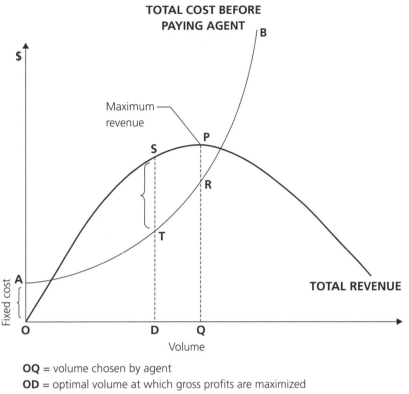

OQ = volume chosen by agent
OD = optimal volume at which gross profits are maximized
PQ = maximum sales revenue
ST = maximum gross profits
PR = gross profits based on policy chosen by agent

Figure 16.1 The effect of the suboptimal pricing decision made by the sale agent.

Point to consider.   Are there any industries in which the firm can delegate pricing authority and yet compensate the sales agent based on sales revenue?

Consider any industry in which marginal costs are approximately zero. For example, suppose the product is an information product (e.g., a software program). Suppose the firm delegates pricing authority to the sales agent. Since the only costs involved (before paying the sales agent) are fixed, any pricing policy that maximizes sales revenue will also maximize gross profits. Hence the firm should compensate the sales agent based on sales revenue.

For most industries, marginal costs are zero. Hence, in general, the firm should not use a sales revenue–based compensation plan when it delegates pricing authority.

Point to consider.   Suppose a company's district sales manager determines the sales call policies of the sales agents in her territory. What compensation system should the firm use for the district sales manager?

If the firm uses a revenue-based compensation plan for the district sales manager, the manager will choose sales call policies that produce market shares (both volume-based and revenue-based) that are too high. Hence the firm should pay the district sales manager using a *profit-sharing plan*.

Point to consider.   Suppose the firm allows the sales agent to entertain clients in order to obtain business. Should the firm pay these selling expenses? Assume that a linear profit-sharing contract is optimal.

Suppose the optimal contract for the firm is to pay the sales agent a fixed wage plus 10% of *net* profits. If the sales agent is paid commissions on the basis of sales revenue, the sales agent will attempt to maximize sales revenue. Consequently, the sales agent will overspend on entertainment. Hence the firm's volume-based and revenue-based market shares will be too high, and the firm's profits will be too low.

To address this problem, the firm should share sales expenses with the agent. Specifically, given the optimal contract in our example, the firm should absorb 90% of the selling expenses and require the sales agent to pay the remainder of the selling expenses (10%).

▲ 16.7 How Will the Internet Affect the Firm's Sales Force Compensation Plan?

Because of recent changes in technology, many firms are using multiple channels (e.g., a sales force and the Internet) to sell their products. Hence the firm needs to coordinate its marketing policies across these channels.

Suppose a firm has been selling its product through a sales force. It is now planning to use two channels: a sales force and the Internet. Assume that the sales agent's effort is observable, the sales agent has no control over price, and the firm's policies do not have an impact on the volatility of sales volumes. Suppose that the optimal compensation plan is linear, and marginal costs are constant.

▲ How should the firm revise the compensation plans for its sales force?

Pre-Internet Compensation Plan

Since the optimal profit-sharing plan is linear and marginal costs are constant, the optimal policy for the firm is to pay the sales agent a base wage plus a fixed percentage of sales revenue generated. As previously discussed, this percentage depends only on the risk attitudes of the firm and the sales agent; in particular, it does not depend on the sales agent's productivity.[5]

Post-Internet Compensation Plan

Since the commission rate on gross profits generated is unchanged, the firm only needs to change the base wage rate for the sales agent after it uses the Internet as a channel.

We distinguish two scenarios.

Case 1.   Suppose the Internet decreases the sales agent's productivity. For example, the firm sells standardized industrial parts. Hence buyers who use the Internet to make purchases will not purchase via the sales force. Since the profit-sharing rate should be unchanged after the firm uses the Internet and the sales agent's productivity has been decreased, the sales agent's expected commission income will be decreased. Furthermore, since the firm's use of the Internet does not change the *volatility* of demand, the volatility of the sales agent's commission earnings will remain unchanged. If the sales agent's fixed wage is the same as before, the sales agent will be worse off, since the agent's expected income will fall and the volatility of income is unchanged. Thus, *the firm will need to increase the sales agent's fixed wage after it uses the Internet.*

Case 2.   Suppose the Internet increases the sales agent's productivity. For example, consider a firm that markets sophisticated industrial products that are customized to meet the specifications of particular customers. Then, the main function of the Internet is to generate product awareness. Once potential customers become aware of the firm's product offering, they contact a sales agent, who, in turn, has a significant effect on their purchasing decision. (In our example, the Internet affects only the sales agent's productivity but not the volatility of sales.) Hence, following the same reasoning as before, it follows that *the firm should decrease the sales agent's fixed wage after it uses the Internet.*

Fusion for Profit Maxim

The firm should decrease (increase) the sales agent's fixed wage if the Internet increases (increases) the sales person's productivity. If the firm uses a linear profit-sharing plan, there is no need for the firm to change the profit-sharing rate.

Point to consider.   Suppose the firm's Internet strategy increases demand uncertainty for sales generated by the sales agent. How should the compensation contract be revised?

We need to distinguish different scenarios based on how the Internet affects the sales agent's productivity.

Case 1.   Suppose the Internet decreases the sales agent's productivity and simultaneously increases the uncertainty in sales generated by the sales agent. Since the profit-sharing rate is unchanged, the sales agent's commission income will be more uncertain than before the firm uses the Internet. Consequently, the firm will need to increase the sales agent's fixed wage even more than in the case where demand uncertainty is unchanged.

Case 2.   Suppose the Internet increases the sales agent's productivity and simultaneously increases the uncertainty in sales generated by the sales agent. As in the previous cases, the risk attitudes of the firm and the sales agent (and hence the commission rate) are unaffected by the firm's choice of channels. Hence it is only necessary for the firm to change the fixed wage component of the agent's compensation plan.

However, there are now two opposing effects on the fixed wage. On one hand, the Internet has increased the sales agent's productivity (and hence expected commission income). This suggests that, other factors being equal, the firm should *decrease* the sales agent's fixed wage. On the other hand, the Internet has also increased demand uncertainty for the sales agent and hence increased the volatility in the sales agent's income. Thus, other factors being equal, the firm should *increase* the sales agent's fixed wage to compensate the agent for the additional risk he or she will incur. Consequently, the effect of the Internet on the agent's fixed wage is ambiguous.

Fusion for Profit Maxim

If the firm uses the Internet as an additional channel to sell its product, it needs to revise the compensation plan for the sales agent based on how the Internet affects the sales agent's productivity and the uncertainty in sales revenue generated by the sales agent.

◣ 16.8 What Compensation Plan Should the Firm Use if It Hires the Sales Agent Using a Multiperiod Contract?

In our previous analysis, we have focused on single-period employment contracts. In some cases, firms hire sales agents using multiperiod contracts.

◣ *Suppose the firm hires the sales agent using a multiperiod contract. What compensation policy should the firm use if the mix of customers (e.g., first-time buyers and repeat buyers) changes over time?*

Typically, the sales agent's effort in any given period is allocated to two segments: new buyers and repeat buyers.

Each segment will have a different effect on the firm's long-run profitability. Consequently, the firm needs to correctly allocate sales effort across customer segments both now and in the future. In addition, the firm needs to choose an appropriate multiperiod sales force compensation strategy.

As we discuss below, the optimal multiperiod compensation policy will depend on the firm's current and future strategies (e.g., the firm's changing emphasis on acquiring new customers and on customer retention).

Example: Suppose the firm has hired a sales agent to sell a new industrial product. In particular, the sales agent sells only the new product, the firm determines how the sales agent should allocate his or her time across customers (i.e., the firm chooses the sales call plan), and the new product is launched at the beginning of the first period.

Suppose a *linear profit-sharing plan* is optimal.[6] To focus on essentials, assume that the firm employs the sales agent under a two-period contract. Then, in the first period all customers will be new. However, in the second period, the sales agent will sell to two segments: a new group of customers and repeat customers from the first period.

Note that segmentation is not an issue in the first period because all customers are new. However, in the second period, the firm will need to determine how the sales agent's time should be allocated between customer retention and customer acquisition. For example, if the sales agent spends too little time on old customers, the repeat purchase rate of this segment may be low. Hence the firm's long-run profitability from this segment will suffer. Alternatively, if the sales agent spends too much time on old customers, the firm may forgo profitable opportunities to develop new business.

Given this scenario, the firm should proceed as follows:

1. Coordinate the sales call policies across customer segments in both periods to maximize long-run performance.
2. For each period, choose the appropriate risk-sharing compensation plan for the sales agent.

Suppose the gross profit margin is $50 per unit sold and the contract requires the sales agent to work for a fixed number of hours in each period. Then, in the first step, the firm will decide how the sales agent should allocate his or her time across different customer segments in each time period. In the second step, the firm will choose the optimal multiperiod compensation plan.

Suppose the average numbers of units sold by the agent in different periods are as shown in table 16.3. Note that in the third period, customers do not obtain any sales support because the sales agent does not work for the firm. Consequently, the retention rate drops from 62.5% to 40%, and there are no new purchases.[7]

Suppose the firm's *cost of capital* is 20% per annum. Then, selling 36 units in the third period is equivalent to selling an additional 30 units in the second period (table 16.4). Hence the average cash flows from the firm's sales call policy are equivalent to those from selling 120 units (90 + 30) on average in the second period and 80 units in the first.

Given this scenario, what compensation plan should the firm use for each period? Assume that the multiperiod compensation plan must be chosen at

Table 16.3
Effect of Salesperson's Effort on Sales in Multiple Periods

| | Purchases | | |
	Repeat	New	Total
Average first-period sales		80	80
Average second-period sales	50*	40	90
Average third-period sales	36**	0	36

*Customer retention rate = 62.5%.

**Customer retention rate = 40%.

Table 16.4
Determining the Net Present Value of Future Sales

Average units sold in third period	36
Cost of capital	20%
NPV (of units) in terms of second-period sales	36/(1 + 0.2) = 30

the beginning of the first period and cannot be changed after each period's sales results become available.

Suppose the sales agent's reservation income is $700 per period. Then, the sales agent will work for the firm if he or she is paid a guaranteed wage of $700.

Alternatively, if the firm requires the sales agent to bear some risk, it must pay the agent the *risk-adjusted equivalent* of the agent's reservation income ($700). For simplicity, assume that this reservation income does not change during the two time periods in question.

► *What compensation plan should the firm use in the first period?*

Suppose the optimal compensation policy for the firm is to use the following linear contract: pay the sales agent a fixed wage of $600 plus 5% of gross profits. Note that this contract is equivalent to paying the sales agent a fixed wage of $600 plus a commission of $2.50 per unit on every unit sold (5% of the gross profit margin of $50). Thus, on average, the sales agent will earn an expected income of $800 in the first period (table 16.5).

Note that although the sales agent's expected income in the first period is higher than the agent's reservation income ($700) in that period, the agent's commission income will fluctuate around this value because demand is uncertain. Hence the sales agent is no better off than the agent would have been if the agent had received a guaranteed wage equal to his or her reservation income ($700).

Table 16.5
Determining the Sales Agent's Average units Income in the First Period

Average units sold in first period	80
Commission rate per unit	5% of $50
Average commission	= $200
First-period wages	+ $600
Average first-period income	= $800

Table 16.6
Determining the Sales Agent's Average Commission Income in the Second Period

Average units sold in second period*	120
Commission rate per unit	× $3.33
Average commission income	= $400

*Total purchases in second period + second-period NPV of units sold in third period.

▶ *What commission rate should the firm use in the second period?*

As shown above, because of the customer-retention effect in the third period, the long-run value of selling 90 units in the second period is equivalent to that of selling 120 units in that period (90 sold in the second period + the *net present value* of 36 sold in the third period).[8]

Since the optimal policy for the firm is to pay the sales agent 5% of gross profits, the second-period commission rate per unit sold should be one-third higher than the corresponding first-period commission rate. Thus, the second-period commission rate should be increased to $3.33 per unit ($2.50 × (1 + ⅓)). Given this commission rate, the sales agent's expected commission income in the second period will be $400 (table 16.6).

▶ *What wage should the firm pay the sales agent in the second period?*

The answer depends on the firm's sales call strategy and, in particular, on the degree to which the firm focuses on acquiring new customers or on retaining old customers.

Case 1. Suppose the firm chooses to focus more heavily on customer retention than on customer acquisition in the second period. For instance, the firm is conservative; alternatively, the cost of acquiring new customers in the second period is high.

Then, the variability in gross profit in the second period and the sales agent's commission income in that period could decrease significantly.

If this is the case, *the sales agent's expected income in the second period could be lower than it was for the first period ($800)*. But, as discussed above, optimal risk-sharing requires that the sales agent's expected commission income in the second period ($400) is higher than the expected commission income in the first period ($200). Hence the firm should reduce the agent's second-period wage below $400 (agent's expected income in the first period – agent's expected commission income in the second period = $800 – $400).

Case 2.   Suppose the firm chooses an aggressive sales call policy in the second period and focuses heavily on acquiring new customers. Now, the effect on the sales agent's second-period wage will depend on how aggressive the firm's sales call policy is.

Suppose the variabilities in gross profits and the sales agent's commission income in the second period are considerably higher than the corresponding quantities in the first period. Then, it may be necessary for the firm to increase the agent's fixed wage in the second period *even though the agent's expected commission income is higher than it was in the first period*.

Case 3.   Suppose the firm pursues a mildly aggressive sales call policy that focuses on both customer retention and new customer acquisition. Then, the volatilities of gross profits and commission income will not increase sharply in the second period. Consequently, as in Case 1, the optimal policy for the firm may be to decrease the agent's fixed wage in the second period.

Fusion for Profit Maxim

Suppose the firm uses a multiperiod contract. Then, the firm will need to change the sales agent's compensation plan from period to period. The effect on the sales agent's expected income and commission rates will vary depending on the firm's discount rate and on the extent to which the firm's strategy focuses on customer retention or market growth.

Chapter 16 Key Points

- The optimal sales force compensation plan depends on the risk attitudes of the firm and the sales agent and on whether the sales agent's effort is observable.
- In general, the firm has more wealth than the sales agent. Hence the firm should use a mixed compensation plan that includes a fixed wage component and a profit-sharing plan.
- When the firm chooses the optimal compensation contract in a *competitive labor market*, in general, the sales agent will make a higher expected income than his or her reservation income. However, the sales agent's income will be uncertain.
- Since the firm knows its cost structure and does not wish to share profit information with the sales agent, in many cases the firm can

convert a profit-sharing contract into an equivalent contract where the sales agent's commission is based on sales revenue. The precise form of this contract depends on how costs vary with volume and on whether the firm has a learning curve.

- If the firm delegates any marketing decision-making power (e.g., pricing or selling expenses) to the sales agent, the firm should compensate the sales agent using a profit-sharing plan. In particular, the firms should not use a compensation plan that is based on sales revenue.
- The firm will need to revise its sales force compensation plan when it sells its product through multiple channels, including the Internet and its sales force. The precise effect depends on the complexity of the product, how the Internet affects the sales agent's productivity, and how the Internet affects demand uncertainty.
- When the firm hires a sales agent using a multiperiod contract, it should use different compensation plans over time depending on its strategy (e.g., the relative foci on acquiring new customers and customer retention) and its discount rate.

Model Extensions: How Should the Multiagent/ Multiproduct Firm Reward and Measure Sales Force Performance?

The previous chapter presented a basic framework for how the firm should choose its sales force compensation policy. In this chapter, we focus on the general case where the firm sells multiple products and/or employs multiple sales agents. Here, for simplicity, we will focus on the case where the firm is privately owned. The analysis can be extended to the case where the firm is owned by shareholders.[1]

The information covered in this chapter will be useful when you are faced with the following types of decisions:

- How should my firm compensate sales agents with different levels of experience and productivity and different attitudes toward risk?
- How should my firm coordinate its *market segmentation* policy and its sales force compensation plans?
- How should my firm choose the optimal sales force compensation plan if its sales force is responsible for selling multiple products?
- How should my firm measure the productivity of its sales force?
- How should my firm track changes in sales force productivity over time and accordingly revise its sales force compensation policy?

The following terms will be introduced in this chapter (see glossary for definitions):

asymmetric information   bundle   customer satisfaction
bad turnover   cross-sectional data downside risk

gross profit margin	market segmentation	risk-averse
harvester	menu of contracts	risk aversions
hunter	myopic strategy	sales call policies
income volatility	piece rate	sliding compensation
linear profit-sharing	relationship segment	system
contract	reservation income	time series data
marginal costs	revenue-sharing contract	transaction segment

▶ 17.1 How Should the Single-Product Firm with Multiple Salespeople Compensate Its Sales Force?

We begin with the case of a firm with one product that is sold by multiple sales agents, each of whom is assigned a set of customers or a given geographical territory. For simplicity, assume that *marginal costs* are constant and that all players (i.e., the firm and its sales agents) have constant (but different) *risk aversions*.

> ▶ *How should the firm choose the optimal sales force compensation plan? Assume that the firm sets the prices of its products and determines the* sales call policies *of its agents.*

Suppose all the players (i.e., the firm and its sales agents) have constant *but different* risk aversions across plausible changes in wealth level. Since each sales agent is assigned a separate territory or set of customers and marginal costs are constant, the firm can treat each sales agent as an independent profit center. Hence, the optimal policy for the firm is to pay each sales agent using a *linear profit-sharing contract*.

Since the agents differ in their risk attitudes and productivities, the base wages and profit-sharing rates should differ across agents. Since the firm chooses the sales call policies and knows its own cost structure, the firm can convert the profit-sharing contract for each sales agent into an equivalent *revenue-sharing contract* (see chapter 16).

> ▶ *Suppose the firm has hired two sales agents, Tom and Viv, with equal productivities. However, Tom is more* risk-averse *than Viv. What is the optimal structure of compensation contracts? Assume that the firm assigns Tom and Viv different territories and chooses their sales call policies.*

For the conditions described, the firm can treat each sales agent as an independent profit center. Hence the firm should offer both Tom and Viv linear profit-sharing contracts. However, since Tom and Viv have different risk attitudes, the firm should offer them different compensation contracts.

Since Tom is more *risk-averse* than Viv, the firm should provide Tom with more *downside risk* protection. That is, the firm should pay the more risk-averse sales agent (Tom) a higher fixed wage and a lower profit-sharing rate than the less risk-averse agent (Viv). Thus, Tom will obtain a lower expected income than Viv; however, Tom's income will be less uncertain than Viv's.

Point to consider.   Suppose the firm has two sales agents. Both sales agents have the same productivities and risk attitudes and are assigned exclusive territories or customer segments. The firm assigns one sales agent (Chuck) to a new territory (segment) and the other (Donna) to an established territory (segment) that was previously assigned to another sales agent who has left the company. What compensation plans should the firm use for both sales agents? Assume that marginal costs are constant.

For simplicity, assume that the demand uncertainties in each territory or customer segment are unaffected by sales effort. (This assumption will be relaxed later.) Since marginal costs are constant and the two sales agents operate in mutually exclusive territories or are assigned nonoverlapping customer segments, the firm should treat each sales agent as a separate profit center.

By assumption, both sales agents have the same risk attitudes. *Therefore, optimal risk-sharing implies that the firm should pay each sales agent the same commission rates on sales revenues generated.*

Since Chuck is assigned a new territory, he will sell less, on average, than Donna, who is assigned an established territory. Hence Chuck will obtain a lower expected commission income than Donna.

By assumption, the demand uncertainty is equal for both territories. Hence both sales agents will face identical *income volatilities* when the firm chooses the optimal compensation contract. But both sales agents have equal productivities (*reservation incomes*); in addition, they have identical risk attitudes. Hence optimal risk sharing implies that the firm should pay the sales agent (Chuck) who is assigned a new territory a higher fixed wage than the sales agent (Donna) who is assigned a territory that was previously assigned to another sales agent.

Fusion for Profit Maxim

Suppose two sales agents have the same productivities and risk attitudes and are assigned different exclusive sales territories (customer segments). Then, if the demand uncertainties are the same in both territories, the sales agent who is assigned a new territory (customer segment) should be paid a higher fixed wage than the one who is assigned an established territory (customer segment).

Point to consider.   In the Chuck and Donna example, how should the firm change the compensation contracts if demand uncertainty in the new territory is higher than it is in the established territory?

In general, it is likely that the demand for the firm's product will be more uncertain in the new territory. By assumption, both sales agents (Chuck and Donna) have the same risk attitudes. Hence the firm should offer both sales agents the same profit-sharing rates—*regardless of the fact that demand is more uncertain in the new territory.*[2] Since marginal costs are constant, this implies that the firm should pay both sales agents the same commission rates on sales. However, demand is more uncertain in the new territory than in the established territory. Hence the sales agent who is assigned the new territory (Chuck) will face higher *income volatility* than the sales agent who is assigned an established territory (Donna).

However, both sales agents have the same productivities (reservation incomes). *Consequently, it follows that the sales agent who is assigned a new territory will obtain a higher expected income than the sales agent who is assigned an established territory.*

Note that, since both Chuck and Donna will make the same expected commission incomes, the firm will need to pay Chuck an even higher fixed wage than in the case where demand uncertainty is the same for both territories.

Fusion for Profit Maxim

Suppose two sales agents have the same productivities and risk attitudes and are assigned different exclusive sales territories (segments). Then, if the demand uncertainty in the new territory is higher, the sales agent who is assigned a new territory will earn a higher expected income and face greater income fluctuations than the one who is assigned an established territory.

▶ 17.2 How Does the Firm's Market Segmentation Strategy Affect the Firm's Compensation Plan?

Suppose a firm has two sales agents (Tom and Viv) with equal abilities and the same risk attitudes. Let's say that the firm assigns Tom to a segment in which consumers purchase on a one-shot basis. We say that Tom is assigned to a *transaction segment*. However, the firm assigns Viv to a segment in which customers in the first period are likely to make future purchases. We say that Viv is assigned to a *relationship segment*.

▶ What compensation plans should the firm use for sales agents who are assigned to the transaction and relationship segments?

For simplicity, suppose the optimal *profit-sharing contracts* are linear. Since consumers in the transaction segment purchase on a one-shot basis, short-run and long-run profits are equivalent. Suppose the optimal commission rate for the sales agent in the transaction segment (Tom) is 5% of short-run profit.

▶ *How should the firm pay the sales agent in the relationship segment (Viv)?*

Since consumers in the relationship segment are likely to make future purchases from the firm, the firm's short- and long-run profits are not equivalent. For simplicity, assume that the firm's discount rate is zero. Suppose that, because of repeat purchases by the relationship segment, the long-run profit from this segment is double the short-run profit. Then, the firm should pay Viv a commission rate of 10% (5% × 2) based on short-run profit.

▶ *Should the fixed wage component of the compensation plan be higher or lower for the sales agent in the relationship segment?*

Since the sales agent in the relationship segment (Viv) should be paid a higher commission rate, she will face greater income volatility than the sales agent in the transaction segment (Tom). To compensate Viv for the higher uncertainty in income, the firm will need to choose a contract that allows Viv to earn a higher average income than Tom. However, as discussed, Viv will make a higher expected commission income than Tom. Hence it is unclear whether the firm will need to pay Viv a higher wage than Tom. Note that, if the market for the firm's product is highly cyclical, it may even be necessary for the firm to pay Viv (the sales agent in the relationship segment) a higher base wage than Tom (the sales agent in the transaction segment).

Fusion for Profit Maxim

In general, the firm should use different compensation plans for sales agents who are assigned to different customer segments. Specifically, sales agents who are assigned to relationship customers will make a higher expected income and face greater income fluctuations than sales agents with the same productivities and risk attitudes who are assigned to transaction customers.

Point to consider. Some firms use two types of sales agents: *hunters* and *harvesters*. Hunters are responsible for bringing in new customers, and harvesters for retaining existing customers. Suppose the firm has hired two sales agents with equal productivities: one is a hunter, and the other is a harvester. How should the firm compensate the hunter and the harvester?

In general, the sales generated by a hunter will be more uncertain than the corresponding sales by a harvester. By assumption, both the hunter and the harvester are equally productive. Hence the hunter should make more money on average than the harvester; however, the hunter should also face more risk from income fluctuations.

▶ *The previous analysis assumed that the firm knows the exact rela-*
tionship between short- and long-run profits in the relationship
segment. What will happen if the firm does not know this rela-
tionship with precision?

This scenario is very likely, especially for new products or segments that are
new to the firm. In such cases, there is no previous purchase history to measure the customer retention rate.

▶ *How should the firm proceed?*

One approach is to use estimates of *customer satisfaction* as proxies for repeat
purchase in the relationship segment. Then, use a three-part compensation
formula for sales agents: a fixed wage, a commission based on current sales
revenue, and a commission based on satisfaction (as a proxy for long-run
profits).

In this analysis it is critical to recognize that *satisfaction is an unobserv-*
able quantity and that self-stated satisfaction levels by consumers are not equiva-
lent to the true satisfaction levels.[3]

▶ *The proxies for long-run profit contain measurement error. Is there*
any danger in using these proxies in the compensation plan?

In general, it is better for the firm to use imprecise proxies (e.g., measured
satisfaction) than to ignore them. *The less precise the proxies are, the higher the*
agent's risk and expected income will be.

As the precision in measurement is improved (e.g., by using better market research methodology), the firm will gain. Since the labor market for
sales agents is competitive, the agent will not gain when more precise metrics
become available. Specifically, the agent will continue to earn an income whose
value after adjusting for risk is equal to the agent's reservation income.

Fusion for Profit Maxim

In general, the firm should use proxies for future sales and profits to compensate salespersons who are assigned to relationship customers, even if these
proxies contain error.

▶ **17.3 How Should the Multiproduct Firm Compensate**
Its Sales Force?

So far, we have focused on the single-product firm with multiple sales agents.
In this section, we discuss how the multiproduct firm should compensate its

sales agents. We begin with the case where one agent sells multiple products. Later, we will consider the case where the multiproduct firm employs multiple sales agents.

▶ *Some products are more difficult to sell than others. Should the firm pay higher commission rates on products that are more difficult to sell? Assume that the firm chooses the sales call policy for the sales agent and determines the prices of its products.*

At first glance, it seems reasonable that the firm should pay higher commission rates on products that are more difficult to sell. However, as discussed below, this is not the case.

By assumption, the firm decides how the sales agent should allocate his or her time across customers. In addition, the firm sets the prices of its products. Hence the firm should proceed in two steps:

1. Determine how the sales agent's time should be allocated across customers. This answer will depend on how easy or difficult it is to sell different products and on the profit margins of each product. For example, *it may be optimal for the firm to choose a sales call plan in which the sales agent allocates more time to selling a high-margin product even though the probability of success is low or the time necessary to make a sale is high.*
2. Determine how it should share risk and return with the sales agent.
3. Suppose a linear profit-sharing rule is optimal. Then the firm should pay the agent a fixed wage plus a fixed percentage of gross profits across product lines.

To illustrate, suppose that the sales agent should be paid a base wage of $10,000 plus 5% of gross profits across product lines. Suppose the sales agent sells two products, A and B, with unit gross margins of $100 and $200, respectively. Then, the sales agent should be paid commissions of $5 per unit (profit-sharing rate × unit gross margin) for Product A and $10 per unit for Product B (table 17.1).

Note that the ratio of the commissions paid per unit sales of the two products equals the ratio of the corresponding unit *gross profit margins.*

Table 17.1
Example Showing How the Multiproduct Firm Should Set Commission Rates for Different Products

Product	Commission rate	Gross margin	Commission per unit
A	5%	$100	5% of $100 = $5
B	5%	$200	5% of $200 = $10

> **Fusion for Profit Maxim**
>
> If the firm determines how the sales agent should allocate his or her time, the commission rates for different products should be proportional to the profit margins for those products. These commission rates do not depend on how easy or difficult it is to sell particular products.

► *What will happen if the multiproduct firm pays sales agents commissions based on total sales revenues?*

This policy will lead to inefficient risk sharing, since multiproduct revenues and profits are not perfectly correlated. Note that the multiproduct firm will *lose* if it pays salespersons commissions based on the total revenue generated across products. However, the sales agent will be unaffected because the labor market for sales agents is competitive (i.e., the sales agent will be paid the equivalent of his or her reservation income).

Point to consider. Should firms set sales quotas for particular products or market segments?

The answer depends on whether the firm or the agent chooses the *sales call policy* and on whether the agent and the firm have different market information. Suppose the agent's effort is observable, and the firm and the agent have the same information about the demand for the firm's products. Then, as discussed below, it is redundant for the firm to set quotas for its products.

Example: Consider a large computer manufacturer such as Hewlett-Packard that sells computers and printers to different industries. Suppose Hewlett-Packard and the sales agent have the same market information and that Hewlett-Packard determines the agent's sales call policy. Suppose Hewlett-Packard's strategy is to increase its long-run performance by expanding into a high-growth segment (e.g., computer applications in the banking industry). Then, Hewlett-Packard should proceed as follows:

1. Choose a sales call policy that emphasizes long-term growth (i.e., more sales effort will be directed to the banking industry), and
2. Pay the agent using a commission system based on the gross profit margins of its product line (computers and printers, in our example).

Note that, for this scenario, sales quotas are unnecessary because the agent has no discretion over his or her sales call policy.

Now, suppose the agent determines the sales call policy; in addition, the firm and the agent have different information about the market. *In this case, because the agent's effort is unobservable and the firm and the agent have asymmetric information, it may be necessary for the firm to set sales quotas for particular products/market segments to encourage the sales agent to focus on long-run performance.*

We continue with the Hewlett-Packard example. If the agent's effort is unobservable to Hewlett-Packard, there is no guarantee that the agent will choose the optimal call policy. By assumption, Hewlett-Packard's strategy focuses on computer applications in the banking industry (a high-growth segment). Hence Hewlett-Packard should assign the sales agent a high sales quota for sales to the banking industry.

Fusion for Profit Maxim

The firm does not need to set quotas on the sales of individual products if it chooses the sales agent's call plan. If information is asymmetric or if the firm cannot observe the effort of the sales agent, the firm may need to set sales quotas for particular products so that the sales agent chooses a call plan that is consistent with the firm's strategy.

Point to consider.   The previous analysis assumed that the multiproduct firm has only one sales agent. What compensation plan should the multiproduct firm use if it employs many sales agents?

Suppose the marginal cost of each product in the firm's product portfolio is constant. (This assumption does not imply that all products in the firm's product portfolio have equal marginal costs.) In addition, the multiproduct firm assigns each sales agent an exclusive territory or set of customers. Then, the firm can treat each sales agent as a separate profit center. Hence the previous results for the multiproduct firm with one sales agent will apply to the case where the multiproduct firm has multiple sales agents.

Point to consider.   Suppose two single-product firms (Firm A and Firm B) merge. Assume that both before and after the merger, firms determine the prices of their product(s) and the sales call policies of their respective sales agents. After the merger, the merged firm sells three products: the products made by Firms A and B, respectively, before the merger, and the *bundle* of those products. Furthermore, the two sales forces are integrated (i.e., each sales agent in the merged firm sells all three products). How should the compensation system for the sales force be changed after the merger? Assume that the cost structures of both firms are linear, there are no joint costs, each sales agent is assigned his or her own sales territory or set of customers, and the sales agents have no control over prices.

Prior to the merger, each firm proceeds as follows:

1. Choose the price of its product and the sales call policy for each sales agent, and
2. Pay each sales agent using a combination plan: a wage plus a fixed percentage of sales revenue.

(As discussed previously, the wages and commission rates should vary across sales agents based on their respective productivities and risk attitudes.)

After the merger, the firm needs to set three prices: the price of Firm A's product, the price of Firm B's product, and the price of the bundle. In addition, the merged firm needs to determine the new optimal sales call policies for each agent.

Since the merged firm now sells three products, the firm should not pay commissions based on sales revenues. Instead, *it should pay each sales agent a fixed wage plus a fixed percentage of aggregate gross profits generated (i.e., the sum of profits generated across the product portfolio).*

To illustrate, suppose the optimal unit profit margins after the merger are as follows: $10 for Firm A's product, $20 for Firm B's product, and $25 for the bundle. (Note that, in general, the profit margins for the individual products will change after the merger, since marketing policy should be coordinated to maximize product-portfolio performance.)

Then, the corresponding commissions per unit sold of each product should be in the ratio 10:20:25. As previously discussed, these ratios do not depend on any of the following factors:

- The ease or difficulty of selling the individual products and the bundle,
- The salespersons' productivities, or
- The sales agents' risk attitudes.

Note that, although none of these factors affects the profit-sharing rate, they do affect the firm's marketing policies (e.g., sales call policies). Hence they have an indirect effect on the sales agent's return (expected income) and risk (income volatility).

▶ *Suppose the salesperson sells multiple products for the firm. However, the sales agent determines the sales call policy. In this case, should the profit-sharing plan depend on the difficulty of selling particular products?*

Since the firm has delegated sales force policy to the agent, it may be necessary for the firm to provide the sales agent an incentive by increasing the commission rates on sales of products that are more difficult to sell but generate higher gross profit margins.[4]

Point to consider.   Suppose a Dell sales agent sells both PCs and printers. Purchasers of Dell printers will purchase proprietary replacement cartridges from Dell in the future. What commission rates should Dell use for PC and printer sales?

Suppose Dell's gross profit margin on a PC sale is $80 per unit, and its gross profit margin on a printer sale is $40. Suppose market research has shown that, on average, a consumer who buys a Dell printer will purchase four proprietary replacement cartridges in the future. Let's say that the gross profit margin on replacement cartridges is $15 per cartridge. (For simplicity, assume that the discount rate is zero.) Hence as shown in table 17.2, the

Table 17.2
Dell Example: Profit Margins from Selling a PC, a Printer, and Replacement Cartridges for the Printer

	Profit margin	Calculation
PC	$80	
Printer	$100	($40* + $60**)

* = Profit margin per printer sold.
** = Profit margin for replacement cartridges
(4 replacements × $15 profit margin per cartridge).

Table 17.3
Dell Example: Effect on Dell's Profit Margins If Generic Printer Cartridges Become Available

	Profit margin	Calculation
PC	$80	
Printer	$88	($40* + $48**)

* = Profit margin per printer sold.
** = Profit margin for replacement cartridges
(4 replacements × $12 profit margin per cartridge).

commissions per unit on PCs and on printers should be in the ratio of the corresponding profit margins per unit (80:100).

▶ *How should Dell adjust its commission rates on PC and printer sales if generic replacement cartridges for Dell printers become available in the future?*

Suppose generic replacement cartridges become available for Dell printers. Then, Dell will need to lower the price on its replacement cartridges. Suppose the gross profit margin on replacement cartridge sales is reduced to $12 per unit. Then, as shown in table 17.3, the profit margin generated from a printer sale should be reduced from $100 to $88 (a reduction of 12%).

Thus, as a result of the availability of generic replacement cartridges, the commissions on printer sales should be reduced by 12%.

▶ **17.4 How Should the Multiproduct Firm Measure Sales Force Productivity?**

So far, we have assumed that the firm knows the productivity of its sales agents with certainty. However, in most cases the firm will have incomplete information about how productive its sales agents are.

▶ *Should firms use sales revenue to measure sales force productivity?*

This approach is often used in practice. However, the method is flawed, especially in a multiproduct firm.

Example: Recently, the retail division of Morgan Stanley faced the following problems: low margins and a high proportion of unproductive brokers.[5] Should Morgan Stanley rank brokers in its retail division according to the revenue they generate and drop the bottom performers?

Brokers in the retail division typically sell multiple products with unequal margins. Suppose two hypothetical brokers (Andy and Beth) work for Morgan Stanley. Then Andy, for example, could be generating more revenue across product lines than Beth but producing lower profits. By using a revenue-based measure of productivity, Morgan Stanley would drop Beth even though she contributes higher profits than Andy.

Additionally, for competitive and other reasons, the revenues for some product lines are likely to be more uncertain than those for others. Thus, high revenues for any given product may be due to "good luck" rather than superior productivity.

Consequently, by evaluating its brokers on the basis of total revenues generated across product lines, Morgan Stanley could experience *bad turnover* by losing both unproductive *and* productive brokers.

▶ *If sales revenue is a poor metric to measure sales force productivity, how should the firm measure the productivities of its sales force?*

The sales revenue from a particular product depends on the marketing policies (e.g., price) of the firm and its competitors, the time spent by the sales agent on selling the product, the sales agent's ability (an unobservable quantity), and random fluctuations. As discussed below, it is necessary for the firm to measure each of these effects correctly in order to measure sales force productivity. For the moment, we focus on theoretical issues. Empirical methods for estimating productivity will be discussed later.

Competition

Unless the firm controls for competitive effects, sales is a flawed metric for measuring productivity, even in a single-product firm. Consider two sales agents with equal abilities who sell the same product in different territories (or, equivalently, sell to nonoverlapping customer segments). Assume for simplicity that both sales agents spend equal amounts of time on selling the product in question.

If competition is more severe in one territory (Territory 1) than in the other (Territory 2), on average the sales agent who is assigned to Territory 1 will underperform in terms of sales, even though he or she is as productive as the sales agent assigned to Territory 2.

Uncertainty

Even if competitive effects are identical in both territories, sales are a misleading proxy of productivity. Suppose the firm and its competitors are using identical marketing policies in Territories 1 and 2, and both sales agents have equal abilities. However, sales are uncertain in Territory 1 but are predictable in Territory 2. Then, on average, the firm's sales will be equal in both territories.

Suppose that there is a 50% chance that sales in Territory 1 will be $9,000 and a 50% chance that sales in Territory 1 will be $11,000. Then, the average sales in Territory 1 will be $10,000.

Assume that sales are predictable in Territory 2 and equal $10,000. Now, for purely fortuitous reasons, 50% of the time the sales agent in Territory 1 will appear to be more productive than the sales agent in Territory 2 *even though both sales agents have equal abilities.* Thus, if sales are used as *the* metric to measure productivity, both sales agents will be needlessly exposed to the luck of the draw and the firm will experience bad turnover (i.e., turnover that is unrelated to productivity).

As the example shows, using sales revenue as a metric is likely to have highly undesirable consequences for the firm, especially if demand is highly volatile. The loss to the firm is twofold:

1. It will lose productive *and* unproductive sales agents, and
2. It will incur additional expenses in hiring new sales agents in the future. And, hiring new sales agents is expensive both in dollar terms and in terms of the implicit cost of the time spent by managers in sorting job candidates and interviewing and training them.

Fusion for Profit Maxim

Sales depend on many factors in addition to the sales agent's ability. Hence the firm should not use raw sales as a measure of productivity.

Point to consider.   Suppose customers call in to the Dell Customer Center and are randomly assigned to the next available sales representative. How should Dell measure the productivities of its sales representatives? What compensation plan should Dell use for its sales representatives?

Since customers are randomly assigned to sales representatives, market conditions are similar across these representatives.

Case 1.   Sales Representatives Have No Control over Prices. Suppose the optimal compensation structure is linear. Then, Dell should pay the agent a fixed *piece rate* per each item sold. For example, the agent could be paid $15 for each PC sold and $20 for each printer sold. Since Dell is a multiproduct firm, it should measure the productivity of an agent using the gross profits generated by that agent across product lines.

For products such as printers, the gross profits should include the net present value of future profits from replacement cartridges. For the scenario given, market conditions are constant across sales representatives (customers are randomly assigned to sales representatives). Consequently, Dell can use the gross profits generated by sales agents to rank sales agents according to productivity.

Case 2. Sales Representatives Have Some Control over Prices. For this scenario, Dell should use a *sliding compensation system* in which the commission paid on the sale of a given product (e.g., a PC) is based on the gross profit generated by that sale. Note that, since customers are randomly assigned to sales agents, Dell can use the same method to rank sales agents as in the case where the sales agents have no control over price. That is, it is appropriate for Dell to rank its sales agents according to the gross product-line profits that they generate.

► *Can these compensation schemes be adjusted to improve long-run performance?*

Suppose satisfied customers are more likely to return to Dell in the future to purchase additional products. Then, the compensation contract should be modified by including an additional component based on measured customer satisfaction.[6]

Point to consider. Firms sometimes measure and reward customer representatives at a call center based on the time spent per customer. Is this a good idea?

Suppose customers are randomly assigned to customer service representatives. Since all representatives serve the same mix of customers, the firm can measure short-run efficiency based on the average time that the sales representative spends per customer. However, this strategy is likely to be *myopic*. If call center representatives focus on minimizing the time spent per customer, customer satisfaction will fall. This will reduce the customer retention rate and hence future profits.

► *How can the firm encourage its customer representatives to focus on maximizing long-run performance?*

One method is to use a *three-part compensation plan*: a fixed wage (A), a commission based on the time spent per customer (B), and a component based on measured customer satisfaction (C). *Note that B is inversely related to the average time spent per customer (i.e., the more time spent with the customer, the less the commission). In addition, C is likely to be nonlinear (e.g., at high levels of satisfaction, further increases in satisfaction have very little impact on the customer retention rate).*

As one would expect, the relative importance of each of these three income components (A, B, and C) should differ across industries. For example, C should be a high proportion of the agent's income in industries where customer satisfaction has a critical impact on the customer retention rate and hence on future profits.

Point to consider.   Suppose a multinational firm has set up two call centers abroad: one in India and the other in the Philippines. Customers who need service are randomly assigned to these call centers. Suppose the average time spent per client by call center representatives in the Philippines is lower than the corresponding average times in India. Does it follow that the Philippines center is more efficient?

Consider the following scenario. Suppose that

- The Philippines call center successfully resolves 80% of the cases; however, the corresponding success rate for the India call center is much higher (90%).
- In contrast to the India call center, the Philippines call center transfers a very high proportion of difficult, time-consuming cases to the company's main call center in the United States.
- The cases that the Philippines call center is unable to successfully resolve contain a high proportion of large customers.

As this scenario illustrates, the firm should not use a simplistic measure of efficiency such as the average time spent per customer. Instead, *the firm should use several performance metrics*, including the average time per client and the success rates in resolving customer problems. *These metrics should be adjusted by the difficulty of the cases involved and the economic value generated by particular customer segments.* For example, the firm should distinguish segments by purchase quantity, frequency of purchase, or whether they buy high-margin products.

Fusion for Profit Maxim

The firm is likely to jeopardize its long-run performance by using one-dimensional, cost-based metrics such as the time spent per customer by the customer representative.

▲ *The previous analysis of compensation contracts assumed that the firm knows the sales agents' productivities and risk attitudes. How should the firm design a compensation plan when these conditions do not hold?*

One approach is to proceed as follows. Use proxies of sales productivity (e.g., number of years experience in sales) to form segments of sales agents. For each segment, design a segment-specific *menu of contracts* with different combinations of fixed wages and commissions. For example, the firm could offer the following menu of contracts to a particular sales force segment: a high fixed wage of $5,000 per month plus 2% sales revenue (Contract 1) or a lower fixed wage of $3,000 per month plus a higher percentage of sales revenue, say 4% (Contract 2).

Then, other factors remaining the same, a highly risk-averse agent will be more likely to choose Contract 1. A less risk-averse agent will be more likely to choose Contract 2. Similarly, other factors remaining the same, a more productive agent will be more likely to choose Contract 2 than a less productive agent.

In practice, the menu of contracts should include a choice among several options and not merely two, as in this example. Furthermore, the firm should test the menu of contracts on a pilot basis before implementing the new compensation plan on a national basis.

Example: A large multinational computer manufacturer recently tested this menu-of-contracts approach for compensating its sales force. The following results were achieved in the pilot test: within seven weeks of implementation, sales increased by more than $10 million, and productivity increased by 8%. In addition, sales force satisfaction increased significantly.

► *If sales revenue is a poor metric for measuring a sales agent's productivity, what empirical method should the firm use to measure the productivities of its sales agents?*

Interestingly, the multiproduct firm is in a better position to measure sales force productivity than the single-product firm. The intuition is straightforward: the multiproduct firm has more information than the single-product firm. Specifically, for the multiproduct firm, the *sales data for* each *individual product sold by a given sales agent provides information about that agent's (unobserved) productivity.* Hence it is possible to analyze historical sales data across product lines to obtain unbiased measures of the sales agent's productivity.[7]

Roughly speaking, the methodology is as follows. Given the sales agent's sales history for the firm's product line, the firm can combine sales data across sales agents in any given period (*cross-sectional data*) and over time (*time series data*). By analyzing the pooled data, the firm can estimate the following effects for each product:

- The effect of competition,
- The unobservable effects of the sales agent's ability (productivity), and
- Random disturbances.

The firm can then use these estimates to:

- Correctly measure productivity,
- Rank sales agents by ability, and
- Choose the future sales force policy (e.g., sales call policy, which sales agents to retain, and what compensation contracts to offer them).

Fusion for Profit Maxim

The multiproduct firm with multiple sales agents can objectively measure the abilities (productivities) of its sales agents by analyzing their past sales histories. As discussed previously, the firm should not simply use sales revenues as proxies for productivity.

Chapter 17 Key Points

- The firm with multiple sales agents will often assign agents different customer mixes (e.g., first-time and repeat customers) based on its long-run strategy. In such cases, the firm should adjust its sales force compensation plans to allow for the differences in productivities across customer segments, the demand uncertainties involved, and the effects of the firm's segmentation strategy on the firm's long-run performance.
- If the multiproduct firm determines how the sales agent should allocate his or her time, the firm should choose commission rates that are proportional to the long-run profit margins of different products. The firm should not compensate the sales force on the basis of the total sales revenue generated across products.
- If information is asymmetric or if the firm cannot observe the sales agent's effort, the firm will need to set sales quotas for particular products so that the sales agent chooses a call plan that is consistent with the firm's strategy.
- Sales revenue is a flawed measure of productivity, even in a single-product firm. However, the multiproduct firm with multiple agents can objectively measure the productivities of its sales agents by analyzing their past sales histories.
- One-dimensional measures of productivity (e.g., the average time spent to service a call center customer) should not be used. It is better to use multiple metrics to measure productivity. In addition, it is better to use a multipart compensation plan in which each part is based on a different metric (e.g., customer satisfaction and sales revenue).

IX

How to Allow for Competitive Reaction

18

How to Make Marketing Decisions When Competitors React: A Game-Theoretic Approach

When the firm changes its marketing policies, its competitors are likely to react. In this chapter, we discuss how the firm should make optimal marketing decisions *after* allowing for the effects of competitive reaction. In addition, we discuss how the firm should adapt its marketing decisions when new information becomes available to it or to its competitors in the future. Finally, we discuss how the firm can make optimal decisions after simultaneously allowing for competitive reaction *and* the arrival of new information.

The information covered in this chapter will be useful when you are faced with the following types of decisions:

- How can my firm choose marketing policies after allowing for competitive reaction?
- How can my firm choose the optimal marketing policy for its product when it does not have complete information about competitors' *demand* and *cost structures*?
- How can my firm choose the optimal price for its product when my firm or its competitors have *learning curves*?
- How should my firm revise its marketing policy when a competitor changes its financing decisions?
- How will changes in the spare parts industry affect the prices of durable products that use those spare parts?
- What metrics should my firm use to choose marketing policies after allowing for competitive reaction?

- What empirical methods should my firm use to choose its marketing policies when it has incomplete information about competitors' marketing policies?
- How can my firm make optimal sequential decisions after allowing for competitive reaction and the arrival of new information?
- Can myopic decisions that fail to allow for competitive reaction ever lead to optimal strategies?

The following terms will be introduced in this chapter (see glossary for definitions):

barriers to entry	learning curve	retiring long-term debt
barriers to exit	marginal costs	risk-neutral
behavioral modes	marginal productivity	sequential market
certainty-equivalent profit	market price	entry strategy
competitive industry	market signals	share of voice
complementarity	myopic pricing	signaling
conditional net present	Nash equilibrium	standard net present
value	net present value	value
conditional profits	noncooperative	strategic alliance
cooperative equilibrium	equilibrium	strategic complements
cost structure	payoff matrix	strategic flexibility
demand structure	price discrimination	strategic
discount rate	strategy	interdependence
dominant strategy	price oscillations	strategic price
economies of scale	price sensitivity	advantage
first mover	product life cycle	strategic pricing
flexible pricing	race to the market	strategic substitutes
game theory	reaction curve	sunk costs
joint effect	real options	uniform pricing
late entrants	reservation price	utility

▲ 18.1 What Is the Firm's Objective When Competitors React?

The firm's objective when competitors react depends on the type of market in which the firm operates. In particular, the answer depends on whether the firm is in a *competitive industry* with many players. Alternatively, is the firm in an industry in which only a few firms produce similar products?

▲ What is the firm's objective in a competitive industry?

Suppose the firm is in a competitive industry. Then, many firms produce products of identical quality, consumers are well informed, and there are no *barriers to enter* or *exit* the industry. Hence for any given product design there is one *market price*. Since all prices are determined by the market, the firm should proceed sequentially as follows:

1. Choose which industry or industries to operate in, based on its own competencies,
2. For each industry it enters, choose which quality level(s) to produce, and
3. For each quality level, choose the cost-minimizing technology to produce that product.

Note that, since all market prices are given, the firm can unambiguously maximize its own performance (i.e., profits).[1]

See chapter 7 for a detailed discussion of how to choose marketing strategy in competitive markets.

Fusion for Profit Maxim

Firms in competitive industries can unambiguously maximize their profits without explicitly analyzing competitive retaliation.

▲ *What is the firm's objective when it operates in an industry with few competitors?*

In general, the products sold by different firms in an industry will be similar but not identical. Furthermore, in many industries, only a few firms compete in the marketplace. Hence, in contrast to a competitive industry, firms have control over both product quality *and* price. As discussed below, under these conditions, the firm cannot unconditionally maximize its profits.

Example: Samsung and Sony compete in the DVD player market. Since each firm produces DVD players with different features, the Samsung and Sony DVD players are similar but not identical. Assume that both firms seek to maximize their respective performances and have the same planning horizons (one period).

▲ *Suppose Samsung charges $150 per unit for its DVD player. Let's say that, given this pricing scenario, the optimal policy for Sony is to charge $130 per unit. Suppose Sony's profit under this pricing scenario is $30 million. What will happen to Sony's profits if Samsung charges a higher price ($160 per unit) for its DVD player?*

Suppose that, for this higher price chosen by Samsung, the optimal policy for Sony is to increase the price of its DVD player to $145 (≠ $130). Let's say that, under this scenario, Sony makes a profit of $35 million (≠ $30 million). Note that Sony's profits depend on what price Samsung charges.

As this example shows, Sony's optimal policy and profits depend critically on Samsung's policy. Similarly, Samsung's optimal policy and profits will also depend critically on Sony's policy. Hence the notion of profit maximization is ambiguous.

Fusion for Profit Maxim

In an industry with differentiated products and few players, the concept of profit maximization is ambiguous. The firm can only attempt to maximize its profits conditional on its assumptions about the marketing policies chosen by its competitors.

▲ 18.2 Choosing Optimal Strategies When Competitors React: Basic Methodology

As discussed above, the concept of profit maximization is ambiguous when firms sell differentiated products in an industry with few players. One intuitively appealing way to address this ambiguity is to modify the concept of profit maximization by assuming that each firm seeks to maximize its profits conditional on any policy chosen by its competitor. However, to implement this approach one needs to answer two questions:

1. How can the firm predict what its rival will do in a given situation?
2. How can the firm maximize its *conditional profits* given its beliefs about how the competitor will choose its marketing policies?

We illustrate the methodology below.

How can the firm choose marketing policies that maximize its conditional profits? For simplicity, suppose that the design features (qualities) of the products are fixed and that the only decision variable for each firm is price. Furthermore, assume there any only two firms in the marketplace.

Example: In 1999, both Coca-Cola and Pepsi were using *uniform pricing* policies to sell Coke and Pepsi using vending machines. In December 1999, the CEO of Coca-Cola, M. Douglas Ivester, announced that Coca-Cola was planning to use a *flexible pricing* approach in which it would vary Coke's prices for vending machine sales, based on such factors as the weather and the temperature.[2]

▲ Should Coke have switched to a flexible pricing strategy? How should Pepsi have reacted to Coke's new strategy?

Suppose that each firm could have chosen one of two pricing strategies: uniform pricing (the status quo) or flexible pricing. Hence four scenarios are possible (table 18.1).[3] In table 18.1, the rows correspond to Coke's strategies

Table 18.1
Coke-Pepsi Example: Effects of Competitive Reaction

	Pepsi's strategy	
	Uniform pricing	Flexible pricing
Coke's strategy		
Uniform pricing	(100*, 60**)	(120, 50)
Flexible pricing	(80, 105**)	(130*, 70)

Note: Numbers in parentheses represent profits in millions of dollars; the first entry in each cell indicates Coke's profits and the second Pepsi's profits.
  *Coke's optimal policies conditional on Pepsi's policies.
  **Pepsi's optimal policies conditional on Coke's policies.

and the columns to Pepsi's strategies. For each cell, the first entry denotes Coke's annual profits from vending machine sales, and the second denotes Pepsi's. (All dollar values are hypothetical.) Since this table contains information about firms' strategies and profits, it is known as a *payoff matrix*.

In general, we expect that the vending machine demand for soft drinks will be less *price-sensitive* on hot days than on cold days. Hence, other factors remaining the same, both Coke and Pepsi should charge higher prices on a hot day than on a cold day. Thus, each firm will gain by switching from uniform to flexible pricing—*provided its competitor does not react*. However, this assumption is unlikely to hold.

Hence, after allowing for competitive reaction, it is not obvious whether Coke or Pepsi can increase its profits by switching to a flexible pricing plan. To answer this question, we need to analyze Coke's and Pepsi's conditional profits for each of the four industry pricing scenarios in table 18.1.

Scenario 1: Both Coke and Pepsi Use Uniform Pricing

This is the status quo scenario where both firms use uniform pricing. Suppose Coke's annual profit is $100 million, and Pepsi's is $60 million. (At the time, Coke had considerably more vending machines in place than Pepsi did. Hence the assumption that Coke's profits from vending machines were larger than Pepsi's is reasonable.) This outcome is shown in the (100, 60) cell in table 18.1.

Scenario 2: Both Coke and Pepsi Use Flexible Pricing

Suppose both Coke and Pepsi change from uniform to flexible pricing. Then, each firm should raise its price on hot days and decrease its price on cold days. Given this *price discrimination strategy* over time by both firms, industry profits will increase. However, the gains will differ by firm.

Since at the time, Coke had more vending machines in place than Pepsi, most of the increase in industry profits would have gone to Coke.

Let's say that Coke would have increased its profits to $130 million (> $100 million), and Pepsi would have increased its profits by a smaller amount to $70 million (> $60 million). This outcome is shown in the (130, 70) cell in table 18.1.

Scenario 3: Coke Uses Flexible Pricing and Pepsi Uses Uniform Pricing

Suppose Coke uses flexible pricing, but Pepsi continues to use uniform pricing. Then, compared with Pepsi's price, Coke's price on hot days will be too high, and Coke's price on cold days will be too low. Hence Coke will lose profits on hot days and gain profits on cold days.

Since vending machine traffic on hot days is much higher than it is on cold days, Coke's profits over the year are likely to fall. Correspondingly, Pepsi's annual profits will increase. Let's say that, given the price sensitivities in the market, Coke's annual profits fall to $80 million (< $100 million), and Pepsi's annual profits increase to $105 million (> $60 million). This outcome is shown in the (80, 105) cell in table 18.1.

Scenario 4: Coke Uses Uniform Pricing and Pepsi Uses Flexible Pricing

Similar to Scenario 3, if Pepsi uses flexible pricing, but Coke continues to use uniform pricing, Coke's annual profits will increase and Pepsi's annual profits will decrease. Let's say that Coke's annual profits increase to $120 million (> $100 million), and Pepsi's annual profits decrease to $50 million (< $60 million). This outcome is shown in the (120, 50) cell in table 18.1.

▶ *Given these four scenarios, which pricing policies will Coke and Pepsi choose?*

The answer depends on whether Coke and Pepsi cooperate with each other. We first consider the case where Coke and Pepsi do not cooperate with each other.

Coke and Pepsi Do Not Cooperate with Each Other

Since both firms compete with each other, each firm will seek to maximize its conditional profits for any strategy chosen by its competitor. In table 18.1, we use the notation * to denote Coke's optimal strategies, conditional on what Pepsi does, and ** to denote the corresponding optimal strategies for Pepsi, conditional on what Coke does.

1. Suppose Coke uses uniform pricing. Then, Pepsi should choose uniform pricing to maximize its conditional profits (60 > 50).
2. If Coke uses flexible pricing, Pepsi should use uniform pricing (105 > 70). Note that, regardless of which pricing strategy Coke

uses, Pepsi will use uniform pricing to maximize its conditional profits. We say that uniform pricing is a *dominant strategy* for Pepsi.
3. Suppose Pepsi uses uniform pricing. Then, Coke should use uniform pricing (100 > 80).
4. If Pepsi uses flexible pricing, Coke should also use flexible pricing (130 > 120).

Note that in table 18.1, the only cell that contains both the * and the ** notations is the (100, 60) cell, where both Coke and Pepsi use uniform pricing. We say that this is the *Nash equilibrium*.

To see why the (100, 60) cell is the only possible *noncooperative equilibrium* (i.e., when Coke and Pepsi compete), consider the following. Let's say that Coke introduces flexible pricing. Then Pepsi has two choices. It can follow Coke and use flexible pricing. Alternatively, Pepsi can stay with uniform pricing. Given these choices, Pepsi should stay with uniform pricing, since this pricing policy will maximize its conditional profits (105 > 70).

▶ *However, will this outcome be acceptable to Coke?*

If Coke goes back to uniform pricing, it can obtain a higher profit (100 > 80). Hence both firms will return to the status quo (the (100, 60) cell), where they use uniform pricing. *Note that, because of competitive reaction, neither Coke nor Pepsi can achieve their respective maximum profits ($105 million for Pepsi and $130 million for Coke).*

Coke and Pepsi Cooperate with Each Other

Suppose Pepsi cooperates with Coke when Coke introduces flexible pricing. Then, Pepsi will take the cue from Coke and also use flexible pricing. Hence both firms will end up in the (130, 70) cell. Note that this cooperative solution is a win-win solution for both firms. Thus, compared with the status quo where both firms use uniform pricing, Coke increases its profits from $100 million to $130 million. Pepsi also gains, since it increases its profits from $60 million to $70 million.

Note that only the cells on the diagonal of the payoff matrix (the (100, 60) and the (130, 70) cells in table 18.1) are stable solutions. In our example, the (100, 60) cell is the noncooperative Nash equilibrium, and the (130, 70) cell is the *cooperative equilibrium*.

Fusion for Profit Maxim

Firms that compete with each other cannot unconditionally maximize their profits. However, they can maximize their conditional profits based on their assumptions about the behaviors of competing firms. One useful managerial tool is a payoff table that shows the profits that each player makes for different combinations of strategies chosen by the players in the market.

Point to consider.   The previous analysis implicitly assumed that Coke and Pepsi know each other's cost structures. What will happen if they do not have this information?

At first glance, it might appear that the market will be unstable as each firm revises its marketing policies based on its best "guesses" about its competitor's costs. However, as shown below, this may not be the case. Coke and Pepsi do not need precise numerical information about each other's cost structures. *Each firm only needs to know how its competitor ranks the different outcomes in the payoff table.*

To illustrate let's refer to table 18.2. Let 4 denote the most preferred alternative and 1 the least preferred alternative for each player. For each cell below, the first entry denotes Coke's rank ordering, and the second denotes Pepsi's rank ordering. Based on the qualitative arguments discussed above, the rank-ordered profit outcomes will be as shown in table 18.2.

Suppose Coke and Pepsi do not cooperate with each other. Then, each firm will seek to maximize its conditional profits for any strategy chosen by the competitor.

1. Suppose Pepsi chooses uniform pricing. Since Pepsi knows Coke's rank ordering, Pepsi knows that Coke will choose uniform pricing ($2 > 1$).
2. Pepsi also knows that, if it chooses flexible pricing, Coke will use flexible pricing ($4 > 3$).
3. Similarly, Coke knows Pepsi's rank ordering. Hence Coke knows that Pepsi will always choose uniform pricing.

These conditional decisions imply that both firms will use uniform pricing (the (2, 2) cell).

Table 18.2
Coke-Pepsi Example: Choosing Pricing Strategies When Quantitative Information Is Not Available

	Pepsi's strategy	
	Uniform pricing	Flexible pricing
Coke's strategy		
Uniform pricing	(2*, 2**)	(3, 1)
Flexible pricing	(1, 4**)	(4*, 3)

Note. The first entry in each cell denotes Coke's ranking, and the second entry in each cell indicates Pepsi's ranking (1 = least preferred to 4 = most preferred).
*Coke's optimal policies conditional on Pepsi's policies.
**Pepsi's optimal policies conditional on Coke's policies.

Fusion for Profit Maxim

Markets can reach equilibrium even if firms do not have precise quantitative information about each other. All that is necessary is that each firm knows how the other will rank different strategies.

Point to consider.   We continue with the Coca-Cola example. When Ivester made an announcement to the media that Coke was planning to use flexible pricing for its vending machine sales, what was he trying to do? Why did the stock market react positively to this announcement?

One possibility is that Ivester was sending a *signal* to Pepsi. Specifically, it could be argued that Ivester was trying to move from the noncooperative (2, 2) cell to the cooperative (4, 3) cell. That is, both Coke and Pepsi could have increased their profits if Pepsi had followed Coke and introduced flexible pricing. Note that the positive reaction of the stock market was consistent with this *signaling* hypothesis.

◤ Why did this win-win cooperative outcome not occur?

As reported in the *Wall Street Journal* (17 December 1999), the CEO of Coca-Cola, Ivester, had recently made the following remark to a Brazilian newsmagazine: "Coca-Cola is a product whose *utility* varies from moment to moment. In a final summer championship, when people meet in a stadium to have fun, the utility [*reservation price*] of a cold Coca-Cola is very high. So it is fair that it should be more expensive."

Ivester's remarks generated adverse publicity for Coca-Cola because they were considered insensitive. Consequently, Coke had to backtrack; furthermore, Pepsi was forced into a defensive mode where it stuck to the status quo of uniform pricing. In fact, a Pepsi spokesman declared, "We believe that machines that raise prices in hot weather [flexible pricing] exploit consumers who live in warm climates."

Fusion for Profit Maxim

Public announcements by the CEO of a firm are critical *market signals* because they show that the firm is committed to a particular strategy. If such announcements are executed well, both the firm and its competitor can gain.

◤ 18.3 Choosing Optimal Strategies When Competitors React: Some Refinements

The previous analysis examined the case where each firm has only one marketing decision variable. In our examples, we focused on price. Furthermore, we considered the case where each firm had only two alternatives (e.g., uniform pricing and flexible pricing).

In many cases, however, the firm needs to choose the optimal levels of several marketing decision variables such as price and advertising. Furthermore, for each decision variable, it is likely that the firm has a number of options. Thus, in the Coca-Cola example, each firm can choose many different price levels, not just two. We now show how the earlier methodology can be refined to analyze these cases.

▶ *How can the firm choose the optimal marketing policy when multiple strategies are available? Assume that each firm has only one decision variable.*

To answer this question, we need to introduce the concept of a *reaction curve*.

Example: Consider the computer chip market. For simplicity, we focus on two major players: Intel and AMD. In our example, we assume that the market considers the Intel chip to be somewhat superior to the AMD chip.

As in the Coca-Cola example, each firm (Intel and AMD) will choose its pricing policy conditional on the price chosen by its competitor. As shown below, this set of choices defines the reaction curve for that firm. Note that, in contrast to the Coca-Cola example, both Intel and AMD can choose multiple strategies (prices).

▶ *How can we obtain AMD's reaction curve?*

Consider any price chosen by Intel, say $200 per chip. Given this price, let's say that AMD's optimal policy is to charge $180 (< $200) per chip. Thus the pair (200, 180) corresponds to AMD's optimal price if Intel charges $200 per chip. This market outcome is shown by point F in figure 18.1. Similarly, suppose Intel charges a lower price of $130 per chip. Let's say that AMD's optimal price is now $115 (< $130) per chip. Then, the pair (130, 115) corresponds to AMD's optimal price if Intel charges $130 per chip. See point G in figure 18.1.

Using the same methodology, we can determine AMD's optimal prices conditional on different prices that Intel can charge. The set of all such pairs is shown by the curve AEB in figure 18.1. We say that AEB is AMD's reaction curve. Similarly, the curve CED defines Intel's optimal pricing strategies conditional on AMD's pricing strategies. We say that CED is Intel's reaction curve.

Note that the only point that the two reaction curves have in common is E, where Intel charges a price of $150 per chip and AMD charges $140 per chip. We say that E defines the noncooperative Nash equilibrium in the chip market.

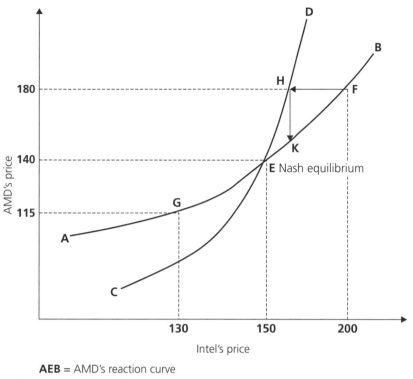

AEB = AMD's reaction curve
CED = Intel's reaction curve

Figure 18.1 Intel-AMD example: Reaction curves when prices are strategic complements.

To see why E is the only equilibrium solution, consider the following heuristic argument. Let's say that Intel charges $200 per chip, and AMD charges $180 per chip (point F in figure 18.1).

▶ Can this set of prices be an equilibrium?

As discussed, each firm maximizes its conditional profits given any policy chosen by its rival. Thus, given AMD's price of $180, Intel will reduce its price below $200 in order to maximize its profits (see point H on Intel's reaction curve in figure 18.1).

▶ What will AMD do now?

Given Intel's lower price (see point H), AMD will reduce its price (see point K on AMD's reaction curve). Note that K is closer to E than F is. This sequence of pricing moves and countermoves will continue. Finally, the market will converge to E, the equilibrium solution.

> **Fusion for Profit Maxim**
>
> The reaction curve defines the firm's optimal policies conditional on any policies chosen by its competitor. The Nash noncooperative equilibrium occurs where the two reaction curves intersect.

▶ *In the Intel-AMD example, why do the reaction curves slope upward?*

Consider any point on AMD's reaction curve. For example, suppose AMD charges $115 per chip, and Intel charges $130 per chip.

Suppose Intel increases its price from $130 to $135 (say). Then, different scenarios are possible:

1. The market for AMD's chip could become less price-sensitive than before, and
2. The market for AMD's chip could become more price sensitive than before.

We examine each of these scenarios below.

Scenario 1

Suppose that when Intel increases its price from $130 to $135, the demand for AMD's chip becomes less price-sensitive than before. Then AMD will follow Intel and also increase its price, though not necessarily by the same amount. Thus, AMD will charge a higher price than $115. Since both prices move in the same direction, AMD's reaction curve is upward sloping. (This is the assumption that we implicitly made in our previous analysis.) We say that AMD's and Intel's prices are *strategic complements*.

Note that the notion of strategic complementarity has nothing to do with the concept of *complementarity*. Thus, the AMD chip and the Intel chip are similar products. Hence they are substitutes—not complements. However, for the scenario above, their prices are strategic complements.

> **Fusion for Profit Maxim**
>
> If the marketing decision variables are strategic complements, the reaction curves will be upward sloping.

▶ *Why is the reaction curve for Intel steeper than the reaction curve for AMD?*

Suppose this is not the case. Following the previous heuristic argument, we can show the following result. Suppose we start from any arbitrary point on AMD's reaction curve. Then the sequence of moves and countermoves will lead to an ever-widening pattern of *price oscillations*.[4] Hence the market can reach equilibrium only if the reaction curve for Intel is steeper than AMD's reaction curve.

Scenario 2

Suppose instead that when Intel increases its price, the market for AMD's chip becomes more price-sensitive. Then, AMD will *reduce* its price when Intel *increases* its price. In this case, AMD's reaction curve will be downward sloping (see figure 18.2). We say that AMD's and Intel's prices are *strategic substitutes*.

▶ *Suppose prices are strategic substitutes. Will Intel's reaction curve be steeper than AMD's?*

One can use the previous heuristic argument to show that, if this is not the case, the equilibrium will not be stable. Hence Intel's reaction curve must be steeper than AMD's.

Note that, *regardless of whether prices are strategic substitutes or* strategic complements, Intel's reaction curve must be steeper than AMD's. If this condition does not hold, the market will not reach equilibrium.

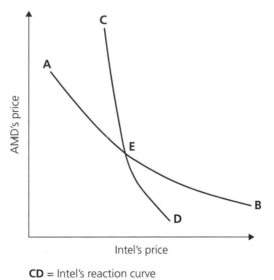

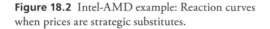

CD = Intel's reaction curve
AB = AMD's reaction curve

Figure 18.2 Intel-AMD example: Reaction curves when prices are strategic substitutes.

Fusion for Profit Maxim

If the marketing decision variables are strategic substitutes, the reaction curves will be downward sloping.

▲   *Are advertising decisions strategic substitutes or strategic complements?*

As in the case of pricing, advertising decisions can be either strategic substitutes or strategic complements. In many cases, the firm should spend less on advertising when its competitor increases its advertising expenditure. The intuition is that higher advertising spending by the competitor will reduce the productivity of the firm's own advertising. For example, the firm's sales volume may depend on its *share of voice* in the marketplace. Hence both advertising reaction curves will be downward sloping. Since the decision variables for both firms (i.e., advertising expenditures) move in opposite directions, we say that the firm's advertising decisions are strategic substitutes.

In contrast, consider an industry in the early phase of the *product life cycle*. Then, higher advertising by a competitor can expand the market and hence increase the productivity of the firm's advertising. In this case, the advertising reaction curves will be upward sloping. We say that the firm's advertising decisions are strategic complements.

Fusion for Profit Maxim

In general, advertising decisions are strategic substitutes, and pricing decisions are strategic complements. However, under certain market conditions, advertising decisions can be strategic complements, and pricing decisions can be strategic substitutes.

▲   *18.4 Some Additional Examples of Optimal Decision Making When Competitors React*

We now use the general theoretical framework to analyze how firms will react to changing market conditions, after allowing for the effects of competitive reaction.

▲   *Suppose the firm's competitor has just introduced a highly effective new commercial for its product. How should the firm and its competitor change their advertising budgets?*

In most cases, the competitor's new commercial will increase the *marginal productivity* of advertising for the competitor. Hence, for any given advertising expenditure by the firm, its competitor should increase its advertising spending.

Strategic Substitutes

Suppose advertising decisions are strategic substitutes (e.g., the industry is in the maturity or decline phase of the product life cycle). Then, the reaction curves for both the firm and its competitor will be downward sloping (figure 18.3). Since the competitor's reaction curve will move upward, and the firm's reaction curve remains unchanged, the competitor will increase its advertising spending, and the firm will *decrease* its advertising (compare points E and F).

Strategic Complements

Suppose advertising decisions are strategic complements. For example, the industry is in the growth stage of the product life cycle. Then, both reaction curves will be upward sloping (figure 18.4). Hence both firms will increase their respective advertising expenditures.

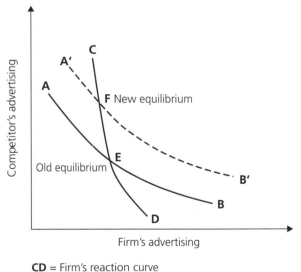

CD = Firm's reaction curve
AB = Competitor's old reaction curve
A'B' = Competitor's new reaction curve

Figure 18.3 Reaction curves when advertising decisions are strategic substitutes.

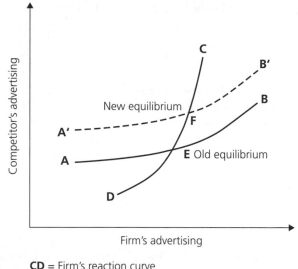

CD = Firm's reaction curve
AB = Competitor's old reaction curve
A'B' = Competitor's new reaction curve

Figure 18.4 Reaction curves when advertising decisions are strategic complements.

Fusion for Profit Maxim

The effect of a change in market conditions on a firm's strategy depends critically on whether the decision variables for the firm and its competitors are strategic substitutes or strategic complements.

▶ *Suppose a major airline* retires some long-term debt. *How will this decision affect prices in the airline industry? Assume that prices are strategic complements.*

For simplicity, consider two firms, Continental and Rival, where Rival consists of all other airlines. As discussed, Continental's reaction curve describes Continental's optimal pricing strategies for any price strategy chosen by Rival. Similarly, Rival's reaction curve describes Rival's optimal pricing strategies for any price strategy chosen by Continental. Since prices are strategic complements, the reaction functions for both Continental and Rival will be upward sloping (figure 18.5).

Now Continental's future fixed costs (i.e., interest payments to bondholders) will fall when Continental retires long-term debt. Since Continental's cash flows are now less risky, Continental is likely to price more aggressively.

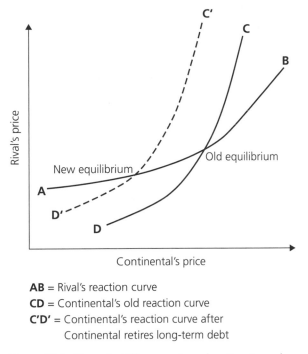

AB = Rival's reaction curve
CD = Continental's old reaction curve
C'D' = Continental's reaction curve after
Continental retires long-term debt

Figure 18.5. Example: Effect on prices when Continental retires long-term debt.

Thus, for any price chosen by Rival, Continental will charge a lower price than before. Hence Continental's reaction curve will move inward, from CD to C'D' (see figure 18.5).

▶ *How will Continental's decision to retire long-run debt affect Rival's reaction curve?*

Since Continental's decision to retire long term debt does not affect Rival's cost structure, Rival's reaction curve, AB, will not change. The net result is that *both Continental and Rival will reduce their prices* after Continental retires some long-term debt.

Fusion for Profit Maxim

In general, a firm's financing decisions (e.g., retiring long-term debt) will affect the marketing strategies chosen by that firm and by its competitors.

Point to consider. Will Continental's market share increase after Continental reduces its long-run debt?

Both Continental and Rival are likely to reduce their prices following Continental's retirement of long-term debt. Hence the effects on Continental's market share (volume-based and revenue-based) are ambiguous.

Point to consider.   Consider two tractor manufacturers, Caterpillar and Komatsu, that compete in the large-tractor market. Suppose a new supplier has emerged that can supply generic spare parts for Caterpillar tractors. How should Caterpillar and Komatsu adjust the prices of their large tractors?

Assume that prices are strategic complements. A similar analysis can be performed if prices are strategic substitutes (figure 18.6).

Since low-priced generic spare parts are now available for Caterpillar's tractors, it is less attractive for Caterpillar to charge low prices for its tractors now in order to make more profits from the sale of high-priced proprietary spare parts in the future. Consequently, for any price chosen by Komatsu, Caterpillar should charge a *higher* price for its tractors than before (i.e., Caterpillar will sell fewer tractors than before). Hence Caterpillar's reaction curve will move to the right from CD to C'D' (see figure 18.6).

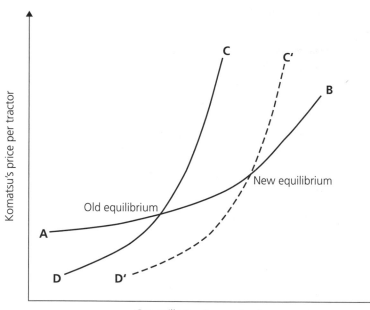

AB = Komatsu's reaction curve
CD = Caterpillar's reaction curve before generic parts are available
C'D' = Caterpillar's reaction curve after generic parts become available

Figure 18.6 Example: Effect of generic spare parts for Caterpillar tractors when prices are strategic complements.

Komatsu's reaction curve, in contrast, is unaffected because generic spare parts are not available for Komatsu tractors. Hence both Komatsu and Caterpillar should increase the prices of their respective large tractors.

Fusion for Profit Maxim

Suppose generic spare parts become available for the firm's durable product. Then, in general, both the firm and its competitors should increase the prices of their durable products when prices are strategic complements.

Point to consider. Suppose generic spare parts become available for Caterpillar's tractors. How will Caterpillar's *discount rate* affect the prices of large tractors?

Suppose Caterpillar's discount rate is high. Then, for any given value of profits from the sale of proprietary spare parts in the future, the effect on Caterpillar's long-run profit (*net present value*) will be reduced. This implies that the effect of generic spare parts will be dampened if Caterpillar's discount rate is high (i.e., in figure 18.6, CD and C'D' will be closer when the discount rate is high).

In other words, the movement in Caterpillar's reaction curve will be less when Caterpillar's discount rate is high (i.e., CD and C'D' will be closer together when the discount rate is high). Consequently, after generic spare parts for Caterpillar tractors become available, *both Caterpillar and Komatsu should increase their tractor prices by smaller amounts when Caterpillar's discount rate is high.*

Fusion for Profit Maxim

Suppose a firm sells durables. Then, the higher the discount rate is, the smaller is the effect of generic spare parts on the price of the durable.

Example: Consider two firms, say Intel and AMD, that compete in a given segment of the computer chip market. Suppose both Intel and AMD have predictable learning curves and demand is stable in this segment. Should Intel and AMD focus on short-run or long-run profits?

Here, the key decision variable for each firm is pricing. For simplicity, assume that each firm can choose one of two prices: a high current price that maximizes the firm's short-run profits (*myopic pricing*) or a low current price that attempts to leverage the firm's learning curve by forgoing some current profits to increase future profits (*strategic pricing*). Furthermore, suppose both firms make their pricing decisions simultaneously.

The market outcomes are listed in table 18.3. In each cell, the first entry is the net present value (NPV) of this computer chip segment for Intel, and

Table 18.3
Intel-AMD Example: A Comparison of Myopic and Strategic Pricing Strategies When There Is a Learning Curve

	AMD	
	Myopic pricing	Strategic pricing
Intel		
Myopic pricing	(800, 100)	(800− −, 100+ +**)
Strategic pricing	(800+ +*, 100− −)	(800+*, 100+**)

Note: Numbers in parentheses represent profits in millions of dollars; the first entry in each cell indicates Intel's profits and the second AMD's profits.
*Intel's optimal policies conditional on AMD's policies.
**AMD's optimal policies conditional on Intel's policies.

the second is the corresponding NPV for AMD. Note that the particular NPV numbers used are purely illustrative. As discussed in the Coca-Cola example, the particular dollar values are not important. *The critical issue is how each firm ranks its NPVs in different cells.*

Suppose both Intel and AMD use myopic pricing to maximize their respective short-run profits. Let's say that the NPVs from these strategies are as follows: $800 million for Intel (the larger player) and $100 million for AMD (the smaller player).

▶ *What will happen if AMD uses myopic pricing but Intel prices strategically to leverage its learning curve?*

Since the AMD and Intel chips are similar but not identical, both AMD and Intel have some flexibility in setting their respective prices. Suppose AMD prices myopically, but Intel prices strategically.

Since Intel is using strategic pricing, for any price charged by AMD, Intel will charge a lower price than it would have charged if both firms had priced myopically. Hence the price differential between the Intel and AMD chips will be wider if Intel prices strategically than when both firms use myopic pricing. Consequently, compared with the case where both firms price myopically, Intel's current sales will increase sharply. Hence Intel's NPV will be considerably greater than $800 million (denoted by 800+ + in table 18.3). Since AMD is using a myopic pricing policy, its chip is "overpriced." Hence AMD's NPV will be significantly less than $100 million (denoted by 100− −).

Similarly, if AMD uses strategic pricing and Intel uses myopic pricing, AMD's NPV will be substantially higher than $100 million (100+ +), and Intel's NPV will be considerably lower than $800 million (800− −).

▶ *What will happen if both Intel and AMD attempt to leverage their respective learning curves by using strategic pricing?*

For this scenario, each firm will increase its NPV because of the future cost reductions that it can achieve. However, the gain to each firm from learning will be less than it would have been if only that firm had used strategic pricing and its competitor had used myopic pricing. Consequently, when both firms use strategic pricing, Intel's NPV will be $800+ million, and AMD's will be $100+ million.

▶ *What pricing strategies will Intel and AMD choose?*

Let's refer back to table 18.4, in which * denotes Intel's optimal strategy conditional on any strategy chosen by AMD, and ** denotes AMD's optimal strategy conditional on any strategy chosen by Intel.

- Suppose AMD chooses myopic pricing. Since 800+ + is greater than 800, Intel should choose strategic pricing.
- Suppose AMD chooses strategic pricing. Since 800+ is greater than 800−, Intel should choose strategic pricing.

Thus, regardless of which strategy AMD picks, Intel should choose strategic pricing. Similarly, regardless of which pricing strategy Intel chooses, AMD should choose strategic pricing.

Note that the only cell that contains the * and ** notations is the one where both firms use strategic pricing. Hence both Intel and AMD should set low prices for their computer chips. The intuition is that by charging a low price, each firm can leverage its learning curve and maximize its long-run profit.

Point to consider.   Suppose Intel has a predictable learning curve for its computer chip, but AMD's learning curve is uncertain. (AMD is a relatively new player in the chip market.) What pricing strategy (myopic or strategic) should each firm choose? Assume that each firm has the same cost of capital.

Since Intel's learning curve is predictable, Intel will obtain a higher NPV from strategic pricing than from myopic pricing, regardless of which pricing strategy AMD chooses. Hence Intel should always choose strategic pricing.

Since AMD's learning curve is uncertain, AMD's pricing strategy will depend on several factors, including the magnitude of uncertainty in learning, the expected gains from future decreases in cost that result from learning, and AMD's cost of capital. Consequently, different scenarios are possible depending on which combination of factors AMD faces.

Scenario 1

Suppose AMD's future cost reductions from using strategic pricing are highly uncertain. Then, other factors being the same, the net present value of these cost reductions will be low, since the cost of capital for high-tech firms such as Intel and AMD is high. Consequently, AMD should choose myopic pricing regardless of which pricing strategy Intel uses.

Scenario 2

Suppose the expected gains to AMD from future cost reductions via learning are high, and the uncertainty in learning is low. Then, it may be worthwhile for AMD to forgo some current profits in exchange for a substantial though uncertain improvement in future profits resulting from the learning curve. Hence, other factors being the same, AMD should price strategically.

Fusion for Profit Maxim

When the learning curve is predictable, the firm should use strategic pricing to maximize long-run profits. When the learning curve is highly uncertain, the optimal policy for the firm may be to focus on short-run profits, especially if the discount rate is high.

▲ 18.5 What Does Competitive Reaction Imply about Data Collection and Data Analysis?

So far, we have focused on theoretical issues. We now discuss empirical measurement.

In general, the firm's data collection and data analysis strategies will depend on whether the firm has information on the past strategies of its competitors. In many cases, the firm will have only partial information about competitors' marketing policies. For example, historical pricing data for competitors' products may be available. However, historical data on competitors' advertising spending on particular products may not.

We shall examine both possibilities. However, for simplicity we begin with the case where the firm has information about the past marketing decisions of its competitors (e.g., prices).

▲ Consider the Coca-Cola example. What empirical analyses should Coke and Pepsi perform in order to choose their optimal marketing policies?

Each firm should recognize that the demand for its product depends on the marketing decisions of its competitor. For instance, Coke's sales will depend on *both* Coke's and Pepsi's prices and advertising strategies. Hence Coke needs to determine the effect of Pepsi's strategies on Coke's past sales.

Similarly, Pepsi needs to estimate how Coke's marketing policies have affected Pepsi's sales in the past. For simplicity, we focus on the case where price is the only marketing decision variable.

Effects of Competitors' Policies

Different scenarios are possible, depending on whether prices are strategic substitutes or strategic complements. For illustrative purposes, we shall consider the case where Coke's and Pepsi's prices are strategic complements. That is, if Coke reduces its price, Pepsi will also reduce its price, though not necessarily by the same amount. Similarly, if Pepsi increases its price, Coke will increase its price to some degree.

Suppose Coke reduced its price last month by $1 per unit. Let's say that Pepsi responded to Coke's price cut by reducing its price by $1.25 per unit. Suppose the result was that Coke increased its sales last month by 5,000 units. Then, the increase in Coke's sales volume (5,000 units) last month is the net result of two opposite effects:

1. The *increase* in volume caused by the reduction in Coke's price (x units), and
2. The *decrease* in volume caused by Pepsi's price cut (y units).

Since Coke's sales volume increased by 5,000 units, x must be greater than 5,000. Note that if Coke does not consider the effect of Pepsi's price on Coke's demand in the past, Coke will *underestimate* the market's price sensitivity to a price cut by Coke.

Strategic Interdependence

Suppose Coke recognizes the problem discussed above. Specifically, Coke measures the *joint effect* of Coke's prices *and* Pepsi's prices on Coke's past sales.

▶ *Will this analysis give Coke the right information about how the market reacts to Coke's prices given any price charged by Pepsi?*

Interestingly, the answer is no. As we have discussed, Coke's optimal price policy depends on the price chosen by Pepsi. However, Pepsi's optimal price policy also depends on Coke's price. Because of this *strategic interdependence*, Coke should simultaneously analyze the demand for *both* Coke and Pepsi. Similarly, Pepsi should also simultaneously analyze the demand for both Pepsi and Coke.

If Coke (or Pepsi) does not perform a simultaneous analysis of demand, it will obtain biased estimates of how prices affect demand. Consequently, it is likely that Coke (or Pepsi) will make poor pricing decisions.[5]

> **Fusion for Profit Maxim**
>
> The firm should measure the joint effect of its own policies and those of its competitors on the sales of its product. In addition, because of strategic interdependence, the firm should simultaneously estimate the demand for its own product *and* the demand for the competitor's product.

► *The previous analysis assumed that each firm can observe the marketing decisions of its competitor. How should each firm proceed if it does not have historical data on the marketing decisions of its competitor?*

In many cases, firms may have incomplete information about the marketing policies chosen by their competitors. Consider the following example.

Example: Both Merck and Pfizer use sales forces to sell their products. However, neither firm knows how much its competitor has spent on its own sales force in the past. How should Merck and Pfizer analyze historical sales data in order to determine the optimal level of spending on its sales force?

Since neither Merck nor Pfizer has information on the marketing decisions of its competitor, the method described earlier cannot be used. One approach for each firm is to proceed as follows:

- Estimate the reaction curve of its competitor,
- Use this information to infer the sales force expenditures that the competitor chose in the past, and
- Apply the standard method discussed earlier to analyze the historical sales data for *both* firms simultaneously, using these imputed values.

To illustrate, suppose Merck spent $10 million on its sales force in March 2006 and obtained a sales revenue of $100 million. The question that Merck needs to answer is: What was Pfizer's sales force expenditure in March 2006?

Suppose the empirically estimated reaction curve for Pfizer shows that, if Merck spent $10 million on its sales force, Pfizer's optimal policy would have been to spend $12 million on its own sales force. Then, Merck can analyze its sales data for March 2006 using this imputed value of $12 million for Pfizer's sales force expenditure in that month. Similarly, Merck can calculate the imputed values of Pfizer's sales force expenditures for other months.

Pfizer can use the same methodology to analyze Merck's empirically estimated reaction function and determine the imputed values of Merck's sales force expenditures for each month in the data set.

Since there are no longer any missing data regarding competitors' marketing policies, Merck and Pfizer can now use the standard methodology (described earlier) to analyze the historical sales data for both firms *simultaneously* and choose their optimal marketing policies accordingly.

> **Fusion for Profit Maxim**
>
> The firm may be able to determine its optimal policies even if it does not have historical data on the marketing policies chosen by its competitors. One approach is to impute the values of the missing data on competitors' marketing policies by assuming that each firm maximizes its profits conditional on the policies chosen by its competitors.

◤ 18.6 How Useful Is the Game-Theoretic Methodology for Marketing Decision Making When Competitors React?

The methodology discussed earlier can be extended to the case where several firms are involved, each firm uses multiple marketing instruments, or information varies across firms. For example, firms may first compete on price and then on advertising. Alternatively, they may compete by simultaneously changing both price and advertising.

In many cases, it is not obvious which behavioral scenario will occur in the market. Firms may react using different marketing variables. Thus, suppose a competitor reduces the price of its product. Then, the firm may react by changing a different decision variable. For example, when the competitor cuts its price, the firm may increase its advertising expenditure but keep the price of its product unchanged. Similarly, a new entrant in an industry may not have accurate information about the cost structures of incumbent firms.

> **Fusion for Profit Maxim**
>
> The *game-theoretic* method can be extended to the case where firms use different marketing instruments and *behavioral modes*.

◤ 18.7 How Can the Firm Make Sequential Decisions after Allowing for Competitive Reaction?

So far, we have focused on the case where firms make decisions at one point of time. However, firms often make sequential decisions. For example, suppose the market contains two competitors. Under one scenario, both firms compete on price first and then set their advertising budgets. Alternatively, both firms could simultaneously compete on price and advertising. Each of these behavioral scenarios has different implications for market behavior.

We now discuss how firms can use the general methodology to make sequential decisions.

Example: Suppose two major global automobile manufacturers, Ford and General Motors, are planning to enter the small SUV market in China. One strategy for each firm is to set up manufacturing facilities in China at the beginning of the first year. An alternative strategy for each firm is to use a sequential decision-making approach.[6] That is, export SUVs from the United States to China in the first year. If the demand for SUVs in China is high, set up manufacturing operations in China at the beginning of the second year. If the demand for SUVs is low, do not enter the China market.

For simplicity, assume that Ford and General Motors simultaneously make their initial decisions to manufacture in China or to export to the Chinese market, both firms produce similar SUVs, and the size of the Chinese SUV market is fixed.

▲ What market entry strategies should Ford and General Motors use?

Suppose both Ford and General Motors are *risk-neutral* and have the same discount rates (20%). Then, each firm seeks to maximize the net present value of its expected future profits. Suppose that, if either Ford or General Motors chooses the export alternative, it will have to spend $70 million to set up the export unit at the beginning of the first year.

Suppose that if the demand for SUVs in China is high, each exporting firm will make a gross profit of $100 million at the end of the first year. If the demand is low, the gross profit for each firm at the end of the year will be $20 million. Assume that each market condition (high or low demand) is equally likely.

Then, the expected gross profit for each firm from export operations at the end of the first year is $60 million ([0.5 × 20] + [0.5 × 100]). Hence the net present value for each firm from export operations in the first year is an expected loss of $20 million:

$$\frac{\text{Expected gross profit at the end of the first year}}{1 + \text{discount rate}} - \text{cost of export operations}$$

$$= \left(\frac{\$60M}{1 + 20\%} \right) - \$70M$$

Suppose the required investment to set up a manufacturing plant in China is $1 billion. Suppose that if demand is high, gross industry profits will be $1 billion per year. However, if demand is low, gross industry profits will be only $200 million per year. As noted earlier, we assume that both market conditions (high or low demand) are equally likely.

Each firm has two alternatives. The first is to set up manufacturing operations directly in China at the beginning of the first year. The second is to proceed sequentially. That is, export to China in the first year. If demand is low, do not enter the China market. If demand is high, set up manufacturing operations in China at the beginning of the second year. Hence four scenarios are possible. These are described in table 18.4.

Table 18.4
Ford-General Motors Example: The Joint Effects of Competitive Reaction and Sequential Decision Making

	General Motors	
	Set up plant in China now	Export to China first
Ford		
Set up plant in China now	(500*, 500**)	(2,000*, −20)
Export to China first	(−20, 2,000**)	(755, 755)

Note: Numbers in parentheses represent profits in millions of dollars; the first entry in each cell indicates Ford's net present value (NPV) or conditional NPV and the second the corresponding values for General Motors.

*Optimal policies for Ford conditional on policies chosen by General Motors.

**Optimal policies for General Motors conditional on policies chosen by Ford.

For each cell, the first entry in the table denotes the net present value or *conditional net present value* where appropriate for Ford. The second entry in each cell denotes the corresponding values for General Motors. To see how these entries are obtained, see the appendix at the end of this chapter.[7]

Let's refer to table 18.4, where * denotes the optimal policies for Ford, conditional on General Motors' policies. Correspondingly, let ** denote the optimal policies for General motors, conditional on Ford's policies. For example, if General Motors chooses to export to China first, the optimal policy for Ford is to set up a plant in China now (2,000 > 755). As shown in table 18.4, the only cell that contains both the * and ** notations is the cell in which each firm sets up a plant in China now. This cell is the Nash equilibrium.

Note that, by assumption, a $1 billion plant is sufficient to meet demand for the optimistic (high) demand scenario. However, because of competition, each firm (Ford and General Motors) will set up a $1 billion plant at the beginning of the first year. Hence competition leads to a *race to the market* and results in significant industry overcapacity.

Fusion for Profit Maxim

The firm can choose optimal sequential marketing decisions after allowing for competitive reaction and the economic value of *strategic flexibility*.[8]

Point to consider.   What strategies should Ford and General Motors choose if they can cooperate?

As discussed in the appendix, both firms should cooperate by forming a *strategic alliance*/partnership. Specifically, the optimal strategy for each firm is to proceed sequentially:

1. In the first step, both firms should export SUVs to China from the United States in the first year and share the risk and return from this joint export operation.

2. If demand in China in the first year is low, neither firm will enter the Chinese market. However, if demand is high, both firms should set up manufacturing operations in China at the beginning of the second year and share the market equally.

As shown in the appendix, the net present value to each firm from the cooperative solution ($765 million) is greater than the net present value from the noncooperative Nash solution ($500 million). Note that both firms gain by cooperating. Thus, both firms share the risk of export operations. In addition, both firms share the benefits from strategic flexibility.

▶ Under what conditions will this cooperative strategy succeed?

This cooperative strategy can work provided Ford and General Motors are the only potential foreign firms to enter the Chinese market. However, there are other potential entrants into the SUV market in China (e.g., Honda and Nissan). Furthermore, given the capital-intensive cost structure of the industry, the *first mover* is likely to have a *strategic price advantage* over *late entrants* (see the discussion for Scenario 2 in the appendix).

Hence, regardless of whether Ford and General Motors cooperate, other competitors such as Honda and Nissan are likely to enter the Chinese market at the beginning of the first year. Consequently, the cooperative strategy may not work.

Fusion for Profit Maxim

Firms can gain by using cooperative sequential market entry strategies, especially when market conditions are uncertain and there are only a few players in the market. However, these cooperative strategies may not work when the industry contains multiple players.

Point to consider.   Can myopic strategies lead to optimal decisions? Consider either firm, say Ford. Ford has two choices:

1. It can set up manufacturing operations in China at the beginning of the first year.
2. Alternatively, it can use a *sequential market entry strategy*. That is, it can export to China in the first year. If demand is low, it will withdraw from the Chinese market. If demand is high, it will set up manufacturing operations in China at the beginning of the second year.

By assumption, Ford acts myopically by failing to consider the effect of General Motors' reactions.

Intuitively, one might expect that myopic decision making will always lead to bad strategies. Interestingly, this is not necessarily the case. In this example, the myopic net present value to Ford from setting up manufacturing operations in China immediately is $2 billion. Similarly, the myopic conditional net present value of using a sequential market entry strategy is only $1.647 billion (< $2 billion). (See the appendix for details.)

Hence, if Ford acts myopically by not allowing for competitive reaction by General Motors, it will set up manufacturing operations in China immediately. *Note that this is the same strategy that Ford would have chosen if it had behaved strategically and allowed for competitive reaction by General Motors.*

Fusion for Profit Maxim

Under certain conditions, myopic decision making may lead to the same policies as strategic decision making that allows for the effects of competitive reaction.

Point to consider.   Suppose management is under pressure by Wall Street to focus on short-run profits. What strategies will Ford and General Motors choose vis-à-vis the Chinese SUV market?

Let's say that Wall Street uses a one-year horizon to value profits. Since Wall Street is myopic, investors value only the cash flows generated in the first year. For simplicity, assume that Wall Street has the same information as Ford and General Motors. Furthermore, suppose the managers of both Ford and General Motors seek to satisfy Wall Street.

Suppose both Ford and General Motors set up manufacturing plants in China at the beginning of the first year. Then, as discussed earlier, the average industry gross profits will be $600 million in the first year. By assumption, Ford and General Motors sell highly similar SUVs in the China market. Hence Wall Street will expect each firm to obtain an average gross profit of $300 million ($0.5 \times 600$) from its China operations at the end of the first year.

Suppose Wall Street values these cash flows from each firm's China operations at X, where X is a positive quantity.

Suppose Ford sets up a plant in China at the beginning of the first year, but General Motors chooses the export alternative. Then, Wall Street expects that Ford will obtain an average profit of $600 million at the end of the first year. Hence Wall Street will value Ford's China operations at $2X$ at the beginning of the first year.

Since General Motors has chosen the export alternative, Wall Street will assign a negative net present value of $20 million to this operation (see earlier discussion). That is, General Motors's stock price will fall by $20 million at the beginning of the first year. Similarly, if General Motors sets up a plant in China at the beginning of the first year and Ford chooses the export alternative, Wall Street will value General Motors's China strategy at $2X$ and will assign Ford's export operation a negative net present value of $20 million.

Suppose both Ford and General Motors export SUVs to China in the first year. Then, Wall Street will assign negative net present values of $20 million to each firm's export operation.

Table 18.5
Ford-General Motors Example: Effect of Wall Street's Valuation

	General Motors	
	Set up plant in China now	Export to China first
Ford		
Set up plant in China now	(X^*, X^{**})	$(2X^*, -20)$
Export to China first	$(-20, 2X^{**})$	$(-20, -20)$

Note: X denotes profits (in millions of dollars); the first entry in each cell indicates Ford's profits and the second General Motors's NPV.
*Ford's optimal policy for any policy chosen by General Motors.
**General Motors's optimal policy for any policy chosen by Ford.

The payoffs for the different scenarios are shown in table 18.5. The first entry in each cell denotes the incremental effect on Ford's stock price. The second entry in each cell denotes the incremental effect on General Motors's stock price.

Note that in table 18.5, the only cell that contains the * and ** notations is the (X, X) cell. Thus, given Wall Street's myopic valuations, both Ford and General Motors will set up manufacturing operations in China at the beginning of the first year.

Interestingly, in spite of Wall Street's myopic valuations, the managers of both Ford and General Motors will choose the optimal long-run strategies for their respective firms (i.e., strategies that allow for competitive reaction and the economic value of strategic flexibility).

Fusion for Profit Maxim

Under certain conditions, firms may choose optimal long-run policies even if investors are myopic and firms seek to satisfy those investors.

▶ Chapter 18 Key Points

- Firms in competitive industries can unambiguously maximize their profits without explicitly analyzing competitive retaliation. However, if the industry has few players, the concept of profit maximization is ambiguous.
- When the market contains few players, different behavioral scenarios are possible. In general, firms will seek to maximize their conditional risk-adjusted profits based on their assumptions about the marketing strategies chosen by their competitors.
- Markets in which firms sell differentiated products can reach equilibrium even if firms do not have precise quantitative information about each other.

- In general, prices are strategic complements, and advertising decisions are strategic substitutes. However, for certain market conditions, prices can be strategic substitutes, and advertising decisions can be strategic complements.
- Suppose generic spare parts become available for a competitor's durable product. Then, both the firm and its competitor should increase the prices of their durable products. Other factors being the same, these price changes will be smaller when firms have high discount rates.
- Suppose the firm and its competitor have predictable learning curves for their new products. Then, both firms should focus on long-run profits and charge low prices initially. However, if the learning curves are uncertain, firms may prefer to focus on short-run profits, especially when the uncertainty in learning and the discount rate are high.
- In order to choose optimal marketing policies, the firm needs to simultaneously estimate the effect of the competitor's marketing policies on its sales and the effect of its own marketing policies on the competitor's sales.
- The firm can make optimal sequential decisions after simultaneously allowing for competitive reaction and the economic value of strategic flexibility.
- Under certain circumstances, firms may choose optimal long-run policies even if investors are shortsighted and managers seek to satisfy those investors.

◣ *Appendix*

We return to the Ford–General Motors example to compute profits for different sequential strategies.

In table 18.A, the first entry in each cell denotes the appropriate net present value or conditional net present value for Ford. The second entry in each cell denotes the corresponding value for General Motors.

The entries in Table 18.A are obtained as follows.

Table 18.A
Ford-General Motors Example: Joint Effects of Competitive Reaction and Sequential Decision Making

	General Motors	
	Set up plant in China now	Export to China first
Ford		
Set up plant in China now	(500*, 500**)	(2,000*, −20)
Export to China first	(−20, 2,000**)	(755, 755)

Note. Numbers in parentheses represent profits in millions of dollars; the first entry in each cell indicates Ford's profits or conditional NPV and the second the corresponding values for General Motors.

*Optimal policies for Ford conditional on policies chosen by General Motors.

**Optimal policies for General Motors conditional on policies chosen by Ford.

Scenario 1: Both Ford and General Motors Set Up Plants in China Now

Suppose both Ford and General Motors set up manufacturing plants in China at the beginning of the first year. Assume that each plant has sufficient capacity to meet demand under the high-demand scenario. Then, each firm will invest $1 billion. As discussed in the chapter, both demand scenarios (profits of $200 million or $1 billion annually) are equally likely. Hence the average industry gross profits will be $600 million per year ([0.5 × 200] + [0.5 × 1,000]).

Since Ford and General Motors produce similar SUVs, each firm will capture approximately 50% of the Chinese market. Hence each firm will obtain an average gross profit of $300 million per year. By assumption, the discount rate for each firm is 20% per annum. Hence, if both Ford and General Motors set up manufacturing operations in China at the beginning of the first year, the net present value of future profits to each firm is $1.5 billion (recurring annual profits of $300 million/discount rate of 20%).

Since each firm invests $1 billion in a manufacturing plant at the beginning of the first year, each firm will obtain a net present value of $500 million (net present value of future profits – investment in manufacturing at the beginning of the first year = $1.5 billion – $1 billion). This market outcome is shown by the (500, 500) cell in table 18.A.

Scenario 2: Ford Sets Up Plant in China Now, General Motors Exports to China First

Suppose Ford is a first mover and sets up manufacturing operations in China at the beginning of the first year. General Motors, on the other hand, chooses a sequential strategy. That is, General Motors exports SUVs from the United States to China during the first year.

▶ *How should Ford and General Motors revise their decisions in the second year after the demand uncertainty has been resolved?*

Consider General Motors first. Suppose the demand for SUVs in China in the first year is high. Given this information at the end of the first year, General Motors would like to set up a manufacturing plant in China at the beginning of the second year. However, Ford has already established a plant of sufficient capacity to meet the entire market demand.

Thus, if General Motors sets up a plant in China in the second year, Ford will cut the prices of its SUVs sharply. In fact, since Ford's investment is *sunk*, Ford can cut its SUV prices in the second year drastically to the point where its *marginal costs* of SUVs are just covered. *Consequently, even if the high demand scenario occurs, it is too late for General Motors to set up manufacturing operations in China.*

Note that, because of Ford's preemptive strategy in the first year, General Motors will obtain zero cash flows from the second year onward. Hence the economic value to General Motors depends entirely on the cash flows in the first year. Specifically, General Motors will obtain a net present value of $50 million from its export earning in the first year:

$$\frac{\text{average annual profits in the first year}}{1 + \text{discount rate}} = \frac{0.5(20 + 100)}{1 + 20\%}.$$

General Motors will also incur an investment of $70 million at the beginning of the first year to set up export operations. Hence General Motors will obtain a negative net present value of $20 million.

▶ *What will Ford do once the demand uncertainty is resolved at the end of the first year?*

Even if demand is low, the gross annual profit ($200 million) is positive. *Hence Ford will remain in the Chinese market, regardless of whether demand is high or low.* Since Ford will not revise its decision at the end of the first year, the *standard net present value* calculation for valuing the project is appropriate. Since Ford is the only player in the market from the first year onward, and Ford expects to not revise its decisions, Ford will obtain all the industry profits every year from the first year onward (average value = $600 million per year).

This implies that the net present value of these profits to Ford at the beginning of the first year is $3 billion (average annual industry profits/discount rate = $600 million/20%). Since Ford incurs an investment of $1 billion at the beginning of the first year to set up a plant in China, the net present value of this strategy to Ford is $2 billion ($3 billion − $1 billion). This outcome is shown in the (2000, −20) cell in table 18.A.

Scenario 3: Ford Exports to China First, General Motors Sets Up Plant in China Now

Given the symmetry of the problem, we see that the net present value to Ford is a loss of $20 million. Furthermore, the net present value to General Motors is $2 billion. This outcome is shown in the (−20, 2000) cell in table 18.A.

Scenario 4: Both Ford and General Motors Export to China First

Suppose both Ford and General Motors export SUVs to China in the first year. At the end of the first year, demand uncertainty is resolved. If demand is low, both firms will leave the China market, and no further cash flows will be generated. If demand is high, both firms will set up manufacturing operations in China at the beginning of the second year. Note that each firm pursues a conditional manufacturing strategy based on the demand in the market. We say that each firm has strategic flexibility.

▶ *The remaining question is: What cash flows will Ford and General Motors obtain in the second year and thereafter when demand is high?*

Since both firms enter the market simultaneously at the beginning of the second year, neither firm has a first-mover advantage. In particular, since both firms produce similar SUVs, the industry gross profits ($1 billion per year for the high demand scenario) will be equally divided between Ford and General Motors. Thus, each firm will make an annual gross profit of $500 million (0.5 × 1,000) per year from the second year onward.

Since each firm knows that its competitor will also set up manufacturing operations in China at the beginning of the second year, each firm will set up a smaller plant than if it had set up manufacturing operations in China at the beginning of the first year. Suppose the required investment for each firm is $640 million. (We assume that there are *economies of scale* in manufacturing. That is, if plant capacity is doubled, the required investment will increase by a factor of less than two.)

▶ *What is the net effect of these sequential decision strategies?*

Both firms face demand uncertainty when they export to China in the first year. Hence each firm will obtain a negative net present value of $20 million from export operations regardless of whether demand is low or high (see Scenario 2 above). The cash flows from the second year onward are conditional on how demand uncertainty is resolved in the first year.

Suppose demand in the first year is low. Then, both firms will leave the China market at the end of the first year. Hence there will be no cash flows from the second year onward. Thus, for each firm the conditional net present value of cash flows from the second year onward is zero. If *demand is high*, each firm will invest $640 million at the beginning of the second year and make annual gross profits of $500 million per year from the second year onward. The conditional net present value to each firm from this strategy measured at the beginning of the second year is $1.86 billion ([annual gross profits from the second year onward/discount rate] − investment of $640 million at the beginning of the second year = [500/0.2] − 640).

The present value of these cash flows at the beginning of the first year is $1.55 billion:

$$\frac{\text{conditional net present value}}{(1 + \text{discount rate})} = \frac{\$1.86\ \text{billion}}{(1 + 20\%)}$$

Hence, if demand is high, the conditional net present value of cash flows to each firm from the second year onward is $1.55 billion.

By assumption, each market condition (low and high demand) is equally likely. Hence the conditional net present value of cash flows to each firm from the second year onward after allowing for strategic flexibility is $775 million ([50% × 0] + [50% × $1.55 billion]).

Since the net present value of cash flows for each firm in the first year is a loss of $20 million, each firm will obtain a value of $755 million ($775 million − $20 million). This outcome is shown in the (755, 755) cell in table 18.A.

Note that a $1 billion plant is sufficient to meet the maximum demand in the Chinese market. Hence competition leads to a race to the market and results in significant industry overcapacity (100% in the example).

▶ What will happen if Ford and General Motors cooperate?

Suppose Ford and General Motors cooperate by forming a fifty-fifty strategic alliance/partnership, in which each firm exports SUVs to China in the first year. Given this cooperative strategy, both firms will share equally the risk of export operations in the first year. Hence each firm will obtain a negative net present value of $10 million from its export operations in the first year.

If demand in the first year is low, both firms will leave the China market at the end of the year. Hence all cash flows from the second year on will be zeros. If demand is high, Ford and General Motors will share the market equally. Hence each firm will set up a plant worth $640 million in China at the beginning of the second year and make an average annual profit of $500 million from the second year onward.

As discussed above for Scenario 4, the conditional net present value of these cash flows from the second year onward is $775 million. Since the net present value to each firm of the cash flows in the first year is a loss of $10 million, each firm will obtain a value of $765 million ($775 million − $10 million) when both firms cooperate. Note that both Ford and General Motors will gain considerably under this cooperative strategy. Specifically, each firm's value will increase from $500 million (noncooperative solution) to $765 million (cooperative solution).

Furthermore, resources will not be wasted. Thus, if demand in the first year is low, neither Ford nor General Motors will set up manufacturing operations in China. If demand in the first year is high, both firms will set up plants to manufacture SUVs in China in the second year. Since each firm will set up a plant to meet half the market demand for SUVs, there will be no excess capacity.

▶ What will happen if Ford uses a sequential decision-making approach but behaves myopically (i.e., Ford does not consider competition by General Motors)?

Suppose Ford sets up manufacturing operations in China at the beginning of the first year. Then, it will invest $1 billion at the start of the first year. Since

Ford behaves myopically, it does not consider competition. Consequently, Ford assumes that it can make an average gross profit of $600 million at the end of the first year and at the end of every year thereafter. The net present value of this strategy is $2 billion ([average annual profit/discount rate] − investment in plant = [600/0.2] − 1,000).

Suppose instead that Ford uses a sequential strategy and exports to China in the first year. If demand is low in the first year, Ford will leave the Chinese market at the end of the year. Hence the cash flows from the second year onward will be zeros. Thus, the net present value from these cash flows is zero. If demand is high, Ford will invest $1 billion to set up manufacturing facilities in China at the beginning of the second year.

Given this strategy and its myopic assumption that there is no competition, Ford expects that it will earn an average gross profit of $1,000 million every year, from the end of the second year onward. The net present value of these cash flows measured at the beginning of the second year is $4 billion ([average annual gross profit/discount rate] − investment in plant = [1,000/0.2] − 1,000). If demand in the first year is low, Ford will not enter the Chinese market. Hence the cash flows from the second year onward will be zeros.

Since the high- and low-demand conditions are equally likely, the conditional net present value of expected cash flows from the second year onward measured at the beginning of the second year is $2 billion ([0.5 × 4] + [0.5 × 0]). Since the discount rate is 20%, the conditional net present value of these cash flows at the beginning of the first year is $1.667 billion ($2 billion/1.2).

As discussed, the net present value to Ford from export earnings in the first year is a loss of $20 million. Hence the value to Ford of this sequential strategy is $1.647 billion ($1.667 billion − $20 million). Note that the value from the sequential market entry strategy ($1.647 billion) is less than the net present value of setting up manufacturing operations in China at the beginning of the first year ($2 billion). Hence Ford will set up manufacturing operations in China at the beginning of the first year.

Interestingly, this myopic strategy is the same strategy that Ford would have chosen *after* allowing for *both* competitive reaction and the economic value of strategic flexibility.

X

Other Applications of Fusion for Profit

19

Measuring and Building Brand Equity

One of the key objectives of marketing is to differentiate the firm's products from competitive brands. Loosely speaking, the firm's goal is to develop *brand equity*. (A more formal definition will be given later in the chapter.) This raises a number of interesting questions. From a *Fusion for Profit* viewpoint, how can one measure the dollar value of brand equity? From a strategic viewpoint, what marketing strategies should the firm use to build and sustain its brand equity in the marketplace? This chapter addresses these issues.

The information covered in this chapter will be useful when you are faced with the following types of decisions:

- Under what conditions does my firm's product have brand equity?
- If my firm's product has brand equity, should my firm price its product higher than similar products in the marketplace?
- Which method or methods should my firm use to measure the dollar value of the brand equity of its product?
- Should my firm use financial data, behavioral data, or a combination of metrics to estimate the brand equity of its product?
- How does the name of my firm's product affect the product's brand equity?
- How does competitive behavior affect the brand equity of my firm's product, and how can my firm measure these effects?

- What strategies should my firm use to build and sustain the brand equity of its products?
- How can my firm coordinate its positioning strategy and its marketing policy in order to build brand equity?

The following terms will be introduced in this chapter (see glossary for definitions):

behavioral modes	growth-adjusted	positive brand
brand equity	multiplier	equity
brand identity	installed base effect	price premium
cash flows	latent class methodology	price sensitivity
central information-	multiplier method	product positioning
processing	Nash equilibrium	reaction function
certainty equivalent (CE)	negative brand equity	repeat purchase rate
choice experiment	net present value	reservation price
conjoint experiment	(NPV)	reverse engineering
demand dynamics	perceived benefits	risk-adjusted return
diffusion	perceptual mapping	risk-averse
discount rate	studies	strategic pricing
fixed costs	peripheral information-	Tobin's q-ratio
focus group	processing	word of mouth

▶ 19.1 When Does Brand Equity Exist?

To answer this question, we need to first define brand equity.

▶ What is brand equity?

Suppose the industry contains two products with the same attributes and attribute levels: one is unbranded (generic), and the other is branded. Then, roughly speaking, the branded product has brand equity if it is more profitable than the generic product. The concept can be easily generalized to industries with multiple products. (We shall refine this concept shortly.)

▶ What conditions are necessary for brand equity to exist?

For simplicity, suppose there are two products in the market: a generic and a branded product. In particular, both products contain identical combinations of the same set of attributes. Suppose all consumers are able to evaluate both products with certainty; in addition, all consumers have the same perceptions about each product's attributes or benefits. Then, for any given consumer, the willingness to pay will be identical for both products. Consequently, the branded product will have no advantage over the generic. We say that there is no brand equity.

Now, suppose that at least some consumers are uncertain in their evaluations of the generic and/or branded products. Specifically, suppose consumers in this segment have higher uncertainty about the attributes or benefits provided by the generic than in those provided by the branded product. Suppose consumers in this segment are *risk-averse*. Since purchasing the generic product results in highly uncertain gains, this segment's willingness to pay for the generic will be lower than its willingness to pay for the branded product, *even though both products contain identical combinations of attributes*. If this is the case, it is possible that the branded product will have an advantage over the generic. We say that brand equity *may* exist. (As discussed later, this "willingness to pay" condition is not sufficient for brand equity to exist.)

Alternatively, suppose some consumers believe that the benefits provided by the branded and generic products are different, even though the two products contain identical combinations of attributes. Let's say that, for this consumer segment, the *perceived benefits* provided by the branded product are greater than those provided by the generic. For example, many consumers are willing to pay more for branded cold medications than for store brands that are clones of the branded products. If this is the case, it is also possible that the branded product has brand equity.

Fusion for Profit Maxim

For brand equity to exist, a necessary condition is that some consumers are willing to pay a higher price for a branded product than for an identical generic product. This condition will be satisfied if some consumers are more confident in their evaluations of a branded product than they are in their evaluations of a generic product with the same combination of attributes. Alternatively, for some consumers the perceived benefits provided by the branded product are higher than those from the generic product.

▶ 19.2 How Does the Name of a Product Affect Brand Equity?

A product's name can have a major effect on the product's brand equity, regardless of the type of product. These effects can range from extremely positive to extremely negative. Consider the following examples.

Positive Effect on Consumers

A men's retail clothing store formerly known as Casual Male Big & Tall was renamed Casual Male XL. *Focus group* studies had shown that nonbuyers from the store perceived the old name negatively. In contrast, non-buyers felt that the new name inspired confidence. Subsequent to the name change, store traffic increased significantly, and the store became highly profitable.[1]

Negative Effect on Consumers

Several years ago, the Vicks Health Care Division used the name Vicks Versus 3 to introduce a new product that it positioned as a multicondition remedy for three conditions: colds, sinuses, and allergies.[2] The new product was highly similar (in terms of ingredients) to an existing product in the market, Dristan.

When Vicks Versus 3 was test-marketed, consumers were confused. Some consumers were unclear whether "Versus 3" referred to three other medicines or to three companies. For some consumers, the name Vicks Versus 3 created an antagonistic image that was contrary to the prevailing image of Vicks as 'good, old, reliable, and nurturing.'

Vicks Versus 3 did not succeed in the market.

Neutral Effect on Consumers

Several years ago, a well-known chemical company, Rohm and Haas, added a new solid-form product to its liquid biocide product line. At the time it introduced the new product, Rohm and Haas was the market leader in the liquid biocide market, where it sold its brand, Kathon MW, to formulators. These formulators used Kathon MW as an input to prepare maintenance packages of liquid biocide and metalworking fluids they sold to large end users. Since these end users were unaware that the maintenance packages they purchased from formulators contained Kathon MW, Kathon MW did not have brand equity among these end users.

Since Kathon MW did not have any brand equity to begin with among any end users, including the new target segment of small end users, the name Kathon MW did not provide any demand leverage for Kathon MWX. An additional factor was that the name Kathon MWX did not convey any information about product benefits to end users. This was problematic, since, in contrast to the end-user group for the old product (Kathon MW), the end-user group for the new product (Kathon MWX) contained a very high proportion of uninformed consumers.

Since Kathon MWX's sales were poor, Kathon MWX was withdrawn from the marketplace.[3]

Customer Confusion

Chery Automobile, a Chinese company, has a similar name to Chevy, which is a nickname for the Chevrolet brand. General Motors has argued that the name Chery has led to consumer confusion and allowed Chery to benefit from the brand equity of the Chevrolet brand.

Multiproduct Effects

The name of a product or company can have significant multiproduct effects.

Example 1: In January 2007, Apple Computers Inc., changed its name to Apple, Inc., on the same day that it announced the launch of two new products, the iPhone and Apple TV. Apple's goal was to leverage the *positive brand equity* of its computers in the new consumer electronic product categories that it was entering.

Example 2: After its recent acquisition of Cingular, AT&T replaced the Cingular brand name with the AT&T name. The parent company's logic for the renaming strategy was that, even though Cingular was a newer name and appealed to young consumers, the name AT&T had brand equity across a wide array of products such as land lines, cell phones, cable TV, and Internet access. Hence, management expected that this brand equity would carry weight in the new markets AT&T was entering.

Fusion for Profit Maxim

A product's name can have a significant effect on the product's financial performance. These effects can range from positive to negative.

Point to consider.   How should the firm determine the effect of its product name on brand equity?

The firm can use different methods to determine how the brand name of a product affects the demand for the product and hence brand equity.

One approach is to conduct a *conjoint* study or a *choice-based experiment* using respondents from the target segment. Specifically, the firm can measure the effect of different profiles (i.e., combinations of product attributes, prices, and product names) on consumers' preferences, intentions, or choices.

Another approach is to conduct a study to determine the effect of different product names on consumers' perceptions in the target segment. This approach can be especially useful for products that are very similar in terms of physical attributes (e.g., cold medications) but are perceived very differently in terms of consumer benefits.

Note that these research methods can be used together because they provide complementary types of information about the effect of product name on consumer behavior and hence on brand equity. (For a detailed discussion of these methods, see chapter 8.)

▶ *Suppose the brand name has a positive effect on* reservation prices *for the branded product for a consumer segment. Does it follow that the branded product has positive brand equity?*

Consider the toothpaste industry. Suppose the brand name (e.g., Crest) has a positive effect on reservation prices for the brand (i.e., the willingness to pay) for at least some consumers. As we discuss below, this condition is not sufficient to ensure that Crest has positive brand equity.

Example: Suppose Crest has to advertise heavily to persuade consumers that Crest is superior (i.e., to increase consumers' reservation prices for Crest) to a generic product with the same combination of product attributes. Suppose the additional gross profits generated by advertising are less than the advertising costs. If this is the case, Crest's *brand equity will be negative*.

◣ Can market conditions change brand equity?

New information can have a significant effect on brand equity.

Example: Suppose a branded blood pressure medicine has just been found to have serious side effects. Then, if that brand name is used to sell another medication, the brand equity will be negative.

Fusion for Profit Maxim

The condition that a brand name has a positive effect on reservation prices for a consumer segment does not guarantee that the branded product has brand equity. Under certain conditions, brand equity can be negative.

Henceforth we shall assume that brand equity is positive.

◣ 19.3 Brand Name and Pricing Strategy

Suppose the brand name has a positive effect on reservation prices for the brand in question.

◣ Does this mean that the price of the branded product should be higher than the corresponding price of a generic product with identical attributes?

At first glance one might conclude that, since consumers' willingness to pay is higher for a branded product, the manufacturer of the branded product should always charge a *price premium* over an equivalent generic. However, as we discuss below, this conclusion is not always correct.

Single-Period Example

Suppose there are two firms that have developed identical software programs. One firm, Clonedike, is a newcomer in the marketplace and is unknown. We refer to Clonedike's software program as a "generic" product. The second firm, Inventeev, is an established firm that has a strong reputation in the marketplace for software. We refer to Inventeev's software program as a "branded" product.

Suppose there are two market segments (Segments A and B) of equal size. For simplicity, assume that the marginal costs of the software are zero (e.g., each firm sells its software through the Internet), each segment contains 1 million individuals, and both firms have the same planning horizons (one period). Suppose consumers' reservation prices for the Clonedike and Inventeev software programs are as shown in table 19.1.

Because Clonedike is unknown in the marketplace and Inventeev is an established brand, each segment's reservation price for Inventeev is higher than its reservation price for Clonedike. Assume that Segment B ("novices") is highly uncertain about the product quality of Clonedike's software program, whereas Segment A ("experts") is not. Consequently, Segment B is willing to pay a larger premium ($40 = $80 – $40) than Segment A ($10 = $100 – $90) to purchase the branded product, Inventeev, instead of the generic, Clonedike.

To focus on essentials, we compare two cases: Clonedike develops the generic software program (Case 1), and Inventeev develops the branded software program (Case 2).

► *What prices should Clonedike and Inventeev charge for their respective software programs?*

Case 1.   Suppose Clonedike is the only firm in the market that has developed the new software program. Then Clonedike should charge a high price ($90 per unit) and sell to Segment A only (table 19.2).

Case 2.   Suppose, instead, that Inventeev is the only firm that has developed the new software program. Then Inventeev should charge a lower price ($80) and sell to both segments (table 19.2).

Table 19.1
Clonedike-Inventeev Example: Reservation Prices for Different Segments

Segment	Reservation price for Clonedike	Reservation price for Inventeev
A (experts)	$90	$100
B (novices)	$40	$80

Table 19.2
Clonedike-Inventeev Example: Optimal Pricing Strategies

	Clonedike (Case 1)			Inventeev (Case 2)	
Price	Units sold	Gross profits	Price	Units sold	Gross profits
$90*	1M	$90M	$100	1M	$100M
$40	2M	$80M	$80**	2M	$160M

*Optimal price charged by Clonedike.
**Optimal price charged by Inventeev.

Note that the branded product, Inventeev, makes a higher gross profit ($160 million) than the unbranded product, Clonedike ($90 million). *However, Inventeev charges a lower price ($80 per unit) than Clonedike does ($90 per unit).*

▶ *Why does Inventeev charge a lower price for its branded product even though all consumers are willing to pay a premium for Inventeev's software program?*

The reason has to do with *price sensitivity*. Consider Inventeev. By reducing its price from $100 per unit to $80 per unit (a 20% reduction in price), Inventeev can double the number of units it sells from 1 million to 2 million (a 100% increase). In contrast, for Clonedike to double the number of units it sells from 1 million to 2 million (a 100% increase), Clonedike has to reduce its price drastically from $90 per unit to $40 per unit (a 55.6% decrease). Since the demand for Inventeev is more responsive to price reductions than the demand for Clonedike, Inventeev should choose the low-price strategy, *even though all consumers are willing to pay a premium to purchase Inventeev.*

Fusion for Profit Maxim

Brand equity does not imply that the branded product should charge a price premium over an equivalent generic product.

Multiperiod Example, Frequently Purchased Products

Suppose two firms have developed identical new detergents. One firm, the Plato Corporation, is unknown. We shall refer to Plato's detergent as a generic. The second is a well-known firm (e.g., Procter & Gamble). Assume that both Procter & Gamble and Plato seek to maximize their respective *net present values* (NPVs) and have the same planning horizons (two periods).

Suppose market research has shown that consumers are willing to pay a higher price for the Procter & Gamble detergent than for the detergent made by Plato. Furthermore, the customer satisfaction level after product use (and hence the *repeat purchase rate*) for Procter & Gamble's new brand of detergent is higher than that for Plato's generic detergent. Let's say that the optimal prices that maximize the NPV for the generic detergent, Plato, are as follows: $4 per unit (first period) and $6 per unit (second period).

▶ *What pricing strategy should Procter & Gamble use to maximize its NPV?*

Given the customer satisfaction scenario (*demand dynamics*) above, the optimal policy for Procter & Gamble may be to charge a first-period price that is lower than Plato's ($4 per unit). By "underpricing" in the first period, Procter & Gamble will forgo some first-period profits in order to increase its customer base in the future.

However, because of the high repeat rate by first-period customers, Procter & Gamble will increase its second-period profits. Note that Procter & Gamble should charge a "negative" price premium in the first period even though consumers are willing to pay higher prices for the Procter & Gamble brand than for a generic detergent with the identical combination of attributes.

Fusion for Profit Maxim

The optimal multiperiod strategy for a frequently purchased branded product may be to charge a "negative" price premium when it introduces a new product into the marketplace.

Multiperiod Example, Durable Products

Suppose two mobile phone manufacturers have developed identical new mobile phones with new Internet connectivity features. For example, the new mobile phones allow more efficient downloading of videos and photos from the Internet. The first firm, Tango, is unknown. However, the second is a well-known firm, Churly. Suppose both firms have the same cost structures; in addition, both firms seek to maximize their respective NPVs and have the same planning horizons (two periods).

▶ *What pricing strategies should Tango and Churly use?*

Suppose that, for any given first-period sales volume, the Churly phone will generate more *word-of-mouth* activity than Tango's phone. Alternatively, suppose the Churly phone has a higher *installed base effect*. That is, for any given volume sold in the first period (the installed base), the reservation prices for consumers in the second period increase more for the Churly phone than for the Tango phone.

Then, other factors being held constant, Churly will gain more from stimulating word-of-mouth activity or from leveraging the installed base effect. Hence Churly should charge a lower price in the first period than Tango, *even though consumers' reservation prices for the Churly product are higher than those for the Tango product.*

Fusion for Profit Maxim

Regardless of whether the product is a durable or not, the price premium charged by a product is not a good proxy for brand equity.

▶ 19.4 Strategies for Building Brand Equity

As discussed above, brand equity can help to increase the firm's long-run performance. This leads to a basic question.

▶ What branding strategies can the firm use to build brand equity?

The firm needs to make two basic decisions: What product name and *product positioning* strategy should it use? We have already discussed methods for determining the effect of product name on consumer behavior.[4] In this section, we focus on how to use product positioning strategy to build brand equity.

Example: Suppose Toyota is the first automobile manufacturer to develop a commercially viable hydrogen-powered car. Furthermore, Toyota's technology is patented. Then, assuming that the new hydrogen-powered car is well accepted by the marketplace, Toyota will enjoy excess profits from its new car for several years.

▶ What will happen once a clone ("generic") is introduced by a competitor, say Nissan?

Brand equity at any point in time is the difference between the net present values of the branded product and the net present value of the generic. Hence, if consumers in the future believe that the branded and the generic hydrogen-powered cars are identical, Toyota will have no brand equity when Nissan introduces its clone.

▶ What steps can Toyota take to build brand equity when it introduces its branded hydrogen-powered car into the marketplace?

The first step for Toyota is to recognize that its technology for producing the hydrogen-powered car will be imitated in the future. Hence, if consumers process information in terms of physical attributes, Toyota will have zero brand equity in the future when competitors (Nissan in our example) clone its hydrogen-powered car.

To address this problem, Toyota should use a long-run branding strategy based on product positioning. Specifically, Toyota should encourage consumers to process information in terms of the perceived and intangible benefits provided by its hydrogen-powered car. Furthermore, Toyota should establish a *brand identity* among consumers for its hydrogen-powered car.

If these product-positioning strategies are successful, consumers in the future will perceive the Toyota hydrogen-powered car as superior, *even though clones may offer the same combination of physical attributes in the future.* Hence Toyota will be able to establish and maintain brand equity in the long run.

Note that Toyota faces a potential dilemma. In the short run, it may be easier and more profitable for Toyota to encourage consumers to focus on objective product attributes that differentiate its hydrogen-powered car from competitive cars in the marketplace. However, in the long run this strategy may not be optimal for Toyota because this strategy has encouraged consumers to process information in terms of objective physical attributes (which can be easily copied by competitors) rather than in terms of intangible benefits (which are more difficult for competitors to copy).

Fusion for Profit Maxim

To develop and sustain brand equity, a branded product should use a product positioning strategy that encourages consumers to process information in terms of perceived benefits. In addition, the firm should establish a *brand identity* (e.g., an emotional link between the branded product and consumers), especially when consumers process information peripherally. This branding strategy may require the firm to trade off short-run for long-run profits.

▶ *What methods can the firm use to implement the branding strategy described above to develop brand equity?*

We continue with the Toyota example. Suppose Toyota has developed a branding (product positioning) strategy for its new hydrogen-powered car. Given the nature of the product, some consumers are likely to be more uncertain about the benefits of the new car than others. Furthermore, consumers are likely to put different emphases on different product benefits. For example, some consumers may place primary emphasis on performance, whereas others place primary emphasis on reliability.

▶ *Given this scenario, how can Toyota develop an appropriate product positioning strategy to build brand equity for the new car?*

Toyota can follow a standard approach—that is, conduct *conjoint experiments* to measure the effect of product design, price, and brand name on consumers' preferences. In addition, Toyota can conduct separate studies (e.g., *perceptual mapping studies*) to determine how different brands are perceived in the marketplace.

Alternatively, Toyota can use an integrated model[5] that simultaneously estimates these linkages among product attributes, perceptions, and preferences (or choices) using information from *one* comprehensive study. The integrated model has two parts, both of which should be estimated simultaneously.

The first part of the integrated model quantifies how consumers transform information about the objective *observable* physical attributes of the new car such as horsepower into *unobservable and uncertain* subjective benefits such as reliability. The second part of the model quantifies how these subjective benefits affect consumers' preference and choices. *A key advantage of the integrated model is that it allows one to estimate the consumer's information-processing model while simultaneously allowing for consumers' perceptual errors and for measurement errors in survey data.*[6]

Once these results have been obtained, the firm (e.g., Toyota) can quantify the joint effect of different marketing mix and branding strategies on consumer behavior. Consequently, the firm can choose a branding strategy that will increase brand equity.

Note that the two-step, integrated model should be estimated differently, depending on the firm's prior knowledge of the market. In our example, suppose Toyota has sufficient market information to form segments a priori. Then, the model should be estimated separately for each segment and the results aggregated across segments.

Alternatively, suppose Toyota cannot form segments a priori. In this case, the two-step model should be extended so that one can identify the unobserved segments and simultaneously estimate the model for each segment.[7]

Fusion for Profit Maxim

The firm can use an integrated methodology to implement a branding (product positioning) strategy. This method will allow the firm to simultaneously measure the relationships among product attributes (including brand name) and perceptions and among perceptions and preferences or choices.

▲ 19.5 How Can the Firm Measure Brand Equity?

A variety of methods have been proposed to measure brand equity. These methods range from those that are based on market share to those that are based on published financial data to methods that are based on consumer experiments or behavioral data.

▲ 19.6 Should the Firm Use a Brand's Market Share to Measure Brand Equity?

As discussed in detail in chapter 4, high market share does not imply high profitability. For example, the firm may have had to invest heavily in advertising to obtain a high market share. Similarly, high market share does not imply high future profitability in a declining market.

Fusion for Profit Maxim

A brand's market share is not a good proxy for brand equity.

▶ 19.7 Measuring Brand Equity Using Financial Data: The Net Present Value Method

As noted earlier, an alternative way to measure brand equity is in terms of the value of the long-run profits from that brand (i.e., the net present value of the future earnings from that brand).

▶ Is it necessary to consider uncertainty in measuring brand equity?

If the firm uses net present value to measure brand equity, it should explicitly consider the effect of uncertainty on brand equity. However, one has to be careful in measuring the effect of uncertainty on brand equity.

Example: Suppose there are two types of paper towels in the market: generic (Economo) and branded (Croesus). Let's say that both types of paper towel contain identical combinations of product attributes. To focus on essentials, assume that the investment levels for both Economo and Croesus are identical. Furthermore, assume a one-period model. (We will discuss multiperiod effects later.)

For simplicity, assume that the expected profit for Economo in the next period is $60 million. Correspondingly, the expected profit for Croesus in the next period is $84 million. Suppose the *risk-adjusted return* or *discount rate* for Economo is 20% per period.

▶ Is it appropriate to estimate brand equity as follows?

Compared with Economo, Croesus provides an incremental increase in expected profits of $24 million ($84 million – $60 million). Hence the incremental net present value (brand equity) of Croesus is $20 million:

$$\frac{\text{increase in expected profit}}{(1 + \text{discount rate})} = \frac{24}{(1 + 20\%)}.$$

At first glance, this method for measuring brand equity appears to be reasonable. However, this measure is likely to *overstate* brand equity. For example, the demand for the branded paper towel, Croesus, may fluctuate more over the business cycle than the demand for the generic (Economo). Consequently, the risk-adjusted rate of return for the branded product (Croesus) will be higher than the corresponding return for the generic (Economo).

Suppose the risk-adjusted discount rate for the branded product, Croesus, is 25% (> 20%). Then, the NPV of Croesus is $67.2 million ($84 million/1.25), and the NPV of Economo is $50 million ($60 million/1.20).

Hence the brand equity of Croesus is $17.2 million (NPV of Croesus – NPV of Economo). *Note that the brand equity ($17.2 million) for the branded* *paper towel, Croesus, is not the same as the estimate of brand equity discussed earlier ($20 million).*

Fusion for Profit Maxim

Brand equity should not be measured by simply comparing the expected profits of the branded and generic products. These expected profit values should be adjusted to allow for the differential risks for both types of product.

▶ *Some analysts compute brand equity by multiplying the excess profits of the branded product by a multiplier. How useful is this valuation method?*

This *multiplier method* is based on the intuitive idea that brand equity is the long-run value of a brand. Specifically, the multiplier method defines:

net present value (long-run value) of a brand = excess annual profit × multiplier.

We continue with the paper towel example. Suppose the stock market expects the branded product, Croesus, to produce a recurring annual expected profit that is $20 million higher than the corresponding expected profit for the generic, Economo. In addition, suppose the multiplier is 5. Then, according to the multiplier valuation method, the value of the Croesus brand (net present value) is $100 million (excess annual profit of Croesus × multiplier = $20M × 5).

At first glance, this multiplier method appears to be reasonable. However, it can lead to misleading estimates of brand equity.

Risk Factors

As discussed above, one should not compute the excess profits for a branded product without making the appropriate adjustments for risk—*even within a given industry.* Specifically, financial risk is likely to vary across market segments (e.g., sales for the branded product may be more volatile over the business cycle). Hence, other factors being the same, different multipliers should be used for Croesus and Economo.

Suppose the stock market expects Croesus to produce a recurring expected annual profit of $10 million. In addition, the risk-adjusted return for Croesus is 20% per annum. Then, the correct multiplier for Croesus is 5 (1/20%). Consequently, the net present value of Croesus is $50 million (expected annual profit × multiplier for Croesus = $10M × 5).

Suppose the stock market expects Economo to produce an expected annual profit of $4 million; in addition, the risk-adjusted return for Economo is 10% per annum ($< 20\%$). Then, the multiplier for Economo is 10 ($1/10\%$). Consequently, the net present value of Economo is $40 million (expected annual profit for Economo × multiplier for Economo = $4M × 10). Since Croesus has a net present value of $50 million, and Economo has a net present value of $40 million, the brand equity of Croesus is $10 million (the difference between the two NPVs).

Note that the correct value of brand equity for Croesus ($10 million) is considerably lower than the values that one would have obtained by using a common multiplier across brands. Thus, the incremental annual expected profit generated by Croesus is $6 million (expected annual profit for Croesus − expected annual profit for Economo = $10 million − $4 million). If a multiplier of 5 had been used, the estimated brand equity for Croesus would have been $30 million ($> $10 million). If a multiplier of 10 had been used instead, the estimated brand equity would have been $60 million ($>> 10$ million). Both these numbers are dramatically higher than the correct value of brand equity for Croesus ($10 million).

Fusion for Profit Maxim

The multiplier that is used to measure brand equity should be adjusted to reflect the risk of the brand in question.

Growth Rates

The multiplier should accurately reflect growth rates. If the generic and branded products target different segments (e.g., the generic caters to the informed segment, and the branded product to the uninformed segment), the growth rates for both products are likely to differ over their respective product life cycles. Hence it is necessary to use different multipliers for generic and branded products. In particular, one should not measure brand equity by multiplying the excess profits of the branded product by a standard multiplier.

▶ *How can one adjust the multipliers to allow for differential growth rates?*

We illustrate the methodology using the paper towel example.

Suppose the expected annual growth rate in profits for Croesus is 10%, and the risk-adjusted annual rate of return is 20%.[8] Then, the *growth-adjusted multiplier* for Croesus is 11:

$$\frac{(1 + \text{expected annual growth rate})}{(\text{risk-adjusted annual return} - \text{expected annual growth rate})} = \frac{(1 + 10\%)}{(20\% - 10\%)}$$

Thus, if the expected annual profit for Croesus in the next year is $15 million, the net present value of Croesus will be $165 million (expected annual profit for Croesus in the first year × growth-adjusted multiplier = $15M × 11).

Similarly, suppose the expected annual growth rate in profits for Economo is 5%, and the corresponding risk-adjusted annual rate of return is 10%. Then, the growth-adjusted multiplier for Economo is 21. Thus, if the expected annual profit of Economo in the next year is $5 million, the net present value of Economo will be $105 million ($5M × 21).

Since the net present value of Croesus is $165 million, and the corresponding net present value of Economo is $105 million, the brand equity of Croesus is $60 million ($165M – $105M).

Note that the multiplier for a given product should reflect both the expected growth rate for that product and that product's risk-adjusted return. Thus, even though the anticipated growth rate for the branded product (Croesus) is *almost double* that for the generic (Economo), the multiplier for Croesus (11) *is much lower* than that for Economo (21).

Fusion for Profit Maxim

The multiplier that is used to measure brand equity should be adjusted for that brand's risk and growth rate. Since these factors vary across brands, the firm should not use industry-specific multipliers to measure brand equity.

Point to consider. What additional factors should the firm consider when using financial data to measure brand equity?

As noted earlier in this chapter, a branded product may choose *strategic pricing* in order to stimulate market growth in the future. The firm's marketing decisions can affect future growth rates (i.e., the growth rates are not fixed). In addition, brand equity can affect the performances of other products in the firm's product portfolio.

We discuss these factors below.

Multiperiod Effects

Suppose the branded product uses low prices to enter a given industry. For example, suppose the firm's strategy focuses on increasing long-run profits by developing repeat purchase business from initial customers. Alternatively, the branded product charges low prices initially in order to increase future profits by stimulating *diffusion*. Then, the excess profits earned by the branded product early in its product life cycle will be too low. Hence, other factors being the same, the multiplier approach is likely to understate the branded product's brand equity.

Marketing Policies and Growth Rates

In our discussion we assumed that the market growth rates were fixed. In practice, the firm may be able to influence the growth rate of the market through its marketing policies (e.g., pricing and advertising). In principle, the basic methodology can be extended to capture these effects.

Multiproduct Effects

The multiplier approach we have discussed focused on measuring the brand equity of one product. In principle, the multiplier approach can be extended to the multiproduct firm. For example, one can allow for the additional profits that the branded product *could make* by introducing line extensions in the future or by entering into co-branding contracts with other firms.[9]

Fusion for Profit Maxim

When using financial data to measure brand equity, the multiplier should be adjusted to allow for multiperiod and multiproduct effects.

◣ 19.8 Measuring Brand Equity Using Financial Data: Tobin's q-Ratio Method

One popular way to measure brand equity using publicly available financial data is based on *Tobin's* q-*ratio*.[10]

◣ What is Tobin's q-ratio? Is this ratio a good proxy for brand equity?

The Tobin's q-ratio for the firm is defined by the following quantity:

$$q = \frac{\text{market value of the firm's equity} + \text{market value of the firm's debt}}{\text{estimated replacement cost of the firm's assets}}$$

Thus, suppose the firm's equity has a market value of $2 billion, and the firm's debt has a market value of $1 billion. Then the firm is worth $3 billion. Suppose that, at current market prices, it is necessary to spend $1.5 billion to "clone" the firm's assets. Then, q has a value of 2 ($3B/$1.5B).

The intuition behind the q-ratio is simple. If q has a value greater than 1, further investment is profitable, since the firm's assets are worth more than the cost of replacing them. If q is less than 1, the firm should stop investing, since the firm's assets are worth less than their replacement cost. In fact, when *q* is less than 1, it may be cheaper for the firm to acquire assets through mergers rather than by purchasing new assets.

Note that the q-ratio is measured at the firm level: it does not apply to individual brands produced or sold by the firm. Hence the firm should not use the q-ratio to determine the brand equities of individual brands in its product portfolio.

Example: Suppose Procter & Gamble has a *q*-ratio of 2. This implies that Procter & Gamble should expand its operations overall. However, it does *not* mean that Procter & Gamble should expand its operations for any particular product (e.g., Crest toothpaste). Nor does the *q*-ratio provide any information about the brand equity of Crest toothpaste.

Fusion for Profit Maxim

Tobin's *q*-ratio should not be used to measure the brand equity of individual brands in the firm's portfolio. It is preferable to use other methods that are based on brand-specific information.

▶ 19.9 Measuring Brand Equity in a Competitive Market Using Behavioral Data

So far, we have focused on how to use market-level data (e.g., market shares) and financial data (e.g., profits) to measure brand equity. In this section, we ask a different question.

▶ Should the firm use consumer behavior studies to measure brand equity?

For simplicity, assume that there are two products: a generic and a branded product. Initially, we shall assume that all consumers are aware of both products. (We will relax this assumption later.) Then the following experimental methodology can be used.

Step 1.   Choose a representative sample of consumers. If possible, distinguish segments based on knowledge of the market. However, this a priori segmentation is not necessary.

Step 2.   Conduct a *choice experiment* to determine the joint distribution of reservation prices of these consumers for the branded product and for the generic.[11]

Step 3.   Use cost data for the branded product and the results from Step 2 to determine the branded product's optimal price for any given price chosen by the generic product (the branded product's *reaction function*).

Step 4.   Use cost data for the generic product and the results from Step 2 to determine the optimal price of the generic for any given price chosen by the branded product (the generic product's reaction function).

Note that the costs for the generic and the branded products need not be the same even though both products are physically identical. For example, the branded product may be able to take advantage of quantity discounts on raw materials if its volume is sufficiently high.

Step 5.   Combine the results from Step 3 and Step 4 to determine the prices charged by the generic and the branded product (the *Nash equilibrium*).

Step 6.   Determine the expected profits of the generic and the branded products, after allowing for differential purchase quantities across consumers. (The problem simplifies considerably for durables because each buyer purchases the same quantity: one unit.)

Step 7.   Determine the net present values of the expected profits for the generic (X) and the branded product (Y) using the appropriate risk-adjusted returns and expected growth rates for each product.

Step 8.   Brand equity for the branded product $= Y - X$.

Example: Consider a pharmaceutical product for alleviating problems caused by stomach ulcers. Suppose there are two products with identical combinations of attributes; one is branded, and the other is generic.

Suppose the Nash equilibrium is as follows: the price of the branded product is $10 per dose, and the price of the generic is $7 per dose. Suppose the marginal costs per dose are $3 for each product. Then, the gross profit margin for the branded product is $7 per dose, and the corresponding gross profit margin for the generic is $4 per dose.

Suppose the Nash equilibrium implies that the average annual quantities sold are as follows: 3 million doses of the branded product and 1 million doses of the generic. Then, the average annual gross profit margin generated by the branded product is $21 million (unit profit margin × average number of doses sold annually $= $7 × 3 million), and the corresponding average annual gross profit margin generated by the generic is $4 million ($4 × 1 million).

For simplicity, assume that the market is not growing.

In general, the *cash flows* for the branded product *are likely* to be more risky than those for the generic. Suppose the risk-adjusted annual return for the generic is 15%, and the risk-adjusted annual return for the branded product is 20% (> 15%). Then, the net present value of the branded product is $105 million:

$$\frac{\text{average annual gross profit margin}}{\text{risk-adjusted rate of return for the branded product}} = \frac{\$21M}{20\%}$$

and the corresponding net present value for the generic is $26.67 million. Hence the brand equity of the branded product is the difference in the net present values ($78.33 million $= $105M − $26.67M).

Fusion for Profit Maxim

Data from behavioral studies can be used in economic models of competition to estimate brand equity.

Point to consider.   Suppose *fixed costs* are identical for the branded and generic products. Will the level of fixed costs have any effect on brand equity?

Intuitively, one might expect that, since both the branded product and the generic have the same fixed costs, the particular values of those fixed costs should have no effect on brand equity. However, this is not the case. The reason is that, in many cases, the risk-adjusted return for the branded product will be higher than the corresponding risk-adjusted return for the generic. Hence fixed costs of any given magnitude are likely to have a *smaller* negative effect on the net present value of the branded product. One implication is that, other factors being the same, brand equities will be higher in industries with high fixed costs.

▶ *What additional factors should the firm consider when using this behavioral methodology for measuring brand equity?*

The firm may need to adjust the basic methodology to address the following issues.

Measuring Profits

Product-specific cost data may not be available for competitors' brands, since firms' profit and loss statements typically provide only total costs across the firm's product line. Hence the firm may have to use *reverse engineering* or "guesstimates" to determine competitors' costs. Furthermore, future costs for the firm and its competitors may be uncertain, since input prices fluctuate over time.

One approach is to use estimates of the *certainty equivalents* of future input prices wherever possible (e.g., using the appropriate futures prices for those inputs).

Product Design and Product Name

The basic model described above implicitly assumes that the product designs and product names are fixed for the branded and generic products. This assumption can be relaxed.[12]

Marketing Mix

The basic model assumes that firms use only price as a competitive tool. In practice, firms may use additional marketing instruments such as advertising.

In addition, firms may use different *behavioral modes*. For example, they may cooperate in some dimensions (e.g., pricing) but compete in others (e.g., advertising). In such cases, the market equilibrium (and hence the estimates of brand equity) will change depending on the behavioral modes that the firms choose. Furthermore, behavioral modes are likely to vary across industries, depending on the cost and demand structures for those industries. This adds complexity to the model; however, the basic modeling approach can still be used.

Awareness

The basic model assumed that all consumers are fully aware of the generic and the branded product. This assumption may not hold. Thus, in general, there are four consumer segments:

1. Those who are aware of both products,
2. Those who are aware of the branded product only,
3. Those who are aware of the generic product only, and
4. Those who are unaware of both products.

To address this problem of differential awareness levels across segments, the choice experiment in Step 2 should be modified. One approach is to classify consumers into one of the four segments using self-stated awareness data (e.g., "Do you know about Brand Z?"), conduct the choice experiment for Segments 1, 2, and 3 using an appropriate experimental design, and aggregate the results across segments to determine the joint distribution of reservation prices in the population.

Once this is done, the results can be used to perform the subsequent steps (Step 3 onward). Note that, since each firm now has two decision variables (price and advertising), the computation of the Nash equilibrium will be more complicated.

Multiple Products

The choice experiment to measure reservation prices (Step 2) should explicitly allow for multiple products sold by the firm. This extension is especially important when a significant fraction of the firm's consumers purchase more than one type of product from the firm.

Example: Consider a firm such as Pepperidge Farm that has multiple product lines. If the choice experiment to measure reservation prices (Step 2) considers only one product line (e.g., cookies) made by Pepperidge Farm, the estimated brand equity will be too low.

Multiple Firms

The basic model assumes that there are only two products: a branded product and a generic. In reality, the industry is likely to contain a number of brands. In principle, the basic model can be extended to allow for this, but the estimation will be more complex.

Future Product-Line Extensions

As noted earlier, the estimates of brand equity are based on the firm's current product line only. Hence these estimates are a lower bound on the value of the firm's brand equity.

Fusion for Profit Maxim

By using a hybrid behavioral model that combines game theory and finance, the firm can measure brand equity by simultaneously allowing for uncertainty, multiple decision variables, multiple products, and multiple firms in an industry.

► *Is it necessary to explicitly consider consumer perceptions when estimating brand equity?*

Perceptions can vary across consumers, since different consumers may use different information-processing strategies. Thus, some consumers use *central information-processing*. That is, they first transform information on the physical attributes of a product into perceptions (perceived benefits), which in turn drive their preferences and choices.

Other consumers *process information peripherally*. That is, they do not filter information about brands through a perceptual lens. Rather, the brand stimulus affects their preferences and choices directly.[13]

At first glance, one might conclude that it is necessary to allow for these differential information-processing strategies when one estimates the reservation prices in the choice experiment (Step 2).

As previously discussed, this type of information can be very useful to the firm in choosing an integrated marketing policy that includes product design, pricing, and the advertising message.[14] However, this level of detailed information about consumers' information-processing strategies is not essential in order to measure brand equity.[15]

Chapter 19 Key Points
- For brand equity to exist, consumers must perceive products differently even if they are identical. Alternatively, consumers must be uncertain in their evaluations of different products.
- The condition that a brand name has a positive affect on reservation prices for a consumer segment does not guarantee that a branded product has brand equity. Under certain conditions, brand equity can be negative.

- Brand equity does not imply that the branded product should always charge a price premium over an unbranded product with the same combination of attributes.
- To develop and sustain brand equity, a branded product should encourage consumers to process information in terms of perceived benefits. This product positioning strategy may require the firm to trade off short-run and long-run profits.
- A brand's market share is not a good proxy for brand equity.
- The multiplier method for measuring brand equity should be adjusted to allow for differential growth rates and risks for branded and unbranded products. One implication is that the firm should not use industry-specific multipliers to compute brand equities.
- Tobin's q-ratio is not a good proxy for measuring brand equity in multiproduct firms.
- When using financial data to measure brand equity, the multiplier should be adjusted to allow for multiperiod and multiproduct effects.
- By using a hybrid behavioral model that combines game theory and finance, the firm can measure brand equity by simultaneously allowing for uncertainty, multiple decision variables, multiple products, and multiple firms in an industry.

20

How Marketing Policy Affects Consumer Well-Being and Social Welfare

This chapter addresses a fundamental but neglected area in the marketing literature: How does the firm's marketing policy affect *social welfare*? Consider the following examples:

- Merck gives out free samples of a new drug to doctors.
- Nestlé advertises to increase awareness of a new food product.
- Gillette gives out free samples of a new razor.
- Apple introduces new models of the iPod and phases out old models.
- Comcast introduces a new *bundling* plan in which it offers consumers a bundle consisting of Internet service, cable service, a cell phone, and a fixed line.

These policies raise some interesting questions: Are marketing policies that maximize shareholder wealth good for consumers? Are these policies good for society as a whole? What metrics should one use to answer these questions? Under what conditions is it necessary for the antitrust division of the government to intervene in the market so that social welfare is improved? As discussed in this chapter, the answers to these questions are not always what one might expect.

The information covered in this chapter will be useful when you are faced with the following issues:

- How does my firm's pricing policy for a durable product affect consumer well-being and social welfare?

- If my firm gives out free samples of a nondurable product, will consumers and society gain in the long run?
- If my firm uses *strategic pricing* based on *cost* or *demand dynamics*, how will this policy affect consumers and society in the long run?
- If my firm's price-advertising strategy is based on creating product awareness, how will this strategy affect consumer well-being and social welfare?
- If my firm's price-advertising strategy informs consumers about product attributes or benefits, how will this strategy affect consumer well-being and social welfare?
- If my firm uses a mixed advertising strategy based on increasing product awareness and on providing information about product benefits or performance, how will this strategy affect consumer well-being and social welfare? And, how will these effects vary over the *product life cycle*?
- If my firm offers consumers more choices by introducing a mixed bundling plan, will consumers gain?
- If my firm introduces new durable products sequentially over time, will consumers and society gain? And, how will the existence of *secondhand markets* for used products affect consumer well-being and social welfare?

The following terms will be introduced in this chapter (see glossary for definitions):

anticompetitive effect	first-generation buyers	price skimming
awareness effect	full upgrade	producer welfare
bundling	innovation	product life cycle
choice experiment	joint distribution of	pure bundling strategy
consumer information	reservation prices	quality-adjusted cost
structure	joint industry profits	ratios
consumer surplus	learning curve	quantity discounts
consumer welfare	mature product	reservation price
cost dynamics	mixed bundling	reservation price
demand dynamics	strategy	effect
dynamic pricing policy	myopic pricing	salvage value
economic value	net present value	secondhand market
firms	partial upgrade	social welfare
first-degree price	price discrimination	socially neutral
discrimination	strategy	strategic pricing
strategy	price insensitive	uniform pricing plan

▶ 20.1 What Is Social Welfare and How Is It Measured?

To analyze how the firm's marketing policies affect consumers and society as a whole, we need to define the well-being of consumers and of society. The standard theory goes as follows.

Table 20.1
Toyota Example: Optimal Policy Using Uniform Pricing

	Units sold	Total revenue	Cost per unit	Total cost	Total profit
$20,000	1M	$20B	$7,000	$7B	$13B
$16,000*	2M	$32B	$7,000	$14B	$18B
$10,000	3M	$30B	$7,000	$21B	$9B

*Toyota's optimal policy if it uses uniform pricing.

Society consists of *firms* and consumers. Firms produce and sell services. Consumers purchase and use those services. Hence the social welfare from a given marketing policy is defined as the sum of the benefits of that policy (profits) to the owners of the firm and the net gain to all consumers in the marketplace. (The net gain to consumers will be defined shortly.)

The concept of social welfare is best illustrated with an example.

Example: Suppose Toyota can sell its Scion brand of automobile to three segments: A, B, and C. For simplicity, assume that each segment is of equal size, 1 million, and that each consumer will purchase at most one car. Suppose Toyota's unit cost per Scion is $7,000 and that the *reservation prices* (willingness to pay) for segments A, B, and C, respectively, are as follows: $20,000, $16,000, and $10,000.

If Toyota charges each consumer the same price, we say that Toyota is using a *uniform pricing plan*. Since Toyota's goal is to maximize its profits, it should charge a price of $16,000 per car and make a profit of $18 billion by selling to Segments A and B only (table 20.1).

▶ *What is the effect of Toyota's uniform pricing policy on consumers' well-being?*

Suppose Toyota uses uniform pricing. Then, each consumer in Segment A is willing to pay $20,000 for the Scion but pays only $16,000. Hence each consumer in Segment A obtains a *consumer surplus* or net benefit of $4,000. Thus, Segment A as a whole obtains a net consumer surplus of $4 billion (customers in that segment × net benefit to each customer = $1M × $4,000).

Each customer in Segment B, in contrast, pays a price that is equal to his or her reservation price ($16,000). Hence Segment B obtains a net consumer surplus of zero.

Customers in Segment C do not buy the Scion, since the price ($16,000) is higher than their reservation prices ($10,000). Hence Segment C's net surplus is also zero.

Thus, the total consumer surplus to buyers as a group (Segments A, B, and C combined) is $4 billion. Since, by charging $16,000 per car, Toyota

Table 20.2
Toyota Example: Comparing Policies That
Provide the Same Levels of Social Welfare

Policy	Profit	Consumer surplus	Social welfare
X	$18B	$4B	$22B
Y	$22B	$0	$22B

makes a profit of $18 billion, the social welfare if Toyota uses a uniform pricing strategy is $22 billion (Toyota's profit + total surplus to consumers as a whole = $18B + $4B).

Fusion for Profit Maxim

The social welfare from a given marketing policy = profits + net consumer surplus.

Point to consider.   What does the standard measure of social welfare imply about the gains to consumers and the owners of the firm?

The standard measure of social welfare implies that the division of gains among consumers and the owners of the firm is irrelevant, *as long as the total value is unchanged.* This measure of social welfare may not be acceptable to all groups in society.

In the Toyota example, suppose Toyota can choose two marketing policies (Policy X and Policy Y). Suppose each policy leads to the same social welfare ($22 billion). However, the division of gains is as given in table 20.2.

Then, according to the standard definition of social welfare, society should be indifferent to which policy Toyota chooses. However, consumer advocates will prefer Policy X, since this policy provides consumers with a larger gain (consumer surplus). In contrast, investors in the stock market will prefer Policy Y, since this policy leads to higher profits.

▲ 20.2 Is Profit Maximization Compatible with Maximizing Social Welfare?

We continue with the Toyota example. Suppose Toyota uses a uniform pricing plan. As discussed, if Toyota maximizes its profits, it will charge a price of $16,000 for the Scion, sell 2 million units, and make a profit of $18 billion.

▶ *Will this uniform pricing policy maximize social welfare?*

Each consumer in Segment C is willing to pay up to $10,000 to buy a Scion. However, it costs Toyota only $7,000 to produce each additional Scion. Hence if Toyota were to sell more Scions, an additional gain of $3,000 could be created for each consumer in Segment C. In fact, if Toyota were to sell 3 million Scions instead of only 2 million units, an additional social gain of $3 billion could be created (number of consumers in Segment C × net economic benefit to each consumer in Segment C = 1 million × $3,000).

Fusion for Profit Maxim

Social welfare will not be maximized if the firm uses uniform pricing and maximizes its profits. The firm will produce fewer units than the socially optimal value.

▶ *Is there a way to reconcile the firm's goal of profit maximization and society's goal of maximizing social welfare?*

We continue with the Toyota example. Suppose Toyota can charge each segment its reservation price. We say that Toyota is using a perfect *first-degree price discrimination strategy*. Since the reservation price for each consumer is higher than the cost of producing each additional Scion ($7,000), Toyota should sell to all three segments. Hence Toyota will produce the socially correct number of Scions (3 million units).

▶ *How will this first-degree price discrimination strategy affect social welfare?*

As previously discussed, under uniform pricing the following results would have occurred:

1. Toyota would have sold the Scion to Segments A and B,
2. Consumers in Segment A would have obtained a net consumer surplus of $4 billion, and
3. Toyota would have obtained a profit of $18 billion.

Consequently, if Toyota uses uniform pricing, social welfare will be $22 billion (Toyota's profit + consumer surplus across all three segments = $18B + $4B + $0 + $0). However, if Toyota uses a first-degree price discrimination strategy, the following results will occur (table 20.3):

1. Toyota will sell the Scion to all three segments,
2. Toyota will charge each segment its reservation price for the Scion. Hence the net consumer surplus across all three segments will be zero, and
3. Toyota will obtain a profit of $25 billion.

Table 20.3
Toyota Example: How Perfect First-Degree Price Discrimination Affects Social Welfare

Segment	Price paid	Units sold	Revenue	Cost per unit	Cost	Profit	Consumer surplus	Profit + consumer surplus
A	$20,000	1M	$20B	$7,000	$7B	$13B	$0	$13B
B	$16,000	1M	$16B	$7,000	$7B	$9B	$0	$9B
C	$10,000	1M	$10B	$7,000	$7B	$3B	$0	$3B
Social welfare								$25B

Note. Prices paid were same as reservation prices.

Hence, if Toyota uses a first-degree price discrimination strategy, social welfare will be $25 billion—a net improvement of $3 billion ($25 B − $22 B) over the social welfare under the uniform pricing strategy.

Fusion for Profit Maxim

Social welfare and profit maximization are compatible if the firm can use a perfect first-degree price discrimination strategy. This strategy will always increase the firm's profits. However, consumers will be worse off, since all consumer surpluses will be reduced to zero.

Point to consider.   Firms that sell durable products often reduce their prices over time. How will this strategy affect consumer and social welfare?

To focus on essentials, suppose the discount rate is zero and there is no market growth. Furthermore, consumers who do not buy in any time period remain in the market in the future and behave myopically. That is, they will buy the Scion in any given time period provided the net gain from purchase is zero or positive. (This assumption will be relaxed later.)

We continue with the Toyota example. Given this scenario, Toyota should use a *dynamic pricing policy* and should charge the following prices:

1. $20,000 in the first period,
2. $16,000 in the second, and
3. $10,000 in the third.

Since each consumer will pay his or her reservation price for the Scion, this strategy will lead to a net consumer surplus across segments of zero. Hence, Toyota's net profits will be as follows:

1. $13 billion (first period),
2. $9 billion (second period), and
3. $3 billion (third period).

Since the discount rate is zero, the net present value of Toyota's profits will be $25 billion. Thus, Toyota's price strategy (known as *price skimming*[1]) will increase Toyota's profit, remove all consumer surpluses, and maximize social welfare.

Fusion for Profit Maxim

If the firm uses a price-skimming policy, social welfare will be maximized. However, consumer surplus will be zero, and all the benefit will accrue to the firm in the form of profits.

▲ **20.3 Do Consumers and Society Gain When Firms Give out Free Samples?**

Many firms give out free samples. The pharmaceutical industry routinely gives out free samples of medicines to doctors. More recently, pharmaceutical firms have been giving out free samples of medicines (where permissible by law) to consumers. Newspapers and magazines often give free trial offers before charging customers a subscription fee. Software companies provide the basic software free in the hope that consumers will pay for enhanced software features.

At first glance, it might appear that consumers and society will always gain when the firm gives out free samples. *However, this conclusion is not always correct.*[2]

Example: Suppose a pharmaceutical firm, say Merck, discovers a new prescription drug that can control both high blood pressure and high cholesterol. (For simplicity, assume that both society and Merck have two-period planning horizons and that the discount rates for both society and Merck are zero.)

Then, the social welfare from any marketing policy chosen by Merck is defined by Merck's total profits + total consumer surplus, where total profits = (profit in the first period + profit in the second period) and total consumer surplus = (consumer surplus in the first period + consumer surplus in the second period).

By assumption, Merck chooses to distribute free samples of the new drug to doctors. Hence, by definition, Merck's total profit from using a free sample policy is greater than the corresponding total profits from not doing so. Let us refer to the latter strategy as "myopic."

▲ *What will happen to consumer surplus if Merck gives out free samples in the first period and charges for the drug in the second period?*

Since consumers do not pay for the product in the first period, the consumer surplus in the first period will be higher than if Merck chooses a myopic policy. However, the effect of free samples on consumer surplus in the second period is more interesting.

Consider the following scenario for the second period. Suppose consumers who use Merck's free samples in the first period conclude that the new drug is highly superior to existing products. As a result, the demand for the new drug in the second period becomes very *price insensitive*. Then, Merck can charge a very high price for the new drug in the second period. Consequently, the number of doses sold in the second period could be very low. Hence it is possible that consumer surplus in the second period could be much lower than it *would have been* if Merck had used a myopic policy (i.e., charged consumers for the drug in the first period).

This implies the following result: the *net consumer surplus* (consumer surplus in the first period + consumer surplus in the second period) *could fall* when Merck distributes free samples in the first period. Suppose the decrease in net consumer surplus (first period + second period) outweighs the increase in Merck's profits (first period + second period). Then, social welfare will be lower when Merck gives out free samples.

▶ *What is the intuition behind this result?*

By giving out free samples in the first period, the firm is able to charge high prices in the second period. If the reduction in volume in the second period is sufficiently large, consumers in the second period could lose heavily. Hence, even though consumers gain in the first period, they lose overall.

Fusion for Profit Maxim

If the firm gives out free samples of its products, consumers and society *do not* necessarily gain in the long run.

▶ ### 20.4 Do Consumers and Society Gain When the Firm Has a Learning Curve?

When the firm has a *learning curve*, it has an incentive to behave strategically by increasing short-run volume to achieve future cost reductions. How will this strategic behavior affect consumers, profits, and social welfare?

Example: Suppose AMD has developed a new multifunctional computer chip that is suitable for the next generation of cell phones. For simplicity, consider a two-period model. In addition, assume that there is no market growth in demand and that AMD's discount rate is zero.

Suppose AMD has a learning curve in manufacturing the new chip. That is, the unit cost per chip in the second period depends on the number of chips produced in *both* the first and the second time periods. Now, the social welfare from any marketing policy that AMD chooses is defined by:

social welfare = (AMD's profit in the first period + AMD's profit in the
                 second period) + (consumer surplus in the first period +
                 consumer surplus in the second period).

Or equivalently,

social welfare = AMD's total profit + (consumer surplus in the first
                 period + consumer surplus in the second period).

We will compare the welfare effects of two policies: myopic and strategic.

1. Under the myopic policy, AMD proceeds sequentially. That is, AMD sets the first-period price to maximize its first-period profits and then sets the second-period price conditional on this strategy.
2. Under the strategic policy, AMD coordinates its price policies over the two periods to maximize its total profit.

▶ *Because of the learning curve, AMD's total profit under the strategic pricing policy will be higher than the corresponding total profit under the myopic policy. But, what is the effect of the strategic pricing policy on consumer surpluses in the first and second periods?*

When AMD prices strategically, it will sell a higher volume (i.e., charge a lower price) in the first period in order to lower future costs via the learning curve. Hence consumer surplus in the first period will increase.

Since AMD has now accumulated more experience in the first period, it will become more efficient in the second period than it would have been if it had priced myopically in the first period. This implies that, other factors being the same, the strategic price in the second period *will also be lower* than the corresponding myopic price in that period. That is, AMD will sell more chips in the second period when it behaves strategically. Consequently, consumer surplus will increase in the second period as well.

These results imply that all constituencies (AMD's shareholders, AMD's consumers, and society) will gain when AMD prices strategically based on the learning curve.

Fusion for Profit Maxim

When the firm chooses its marketing policy based on the learning curve, consumers and shareholders will be better off. Hence social welfare will increase.

▶ 20.5 Do Consumers and Society Gain When There Are Demand Dynamics?

This problem is similar to the case where the firm gives out free samples of its product in the first period and charges for the product in subsequent periods.

Example: Suppose Colgate-Palmolive has developed a new shampoo, Shimmerz. We will compare the welfare effects of myopic and strategic pricing. Under *myopic pricing*, Colgate-Palmolive maximizes its profits period by period. Under strategic pricing, Colgate-Palmolive coordinates its pricing policies over time to maximize long-run profits.

Suppose Colgate-Palmolive uses strategic pricing. That is, it charges a low introductory price for Shimmerz in order to obtain a high trial rate and hence increase future demand.

Then, in the first period, Colgate-Palmolive will charge a lower price, sell a higher volume, and obtain lower profits than it would have obtained under myopic pricing (i.e., the strategy that maximizes profits in the first period). Since Colgate-Palmolive charges a lower price in the first period when it chooses its marketing policy strategically, first-period consumers will gain.

▶ However, will consumers in the second period gain when Colgate-Palmolive prices strategically in the first period?

The answer to this question depends critically on what happens to price and volume in the second period. In many cases, for frequently purchased products, second-period consumers (including repeat purchasers from the first period) will be better off, since volume will increase. However, as in the case where the firm gives out free samples, it is possible that strategic pricing could make consumers in the second period worse off than under myopic pricing.

Consider the following scenario. Suppose strategic pricing reduces price sensitivity significantly in the second period. Consequently, Colgate-Palmolive raises prices significantly in the second period, leading to a sharp reduction in volume. If this occurs, second-period consumers (including repeat purchasers from the first period) will be worse off when Colgate-Palmolive uses strategic pricing. Hence *the effect of strategic pricing on consumer well-being and social welfare is ambiguous.*

Fusion for Profit Maxim

Suppose there are demand dynamics and the firm chooses its marketing policy to maximize long-run profits. Then, the effect on consumer well-being and social welfare is conditional.

Table 20.4
How Strategic Pricing Affects Social Welfare

Effect of strategic pricing	Consumer surplus (period 1)	Consumer surplus (period 2)	Total consumer surplus	Total profits	Social welfare
Learning curve	Increase	Increase	Increase	Increase	Increase
Demand dynamics	Increase	Often increase	Often increase	Increase	Often increase
Combined effect	Increase	Often increase	Often increase	Increase	Often increase

Point to consider.   Suppose the firm has a learning curve, and demand dynamics exist. How will strategic pricing affect consumer well-being and social welfare?

Combining the results from our previous analyses on the learning curve and demand dynamics, we obtain the following results. The firm increases its long-run profits when it prices strategically; in addition, consumers in the first period gain. In many cases, consumers in the second period will also gain. For this scenario, *strategic pricing will lead to higher long-run profits and consumer surplus.* Consequently, strategic pricing will lead to higher social welfare.[3] These results are summarized in table 20.4.

Point to consider.   Will strategic pricing increase social welfare under uncertainty? How will competitive behavior affect the social welfare impact of strategic pricing?

The previous analyses assumed that the firm knows its cost and demand structures with certainty; furthermore, we did not consider competition. We now relax these assumptions.

Example 1: Suppose the firm has a strong and proprietary learning curve. Then, the optimal strategy for the firm may be to proceed as follows. Invest heavily in a plant with high capacity, and price strategically to accumulate experience rapidly to lower future costs. Once this is achieved, the firm can lower price and drive out competitors in the future. This strategy is *anticompetitive* and could reduce social welfare.

Example 2: Suppose the learning curve is highly uncertain. Then, strategic pricing may not lead to the anticipated reductions in future cost savings. Consequently, the firm may go bankrupt: witness the dot-com debacle of the 1990s. Thus, strategic pricing may not lead to an improvement in social welfare in the long run.

▶ 20.6 Are Quantity Discounts Good for Consumers and for Society?

On the surface, it might appear that consumers will always gain when the firm offers *quantity discounts*. After all, heavy users of the firm's product—who clearly value the firm's product highly—will get a price break if the firm offers quantity discounts. Hence they should be better off.

Interestingly, this result may not occur. As shown below, by offering a quantity-discount pricing plan, the firm can simply transfer consumer surplus to itself in the form of additional profit. Hence, consumers as a group may be worse off when the firm offers quantity discounts.[4]

Example: Suppose John Deere has two potential buyers for a new tractor it is planning to introduce into the marketplace. The first potential buyer, Alpha, is small and is willing to purchase one of the new John Deere tractors for a maximum price of $50,000. The second buyer, Beta, is larger. Specifically, Beta is willing to purchase one John Deere tractor for $50,000 but will purchase two tractors if the price is reduced to $40,000 per tractor. Assume that John Deere's marginal cost of producing each new tractor is $10,000.

Suppose John Deere charges a fixed price per tractor. We say that it is using a uniform pricing strategy. Then, John Deere can charge a price of $50,000 (Strategy 1) or $40,000 (Strategy 2).

As shown in table 20.5, the optimal policy for John Deere is to choose Strategy 2; in other words, to charge a price of $40,000 per tractor and to sell three tractors. If John Deere chooses this strategy, it will make a profit of $90,000.

▶ What is the effect on buyers?

As shown in table 20.6, Alpha will buy one tractor and obtain a surplus of $10,000 (reservation price of one tractor − price paid for one tractor =

Table 20.5
John Deere Example: John Deere Charges a Fixed Price per Tractor

	Price	Units sold	Revenue	Cost	Profit
Strategy 1	$50,000	2	$100,000	$20,000	$80,000
Strategy 2	$40,000*	3	$120,000	$30,000	$90,000

*Policy chosen.

Table 20.6
John Deere Example: Consumer Surplus If John Deere Charges a Fixed Price per Tractor

Buyer	RP (1st unit)	RP (2nd unit)	Total RP	Price per unit	Units bought	Amount paid	Consumer surplus
1	$50,000	$0	$50,000	$40,000	1	$40,000	$10,000
2	$50,000	$40,000	$90,000	$40,000	2	$80,000	$10,000
Total							$20,000

Note. RP, reservation price.

$50,000 – $40,000). Beta will buy two tractors and obtain a surplus of $10,000 (reservation price of two tractors – amount paid for two tractors = $90,000 – $80,000). Thus, if John Deere uses a uniform pricing policy, the total consumer surplus to buyers is $20,000 (surplus to Alpha + surplus to Beta).

Hence, the social welfare if John Deere uses uniform pricing is $110,000 (John Deere's profit + net consumer surplus = $90,000 + $20,000).

▶ How can John Deere improve its profits?

John Deere can improve its profits by using the following quantity-discount policy: charge a price of $50,000 for one tractor and offer a $10,000 discount on the purchase of the second.

Given this quantity-discount schedule, Alpha will buy 1 tractor for its reservation price ($50,000). Hence Alpha will obtain zero consumer surplus.

Beta is willing to pay up to $90,000 for two tractors. Hence, given John Deere's quantity-discount policy, Beta will spend exactly this amount to buy two tractors. Specifically, Beta will buy the first tractor for $50,000 and the second for $40,000. Note that Beta's consumer surplus will also be reduced to zero.

▶ What will happen to John Deere's profits?

By using this quantity-discount policy, John Deere can transfer all the consumer surplus in the market ($20,000) to itself. Hence John Deere's profit will increase from $90,000 to $110,000 (table 20.7).

▶ How will John Deere's quantity-discount policy affect social welfare?

Interestingly, John Deere's quantity-discount policy is *socially neutral. All that happens is a transfer of consumer surplus from buyers as a group to John Deere* (table 20.8).

Fusion for Profit Maxim

Consumers as a group may be worse off if the firm uses a quantity-discount policy. Furthermore, a quantity-discount policy may be socially neutral.

▶ 20.7 Does Advertising Make Consumers and Society Better Off?

The answer to this question depends on how advertising affects consumer awareness and/or consumers' reservation prices.[5] We consider different scenarios below.

Table 20.7
John Deere Example: Effect on Profits If John Deere Offers Quantity Discounts

Buyer	RP (1st unit)	RP (2nd unit)	Total RP	Price (1st unit)	Price (2nd unit)	Units bought	Total price	Consumer surplus	Cost per unit	Cost	Profit
1	$50,000	$0	$50,000	$50,000	$40,000	1	$50,000	$0	$10,000	$10,000	$40,000
2	$50,000	$40,000	$90,000	$50,000	$40,000	2	$90,000	$0	$10,000	$20,000	$70,000
Total						3	$140,000			$30,000	$110,000

Note. RP, reservation price.

Table 20.8
John Deere Example: Effect of Quantity-Discount Policy on Social Welfare

Pricing policy	Consumer surplus	Profit	Social welfare
Uniform pricing	$20,000	$90,000	$110,000
Quantity discount	$0	$110,000	$110,000

Advertising Affects Only Awareness

Suppose the only role of advertising is to increase product awareness; in particular, the advertising message contains no information about price.

How will advertising affect consumer well-being and social welfare?

Example: Suppose Microsoft introduces a new type of software called Virtuoso into the marketplace. Let's say that there are two consumer segments (A and B), each of equal size, 1 million. Suppose the marginal cost of production for Virtuoso is zero (a reasonable assumption for software). Let's say that the reservation prices for Virtuoso are as follows: $100 per unit (Segment A) and $70 per unit (Segment B).

Suppose only the segment with high reservation prices (Segment A) is aware of Virtuoso when Microsoft does not advertise. Hence, if Microsoft does no advertising, it will sell 1 million units of Virtuoso to Segment A at a price of $100 per unit and make a net profit of $100 million. Since consumers in Segment A pay their reservation prices ($100), Segment A obtains zero consumer surplus (table 20.9).

Since consumers in Segment B are unaware of Virtuoso, they do not purchase Virtuoso. Hence Segment B also obtains zero consumer surplus. Consequently, the net consumer surplus across both segments is zero.

Hence, if Microsoft does not advertise Virtuoso, social welfare (profits + net consumer surplus) is equal to Microsoft's profit from Virtuoso ($100 million).

Now, suppose Microsoft can use an advertising campaign to make the segment with lower reservation prices (Segment B) aware of Virtuoso. Let's say that this advertising campaign will cost Microsoft $20 million.

Table 20.9
Microsoft-Virtuoso Example: Effect on Social Welfare If the Segment with Low Reservation Prices Is Not Aware of Virtuoso (No Advertising for Virtuoso)

	Awareness	RP	Units sold	Price per unit	Consumer surplus	Revenue	Advertising expenditure	Profit	Social welfare
Segment A	Yes	$100	1M	$100	$0	$100M	$0	$100M	$100M
Segment B	No	$70	0	$100	$0	$0	$0	$0	$0

Note. RP, reservation price.

Table 20.10
Microsoft-Virtuoso Example: Effect on Microsoft's Profits and Social Welfare When Microsoft Advertises to the Unaware Segment with Low Reservation Prices

	Awareness	RP	Units sold	Price per unit	Consumer surplus per unit	Revenue	Profit	Social welfare
Segment A	Yes	$100	1M	$70	$30	$70M	$70M	$100M
Segment B	Yes	$70	1M	$70	$0	$70M	$70M	$70M
Advertising expenditure							–$20M	–$20M
Totals			2M		$30M	$140M	$120M	$150M

Note. RP, reservation price.

▶ *What price should Microsoft charge for Virtuoso if it uses this advertising strategy?*

Suppose Microsoft advertises. Since all potential consumers will now become aware of the availability of Virtuoso, the optimal strategy for Microsoft is to reduce the price from $100 per unit and sell to both segments (table 20.10). Specifically, Microsoft should charge $70 per unit, sell 2 million units, and make a gross profit of $140 million. Since Microsoft now incurs an advertising cost of $20 million, it will make a net profit of $120 million on Virtuoso (gross revenue from both segments – advertising cost).

▶ *What is the effect of advertising on consumers?*

Since both segments now buy Virtuoso at a price of $70 per unit, each consumer in Segment A obtains a consumer surplus of $30 (reservation price – price paid = $100 – $70). Hence, in aggregate, consumers in Segment A obtain a consumer surplus of $30 million (number of customers in Segment A × surplus per customer = 1M × $30).

Since all consumers in Segment B pay their reservation prices, they obtain consumer surpluses of zero. Hence the aggregate consumer surplus across both segments is $30 million (consumer surplus for Segment A + consumer surplus for Segment B = $30M + $0).

▶ *What is the effect of advertising on social welfare?*

Virtuoso's profits increase from $100 million to $120 million. Hence Microsoft's stockholders gain (See table 20.10.). The net consumer surplus increases from zero to $30 million. Hence consumers also gain. Since both constituencies (stockholders and consumers) gain, social welfare increases. Specifically, when Virtuoso advertises, social welfare increases from $100 million to $150 million (a 50% increase).

> **Fusion for Profit Maxim**
>
> Suppose advertising increases awareness among consumers with low reservation prices. Then, the firm should reduce prices. Consequently, profits will increase, consumers will gain, and social welfare will increase.

Point to consider. In the Microsoft-Virtuoso example, suppose only consumers with low reservation prices ($70 per unit) are aware of Virtuoso when Microsoft does not advertise. Furthermore, all consumers with high reservation prices ($170 per unit) are unaware of Virtuoso.

Let Segment C denote the segment with low reservation prices for Virtuoso ($70 per unit) and Segment D the segment with high reservation prices ($170 per unit). By assumption, if Microsoft does not advertise, only customers in the segment with low reservation prices (Segment C) are aware of Virtuoso (table 20.11).

Given this scenario, Microsoft should charge $70 per unit for Virtuoso, all consumers in Segment C will buy the product, and Microsoft will make a gross profit of $70 million (number of consumers in Segment C × price) (see table 20.11).

Since all consumers pay a price that is equal to their reservation prices, the net consumer surplus is zero. Hence social welfare is $70 million (Microsoft's profits + net consumer surplus = $70M + $0).

▶ *How will advertising affect consumer and social welfare? Assume as before that Microsoft will need to spend $20 million on advertising to make the market fully aware that Virtuoso is available.*

Now, advertising makes the segment with high reservation prices, Segment D (1 million customers), aware of Virtuoso. Hence Microsoft has two choices: charge $70 per unit as before, or increase the price to $170 per unit.

Suppose Microsoft continues to charge the low price of $70 per unit after it advertises. Then, Microsoft will sell 2 million units of Virtuoso and make a net profit of $120 million (> $70 million).[6] Now, each consumer in

Table 20.11
Microsoft-Virtuoso Example: Effect on Microsoft's Profits When Microsoft Does Not Advertise Virtuoso

	Awareness	RP	Units sold	Price per unit	Consumer surplus	Revenue	Advertising expenditure	Profit	Effect on social welfare
Segment C	Yes	$70	1M	$70	$0	$70M	$0	$70M	$70M

Note. RP, reservation price.

Segment D will obtain a consumer surplus of $100 (reservation price − price paid = $170 − $70). Hence Segment D will obtain a consumer surplus of $100 million. However, each consumer in Segment C will pay his or her reservation price ($70). Hence Segment C obtains zero consumer surplus. Consequently, the net consumer surplus across segments will be $100 million (table 20.12).

Hence social welfare will be $220 million (Microsoft's profit + net consumer surplus = $120M + $100M). Note that this is a *substantial increase over the social welfare ($70 M) if Virtuoso does not advertise* (see table 20.11).

Alternatively, Microsoft can raise the price of Virtuoso to $170 per unit after it advertises. In this case, it will sell 1 million units of Virtuoso to Segment D and make a net profit of $150 million. However, the net consumer surplus across segments will be zero. Hence social welfare will be $150 million (Microsoft's profits + net consumer surplus) (table 20.13).

Table 20.12

Microsoft-Virtuoso Example: Effect on Microsoft's Profits and Social Welfare When Microsoft Advertises to the Unaware Segment with High Reservation Prices and Charges a Low Price

	Awareness	RP	Units sold	Price per unit	Consumer surplus per unit	Revenue	Profit	Effect on social welfare
Segment C	Yes	$70	1M	$70	$0	$70M	$70M	$70M
Segment D	Yes	$170	1M	$70	$100	$70M	$70M	$170M
Advertising expenditure							−20M	−$20M
Totals						$140M	$120M	$220M

Note. RP, reservation price.

Table 20.13

Microsoft-Virtuoso Example: Effect on Microsoft's Profits and Social Welfare When Microsoft Advertises to the Unaware Segment with High Reservation Prices and Charges a High Price

	Awareness	RP	Units sold	Price per unit	Consumer surplus	Revenue	Profit	Effect on Social welfare
Segment C	Yes	$70	1M	$170	$0	$0	$0M	$0M
Segment D	Yes	$170	1M	$170	$0	$170M	$170M	$170M
Advertising expenditure							−$20M	−$20M
Totals						$170M	$150M	$150M

Note. RP, reservation price.

▶   *Which price-advertising strategy should Microsoft choose?*

Microsoft should advertise and increase the price of Virtuoso to $170 per unit because this strategy leads to a higher profit ($150 million) than the profit ($120 million) from the alternative strategy of advertising and charging a low price (table 20.14).

Note that there is a conflict between maximizing profits and maximizing social welfare (see table 20.14). From a social viewpoint, Microsoft should spend $20 million on advertising and charge a low price ($70 per unit) for Virtuoso. However, *to maximize shareholder value, Microsoft should spend $20 million on advertising and charge a high price ($170 per unit).*

Fusion for Profit Maxim

Suppose advertising increases awareness among consumers with high reservation prices. Then, profit maximization may conflict with maximizing social welfare.

Point to consider.   In the Microsoft-Virtuoso example, suppose some customers in each segment are unaware of Virtuoso. What is the likely impact of advertising on consumers and social welfare? Assume that Microsoft cannot selectively target customers in each market segment. Furthermore, suppose Microsoft and society are risk-neutral (i.e., Microsoft's shareholders seek to maximize their expected incomes, and consumer well-being is given by the expected consumer surplus from any marketing policy chosen by Microsoft). How will the results change if Microsoft can selectively target customers in both segments?

Selective Targeting Not Possible

We begin with the case where Microsoft cannot selectively target customers in both segments. Hence advertising increases the average sizes of the aware groups in each segment *by the same proportion.*

Table 20.14
Microsoft-Virtuoso Example: Effect of Microsoft's Strategy on Social Welfare When Microsoft Advertises to Reach the Unaware Segment with High Reservation Prices

Price	Units sold	Revenue	Advertising cost	Net profit	Consumer surplus	Social welfare
$170	1	$170	$20	$150	$0	$150
$70	2	$140	$20	$120	$100	$220

Note. All values except price are in millions.

As illustrated in the example below, the following results will occur. Microsoft will increase its profits after it advertises. However, *Microsoft will not change the price of Virtuoso*. If consumer surplus in the no-advertising case is zero, it will remain zero after Microsoft advertises. If consumer surplus in the no-advertising case is positive, it will increase after Microsoft advertises. Regardless of which scenario occurs, *social welfare will increase when Microsoft advertises*.

Example: Suppose Segments E and F each contain 2 million customers. Each customer in Segment E has a reservation price of $100 for Virtuoso, and each customer in Segment F has a lower reservation price of $70. Suppose Microsoft believes that, on average, 500,000 customers in each segment are already aware of Virtuoso even if it does not do any advertising. Then, if Microsoft does not advertise Virtuoso, it will charge a price of $70 per unit and make a gross profit of $70 million ([500,000 + 500,000] × $70). Each buyer in Segment E will make a surplus of $30 (reservation price − price paid = $100 − $70), and each buyer in Segment F will make a surplus of zero ($70 − $70) (table 20.15).

Hence Segment E will obtain a consumer surplus of $15 million (number of aware consumers in Segment E × consumer surplus per buyer in Segment E = 500,000 × $30), and Segment F will obtain a consumer surplus of zero (500,000 × $0).

Consequently, the social welfare from Virtuoso's sales to Segment E (gross profits from Segment E + consumer surplus to Segment E = $35M + $15M) is $50 million. Correspondingly, the social welfare from Virtuoso's sales to Segment F is $35 million ($35M + $0). Hence the overall social welfare generated by Virtuoso is $85 million ($50M + $35M).

Let's say that Microsoft can maximize its expected net profits by spending $15 million on advertising. (By assumption, Microsoft cannot selectively target customers in each segment.) Hence, when Microsoft spends $15 million on advertising, on average, the number of aware customers in each segment will increase by the same proportion. Let's say that, on average, if Microsoft spends $15 million on advertising, the number of aware customers in each segment will increase by the same proportion, from 500,000 to 1 million.

Table 20.15

Microsoft-Virtuoso Example: Social Welfare When Microsoft Does Not Advertise and Some Consumers in Each Segment Are Unaware of Virtuoso

	RP	Price per unit	Consumer surplus per unit	Units sold	Consumer surplus	Advertising expenditure	Revenue	Effect on social welfare
Segment E	$100	$70	$30	0.5M	$15M	$0	$35M	$50M
Segment F	$70	$70	$0	0.5M	$0	$0	$35M	$35M
Totals				1M	$15M		$70M	$85M

Note. RP, reservation price.

▶ *What price-advertising policy should Microsoft use, and how will this affect consumer and social welfare?*

Since Microsoft cannot selectively target customers in different segments, advertising simply increases the size of each market segment by the same proportion. *That is, advertising does not change the mix of customers.* Hence the optimal policy for Microsoft is to continue to charge a price of $70 per unit when it advertises.

Note that advertising has doubled the size of each market segment (i.e., the units sold have increased from 0.5M to 1M in each segment). Hence, advertising doubles the consumer surplus in the market from $15 million to $30 million (table 20.16). Since advertising increases both the expected consumer surplus across segments and Microsoft's expected profits, social welfare will increase.

▶ *What will happen if the net consumer surplus before Microsoft advertises is zero?*

In this case, since advertising leaves the customer mix unchanged, Microsoft will continue to charge the same price for Virtuoso as it did before. Hence the net consumer surplus across segments will remain at zero. Consequently, the following results will occur after Microsoft advertises: Microsoft's profits will increase, consumers will be unaffected, and social welfare will increase.

Fusion for Profit Maxim

The effect of advertising on consumer and social welfare depends on *how advertising changes the mix of aware customers* in different segments. If the mix remains unchanged, the firm will not change its pricing policy when it advertises, and social welfare will increase.

Table 20.16
Microsoft-Virtuoso Example: Effect on Social Welfare When Microsoft's Advertising Cannot Selectively Target Unaware Consumers in Different Segments (Optimal Advertising)

	RP	Price per unit	Consumer surplus per unit	Units sold	Consumer surplus	Revenue	Effect on social welfare
Segment E	$100	$70	$30	1M	$30M	$70M	$100M
Segment F	$70	$70	$0	1M	$0	$70M	$70M
Advertising expenditure						–$15M	–$15M
Totals				2M	$30M	$125M	$155M

Note. RP, reservation price.

Selective Targeting

Suppose Microsoft has done market research and conducted a market segmentation study. Let's say that the results show that customers whose annual incomes are greater than $70,000 are more likely to belong to the segment with high reservation prices for Virtuoso.

Then Microsoft should choose a media plan that selectively reaches customers in this target segment. Hence advertising will change the mix of customers; in particular, the *proportion* of customers who belong to the target segment will increase when Microsoft advertises. *This implies that Microsoft should increase the price of Virtuoso when it advertises.*

Consequently, it is quite possible that net consumer surplus will fall after Microsoft advertises Virtuoso. Indeed, *if the reduction in the number of units sold is sufficiently large when Microsoft raises its price, it is possible that social welfare will decrease.*

Fusion for Profit Maxim

If advertising changes the mix of aware customers in different segments, the firm may charge a higher price when it advertises. In this case, it is possible that social welfare will decrease when the firm advertises.

Advertising Affects Reservation Prices

To focus on essentials, assume that all consumers are aware of the product. However, they have incomplete information about the product's benefits. Hence advertising has an impact on consumers' reservation prices.

Suppose advertising makes the market less price-sensitive. Then, it is likely that the firm will increase the price of its product. If the price increase is large, the number of units sold could decrease sharply. In this case, it is quite possible that consumers and society will be worse off when the firm advertises.

We continue with the Microsoft-Virtuoso example.

Suppose there are two segments that are potential buyers of Virtuoso. However, *both segments are aware of Virtuoso even if Microsoft does not advertise.* Suppose each segment contains 1 million customers. Let's say that the reservation prices before Microsoft advertises are as follows: $100 per unit (Segment G) and $70 per unit (Segment H). Suppose Microsoft does not advertise Virtuoso. Then Microsoft should charge a price of $70 per unit and sell 2 million units (table 20.17).

Hence Microsoft's net profit will be $140 million, the net consumer surplus will be $30 million, and social welfare will be $170 million (Microsoft's profit + net consumer surplus).

Table 20.17

Microsoft-Virtuoso Example: Effect on Social Welfare If All Consumers Are Aware of Virtuoso and Microsoft Does Not Advertise

	RP	Price per unit	Consumer surplus per unit	Units sold	Consumer surplus	Revenue	Effect on social welfare
Segment G	$100	$70	$30	1M	$30M	$70M	$100M
Segment H	$70	$70	$0	1M	$0	$70M	$70M
Advertising expenditure						$0	$0
Totals				2M	$30M	$140M	$170M

Note. RP, reservation price.

Suppose Microsoft advertises Virtuoso, and the advertising message explains in detail how consumers can use Virtuoso to perform multiple tasks. Suppose the advertising cost is $10 million. *Since advertising informs customers about how they can use Virtuoso, their reservation prices will increase.*

Suppose Segment G's reservation price increases from $100 to $170 (a large increase), and Segment H's reservation price increases from $70 to $80 (a smaller increase) (table 20.18). Then Microsoft should charge a price of $170 per unit and sell 1 million units to Segment G.

Hence Microsoft will make a net profit of $160 million (gross profits – advertising cost = $170M – $10M). Since Segment G pays its reservation price, the net consumer surplus across segments will be zero. Hence social welfare will be $160 million (Microsoft's profits + consumer surplus = $160M + $0).

Note the effect of Microsoft's advertising. Microsoft's shareholders will be better off, since Microsoft increases its profits from $140 million to $160 million. The price of Virtuoso will increase from $70 to $170 per unit. Consumers will be worse off, since the net consumer surplus across segments will be reduced from $30 million to zero. And, social welfare will decrease from $170 million to $160 million.

Fusion for Profit Maxim

If advertising increases consumers' reservation prices, social welfare could decrease.

◤ 20.8 How Does Advertising Affect Consumer Well-Being and Social Welfare over the Product Life Cycle?

All products go through different phases: introduction, growth, maturity, and decline. We say that products go through a product life cycle. As

Table 20.18
**Microsoft-Virtuoso Example: Effect on Social Welfare If All Consumers Are
Already Aware of Virtuoso and Microsoft Advertises to Increase Consumers'
Reservation Prices (Optimal Advertising)**

	RP	Price per unit	Consumer surplus per unit	Units sold	Consumer surplus	Revenue	Effect on social welfare
Segment G	$170	$170	$0	1M	$0	$170M	$170M
Segment H	$80	$170	$0	0	$0	$0	$0
Advertising expenditure						–$10M	–$10M
Totals				1M	0	160M	$160M

Note. RP, reservation price.

one would expect, advertising is likely to have different roles over the life cycle.

For instance, the proportion of aware and informed consumers is likely to increase over time as the product goes through its life cycle. Hence the impact of advertising on social welfare over the product life cycle will depend on two factors:

1. How advertising affects awareness (the *awareness effect*), and
2. How advertising affects consumers' reservation prices (the *reservation price effect*).

In the early part of the product life cycle, both the awareness and reservation price effects are likely to be strong, especially for a product that is new to the market. Thus, advertising is necessary to increase awareness. In addition, advertising is necessary to inform consumers about the benefits of the new product and hence increases consumers' reservation prices. Hence the awareness effect is likely to be strong, since many consumers do not know about the product's existence. As discussed, other factors remaining the same, this awareness effect tends to lead to *higher* social welfare because the firm charges a lower price.

However, depending on the product, the reservation price effect could also be strong. For instance, advertising could increase consumers' reservation prices and reduce the price sensitivity of the market. If this effect is sufficiently strong, the firm could increase prices and reduce volume sharply. Consequently, other factors remaining the same, the reservation price effect could lead to *lower* social welfare.

Note that the effect of advertising on social welfare will depend on whether the awareness effect is stronger or weaker than the reservation price effect. These effects are likely to vary by product type and the phase of the product life cycle (i.e., introduction, growth, *maturity*, or decline).

Fusion for Profit Maxim

The effect of advertising on consumer well-being and social welfare depends on the awareness and reservation price effects. These effects are likely to vary over the product life cycle and across products.

▲ 20.9 Is Competitive Advertising Good or Bad for Consumers and for Society?

So far, we have focused on the effects of advertising by the firm without considering the effects of advertising by competitors. How will competitive advertising affect consumer well-being and social welfare?

In general, the answer will depend on how competitors' pricing and advertising strategies affect the awareness levels and reservation prices for *both the competitors' products and those produced by the firm.* For simplicity, we focus on the case where the firm has only one competitor. Both firms produce similar but not identical products.

Example: Consider the liquid detergent industry. Suppose the Pristeen Company produces a high-quality detergent (Brand A), and its competitor, the Murkee Company, produces a lower-quality detergent (Brand B).

Suppose the market contains 2 million identical consumers whose reservation prices for Brands A and B, respectively, are $10 and $8 per unit. For simplicity, assume that the marginal costs for both brands are very small (approximately zero) and that all consumers are aware that both brands are available in the marketplace. In addition, each consumer will purchase at most one unit every month.

Then, in the absence of advertising, Brand A should charge a price of $10 per unit and sell 1 million units every month. Thus, Brand A will make a monthly profit of $10 million. Similarly, Brand B should charge a price of $8, sell 1 million units every month, and make a monthly profit of $8 million (table 20.19).

Since each consumer pays his or her reservation price, the net consumer surplus across both brands is zero. Consequently, the social welfare when neither firm advertises is $18 million per month (profit for Brand A + profit for Brand B = $10M + $8M).

We now show that, depending on the price and advertising strategies that different firms choose, *competitive advertising can either increase or decrease social welfare.*

Advertising by the High-Quality Product

Suppose the high-quality brand (Brand A) advertises to consumers and educates them about the benefits from using Brand A. For example, Pristeen

Table 20.19
Pristeen-Murkee Example: Effect on Social Welfare If Neither Firm Advertises

Brand	RP per unit	Units sold per month	Price per unit	Consumer surplus	Profit	Social welfare
A	$10	1M	$10	$0	$10M	$10M
B	$8	1M	$8	$0	$8M	$8M
Advertising expenditure					$0	$0
Totals					$18M	$18M

Note. RP, reservation price.

runs an advertising campaign that costs $3 million per month and that contains the following message: "An independent product-testing agency has found Brand A to be gentler on delicate fabrics than Brand B." The result is that the reservation prices for all consumers for Brand A increase from $10 to $12 per unit.

▲ *What pricing strategy should Pristeen use?*

Pristeen should charge a price for Brand A that is slightly less than $12 per unit so that each consumer obtains a small positive surplus by purchasing Brand A (table 20.20). Thus, all consumers will buy Brand A. Hence Pristeen will obtain a gross monthly revenue of $24 million (approximately) and a net monthly profit of $21 million (approximately) after paying the cost of advertising ($3 million). Note that consumers will obtain a net consumer surplus of zero (approximately), and Brand B will leave the market.[7] Hence the social welfare when Brand A advertises is approximately $21 million per month (Brand A's profit + net consumer surplus).

Note that advertising by the high-quality product (Brand A) increases social welfare from $18 million to $21 million per month. However, *the benefits* from the increase in social welfare are highly skewed. The only party that gains as a result of advertising is Pristeen, which increases its profits on Brand A from $10 million to $21 million per month. However, consumers are no better off than in the case where Brand A does not advertise.

Advertising by the Low-Quality Product

Suppose the low-quality brand (Brand B) advertises using the following message: "An independent product-testing agency (e.g., *Consumer Reports*) has found that Brand B's performance has been underrated in the past."

Let's say that after being exposed to this ad, all consumers increase their reservation prices for Brand B to $9 per unit. As in the previous example, suppose the cost of advertising is $3 million per month.

Table 20.20
Pristeen-Murkee Example: The Effect on Social Welfare If the High-Quality Brand (Brand A) Advertises

	RP per unit	Units sold per month	Price per unit	Consumer surplus per unit	Profit	Social welfare
Brand A	$12	2M	$11.99	$0.01	$23.98M	$23.98M
Advertising expenditure					−$3M	−$3M
Totals					$20.98M	$20.98M

Note. RP, reservation price.

Given this advertising message strategy, Brand B should charge a price just below each consumer's reservation price for Brand B ($9) (table 20.21). Hence all consumers will buy Brand B, the net consumer surplus will be zero (approximately), Brand B will make a profit of approximately $15 million per month, and Brand A will leave the market. (This time, assume that Pristeen is small and does not wish to enter a price war with its larger competitor, Murkee.)

Note that, in contrast to the previous case, society will be worse off when the firm advertises. Interestingly, even though industry prices have fallen, social welfare will be *reduced* from $18 million to $15 million per month.

Fusion for Profit Maxim

The effect of advertising on social welfare depends on how competitors' price and message strategies affect the awareness levels and reservation prices for the products that compete in the marketplace. A decrease in market prices does not imply that social welfare has increased.

Point to consider.   Suppose consumers are fully informed about both products, and no advertising is done. What strategy should the firms use? How will these strategies affect consumer and social welfare?

When neither firm advertises, Brand A makes a profit of $10 million per month, and Brand B makes a profit of $8 million per month. Hence the *joint industry profits* are $18 million per month.

Suppose Pristeen buys Brand B from Murkee and takes it off the market. After the acquisition, consumers who wish to purchase Brand B will have no alternative but to buy Brand A for $10 per month. Hence Brand A's profit will double from $10 million to $20 million per month. Note that, as a result of the acquisition, the joint industry profits will increase from $18 million

Table 20.21
Pristeen-Murkee Example: The Effect on Social Welfare If the Low-Quality Brand (Brand B) Advertises

	RP per unit	Units Sold per month	Price per unit	Consumer surplus per unit	Profit	Social welfare
Brand B	$9	2M	$8.99	$0.01	$17.98M	$17.98M
Advertising expenditure					−$3M	−$3M
Totals					$14.98M	$14.98M

Note. RP, reservation price.

per month to $20 million per month. Hence Pristeen can pay a premium of up to *25%* to purchase Brand B, where,

$$\text{percentage premium} = \frac{\text{increase in profit to Brand B after the acquisition}}{\text{profit of Brand A before the acquisition}}$$

▶ How will this acquisition affect consumers and society?

Paradoxically, despite the *anticompetitive effect* of the acquisition, social welfare will increase from $18 million per month to $20 million per month (an 11.1% improvement). However, the benefits will be skewed. All the gain will be in the form of additional profits to Pristeen; the net consumer surplus will remain unchanged.

Note that Murkee could apply the same logic to acquire Brand A. Thus, after the acquisition, Murkee would drop Brand B from the market. Following the same logic as above, we see that Murkee can pay a premium of up to *20%* to purchase Brand A where,

$$\text{percentage premium} = \frac{\text{increase in profit to Brand B after the acquisition}}{\text{profit of Brand A before the acquisition}}$$

This example provides a simple explanation of why two firms in a given industry may attempt to acquire each other at the same point in time. (For a detailed discussion of mergers and acquisitions, see chapter 22.)

Point to consider. What empirical method or methods can one use to determine if advertising increases or decreases social welfare?

The key issue is to determine how advertising affects awareness and reservation prices. There are two complementary approaches. The first approach is to analyze historical data and to estimate the demands for the relevant products using such variables as prices and advertising expenditures for different competitors. Once the demand structure has been estimated, one can compute the relevant consumer surpluses.[8]

If cost information is available, one can compute the joint profits of the industry. Social welfare can then be obtained simply as the sum of the net consumer surpluses across firms and industry profits.

However, despite its simplicity and intuitive appeal, this approach is not always feasible. For example, insufficient historical data may be available to estimate demand (e.g., the product in question is a high-tech product that becomes obsolete rapidly in the marketplace).

The second approach is to conduct a *choice experiment* in which subgroups of consumers are exposed to different advertising messages and price treatments.

For simplicity, assume that there are two brands in the market, SuperG and Maximus. Then, one can analyze the product choices of three matched samples of consumers from the target segment using different combinations of prices for those who are exposed to advertising by SuperG (Group 1), those who are exposed to advertising by Maximus (Group 2), and those who are exposed to advertising messages by both SuperG and Maximus (Group 3).

The results from the choice experiment can be analyzed to determine how industry-level advertising affects the *joint distribution of reservation prices* for the relevant products.[9] Once we have measured the effect of industry advertising on the joint distribution of reservation prices, we can estimate consumer and social welfare using the same methodology as in the first approach discussed above.

◣ 20.10 How Does Product Bundling Affect Consumer Well-Being and Social Welfare?

Suppose a firm markets two products. If the firm *only* sells both products together, we say that the firm is using a *pure bundling strategy*. If the firm sells three products (each product separately and the bundle), we say that the firm is using a *mixed bundling strategy*. Typically, the firm's profits will increase when the firm uses a product bundling strategy.[10] However, as shown below, consumers may be worse off.

Interestingly, this result can occur *even if the firm chooses a mixed bundling plan that offers the consumer more choices* (i.e., the consumer can purchase each product separately or the bundle). We begin with the case where the firm offers a pure bundling plan (i.e., the firm does not provide the consumer with the opportunity to purchase the products individually).

Pure Bundling Plan

Consider a communications company (e.g., Verizon) that sells two products: Internet access and cable service. Suppose there are three segments of equal size (1 million) whose monthly reservation prices (RPs) for Verizon's Internet and cable services are as shown in table 20.22.

For simplicity, assume that all marginal costs are zero. We first consider the case where Verizon prices Internet and cable services separately.

Separate Pricing.   Suppose Verizon has two managers, each of whom is treated as a separate profit center. One is responsible for Internet services and the other for cable. Since each manager acts independently of the other, each manager will set price to maximize the profit from his or her product.

Thus, each manager will charge $20 per month for his or her service (table 20.23). Hence Verizon will make monthly profits of $40 million from the Internet and cable markets, respectively. Thus, Verizon's monthly product-line profit from the cable and Internet services will be $80 million.

Given this product-line pricing plan, Segments A and B will purchase Verizon's Internet service. Each consumer in Segment A will obtain a monthly surplus of $10 from this purchase (reservation price of consumer in Segment

Table 20.22
Verizon Example: Reservation Prices for Internet Service, Cable, and the Bundle

Segment	Internet	Cable	Bundle
A	$30	$10	$40
B	$20	$20	$40
C	$10	$30	$40

Table 20.23
Verizon Example: The Effect on Social Welfare When Managers Choose Policies Independently

Price	Demand	Revenue	Consumer surplus	Social welfare
Internet				
$30	1M	$30M	$0	$30M
$20*	2M	$40M	$10M	$50M
$10	3M	$30M	$30M	$60M
Cable				
$30	1M	$30M	$0	$30M
$20*	2M	$40M	$10M	$50M
$10	3M	$30M	$30M	$60M

*The pricing plans when managers act independently.

A – price of Internet service = $30 – $20). However, each consumer in Segment B will obtain a surplus of zero because the monthly price the consumer pays equals the consumer's monthly reservation price ($20). Thus, the net monthly consumer surplus generated by Verizon's Internet service will be $10 million, and the net monthly social welfare generated will be $50 million (Verizon's monthly profit for Internet service + monthly consumer surplus across segments for the Internet service = $40M + $10M).

Similarly, Verizon's cable service manager will charge $20 per month for cable service. Each consumer in Segment C will obtain a monthly surplus of $10 from this purchase (reservation price of each consumer in Segment C – price paid for cable service = $30 – $20), and each consumer in Segment B will obtain a surplus of zero because the monthly price the consumer pays equals the consumer's monthly reservation price ($20). Hence, the net monthly consumer surplus generated by Verizon's cable service will be $10 million, and the net monthly social welfare generated will be $50 million (Verizon's monthly profit for cable service + monthly consumer surplus across segments for the cable service = $40M + 10M).

Thus, if Verizon prices its Internet and cable services separately, Verizon will make a monthly product-line profit of $80 million ($40M + $40M), consumers will obtain a net monthly surplus across product lines of $20 million ($10M + $10M), and social welfare will be $100 million per month (Verizon's aggregate profits across product lines + net consumer surplus generated across product lines = $80M + $20M).

Bundling.   Now, suppose Verizon's Internet and cable managers coordinate their pricing strategies. What product-line pricing policy should Verizon use to maximize product-line performance?

Since all consumers have a common reservation price for the bundle ($40 per month), Verizon should use a pure bundling plan. Specifically, it should only offer an Internet-cable bundle for $40 per month. That is, consumers will no longer be able to purchase the Internet or cable services separately.

The result is that all three segments will purchase the bundle, and Verizon will make a monthly profit of $120 million (number of customers × profit per customer) (table 20.24).

Table 20.24
Verizon Example: Effect on Social Welfare If Verizon Uses a Pure Bundling Strategy

	Separate pricing	Pure bundling
Verizon's product-line profits	$80M	$120M
Consumer surplus across product lines	$20M	$0
Social welfare	$100M	$120M

▶ *What is the impact of Verizon's pure bundling plan on consumer well-being and on social welfare?*

Consumers will be worse off, since consumer surplus is reduced from $20 million to zero. However, social welfare increases from $100 million to $120 million.

Fusion for Profit Maxim

When the firm uses a pure bundling plan, consumers are likely to be worse off. However, profits and social welfare increase.

Mixed Bundling Plan

In the Verizon example, suppose the monthly reservation prices are as shown in table 20.25.

Suppose the managers for the Internet and cable services act independently. Then, each manager will charge $20 per month for his or her service, Verizon will make a monthly product-line profit of $80 million, consumers will obtain a surplus of $20 million per month, and social welfare will be $100 million per month (table 20.26).

Table 20.25
Verizon Example: Reservation Prices for Internet Service, Cable, and the Bundle

Segment	Internet	Cable	Bundle
A	$30	$5	$35
B	$20	$20	$40
C	$5	$30	$35

Table 20.26
Verizon Example: The Effect on Social Welfare When Managers Act Independently

Price	Demand	Revenue	Consumer surplus	Social welfare
Internet				
$30	1M	$30M	$0	$30M
$20*	2M	$40M	$10M	$50M
$5	3M	$15M	$40M	$55M
Cable				
$30	1M	$30M	$0	$30M
$20*	2M	$40M	$10M	$50M
$5	3M	$15M	$40M	$55M

*⁺The pricing plans when managers act independently.

► *What will happen if Verizon's Internet and cable managers coordinate their pricing policies to maximize product-line performance?*

Now, the optimal policy for Verizon is to use the following mixed bundling plan: charge $30 per month for the Internet service, $30 per month for cable, and $40 per month for the bundle.

The rationale is as follows:

- Consumers in Segment A value Verizon's Internet service highly but not cable. Hence it is optimal for Verizon to sell these consumers only the Internet service and charge them a high price ($30 per month).
- Consumers in Segment C value Verizon's cable service highly but not the Internet service. Hence it is optimal for Verizon to sell these consumers only the cable service at a high price ($30 per month).
- Consumers in Segment B value both Verizon's Internet and cable services moderately ($20 per month for each service). Hence it is optimal for Verizon to sell these customers the bundle at a price of $40 per month.

► *What is the effect of Verizon's mixed bundling plan on consumer well-being and on social welfare?*

Each consumer now pays his or her reservation price for the product or products he or she purchases (Internet, cable, or the bundle). Hence all consumer surpluses will be zero.

Verizon's monthly profits will be as follows: $30 from each customer in Segment A, $40 from each customer in Segment B, and $30 from each customer in Segment C. Since each segment contains 1 million customers, Verizon's monthly product-line profit will be $100 million ([$30 × 1M] + [$40 × 1M] + [$30 × 1M]). Hence monthly social welfare will be $100 million (Verizon's product-line profit + consumer surplus across product lines = $100M + $0 + $0 + $0). See table 20.27.

Note that Verizon's mixed bundling plan is socially neutral (i.e., social welfare is the same as it was when Verizon priced each service separately).

Table 20.27
Verizon Example: The Effect on Social Welfare When Managers Coordinate Their Policies and Use a Mixed Bundling Strategy

	Separate pricing	Mixed bundling
Verizon's product-line profits	$80M	$100M
Consumer surplus across product lines	$20M	$0
Social welfare	$100M	$100M

Fusion for Profit Maxim

Mixed bundling can be socially neutral. However, consumers are likely to be worse off.

▶ 20.11 Do Consumers and Society Gain When the Firm Introduces New Models of Its Product over Time?

The firm's new product policy and the effect on consumer well-being and social welfare depend crucially on the type of *consumer information structure* (discussed later) *and* on the costs and qualities of the old and new models. In addition, the firm's policy depends on whether there is a secondhand market for used products.

In our analysis we consider a two-period model. Suppose a firm can produce two qualities (low and high) of a durable product; in particular, each product is produced under constant cost conditions. For simplicity, assume that the firm uses the following product introduction strategy. Sell the low-quality product in the first period. In the second period, discontinue the low-quality product and replace it with the high-quality product.[11]

In our analysis, we first consider the case where there are no secondhand markets (first scenario). Later, we shall extend the analysis to the more general case where secondhand markets exist (second scenario). Note that the first scenario is appropriate for information goods such as software (e.g., consumers do not wish to buy an old version of Windows); the second scenario is appropriate for physical products such as automobiles for which active secondhand markets exist.

No Secondhand Markets

A critical factor is whether all or only a fraction of the buyers of the low-quality product (*first-generation buyers*) upgrade to the high-quality product in the second period. We refer to these scenarios, respectively, as *full upgrade* and *partial upgrade*. Which upgrade scenario occurs depends on a number of market conditions:

1. The type of consumer information structure (i.e., whether or not the firm can identify first-generation buyers in the second period).
2. The *quality-adjusted cost ratios* of the old and new products. If the quality-adjusted cost ratio of the new model is much lower (higher) than the corresponding ratio for the old model, we say that the *innovation* is major (minor). If the quality-adjusted cost ratio of the high-quality product is somewhat higher than the corresponding ratio for the low quality product, we say that the innovation is moderate;

3. The rate at which product quality deteriorates over time;
4. The market growth rate; and
5. The discount rate.

To determine the effect of the firm's new product introduction policy on social welfare, we define

- *Consumer welfare* as the net present value of the appropriate consumers' surpluses,
- *Producer welfare* as the net present value of the firm's profits, and
- Social welfare as the sum of consumer welfare and producer welfare.

As we discuss below, the firm should use a *price discrimination strategy* when it sells the high-quality product in the second period.

Example: Consider a consumer whose reservation prices for new units of the low- and high-quality products, respectively, are $100 and $180. Suppose each new unit of the durable product has an economic life of two periods; furthermore, the value to the consumer of each new unit depreciates at a constant rate over time.[12]

Suppose the consumer purchases a new unit of the low-quality product at the beginning of the first period. Since the unit depreciates by 50% every year, its *economic value* to the consumer at the beginning of the second period will be $50. Consequently, this consumer's reservation price for the high-quality product at the beginning of the second period will be the incremental value of this purchase, $130 (reservation price of a new unit of the high-quality product – value to the consumer of a used unit of the low-quality product at the beginning of the second period = $180 – $50).

In contrast, if this consumer is a first-time buyer in the second period, his or her reservation price for a new unit of the high-quality product will be much higher ($180). *Note that upgraders in the second period have a lower willingness to pay ($130 per unit) for the high-quality product than similar first-time buyers in that period ($180 per unit).* Hence the firm has an incentive to use a price discrimination strategy in the second period.

In our example, the firm may gain by charging a "normal" price of $180 for a new unit of the high-quality product in the second period and offering buyers from the first period an "upgrade discount" of $50 for purchasing a new unit of the high-quality product in the second period.

▶ *Suppose the firm uses a price discrimination strategy when it follows a sequential new product introduction policy and introduces the high-quality product in the second period. How will this strategy affect consumer well-being and social welfare?*

The answer depends critically on whether the innovation is minor, moderate, or major. In addition, it depends on whether or not the firm can identify first-period buyers in the second period (i.e., on the information structure in the market).

The intuition is as follows. Suppose the firm can identify first-period buyers in the second period. Then, the firm needs to choose three prices (the price of the low-quality product in the first period, the price of the high-quality product in the second period, and the upgrade discount to first-period buyers in the second period) so that it maximizes the *net present value* of its profits.

Suppose the innovation is major. That is, the improvement in product quality is large compared with the incremental increase in the cost of producing the higher quality product.

▲ *What pricing plan should the firm use if it can use a price discrimination strategy (i.e., offer first-period buyers an upgrade discount for purchasing the high-quality product in the second period)?*

Since the improvement in product quality is large (the innovation is major), other factors being the same, buyers in the first period will have a higher willingness to pay for the high-quality product in the second period. To take advantage of this, the firm should increase the pool of potential upgraders in the second period. Hence the firm should charge a lower price for the low-quality product in the first period. Since the firm will sell more units of the low-quality product in the first period at a lower price, buyers in the first period will gain.

▲ *What will happen in the second period?*

Since the pool of potential buyers (upgraders + new buyers) will be larger in the second period, the firm should charge a lower regular price in the second period. Hence new buyers will gain. Since upgraders from the first period also pay a lower price than they would have paid if the firm had used a uniform pricing strategy, upgraders will also gain.

In sum, the net present value of the total consumer surplus (consumer surplus to first-period buyers + consumer surplus to upgraders in the second period + consumer surplus to new buyers in the second period) will increase. Furthermore, the firm will increase its net present value (producer welfare) by using a price discrimination strategy. Consequently, social welfare (producer welfare + net present value of consumer surplus) will increase.

Interestingly, if the innovation is minor, social welfare will *decrease* if the firm offers upgrade discounts. However, if the innovation is moderate, the effect of price discrimination on social welfare is less well defined.[13]

Fusion for Profit Maxim

The effect of the firm's sequential new product introduction policy on consumer well-being and social welfare depends on the magnitude of the innovation (minor, moderate, or major) and on the consumer information structure. If there are no secondhand markets and the innovation is major, price discrimination can make all constituencies (the firm, consumers, and society) better off.

Secondhand Markets

Suppose there is an active secondhand market for the firm's low-quality product in the second period. In this case, the effects of the firm's new product policy on the firm's prices, profits, net consumer surplus, and social welfare are more complicated.

Consider the firm's pricing strategy in the second period when secondhand markets exist for used units of the low-quality product. On the one hand, the firm will gain because the secondhand market allows first-period buyers to obtain a *salvage value* when they resell their units of the old model. This "discount" effect makes it more attractive for buyers of the low-quality product in the first period to upgrade to the high-quality product in the second. On the other hand, the firm will lose because the supply of used units of the low-quality product on the secondhand market will cannibalize sales of the high-quality product.

Thus, the *effects of secondhand markets* on the firm's prices, profits, consumer surpluses, and social welfare are conditional and *depend critically* on the precise set of market conditions that prevail. These conditions include the cost structures of the high- and low-quality products; whether the innovation is minor, moderate or major; and the market growth rate.[14]

Fusion for Profit Maxim

If there are secondhand markets, we need precise quantitative information on cost and demand in order to determine how the firm's new product introduction policy affects profits, consumers, and social welfare.

Chapter 20 Key Points

- The social welfare from a marketing policy = profits + net consumer surplus.
- If the firm can use a perfect price discrimination strategy, profit maximization will lead to optimal social welfare. However, all the gain will accrue to the firm.
- If the firm gives out free samples of its products, consumers and society do not necessarily gain in the long run.
- If the firm uses strategic pricing based on the learning curve, all constituencies (shareholders, consumers, and society) will gain.
- Under certain conditions, consumers may be worse off when the firm uses a quantity discount pricing plan.
- In general, the impact of advertising on consumer and social welfare depends on how advertising changes the mix of aware customers in

different segments (the awareness effect). In addition, the impact of advertising depends on how advertising changes consumers' reservation prices (the reservation price effect). These effects vary over the product life cycle and across products.

• In a competitive market the effect of advertising on social welfare depends on how competitors' price and message strategies affect the awareness levels and reservation prices for the products that compete in the market. A decrease in market prices does not imply that society is better off.

• If the firm introduces a mixed bundling plan, consumers may not gain even though they have more choices than before.

• If the firm introduces new products sequentially, the effects on consumers and social welfare depend on the magnitude of the degree of innovation (minor, moderate, or major) and on whether secondhand markets for used products exist.

21

Internet Marketing

The Internet has had a major effect on the economy and on industry structure, in particular. Consumers can obtain information more cheaply and efficiently than before; in addition, this information is available on a real-time basis.

Advertisers and *search engines* can use new and highly sophisticated methods to measure Internet advertising productivity. In addition, because of the continuing pace of technological innovations in the information sector, firms face new challenges in coordinating their marketing policies across the Internet, conventional media (e.g., TV and magazines), and the sales force. This chapter analyzes some of the implications for advertisers, search engines, consumers, and society.

The information covered in this chapter will be useful when you are faced with the following types of decisions:

- How will the Internet affect my firm's pricing strategy?
- How can my firm coordinate its market segmentation policy with its Internet advertising strategy?
- How will the Internet affect the competitive landscape for my firm in the *business-to-business* (B to B) *market?*
- How can my firm use the Internet to reduce the degree of *commoditization* in the industry in which it operates?
- How will the Internet affect the competitive landscape for my firm in the *business-to-consumer* (B to C) *market?*

- What advertising message strategy should my firm use for Internet advertising?
- How should my firm measure the productivity of its Internet advertising?
- Is Internet advertising a substitute for or a complement to traditional advertising media?
- How should my firm develop a multimedia plan that includes Internet advertising?
- How should search engines price Internet advertising? Does it make sense for them to use *auctions*?
- How much should my firm bid to advertise on a particular search engine?
- How should my firm coordinate its Internet and sales force strategies?
- How will Internet advertising affect consumer well-being and *social welfare*?
- How will the Internet affect the advertising industry in the future?

The following terms will be introduced in this chapter (see glossary for definitions):

auctions	economies of scope	one-stop shopping
behavioral targeting	electronic exchange	price dispersion
B to B marketing	equilibrium	price sensitivity
B to C marketing	fixed costs	profit-sharing plan
bricks-and-mortar	gross margins	reach
stores	gross profits	reservation price
bundling	gross rating points	risk-averse
clickthrough fraud	(GRPs)	risk-neutral
clickthroughs	law of one price	search engine
commoditization	linear wage-commission	segmented equilibrium
complements	compensation plan	social welfare
conquest advertising	marginal cost	substitutes
consumer surplus	market skimming	transaction costs
cost structure	media interaction effects	value-added bundle
dynamic search	me-too product	Vickrey auction
behavior	mixed bundling	volatility
economies of scale	strategy	winner's curse

▶ *21.1 How Does the Internet Affect Prices?*

We begin with a basic question: Will the Internet lead to lower prices?

Suppose the Internet allows the firm to expand its market and to benefit from *economies of scale* in production. These demand-expansion and cost-reduction effects suggest that the firm should charge *lower* prices on the Internet.

But now suppose the Internet allows the firm to reduce the *price sensitivity* of demand for its products by controlling the order in which information is presented to the consumer. For example, if the firm sells a highly differentiated product, it can present product attribute information before presenting information regarding prices. This effect suggests that the firm should charge *higher* prices on the Internet.

If all these effects are simultaneously present, the effect of the Internet on prices is not obvious. One implication is that it will become even more important than before to coordinate policies across different functional areas in the firm (e.g., production, procurement, and marketing).

Fusion for Profit Maxim

The effect of the Internet on prices will depend on the firm's *cost structure*, advertising message strategy, and segmentation policy. Consequently, different functional areas including marketing and finance should be involved in developing a coordinated Internet strategy that maximizes performance.

▶ *It is inexpensive to establish Web sites. Does it follow that the Internet will make the marketplace more competitive?*

The degree of competitiveness in the market depends on the type of product in question. The critical factors for the single-product firm are economies of scale, particularly in information dissemination. Correspondingly, the key theoretical factors for the multiproduct firm are scale economies and *economies of scope*, particularly those that result from selling multiple products to a common set of consumers.

Economies of Scale

Consider a single-product firm in any given industry. Initially, suppose the Internet is not available. Assume that, for this industry structure, there are significant economies of scale in the dissemination of information via traditional advertising media such as television and print. Furthermore, suppose that consumers for the product in question have different tastes and preferences for different product variants (qualities).

Then, since the only advertising media that are available are the traditional formats such as television and print, firms in the industry are likely to neglect segments that are not sufficiently large.

For instance, consider a segment for which consumers' *reservation prices* do not increase much when product quality is improved. If this segment is sufficiently small and if information costs are a significant fraction of total costs, firms are likely to ignore this segment—*even if there are strong economies of scale in production.*

► *How will the Internet affect such an industry?*

Suppose the *fixed costs* of establishing a Web site are low, and the *marginal costs* of maintaining a Web site are also small. Then the Internet will substantially reduce or even eliminate the advantages to large firms of economies of scale in information.

Consequently, it may now be feasible for firms, small or large, to make profits by selling to niche segments that have traditionally been neglected. Hence the Internet can make the product market more competitive than before.

Economies of Scope

Consider a large multiproduct Internet firm (e.g., Amazon). To focus on essentials, suppose Amazon does *not* have a superior cost structure to competing Internet firms that specialize in particular products. However, suppose there are economies of scope in demand. Then, in general consumers' reservation prices for the bundle of products sold by Amazon (a multiproduct firm) will be more similar than the reservation prices for the individual products in the bundle. (For a detailed discussion of *bundling*, see chapter 9.)

This high degree of similarity in consumers' reservation prices for bundles will provide a *one-stop shopping* advantage to Amazon. Specifically, by selling individual products separately and simultaneously selling assortments of products, Amazon will be able to use a *mixed bundling strategy* to squeeze out firms that specialize in particular products—*even though it may not have any cost advantage over those competitors.*

Consequently, small and niche firms can now be at a disadvantage and may even be forced to leave the industry. Thus, by providing multiproduct firms with economies of scope, the Internet can make the market less competitive than before.

Fusion for Profit Maxim

The effect of the Internet is likely to be industry-specific. In particular, the answer will depend on the combined effects of economies of scale, economies of scope, and on whether buyers purchase value-added services from vendors. Large Internet retailers may obtain a one-stop shopping advantage by using a mixed bundling strategy.

► *The Internet has led to a substantial reduction in search costs for consumers in many industries. Does this imply that prices in these industries will converge?*

To answer this question one needs to analyze the joint effect of several factors, including sales taxes and transportation costs. In contrast to sales at *bricks-and-mortar stores*, Internet sales are often not subject to sales taxes. However, Internet sales of physical products will require the firm to incur transportation costs in getting the product to the consumer. Consequently, bricks-and-mortar stores and Internet stores will need to set different prices for the same merchandise.

Example: Suppose a bricks-and-mortar branch of Barnes & Noble charges $100 for a particular book in New Jersey. Then, the net price to that consumer is $107, including sales tax. (The current sales tax rate in New Jersey is 7%.)

▶ How much should Barnes & Noble charge for this book on its Web site?

Suppose Barnes & Noble's transport cost of shipping this book to the buyer in New Jersey is $5. Furthermore, suppose Barnes & Noble's return policies for the book are identical, regardless of whether the consumer buys the book on the Internet or at a bricks-and-mortar store.

Then, *equilibrium* requires that the net prices of the book (including sales tax where applicable) to the consumer should be the same for both channels. Hence Barnes & Noble should price the book higher ($102) on the Internet (Internet price + transport cost = bricks-and-mortar price + sales tax ≡ $102 + $5 = $100 + 7%).

Fusion for Profit Maxim

Internet retailers and bricks-and-mortar retailers will need to charge different prices for the same product because of transport costs and sales taxes.

▶ 21.2 Will the Internet Lead to Commoditization?

Intuitively, one might expect that the Internet would lead to greater commoditization in all industries. However, as discussed below, the answer is not clear-cut. In our discussion, we will distinguish the cases where firms sell to consumers via the Internet (the *B to C market*) and where firms sell to other firms (the *B to B market*). But first we must address a basic question.

▶ How can one measure commoditization?

Suppose consumers believe that the products made by competing firms in an industry are of identical qualities. Furthermore, all consumers are fully informed about product availability (i.e., there are no search costs).

Given this scenario, all firms in the industry will be forced to charge the same price. Equivalently, there will be no *price dispersion* across products in the industry. We say that the *law of one price* holds; alternatively, the industry is commoditized.

In general, firms in an industry sell products that consumers may perceive to be similar but not of identical quality. In many cases, consumers are likely to be imperfectly informed about prices and product qualities. In addition, consumers face search costs in obtaining information about products in the industry, including the channels through which they can purchase these products. Hence prices will vary to some extent across firms and channels. We say that there is price dispersion in the market. It is incorrect, however, to define commoditization in terms of price dispersion alone.

Example: Suppose the average price of a Mercedes Benz 500 SL sports car is $120,000, and the price dispersion is $6,000;[1] in addition, the average price of a Toyota Corolla is $15,000, and the corresponding price dispersion is $1,000. Then, the price dispersion for the Mercedes Benz ($6,000) is six times larger than that of the Toyota Corolla ($1,000).

Hence, by using price dispersion alone to measure commoditization, one would conclude that the market for the Toyota Corolla is more commoditized than that for the Mercedes. However, this conclusion is inappropriate, since the average price of the Mercedes Benz ($120,000) is *eight* times larger than the corresponding average price of the Toyota Corolla ($15,000).

To address this issue, it is necessary to define the degree of commoditization by using *both* price dispersion *and* the average price. In our discussion, we will use the following definition:

$$\text{commoditization index} = \frac{\text{average price}}{\text{price dispersion}}$$

Note that, in the special case where an industry is fully commoditized, the law of one price holds (i.e., price dispersion is zero). Hence the commoditization index will be infinitely large.

Using this definition, we obtain the following commoditization indices in our example: 20 (Mercedes) and 15 (Toyota Corolla). Hence the market for the Toyota is *less* commoditized than that for the Mercedes. Note that, to understand the effect of a shift in industry structure (e.g., the advent of the Internet) on the degree of commoditization in a market, it is necessary to determine how the structural shift affects *both* average price and price dispersion.

Fusion for Profit Maxim

The degree of commoditization in an industry depends on both the average price of products in that industry and the degree of price dispersion.

▲   *Will the Internet lead to the commoditization of the B to C (business-to-consumer) market?*

Example: Suppose an expensive brand of furniture is sold by two retailers: one is an Internet retailer, and the other a bricks-and-mortar retailer.

▲   *Will both furniture retailers charge the same prices for identical models?*

The products sold by both retailers are not equivalent. Suppose the bricks-and-mortar retailer sells a bundle (product plus after-sales service), whereas the Internet retailer sells the product only. Note that the product offerings of both retailers are not equivalent, even though the physical products are. Consequently, other factors being the same, the service-conscious or *risk-averse* segment will purchase the bundle (furniture plus after-sales service) from the bricks-and-mortar retailer. In contrast, the price-conscious or less risk-averse segment will purchase the furniture from the Internet retailer.

Since the bricks-and-mortar retailer sells a bundle (product plus after-sales service), whereas the Internet retailer sells only the product, the bricks-and-mortar retailer should charge a higher price than the Internet retailer.[2] We say that there is a *segmented equilibrium.*

This implication is not surprising. After all, even before the advent of the Internet, full-service department stores charged higher prices than no-frills discount stores did for the same merchandise.

Fusion for Profit Maxim

The Internet may not lead to greater commoditization in the B to C market, since products sold through the Internet are not equivalent to the same products sold via bricks-and-mortar retailers.

▲   *Will the Internet lead to the commoditization of the B to B (business-to-business) market?*

The Internet can lead to either increased or decreased commoditization, depending on the structure of the B to B market.

Increased Commoditization

Consider an industry where neither manufacturers nor distributors have economies of scale or economies of scope. Suppose buyers purchase similar quantities of the product through distributors. However, they have different search costs for obtaining information. Then, prior to the availability of the Internet, there will be some price dispersion across distributors *even for the same brand.* Since the law of one price does not hold, the market is not commoditized.

▶ How will the Internet affect the degree of commoditization in the industry?

The Internet will allow manufacturers to reduce the cost of providing information to buyers. For example, it may be more efficient to provide product or brand-related information over the Internet rather than through a sales force. Buyers will also incur lower search costs than before in obtaining information; more important, buyers will now have similar (identical) search costs.

By assumption, there are no economies of scale or economies of scope in the market. Since manufacturers incur lower information costs in reaching consumers, average prices in the industry will fall. In addition, since buyers have lower search costs, the price dispersion in the market across brands and channels will also be reduced. But margins are low even before the Internet, since neither manufacturers nor distributors have economies of scale. Hence, for this scenario, it is likely that the effect of the reduction in price dispersion will be stronger than the effect of the reduction in average price.

Consequently, the commoditization index (new average price/new price dispersion) is likely to increase. In other words, the Internet will lead to increased commoditization of the industry.

Decreased Commoditization

The previous example showed how the Internet can lead to increased commoditization in an industry where neither manufacturers nor distributors have economies of scale or scope. Now, consider an industry such as semiconductors in which there are strong economies of scale and economies of scope in manufacturing and distribution, buyers purchase dissimilar quantities, and demand is highly uncertain.

▶ What is the structure of the semiconductor industry prior to the Internet?

As discussed below, the market will not be commoditized prior to the Internet. That is, the price for any given brand of semiconductor will vary across channels and buyer segments. Assume that the market for any semiconductor manufacturer consists of three buyer segments: heavy users, medium users, and light users. Furthermore, small and large manufacturers use different product and pricing strategies and channels of distribution. Since economies of scale and economies of scope are significant, the following scenario is likely.

Large manufacturers will sell directly to heavy users using specialized sales forces. However, they will use a limited number of large franchised distributors to sell to medium users and to efficiently monitor demand fluctuations in the market. Light users will be served by a potentially large group of small unfranchised distributors.

To prevent business from being siphoned away from their large franchised distributors to unfranchised distributors, large manufacturers will provide a product warranty only on those units of their brand that are sold by franchised distributors. Thus, the units sold by franchised and unfranchised distributors are not comparable.

In many cases, the franchised distributors for large semiconductor manufacturers will focus on selling *value-added bundles* to medium users (e.g., packages of semiconductors and engineering assistance to help users design and manufacture products using semiconductors). This segment is likely to be less price-sensitive than the segment of heavy users.

Unfranchised distributors, in contrast, will sell the large manufacturer's semiconductors on a stand-alone basis to light users. This segment is generally highly price-sensitive; in particular, buyers in this segment are likely to be more willing than those in the other segments to incur search costs to find the lowest price for any given brand (product).

Since large manufacturers dominate the medium- and heavy-user segments, small manufacturers will focus on the light-user segment and use a more specialized channel strategy than large manufacturers. Specifically they will use small distributors to sell their brands to the light-user segment.

Given this industry structure in the absence of the Internet, the price dispersion in the market across channels and brands will be significant. Note that, because large manufacturers do not provide warranties on those units of their products that are sold by unfranchised distributors, the price dispersion *across* distribution channels and brands is likely to be high.

► How will the Internet affect prices in the semiconductor industry?

Large manufacturers will continue to directly target the heavy-user segment using their sales forces. Consequently, the prices paid by heavy users will not change significantly.

Large manufacturers will also continue to target medium users through large distributors. These distributors are not likely to change their strategy of focusing on selling value-added bundles to medium users. However, they may now find it more efficient to use the Internet rather than their sales forces to provide selected product- or brand-related information to current or potential buyers.

Thus, since the purchase decisions of medium users are primarily driven by value, the prices paid by medium users for brands made by large manufacturers will also remain largely intact.

The primary effect of the Internet will be on the prices paid by the light-user segment. The number of small distributors who serve the light-user segment is likely to increase, since the cost of reaching and informing

Table 21.1
Effect of the Internet on Commoditization in the
Semiconductor Industry Example

Segment	Average price	Price dispersion
Heavy users	Unchanged	Unchanged
Medium users	Unchanged	Unchanged
Light users	Reduced	Reduced

customers is now lower than before. In addition, all buyers, including those who purchase from small distributors, now have more similar information than before.

The net result is that the average price paid for a given brand by light users is likely to fall; in addition, the price dispersion for that brand across light users will be reduced. Table 21.1 summarizes these results.

▶ *What is the likely net effect of these changes on the degree of commoditization in the semiconductor industry?*

Suppose light users do not account for a significant proportion of total sales across segments (heavy, medium, and light users). Then, the commoditization index (which is measured across all segments) will be approximately the same as it was before firms began using the Internet. If light users account for a significant proportion of industry sales, the key issue is how the Internet will affect average prices and price dispersions in this segment. Consequently, different scenarios are possible.

Example: Suppose the average price paid for a manufacturer's brand by light users falls sharply when that manufacturer uses the Internet as a channel. However, the corresponding reduction in price dispersion is small.[3]

Given this scenario, the commoditization index (average price/price dispersion) will decrease. Thus, the industry will become less commoditized than before.

Other scenarios can be constructed where the industry becomes more commoditized than before.

Fusion for Profit Maxim

The Internet can lead to increased or decreased commoditization in the B to B market depending on how the Internet affects average prices and price dispersion. These effects in turn will depend on whether the industry has economies of scale and economies of scope and on how purchase quantities and search costs vary across buyers.

▶ *21.3 The Internet and Advertising Message Strategy*

As discussed below, Internet advertising has significant implications for advertising message strategy.

▶ *How will the Internet affect the firm's advertising message strategy?*

The Internet provides an important message strategy advantage over conventional advertising media. The firm can present information sequentially; furthermore, this sequence can be customized to particular individuals or market segments based on their decision processes and prior information-search behavior.

Consider two firms, one of which produces a branded product, Alpha, and the other a generic version, Genalpha, of the same product. Then, each firm should use a different Internet advertising message strategy. Thus:

1. The branded product, Alpha, should focus on presenting product-related information so that consumers' reservation prices are increased and/or consumers' price sensitivities are kept low.
2. In contrast, the generic, Genalpha, should focus on providing price-related information so that price sensitivities are increased.

Regardless of whether the product is branded, the firm is likely to achieve additional benefits by customizing the information to particular individuals or segments based on their prior information-search behavior.

Fusion for Profit Maxim

The Internet allows firms to improve their performance by customizing their advertising messages to particular customers and choosing the sequence in which information is made available to those customers. In general, branded products should present attribute-based information first, whereas generics should present price information first.

▶ *21.4 Measuring the Productivity of Internet Advertising*

The Internet allows firms to use new and sophisticated metrics to measure advertising productivity. We discuss some of the implications below.

▶ *How should the firm measure the productivity of its Internet advertising? Assume that the firm advertises only on the Internet and measures advertising productivity using advertising exposures as a metric.*

As discussed in chapter 14, standard measures of advertising exposure such as *reach* and *gross rating points* (GRPs) in conventional media such as magazines, newspapers, and TV are fraught with error. Furthermore, these metrics are not generally available at the level of the individual consumer. In contrast, the Internet allows firms to measure advertising exposure using cleaner metrics such as the number of *clickthroughs* on a particular ad or the number of page views. In addition, this information is available at a disaggregate level.

Hence, in principle, the firm can determine how effective these metrics (e.g., clickthroughs) are in generating sales at different levels (individual, segment, or market).

One potential problem with using the number of clickthroughs to measure advertising exposure on the Internet is *clickthrough fraud*. For example, a firm's competitors can inflate the number of clickthroughs for the firm's ads by paying a third party to keep clicking on the firm's ads. This way, the firm that advertises on the Internet is likely to conclude that its Internet advertising is not productive. That is, even though the firm's ads lead to a large number of clickthroughs, the subsequent effect on sales at the market level is poor. (Later in this chapter, we will discuss how clickthrough fraud is likely to affect the demand and supply of Internet advertising.)

Although clickthrough fraud can pose problems, the clickthrough metric provides several important advantages. Unlike commonly used measures of advertising exposure for conventional media (e.g., recall), clickthrough data are objective. That is, they are not subject to self-reporting error. Furthermore, clickthrough data can be refined to obtain a more precise measure of how effective Internet advertising exposures are. For example, for any individual, one can weight each clickthrough by the time that the individual spent on a particular Web page.

Fusion for Profit Maxim

In general, measures of advertising exposure for the Internet will be more accurate than those for conventional media.

▶ *Suppose the firm uses a mixed media plan including Internet advertising. Will the firm obtain more accurate estimates of how its media plan affects sales? Assume that there is no clickthrough fraud.*

For simplicity, consider the case of a firm that uses two media: Internet advertising on Yahoo, and TV advertising on *60 Minutes*. The approach can be generalized to the case where the firm uses a multimedia plan, including Internet advertising.

Let's say that the firm varies its media spending over time using these two media. Specifically, the firm uses the number of clickthroughs on the Yahoo Web site to measure advertising exposures in that medium. In addition, it uses reach to measure advertising exposure on the *60 Minutes* TV show.

By assumption, there is no clickthrough fraud. Hence the measures of advertising exposure on Yahoo will not contain any measurement error. In contrast, TV reach is measured using a sample of individuals or households. Hence the measures of reach on *60 Minutes* are only *estimates* of advertising exposure. In the best-case scenario, these TV reach measures will be correct on average (i.e., unbiased). Suppose this is the case.

► **Will the firm be able to accurately measure the effect of its media plan on sales?**

Interestingly, the answer is no—*even though the advertising exposure data for both media are correct on average.* The intuition is that, even though the TV reach measures are unbiased, they are still imprecise. Consequently, in general, the effects of *both* Internet advertising and TV advertising on the firm's sales will be biased.[4]

Fusion for Profit Maxim

The Internet does not provide a panacea for measuring advertising productivity when the firm uses a mixed advertising plan that includes conventional media and Internet advertising.

► **Is Internet advertising a substitute or a complement for traditional advertising media?**

Internet advertising and traditional advertising media can be either *substitutes* or *complements.*

Substitutes

Suppose the Beta company plans to introduce a new *"me-too"* soap, Lavex, in the market. Let's say that Beta has already determined its advertising budget for Lavex. In addition, since Lavex is a low-involvement me-too product, Beta's advertising goal is to maximize awareness of Lavex among consumers in the target segment.

Since both the Internet and traditional advertising media can create awareness, Beta can use either medium. Hence Internet advertising and traditional media are substitutes.

Complements

Consider a large computer manufacturer such as Dell that uses a multimedia strategy to launch a new laptop model that is differentiated from extant products in the market.

For simplicity, suppose Dell uses a media plan consisting of TV and Internet advertising. Since a laptop is a high-involvement product and Dell's new laptop is differentiated from other currently available laptops in the market, Dell has two objectives: to create brand awareness and to provide product-specific information.

Thus, Dell can use national TV advertising to create brand awareness among consumers in the target segment. Suppose the Dell TV advertisement, in turn, is designed to encourage viewers to obtain additional product-specific information on the new laptop by visiting a special Dell Web site that is dedicated to the new laptop.

Given Dell's advertising strategy, traditional advertising media (TV in our example) will make Internet advertising more productive. We say that traditional media and Internet advertising are complements. Note that Dell's TV advertising makes Dell's Internet advertising more productive, but not vice versa. Hence the *media complementarity effects are asymmetric.*

Fusion for Profit Maxim

Traditional media and Internet advertising can be substitutes or complements. If they are complements, these effects need not be symmetric.

▶ *Suppose a firm uses a multimedia advertising plan that combines traditional media and Internet advertising. Is it necessary to develop new empirical methods to measure the productivity of this mixed advertising plan?*

As discussed, traditional media and Internet advertising media can be substitutes or complements; in addition, the complementarity effects may be asymmetric. These effects can be captured empirically.[5]

▶ ### 21.5 How Much Should the Firm Be Willing to Spend on Internet Advertising?

Our previous discussion focused on metrics for measuring the productivity of Internet advertising. We now ask a different but related question.

▶ *How much should a firm be willing to spend to advertise on an Internet search engine such as Google?*

The answer to this question depends on several factors, including whether the firm is a multiproduct firm or not, the firm's risk attitude, whether the firm is using a multimedia advertising policy, and the length of the firm's planning horizon.

Single-Product Firm

One way of estimating the *gross profits* that the Internet ad on Google will generate is to proceed as follows. First, estimate the number of clickthroughs that the ad will generate. Next, estimate the proportion of clickthroughs that will lead to a purchase. Finally, use these results to determine the increase in *gross margins* for the product.

To illustrate, consider a hypothetical privately held computer firm, Megatech, that sells servers online. For simplicity, assume that Megatech does not use any other channels. (This assumption will be relaxed later.)

▶ *How should Megatech proceed if it is* risk-neutral?

Since Megatech is *risk-neutral*, it should choose marketing policies that maximize its expected profits.

Suppose Megatech advertises a new model of server on the Internet and has the following expectations. By advertising on Google:

- On average, Megatech will obtain 50,000 clickthroughs, and
- On average, 0.1% of these clickthroughs will result in a purchase.

Thus, the expected number of additional servers that Megatech will sell by advertising on Google is 50 (average number of clickthroughs × average conversion rate of clickthroughs = 50,000 × 0.1%).

▶ *Suppose the gross profit margin on the new server is $400 per unit. What is the maximum amount that Megatech should be willing to spend to advertise the new server on Google?*

Since Megatech is risk-neutral, it should choose its marketing policies to maximize the expected gross profits generated. Consequently, Megatech should be willing to pay up to $20,000 (gross profit per server × expected number of additional servers sold = $400 × 50) for the advertising slot on Google.

▶ *How should Megatech proceed if it is* risk-averse?

If Megatech is risk-averse, it should choose its marketing policies based on how these policies affect both expected profits *and* fluctuations in profits.

In our example, the number of clickthroughs that Megatech can obtain by advertising on Google is uncertain. Specifically, the number of clickthroughs can be above or below the average value of 50,000. Similarly, the actual proportion of clickthroughs that result in purchase is also uncertain. Specifically, this proportion can be above or below the average conversion rate of 0.1%. Hence the realized gross profit from advertising on Google will fluctuate around the average gross profit generated ($20,000).

Since the gross profit generated by advertising on Google is uncertain and Megatech is risk-averse, the maximum amount that Megatech should be willing to pay to advertise on Google will be less than the average gross profit ($20,000).

Fusion for Profit Maxim

The advertiser's willingness to pay for Internet advertising depends on the advertiser's attitude toward risk.

▶ *How should the advertiser determine the value of advertising in a given slot on a particular search engine?*

The answer depends on the firm's media plan.

Single-Medium Case.   Suppose the advertiser has previously advertised on a particular search engine. Then, it can track the *dynamic search behavior* of each individual who has been exposed to that advertisement. For example, the advertiser can track the number of visits to its Web site by each of these individuals and the durations and patterns of each visit. The advertiser can now use standard methods to determine the incremental sales and profits generated by the Internet ad. (See chapter 14 for a discussion.)

Multiple-Media Case.   Suppose the advertiser simultaneously uses several online media (e.g., Yahoo and Google). Then, it is likely that some customers will use both search engines. Because of this overlap, the advertiser cannot separately measure the productivities of each search engine as in the single-medium case. In such cases, the firm can use an interaction model to measure the productivities of each search engine. Note that the audience duplication effects can be positive or negative.[6]

Fusion for Profit Maxim

The firm's willingness to pay for Internet advertising will depend on whether the firm uses a multimedia plan that combines the Internet and conventional media.

Point to consider.   Suppose two firms of different sizes have the same expectations regarding the productivity of Internet advertising. Will both firms have the same willingness to pay for advertising on the Internet?

The answer depends on the ownership structures and risk attitudes of the firms. For example:

1. Suppose both firms are privately held. Then, the smaller firm is likely to be more risk-averse than the larger one. Hence, other factors

remaining equal, the smaller firm will have a lower willingness to pay for Internet advertising.

2. If both firms are 100% owned by stockholders, the risk to shareholders will be unaffected by the sizes of the firms. Hence both firms should have the same willingness to pay for the Internet ad.

Fusion for Profit Maxim

The privately held firm's willingness to pay for Internet advertising depends on the size of the firm (a proxy for the risk attitude of the owner). The publicly held firm's willingness to pay for Internet advertising does not depend on the size of the firm.

Multiproduct Firm

Suppose the firm's products are complementary. Then, the firm should be willing to pay more to advertise on the Internet, regardless of the firm's risk attitude. To focus on essentials, we consider the risk-neutral firm.

In the Megatech example, suppose Megatech is risk-neutral and expects that, of those who buy the new server, on average 10% will buy a service contract on the server for one year. Suppose the gross profit margin on this service contract is $1,000. For simplicity, assume that Megatech's discount rate is zero. Then, the Google ad will, on average, increase Megatech's gross profit by an additional $5,000 (average number of service contracts sold × gross profits per service contract = [50 × 10%] × $1,000). Hence, if Megatech is risk-neutral, it should be willing to pay up to $25,000 (expected profit from servers sold + expected profit from additional service contracts generated = $20,000 + $5,000) to advertise on Google.

Multimedia Advertising

We continue with the Megatech example. Suppose Megatech advertises its new server using two Internet search engines, Google and Yahoo. (For simplicity, assume that there are no multiproduct effects.) Then, there are three groups of potential buyers of the new server: those who see the ad on Google only (Group A), those who see the ad on Yahoo only (Group B), and those who see the ads on both Google and Yahoo (Group C).

If the audience overlap for Google and Yahoo is small (Group C is approximately of size zero), Megatech can proceed as described above and separately evaluate the productivities of the Google and Yahoo ads. If the audience overlap is significant, Megatech will need to jointly evaluate the productivities of advertising on Google and Yahoo.[7]

Fusion for Profit Maxim

The advertiser's willingness to pay for Internet advertising depends on the firm's risk attitude, whether or not the firm is a multiproduct firm, whether the firm is using a multimedia advertising policy, and the length of the firm's planning horizon.

▶ 21.6 How Should Search Engines Price Internet Advertising?

As discussed above, the Internet allows firms to use different metrics to measure advertising productivity. This raises an interesting question.

▶ Should Internet search engines, such as Google, price Internet advertising differently from traditional media?

Technology has led to two major structural changes in the advertising industry:

1. The Internet allows the firm to measure the intermediate productivity of advertising much more accurately than the corresponding measures for conventional media. (For instance, clickthroughs are much more accurate metrics than recall, reach, and awareness.)
2. In contrast to conventional media, the Internet allows advertisers and search engines to continuously renegotiate advertising contracts in real time and to do so with low *transaction costs*.

Consequently, as discussed below, Internet search engines should price advertising differently from traditional media.

Effect of Measurement Error

As we have seen earlier (Chapter 14), advertising works in two steps: it affects an intermediate measure such as reach (Step 1). This intermediate measure affects sales (Step 2).

In our analysis, we will use a key result: in general, both parties in a contract should share risk and return.[8] (For a detailed discussion of risk-sharing contracts, see chapters 15 through 17.)

We begin with the case where the advertiser uses a conventional medium, say, a newspaper. Then, under the typical contract, the advertiser pays the newspaper a fixed fee for placing an ad. Since the newspaper's income does not depend on any of the outcomes (e.g., reach or sales), *the advertiser bears all the risk.*

Now suppose the firm advertises on the Internet. As discussed, the relationships between advertising and clickthroughs (Step 1) and between clickthroughs and sales (Step 2) are both uncertain. However, in contrast to conventional media, the intermediate measure of advertising effectiveness (the number of clickthroughs) can be measured fairly accurately. Hence, as we discuss below, the contract between the search engine and the advertiser can be improved.

Thus, suppose the search engine charges the advertiser an amount based on the number of clickthroughs for the advertiser's product. Note that, at the time that the contract is chosen, the number of clickthroughs is uncertain. Consequently, under this contract the search engine bears some risk (Step 1 above). However, the risk sharing between the advertiser and the search engine is incomplete. Specifically, *the advertiser bears all the risk from the uncertain effect of clickthroughs on sales (Step 2 above) and hence on gross profits.*

Fusion for Profit Maxim

Internet advertising allows more efficient risk sharing between advertisers and search engines than advertising in conventional media. However, contracts based on clickthroughs will lead to incomplete risk sharing.

Point to consider.   Is there a better contract for pricing Internet advertising than a contract that is based on the number of clickthroughs?

The answer to this question depends on whether the advertiser sells multiple products and/or uses multiple media.

Single-Product Firm, Single-Medium Plan

We continue with the Megatech example. Suppose Megatech sells only one product and uses only one medium (e.g., it advertises exclusively on Google). Let's say that both Megatech and Google have the same information on how advertising affects clickthroughs (Step 1) and how clickthroughs affect Megatech's sales (Step 2).

Then, it is possible to design a full risk-sharing contract that is superior to one in which Megatech pays Google based on the number of clickthroughs. Specifically, both parties can use a profit-sharing contract in which Megatech pays Google a fixed fee plus a share of gross profits generated by the Internet advertising.[9]

Single-Product Firm, Multimedia Plan

Consider the following scenario. Suppose Megatech uses a multimedia schedule when it advertises on Google. For example, suppose Megatech uses several Internet search engines simultaneously or uses a combination of conventional media and Internet advertising.

Then, Megatech's profits will depend on a number of factors that Google will not be able to observe. Specifically, Google will have incomplete information about Megatech's advertising productivity. For example, Google will not know the *total* number of clickthroughs for Megatech's Internet advertising across different Web sites during any given time period. Nor will Google know the reach that Megatech obtains using conventional media advertising during that period. Consequently, because of this information asymmetry, a profit-sharing contract between Google and Megatech will not be optimal.

Alternatively, regardless of whether Megatech uses a multimedia plan, suppose Megatech charges consumers different prices after they have seen the advertisement on Google. Now, the relationship between clickthroughs on Google and the consequent sales revenue is under Megatech's control. Importantly, Google will not know how advertising on its Web site affects Megatech's sales revenue *even if Google were to know the number of click-throughs on the Google Web site with certainty*. Consequently, as in the multimedia case, a *profit-sharing plan* will not be optimal.

Multiproduct Firm

The problems discussed above will be compounded. Hence a profit-sharing plan between the advertiser and Google will not be optimal.

Fusion for Profit Maxim

Under certain circumstances, optimal risk-sharing between the advertiser and the Internet search engine can be achieved by using profit-sharing contracts.

▲ *How should an Internet search engine price its advertising when the advertiser uses multiple media, sells multiple products, or independently determines its marketing policy (e.g., price)?*

For this scenario, each advertiser will have a different reservation price for a particular ad placement on the search engine (e.g., an ad to be run on a particular day for a specified length of time). One way for the search engine to take advantage of these differential reservation prices across advertisers is to auction its ad placements.

Example: Suppose there are two potential advertisers for a particular ad slot on Google, say Hewlett-Packard and Sony. Specifically,

- Hewlett-Packard is planning to advertise a new printer model on Google. Then, Hewlett-Packard's long-run profits will come from selling the printer and from selling printer cartridges in the future to current printer buyers.
- Sony is planning to advertise a new model of digital camera with no add-on features. Then, in contrast to Hewlett-Packard, Sony will earn profits only from onetime sales of its new product (digital cameras).

For simplicity, assume that both Hewlett-Packard and Sony are risk-neutral. In addition, suppose the profit margins on the Hewlett-Packard printer and on the Sony digital camera are equal, both companies expect to obtain the same number of clickthroughs from an ad placement on Google, the conversion rates from clickthroughs to purchase are equal for the printer and the digital camera, and each firm uses only one medium (Google).

Then, the long-term average gross profit from an ad placement on Google (before paying advertising costs) will be higher for Hewlett-Packard than it is for Sony. Consequently, Hewlett-Packard should be willing to pay more for the ad placement on Google.

Fusion for Profit Maxim

Other factors being the same, firms that sell complementary products should be willing to pay more to advertise on the Internet.

▶ What type of advertising contract should Google use?

Ideally, Google would like to set the price of the advertising slot to equal Hewlett-Packard's reservation price (i.e., its maximum willingness to pay). However, Google does not know this value. Hence, as a "second-best" solution, Google can auction the advertising slot. When Google uses this strategy, Hewlett-Packard will outbid Sony and purchase the advertising slot.

▶ What are the potential gains and losses to Google and advertisers if Google auctions its ad placements?

Auctions are a mixed blessing for all parties.

The Advertiser. As in any auction, the buyer is concerned about over-bidding (i.e., the *winner's curse*). One way for Google to alleviate this problem for the advertiser is by pricing ad placements on its Web site using the second-price *Vickrey auction* method. That is, the highest bidder (the winner) pays an amount equal to the second-highest bid.[10]

In the Google example, suppose Sony's maximum bid for the ad is $15,000, and the corresponding value for Hewlett-Packard is $25,000. Then Hewlett-Packard will win the auction and pay Google $15,000 for the ad spot.

Note that the Vickrey auction method alleviates the problem of overbidding. However, it does not address the issue of optimal risk-sharing. Thus, when the auction method is used, the winner pays a flat fee for the ad. Hence *the advertiser bears all the risk as it does when it advertises uses a conventional medium.* When the Vickrey auction method is used, the winner does not pay its reservation price. Hence Google will underprice to some degree (here, Google will have "underpriced" the ad slot by $10,000 ≡ Hewlett-Packard's reservation price for the slot – Sony's reservation price for the ad slot). In practice, there will be many bidders, and not just two as in this example. Hence the effect of underbidding will be substantially reduced.

The Optimality of the Auction Method.   The auction method for pricing Internet ads is a double-edged sword. We continue with the Google example. On the one hand, the auction methodology will allow Google to *skim the market.* That is, Google can ration scarce resources (ad space on its Web site) according to the reservation prices of its advertisers. On the other hand, when Google uses the auction method, all the risk is borne by the advertiser. This reduces advertisers' reservation prices and hence reduces the gains to Google from skimming the market. Thus, *some form of risk-sharing contract may be superior to the auction method.*

Fusion for Profit Maxim

A search engine can skim the market by using the auction methodology to sell Internet advertising. However, this method can lead to suboptimal risk-sharing because the advertiser bears all the risk.

Point to consider.   Should a small Internet search engine price its advertising space differently from industry giants such as Yahoo?

The small search engine firm is likely to be highly risk-averse in comparison to Yahoo. Hence, the optimal contract for the small search engine may be to charge a flat fee for its advertising space. The only remaining question is how the small search engine can take advantage of the differential reservation prices among potential advertisers. To address this problem, the small Internet search engine can use the Vickrey auction methodology. That is, the winner pays a price equal to the second-highest bid.

In contrast, since Yahoo is a large firm, it should be more willing to take risks than a small search engine. Consequently, Yahoo may prefer to enter into a profit-sharing agreement with the advertiser. (See previous discussion on the pros and cons of profit-sharing contracts for pricing Internet advertising.)

Fusion for Profit Maxim

The Vickrey auction methodology for selling Internet advertising may be more appropriate for small Internet search engines than for larger Internet firms.

▶ 21.7 How Should the Firm Coordinate Its Internet Advertising and Sales Force Strategies?

The previous analysis focused on how Internet advertising can affect the productivities of conventional media and vice versa. However, many firms use *both* advertising and a sales force to provide information to customers. This raises an important question.

▶ *How can the firm coordinate its Internet advertising and its sales force strategies?*

The key issue is the following. Depending on the industry and the firm's strategy, Internet advertising and the firm's sales force can be either complements or substitutes.

Example: Consider a large industrial firm, Goliath, that focuses on building long-run relationships with customers. Then, the optimal strategy for Goliath could be to use an Internet Web site to create awareness among potential clients. In particular, the Web site could direct these clients to particular salespersons in the firm, depending on the clients' particular needs. If Goliath uses this strategy, Internet advertising will make its sales force more productive. That is, Goliath's sales force and Internet advertising are complementary.

Alternatively, Goliath may prefer to use a segment-specific strategy. Thus, Goliath could be using its most productive sales personnel to target key customer accounts and using the Internet to reach less important segments (e.g., low-volume purchasers). Now Goliath's sales force and Internet advertising are likely to be independent or even substitutes.

▶ *How can Goliath coordinate its Internet and sales force strategies?*

If sufficient historical data are available, Goliath can estimate the relationship among sales, Internet advertising, and sales effort, regardless of how they interact with each other (e.g., whether they are complements or substitutes). The methodology is the same as that for measuring the effects of a standard multimedia plan for conventional media such as TV and newspapers.[11]

▶ *Suppose that, in the past, Goliath has sold via a sales force only. Now, Goliath plans to sell via both a sales force and Internet advertising. How should Goliath revise its sales force compensation plans?*

The critical issues are twofold:

1. Are Internet advertising and sales force efforts substitutes, complements, or independent?
2. How will Internet advertising affect the *volatilities* of Goliath's sales and gross profits?

Depending on how strong these effects are, Goliath will need to revise its sales force compensation plans accordingly.

Suppose Goliath has many salespersons, each of whom is assigned a separate geographical area or set of customers. Suppose Goliath determines the sales call policies of all its agents. In addition, Goliath uses a *linear wage-commission compensation plan* in which each salesperson is paid a base salary and a fixed percentage of the sales revenues that he or she generates. (These fixed wages and commission rates need not be the same across sales agents.)

Then, for the given scenario, Goliath can treat each salesperson as a separate profit center. Furthermore, the optimal commission rate for any given salesperson will depend only on the risk attitudes of Goliath and that salesperson.[12]

▶ *How should Goliath revise the sales force compensation plan if Internet advertising increases each salesperson's productivity (not necessarily by the same amounts) but has no impact on the volatility of sales?*

For this scenario, the effects of Internet advertising and the sales force are independent. Furthermore, as mentioned above, Goliath can treat each salesperson as a separate profit center. Since the Internet advertising and sales force effects are independent, Goliath can proceed sequentially. First, determine the optimal level of Internet advertising, and second, revise each salesperson's contract separately, since each salesperson can be treated as a separate profit center.

To illustrate how this works, suppose Goliath has two salespersons, Theo and Aida, each of whom is equally productive. However, Theo is more risk-averse than Aida. Since Theo is more risk-averse than Aida, Goliath pays Theo a *higher* annual base salary ($50,000) but only 3% of sales revenue, whereas Goliath pays Aida a *lower* annual base salary of $40,000 plus a higher commission rate (5.5%) on sales revenue.

Let's say that, before Goliath advertises on the Internet, both Theo and Aida can produce average sales revenues of $500,000. Then, Theo's expected commission income is $15,000 (commission rate × average sales revenue = 3% × $500,000), and Aida's expected commission income is $27,500 (5.5% × $500,000). Hence, Theo's expected income is $65,000 ($50,000 + $15,000), and Aida's expected income is $67,500 ($40,000 + $27,500).[13]

By assumption, the risk aversions of all players (Goliath, Theo, and Aida) remain unchanged after Goliath advertises on the Internet. Hence Theo's commission rate should remain at 3% of Theo's sales revenue, and Aida's commission rate should remain unchanged at 5.5% of Aida's sales revenue.

▶ *Suppose Internet advertising significantly increases sales in the customer segment to which Theo is assigned. How should Goliath change Theo's compensation plan?*

Let's say that, because of Goliath's Internet advertising, Theo can now produce an average sales revenue of $600,000 (> $500,000). Then Theo's expected commission income will increase from $15,000 to $18,000 ($600,000 × 3%)—an increase of $3,000. However, by assumption, the volatility of Theo's sales (and hence of Theo's commission income) will be unaffected by the Internet. Furthermore, by assumption, Theo's risk attitude is the same as before.

Since Goliath needs to pay Theo only the equivalent of his reservation income, the only change that Goliath needs to make to Theo's compensation plan is to reduce his annual base salary by $3,000. Note that, both before and after Goliath advertises on the Internet, Theo will make the same expected income ($65,000). In addition, he will face the same volatility in income in both cases. Consequently, Theo will make the equivalent of his reservation income regardless of whether Goliath advertises on the Internet.

▶ *Suppose Internet advertising also increases sales in the customer segment to which Aida is assigned. How should Goliath change Aida's compensation plan?*

Let's say that the increase in sales in Aida's customer segment is less than the increase in Theo's segment. Suppose Aida can now produce an average sales revenue of $550,000 (< $600,000). Then, Aida's expected commission income will increase from $27,500 to $30,250 ($550,000 × 5.5%)—an increase of $2,750.

Since Goliath needs to pay Aida only the equivalent of her reservation income, the only change that Goliath needs to make to Aida's compensation plan is to reduce her annual base salary by $2,750.

Note that, both before and after Goliath advertises on the Internet, Aida will make the same expected income ($67,500). In addition, Aida faces the same volatility in income in both cases. Consequently, Aida also makes the equivalent of her reservation income regardless of whether Goliath advertises on the Internet.

▶ *In our analysis, we assumed that Internet advertising helped to increase sales in both territories. What will happen if Internet advertising cannibalizes sales in both territories?*

In this case, Goliath will need to increase the base salaries for Theo and Aida by the amounts necessary to ensure that they earn the equivalent of their reservation incomes.

Fusion for Profit Maxim

Firms that sell via the Internet and a sales force should coordinate their Internet budgets and sales force compensation plans to obtain the optimal risk-return combination.

Other scenarios can be examined similarly (e.g., the Internet changes both the expected sales and the volatility of sales for each agent).

▶ **21.8 How Does the Internet Affect Social Welfare?**

So far we have focused on how the Internet affects the firm's profits. We now ask a different question: What is the impact of the Internet on consumers' well-being and on social welfare?

One cannot answer this question precisely without industry-specific cost and demand data. Following is a qualitative discussion of how some general cost and demand factors will affect consumers' well-being and social welfare.[14]

Search Costs

The Internet is an efficient vehicle for obtaining product information. Since Internet advertising allows consumers to obtain information more efficiently and reduce their search costs, the Internet should increase consumer well-being (*consumer surplus*).

The Internet is also an efficient vehicle for information dissemination by firms. Hence the firm, in turn, can increase its profitability by using a more efficient media plan. For instance, the firm can switch a part of its advertising budget from conventional media to the Internet. These effects imply that social welfare (consumer surplus + profits) should increase.

Price Sensitivity

The Internet allows the firm to control the order in which it provides information to consumers. For example, the firm can send consumers to different Web pages depending on the pattern of clickthroughs. This will affect price sensitivity.

Thus, branded products will be able to reduce the price sensitivities for their brands by focusing primarily on product-related information and downplaying price information. In contrast, generics can use the opposite strategy and provide information paths on the Internet that are likely to increase consumers' price sensitivities.

Because of these divergent effects on price sensitivity, the effects of Internet advertising on consumer and social welfare are likely to be ambiguous.

Economies of Scale

As discussed earlier, the Internet can reduce the cost disadvantages of small firms, especially in those industries where information costs are significant. This will allow both extant firms in the industry and new entrants to make profits by selling their products to underserved or neglected market segments. Consequently, for such industries, consumers will be better off, industry-wide profits will increase, and social welfare will be augmented.

Economies of Scope

If economies of scope are significant, the Internet will allow the multiproduct firm to use a bundling strategy to reduce competition and increase profits. Thus, the Internet could make consumers worse off. However, social welfare is the sum of profits and consumer surpluses across products. Hence social welfare could increase if the increase in firms' profits outweighs the reduction in consumers' surpluses across product lines.[15]

Fusion for Profit Maxim

The effect of the Internet on consumer well-being and social welfare is likely to be industry-specific and will depend on the magnitudes of search costs, economies of scale, economies of scope, and price sensitivities in those industries.

▶ 21.9 How Will the Internet Affect the Advertising Industry in the Future?

As discussed, the Internet has led to fundamental and rapid changes in the structure of the advertising industry. These changes are likely to continue in the future as further improvements in Internet technology make new modes of advertising delivery and advertising pricing possible.

Conquest Advertising

Because of recent changes in Internet technology, advertisers can purchase advertising space immediately adjacent to editorial content about a competitor's product. This tactic, known as *conquest advertising*, allows the firm to preempt a competitor by reducing the probability that consumers will purchase the competitor's product.

Web sites are presently using differentiated strategies to sell conquest advertising. For example, some Web sites such as Edmunds.com ban advertisers from buying out the entire ad inventory adjacent to reviews about their own brands. Other Web sites such as Yahoo Finance give firms the opportunity to stop conquest ads by their competitors. To accomplish this, a firm can preempt a competitor by matching the ad price offered by the competitor and buying the ad space for itself.

Since Web sites are using dissimilar pricing strategies, it is difficult to predict a priori how conquest advertising will affect the advertising industry in the future.[16]

Behavioral Targeting

At present, advertising based on keywords is a major source of advertising revenue for many Internet search engines. For example, according to the Interactive Advertising Bureau (IAB), keyword search accounted for 40% of Google's revenue in 2006.

Now, because of recent advances in Internet technology, sellers of online advertising can track users' online actions in detail. Consequently, advertisers can customize their advertising to each individual based on that individual's Web-surfing behavior. This advertising strategy is known as *behavioral targeting*.

Example: Suppose an individual in Dallas is browsing for hybrid cars on the Yahoo Autos Web site. Then, Yahoo's SmartAds' platform allows an automobile manufacturer (say Toyota) to showcase a particular hybrid model to that individual. In particular, Toyota can customize the ad by providing the individual with information about a specific Toyota dealer or dealers in Dallas. Furthermore, Toyota can use its knowledge of that individual's prior Web-surfing behavior to provide tailor-made, product-related information that is relevant to the individual. Similarly, the SmartAds platform will soon allow users to purchase items within the ad unit, without having to click through to another Web site.[17]

Behavioral targeting is likely to have significant effects on the evolution of the advertising industry. On the demand side, behavioral targeting allows advertisers to use a highly customized advertising message strategy. On the supply side, Internet search engines will need to diversify their product portfolios beyond a specialized platform that is based primarily on keyword search. For example, Google recently acquired DoubleClick in order to increase its presence in the online display advertising market. The net result is likely to be a decrease in the relative importance of keyword search advertising in the future.

Electronic Exchanges

Electronic exchanges have recently emerged as brokers to match ad buyers with sellers of unused ad space. By creating a market with a large number of ad sellers, these exchanges allow advertisers to purchase highly targeted ads across different Web sites. Typically, the exchanges collect payments for the ads from the advertisers, deduct a commission, and pass along the remainder to the appropriate Web sites.[18]

The growth of electronic exchanges is likely to have far-reaching effects on the advertising industry in general and on conventional advertising in particular. For example, space on conventional media such as TV and radio will be increasingly sold on electronic exchanges.

However, the net effect of these changes on the supply and demand for advertising is difficult to predict a priori. A critical unknown is what percentage of advertising space sellers of conventional and Internet advertising will make available for sale through the electronic exchanges. For example, on the supply side, the major TV networks may decide to only sell "surplus" ad inventory on the exchanges and sell premium ad space directly to large ad buyers.

Similarly, on the demand side, large buyers may conclude that ad inventory sold via the exchanges is commoditized. If this is the case, the bulk of the buyers on the exchange will consist of small and medium-sized firms. Hence, for the scenario described, a segmented equilibrium will emerge in which primarily small and medium-sized firms will participate in the electronic exchange market, whereas large firms (buyers and sellers) will directly negotiate with one another.

Another key factor that will affect the evolution of the electronic exchange market is critical mass. Suppose it turns out that electronic exchanges can benefit from economies of scale only if the numbers of buyers and sellers are sufficiently large. Then, in the future, small electronic exchanges will have to merge with one another to be efficient. Alternatively, electronic exchanges will be purchased by large Internet firms such as Google, which have the customer base and resources necessary to leverage economies of scale and economies of scope. If this is the case, the electronic exchange market will be dominated by a few large players (e.g., Google and Yahoo).

Other Intermediaries

Buying online advertising can be a daunting task to buyers (especially small and medium-sized firms), since the number of potential media alternatives is enormous. In addition, small and medium-sized firms are likely to incur high transaction costs by directly seeking to obtain the best advertising deals in the market. Hence it is very likely that specialized Internet firms will emerge to help online advertisers to choose optimal media planning and message strategies across conventional media and the Internet.

Metrics

The metrics used by the Internet industry are changing rapidly. For example, Nielsen recently decided to eliminate its rankings of Web sites based on page views. Instead, Nielsen will now rank Web sites based on total minutes spent at those sites. This change of metric has a major effect on the reported rankings. For example, based on page views, AOL currently would be ranked sixth. However, based on total minutes, AOL would be ranked first.[19]

Neither measure (page views or total minutes) is a perfect proxy for advertising productivity. For example, if one uses page visits as the metric, one is ignoring whether the user clicked and closed the page immediately or whether the user left the page open for a period of time and then navigated to other pages on the site being evaluated. Similarly, if one uses the time spent on a page as the metric, one will not know if the users left the page open in the background while looking at another window or if they left the machine running while they were away.

Since Nielsen is a market leader, and the new metric for measuring advertising productivity will affect the rankings of sites dramatically, one can expect significant changes in how Internet advertising will be priced in the future. (For a detailed discussion of how error in measuring advertising productivity affects advertising policy, see chapter 14.)

Advertising Rates

The changes in supply and demand discussed above are likely to have a significant effect on the structure of advertising rates and especially on how advertising rates vary over time. (For a discussion of how to make decisions when advertising rates are uncertain, see chapter 14.)

Fusion for Profit Maxim

The Internet is likely to have far-reaching consequences for the evolution of the conventional and Internet advertising industries in the future. These changes will depend on the growth rates of conquest advertising, behavioral targeting, and electronic exchanges to sell advertising space. In addition, they will depend on the new metrics that will be introduced in the future to measure the productivity of Internet advertising.

Chapter 21 Key Points

- The effect of the Internet on prices will depend on the firm's cost structure, advertising message strategy, and segmentation policy. Consequently, different functional areas, including marketing and finance, should be involved in developing a coordinated Internet strategy that maximizes performance.
- The effect of the Internet on prices is likely to be industry-specific. In particular, the answer will depend on the combined effects of economies of scale, economies of scope, and whether buyers purchase value-added services from vendors.
- The Internet may not lead to greater commoditization in the B to C market, since a product sold through the Internet is not equivalent to the same product sold via bricks-and-mortar retailers.
- The Internet can lead to increased or decreased commoditization in the B to B market depending on how the Internet affects average prices and price dispersion for the industry in question. These effects, in turn, will depend on whether the industry has economies of scale and economies of scope, and on how purchase quantities and search costs vary across buyers.
- The Internet allows firms to improve their performance by customizing their advertising messages to particular individuals and choosing the sequence in which information is made available to those individuals. In general, branded products should present attribute-based information first, and generics should present price information first.

- In general, a firm that uses only Internet advertising will be able to measure advertising productivity more accurately. However, this conclusion may not hold for firms that use a mixed advertising plan involving conventional media and Internet advertising.
- Traditional media and Internet advertising can be substitutes or complements. If they are complements, these effects need not be symmetric.
- The advertiser's willingness to pay for Internet advertising depends on the firm's risk attitude, whether or not the firm is a multiproduct firm, whether the firm is using a multimedia advertising policy, and the length of the firm's planning horizon.
- Internet advertising allows more efficient risk-sharing between advertisers and search engines than advertising in conventional media. Under certain circumstances, optimal risk-sharing between the advertiser and the Internet search engine can be achieved by using profit-sharing contracts.
- A search engine can skim the market by using the auction methodology to sell Internet advertising. However, this method is likely to lead to inefficient risk-sharing because the advertiser bears all the risk.
- The Vickrey auction methodology for selling Internet advertising may be more appropriate for small Internet search engines than for larger Internet firms.
- Firms that simultaneously sell via a sales force and the Internet should coordinate their Internet budgets and sales force compensation plans to obtain the optimal risk-return combination for the owners of the firm.
- The effect of the Internet on consumer well-being and social welfare is likely to be industry-specific and will depend on the magnitudes of search costs, economies of scale, economies of scope, and price sensitivities in those industries.
- The future effect of the Internet will depend on the new metrics that will be introduced over time, and on the growth rates of conquest advertising, behavioral targeting, and electronic exchanges to sell advertising space.

22

Mergers and Acquisitions

The pace of *mergers* and *acquisitions* has accelerated in recent years, both nationally and internationally. Although there is a vast literature in this area, the discussion is often highly specialized by discipline (e.g., accounting, finance, and strategy).

In this chapter, we take a different approach. In particular, we emphasize the *marketing-finance interface*. Furthermore, we discuss how firms can combine *game theory* and behavioral studies to determine how they should value mergers and acquisitions.

The information covered in this chapter will be useful when you are faced with the following types of decisions:

- When should my firm merge with or acquire another?
- What are the potential gains and costs to my firm from a merger or acquisition?
- What can my firm learn from the history of postmerger performance?
- Should my firm use a *focused acquisition strategy* or form *strategic alliances* with other firms?
- How will a strategic alliance affect the value of my firm?
- How should my firm determine the value of a brand it is planning to acquire?
- Should my firm use standard *brand equity* measures when it bids to acquire another firm?

- Does it make sense for a brand with no brand equity to acquire a brand with high brand equity?
- How will mergers and acquisitions by *private equity firms* and *hedge funds* affect different industries and the economy?
- What issues should my firm consider if it is planning an international merger?

The following terms will be introduced in this chapter (see glossary for definitions):

a priori segmentation	economies of scope	mixed bids
acquisitions	financial leverage	mixed bundling
administrative	financial synergy	strategy
synergies	focused acquisition	performance fees
asymmetric information	strategy	private equity firms
bad turnover	game theory	profitability
bankruptcy	hedge funds	reservation price
bondholders	intangible assets	risk-adjusted rate of
brand equity	internal transfer price	return
carried interest	joint distribution of	segmented equilibrium
core competencies	reservation prices	social welfare
cost of capital	joint profits	strategic alliance
cost structure	marginal cost	strategic business unit
customer relationship	market power	(SBU)
management (CRM)	marketing-finance	supply chain
demand structure	interface	synergy
differential tax rates	maximum percentage	tapered vertical
discount rate	premiums	integration
economies of scale	mergers	winner's curse

▶ **22.1 The Rationale for Mergers and Acquisitions**

Although there are important legal distinctions between mergers and *acquisitions*, for present purposes we can use the two terms interchangeably.

▶ *We begin by asking a fundamental question: Why do mergers and acquisitions take place?*

The conventional view is that the managers of the acquiring firm purchase other firms in order to increase the wealth of the owners of the firm. However, there is a less altruistic explanation.

In general, the cash flows of the acquiring and acquired firms will not be perfectly correlated. This implies that, by acquiring another firm, managers may be able to reduce the risk of their own earnings *even if this strategy does not increase the owners' wealth*. Thus, there may be a potential conflict of interest between management and ownership.

In our analysis, we shall focus primarily on how mergers and acquisitions affect the wealth of the owners of the acquiring and acquired firms. In particular, we shall distinguish between privately and publicly held firms.

Fusion for Profit Maxim

The fiduciary duty of managers is to increase the wealth of the owners of the firm. However, managers may use mergers and acquisitions to reduce their own financial risks rather than increase the wealth of the owners of the firm.

▶ 22.2 The Potential Gains from Mergers

We begin with the case where both the acquiring and the acquired firms are publicly held.

Suppose the acquiring firm has a stock value of $500 million and the acquired firm has a stock value of $300 million. Then, the merger will add value to the stockholders of the acquiring firm only if the merged firm is worth more than the sum of the separate stock values before the merger ($800 million).

▶ Under what conditions will mergers add value to the acquiring company?

The merger must lead to increased *market power* in the product market or in the *supply chain*, *economies of scope*, or other *synergies*.

Market Power

Mergers can increase market power in several ways. Suppose two large consumer product companies such as Procter & Gamble and Colgate-Palmolive merge. Alternatively, suppose NetFlix and Blockbuster merge in the movie and DVD rental industry. These mergers can add value to the acquiring firms in two ways:

1. Even if the *cost structure* is unaffected by the merger, the merged firm will be able to coordinate prices across product lines. Hence *joint profits* will increase.
2. If the merged firm is large enough, it may be able to cut costs by reducing the prices it pays to firms from which it purchases raw materials and other inputs. Thus, by achieving market power over suppliers, the merged firm will be able to further increase its profits.

A merger can also help the acquiring firm to increase its market power in the supply chain, especially if the acquired firm controls a scarce resource.

Example: Suppose Google uses a unique software program provided by a vendor who has a patent on this product. Then, Google may be able to increase its profits by acquiring the vendor and controlling the availability of the software program to other firms. Note that, in general, there is no gain to the firm from purchasing a vendor if close substitutes for the vendor's product are readily available in the market.

Firms at different levels in the supply chain may have unequal bargaining powers because of *asymmetric information*. One strategy for the firm to improve its *profitability* is to reduce this information asymmetry by acquiring another firm at a different level in the supply chain or channel of distribution.

Example: Suppose a major oil company (e.g., Exxon) acquires a small tanker company in order to accurately determine the cost structure of the oil tanker business. This strategy—known as *tapered vertical integration*—will put Exxon in a superior bargaining position when it negotiates contracts with other oil tanker companies to transport crude oil.

Economies of Scope

Economies of scope imply that the multiproduct firm has an advantage over firms that specialize in individual products. These advantages can accrue because of both demand and cost factors. We consider these in turn.

Suppose two firms sell different products. However, they sell to a common set of customers. In this case, the economies of scope are driven by demand.

Example: Comcast sells cable television service, and Vonage sells an Internet phone service. Hence, there are three segments of buyers:

1. Those who buy their cable service from Comcast,
2. Those who buy their Internet phone service from Vonage, and
3. Those who buy both services.

Now, if Comcast acquires Vonage, Comcast may be able to increase joint profits by using a *mixed bundling strategy*. That is, the merged firm will sell a product line of three products: cable television, Internet telephone service, and a bundle of cable and Internet telephone services.[1]

Suppose a multiproduct firm has a cost advantage over firms that specialize in particular products. In this case, the economies of scope are driven by cost.

Example: Let's say that one firm specializes in computers and the other in printers. Suppose both firms use salespersons to sell their products to business users. Then, other factors being the same, a merger will allow the merged firm to become more efficient by combining the two sales forces and making each salesperson responsible for selling both computers and printers. Since the merged firm will obtain economies of scope based on cost, joint profits should increase after the merger.

Other Synergies

Mergers can increase joint profits in several other ways. For example, the merged firm may gain from *economies of scale* in administrative costs. We say that the merger leads to *administrative synergies.*

If the cash flows of the merging companies are not highly correlated (better yet, if they are uncorrelated or negatively correlated), the probability of *bankruptcy* for the merged firm will be lower than the corresponding probabilities for the merging companies. Consequently, a merger will lead to lower risk for *bondholders* of the merged firm.[2]

Since the firm's bonds will be less risky after the merger, shareholder value will increase. Alternatively, a firm may merge with another for tax reasons, specifically to take advantage of the acquired firm's accumulated losses. These are examples of *financial synergy.*

Note that these sources of postmerger gain are unrelated to those that accrue to the multiproduct firm from economies of scope.

Fusion for Profit Maxim

Mergers can add value to the acquiring firm if they increase the firm's market power in the marketplace or in the supply chain, leverage economies of scope, or lead to other synergies.

▲ *22.3 Do Intangible Assets Add Value in a Merger?*

The current stock price of a company implicitly includes the values of the firm's *intangible assets* such as its managerial and R&D personnel. Hence, intangible assets can add value only if they lead to postmerger synergy or if the acquiring firm has superior information to the stock market.

Example: Consider Lenovo's 2005 acquisition of IBM's PC business for $1.75 billion. Lenovo paid a premium to acquire the intangible assets in IBM's PC business, including IBM's managerial and technical personnel. This strategy of purchasing intangible assets at a premium can add value to Lenovo only if two conditions hold simultaneously:

1. IBM's managerial and technical know-how are transferable to Lenovo. This condition may not hold if IBM's and Lenovo's product lines are dissimilar, the overlap in technology across both firms is limited, or the managerial skills to market both firms' products are significantly different. For instance, both firms could be serving distinct market segments that require different marketing skills, including the use of different channels of distribution.
2. The intangible assets that Lenovo acquires from IBM remain with Lenovo after the merger. For example, the anticipated postmerger gains

to Lenovo will not occur if key technical and managerial personnel from IBM's PC unit leave after the acquisition.

Fusion for Profit Maxim

An acquisition strategy that focuses on the purchase of goodwill or intangible assets from the acquired firm does not guarantee that the shareholders of the acquiring firm will increase their wealth.

Point to consider.   Suppose two major firms sell differentiated products in the same industry. Does it make sense for the less profitable firm to acquire the more profitable firm? Assume that cost conditions remain unchanged after the merger.

When two major firms in an industry merge, the merged firm increases its market power. Hence *each firm should attempt to acquire* the other, regardless of whether its current profitability is high or low.

Example: Suppose NetFlix is presently making annual profits of $100 million, and Blockbuster is making annual profits of $400 million. For simplicity, assume that each firm has the same annual *discount rate* (say 10%) and that these discount rates do not change after the merger. Furthermore, assume there is no market growth.

Then, before the merger, NetFlix stock will be worth $1 billion (annual profits/NetFlix's discount rate). Similarly, Blockbuster stock will be worth $4 billion. Hence both companies will have a combined premerger stock value of $5 billion.

▲ What will happen after the merger?

The joint annual profits for NetFlix and Blockbuster before the merger are $500 million. Since the merger leads to increased market power, postmerger joint profits will be larger than $500 million per year. Suppose the postmerger joint profits increase to $600 million per year.

Then, the merged firm will be worth $6 billion (joint annual profits after the merger/discount rate = $600M/10%). Suppose the brokerage costs and fees to complete the merger are $300 million. Then, the value of the merged firm after paying these onetime brokerage expenses is $5.7 billion (value of long-run profits of the merged firm − brokerage expenses paid to complete the merger = $6B − $300M).

Since the merger increases the combined value of both firms by $700 million ($5.7B − $5B), each firm should be willing to buy the other. Specifically, NetFlix should be willing to pay up to $4.7 billion to buy Blockbuster (value of the merged firm after paying onetime brokerage expenses − NetFlix's current stock value = $5.7B – $1B). Similarly, Blockbuster should be willing to pay up to $1.7 billion ($5.7B – $4B) to buy NetFlix.

Note that the maximum dollar merger premium that either company should be willing to pay to acquire the other is the same ($700M).

The *maximum percentage premiums*, however, will differ between the firms. As discussed, Blockbuster has a premerger value of $4 billion. Since NetFlix should be willing to pay a premium of up to $0.7 billion to acquire Blockbuster, the maximum percentage premium that NetFlix should be willing to pay to Blockbuster's shareholders is 17.5% ($0.7B/$4B).

Similarly, NetFlix has a premerger value of $1 billion. Since Blockbuster should be willing to pay a premium of up to $0.7 billion to acquire NetFlix, the maximum percentage premium that Blockbuster should pay to NetFlix's shareholders is 70% ($0.7B/$1B).

Fusion for Profit Maxim

When two major firms in a differentiated industry merge, the merged firm will increase its market power. Hence each firm should be willing to buy the other, regardless of whether its current profits are high or low, or whether the acquiring firm is the market leader.

▶ *Suppose two firms make separate bids to acquire a third. Assume that the first makes a bid of $2 billion, and the second makes a bid of $2.5 billion. Which bid should the managers of the third firm accept?*

The answer depends on the offers. If both transactions are all-cash, the higher bid by the second firm is clearly superior. However, consider the following scenario. Suppose the $2 billion offer by the first firm is all cash, and the $2.5 billion offer by the second firm is a *mixed bid* of $1 billion in cash plus stocks that are currently valued at $1.5 billion. Then, since future stock returns are uncertain, it is possible that the all-cash $2 billion bid is superior for the acquired firm, *even though the value of the mixed bid ($2.5 billion) is higher*.

In practice, many merger offers are mixed bids containing different combinations of cash and stock. Hence the boards of acquired companies often have considerable discretion in deciding what is best for their stockholders.

Fusion for Profit Maxim

The value of a merger offer to the acquired firm depends on whether the offer is all-cash or a mixed bid containing both cash and stocks. A lower all-cash bid may be superior to a risky mixed bid that has a higher current market value.

Point to consider.   In many cases, financial advisers are paid a flat one-time fee for their services in arranging a merger. Is this type of contract good for shareholders?

By assumption, each financial adviser is paid a flat fee. Hence, all the risk is borne by the acquiring and acquired firms. A better strategy for each firm (acquiring or acquired) may be to pay its financial adviser(s) on a performance basis. For example, each firm could use a combination compensation strategy in which it pays its financial advisers a lower flat fee plus a number of shares in the merged firm. This way, risk sharing will be improved across all parties (the acquiring firm, the acquired firm, and their respective financial advisers). (See chapters 15 through 17 for a discussion of optimal risk-sharing contracts.)

An additional advantage of using a combination compensation strategy is that the market for financial advisers could become more efficient. Thus, a high-quality financial adviser should be more willing to take the mixed compensation plan (a combination of a flat fee plus shares in the merged firm) than a low-quality financial adviser. Hence a *segmented equilibrium* could occur in the merger market. That is, more productive financial advisers would be paid using a mixed compensation plan. Less productive financial advisers would be paid on a onetime fee basis.

Fusion for Profit Maxim

In general, merging firms should use performance-based contracts to pay their respective financial advisors.

▲ 22.4 Do Mergers Work?

So far, we have discussed the theory of mergers. We now ask a fundamental question: Do stockholders gain from mergers?

In general, the effects are different for the acquired and the acquiring firms. In most cases, it is necessary for the acquiring firm to pay a premium to purchase the acquired firm. Hence shareholders of the acquired firm gain, since they receive a premium. However, history shows that, on average, mergers do not increase the wealth of the shareholders of the acquiring firm.

▲ Why do most mergers fail to add value to the shareholders of the acquiring firm?

There are several explanations.

Winner's Curse

Potential buyers may have engaged in a bidding war prior to the merger. Hence the acquiring firm may have paid too much. This phenomenon is known as the *winner's curse.*

Example: China Mobile recently withdrew its offer to buy Millicom International Cellular for $5.3 billion. According to a number of analysts and dealmakers, if the deal had gone through, China Mobile would have overpaid to acquire a heterogeneous group of assets that would have been difficult to manage.[3]

Synergies

The acquiring firm may have formed wrong expectations about the gains from postmerger synergy. For instance, on the cost side, the acquiring firm may have underestimated the coordination costs of running the larger organization resulting from the merger. On the demand side, the acquiring firm may have incorrectly estimated consumers' *reservation prices* (willingness to pay) for product bundles to be sold after the merger. Given these scenarios, postmerger performance will be lower than anticipated.

Example: Major readjustments may be necessary after a merger if the corporate cultures of the acquiring and acquired firms are significantly different. Thus, prior to Procter & Gamble's acquisition of Gillette in 2005, Procter & Gamble typically made key managerial decisions based on consensus. In sharp contrast, Gillette's management typically had a free hand in decision making. After the merger, Procter & Gamble's new management had to make significant adjustments to its decision-making processes. Additional problems were caused when Procter & Gamble merged the two sales forces after the merger with Gillette. Historically, the two sales forces had competed vigorously in the marketplace.[4]

Productivity

The acquiring firm may have paid too much attention to the "numbers" and failed to factor in the human element. For example, acquiring companies often impose their own metrics for measuring and rewarding performance in the merged firm. The consequences can be drastic. Productive managers may leave. In addition, the morale of those who remain can fall. Consequently, both postmerger productivity and performance may be reduced, sometimes dramatically.

Scope of Postmerger Gains

When firms merge, most of the gains (if any) tend to be highly localized. That is, the performance gains occur only in limited areas of the merging firms (often at the *strategic business unit* level) that have joint costs or share a common customer base. Hence mergers often have a very small impact on overall corporate performance.[5]

Fusion for Profit Maxim

Mergers may fail to deliver value to the acquiring firm because of the winner's curse, overoptimistic estimates of the gains from synergies, biased estimates of consumers' reservation prices, and underestimates of postmerger coordination and adjustment costs.

► *History shows that most mergers do not add value. So why do mergers persist?*

There are several reasons for this phenomenon. The management of the acquiring firm may erroneously believe that it is superior to the management of the acquired firm. Alternatively, the managers of the acquiring firm may overestimate the gains from postmerger synergy or underestimate coordination or other postmerger costs.

Finally, as previously noted, the managers of acquiring firms may merge with other firms to reduce the risk of their own earnings rather than to add value to the shareholders of the acquiring firm.

► *22.5 Alternative Acquisition Strategies*

As discussed above, many mergers do not lead to an increase in performance of the merged firm. This raises an interesting question: since many mergers fail, what acquisition strategy (if any) should firms pursue?

In general, apart from pure tax considerations, it is not wise for a firm to merge with or acquire another firm unless at least one of the following conditions holds:

1. The acquiring firm can increase its market power or bargaining power in the supply chain, or
2. The acquiring firm can achieve significant postmerger synergies in different dimensions (e.g., finance, administration, and marketing).
   In addition, the expected postmerger coordination costs should be less than the anticipated gains from the merger.

These conditions do not hold in many cases. Furthermore, many of the anticipated postmerger costs and benefits are difficult to quantify, especially when the acquired company has many divisions or product lines or operates in many countries.

In view of these potential problems that stem from outright mergers, the firm may be better off using a focused acquisition strategy or forming a strategic alliance with another firm.

Focused Acquisition Strategy

Since history shows that most postmerger performance gains are confined to subunits of the firm and are not company-wide, a better approach for the acquiring firm may be to pursue a narrower and more focused acquisition strategy.

Thus, the acquiring firm should first choose a strategic focus. For example, it could identify a critical *strategic business unit (SBU)* where it seeks to develop a long-run differential advantage over competitors. Then, it should search for and acquire specialized firms or brands that provide complementary resources (technical, managerial, or otherwise) to the relevant SBU so that this SBU's performance can be improved.

In general, a focused acquisition strategy will be superior to the merger strategy of first acquiring another company, then getting rid of unwanted or unprofitable product lines or divisions, and paying financial advisers substantial fees for arranging these sales.

Finally, a focused acquisition strategy is likely to be superior to a merger strategy because it forces management to devote its time and attention to its primary task: choosing strategies that maximize shareholder wealth.

Example: Over the last few years, IBM has acquired a large number of specialized software firms. The strategy is to capture market share rapidly by using IBM's large sales force to sell the software. This is an example of a focused acquisition strategy to benefit from synergy.[6]

Strategic Alliances

Sometimes, firms have complementary skills in certain dimensions such as marketing, production, or efficiently reaching particular markets or customer segments. In such cases, these firms may find it mutually advantageous to form strategic alliances to cooperate in the relevant domain where their skills overlap.

Example 1: General Motors used this approach to form highly focused strategic alliances with narrow scopes (e.g., the joint development of a particular model of car) with its Japanese and European competitors.[7]

Example 2: PepsiCo recently announced a partnership with Ocean Spray Cranberries to develop beverages that further strengthen PepsiCo's position in the noncarbonated, noncola drink market.[8]

▶ *Do strategic alliances increase the share values of the partnering firms?*

In general, the stock market does not react positively to strategic alliances in the short run. The exception is when the stock market perceives that the strategic alliances will leverage the *core competencies* of the partnering firms.

The long-run effects of strategic alliances are less clear. The reason is that, at the time the strategic alliance is announced, the stock market is unlikely to be fully informed about the future strategic options that could result for any of the partnering firms in the strategic alliance. These strategic options include the development of new products and entry into new markets.[9]

> **Fusion for Profit Maxim**
>
> A strategy that is based on focused acquisitions or strategic alliances may be superior to one based on mergers and acquisitions.

▶ 22.6 Brand Equity and Mergers

Sometimes a firm acquires a competitor in order to leverage the competitor's brand equity. Is this a good strategy? If so, how should each firm measure brand equity?

▶ *Suppose a multiproduct firm plans to sell one of its brands to a rival firm that competes in the same product category. How should the acquiring and acquired firms value this brand?*

For simplicity, assume that prior to the acquisition, neither firm has any economies of scope for the brands in question. Then each firm can evaluate the profitability of its brand independently of the remaining products in its product line. Given this scenario, the acquiring firm should proceed as follows:

1. Determine the *joint distribution of reservation prices* among consumers for both brands,[10] and
2. Use this information to determine the maximum product-line profits if both firms coordinate the pricing policies of their respective brands, and
3. Compare this value of joint profits to the acquiring firm's current profits and determine the maximum price that the acquiring firm should be willing to pay to acquire the other brand.

The firm that is planning to sell its brand should also perform the same analysis to determine the gain from selling its brand.

Example: Both Samsung and Sony manufacture and sell high-definition TVs (HDTVs). For simplicity, assume that both firms have excess capacity, know each other's *cost* and *demand structures*, and that these HDTV models will become obsolete in one year. Furthermore, there are no other competitors in the market. (This assumption will be relaxed later.)

▶ *Should Samsung buy Sony's HDTV brand, or should Sony buy Samsung's HDTV brand? If so, how should each firm determine the dollar value of the HDTV brand to be acquired?*

Suppose there are three segments, each of which contains 1 million households. Suppose the reservation prices (RPs) for the Samsung and Sony HDTVs are as shown in table 22.1.

Table 22.1
Samsung-Sony HDTV Example: Reservation Prices

Segment	Samsung HDTV	Sony HDTV
1	$1,200	$1,000
2	$1,100	$800
3	$700	$600

Note. One million households in each segment.

Note that each segment has a higher reservation price for the Samsung HDTV than for the Sony HDTV. Thus, all consumers agree that the Samsung HDTV has superior quality to the Sony HDTV. Suppose the *marginal cost* of the Samsung HDTV is $300 per unit, and the corresponding marginal cost for the Sony HDTV is $200 per unit.

Now, Samsung can choose one of three prices ($1,200, $1,100, or $700 per unit). Similarly, Sony can choose one of three prices ($1,000, $800, or $600 per unit). Thus, there are nine feasible price combinations.

The first step is to determine the profits made by the Sony and Samsung brands for each of the nine price combinations. We now explain how these profit values are obtained. Suppose Samsung charges $1,100 per HDTV unit, and Sony charges $800. Given these prices, each consumer will choose the HDTV brand that maximizes his or her net economic benefit (reservation price – price). If the maximum net economic benefit from purchasing the Sony or the Samsung HDTV is negative, the consumer will not buy an HDTV set.

Segment 1. If a consumer in this segment purchases the Samsung HDTV unit, he or she will obtain a surplus of $100 (reservation price for a consumer in Segment 1 for the Samsung HDTV unit – price of Samsung HDTV unit = $1,200 – $1,100). If this consumer purchases the Sony, he or she will obtain a larger surplus of $200 (reservation price for a consumer in Segment 1 for the Sony HDTV unit – price of the Sony HDTV unit = $1,000 – $800). Since consumers seek to maximize their net economic benefits, all consumers in Segment 1 will buy the Sony, *even though they all agree that the Samsung is superior.*

Segment 2. Given the prices for the Samsung ($1,100 per unit) and the Sony ($800 per unit), each consumer in Segment 2 will obtain zero surpluses if he or she buys either the Sony or the Samsung. Since these consumers are indifferent to the Sony and the Samsung, half of them will buy the Sony, and half will buy the Samsung.

Segment 3. For the prices given, consumers in Segment 3 will obtain negative consumer surpluses from purchasing either the Sony or the Samsung. Hence none of these consumers will buy an HDTV.

In our example, each segment contains 1 million households. Hence the following results will occur if Samsung charges $1,100 per unit and Sony charges $800 per unit (table 22.2).

Table 22.2
Samsung-Sony HDTV Example: Segment-Level Demands
If Samsung Charges $1,100 per Unit and Sony Charges
$800 per Unit

Segment	Samsung units bought	Sony units bought
1	0	1,000,000
2	500,000	500,000
3	0	0
Total	500,000	1,500,000

Table 22.3
Samsung-Sony Example: Payoffs to Samsung and Sony Corresponding
to Different Pricing Strategies Chosen by Each Competitor

	Sony		
	P = $1,000	P = $800	P = $600
Samsung			
P = $1,200	($450M, $400M)	($0, $1,200M**)	($0, $1,200M**)
P = $1,100	($1,600M*, $0)	($400M, $900)	($0, $1,200M**)
P = $700	($1,200M, $0)	($1,200*, $0)	($1,000M*, $200M**)

Note: P, price. The first entry in each cell indicates Samsung's profits and the second Sony's
profits.
*The optimal strategy for Samsung for any price chosen by Sony.
**The optimal strategy for Sony for any price chosen by Samsung.

At these prices ($1,100 for Samsung and $800 for Sony), the gross margins are $800 per unit for Samsung and $600 per unit for Sony. Hence Samsung will make a gross profit of $400 million (units sold × gross margin per unit), and Sony will make a gross profit of $900 million (table 22.3). The gross profit levels for Samsung and Sony in the cells corresponding to the other price combinations can be obtained similarly. In each cell in table 22.3, the first entry denotes Samsung's profits, and the second denotes Sony's profits.

Before either Sony or Samsung acquires the other's HDTV brand, Sony and Samsung are competitors in the HDTV market. To determine the pre-acquisition values of the Sony and Samsung HDTV brands, we proceed as follows.

Consider any price charged by Sony (say). Let's say that Sony charges $1,000 per HDTV. Then, Samsung should charge $1,100 per unit to maximize its profits. Similarly, consider any price charged by Samsung, say $1,100 per HDTV. Then, Sony should charge $600 per unit to maximize its profits.

Since Sony and Samsung do not cooperate with each other, the equilibrium prices prior to the acquisition will be as follows. Sony will charge a price of $600 per unit, and Samsung will charge $700 per unit.[11]

Given these market prices, Samsung's profit before a merger is $1 billion (gross margin per unit × units sold = $500 × 2M). Similarly, Sony's profit is $200 million. Hence the total industry profits before a merger are $1.2 billion.

Suppose Samsung buys the Sony HDTV brand. Then, Samsung will price its HDTV line to maximize product-line profits. As table 22.3 shows, the maximum joint profit will increase from $1.2 billion to $1.6 billion. Specifically, to achieve this result, it is necessary to sell Samsung HDTVs for $1,100 per set and to drop the Sony HDTV from the market.

▲ *How much should Samsung be willing to pay to buy the Sony HDTV brand?*

By acquiring the Sony HDTV brand, Samsung can increase its profits from $1 billion to $1.6 billion. Hence Samsung should be willing to pay up to $600 million to purchase the Sony HDTV brand. Note that, prior to the acquisition, Sony's brand is worth $200 million. Hence, Samsung should be willing to pay a substantial premium of $400 million (200%) to buy the Sony HDTV brand name *even though it is of lower quality than its own HDTVs.*

▲ *Should Sony be willing to pay a premium to buy the Samsung HDTV brand?*

If Sony buys Samsung's HDTV brand, it can increase its profits from $200 million to $1.6 billion. Hence Sony should be willing to pay up to $1.4 billion (joint profit after the acquisition – current profits from Sony HDTV = $1.6B – $200M) to acquire the Samsung brand.

Fusion for Profit Maxim

In order to determine the value of acquiring another brand, the acquiring firm needs to determine the joint distribution of reservation prices for its own brand and the brand to be acquired. The optimal strategy for a high-quality brand may be to acquire a low-quality brand in a given product category and vice versa.

Point to consider.   Suppose Sony buys the Samsung HDTV brand. How will this affect consumer and *social welfare?*

Before the acquisition, both Sony and Samsung charge low prices for their HDTVs because of competition. Consequently, Segments 1 and 2, respectively, make consumer surpluses of $500 million and $400 million. Hence the total consumer surplus is $900 million. As discussed earlier, the total industry profits are $1.2 billion. Thus, social welfare is $2.1 billion (the sum of industry profits and total consumer surplus = $1.2B + $900M).

After acquiring Samsung's HDTV brand, Sony should raise the price of the Samsung HDTV from $700 to $1,100 per unit; in addition, it should drop the Sony HDTV from the market. Hence Segment 1 will obtain a lower surplus $100 million ([Segment 1's reservation price for Samsung – price of Samsung] × number of households in Segment 1 = [$1,200 – $1,100] × 1M), and the other segments will make zero surpluses. The result is that total consumer surplus will be only $100 million. As discussed, after the acquisition, industry profits will increase from $1.2 billion to $1.6 billion. Hence social welfare will be reduced to $1.7 billion (< $2.1B).

Note that the brand acquisition will lead to increased profits (and stock prices) because the acquiring firm can coordinate prices across brands. However, consumers will be worse off, since the total consumer surplus will be reduced from $900 million to $100 million. In addition, the *increase* in industry profits after the acquisition ($0.4B) will be less than the *decrease* in consumer surplus ($0.8B). Hence social welfare will decrease after the acquisition.

▲   *Suppose Samsung buys the Sony HDTV brand. Will this change the welfare implications of the acquisition?*

Both firms will choose the same pricing strategies after the brand acquisition. Hence the net impact on industry profits and consumer surplus will be the same, regardless of which brand buys the other. Consequently, the social welfare results will be unchanged regardless of whether Samsung buys the Sony HDTV brand or vice versa.

Fusion for Profit Maxim

In general, the effect of an acquisition on consumer well-being and on social welfare does not depend on which firm acquires the other.

Point to consider.   In the HDTV example, how would the brand valuations change if marginal costs were zero (e.g., the brands in question were specialized software programs)?

Proceeding as before, we obtain the profitabilities shown in table 22.4 for Samsung and Sony for each price combination. Thus, prior to the acquisition, Samsung charges a price of $700 per unit and makes a profit of $1.75 billion. Sony charges $600 per unit and makes a profit of $300 million.

Table 22.4
Samsung-Sony Example: Payoffs to Samsung and Sony Corresponding to Different Pricing Strategies Chosen by Each Competitor When Marginal Costs Are Zero

	Sony		
	P = $1,000	P = $800	P = $600
Samsung			
P = $1,200	($600M, $500M)	($0, $1,600M**)	($0, $1,800M**)
P = $1,100	($2,200M*, $0)	($550M, $1,200)	($0, $1,800M**)
P = $700	($2,100M, $0)	($2,100*, $0)	($1,750M*, $300M**)

Note: P, price. The first entry in each cell indicates Samsung's profits and the second Sony's profits.
*Denotes the optimal strategy for Samsung for any price chosen by Sony.
**Denotes the optimal strategy for Sony for any price chosen by Samsung.

Suppose Samsung acquires the Sony HDTV brand. Then, Samsung can increase its profits from $1.75 billion to $2.2 billion. Hence Samsung should be willing to pay up to $450 million ($2.2B – $1.75B) to acquire the Sony HDTV brand. Similarly, if Sony acquires the Samsung HDTV brand, Sony can increase its profits from $300 million to $2.2 billion. Hence Sony should be willing to pay up to $1.9 billion ($2.2B – $300M) to acquire the Samsung HDTV brand.

Note that, compared with the case where marginal costs are positive, Samsung's valuation of the Sony brand name has been *reduced* from $600 million to $450 million. In contrast, Sony's valuation of the Samsung brand name has *increased* from $1.4 billion to $1.9 billion.

> **Fusion for Profit Maxim**
>
> The cost structures of both the acquiring and the acquired firms have a critical effect on brand valuations for acquisitions.

▶ *Firms sometimes use the concept of brand equity to value brands that they are planning to acquire. Is this a reasonable method?*

The firm that is planning an acquisition needs to exercise caution in how it values brands. We return to the HDTV example. To focus on essentials, suppose the Sony and Samsung HDTV sets contain the same combinations of features. However, let's say that behavioral studies have shown that consumers are willing to pay a higher price for the Samsung HDTV set (i.e., Samsung has brand equity).[12]

Using this definition of brand equity, one would conclude that Sony should pay a premium to acquire the Samsung HDTV brand. As our example shows, this is indeed the case. However, this definition of brand equity also implies that Samsung should not buy the Sony HDTV brand name because Sony does not have any brand equity in this market.

As discussed above, this is not the case. As we have shown, Samsung should also be willing to pay a premium to acquire the Sony HDTV brand name, *even though the Sony product does not have brand equity.*

Fusion for Profit Maxim

Brand valuation should be based on an analysis of the cost structures for both the acquiring and the acquired brands, the joint distribution of reservation prices for both brands, and an explicit analysis of competitive reactions. It may be optimal for a high-quality brand with high brand equity to pay a premium to buy a low-quality brand.

Point to consider.   How should a firm measure the value of a brand that it is planning to acquire?

So far, we have focused on the theoretical structure of the brand valuation problem. However, to empirically determine the dollar value of a brand, the manager needs to consider a number of additional factors, as discussed in the following sections.

Segmentation

Separate analyses may be necessary for different types of consumers (e.g., light or heavy users). This is straightforward provided *a priori segmentation* is possible. If a priori segmentation is not possible, one can use a choice-based methodology to infer consumers' reservation prices for the brands in question.[13] As the HDTV example illustrates, information about the joint distribution of reservation prices across brands can be combined with the cost data for the relevant brands to determine brand values for both the acquiring and the acquired firms.

Competition

For simplicity, the HDTV example assumed that the market consisted of only two brands: the acquiring and the acquired brands. In most practical applications, the market will include several competitors. Furthermore, these competitors are likely to react after one brand acquires another.

► *How will competitive reaction in a market with multiple brands affect the brand valuations of the acquiring and the acquired brands?*

To address this problem, it is necessary to estimate the joint reservation prices of the two brands in question *and* key competing brands. The brand valuation analysis should then be performed using the joint distribution of reservation prices for *all* these brands.

Example: Suppose there are three firms in the HDTV market, Samsung, Sony, and Toshiba, and that the current market prices are $700 per unit for Samsung, $600 for Sony, and $550 for Toshiba. Suppose Samsung is planning to purchase the Sony HDTV brand. Then, Samsung should first determine the joint reservation prices of consumers for all three brands. Using this information, Samsung can determine the value of the Sony HDTV brand by analyzing different scenarios.

Suppose Samsung is presently making a profit of $1 billion. Then, the most optimistic scenario for Samsung is the following. Samsung acquires the Sony HDTV brand, Toshiba keeps its price unchanged, and Samsung prices the Samsung and Sony HDTVs to maximize its product-line profits (profits from Samsung + profits from Sony).

Suppose Samsung's product-line profit for this scenario after the acquisition is $1.5 billion. Then, the maximum amount that Samsung should pay to acquire the Sony HDTV brand name is $500 million ($1.5B – $1B). Note that, since Toshiba does not react under this scenario, this value ($500M) is the upper bound on Samsung's valuation of the Sony HDTV brand.

In practice, Toshiba is likely to change its HDTV prices after Samsung acquires the Sony HDTV brand. Hence the gain to Samsung will be less than $500 million. In view of this, Samsung's management can proceed as follows. Suppose they expect Toshiba to cut its price to $500 per unit after Samsung acquires the Sony brand.

► *Given that Toshiba is likely to charge $500 per unit following Samsung's acquisition of the Sony brand, what prices should Samsung charge for the Samsung and Sony brands to maximize product-line performance?*

Samsung should coordinate the prices of the Samsung and Sony HDTV brands to maximize joint profits on the assumption that Toshiba will reduce its price to $500 per unit. Suppose Samsung's product-line profit for this scenario is $1.3 billion. Then, Samsung should value the Sony HDTV brand name at $300 million ($1.3B – $1B). More complicated competitive scenarios can be examined using the same approach.[14]

Fusion for Profit Maxim

Standard measures of brand equity can provide misleading estimates of brand value to both the acquiring and the acquired firm. A better approach for both firms is to estimate the dollar values of brand equity using a game-theoretic model that is based on information about consumers' reservation prices for different brands and cost data for those brands.

Point to consider. What name should a merged firm use if both the acquiring and the acquired firms have brand equity?

This is an interesting question. One strategy is to choose a branding strategy that leverages the brand equities of *both* firms.

Example: When Procter & Gamble (P&G) acquired Gillette in 2005, each company had significant brand equity. At the time, P&G's Crest was the world's number one toothpaste and Gillette's Oral-B was the world's number one toothbrush.

To leverage the brand equities of both firms, the acquiring firm (P&G) chose a "subbranding" strategy in 2007. Thus, P&G had previously added the phrase Pro-Health to the names of the new Crest mouthwash and toothpaste products it had recently introduced in the market. P&G now extended this subbranding strategy to the Oral-B product line (formerly owned by Gillette). Specifically, in order to leverage the brand equity of Oral-B in the toothbrush market, P&G introduced a new toothbrush that it had recently developed under the name Oral-B Pulsar Pro-Health.[15]

▶ 22.7 The Roles of Private Equity Firms and Hedge Funds

Private Equity Firms

Private equity firms are limited partnerships or limited liability companies whose goal is to acquire target companies using debt and funds committed by institutional investors (e.g., pension funds) and wealthy private investors. The theory is that, by acquiring the targeted firms, private equity firms can achieve superior financial results for their investors. The rationale for this conclusion includes the following arguments:

Efficiency. The current managements of target companies are inefficient. For example, the target companies may have excessively high cost structures, serve unprofitable market segments, produce the wrong product mix, or use incorrect discount rates to allocate resources across product lines.

Management Skills. Management skills are generic and not industry-specific. That is, regardless of which industry or industries the target company is in, the manager of the private equity firm (general partner) has superior management skills to the current management of the target company.

Speed of Decision Making. The general partner of a private equity firm can implement policy changes faster than managers of large corporations who are constrained by the bureaucratic and hierarchical structures of their organizations. This can be a critical advantage to private equity firms, especially if the target company is in an industry facing rapid changes in technology or demand.

Wall Street.   Private equity firms are limited partnerships; consequently, they are not required to publicly reveal information, including the returns on their investments. Hence they have more flexibility in choosing long-run strategy (e.g., they are not under pressure to meet Wall Street's quarterly profit expectations).

Regulation.   Since private equity firms are partnerships, they are less regulated than corporations that are owned by stockholders. Hence general partners have greater strategic flexibility than managers of corporations.

Incentive Plans.   The general partner's interests are coaligned with those of the other investors in the private equity firm. Specifically, the general partner is a coinvestor; in addition, the general partner's compensation includes a *performance-based fee* (i.e., a share in the excess profits that the private equity firm makes over a hurdle rate of return).

Investors' Horizons.   Private equity funds are heavily financed by such institutional investors as pension funds and endowments. Since these investors have long planning horizons, private equity firms can focus on long-run performance.

These arguments are not new. Hence the following question is moot: Why have private equity firms been particularly active in recent acquisitions?

The key factors are that debt has been relatively cheap in recent years; in addition, large pools of capital have been available for investment, especially from institutional investors. This combination has allowed private equity firms to increase their resources sharply by taking on substantial amounts of debt at low cost. Consequently, by increasing their *financial leverage*, private equity firms have been able to provide investors with the potential to earn very high returns. (The downside of this leverage-based strategy is that losses are amplified when investments perform badly.)

These potential gains have been magnified by the current tax structure. Specifically, because private equity firms are structured as limited partnerships, the performance-based fees (known as *carried interest*) paid to general partners are currently taxed at the lower capital gains rate (15%) rather than at the higher ordinary income tax rate (35%).[16]

Hedge Funds

Hedge funds are similar to private equity firms in that both types of legal entity are limited partnerships of institutional investors (e.g., pension funds) and wealthy private investors. In addition, both rely heavily on debt financing and participate actively in the corporate takeover market. However, there are two important differences.

Hedge funds can have multiple objectives. Consequently, they invest in a wide class of disparate assets with different risk-return combinations (e.g., stocks, options, and foreign currencies). In contrast, private equity firms have only one objective: to take over target companies. Additionally, investors in a hedge fund can enter or leave the fund easily. However, investors in a private equity firm are locked in for the entire term of the limited partnership (which can extend up to ten years).

As discussed above, in recent years the cost of debt has been low, and institutional investors have had significant pools of capital available for investment. Furthermore, the *performance fees* of hedge fund managers are also taxed in the same way as those paid to the general partners of private equity firms (see above). This combination of factors has encouraged hedge funds, like private equity firms, to be active in the takeover market. Specifically, many hedge funds have used financial leverage to acquire companies or to insist on management changes in companies where they take large stakes.

▶ **What is the likely effect of the acquisition activities of private equity firms and hedge funds?**

The acquisition activities of private equity firms and hedge funds are likely to have significant effects on investors and the economy.

Effect on Investors. In theory, the general partners of private equity firms and hedge fund managers should choose target companies and postacquisition strategies that maximize long-run returns for their investors. However, postacquisition strategies are likely to have asymmetric effects on costs and revenues.

The gains from immediate cost reductions are predictable. In contrast, the potential gains from revenue generation in the future are uncertain. Furthermore, because of the current tax code, general partners and hedge fund managers pay a low capital gains tax rate (15%) rather than a higher ordinary income tax rate (35%) on the performance fees (carried interest) that they are paid.

The net result is that the general partners of private equity firms and hedge fund managers have an incentive to choose postacquisition strategies that focus on predictable cost reductions via layoffs and spin-offs (e.g., selling unprofitable units or divisions of the acquired firm) rather than on generating uncertain future revenues by focusing on R & D, new product development, and *customer relationship management (CRM)*. Hence private equity firms and hedge funds may choose postacquisition strategies that focus on short-run rather than on long-run results.

Macroeconomic Effects. At the macroeconomic level, acquisitions by private equity firms and hedge funds could have a destabilizing effect on the economy. If there is a recession, high levels of debt financing by private equity firms and hedge funds will increase the probabilities that the acquired firms will become bankrupt. In addition, it may be necessary for these firms to sell off assets at distress prices in a recession in order to service debt. If these effects are sufficiently strong, the economy will become more unstable.

Fusion for Profit Maxim

Private equity firms and hedge funds use financial leverage to acquire companies. Given the current tax code and compensation structures, the general partners of private equity firms and the managers of hedge funds have an incentive to take large risks and focus on short-run results. These acquisition activities could lead to wider macroeconomic fluctuations.

▶ 22.8 International Mergers

Recently, the pace of international mergers has increased. This raises an interesting question: Are there any special issues to consider in evaluating international mergers?

When evaluating international mergers, several issues should be considered, including postmerger adjustment, asymmetric information, *differential tax rates*, corporate culture, and the appropriate *cost of capital*.

Postmerger Adjustment

Postmerger adjustment may be more difficult for international mergers because management styles/corporate cultures and organizational structures are likely to vary considerably across countries. Furthermore, these adjustments are likely to take more time than they would for domestic mergers. These postmerger adjustment problems are likely to be exacerbated if the merging firms come from countries where different languages are spoken.

Example: Suppose the acquiring firm is a highly centralized foreign firm, whereas the acquired firm is a decentralized U.S.-based firm. Then, it is very likely that after the merger the foreign firm will continue to use a centralized approach, impose its corporate culture on the U.S.-based firm, and change the performance and reward metrics accordingly. This could lead to *bad turnover*. For example, the most productive managers from the U.S.-based firm could leave after the merger.

Differential Tax Rates

Taxes are an important consideration in international mergers.

Example: Suppose a large U.S.-based pharmaceutical firm acquires an Indian firm that produces generics. After the merger, the Indian firm produces drugs that will be marketed in the United States by the U.S.-based parent. Then, the value added from this merger will depend critically on the *internal transfer price* for the drug (i.e., the price that the Indian subsidiary will charge the U.S.-based parent company) and on the appropriate corporate tax rates in India and the United States.

Asymmetric Information

As discussed previously, even in domestic mergers, it is difficult for acquiring firms to accurately estimate postmerger costs and benefits, especially when the acquired firm has multiple divisions or product lines. Furthermore, especially since there is no a priori guarantee that the merger will occur, the candidate firm to be acquired may be unwilling to provide detailed cost and revenue information to the acquiring firm (e.g., the market value of its current inventory or information about its current production processes and associated cost structures). This problem of asymmetric information is likely to be worse for international mergers.

Example: Consider the unsuccessful attempt in 2005 by the Chinese manufacturer Haier to acquire the U.S.-based manufacturer Whirlpool. Because of asymmetric information (Haier was a relative newcomer in the U.S. marketplace), Haier was at a comparative disadvantage to rival U.S.-based bidders for Whirlpool. Hence it is possible that Haier's bid was too high.

Corporate Culture

Firms in certain countries are culturally slow to make decisions. In addition, management may be excessively cautious and overly focused on solving immediate internal problems. Finally, these firms may not have specialized teams that deal with mergers and acquisitions. Because of this combination of circumstances, such firms will be at a relative disadvantage with respect to successfully completing international mergers.[17]

Cost of Capital

The international capital market is not perfect. Hence firms in different countries may be willing to pay different merger premiums to acquire the same target firm, *even if they have the same expectations about postmerger synergies and cash flows.*

Example: Suppose the U.S. stock market expects Shringar, a hypothetical U.S.-based cosmetic company, to make an average annual profit of $50 million. (For simplicity, assume that there is no market growth.) Suppose Shringar's implicit *risk-adjusted rate of return* to U.S. stockholders is 10% per annum. Then, the U.S. stock market will value Shringar at $500 million (Shringar's expected annual profits/Shringar's risk-adjusted rate of return = $50M/10%). Suppose all firms, including foreign firms, expect that no synergies will occur if they buy Shringar.

Now, suppose a large Chinese firm has excess dollar reserves or has limited investment opportunities in the Chinese market. Specifically, suppose the risk-adjusted rate of return for the Chinese firm is 8% percent per annum (< 10%). Then, even though the Chinese firm does not anticipate any postmerger synergies, it should be willing to pay up to $625 million (expected annual cash flows for Shringar/Chinese firm's risk-adjusted rate of return = $50M/8%) to purchase Shringar. Note that, purely because it has a lower cost of capital than U.S. firms, the Chinese firm should be willing to pay a premium of up to $125 million (25% higher than the current stock price of Shringar, $500 M) to purchase Shringar.

Point to consider.   Suppose the Chinese firm anticipates obtaining postmerger synergies by acquiring the U.S.-based cosmetic company. Should the Chinese firm use its cost of capital to determine the merger premium that it is willing to pay for the acquisition?

In all likelihood, the Chinese firm will have limited knowledge about cost and demand conditions for the U.S.-based cosmetic company (e.g., the channels of distribution and advertising strategy). Hence, the firm is likely to be highly uncertain about the magnitudes of the postmerger synergies from the acquisition.

These uncertainties are likely to be much higher than the demand and cost uncertainties that the Chinese firm faces in its local markets. Hence the Chinese firm should use a higher rate of return than its cost of capital (8% in the Shringar example) to value the target U.S.-based firm. Note that if the Chinese firm uses its cost of capital to determine the merger premium, it is likely to overbid to acquire the U.S.-based firm.

Fusion for Profit Maxim

International mergers pose special difficulties because of such factors as differential tax rates across countries, asymmetric information regarding economies of scope, and postmerger adjustment costs across countries.

Chapter 22 Key Points

- The fiduciary duty of managers is to increase the wealth of the owners of the firm. However, managers may use mergers and acquisitions to reduce their own financial risks rather than to increase the owners' wealth.
- Mergers can add value to the acquiring firm if they increase the firm's market power in the product market or in the supply chain, leverage economies of scope, or lead to other synergies.
- An acquisition strategy that focuses on the purchase of goodwill or intangible assets from the acquired firm may not increase shareholder value for the acquiring firm.
- When two major firms in a differentiated industry merge, the merged firm will increase its market power. Hence each firm should be willing to buy the other, regardless of whether its current profits are high or low or whether it is the market leader.

- In general, merging firms should use performance-based contracts to compensate their respective financial advisers.
- Mergers may not provide any gains to the acquiring firm because of the winner's curse, management's overoptimistic estimates of the gains from synergies, management's underestimates of postmerger coordination and adjustment costs, and biased estimates of consumers' reservation prices for individual products and bundles.
- The corporate-level gains from mergers are often small because the benefits from economies of scope occur in limited areas of the merged firm.
- A strategy that is based on focused acquisitions or strategic alliances may be superior to one that is based on mergers and acquisitions.
- Standard measures of brand equity can provide misleading estimates of brand value to both the acquiring and the acquired firm. A better approach for both firms is to estimate the dollar value of brand equity using a game-theoretic model that is based on information about consumers' reservation prices for different brands and cost data for those brands.
- Private equity firms and hedge funds use financial leverage to acquire companies. Given the current tax code and compensation structures, the general partners of private equity firms and the managers of hedge funds have an incentive to take large risks and focus on short-run results. These acquisition activities could lead to wider macroeconomic fluctuations.
- International mergers pose special difficulties because of such factors as differential tax rates across countries, asymmetric information regarding economies of scope and postmerger adjustment costs, cultural and language differences, and asymmetric costs of capital across countries.

23

How to Choose Optimal International Marketing Strategies

Many firms have international operations. Even firms that operate domestically are likely to purchase raw materials from abroad or to outsource some of their activities. These activities raise fundamental questions that go well beyond the purview of standard marketing theory. These include the impact of the firm's international activities on the *marketing-finance interface*, organizational structure, incentive plans, performance metrics, and coordination within the firm. This chapter addresses some of these issues.

The information covered in this chapter will be useful when you are faced with the following types of decisions:

- What are the major pitfalls in international marketing?
- Under what conditions are international marketing strategies likely to succeed?
- How should my multiproduct firm allocate resources across countries?
- When does *international diversification* add value to a publicly held firm?
- When does international diversification add value to a privately held firm?
- When should my firm use a standardized product design across countries, and when should my firm customize its products?

- What analytical methods should my firm use to determine an international product design strategy?
- What decisions should my firm delegate to its country managers?
- How should my firm compensate its country managers so that they focus on maximizing long-run performance for the parent company?
- When should my firm use a country-manager-based organizational structure?
- What currency should my firm use to compensate its country managers?
- How should my firm choose the optimal *outsourcing* strategy?
- When is it optimal for my firm to use a hybrid outsourcing strategy?
- What metrics should my firm use to measure the performance of an outsourcing center?
- How should my firm compensate the employees and the managers of outsourcing centers?
- What strategies should my firm use to increase the retention rate of key personnel at an outsourcing center?
- When should my firm diversify its outsourcing centers across countries?

The following terms will be introduced in this chapter (see glossary for definitions):

after-tax operating cash flow
asymmetric information
bad turnover
brand equity
bundling
cash flows
core competencies
cost center
cost of capital
cross-selling
customer loyalty
customer satisfaction
cyclicality
discount rate
economic concept of opportunity cost
economic cost
economies of scale
economies of scope
experience curve
group hedging policies

hurdle rates
hybrid organizational structure
infrastructural support
intellectual property
international diversification
latent class methodology
learning curve
linear profit-sharing contract
lumpy investment strategy
market development organizations (MDOs)
market segmentation
marketing-finance interface
me-too product
mixed bundling strategy

mixed outsourcing strategy
monopoly pricing
outsourcing
price skimming
product positioning
profit center
profit-sharing compensation plan
progressive profit-sharing plan
real options
required rate of return
reservation price
stock options
strategic flexibility
systematic component of cash flows
tax shield
time-additive utility
uptime probability
valuation
volatility

▲ 23.1 Is It Necessary to Develop a Separate Theory of International Marketing?

The firm's marketing policies should vary across countries based on such factors as international differences in consumer preferences, cost structures, distribution channels, and competition. However, as we will discuss, this does *not* imply that we need a separate theory of international marketing.

One fundamental difference between domestic and international operations is that the latter involve transactions in different currencies. This has important ramifications for the multinational firm in such areas as resource allocation, organizational structure, and performance metrics. We will address these policy implications later.

Fusion for Profit Maxim

In general, optimal marketing strategies will vary across countries. However, this does not imply that we need a separate theory of international marketing.

▲ 23.2 What Are the Major Pitfalls in International Marketing?

The major pitfalls in international marketing are twofold:

1. In many cases the management of a multinational firm simply transplants successful domestic strategies to foreign markets. These strategies may not succeed in foreign markets because consumer preferences, cost structures, distribution channels, and competition are radically different from those in the domestic market.
2. It is all too easy for the multinational firm to lose sight of the critical *economic concept of opportunity cost.*

Consider the following examples.

Pricing

It may be necessary for firms to use different pricing strategies across different countries.

Example: Prior to entering the Chinese market several years ago, many large mobile phone companies such as Nokia had successfully used a *price-skimming* strategy in Europe to maximize their long-run profits. That is, they introduced new models of mobile phones at high prices and systematically lowered these prices over time. These price-skimming strategies were successful because there was no danger from copycat products. Furthermore, mobile phone manufacturers could practice *monopoly pricing* because their *intellectual property* was well protected.

When the mobile phone companies attempted to use price-skimming in the Chinese market, this previously successful strategy failed because the necessary conditions for success did not hold: copycat products soon flooded the Chinese market, and intellectual property was not well protected.

Product Placement

The optimal placement for a product in a retail store can vary across countries.

Example: A large UK do-it-yourself chain, B&Q, displays its electrical products (sockets, cables, conduits, and switches) in its UK retail outlets by end use, not by brand. When B&Q used the same merchandising approach in its Chinese retail stores, sales were very low. The problem was that, in contrast to the United Kingdom, buyers of these products in China were tradesmen and not consumers. And, tradesmen were loyal to brands. Hence it was inappropriate to categorize electrical products by function. When B&Q realized this, it reorganized the display by brand, and sales went up immediately by 40% to 50%.[1]

Consumer Preferences

Expanding to a foreign country can be unsuccessful if the parent company does not adapt its strategy based on consumer preferences in that country.

Example 1: Wal-Mart, the giant multinational retailer, recently retreated from the German market and sold all its 85 stores in Germany to a local competitor, Metro. An important factor that contributed to the company's departure from the German market was that Wal-Mart had not paid sufficient attention to differences in consumer preferences in Germany and in the United States. Hence Wal-Mart did not choose the right product mix in Germany.

For example, German customers reacted negatively to the U.S. custom of having store employees bag customers' groceries because they did not want strangers handling their food.[2] Furthermore, due to lack of sufficient storage space at home, German consumers were less interested in making bulk purchases than American consumers.

Example 2: In the early 1990s the Campbell Soup Co. unsuccessfully attempted to enter the Chinese market by selling the standard condensed soups that it sold elsewhere. This strategy did not work in China because the soups were not tailored to local tastes and cooking customs.

Recently, Campbell has attempted to reenter the Chinese market using a country-specific strategy. Thus, Campbell has reformulated its soup products to better match the tastes of Chinese consumers (e.g., the broths sold in China are stronger than Campbell's standard soup products). In addition,

Campbell is adapting its marketing campaign to local conditions. For example, because mobile phones are so common in China, Campbell will send text messages reminding people to purchase its broth products.[3]

Competition

Firms sometimes behave as market leaders in countries where they are relatively small players. This strategy can lead to poor results. To illustrate, we continue with the Wal-Mart example.

Wal-Mart is the dominant player in many countries where it has retail operations. Hence, in general, Wal-Mart has been able to successfully apply its business model of low pricing in those countries by leveraging its enormous buying power to obtain major cost efficiencies via *economies of scale* and *economies of scope*.

In Germany, however, Wal-Mart was a relatively small player in the marketplace. Thus, a local competitor, Aldi, had 4,000 stores, whereas Wal-Mart had only 85. Since Wal-Mart's key local competitors such as Aldi had lower costs in logistics and advertising, they could successfully undercut Wal-Mart's prices. Consequently, Wal-Mart's business model of charging low prices did not succeed. Because of this strategic miscalculation, Wal-Mart was forced to leave the German market.[4]

Opportunity Cost

Standard proxies for profitability can be misleading indicators of performance.

Example: A large European manufacturer was satisfied that its sales in China were increasing at an impressive annual growth rate of 40%. However, the Chinese market for the product category in question was expanding at double this rate (80%). Thus, although the company's China operations were highly profitable, the company was actually doing extremely poorly vis-à-vis its competitors.[5]

Core Competencies

Firms sometimes assume that, when they go abroad, they should serve the same market segments that they have successfully targeted domestically. This market entry strategy can provide a major advantage: it allows the firm to leverage its *core competencies* and skills. However, it can easily lead to lost opportunities. And, these can be very expensive in the long run.

Example: Many multinational firms have focused exclusively on the premium segment of the Chinese market. As a result, they have concentrated heavily on large cities such as Beijing and Shanghai.

These policies could be flawed in the long run. For many products (e.g., fast-moving consumer goods such as shampoo and toothpaste), the medium- and low-end segments in China are very large; more important, they are growing rapidly. Furthermore, medium-sized cities (the so-called Tier 2 and Tier 3 cities) offer substantial profit opportunities.

Fusion for Profit Maxim

In general, multinational firms should not merely replicate successful domestic marketing strategies when they go abroad.

▶ 23.3 Under What Conditions Will International Marketing Strategies Succeed?

Firms should carefully analyze foreign markets and, where necessary, adapt their marketing policies to suit foreign market conditions. In some cases, it may even be desirable for the firm to radically change its product positioning strategy when it goes abroad. Consider the following examples.

Product Design

To succeed in international markets, the firm may have to adapt or change product designs that have been successful domestically.

Example 1: When the major international automobile manufacturers entered the Chinese market, many aimed at the premium segment. Contrary to this approach, General Motors developed a small, no-frills SUV that was priced low and targeted at the low- to middle-income segments. This SUV has been extremely successful in the Chinese market.

Example 2: Until recently, the small refrigerator market in the United States had been neglected by the major manufacturers. A Chinese firm, the Haier Group, recognized this gap in the U.S. market and developed a line of compact refrigerators that was designed to meet the tight space constraints of college students who lived in campus dormitories. Haier's U.S. market entry strategy has been extremely successful. In fact, Haier has now diversified its product line in the United States well beyond the small refrigerator market.

Product Positioning

A firm may gain by changing its product positioning strategy when it enters an international market.

Example: In the United States, Pizza Hut is regarded as a lower-end restaurant chain. However, when Pizza Hut entered the Chinese market, it chose a radically different product positioning strategy: Pizza Hut marketed itself as a premium restaurant chain and priced its products accordingly. This strategy has been highly successful in China.

> **Fusion for Profit Maxim**
>
> International markets can be radically different from the domestic market. In some cases, it may be necessary for the firm to choose a radically different product design and/or product positioning strategy when it enters a foreign market.

▶ 23.4 How Should the Multinational Firm Allocate Resources across Countries?

A key issue is what rate of return the firm needs to make by investing in a particular country.

▶ *Should the multinational firm use its* cost of capital *to determine the value of international marketing opportunities?*

At first glance, the firm's cost of capital is an appealing metric for assessing international marketing opportunities because it is an objective company-wide benchmark *discount rate*. However, by using this criterion, the firm is likely to choose poor marketing strategies—regardless of whether the firm is purely domestic or has multinational operations.

Example 1: Suppose Toyota needs to decide how to allocate marketing resources internationally for its Lexus division. Then, the *cash flows* that the Lexus operation in any given country generates will be affected by at least three sources of risk in that country: competition, *cyclicality*, and such factors as unanticipated changes in regulatory conditions or in interest rates.

Since these conditions are likely to vary across countries, Toyota should use country-specific *hurdle rates* for allocating resources to its international Lexus operations and not Toyota's cost of capital.

For instance, suppose regulatory conditions are less predictable in the United States than in China. Then, other factors being equal, Toyota should use a higher hurdle rate for its Lexus operations in the United States than for the corresponding operations in China. If Toyota uses the same *required rate of return* (e.g., its *cost of capital*) for both Lexus operations, the Lexus unit in China will subsidize the Lexus unit in the United States. Hence Toyota will overinvest in its Lexus operations in the United States. Correspondingly, Toyota will underinvest in its Lexus operations in China.

Another problem with using the firm's cost of capital is that most firms produce multiple products. Furthermore, each product involves a different degree of risk. This implies that the required rate of return should vary across products within any given country. It also implies that, in general, the multinational firm should use different discount rates across countries—*even for the same product.*

Example 2: Suppose Procter & Gamble (P&G) has been selling a particular line of shampoo products in the United States for several years. In particular, suppose that in the U.S. market the demand for this product line is fairly stable compared with the demands for other product lines sold by P&G. Suppose P&G's cost of capital for its U.S. operations is 10% per annum. Then, P&G's discount rate for the shampoo product line in the United States should be lower than P&G's cost of capital. Let's say that the appropriate discount rate for P&G's shampoo line in the United States is 8% per annum (< 10% per annum).

Now, suppose P&G is planning to introduce this established line of shampoo products into a rapidly growing foreign market with high demand uncertainty, say China. Then, the appropriate discount rate is likely to be higher than 8% per annum. Indeed, given the magnitude of the demand uncertainty in the China market, the appropriate discount rate for the shampoo product line in China *could even be higher* than P&G's cost of capital.

Fusion for Profit Maxim

The firm's cost of capital is a poor metric for allocating resources internationally. If the firm uses this metric, its investments in low-risk markets will subsidize those in high-risk markets.

▶ *Suppose the multinational firm is comparing two new product opportunities, one domestic and the other international. What additional difficulties, if any, will the firm face in valuing international marketing opportunities?*

International marketing involves additional risks such as political risk and the risk of having intellectual property stolen. These risks will increase the appropriate discount rate for the international marketing opportunity in question.

Fusion for Profit Maxim

Foreign investments often entail additional types of country-specific risk that the firm does not face in its domestic market. Hence the multinational firm's required rate of return should vary from country to country.

▶ *Does international diversification increase shareholder value?*

The effect of international diversification depends on the ownership structure of the firm and on the firm's international marketing strategies.

Publicly Owned Firms

We begin with the case of a publicly owned firm that has purely domestic operations.

▲ *Is the firm an efficient mechanism for helping its shareholders reduce risk by diversifying?*

The firm's shareholders are free to choose their own portfolios, including owning foreign stocks. Hence, if the firm diversifies internationally, unless the firm introduces new market opportunities (discussed shortly), shareholders will not be able to reduce their risk.

▲ *What will happen if the publicly owned firm diversifies internationally?*

The effect on shareholder value will depend on the firm's international marketing strategy.

Example 1: Suppose a U.S.-based firm (say, American Standard) uses a "me-too" strategy and sets up manufacturing operations in a foreign market, say France. That is, American Standard sets up a plant in France to manufacture and sell products that are similar to those already available in the French market.

Now, prior to American Standard's entry into the French market, its shareholders already have the opportunity to diversify internationally by buying any shares they want—including American Standard shares and those of competing French firms. Since American Standard's *me-too product* is similar to those that are already available in the French market, the uncertainty in the cash flows it generates will be similar to the corresponding uncertainties for those competing products in the French market. Consequently, this market entry strategy in France will not help American Standard's shareholders reduce their risk.

▲ *What does this imply for American Standard's shareholders?*

Since the product is a me-too product, American Standard's shareholders will gain if and only if the expected returns from American Standard's French operations are *higher* than the corresponding expected returns from existing French firms (e.g., if American Standard can produce its products more efficiently in France than competing indigenous firms in the French market).

> **Fusion for Profit Maxim**
> Other factors being the same, a publicly owned multinational firm will not gain from international diversification if it uses a me-too market entry strategy.

Example 2: In contrast, consider a U.S.-based automobile firm (e.g., Ford) that enters a foreign market (say, India) using a marketing strategy that is differentiated from those of its competitors in that market. Now, by entering the Indian market, Ford will provide investors with a new market opportunity that did not exist before. Hence this market entry strategy can affect both the expected return and the risk to shareholders who own Ford stock.

◤ How will Ford's India strategy affect its share value?

By entering the India market with a differentiated strategy, Ford will change the set of investment opportunities available to investors. Consequently, investors will rebalance their portfolios, and stock prices will change accordingly. Specifically, Ford's stock price will increase *if and only if* the gain from the increase in Ford's expected returns by entering the Indian market outweighs the impact of the change in risk after investors have adjusted their portfolios.

To illustrate, suppose investors expect Ford's India strategy to produce the same average return as its current operations. Now, different scenarios are possible depending on the particular marketing strategy and segmentation policy that Ford has chosen in India.

For example, suppose Ford plans to produce and sell luxury cars in the Indian market. If the demand in this sector is highly cyclical, Ford's risk could increase. Consequently, since Ford's average return is unchanged (by assumption), Ford's stock price will fall.

In contrast, suppose Ford plans to produce cars aimed at the Indian middle class. Then, if the demand in this segment is less cyclical, Ford's risk could decrease. Consequently, since Ford's average return is unchanged (by assumption), Ford's stock price will increase.

Fusion for Profit Maxim

A publicly owned multinational firm may gain or lose from international diversification, depending on how its marketing strategy affects the firm's incremental risk and return.

Privately Owned Firms

If the firm is privately owned, international diversification will affect *both* the firm's expected return and its risk, *regardless of the market entry strategy that the firm chooses*. To see why this is the case, consider the simplest case where the privately owned firm uses a me-too international marketing strategy.

In the American Standard example above, suppose the firm is privately held by a U.S.-based owner (say, Sam Smith). What will happen if Sam Smith uses a me-too strategy to enter the French market?

Sam Smith's uncertain cash flow from setting up a French operation is the sum of three effects:

1. The expected cash flow generated,
2. A systematic component (which is uncertain and can be positive or negative), and
3. A random component (which is also uncertain and can be positive or negative).

As discussed below, each of these three components will have a separate effect on *valuation* for Sam Smith.

Stockholders of publicly traded firms in France are only fractional owners of those firms. However, Sam Smith is the 100% owner of his French operation. This concentration of ownership has a critical effect on valuation.

Sam Smith has chosen a *lumpy investment strategy* (100% ownership of the French operation) that precludes him from diversifying across French firms. Consequently, in contrast to investors who own shares in French firms, he cannot eliminate the random component of the cash flows generated by his French operation.

Furthermore, because of his 100% ownership strategy, Sam Smith cannot reduce the effect of the *systematic component of the cash flows* generated from his French operations by diversifying across firms in France or elsewhere. Hence, regardless of whether Sam Smith chooses a me-too international marketing strategy, international diversification will *always* affect *both* the expected return and the risk of his portfolio.

Fusion for Profit Maxim

In general, international diversification will have an effect on the value of a privately held firm, regardless of whether the firm uses a me-too market entry strategy.

23.5 Should the Multinational Firm Change Its Product Design across Countries?

The answer to this question depends on the cost and demand structures for the products in question.

Standardized Product Design

On the demand side, suppose the distributions of *reservation prices* (i.e., consumers' willingness to pay) for products with a given set of design features are very similar across countries. On the cost side, suppose there are economies of scale or the firm has a steep *experience curve*. (The experience curve pertains to any aspect of cost including advertising, and not just to cost efficiencies in manufacturing.)

Then, other factors being equal, the firm should choose the same standardized product design across countries.

Country-Specific Product Design

Suppose the distribution of reservation prices for products with a given set of design features varies significantly across countries. In addition, the firm uses a flexible modular design process to manufacture its products. Hence there are no economies of scope in production; nor does the firm benefit from economies of scale or an experience curve.

Then, other factors being equal, the firm should choose different product designs for different countries.

Fusion for Profit Maxim

The firm should choose a standardized or a country-specific product design strategy depending on the structure of consumers' reservation prices across countries and cost conditions for products of different qualities. Hence the optimal product design strategy will vary across countries and industries.

▶ *What methodology should multinational firms use to determine the product designs to offer in a given country?*

The first step for the multinational firm is to estimate how consumers' reservation prices vary with different product qualities (i.e., combinations of product attributes).[6] For this step to provide managerially useful results and to make optimal decisions, the firm should pay special attention to *market segmentation*. (See chapter 8 for a discussion of how to measure reservation prices.)

In many cases, especially for a planned entry into a new foreign market, the market segments and buying behavior patterns are likely to be very different from those in the domestic market. In such cases, the firm's prior knowledge of market segmentation from the domestic market could be highly misleading in the foreign market. Hence it may be necessary to use post hoc (*latent class*) segmentation methods that allow the firm to identify these (unobservable) segments.[7]

Once the demand structure has been estimated, the firm can combine these data with cost information to determine the optimal number of product variations to offer and what product features to incorporate in each. If the firm offers several product variants, it will be necessary to quantitatively measure how product design changes affect total costs. In particular, the firm will need to determine the gains from economies of scale for a given product design and economies of scope.

From an organizational viewpoint, optimal results can be obtained only if the firm's marketing, engineering, and production personnel work closely together as a team. The coordination task will be made more difficult if the groups are situated in different countries.

Fusion for Profit Maxim

The firm should quantify the links among product design and consumers' reservation prices in different countries, paying particular attention to market segmentation. This segment-specific information can be combined with cost data to determine the number of product designs to offer in a given country.

▶ 23.6 What Is the Role of Country Managers and How Should the Parent Company Measure and Reward Them?

Many multinational firms use country managers to manage their operations abroad. Hence the multinational firm faces two fundamental problems:

1. How much decision-making power should the parent company delegate to a country manager?
2. How should the parent company measure and reward the performance of its country managers?

We discuss these issues below.

▶ To what extent, if any, should the parent company delegate decision-making authority to its country managers?

The parent company's decision to delegate or to partially delegate decision-making authority to its country managers depends on a number of factors. These include country-specific cost and demand conditions (e.g., wages and consumer tastes differ across countries), competitive market structures (e.g., the firm may have a monopoly in one market but not in others), and whether the firm produces one or multiple product lines.

Firms with One Product Line

Suppose the firm produces one product line only, and any of the following cost conditions holds. For any given product design, there are significant economies of scale, or the *learning curve* is steep. (These cost advantages can occur in a number of areas, including manufacturing, advertising, or information management.) On the demand side, suppose consumer preferences and incomes are similar across countries.

Under these conditions, the optimal policy for the firm is to pursue a similar strategy across countries. Hence, it is unnecessary for the parent company to delegate decision-making authority to country managers.

Firms with Multiple Product Lines

Suppose the firm produces multiple product lines, and economies of scope are significant. For example, the multiproduct firm has a cost advantage over firms that specialize in particular products. Similarly, on the demand side, suppose that the multiproduct firm has an advantage over its more specialized competitors. For instance, the firm can use *bundling* strategies to increase profits. In addition, suppose the reservation prices for the firm's products (including bundles) are similar across countries.

Given these cost and demand scenarios, the parent company could gain by using a globalization strategy. In this case, the head office should determine the mix of products and product designs to be offered internationally. In addition, the head office should choose the common marketing policies to be followed across countries. Consequently, it is unnecessary for the parent company to delegate decision-making authority to the country managers.

In general, however, these limiting market conditions are unlikely to hold simultaneously. Hence the multinational firm may need to partially delegate decision-making authority to country managers. Following are some factors to consider.

Income Differences

Even if consumers in different countries have similar preferences for a given product design, they are likely to respond differently to prices because their incomes differ. Thus, it may be necessary for the firm to use country-specific pricing policies for any given product design.

To illustrate, suppose a U.S.-based pharmaceutical company sells a patented drug domestically and internationally. Then, the company should charge a lower price for the patented drug in a developing country (e.g., Indonesia) than the price it charges in a developed country (e.g., Germany).

Differences in Demand Structure

On the demand side, for many products (e.g., cough drops) consumers' preferences (in this case, taste) are likely to vary considerably across countries. In addition, consumers in different countries may react differently to a given advertising message strategy. Hence it may be necessary for the firm to use different product designs and advertising policies across countries.

Cost Conditions

Cost conditions are likely to vary across countries and even within a given country.

Example: Consider a soft drink manufacturer such as Coca-Cola. For logistical reasons, it is desirable for Coca-Cola to set up manufacturing plants close to the demand centers that it serves. Since cost conditions vary across countries, other factors being equal, Coca-Cola should use a country-specific pricing policy.

Indeed, since cost conditions vary even within a country (e.g., China), Coca-Cola should charge different prices for the same product (e.g., Coke) in different cities and towns in China, depending on the manufacturing, transport, and channel costs in those markets.

Competition

Competitive conditions vary across countries. For instance, the parent company may be a market leader at home but a late entrant in a particular foreign market. Hence it may be necessary for the firm to use different marketing policies domestically and abroad, even if the product design is common for both domestic and foreign markets.

Asymmetric Information

Local managers may have superior knowledge about cost and demand conditions in their countries. Hence it may be necessary for the parent company to leverage this knowledge and adapt its marketing policies accordingly.

Example 1: Google, the world's largest Internet search engine, is presently only the second-largest Internet search engine in China. To achieve its goal of becoming the market leader in China, Google recently announced that it was planning to give its China operations greater autonomy.[8]

Example 2: News Corp. is planning to use an even more radical market entry mode than Google to enter the Chinese market. Specifically, News Corp.'s affiliate in China, MySpace China, will be run by a Chinese company that is controlled by local management who will have the "sole right to decide on the operating model, the technology platform, as well as the product strategy [for MySpace China]."[9]

In summary, full-scale globalization strategies are rarely optimal. In general, the parent company should partially delegate decision-making authority to country managers.

> **Fusion for Profit Maxim**
>
> The decision to use a full-scale globalization strategy or to partially delegate decision-making authority to country managers depends on country-specific cost and demand conditions, on competitive market structures, and on whether the firm produces one product line or multiple product lines.

► *How should the multinational firm compensate its country managers?*

As discussed, in most cases the parent company should partially delegate decision-making power to country managers. This implies that country managers should be paid according to a *profit-sharing compensation plan*. (See chapters 15 through 17 for a discussion of optimal risk-sharing contracts.)

► *What type of profit-sharing plan should the parent company use to compensate its country managers to encourage them to maximize long-run performance?*

One approach is to include *stock options* in the country manager's compensation plan. However, this method will not provide the optimal incentives because the value of the stock options is based on the performance of the *entire* company, and not on that of the country manager alone.

Example: Consider the country manager of Citibank's operations in Singapore. Since Singapore constitutes only a small part of Citibank's global operations, superior performance by the Singapore country manager will have a small effect on Citibank's stock price. Hence the stock option plan will not provide the right incentives to Citibank's country manager for Singapore.

In such cases, a better approach for the parent company may be to tie the country manager's compensation plan to the long-run performance of the company's operations in that country.

> **Fusion for Profit Maxim**
>
> In general, the parent company should pay country managers based on country-specific metrics of performance and not on measures of the overall performance of the parent company.

► *How can the parent company provide an incentive to a country manager to focus on long-run performance?*

We continue with the Citibank example. In 1989 Citibank planned to launch its credit cards in a number of countries in the Asia-Pacific region.

The parent company strongly supported this policy, even though it would lead to huge short-run losses. The parent company's logic was as follows. Once customers in the Asia-Pacific region began using Citibank's credit card service, they would purchase additional financial services from Citibank in the future. And, this *cross selling* would generate significant long-run profits for Citibank.

A critical problem, however, was the high cost ($35 million per year) of the *infrastructural support* needed for the new product launch (e.g., the cost of computer systems, software development, and customer support). Predictably, the country managers in the Asia-Pacific region did not support this strategy because it would reduce their short-run profits.[10]

▶ **What performance metrics and reward structure could the parent company have used to win the support of country managers?**

One approach for the parent company would have been to use the following performance metrics and reward structure.

User Fee Structure

The parent company could have subsidized country managers by absorbing the fixed cost of the infrastructural support ($35 million per year) and charging them user fees based on the intensity with which they used these infrastructural services.

For example, the parent company could have charged country managers a fee each time they used these services. These charges could have been adjusted based on such metrics as the time required to process each transaction in the centralized computer system, the computer space used, and so on. Note that, because of the subsidized user fee structure, each country manager would have been able to generate positive short-run profits rather than losses.

Fusion for Profit Maxim

The parent company may need to subsidize country managers when it launches a new product internationally, especially when the investment in centralized infrastructure is high.

Partial Delegation

The parent company could have partially delegated decision-making authority to country managers. Thus, the parent company could have negotiated the advertising budget for each country with the appropriate country manager and delegated pricing authority—within limits—to that individual.

For example, consistent with the strategic positioning chosen by the parent company (i.e., to position its credit card as a premium product), the parent company could have allowed country managers some latitude in setting the annual and transaction-based fees that credit card customers would pay in their countries.

Profit-Sharing Plan

As discussed in chapter 16, the firm should use a profit-sharing plan to compensate an employee whenever it delegates decision-making to that employee. Hence, in order to implement the partial delegation strategy, the parent company should have set up a profit-sharing plan for the country manager.

Note that, in general, country managers are likely to have better information about local market conditions than headquarters. Furthermore, the country manager's effort is likely to be unobservable to corporate managers. To address this incentive problem, the parent company should have paid its country managers according to a *progressive profit-sharing plan* in which the profit-sharing rate increases with profits. (For a detailed discussion of non-linear compensation contracts, see chapter 16.)

Multiperiod Effects

The parent company's strategy was to first sell credit cards to customers in any given country and then cross-sell new financial services to them in the future. Hence for any country, the strategy chosen in the introductory period was likely to have had a major effect on future profits in that country. We now discuss the impact of such multiperiod effects on the compensation plans for country managers.

Point to consider.   Suppose the parent company plans to discontinue its credit card operations in a given country if the first-period profits from these operations are not sufficiently high. How should the parent company modify the compensation plans for country managers?

We continue with the Citibank example. Consider a two-period model for any country (e.g., Australia). For simplicity, assume that the parent company chooses the strategy for its subsidiary. The analysis can be extended to the case where the parent company delegates some decision-making authority to the country manager.

Suppose the demand for the bank's credit cards in Australia is uncertain. Specifically, two demand conditions are possible: high and low. Each has a probability of 50%. If the demand in the first period is low, the Australian subsidiary will make a profit of $4 million. Correspondingly, if the demand in the first period is high, the Australian subsidiary will make a profit of $12 million. Hence the average gross profit generated by the Australian operation in the first period is $8 million ([$4M × 50%] + [$12M × 50%]).

Suppose the demand uncertainty for credit cards in Australia will be resolved at the end of the first period. That is, the parent company will know for sure whether the demand for credit cards in Australia is low or high. If the demand is low, the parent company will discontinue its credit card operations in Australia at the end of the first period. Hence the cash flow from credit card operations in the second period will be zero. If the demand is high, the parent company will expand its credit card operations in Australia.

Given this scenario, the second-period compensation plan for the country manager should depend on the parent company's strategy if it continues its credit card operations in Australia in the second period. Suppose the parent company's second-period strategy in Australia will focus heavily on acquiring new credit card customers. (This assumes that demand in the first period is high.)

Because *cross-selling* to credit card customers from the first period is highly profitable, the expected profits in the second period from this segment will increase. However, because this second-period strategy is aggressive, the aggregate profits from credit card operations in the second period could be more uncertain than those in the first. Assume that this is the case. Other scenarios can be examined similarly.

For simplicity, assume that the parent company uses a *linear profit-sharing contract* to compensate the country manager for Australia; furthermore, the profit-sharing rate is constant over time.[11] In addition, suppose that, even if the parent company discontinues its credit card operations in Australia in the second period, it will continue to employ the country manager for Australia elsewhere.

Let's say that the optimal first-period contract for the parent company is to pay the country manager in Australia a base salary of $300,000 plus 2% of gross profits in Australia in that period. Then, the country manager in Australia will obtain an expected income of $460,000 in the first period ($300,000 + 2% of $8M). Note that, since profits are uncertain, the country manager's income for the first period will fluctuate around this expected value ($460,000).

▲ *How should the parent company compensate the country manager in the second period? Assume that the country manager's reservation income is the same in both periods.*

Let's say that demand in the first period is high. Given this outcome, the parent company plans to pursue an aggressive expansion strategy in Australia. Suppose the second-period strategy will focus heavily on acquiring new credit card customers. Let's say that this strategy will provide an average second-period profit of $18 million (> $12M). However, because this second-period strategy is aggressive, the *volatility* of profits from credit card operations (including profits from cross-selling) will increase.

By assumption, the profit-sharing rate in the second period is the same as that in the first period (2%). Hence the country manager's expected income from profit sharing in the second period will be $360,000 (2% of $18M). Furthermore, the country manager's reservation income is the same in the first and second periods. Consequently, since the second-period cash flows are more uncertain than those in the first, the country manager's expected income (base salary plus 2% of profits) in the second period must be *greater* than the corresponding expected income in the first period ($460,000). Since the manager's expected income from profit sharing in the second period is $360,000, this implies that his or her base salary in the second period must be *at least* $100,000 ($460,000 − $360,000).

Note that, if the second-period strategy is sufficiently aggressive, the variability in second-period profits could be considerably higher than the corresponding variability of profits in the first period. If this is the case, the country manager's expected income in the second period will be considerably higher than his or her expected income in the first period ($460,000). Hence it may be necessary for the parent company to *increase* the country manager's base salary in the second period.

Fusion for Profit Maxim

If the parent company changes its strategy over time, it should adjust the country manager's compensation plan periodically. These adjustments are necessary so that the parent company can choose an optimal risk-sharing contract for compensating the country manager.

▶ 23.7 What Organizational Structure Should the Multinational Firm Use?

Because of the radical and ongoing changes in technology worldwide, geographical barriers have become much less important than before. For example, information can be transmitted across countries rapidly and at low cost. We now discuss the organizational implications for the multinational firm.

▶ Will the traditional country-manager-based or geography-based organizational structures become obsolete?

Traditionally, many multinational firms have used some variant of the following *hybrid organizational structure*. Domestic operations were organized along product lines, while international operations were organized geographically, based on regions or countries.

Recently, a number of major multinational firms such as General Motors and Procter & Gamble (P&G) have eliminated this traditional hybrid organizational structure and reorganized all their operations, whether domestic or international, along product lines.

For General Motors, the primary anticipated gains from changing to a product-based global organizational structure have been those from obtaining greater efficiencies via economies of scale in product design and sourcing raw materials, leveraging the learning curve more fully, harnessing economies of scope in production, achieving more efficient distribution, and reducing coordination costs across countries.

For P&G the motivation to shift to a product-based global organizational structure was different. Thus, P&G concluded that its traditional geography-based (country-based) organizational structure had led to two major problems in the past:

1. The speed with which P&G had introduced new products worldwide had slowed down considerably. Consequently, global performance had been reduced and profitable opportunities missed.
2. The traditional geography-based organizational structure had negatively affected P&G's profits because it had reduced P&G's ability to negotiate optimal worldwide contracts with large multinational retailers such as Wal-Mart that operated in many countries where P &G was present.

◣ *In view of the changes in the world market, should all firms restructure their international operations along product lines and eliminate geography- or country-based organizational structures?*

The answer to this question depends on whether the firm has a single product line or multiple product lines. Suppose any of the following market conditions holds for the firm with a single product line:

- Consumers' preferences vary considerably across countries,
- The benefits from economies of scale are not significant,
- The optimal channel and advertising policies vary from country to country,
- Competition varies significantly across countries (e.g., the firm is a pioneer in one country and a late entrant in another), and
- Centralized manufacturing and other operations lead to significant transport and coordination costs across countries.

Alternatively, suppose one or more of the following conditions holds for the multiproduct firm:

- The product line is narrow, and
- Economies of scope are country-specific (e.g., the optimal bundling policy for a group of products varies geographically).

Then, a traditional country-manager-based or geography-based organizational structure may be superior to one where all global operations are organized along product lines.

Note that multinational firms should not view the choices among product-based and region-based organizational structures as if they are mutually exclusive. A hybrid organizational structure may provide superior results.

Example: Procter & Gamble is sensitive to the need to adapt its marketing plans for any given product group to geography-based and country-specific market conditions, including differences in consumer behavior, channel structures, sourcing, and competition.

Thus, when Procter & Gamble reorganized its worldwide operations around product groups, it also set up *market development organizations* (MDOs) at both the regional and country levels to provide key region- and country-specific information to the global product-based units and to collaborate with those units to develop customized marketing plans on a geographical or country-specific basis.

Note that merely changing the organizational structure of the multinational firm is no guarantee of superior performance.

Fusion for Profit Maxim

In general, multinational firms should develop hybrid organizational structures that are both country-based and product-based. The optimal organization structure will depend on a number of factors, including economies of scope, transport costs, and differences in consumer preferences across countries for particular product designs.

▶ **Which currency should the multinational firm use to compensate country managers?**

This is a complex and controversial issue. In general, the answer depends on a number of factors, including whether or not the parent firm sets up independent foreign subsidiaries, whether the parent firm delegates both financial and marketing decision-making authority to country managers, and whether or not the parent firm coordinates *group hedging policies* on an international basis.[12]

One administratively simple and efficient method is to compensate the country manager in local currency. Specifically, the country manager can be paid using a four-part compensation formula that consists of:

1. A base wage,
2. A share of the net present value of the *after-tax operating cash flow* generated by the foreign country (A),
3. A share of the net present value of the *tax shield* provided by debt raised in the foreign country (B), and

4. A share of the value of the subsidiary's *real options* in the foreign country.[13]

In general, the multinational firm will need to customize these compensation plans. Specifically, because market conditions (including risk and the values of real options) vary across countries, the proportions of a country manager's incomes from each of the four parts in the compensation formula should vary across countries.

Fusion for Profit Maxim

Multinational firms can use a variety of methods to compensate country managers, depending on which functions (including financing) the parent company delegates to the country manager. One administratively simple and efficient method is to pay each country manager in local currency based on a customized, four-part compensation formula that varies from country to country.

▲ 23.8 How Should the Firm Choose and Implement the Optimal Outsourcing Strategy?

In recent years, many firms have increased the degree to which they use outsourcing. The primary motivation for most firms has been to reduce costs by employing lower-paid foreign workers. However, some firms such as Dell and Gateway have begun to shift the focus from cost reduction to such business functions as product development and design.[14]

▲ Should outsourcing strategies vary across industries?

Consider the following examples.

Example 1: Suppose Citibank is risk-neutral and can achieve daily savings of $8,000 by outsourcing its IT operations to a foreign country (say, India). Let's say that if Citibank chooses this strategy, the probability of a breakdown in IT services during any given day will increase by 0.1%. Suppose the *economic cost* (direct cost + hidden cost) of such an IT breakdown is $10 million.

Then, if Citibank outsources its IT operations to India, the gain that will accrue to Citibank from cost savings ($8,000 per day) will be lower than the increase in expected costs because of a higher probability of breakdowns (0.1% × $10 M = $10,000 per day). Hence Citibank should not outsource.

Example 2: Suppose General Electric is risk-neutral and is also planning to outsource its customer service function for major appliances sold in the United States to a foreign country. Suppose the foreign outsourcing center will reduce General Electric's operating costs but will provide a lower level of customer service than the corresponding domestic unit in the United States.

Now, in contrast to the Citibank example, a "breakdown" (i.e., a failure to provide a high level of customer service) will not have a catastrophic impact on General Electric's future performance. Consequently, it is possible that the gain to General Electric because of the expected cost savings from outsourcing will outweigh the increase in expected costs (including hidden costs) it will incur because of a reduced level of customer service. Hence General Electric should outsource its customer service function.

Fusion for Profit Maxim

Hidden costs can vary considerably across industries. Hence it may be optimal for firms in different industries to use different outsourcing strategies even if they incur the same outsourcing costs and obtain the same accounting gains from outsourcing.

▶ Should firms focus on cost minimization when they make outsourcing decisions?

Cost minimization via outsourcing may not lead to optimal long-run results, especially if this policy conflicts with the firm's product differentiation strategy.

Example: Recently, Dell attempted to reduce its outsourcing costs by trimming the level of customer service provided by its call centers abroad. Following Dell's change in customer-service policy, *customer satisfaction* fell sharply.

When management realized that this cost-cutting strategy was inconsistent with Dell's product differentiation strategy based on providing excellent customer service, it hired 2,000 new sales and support staff and retrained 5,000 others.[15]

Fusion for Profit Maxim

Depending on the firm's product differentiation strategy, it may be inappropriate for the firm to make outsourcing decisions based on cost minimization.

▶ To what extent should the firm outsource?

The firm should not view outsourcing as an all-or-nothing decision.

Example: Suppose a large computer manufacturer such as Hewlett-Packard sells two server models: a low-priced, entry-level model, and a high-priced, sophisticated model. Then, Hewlett-Packard should choose a segment-specific customer service strategy.

Specifically, Hewlett-Packard should use outsourcing to provide a standardized level of customer service for its low-end server model. In contrast, Hewlett-Packard should use skilled domestic personnel to provide customized service for its high-end server model.

The reason is that customers' informational and service needs for the low-end server segment are likely to be fairly similar. However, high-end users are likely to have greater and more varied information and service needs, depending on the complexities and ranges of their server applications. Consequently, Hewlett-Packard should use a *mixed outsourcing strategy*.

Fusion for Profit Maxim

Depending on the firm's market segmentation strategy, it may be optimal for the firm to use a mixed outsourcing strategy

---

▶ What metrics should the firm use to measure the performance of an outsourcing center?

When the firm outsources, it should choose performance metrics that lead to and reward behavior that maximizes long-run performance.

Example 1: Suppose a company in the service sector (e.g., AT&T) measures the efficiency of a call center operator using the following statistic: the number of customers served per hour. This metric is likely to lead to dysfunctional behavior and poor long-run performance.

Consider two call center operators, Betty and Joe, who work in the same AT&T call center abroad. Suppose that, on average, Betty processes 100 customer calls during an eight-hour shift. Of these, 5 are not successfully resolved. On average, Joe processes 120 customer calls during an eight-hour shift. Of these, 40 are not successfully resolved.

Since Joe processes more customer calls per hour than Betty, AT&T will erroneously conclude that Joe is more efficient. However, the fact is that, for any given time period, the customer dissatisfaction level for Joe is much higher than it is for Betty.

▶ What will happen in the long run?

AT&T will hire and reward a large number of Joe-types and retrench Betty-types. The result will be a high level of customer dissatisfaction, low repeat purchase rates, and a reduction in AT&T's long-run profits.

To address this problem, AT&T should measure the productivity of its call center operators by using at least two measures: the number of customers served in a given time period, and the type of outcome (e.g., whether or not the problem was resolved).

These measures can be refined using additional metrics that are more closely related to long-run performance. For instance, AT&T can conduct surveys to gauge customers' satisfaction with its call center operators. In addition, AT&T can adjust the outcome data to reflect the value of a given customer. For example, the data can be adjusted on the basis of *customer loyalty* or the revenue generated by that customer in the past.[16]

Example 2: Suppose a firm (say, Microsoft) has outsourced its data-processing functions abroad. In particular, suppose Microsoft requires the manager of its offshore center to keep its data-processing system running with a very low probability of a breakdown (i.e., a very high *uptime probability*).

Assume that Microsoft is risk-neutral and specifies a minimum uptime probability of 99.98% (i.e., a maximum breakdown probability of 0.02%) for the data-processing system. In addition, the expected economic cost of downtime is $3 million.

Suppose that by reorganizing its operations, the offshore center can reduce Microsoft's outsourcing costs by $400 per day. However, to achieve this cost reduction, the probability of system breakdown will increase by 0.01% (from 0.02% to 0.03%).

▶ Should Microsoft reorganize the offshore center?

If the offshore center is reorganized, Microsoft will save $400 per day. However, since this strategy will reduce system reliability, the expected cost of downtime will increase by $300 per day (increase in breakdown probability × cost of downtime = 0.01% × $3M). The net result is that, by reorganizing the offshore center, Microsoft can increase its expected profit by $100 per day.

▶ However, will the offshore manager have an incentive to choose this reorganization strategy?

Since the manager's performance is measured solely on the basis of uptime probability, he or she has no incentive to choose a reorganization strategy that increases the probability that the system will break down.

▶ How can Microsoft address this problem?

Microsoft can address this issue by using multiple metrics to evaluate performance. In this case, Microsoft should evaluate the manager of the offshore center using two criteria: uptime probability and the cost of running the center.

Fusion for Profit Maxim

The firm should use multiple metrics to measure and reward the performance of the manager of its offshore operations. Focusing on cost only will lead to poor long-run results.

▶ Should the firm own outsourcing centers, or should it use outside vendors?

In general, the firm has a choice of whether to own outsourcing centers, contract with outside vendors to supply the services in question, or pursue a mixed outsourcing strategy. By owning outsourcing centers abroad and employing its own personnel at these centers, the firm can gain in two ways:

1. The firm can reduce variations in the quality of service that it provides to customers. This can significantly improve the firm's long-run performance, especially if the firm is in an industry in which the repeat purchase probability depends heavily on customer satisfaction with service.
2. The firm can leverage the benefits of the experience curve in providing service, provided it is able to retain personnel in the future. (Strategies for retaining personnel will be discussed in the following section.)

On the other hand, this strategy of owning outsourcing centers will constrain the firm because its fixed costs will be higher. For example, the firm will have to purchase or lease fixed assets abroad.

By outsourcing operations to outside vendors, the firm obtains an important benefit: the ability to revise its decisions in the future (*strategic flexibility*). This can be very important, especially for a firm with limited resources.

Example: Consider a small start-up firm that is planning to launch a new product in the marketplace. Initially, the optimal policy may be to control downside risk by outsourcing certain functions to outside vendors.

If demand is low, the firm can exit the market without having to incur the risk of selling fixed assets at a loss or incurring the cost of breaching contracts. If demand is high, the firm can exercise the option of setting up its own outsourcing center in the future. The firm can perform this analysis by using the real options approach.[17]

▶ Are there conditions under which the firm should use a mixed outsourcing strategy?

As discussed earlier, it may be optimal for the firm to use a mixed outsourcing strategy. Specifically, the firm's choice of outsourcing strategy depends on a number of factors, including:

1. The impact of customer satisfaction on customer retention,
2. How similar service needs are across customer segments,

3. How steep the firm's experience curve is, and

4. How large the economic benefits of strategic flexibility are.

▲ **23.9 What Strategies Should the Firm Use to Retain Personnel It Employs at an Outsourcing Center?**

Suppose the firm trains the personnel it employs at an outsourcing center. In addition, suppose there is a steep learning curve in providing service.

▲ *What policies should the firm use to optimize personnel retention?*

As discussed above, regardless of the ownership structure of the outsourcing center, the firm should use multiple metrics to measure and reward productivity. In addition, the firm should set up incentive schemes such that managers focus on maximizing long-run performance and not on meeting subgoals.

When the firm provides training and/or there is a steep learning curve, the firm should adjust its employment contracts periodically based on these performance metrics. Unless the firm does this, it will experience *bad turnover*. That is, productive employees will leave, and long-run performance will suffer.

Roughly speaking, the impact of the learning curve on the employment contract is as follows. Since customer service is a proxy for future profit, the proportion of the employee's income that is based on current customer satisfaction should be increased.[18]

Fusion for Profit Maxim

When the employee's learning curve is steep, a higher proportion of the employee's income should be based on such customer metrics as customer satisfaction that are proxies of long-run profitability.

▲ *Should the firm diversify its outsourcing centers across different countries?*

The firm's decision to diversify its outsourcing centers geographically depends on the types of products and services that the firm offers, on the degree to which service requirements vary across customer segments, and on dynamic changes in the supply and demand for service personnel in different countries.

Types of Products

Suppose the firm sells a commoditized product. Then, the firm should use low-cost foreign centers to provide service support to its customers. Suppose the firm sells a specialized or customized product. Then, the firm should serve buyers through specialized centers (domestic or foreign) run by highly trained personnel.

Suppose the firm sells two types of products: one is commoditized (e.g., a PC), and the other is highly customized (e.g., a high-end server). Then, the firm should use low-cost foreign centers to serve customers who buy PCs and more specialized, higher-cost centers (foreign or domestic) to serve customers who buy high-end servers.

Customer Service Requirements

Suppose the customers who buy a given product made by the firm (e.g., a particular model of computer server) have different reservation prices for service. For example, it is efficient for high-volume buyers to have their computers serviced by their own full-time technical staff. Hence high-volume buyers have low reservation prices for service provided by the firm. In contrast, low-volume buyers do not have any economies of scale in computer maintenance. Hence low-volume buyers have high reservation prices for service provided by the firm.

Since both segments have different reservation prices for the firm's service, the firm should use a *mixed bundling strategy*. That is, it should sell the server on a stand-alone basis and offer a service contract as an "add-on" feature to interested buyers. Now, only low-volume buyers will buy the service contract.

Note that the previous discussion does not imply that all customers in a given segment should be served by one service center only.

Example: In the computer server example above, let's say that 80% of all technical problems are simple to resolve using a standardized troubleshooting protocol. However, the remaining 20% are difficult to diagnose and fix.

Then, the firm should use a sequential approach for addressing technical problems faced by customers. In the first step, customers who need service should be directed to a low-cost foreign center. If the personnel at this center cannot diagnose or solve the problem in a stipulated period of time (say, 20 minutes), the customer's service request should be transferred to another center (foreign or domestic) where more skilled personnel are available to address the problem.

Supply and Demand of Personnel

The firm's decision on where to locate its outsourcing centers depends critically on the projected changes in demand and supply over time in different countries for the type of labor in question (e.g., service personnel). We present two scenarios below.

Scenario 1.   Suppose the firm sells standardized products, customers' service needs for its products are homogeneous, and training costs are low.

Then, the optimal policy for the firm is to locate its outsourcing centers in countries that are currently cost-efficient. Suppose labor costs increase sharply in the future in the countries where these outsourcing centers are located. Then, the firm should relocate its centers to countries that are more cost-efficient at that time.

Scenario 2.   Suppose the firm sells products for which customers' service needs differ, training costs are high, and there is a steep learning curve in providing service. Now, in contrast to Scenario 1, relocating an outsourcing center—even within a given country—will involve significant incremental costs for the firm. Hence the firm should not locate its outsourcing centers based on current costs alone.

Given this scenario, the firm should make the location decision using a long-run perspective. To take advantage of the learning effect, the firm should keep attrition rates low for key personnel in its outsourcing centers. As discussed, this can only be achieved by using appropriate performance metrics and reward systems that encourage these personnel to focus on long-run performance.

Fusion for Profit Maxim

The firm's decision to geographically diversify its outsourcing centers should be based on a number of factors, including the types of products and services that the firm offers, the degree to which service requirements vary across customer segments, dynamic changes in the supply and demand for service personnel in different countries, and the economic value of strategic flexibility.

▶ *How should the firm measure the performance of the manager of an outsourcing unit?*

As discussed above, the firm should treat its outsourcing units as *profit centers* and not *cost centers*. Consequently, the firm should measure and reward the performance of the manager of an outsourcing center using multiple metrics. Importantly, these metrics should include both accounting and hidden costs that will not show up on the balance sheet, either now or in the future.

Example: Consider a publicly held industrial firm that uses an outsourcing procurement unit to purchase critical parts and components for its products. Suppose the firm treats the outsourcing unit as a cost center. Then, the outsourcing manager will purchase components from those suppliers that charge the lowest prices. However, those suppliers may produce poor-quality components; in addition, they may not deliver on time. Hence, the hidden costs of the outsourcing manager's decisions to the firm could be very high. In the short run, production delays could occur because critical components are not available on time. Hence the firm will lose profits from canceled orders. *Note that these lost short-run profits are hidden and will not show up on the firm's balance sheet.*

In the long run, a high proportion of the products that are sold are likely to break down because critical components are defective. Hence the firm's *brand equity* will be eroded. Finally, if current customers cancel their orders, the firm will forfeit the opportunity to make long-run profits from those customers via repeat orders or the sale of additional products to these customers in the future.

Note that although these lost long-run profits will not be reflected in the firm's balance sheet at any time (either now or in the future), their long-run effect on the firm will be visible and unambiguous: the firm's future stock price will fall.

▶ How can the firm provide an incentive to the outsourcing manager to focus on long-run performance?

One approach is to use a three-part compensation formula that is based on both accounting and hidden costs. Thus, the first part should be tied to procurement costs as a measure of efficiency. The second part should consist of a profit-sharing plan that reflects the effect of the procurement strategy on the firm's current performance. The third part should be based on a metric that reflects the impact of the current procurement policy on the firm's future performance (e.g., the difference between a norm and the proportion of units of the product that are sold and break down in a specified time period after purchase by the consumer).

Given this three-part compensation formula, the outsourcing manager will have an incentive to choose a balanced procurement strategy that focuses on long-run performance. For example, suppose the outsourcing manager chooses a cost-minimization strategy. Then, the manager will jeopardize his or her income from the profit-sharing component (e.g., there will be too many canceled orders if the low-cost supplier does not deliver on time) and from the product performance–based component (e.g., the proportion of defective components in the future will be too high if the low-cost supplier provides low-quality components).

Fusion for Profit Maxim

The parent company should treat an outsourcing center as a profit center and not as a cost center. To implement this approach, the parent company should pay the outsourcing manager using a three-part compensation formula that captures both accounting and hidden costs.

Chapter 23 Key Points

- In general, the firm should not enter foreign markets by simply replicating successful domestic strategies. In some cases, it may be necessary for the firm to choose a radically different product positioning strategy when it enters a foreign market.

- The firm's cost of capital is a poor metric for allocating resources internationally. In general, the required rate of return should vary across both countries and products.
- In contrast to a publicly owned multinational firm, a privately owned multinational firm may gain from international diversification even if it uses a "me-too" market entry strategy.
- In order to choose the optimal product designs and marketing policies internationally, the firm should measure the links among product design variables and consumers' reservation prices, paying particular attention to market segmentation.
- The decision to use a full-scale globalization strategy or to partially delegate decision-making authority to country managers depends on country-specific cost and demand conditions and competitive structures, and on whether the firm produces one product or multiple product lines.
- In general, the parent company should pay country managers on the basis of country-specific metrics of performance and not on the basis of measures of the overall performance of the parent company.
- The parent company may need to subsidize country managers when it launches a new product internationally, especially when the investment in infrastructure is high. In addition, the parent company should adjust the country manager's compensation plan periodically. This is necessary to provide the country manager with an incentive to focus on long-run performance and to efficiently share risk and return among the parent company's shareholders and the country manager.
- In general, multinational firms will need to develop hybrid organizational structures that are both country-based and product-based. The optimal organizational structure will depend on a number of factors, including economies of scope, transport costs, and differences in consumer preferences across countries for particular product designs.
- Because of hidden costs, firms in different industries may need to choose different outsourcing strategies, even if they face the same monetary outsourcing costs and gains.
- The firm's decision to geographically diversify its outsourcing centers depends on a number of factors, including the types of products and services that the firm offers, the degree to which service requirements vary across customer segments, dynamic changes in the supply and demand for service personnel in different countries, and the economic value of strategic flexibility.
- The firm should use multiple metrics to measure and reward the performance of its offshore operations. Focusing on any one metric alone, such as cost minimization, will lead to poor long-run results.
- The parent company should treat an outsourcing center as a profit center and not as a cost center. To implement this approach, the parent company should pay the outsourcing manager using a three-part compensation formula that captures both accounting and hidden costs.

▶ Chapter 1

1. For simplicity, this analysis assumes that General Foods is 100% owned by stockholders. For a technical discussion of how the firm's marketing policies affect A and B and hence the risk premium, see chapter 1 in Jagpal, Sharan (1999), *Marketing Strategy and Uncertainty*, New York: Oxford University Press.

2. In certain cases, the risk premium for a privately owned firm can be lower than that for a publicly owned firm. For example, the wealthy private owners of a hedge fund that purchases a publicly owned firm may be more willing to take risks than the stock market as a whole. In this case, after the acquisition, the *hedge fund* is likely to choose more aggressive marketing policies than the publicly owned firm.

3. See note 2 for an exception.

▶ Chapter 2

1. The classic work on how investors should choose their optimal portfolios was done by Harry M. Markowitz. See Markowitz, Harry M. (1952), "Portfolio Selection," *Journal of Finance*, 7, March, 77–91; and Markowitz, Harry M. (1959), *Portfolio Selection: Efficient Diversification of Investments*, New York: Wiley.

2. The classic work on stock valuation was done by Sharpe. See Sharpe, William F. (1964), "Capital Asset Prices: A Theory of Market Equilibrium under Conditions

of Risk," *Journal of Finance*, 19, September, 425–442. For a brief discussion of stock valuation, see *capital asset pricing model* (CAPM) in the glossary.

3. This assumes that the firm's target market and production technology are fixed. If the firm chooses a different market segment or a new production process to manufacture its products, the required rate of return should vary across marketing policies for the product.

4. We discuss this issue in detail in chapter 18.

5. We will discuss compensation contracts in detail in chapters 15, 16, and 17.

◣ Chapter 3

1. "Motorola Says It Will Post a Loss as Sales Fall Short," *New York Times*, 12 July 2007.

2. "Dell's Colorful Designs for Customers," *Wall Street Journal*, 26 June 2007.

3. See chapter 4 in Jagpal, Sharan (1999), *Marketing Strategy and Uncertainty*, New York: Oxford University Press.

4. Market share is not necessarily a good metric to measure performance. We will discuss this issue in detail in chapter 4.

5. See pp. 160–161 in Miniter, Richard (2002), *The Myth of Market Share*, New York: Crown Business.

◣ Chapter 4

1. Marginal costs are positive except for special cases (e.g., information goods such as software).

2. Caveats to this statement will be discussed later in this chapter.

3. For a technical discussion, see pp. 5–6 in Jagpal, Sharan (1999), *Marketing Strategy and Uncertainty*, New York: Oxford University Press.

4. *New York Times*, 10 August 2005.

5. See pp. 16–19 in Jagpal, Sharan (1999), *Marketing Strategy and Uncertainty*.

6. For simplicity, we assume that the new technological process only decreases future costs. The qualitative results will not change if this assumption is relaxed (i.e., the curve AGB moves downward when the new technological process is introduced).

7. The effect of a high churn rate is analogous to that of low switching costs.

8. *New York Times*, 29 July 2005.

9. "How Wal-Mart's TV Prices Crushed Rivals," *Business Week*, 23 April 2007.

10. For a discussion of segmentation, see chapter 8.

◣ Chapter 5

1. For a technical analysis, see Zhao, Hao, and Sharan Jagpal (2006), "Effect of Secondhand Markets on the Firm's Dynamic Pricing and New Product

Introduction Strategies," *International Journal of Research in Marketing*, 23, 295–307.

2. Zhao, Hao, and Sharan Jagpal (forthcoming), "Upgrade Pricing, Market Growth, and Social Welfare," *Journal of Business Research*.

3. This topic is addressed in greater detail in chapters 9 and 18.

◤ *Chapter 6*

1. This analysis assumes that the private owner of the firm is small. If the privately held firm is owned by wealthy individuals (e.g., the firm is owned by a *hedge fund*), the firm may be more willing to take risk than a firm that is owned by stockholders. In this case, the privately held firm is likely to price the new product more aggressively than a firm that is owned by stockholders.

2. Our present focus is theoretical. In practice, the precise shape of the owner's utility function depends on the owner's risk-return trade-off. This trade-off can be measured experimentally using such methods as *conjoint analysis*. See chapter 8 for a discussion of conjoint analysis.

3. *Constant absolute risk aversion* implies that the owner has an exponential utility function. See chapter 8 in Jagpal, Sharan (1999), *Marketing Strategy and Uncertainty*, New York: Oxford University Press.

4. For a technical discussion of how new product introduction affects cannibalization and market growth, see Zhao, Hao, and Sharan Jagpal (forthcoming), "Upgrade Pricing, Market Growth, and Social Welfare," *Journal of Business Research*.

5. See Koku, Paul S., Sharan Jagpal, and P. V. Viswanath (1997), "The Effect of New Product Announcements and Preannouncements on Stock Price," *Journal of Market Focused Management,* 2, 2, 183–199.

6. This result supports Klein and Leffler's theory that preannouncements are effective strategic tools in the manufacturing sector (Standard Industrial Code [SIC] 390). See Klein, B., and K. B. Leffler (1981), "The Role of Market Forces in Assuring Contractual Performance," *Journal of Political Economy*, 89, August, 615–641.

◤ *Chapter 7*

1. "Chiefs Defend Slow Network for the iPhone," *New York Times*, 29 June 2007.

2. Our example assumes that the product attributes (e.g., horsepower) can be measured on a continuous scale. This assumption is not necessary, since the regression model can include *dummy variables*.

3. We have assumed a linear structure for simplicity. In reality, the relationship between the market price and the product design attributes is likely to be nonlinear. For a theoretical discussion, see Rosen, Sherwin (1974), "Hedonic Prices

and Implicit Markets: Product Differentiation in Pure Competition," *Journal of Political Economy*, 82, 34–55.

4. Since the firm has no control over price, marginal revenue equals price. However, profit maximization implies that marginal revenue must equal marginal cost. Hence the firm will choose that volume for which the marginal cost is $32,000.

5. Note that since the firm produces two models of automobile, some costs are likely to be shared.

6. See Kalita, J., Sharan Jagpal, and D. Lehmann (2004), "Do High Prices Signal High Quality? A Theoretical Model and Empirical Results," *Journal of Product and Brand Management*, 13, 4, 279–288.

▲ Chapter 8

1. See Infosino, William J. (1986), "Forecasting New Product Sales from Likelihood of Purchase Ratings," *Marketing Science*, 5, 372–384, p. 375.

2. Jagpal, Sharan, K. Jedidi, and M. Jamil (2007), "MCT: A Multibrand Concept-Testing Methodology for New Product Strategy," *Journal of Product and Innovation Management*, 24, 1, 34–51.

3. The MCT methodology allows both the directions and the magnitudes of the biases to vary across different brands. In addition, it allows for halo effects (i.e., the biases for different brands can be correlated, either positively or negatively).

4. Part-worth conjoint models assume that each attribute has a separate effect on preference. However, this assumption is not necessary. For a discussion of more general methods for measuring preferences, see chapter 4 in Jagpal, Sharan (1999), *Marketing Strategy and Uncertainty*, New York: Oxford University Press.

5. Other variations can be used. For example, the conjoint results can be adjusted to allow for probabilistic choice behavior by consumers.

6. For a detailed discussion and review of the conjoint methodology, see chapter 4 in Jagpal, Sharan (1999), *Marketing Strategy and Uncertainty*.

7. This is the standard definition of reservation price. Alternative definitions have been proposed in the literature. For a discussion, see Jedidi, K., and S. Jagpal (forthcoming), "Willingness to Pay: Measurement and Managerial Implications," in Vithala Rao, ed., *Handbook of Research in Pricing*, Northampton, Mass.: Edward Elgar Publishing.

8. In practice, Toshiba will not leave its price unchanged at $130 when Sony enters the market. For a discussion of pricing strategies when competitors react, see chapter 18.

9. Suppose the measured reservation price = x (true reservation price) + error, where x is a constant whose value is greater than one. That is, on average, consumers tend to overstate their reservation prices for Gloo-Glock. Then, the variability of measured reservation prices = x^2 (variability of true reservation prices) + variability of error. Note that x is greater than one. Hence, the greater the degree to which consumers tend to overstate their reservation prices, the greater is the variability of measured reservation prices.

10. Suppose the measured reservation price $= x$ (true reservation price) $+$ error. Since consumers tend to understate their reservation prices, x will be a positive constant between zero and one. Then, the variability of the measured reservation prices $= x^2$ (variability of true reservation price) $+$ variability of error. Hence, if x is sufficiently small (close to zero, for example), the variability of the measured reservation prices *could be less* than the variability of the true reservation prices.

11. See Jedidi, K., Sharan Jagpal, and P. Manchanda (2003), "Measuring Heterogeneous Reservation Prices for Product Bundles," *Marketing Science*, 22, 1, 107–130.

12. See Jedidi, K., Sharan Jagpal, and P. Manchanda (2003).

13. See Jedidi, K., Sharan Jagpal, and P. Manchanda (2003).

14. For technical details, see Jedidi, K., Sharan Jagpal, and P. Manchanda (2003).

15. The only change that is necessary is to express the reservation price of each brand (dependent variable) as a function of the attributes of that product (explanatory variables). In general, this relationship can be nonlinear.

16. The only change that is necessary is to include brand effects as additional explanatory variables in the choice model.

17. See Jedidi, K., Sharan Jagpal, and P. Manchanda (2003).

18. For a succinct review of the different types of auctions available and a comparison of their advantages and disadvantages, see Jedidi, K. and S. Jagpal (forthcoming), "Willingness to Pay: Measurement and Managerial Implications," in Vithala Rao, ed., *Handbook of Research in Pricing*, Northampton, Mass.: Edward Elgar Publishing.

19. For a detailed comparison of the different methods for measuring reservation prices, including different types of auction, see Jedidi, K. and S. Jagpal (forthcoming), "Willingness to Pay: Measurement and Managerial Implications," in Vithala Rao, ed., *Handbook of Research in Pricing*.

20. For a technical discussion of how to estimate the two-step linkage from physical attributes to perceptions (Step 1) and from perceptions to preference and/or choice (Step 2), see chapter 4 in Jagpal, Sharan (1999), *Marketing Strategy and Uncertainty*.

21. For details, see chapter 4 in Jagpal, Sharan (1999), *Marketing Strategy and Uncertainty*.

22. One popular STM model is ASSESSOR. See Silk, Alvin J., and Glen L. Urban, (1978), "Pre-Test-Market Evaluation of New Packaged Goods: A Model and Measurement Methodology," *Journal of Marketing Research*, 15, 171–191.

23. In general, one can use the STM results to compute revenue-based market shares by using the appropriate weights for different prices across brands and different usage rates across brands or segments.

24. By conducting additional research, Slick can obtain more insight into which marketing decisions are responsible for the low trial rate.

25. This answer will depend on the frequency with which the consumer purchases the product. Consequently, the time period necessary to obtain stable test market results will vary by industry.

▲ Chapter 9

1. Note that consumers in Segment B will not purchase Crest at a price of $3.00, since their reservation price for Crest is only $1.50.

2. See chapter 20 for a detailed discussion of how marketing policy affects social welfare.

3. See chapter 8 for a discussion of methods for obtaining unbiased estimates of reservation prices.

4. Suppose consumers' self-stated reservation prices are unbiased. Then, for each consumer, the following holds true: self-stated reservation price = true reservation price + error, where the error term is random. Hence variance (self-stated reservation price) = variance (true reservation price) + variance (error). Thus, variance (self-stated reservation price) > variance (true reservation price).

5. For a detailed discussion of this methodology, see chapter 8 and Jedidi, K., S. Jagpal, and P. Manchanda (2003), "Measuring Heterogeneous Reservation Prices for Product Bundles," *Marketing Science*, 22, 1, 107–130.

▲ Chapter 10

1. As shown earlier, the maximum gross channel profit is $30,000. See table 10.1.

2. See chapter 20 for a detailed discussion of social welfare.

3. "Top 5ive Supermarket Tricks," *Personal Finance*, 6 July 2006.

4. As shown earlier in the Coca-Cola example, the maximum economic profit in the channel is $20,000 if no advertising is done.

5. See price calculations done in the Wal-Mart example.

6. For a discussion of compensation contracts under uncertainty, see chapters 15, 16, and 17.

7. In general, the Internet price and the price charged by the distributor need not be the same. For example, consumers may be willing to pay a price premium to purchase from the distributor for a variety of reasons (e.g., the opportunity to examine the product before purchase). For a detailed discussion of Internet marketing, see chapter 21.

8. "Rohm and Haas (A)," *Harvard Business School*, 9–587-055.

9. For a detailed analysis of this problem, see chapter 4 in Jagpal, Sharan (1999), *Marketing Strategy and Uncertainty*, New York: Oxford University Press.

10. "Zero Is Coke's New Hero," *Wall Street Journal*, 17 April 2007.

▲ Chapter 11

1. Alternative definitions of reservation prices have been proposed in the literature. For example, some authors define reservation price as a range of prices that are acceptable to the consumer. For a detailed review of the literature, see

Jedidi, K., and S. Jagpal (forthcoming), "Willingness to Pay: Measurement and Managerial Implications," in Vithala Rao, ed., *Handbook of Research in Pricing*, Northampton, Mass.: Edward Elgar Publishing.

2. This analysis assumes a given set of prices for the Toyota Camry and the Honda Accord. In reality, both Toyota and Honda will choose their prices after allowing for the effects of competitive retaliation by their competitors. We will discuss the effects of competitive reaction in detail in chapter 18.

3. Some authors define the magnitude of a price change on the basis of the percentage change in price. Others define the magnitudes of price changes based on the absolute values of the price changes.

4. If the behavioral theory is correct, in general the variability of the reservation prices (AU + TU) will be larger than the variability of the acquisition utilities of consumers (AU). That is, the standard economic theory will understate the differences in willingness to pay across customers and will therefore mismeasure demand. This result is based on the assumption that acquisition utility and transaction utility are uncorrelated. However, suppose AU and TU are positively correlated. Then, the degree to which standard economic theory understates the differences in willingness to pay across customers will be more severe.

5. "Chrysler's 'Employee Discount' of Last Summer Could Be Revived," *New York Times*, 23 June 2006.

6. "Inquiry Looks into Airline Price-Fixing," *New York Times*, 23 June 2006.

7. For a theoretical discussion, see Jagpal, Sharan, and Hao Zhao (2004), "A Dynamic Satisfaction Model: Risk Aversion and Prospect Theory," Marketing Science Conference, The Netherlands.

8. This policy change is not always optimal. For example, suppose that in the downturn only loyal customers will remain with the company. Since these customers are less price sensitive, the optimal policy for the firm may be to *increase* prices.

9. This transaction utility will be reduced to the extent that the industry as a whole reduces prices in an economic downturn. Thus, other factors being constant, the more commoditized an industry is, the less important the transaction utility will be in an economic downturn.

10. As discussed earlier, conventional economic theory implicitly assumes that all transaction utilities are zeros.

11. For simplicity, the analysis assumes that Joe's reference point is constant (i.e., it does not change after Joe receives a bonus).

12. For a detailed discussion of compensation plans, see chapters 15, 16, and 17.

13. This analysis assumes that Laura's reference point remains at $100,000 at the end of the first day. If Laura's reference point increases to $105,000 at the end of the first day, the loss in the second day (–$10,000) will be higher than it would have been (–$5,000) if the reference point had remained unchanged. Hence Laura will be even worse off.

14. For a detailed comparison of methods to measure acquisition utility (AU), see Jedidi, K., and S. Jagpal (forthcoming), "Willingness to Pay: Measurement and Managerial Implications," in Vithala Rao, ed., *Handbook of Research in Pricing*.

15. These measurement problems can be addressed. However, sophisticated methods are necessary. See chapter 4 in Jagpal, Sharan (1999), *Marketing Strategy and Uncertainty*, New York: Oxford University Press.

16. For a detailed comparison of methods to measure acquisition utility (AU), see Jedidi, K., and S. Jagpal (forthcoming), "Willingness to Pay: Measurement and Managerial Implications," in Vithala Rao, ed., *Handbook of Research in Pricing*. For a discussion of methods to measure transaction utility (TU) and reference points (RF), see chapter 4 in Jagpal, Sharan (1999), *Marketing Strategy and Uncertainty*.

◤ *Chapter 12*

1. One advantage of this approach is that media planning is facilitated, since media exposure data are readily available showing the demographic profiles of those who are exposed to a particular media vehicle (e.g., those who watch the national news on NBC every night).

2. Consumers first rank-order product attributes (e.g., horsepower, braking distance, quality of the sound system) based on the importance of these attributes. In the next step, they choose the car that obtains the highest score for the most important attribute, say, horsepower. If two or more products are tied on horsepower, compare these cars using the scores for the attribute ranked second in importance, say, braking distance. Then, pick the car(s) with the highest score on braking distance. If there are ties, compare the remaining cars based on the quality of their sound systems and pick the car with the highest score. If two or more brands are tied, continue this process using other ranked attributes until only one brand is left. This is the brand that is chosen.

3. We will discuss the managerial implications of Internet advertising in detail in chapter 21.

4. A major issue is how to measure the dollar value of brand equity. We discuss measurement methods in chapter 19.

5. For a technical discussion, see chapter 4 in Jagpal, Sharan (1999), *Marketing Strategy and Uncertainty*, New York: Oxford University Press.

6. The critical issue here is to determine how the brand name affects consumers' reservation prices for the products in question. For a technical discussion, see Jedidi, K., S. Jagpal, and P. Manchanda (2003), "Measuring Heterogeneous Reservation Prices for Product Bundles," *Marketing Science*, 22, 1, 107–130.

7. See "Vicks Health Care Division. Project Scorpio (B)," *Harvard Business School*, 582–040.

8. With the advent of Web sites such as YouTube, word-of-mouth activity potentially wields even greater power today than in the past.

9. See "Vicks Health Care Division. Project Scorpio (B)," *Harvard Business School*, 582–040.

10. For a technical discussion, see chapter 4 in Jagpal, Sharan (1999), *Marketing Strategy and Uncertainty*.

11. For a detailed discussion, see chapters 3 and 7 in Jagpal, Sharan (1999), *Marketing Strategy and Uncertainty*.

12. See "Vicks Health Care Division. Project Scorpio (A)," *Harvard Business School*, 582–039.

13. If the firm can identify the novice and expert segments a priori, it can directly use the methodology developed in chapter 4 of Jagpal, Sharan (1999), *Marketing Strategy and Uncertainty*. In some cases, especially for radically new products, the firm may not have sufficient knowledge to form these segments a priori. Hence it will be necessary to use a more sophisticated *latent-class methodology* that allows one to classify consumers into unobservable segments. Loosely speaking, the latent-class methodology will allow the firm to determine which consumers belong to the expert and novice segments. In addition, this method will allow the firm to measure how different advertising message strategies affect each segment's uncertainties in evaluating the new product. For a new product model that uses the latent-class methodology, see Jagpal, Sharan, K. Jedidi, and M. Jamil (2007), "MCT: A Multibrand Concept-Testing Methodology for New Product Strategy," *Journal of Product and Innovation Management,* 24, 1, 34–51.

14. This analysis assumes that incumbent firms have reputations to protect in the long run. Thus, we preclude fly-by-night companies that can succeed in the short run by mimicking the high-quality firm's strategy.

15. For details regarding the experimental design and data-analysis methodology, see Jagpal, Sharan, K. Jedidi, and M. Jamil (2007).

16. See Jagpal, Sharan, K. Jedidi, and M. Jamil (2007).

▲ **Chapter 13**

1. For a discussion of how to measure certainty-equivalent demands using historical data, see Jagpal, Sharan, and I. Brick (1982), "The Marketing Mix Decision under Uncertainty," *Marketing Science*, 1, 1 (Winter), 79–92.

2. See Dorfman, Robert, and Peter O. Steiner (1954), "Optimal Advertising and Optimal Quality," *American Economic Review*, 44, 5, 826–836.

3. It can be shown that the Dorfman-Steiner theorem holds under uncertainty as well. In this case, the firm will choose its promotional policy such that the following condition holds:

$$\frac{\text{advertising expenditure}}{\text{promotion expenditure}} = \frac{\text{risk-adjusted advertising elasticity}}{\text{risk-adjusted promotion elasticity}}.$$

4. See chapter 6 in Jagpal, Sharan (1999), *Marketing Strategy and Uncertainty*, New York: Oxford University Press.

5. For a discussion of how one can measure certainty-equivalent demand using historical data, see Jagpal, Sharan, and I. Brick (1982).

6. See Nerlove, Marc, and K. J. Arrow (1962), "Optimal Advertising under Dynamic Conditions," *Economica*, 29, 129–142.

7. See pp. 144–152 in Jagpal, Sharan (1999), *Marketing Strategy and Uncertainty*.

8. This implication of the Nerlove-Arrow model has led to a spirited debate in the subsequent literature. For a discussion of alternative models, see chapter 6 in Jagpal, Sharan (1999), *Marketing Strategy and Uncertainty*.

9. For a detailed discussion, see pp. 152–159 in Jagpal, Sharan (1999), *Marketing Strategy and Uncertainty*.

10. For a detailed discussion of price-advertising strategies for the privately and publicly held firms under uncertainty, see pp. 152–159 in Jagpal, Sharan (1999), *Marketing Strategy and Uncertainty*.

11. For a discussion of the methodology, see pp. 179–181 in Jagpal, Sharan (1999), *Marketing Strategy and Uncertainty*.

▲ *Chapter 14*

1. Experimentation is not a panacea for measuring advertising productivity. Specifically, although the firm can control its own marketing policies in the experiment, it cannot control the marketing policies of its competitors.

2. The reader who is interested in the experimentation approach for measuring advertising productivity should refer to any standard book on experimental design and analysis. For example, see Box, George E. P., Stuart Hunter, and William G. Hunter (2005), *Statistics for Experimenters: Design, Innovation, and Discovery*, 2nd ed., New York: Wiley.

3. For an in-depth treatment of technical issues in measuring advertising productivity using historical data, see chapter 6 in Jagpal, Sharan (1999), *Marketing Strategy and Uncertainty*, New York: Oxford University Press.

4. The degree of involvement is likely to vary across consumers for any given product category. For example, heavy users of a product (e.g., beer) are likely to have a higher degree of purchase involvement with beer purchase than light users. Consequently, heavy users may have a lower threshold than light users. Similarly, the degree of involvement for any given product may be context-specific. To illustrate, consider a consumer who is planning to purchase a bottle of wine. This consumer may have a lower degree of purchase involvement if the wine is to be consumed personally than if it is to be given as a gift to a friend on a special occasion.

5. See Simon, Hermann (1982), "ADPULS: An Advertising Model with Wearout and Pulsation," *Journal of Marketing Research*, August, 353–363.

6. For details, see pp. 176–179 in Jagpal, Sharan (1999), *Marketing Strategy and Uncertainty*.

7. See Jagpal, Sharan, and Baldwin S. Hui (1980), "Measuring the Advertising-Sales Relationship: A Multivariate Time Series Approach," in J. Leigh and C. Martin, Eds., *Current Issues and Research in Advertising*, Ann Arbor: University of Michigan, Division of Research, 211–228.

8. The bias in the estimated advertising productivities can be severe in nonlinear models. For a theoretical discussion, see pp. 168–169 in Jagpal, Sharan (1999), *Marketing Strategy and Uncertainty*.

9. The reason is technical. This is a classic error-in-variables problem in which the regressor is unbiased but is measured with error. See, for example, chapter 10 in Johnston, J. (1984), *Econometric Methods*, 3rd ed., New York: Wiley.

10. The qualitative results for the multiple-media case will be the same as those for the single-medium case in the special case where the rating scores for all media are uncorrelated. However, this scenario is very unlikely for a number of reasons, including audience duplication across media.

11. "How Many See the Spots? Soon, Ad Buyers Will Know," *New York Times*, 12 July 2006.

12. Note that, for Case 1, the old Nielsen estimates are unbiased to begin with. Since the new Nielsen scores are also unbiased but are less volatile than the old scores, the average estimates of advertising productivity will increase. See table 14.6.

13. "TV Networks Gain in 'Upfront' Ad Deals," *Wall Street Journal*, 18 June 2007, B4.

14. See chapter 18 for a discussion of how to choose marketing policy in the face of competitive reaction.

15. This analysis implicitly assumes that the owners of Alpha have limited wealth and are risk-averse. Suppose, however, that Alpha is owned by wealthy individuals with a high tolerance for risk. For example, Alpha is a *private equity firm* owned by pension funds and wealthy individual investors. Then, the volatility of profits does not matter much to Alpha's owners. Hence Alpha will behave like a risk-neutral firm. Note that, for this scenario, Alpha and Beta will choose similar advertising purchasing strategies. Hence, in this case, ownership structure is irrelevant.

16. The actual monthly sales are the sum of A, B, C, and D (a random effect that captures the effect of other factors that are not explicitly included in the media mix model).

17. The model implicitly allows threshold effects to vary across media. Furthermore, by construction, the model allows equivalent dollar expenditures in different media to have different effects on sales. Hence the model implicitly allows for qualitative differences across media. For example, advertising in one medium may be more credible than advertising in another.

18. Note that, since the specification can allow for general threshold and nonlinear effects for a given medium, it is consistent with *both* reach models (which assume that only the first advertising exposure in a medium matters) and GRP models (which assume that both reach and frequency for the advertising medium matter).

19. For a technical discussion, see chapter 7 in Jagpal, Sharan (1999), *Marketing Strategy and Uncertainty*.

◤ Chapter 15

1. See chapter 2.

2. Alternatively, the firm can pay the manager a bonus if the manager's performance exceeds an internally specified target or goal. In general, however, the stock

option plan is superior to bonus schemes because share prices are determined by the market.

3. For a discussion, see the P&G example on *cross-couponing* in chapter 9.

▲ Chapter 16

1. See Jagpal, Sharan (1983a), "Optimal Sales Force Compensation under Uncertainty: Part I," Working Paper, Rutgers Business School; and Jagpal, Sharan (1983b), "Optimal Sales Force Compensation under Uncertainty: Part II," Working Paper, Rutgers Business School.

2. This assumption implies that both the firm and the sales agent have exponential utility functions. For a technical discussion, see chapter 8 in Jagpal, Sharan (1999), *Marketing Strategy and Uncertainty*, New York: Oxford University Press.

3. See chapter 8 in Jagpal, Sharan (1999), *Marketing Strategy and Uncertainty*.

4. For a technical discussion, see chapter 8 in Jagpal, Sharan (1999), *Marketing Strategy and Uncertainty*.

5. The optimal profit-sharing plan is linear if the firm and the sales agent have exponential utility functions. See chapter 8 in Jagpal, Sharan (1999), *Marketing Strategy and Uncertainty*.

6. The compensation plan in each period will be linear if both the firm and the sales agent have *time-additive exponential utility functions*. For technical details, see pp. 280–282 in Jagpal, Sharan (1999), *Marketing Strategy and Uncertainty*.

7. This analysis implicitly assumes that the firm has historical data on the relationship between sales effort and customer retention.

8. Note that, because the firm's cost of capital is 20%, selling 36 units in the third period is equivalent to selling 30 units in the second period.

▲ Chapter 17

1. See Jagpal, Sharan (1983a), "Optimal Sales Force Compensation under Uncertainty: Part I," Working Paper, Rutgers Business School; and Jagpal, Sharan (1983b), "Optimal Sales Force Compensation under Uncertainty: Part II," Working Paper, Rutgers Business School.

2. The optimal profit-sharing rates for both sales agents are equal because each agent has the same attitude toward risk. For a theoretical discussion, see chapter 8 in Jagpal, Sharan (1999), *Marketing Strategy and Uncertainty*, New York: Oxford University Press.

3. For a detailed discussion of how to perform this analysis and develop appropriate compensation plans when satisfaction is measured with error, see pp. 242–245 in Jagpal, Sharan (1999), *Marketing Strategy and Uncertainty*.

4. As previously discussed, if the firm chooses the price of its products and the sales call plans for its sales agents, the commissions per unit for different products should be proportional to the corresponding gross margins for those products.

5. *New York Times*, 29 July 2005.

6. For a discussion of how to measure customer satisfaction and how to include these measures in the compensation contract, see chapter 8 in Jagpal, Sharan (1999), *Marketing Strategy and Uncertainty*.

7. The methodology is developed on pp. 254–260 in Jagpal, Sharan (1999), *Marketing Strategy and Uncertainty*.

◣ Chapter 18

1. This concept of profit maximization also applies under uncertainty. In this case, however, the firm should maximize the *certainty equivalent of its profits*. If the firm has a long planning horizon, it should maximize the certainty equivalent of its long-run profits (i.e., net present value).

2. See "Coca-Cola's New Vending Machine (A): Pricing to Capture Value, or Not?" *Harvard Business School*, 9-500-068.

3. The assumption that each firm can choose only one of two pricing strategies (uniform or flexible pricing) is a simplification. In reality, both Coke and Pepsi can choose from a continuum of prices. We discuss pricing strategies of this type in the next section.

4. Our discussion has been heuristic. Technically, the assumption that Intel's reaction curve is steeper than AMD's is a sufficient condition for the Nash equilibrium to be stable. See p. 193 in Jagpal, Sharan (1999), *Marketing Strategy and Uncertainty*, New York: Oxford University Press; and pp. 23–25 in Fudenberg, Drew, and Jean Tirole (1992), *Game Theory*, Cambridge, Mass.: MIT Press.

5. This problem is known as simultaneity bias. For a detailed discussion, see pp. 174–175 in Jagpal, Sharan (1999), *Marketing Strategy and Uncertainty*.

6. See chapter 2 for a discussion on how to value *real options*.

7. See chapter 2 for a discussion of the real options methodology and how to determine the economic value of *strategic flexibility*.

8. See chapter 2 for a discussion of the economic value of strategic flexibility and the real options methodology.

◣ Chapter 19

1. "Big Changes at a Store for Big Sizes," *New York Times*, 8 July 2006.

2. "Vicks Health Care Division. Project Scorpio (B)," *Harvard Business School*, 582–040.

3. "Rohm and Haas (A)," *Harvard Business School*, 9–587-055.

4. See chapter 8. In our discussion, we focused on the use of choice experiments to estimate how the name of a product affects consumers' reservation prices for that product. Another approach is to estimate the effect of different product names on consumers' perceptions of that product. This approach will be especially useful for products that are undifferentiated in terms of physical attributes (e.g., cold

medications) but are perceived very differently in terms of consumer benefits. For a technical discussion, see chapter 4 in Jagpal, Sharan (1999), *Marketing Strategy and Uncertainty*, New York: Oxford University Press. Both these methods can be used together because they provide complementary types of information about the effect of the product name on consumer behavior and hence on brand equity.

5. See pp. 102–106 in Jagpal, Sharan (1999), *Marketing Strategy and Uncertainty*.

6. The two-step model discussed in the text assumes that consumers use *central information-processing* strategies. That is, they transform objective product-related information into perceived benefits (Step 1) which in turn drive their preferences and choices (Step 2). This assumption will be met in many cases, but it is not necessary. Specifically, the two-step model can capture *peripheral* (one-step) *information-processing* strategies where product-related information (including brand name) has a direct effect on consumers' preferences and choices without being mediated through perceptions. Note that peripheral information-processing can be a very important driver of brand equity, even for durable goods, if "brand identity" or "brand image" has a significant impact on preferences/choices.

7. If the number of segments is small, one can use the *latent-class methodology* developed by Jedidi, Kamel, Sharan Jagpal, and Wayne DeSarbo (1997), "STEMM: A General Finite Mixture Structural Equation Model," *Journal of Classification,* 14, 23–50; and Jedidi, Kamel, Sharan Jagpal, and Wayne DeSarbo (1997), *"Finite Mixture Structural Equation Models* for Response-Based Segmentation and Unobserved Heterogeneity," *Marketing Science,* 16, 1, 39–59. Otherwise, to capture differences among consumers, one can use the random-coefficient method developed by Ansari, Asim, K. Jedidi, and S. Jagpal (2000), "A Hierarchical Bayesian Methodology for Treating Heterogeneity in Structural Equation Models," *Marketing Science,* 19, 4, 328–347.

8. For simplicity, we assume that the cost structure is constant.

9. One method to allow for this type of multiproduct effect is to make a subjective adjustment of the estimate of brand equity. A better approach may be to not make any arbitrary adjustments. Instead, recognize that the computed measure of brand equity is the lower bound on the dollar value of brand equity.

10. Tobin, James (1969), "A General Equilibrium Approach to Monetary Theory," *Journal of Money, Credit, and Banking,* 1, 15–29.

11. For technical details, see Jedidi, K., S. Jagpal, and P. Manchanda (2003), "Measuring Heterogeneous Reservation Prices for Product Bundles," *Marketing Science*, 22, 1, 107–130.

12. The only changes that are necessary are to simultaneously vary product design (i.e., the product attributes and their levels) and product names in the choice experiment and to allow these treatments to affect consumers' reservation prices. For details, see Jedidi, K., S. Jagpal, and P. Manchanda (2003).

13. See chapter 12 for a discussion of different information-processing models.

14. See chapter 12.

15. See chapter 4 in Jagpal, Sharan (1999), *Marketing Strategy and Uncertainty*; and Jedidi, K., S. Jagpal, and P. Manchanda (2003).

▲ **Chapter 20**

1. Note that price skimming has the same effect on consumer and social welfare as perfect first-degree price discrimination (i.e., charging each segment its reservation price).

2. For a technical discussion, see Jagpal, Sharan, and Menahem Spiegel (2004), "Free Samples, Market Structure, Profits, and Welfare," Working Paper, Rutgers Business School.

3. Note that these results can change if the discount rate is not zero.

4. For a theoretical discussion, see Jagpal, Sharan (1982), "Channel Cooperation, Market Leadership, and Social Welfare," Working Paper, Rutgers Business School.

5. For a theoretical discussion, see Jagpal, Sharan (1982), "Advertising, Uncertainty, and Social Welfare," Working Paper, Rutgers Business School.

6. Original profit made by Microsoft.

7. For simplicity, we assume that Murkee is a small company with limited resources. Hence Murkee cannot afford to play a price-cutting game with Pristeen.

8. The demand structure in a market reflects how reservation prices vary in the population. Since the consumer surplus for any consumer equals the difference between that consumer's reservation price and the price he or she pays for the product, one can estimate the net consumer surplus in the population once the market demand structure has been estimated.

9. For a discussion of how to implement the choice-based methodology, see Jedidi, K., S. Jagpal, and P. Manchanda (2003), "Measuring Heterogeneous Reservation Prices for Product Bundles," *Marketing Science*, 22, 1, 107–130.

10. See chapter 9.

11. Under certain conditions, the optimal strategy for the firm may be to introduce both models simultaneously or to leapfrog (i.e., to sell only the high-quality product). For a discussion of these issues and the technical conditions under which it is optimal for the firm to use a sequential product introduction strategy, see Zhao, Hao, and Sharan Jagpal (forthcoming), "Upgrade Pricing, Market Growth, and Social Welfare," *Journal of Business Research*.

12. The life of a durable product depends on its physical condition after use *and* on the rate of technological obsolescence. For example, a PC may be functional after two years but have no economic value at that time because it is obsolete.

13. Zhao, Hao, and Sharan Jagpal (forthcoming), "Upgrade Pricing, Market Growth, and Social Welfare," *Journal of Business Research*.

14. See Zhao, Hao, and Sharan Jagpal (2006), "Effect of Secondhand Markets on the Firm's Dynamic Pricing and New Product Introduction Strategies," *International Journal of Research in Marketing*, 23, 295–307.

▲ **Chapter 21**

1. Price dispersion can be measured in a number of ways. One common metric is standard deviation.

2. To focus on essentials, this analysis does not consider sales tax or transportation costs.

3. Light users are price sensitive. Hence, even before the advent of the Internet, they were willing to incur significant search costs to find the lowest price of any given product. This implies that the pre-Internet price dispersion for any given product in the light-user segment was low. Consequently, it is likely that the Internet will not reduce price dispersion in the light-user segment significantly.

4. In regression models of the type being discussed (i.e., the relationship between sales as a dependent variable and advertising exposures to different media as explanatory variables), error in *even one* of the explanatory variables will bias *all* the results. In general, one cannot determine the directions of these biases, except in the special case where there is no audience overlap across media. However, this scenario is very unlikely, since, a priori, the firm typically uses several media to target its chosen market segments. For a technical discussion of the "error-in-variables" problem, see chapter 10 in Johnston, J. (1984), *Econometric Methods*, 3rd Edition, New York: Wiley.

5. As discussed, intermediate measures of advertising such as reach are likely to contain measurement error. This problem can be addressed by estimating sales response models in which the explanatory variables are the levels of spending in particular media (which are objective) rather than intermediate measures of advertising effectiveness. See chapter 14.

6. See chapter 14 for details.

7. For a discussion of how to measure such *media interaction effects* (which can be positive or negative), see chapter 14.

8. A fixed-fee contract is optimal only in the special case where the principal (advertiser) is risk-neutral, the agent (advertising medium) is risk-averse, and the agent's effort is observable. See chapters 15, 16, and 17.

9. This analysis implicitly assumes that Megatech does not unilaterally change the price of its product before its ad is run on Google.

10. For a detailed discussion of auctions and reservation prices, see Jedidi, K., and S. Jagpal (forthcoming), "Willingness to Pay: Measurement and Managerial Implications," in Vithala Rao, ed., *Handbook of Research in Pricing*, Northampton, Mass.: Edward Elgar Publishing.

11. See chapter 14 for details.

12. This assumes that Goliath and all salespeople have constant risk aversions. Note that these risk aversions need not be the same across all players.

13. Note that, on average, Aida's expected income is higher than Theo's. However, Aida faces greater income volatility.

14. See chapter 20 for a detailed discussion of social welfare.

15. See chapter 9 for a detailed discussion of bundling.

16. "Marketers Try 'Conquesting'—To Get on Rivals' Nerves," *Wall Street Journal*, 7 June 2007, B1.

17. "Online Customized Ads Move a Step Closer," *New York Times*, 12 July 2007.

18. "Selling Web Advertising Space Like Pork Bellies," *Wall Street Journal*, 29 May 2007, Page B1.

19. "Nielsen Revises Its Gauge of Web Page Rankings," *Associated Press*, 10 July 2007.

◣ **Chapter 22**

1. For a detailed discussion of bundling, see chapter 9.

2. This analysis implicitly assumes that the acquiring firm does not take on additional debt to finance the merger. This assumption does not always hold. For example, recently there has been a spate of acquisitions by private equity firms that finance their acquisitions using bonds. For a general discussion of private equity firms, see section 22.7 of this chapter.

3. "Art of the Deal Meets the China Syndrome," *New York Times*, 14 July 2006.

4. "Merger Challenge: Unite Toothbrush, Toothpaste," *Wall Street Journal*, 24 April 2007.

5. For empirical evidence, see Christian, Thomas, and Sharan Jagpal (1988), "Merger-Related Synergy: More Fiction than Fact," Working Paper, Rutgers Business School.

6. "IBM's Deal to Acquire Telelogic Underscores Software Strategy," *Wall Street Journal*, 12 June 2007.

7. "A Big Vision, Only If G.M. Is Willing," *New York Times*, 14 July 2006.

8. "PepsiCo's Earnings Are Up 14%," *New York Times*, 14 July 2006.

9. See Koku, Paul S., Sharan Jagpal, and P. V. Viswanath (1996), "The Impact of New Product Development Alliances on Stock Prices," Working Paper, Rutgers Business School.

10. It is not sufficient to know the separate distributions of consumers' reservation prices for the brands in question. One also needs to know the correlation structure of these reservation prices. See Jedidi, K., S. Jagpal, and P. Manchanda (2003), "Measuring Heterogeneous Reservation Prices for Product Bundles," *Marketing Science*, 22, 1, 107–130.

11. See chapter 18 for a detailed discussion of noncooperative equilibrium in markets with differentiated products.

12. For a detailed discussion of methods to value brand equity, see chapter 19.

13. See Jedidi, K., S. Jagpal, and P. Manchanda (2003).

14. A more complete analysis can be conducted as follows. Suppose there are four brands in the market: A, B, C, and D. Brand A now acquires Brand B. How much should Brand A be willing to pay to acquire Brand B? For simplicity, assume that the product will become obsolete after one period. The first step is to determine the equilibrium market prices for Brands A, B, C, and D when all four brands compete with each other. Suppose Brand A's profit for the period is $700 million. The second step is to determine the new equilibrium when one firm owns both Brands A and B, a second firm owns Brand C, and a third owns Brand D.

Suppose the postacquisition joint profits for Brands A and B for the period are $1.8 billion. Then, the maximum price that Brand A should be willing to pay to acquire Brand B is $1.1 billion (joint profits of Brands A and B after the acquisition – profits of Brand A before the acquisition).

15. "Merger Challenge: Unite Toothbrush, Toothpaste," *Wall Street Journal*, 24 April 2007, A1.

16. As of July 2007, legislation is pending to tax carried interest at the ordinary income tax rate (35%) rather than at the lower capital gains tax rate (15%).

17. "Art of the Deal Meets the China Syndrome," *New York Times*, 14 July 2006.

◣ Chapter 23

1. Desvaux, Georges, and Alastair J. Ramsay (June 2006 Special Edition), "Shaping China's Home-Improvement Market: An Interview with B&Q's CEO for Asia," *McKinsey Quarterly*.

2. "Wal-Mart's German Retreat," *BusinessWeek Online*, 28 July 2006.

3. "Can M'm, M'm Good Translate?" *Wall Street Journal*, 9 July 2007.

4. "Wal-Mart's German Retreat," *BusinessWeek Online*, 28 July 2006.

5. Hoover, William E., Jr. (2006), "Making China Your Second Home Market: An Interview with the CEO of Danfoss," *McKinsey Quarterly*, 1.

6. See chapter 8 for a discussion.

7. See chapter 8 for a discussion of the *latent-class methodology*.

8. "Google Aims to Make Gains in China by Giving Units Greater Autonomy," *Wall Street Journal*, 27 April 2007.

9. "MySpace China, under Local Control, Enters the Fray," *Wall Street Journal*, 27 April 2007.

10. "Citibank: Launching the Credit Card in Asia Pacific (A)," *Harvard Business School*, 9–595-026.

11. This type of linear multiperiod employment contract will be optimal if both the parent company and the country manager have *time-additive exponential utility functions* and the country manager's effort is observable. For a discussion, see pp. 280–282 in Jagpal, Sharan (1999), *Marketing Strategy and Uncertainty*, New York: Oxford University Press. More complicated nonlinear contracts (e.g., progressive compensation plans where the country manager's effort is unobservable to the parent company or the parent company delegates partial decision-making authority to the country manager) can be analyzed using the same approach.

12. For a succinct theoretical discussion of different employment contracts for compensating country managers, see pp. 303–305 and pp. 310–311 in Jagpal, Sharan (1999), *Marketing Strategy and Uncertainty*.

13. For a technical discussion, see chapter 9 in Jagpal, Sharan (1999), *Marketing Strategy and Uncertainty*.

14. "Offshoring Goes on the Offensive," (2004), *McKinsey Quarterly*, 2.

15. "Dell to Use Chip Made by A.M.D.," *New York Times*, 19 May 2006.

16. See chapter 17 for a discussion of appropriate methods.

17. For a discussion of the real options methodology, see chapter 2.

18. See chapter 16 for a detailed discussion of dynamic compensation contracts where the employee's effort affects long-run costs or revenues.

a priori segmentation Forming groups of similar customers based on existing information.

accounting cost The difference between the firm's revenues and the payments that it makes to outsiders. Accounting profit often overstates the true profitability of the firm because it does not consider hidden costs (e.g., the income that the owner gives up by not working for someone else).

acquisition utility (AU) This term is used in the behavioral literature and refers to the dollar value of the benefits provided by using a given product or service. This concept corresponds to the concept of reservation price in economics. *See* reservation price.

acquisitions The firm purchases another firm. This term is often used interchangeably with the term *mergers*. However, there is a legal distinction between mergers and acquisitions.

addressable market The part of the market that the firm targets. *See* served market.

administrative synergies When a merger reduces the combined administrative costs for the merged firms.

adverse selection The informed parties in a contract self-select in a manner that is harmful to the uninformed parties. For example, persons who know that their automobiles are lemons have an incentive to sell these automobiles on the secondhand market. Since potential buyers cannot distinguish good used automobiles from lemons, their willingness to pay for used automobiles is low. If the "lemons" problem is sufficiently severe, the market for used automobiles will disappear.

advertising elasticity   The advertising elasticity of demand measures how responsive sales volume is to a change in advertising expenditure. Suppose that, starting from a given policy, the firm increases its advertising by 1%. If sales volume increases by 3%, the advertising elasticity is 3.

advertising goodwill   The unobservable effect of previous advertising on current sales. Most empirical studies on advertising use ad hoc proxies for this unobservable construct (e.g., last period's sales or a linear combination of sales from a number of previous periods).

advertising-sales ratio   The ratio of advertising expenditure to sales revenue in a given period.

after-tax operating cash flow   The cash flows available to stockholders after the firm has met all its financial obligations.

agency theory   A principal hires an agent to perform a function, but the agent's effort is unobservable to the principal.

agent   Suppose A hires B to perform certain tasks. Then A is the principal, and B is the agent.

aided recall   The researcher gives the subject cues before measuring awareness.

anchoring effect   The effect of a change in an explanatory variable (e.g., advertising) on a dependent variable (e.g., sales) depends on a particular value for the explanatory variable. This value is known as the anchor. For example, suppose the anchor value of advertising for a firm is last month's advertising budget (say $500,000). Then, if the advertising budget this month is increased to $600,000, the effect on sales depends on the deviation from this anchor value (600,000 − 500,000 = actual advertising spending − anchor value of advertising). In general, the anchoring effect is asymmetric for positive and negative deviations from the anchor value.

annual compound return   The investor receives interest on accrued interest. For example, suppose an individual invests $100 for two years at a compound rate of 10% per annum. Then, the amount due at the end of the first year is $110 (principal + interest). Since the investor is paid compound interest, the investor will receive $121 at the end of the second year (110 + 110 × 10% = principal at the end of the first year + interest on this principal).

annual discount rate   The annual rate of return on an investment.

anticompetitive effect   One firm obtains an unfair advantage over other firms in the industry, possibly forcing some competitors to leave the industry.

arbitrage   If someone can buy a product cheaply in one market and sell it in another market for a higher price.

Arrow-Pratt absolute risk aversion coefficient (ARA)   A measure of the premium a risk-averse person or firm is willing to pay to avoid a fair bet (i.e., a bet in which the expected gain is zero). Typically, one assumes that ARA decreases with wealth. However, some argue that ARA can increase with wealth. *See also* certainty equivalent.

assimilation-contrast theory   A theory that argues that large stimuli (e.g., price cuts) will affect current decisions but will not affect future decisions (i.e., the stimuli are "contrasted"). However, moderate stimuli can affect both current and future decisions (i.e., the stimuli are "assimilated" in the future). This theory has important implications for marketing policy, especially for pricing.

asymmetric cash flows   The cash flows from downside risk (below-average cash flows) are significantly different from the cash flows for upside gain (above-average cash flows).

asymmetric information   Two players do not share the same information. Asymmetric information has a major effect on contracts in the firm (e.g., the compensation plan) and on marketing in general. For example, an automobile manufacturer may have superior information about its product quality than the consumer. Hence the firm has an incentive to communicate its superior information to the firm (e.g., by offering an extended warranty on its cars).

auction   *See* reverse auction and Vickrey auction.

audience duplication   Some consumers are exposed to more than one advertising message by the firm during a given time period.

awareness effect   How advertising affects awareness.

B to B marketing   Business-to-business marketing. The firm's customers are other firms.

B to C marketing   Business-to-consumer marketing. The firm's customers are consumers.

bad turnover   Productive rather than unproductive workers leave the firm.

bandwagon effect   The future demand for a product increases with the number of units sold in the past. *See also* network externalities.

bankruptcy   The firm cannot meet its financial obligations to outsiders.

barriers to entry   Incumbents have an advantage over new entrants. Examples include sunk investments, advertising, channels of distribution, and minimum economic scale of operation.

barriers to exit   The firm faces significant losses if it leaves the industry. For example, suppose the firm enters an industry by setting up an expensive, specialized plant to produce a given product. If the firm subsequently leaves the industry because the demand for the product is weak, the market value of the plant will be close to zero.

BCG portfolio model   A strategic planning/resource allocation model that argues that a firm should choose its product mix and allocate its resources based on two factors: the market growth rate and the product's relative market share.

behavioral modes   Firms use different marketing decision variables to compete in the marketplace. For example, if one firm cuts its price, the other firm can increase its advertising (Behavioral Mode A), cut its price (Behavioral Mode B), or simultaneously increase its advertising and cut its price (Behavioral Mode C).

behavioral targeting Advertisers can customize their advertising to each individual based on that individual's Web-surfing behavior.

benefit-based message An advertising message strategy that emphasizes the benefits provided by the product.

Bertrand equilibrium An equilibrium in which firms choose prices simultaneously and do not cooperate. This is a special case of the Nash equilibrium. *See* Nash equilibrium.

Bertrand-Nash equilibrium *See* Bertrand equilibrium.

beta A measure of the risk facing investors who purchase a firm's stock. Specifically, the expected risk premium on the firm's stock = the firm's beta $\times$ risk premium on the market portfolio. Thus, if the firm's beta is 1, the risk that investors face by investing in the firm's stock is the same as the risk that they face by holding the market portfolio. Similarly, if the firm's beta is greater than (less than) 1, the risk that investors face by investing in the firm's stock is greater than (less than) the risk that they face by investing in the market portfolio. In general, the firm's beta depends on the firm's product mix, production decisions (e.g., choice of whether to use a labor-intensive or a capital-intensive production process), and marketing decisions (e.g., choice of target segments). *See also* capital asset pricing model (CAPM) and market portfolio.

bondholders Those who have given or purchased long-term loans to the firm.

bounded rationality Individuals make decisions based on incomplete information because information collection and information processing are costly. *See also* satisficing theory.

brand equity The dollar value of a brand name.

brand extension strategy Using an existing brand name to launch new products.

brand identity What a brand stands for; similar to a brand's positioning.

brand life cycle Brands go through the following phases: introduction, growth, maturity, and decline.

branding Strategies for making a product with a given design more attractive to consumers. In other words, increasing the consumer's reservation price for the firm's product offering. *See also* reservation price.

breakdown rate The probability that a product or system fails to perform.

break-even pricing Choosing a pricing strategy based on the minimum volume needed before the firm begins to make any profits.

break-even sales volume Consider any marketing policy (e.g., price). Then the break-even sales volume is the minimum volume that the firm needs to sell before it makes any profit.

bricks-and-mortar stores Stores located in actual, physical buildings. (As distinct from virtual stores online.)

budgeting rule A heuristic for choosing budgets. For example, set the advertising budget at 10% of the last period's sales revenue.

bundling Suppose the firm sells two products, A and B. Then bundling refers to the practice of selling the package (A + B). Note that the price of the bundle must be less than the sum of the separate prices of A and B. *See also* mixed bundling strategy and pure bundling strategy.

buzz Word-of-mouth activity.

cannibalization Consider a firm that sells two brands of cereal, A and B. Suppose the firm reduces the price of Brand A. Then some consumers who would have bought Brand B before will switch to Brand A. This effect is known as cannibalization.

capacity The volume of production at which unit cost is minimized.

capital asset pricing model (CAPM) According to the CAPM, the average expected return from investing in the firm's stock is equal to the rate of return on a riskless investment plus an excess return that is proportional to the riskiness of the stock (beta). *See also* certainty equivalent and beta.

carried interest A performance-based fee (typically a percentage of the excess profits generated over a hurdle rate of return) paid to the general partner of a private equity firm or the manager of a hedge fund. Presently, this fee is taxed at the capital gains tax rate (15%), which is lower than the corresponding ordinary income tax rate on this amount (35%).

cash cow According to the BCG portfolio model, a product with a high relative market share but a low growth rate. Such products are referred to as cash cows because they are expected to generate significant amounts of cash. *See* BCG portfolio model.

cash flow The difference between the cash received by the firm in a given period and the cash paid out.

cash rebate Money paid back to a customer by the firm after a purchase is made.

category management Choosing marketing policies for several products in a group to maximize performance for that group of products.

central information-processing Consumers transform information on the physical attributes of a product into perceptions (perceived benefits). These perceptions, in turn, drive preferences and choices.

certainty Everything in the market is known at the time a decision is made.

certainty case The decision maker knows all outcomes from choosing any given policy with precision.

certainty equivalent (CE) The guaranteed sum of money that an individual or firm will be willing to accept in exchange for a project with risky cash flows. Thus, suppose a firm has a project in hand and expects to make an average profit of $10 million from the project in the next period. If the firm is risk-averse, it will be willing to sell the project for a smaller sum of money (say, $8 million). We say that the certainty equivalent of the project to this firm is $8 million. Equivalently, we say that the risk premium is $2 million, or the risk-adjusted profit is $8 million.

certainty-equivalent demand   The guaranteed demand level that the decision maker is willing to accept in exchange for an uncertain demand. For example, suppose the expected demand for a given marketing policy is 1,000 units. Then, the certainty-equivalent demand will be less than 1,000 units for a risk-averse owner.

certainty-equivalent profit   The guaranteed profit that the decision maker is willing to accept in exchange for an uncertain profit. For example, suppose the expected profit for a given marketing policy is $10 million. Then, the certainty-equivalent profit will be less than $10 million for a risk-averse owner.

certainty-equivalent revenue   The guaranteed revenue that the decision maker is willing to accept in exchange for an uncertain revenue. For example, suppose the expected revenue for a given marketing policy is $5 million. Then, the certainty-equivalent revenue is less than $5 million for a risk-averse owner.

channel of distribution   A channel of distribution refers to the set of firms that are involved in getting the final product or service to the buyer. For example, suppose a manufacturer sells its products to retailers, who in turn sell the product to consumers. This supply chain network is known as a channel of distribution.

channel stability   The relationship between the firms in the channel of distribution is stable.

choice criteria   The decision rules that the consumer uses in deciding which product or brand to purchase.

choice experiment   A study in which consumers are asked to evaluate different sets of purchase alternatives (choice sets) and choose the best alternatives for each choice set.

choice set   A group of alternatives from which the consumer can choose.

churn rate   The rate at which current subscribers (users) to a service defect to other suppliers.

clickthrough fraud   A firm hires agents to clickthrough on advertising messages that its competitors have posted on the Web. The purpose is to mislead competitors about the effectiveness of their Internet advertising.

clickthroughs   The number of times a computer user clicks on an advertising message posted on the Internet.

closing wealth   The firm's initial wealth plus profits in a given time period.

cluster analysis   A set of techniques for grouping similar objects or consumers. These techniques can be useful for market segmentation.

Coase paradox   Suppose a firm decides to pursue a market skimming policy (i.e., to charge high prices initially and lower them over time). If consumers expect prices to keep falling in the future, they will continually postpone purchase. Because of this paradox, the firm's market-skimming strategy may not work.

cola wars   Whenever Coke increased its advertising expenditure, Pepsi followed suit and vice versa.

commoditization   Commoditization in an industry means that many firms offer products with the same configurations of attributes.

commodity market   A commodity market implies that the law of one price holds in the marketplace. That is, all firms that produce products with the same levels and combinations of attributes need to charge the same prices.

common customers   Overlapping market segments. Some consumers buy more than one product from the firm.

compensatory model   The consumer is willing to give up some of one attribute in exchange for more of another attribute. For example, a consumer may be willing to give up better gas mileage (up to a point) in exchange for a larger car that provides more safety. *See also* trade-off models.

competition-based pricing   Mimicking competitors' prices.

competitive industry   An industry in which many firms produce products of identical quality, consumers are well informed, and there are no barriers to enter or exit the industry.

competitive labor market   The firm knows the productivities of workers. Consequently, the firm pays the worker (e.g., salesperson) an amount that is equivalent to that worker's market value (i.e., the worker's reservation income). *See also* reservation income.

competitive set   Competing brands.

complementarity   *See* complementary products.

complementary products   The reservation price of a bundle is greater than the sum of the reservation prices of products in that bundle. *See also* reservation price.

complements   *See* complementary products. Alternatively, one input (e.g., TV advertising) increases the productivity of another (e.g., Internet advertising).

conditional net present value (NPV)   The net present value after adjusting for the economic value of strategic flexibility.

conditional profits   Profits that vary depending on the marketing policies chosen by a competitor.

conditional reservation prices   The reservation price of Product A depends on whether or not Product B is available to the consumer. *See also* reservation price.

conglomerate merger   A firm purchases another firm that is in an unrelated industry.

conjoint analysis   A statistical and experimental methodology for measuring the relationship among product attributes (including brand name and price) and consumer preferences.

conjunctive models   A consumer will consider a brand only if each attribute exceeds a minimum threshold level for that attribute.

conquesting A firm advertises on an Internet site right next to editorial content about a competitor.

consideration set The set of brands that an individual will select from when making a purchase decision. The consideration set is also known as the evoked set. Consideration sets vary across individuals and may not be well defined, especially when the consumer lacks previous experience with the product category in question. *See also* elimination by aspects.

constant absolute risk aversion A decision maker's willingness to take risks does not depend on his or her wealth.

consumer information structure The firm's knowledge about consumers' identities, such as whether or not the firm can identify previous buyers of its product.

consumer surplus The net gain to a consumer after purchasing a product. Thus, suppose a buyer is willing to pay $10 for a given product, but the market price is $7. Then the buyer obtains a consumer surplus of $3.

consumer welfare The net present value of the appropriate consumers' surpluses. *See also* net present value.

consumers Those who purchase and use services or products generated by firms.

contestable markets New entrants to a market face the same cost conditions as incumbent firms. A firm can enter or exit a market without losing any investment that is specific to that market.

control A baseline measurement against which to compare test results.

controlled purchase experiments Experiments in which one varies conditions and observes the purchase decisions of respondents.

cooperative equilibrium When firms decide not to compete against each other and, instead, choose policies to maximize their joint performance.

core competencies The fundamental strengths of the firm that are difficult for competitors to copy. These strengths can pertain to a number of areas, including technology, managing supply chains, and so on.

corporate cost of capital (CCC) The average rate of return on the total capital (stocks and bonds) invested in the firm.

corporate image advertising Advertising by the firm that is non-product-specific (e.g., advertising whose goal is to improve the perception of the firm).

cost center A unit of the firm whose performance is measured based on cost efficiency and not profits.

cost dynamics Future costs depend on current volume (e.g., the firm learns from experience).

cost of capital *See* corporate cost of capital.

cost structure The relationship between a firm's costs and volume produced.

cost-plus pricing Pricing by using some measure of cost (typically average cost) and adding a percentage to that cost. For example, suppose the average cost is $100 and the percentage added is 30%. Then the price charged is $130 per unit.

coupons   Discounts on purchases that do not vary with volume.

Cournot equilibrium   An equilibrium in which firms simultaneously choose the quantities of output to sell. This is a special case of the Nash equilibrium. *See* Nash equilibrium.

Cournot-Nash equilibrium   *See* Cournot equilibrium.

cross-couponing strategy   Suppose a firm markets two products, A and B (say, soap and detergent). Suppose the firm offers a coupon to those who purchase its brand of soap; specifically, this coupon is valid only for the purchase of the firm's detergent brand. Then the firm is pursuing a cross-couponing strategy.

cross-elasticity   A change in the marketing policy for one product affects the sales of another. For example, suppose Colgate's sales volume increases by 2% if Crest increases its price by 1%. Then, the cross-elasticity of demand for Crest is 2.

cross-product effects   A change in the marketing policy of one product affects the sales of another.

cross-product marketing interdependencies   The marketing policy for one product affects the sales of another.

cross-sectional data   Data across units (e.g., firms or consumers) for the same time period.

cross-selling   Sales of one product help to increase sales of another product made by the firm.

cumulative trial rate   The proportion of consumers who have purchased a specific new product at least once, on or before a particular date.

customer lifetime value   The net present value of the stream of future profits from a given customer. *See also* net present value.

customer loyalty   The repeat purchase rate if other factors are held constant.

customer relationship management (CRM)   Managing customer service and customer satisfaction to achieve optimal long-run results.

customer satisfaction   The degree to which the customer is satisfied. Customer satisfaction has multiple dimensions (e.g., satisfaction with the product and satisfaction with the level of after-sales service).

customized segment-specific message strategies   Choosing advertising message strategies that differ across segments.

cyclical industry   The prices of the firm's inputs (e.g., raw materials) and/or the firm's outputs (e.g., sales) vary depending on how well the economy as a whole is doing.

cyclicality   The degree to which the firm's cash flows vary with general macroeconomic conditions.

data mining   Analyzing data to identify patterns. This approach can be used for various purposes, including market segmentation.

data-intervalling problem   The data collection period does not match the period in which a policy change is effective. For example, suppose the firm collects and analyzes quarterly advertising and sales data. However, the effects of advertising are felt within a week after the advertisement is run.

deferred stock options   The right to purchase up to a specified number of shares at a fixed exercise price during a specified time period in the future. *See also* exercise price.

definition of market   Determination of the set of products or brands against which the firm's product competes.

demand dynamics   Future demand depends on the firm's current and past marketing decisions.

demand structure   The relationship among sales, the firm's marketing policies, and the marketing polices of the firm's competitors.

demand-pull strategy   The firm uses marketing policies that focus directly on the consumer and not on any intermediate firms in the channel of distribution. For example, the firm advertises to consumers and directly sends consumers promotional offers.

demand-push strategy   The firm attempts to increase sales by offering incentives to other firms in the channel of distribution. For example, the firm offers retailers a quantity discount.

demographic segmentation   Forming groups of similar customers based on such vital statistics as gender, income, and age.

dependent variable   One variable causes another. Suppose advertising causes sales. Then, sales is the dependent variable, and advertising is the independent variable.

differential tax rates   Tax rates differ from country to country. Consequently, the firm's optimal policies (including pricing policies) are country-specific.

differentiated oligopoly   An industry containing only a few firms that produce similar, but not identical, products.

diffusion   Those who are aware of the product in a given period inform other individuals about the product.

diffusion rate   The effect of the firm's current policies on future market growth rates.

diminishing returns to advertising   Each successive dollar that is spent on advertising is less effective than the previous dollar.

discount rate   The rate of return that the investor could have obtained by investing in a "similar" product or venture elsewhere.

disintermediation   Bypassing existing channels of distribution.

disjunctive models   A consumer will consider a brand only if the levels of some, but not all, attributes exceed certain minimum threshold levels for those attributes.

dividends   Periodic (e.g., annual) cash payments made by the firm to shareholders.

dog   According to the BCG portfolio model, a product with low market share and a low growth rate. *See* BCG portfolio model.

dominant strategy The firm's optimal strategy is unaffected by strategies chosen by the firm's competitors.

Dorfman-Steiner theorem The ratio of advertising expenditure to sales revenue is equal to the ratio of the advertising elasticity to price elasticity. *See also* advertising elasticity and price elasticity.

downside risk The possible loss associated with following a specific investment (marketing) strategy.

draw *See* irrecoverable draw and recoverable draw.

dual advertising message strategy The firm varies its message strategy across two or more media.

dummy variable An indicator variable used to capture the effect of an explanatory variable in a regression model.

dynamic carryover effects A firm's marketing policies (e.g., advertising) affect both current and future sales.

dynamic pricing policy When a firm coordinates its prices in different periods to maximize its long-run performance.

dynamic search behavior The consumer changes his or her behavior over time, balancing the anticipated gain (e.g., from finding a lower price for the product) with the additional cost of search (e.g., the extra time or money involved).

economic concept of opportunity cost Costs that are paid plus hidden costs. An example of a hidden cost is the implicit cost of investing one's own time or money in an entrepreneurial activity.

economic cost Economic cost = accounting cost + hidden cost. For example, the accounting cost to a retailer of being out of stock is zero. However, the hidden cost is positive. It is the profit that could have been earned on an out-of-stock unit plus the future profits that could have been earned via repeat purchases by that customer who was unable to purchase the out-of-stock unit.

economic fixed costs Costs, including hidden costs, that do not change based on volume (e.g., implicit costs to the entrepreneur of using his or her own funds to run the firm).

economic power Some firms are in a stronger position to negotiate than others. For example, large consumer goods companies such as Procter & Gamble are often in a stronger position to negotiate than most stores that sell their products. In contrast, large retailers such as Wal-Mart are often in a stronger position to negotiate than their suppliers.

economic profit Accounting profit minus all imputed costs not included in revenue or in cost (e.g., the opportunity cost of personal funds invested in the business by the owner and the opportunity cost of his or her labor). In competitive markets, the firm's economic profit (after allowing for risk) is zero.

economic value The net benefit to an agent after considering all costs, including hidden costs.

economic value of waiting for uncertainty to be resolved The increase in net present value by revising decisions based on the arrival of new information. *See also* net present value.

economies of scale Unit costs decrease with volume. For example, fixed costs are high, or inputs can be purchased at volume discounts.

economies of scope The multiproduct firm has an advantage over firms that specialize in particular products. For example, on the demand side, two products may share a common customer base. Alternatively, the costs of a multiproduct sales force are lower than the combined sales force costs of firms that specialize in particular products. Note that economies of scope do not imply economies of scale and vice versa.

efficient markets hypothesis The hypothesis that prices, particularly those of securities (e.g., stocks), fully and accurately reflect all information relevant to predicting future returns. *See also* semistrong form, weak form, and strong form efficient markets hypothesis.

elasticity Elasticity measures how responsive sales are to a change in a marketing policy. For example, suppose the sales of a product increase by 3% when the firm reduces its price by 1%. Then the price elasticity is –3.

electronic exchange Internet brokers who match ad buyers with sellers of unused advertising space on Web sites or on conventional media such as TV and radio.

elimination by aspects The consumer first selects an attribute with a probability that is proportional to that attribute's importance. Next, the consumer eliminates all brands that do not exceed a threshold requirement for that attribute. Note that this model implies that the consideration sets for a given consumer are not fixed. In particular, the consideration set for a consumer varies and depends on the importance of the attributes in question. *See also* consideration set.

entry-deterrence strategies Strategies to discourage competitors from entering the market in the future. For example, the firm may build a new plant whose capacity substantially exceeds current demand.

equilibrium There are no market forces that encourage firms to change their behaviors.

equilibrium cumulative trial rate The upper bound on the proportion of consumers who will ever try a specific new product.

equilibrium repeat purchase rate The fraction of current buyers who will purchase a new product in the future, after consumers have had the chance to experiment and determine their long-run purchase behaviors.

event-study methodology Statistical tools to measure how new information (e.g., a new product announcement or a corporate name change following a merger) affects the returns to stockholders.

evoked set The set of brands that the consumer evaluates when making a purchase. The evoked set is equivalent to the consideration set. *See also* consideration set.

exclusive distributor   When the distributor carries the products of only one manufacturer.

exemplar brand   *See* industry standard.

exercise price   A fixed price per share at which the holder of a stock option has the right to purchase the firm's stock during a given time period.

experience curve   Costs (productivity) in any given period depend on both current and previous production. The firm can benefit from the experience curve in many areas, including production, advertising, and channels of distribution.

experience curve effect   *See* cost dynamics.

experience good   A product whose quality can be determined only after use.

exponential utility function   The only utility function for which the Arrow-Pratt absolute risk aversion coefficient is constant at all wealth levels. *See* Arrow-Pratt absolute risk aversion coefficient.

external cues   A proxy for product quality used by uninformed consumers. *See* also signals.

external reference price   The consumer determines value based on the deviation of the price paid from an external price, for example, the list price of a brand or the "fair" price.

financial cost   What the investor could have made had she invested her money in a different venture with the same risk-return features.

financial leverage   The use of debt to increase the expected return on equity. Financial leverage is defined as the ratio of long-term debt to long-term capital. Since long-term leases require the firm to commit to a set of fixed payments over time, these payments should be included in long-term debt and long-term capital. Thus, financial leverage = (long-term debt + value of leases)/(long-term debt + value of leases + equity).

financial synergy   When the cash flows of the merged firm are less risky than those of the individual firms prior to the merger.

firms   Companies that produce and sell services and/or products.

firm-specific risk   Fluctuations in cash flows that are unrelated across firms. Since investors can eliminate these risks by diversifying, firm-specific risk does not affect a firm's stock value.

first mover   The first firm to enter a new market or to introduce a new product in an industry.

first-degree price discrimination   The firm charges each customer his or her reservation price. *See* reservation price.

first-generation buyers   Suppose a firm first introduces a basic durable product and then introduces a higher quality product at a later point in time. Those consumers who buy the basic product are first-generation buyers.

first-mover advantage theory   A theory that argues that the optimal strategy is to be first to the market.

fixed costs   Costs that do not change based on volume.

fixed wage contract   Compensation is a fixed salary.

flanking strategy   An aggressive policy in which the firm produces products of higher and lower qualities than those of its competitor(s). Consequently, the firm gains market share from both the quality-conscious and price-conscious segments.

flexible pricing   Prices are changed based on market conditions at any given point in time.

focus groups   A small group of consumers or potential consumers that is asked to discuss specific issues pertaining to the potential for successfully introducing a new product into the marketplace (e.g., the level of satisfaction with current products).

focused acquisition strategy   Acquiring a part of another firm based on strategic fit rather than merging with that firm.

forcing contract   A compensation plan in which sales agents are paid only if they meet or exceed their sales quotas.

franchising   The firm gives someone (the franchisee) the right to sell its products.

frequency   The average number of times the target audience is exposed to the firm's advertising message in a given time period.

full upgrade   When all the buyers of the firm's first-generation durable product upgrade to the firm's second-generation (higher quality product) in the future.

game the system   Managers define the market narrowly in order to artificially enhance market share.

game theory   A theory of market behavior in which firms choose their marketing policies based on the marketing policies that they expect their competitors to use.

general equilibrium analysis   Analyzing multiple markets simultaneously. *See also* partial equilibrium analysis.

goodwill   An intangible asset that has a positive impact on the value of the firm. *See also* advertising goodwill.

grim-trigger pricing strategy   A repeated game in which firms that "cheat" (e.g., undercut competitors by charging a low price) are penalized by the other firms in the industry. For example, when a cheater is detected in an undifferentiated oligopoly, the other firm(s) drive it out of business by reducing the price of the product just below the cheater's marginal cost.

gross channel profit   (Retail price − marginal cost per unit of retailer − marginal cost per unit of manufacturer) × volume sold.

gross margin per unit   Price − variable cost per unit.

gross margins   Sales revenue − variable costs.

gross profit margin   Gross margin per unit × volume sold.

gross rating points (GRPs)   The total number of advertising exposures obtained by using a particular media plan. Thus, suppose the media plan reaches 100,000 individuals with an average frequency of 2.5 in a given time period. Then, the GRP for this plan is 250,000.

gross revenue   *See* revenue.

group hedging policies   The corporate headquarters for the multinational firm centralizes currency-hedging operations. *See* hedge.

growth-adjusted multiplier   A multiplier that adjusts for future growth rates. This multiplier is applied to future profits in order to determine net present value, including the value of brand equity.

GRP model   Advertising effectiveness depends on the total number of advertising exposures from a given media plan.

halo effect   The consumer's perceptions of one benefit or attribute affect that consumer's perceptions of other benefits or attributes. For example, the consumer concludes that, by definition, an inexpensive wine is of low quality (negative halo effect) or that a PC with a Pentium chip will be faster than a computer that uses a different type of chip (positive halo effect).

harvester   A sales agent who is responsible for retaining existing customers.

hedge   Buying one currency and selling another in order to reduce risk.

hedge fund   A limited partnership of institutional investors (e.g., pension funds) and wealthy private investors that uses debt to invest in a wide class of assets with different risk-return combinations (e.g. stocks, options, and foreign currencies). Most hedge funds invest primarily in liquid assets and allow investors to enter or leave the fund easily. Recently, hedge funds have become increasingly involved in corporate takeovers and attempts to change corporate management. *See also* private equity firms.

hedonic pricing   All products with the same combinations of attributes and attribute levels must be sold at the same market price.

Herfindahl index   The sum of the squared market shares of all brands in the market. This index is used to measure the degree of market power.

hold-up problem   Suppose a firm enters into a contract with another firm (partner) and makes a relationship-specific investment. Then, the partner can behave opportunistically in the future by threatening to terminate the relationship. By using this "hold-up" threat, the partner can obtain better terms than those initially agreed on in the contract.

horizontal differentiation   Suppose consumers disagree about the meaning of product quality. Consider two soft drinks, A and B. Suppose A is sweeter than B, but B has more carbonation. Then some consumers think that A has superior quality; others think that B has superior quality. We say that the market is horizontally differentiated. *See also* vertical differentiation.

horizontal merger   A firm purchases another firm that is in the same industry. For example, one toothpaste manufacturer acquires another.

hunter   Sales agents who are responsible for bringing in new customers.

hurdle rate   The minimum rate of return that the firm must earn in order to invest in a given project (e.g., a new product launch).

hurdle rate of return   *See* hurdle rate.

hybrid organizational structure   An organizational structure based on multiple criteria (e.g., products and regions).

hybrid sales-based contract A compensation scheme in which the commission rate increases up to a certain point and then goes down.

identification problem A model must be identified before one can estimate the parameters. For example, suppose the demand for a product depends on prices and advertising. If the firm always increases advertising by $x\%$ when it cuts price by $y\%$, it is impossible to estimate the effects of price and advertising using historical data. We say that there is an identification problem.

idiosyncratic risk *See* firm-specific risk.

incentive compatible A methodology that leads consumers to provide responses that are consistent with their true reservation prices. *See also* reservation price.

incentive money The money given to members of the target segment who are chosen to participate in a simulated market test. This money can be either spent by the consumer in the simulated test market or taken home as compensation for participating in the research study.

income shortfall Income that is below the target income.

income volatility Fluctuations in income.

incremental costs Additional costs associated with increased production.

incremental loss of value A reduction in value when a policy is changed. For example, suppose the initial value is $1 million. After a marketing policy change, the value is reduced to $960,000. Then the incremental loss in value is $40,000.

indivisibilities *See* lumpy investment strategy.

industry standard The benchmark against which all competing products are compared.

informative advertising Advertising that creates awareness or provides information about a product's attributes or benefits.

information release events (IREs) *See* product announcements.

inframarginal units The units that the firm could have sold at a higher price. For example, suppose the firm can sell 1,000 units at a price of $7 per unit. If the firm reduces the price to $5 per unit (say), there are 1,000 inframarginal units. Note that the loss in revenue from these inframarginal units ($2,000) is a direct loss in profits that the firm could have earned from selling those units at a higher price.

infrastructural support Fixed equipment (e.g., a computerized information system) that is shared by different units in the firm.

innovation Introduction of a new product. If the quality-adjusted cost ratio of the new model is much lower (higher) than the corresponding ratio for the old model, we say that the innovation is major (minor). If the quality-adjusted cost ratio of the new model is somewhat higher than the corresponding ratio for the old model, we say that the innovation is moderate.

installed base effect The demand in any given period depends on the number of units previously sold (e.g., the demand for fax machines).

intangible assets   A company's assets, such as managerial or R&D personnel or intellectual property, that are not measured on the balance sheet.

intellectual property   Knowledge that is private to the firm.

intention studies   Studies in which (1) consumers are asked to state how likely they are to purchase a product, and (2) consumers' answers are used to forecast product demand.

intention-purchase relationship   How closely consumers' predictions of their purchase behavior match their actual behavior.

intentions data   Consumers' self-stated predictions of how likely they will be to purchase a product.

intermediate quantity   Suppose advertising affects a behavioral variable (e.g., awareness) that, in turn, affects sales. We say that awareness is an intermediate quantity.

internal rate of return (IRR)   The discount rate at which the net present value of a project is zero. *See also* discount rate; net present value.

internal reference price   Consumers use an internal yardstick to determine a benchmark price for a product, for example, a fair price or an expected price.

internal transfer price   The price that one unit of a firm charges other units of the firm for a given product or resource, for example, the price that the parent company charges a subsidiary for a raw material.

international diversification   A firm extends its activities to foreign countries.

inventory holding cost   The cost associated with keeping a product in stock.

irrecoverable draw   The sales agent is paid a fixed sum of money up front. If sales are above a specified level, the firm pays the sales agent an additional amount based on the overage. If sales are below the specified level, the agent does not return any money to the firm. *See also* recoverable draw.

joint costs   Costs that are common to products. For example, two products are sold through the same sales force.

joint distribution of reservation prices   The structure of reservation prices for different products, including the degree to which these reservation prices are correlated. *See also* reservation price.

joint effect   The combined effect of changing two or more marketing decision variables simultaneously.

joint industry profits   The sum of all profits made by competing brands in an industry.

joint profits   The sum of the profits of two or more firms.

joint venture   An enterprise in which two or more firms share risk and return.

junk bonds   Bonds issued to finance a leveraged buyout that are backed by the target company's cash flows. These bonds increase the firm's financial leverage. *See also* leveraged buyout.

just noticeable differences (JNDs) The theory of just noticeable differences implies that there are threshold effects. For instance, if a price cut is too small and does not exceed a threshold level, it will have no effect in the marketplace. Importantly, the threshold effect depends on the relative magnitude of the change and on the absolute magnitude. *See also* threshold effects.

just-in-time (JIT) manufacturing A production system in which inventories of work in progress are minimized because required inputs are delivered to each stage of the manufacturing process exactly when needed.

lag effect A marketing policy affects both current and future sales.

late entrants Firms enter an industry late.

latent class methodology A methodology that allows one to simultaneously determine how many unobserved segments there are, classify respondents into those segments, and determine the model structure for each segment. This method is useful when the firm has limited prior information about how to form segments.

law of one price There is only one market price for products with a given configuration of product attributes and attribute levels. *See also* hedonic pricing.

learning curve By increasing its current volume, the firm will become more efficient in the future.

learning curve effect *See* cost dynamics.

leveraged buyout (LBO) An acquisition in which a large part of the purchase price is financed by debt and the remaining equity is privately held by a small group of investors. *See also* management buyout.

lexicographic choice model The consumer ranks attributes by importance and evaluates brands one attribute at a time. If one brand has the highest score on the most important attribute, that brand is chosen. If two or more brands are tied for first place, the consumer compares them on the next most important attribute and chooses the brand that has the highest score. If the brands are tied, the consumer evaluates them on the third most important attribute and so on until the ties are broken and only one brand is left. That is the brand chosen.

limit pricing Charging a low price to deter potential competitors from entering the market. This strategy implicitly assumes that the potential competitors have incomplete information about the cost and/or demand structure of the industry. For example, they may use the incumbent's price as a signal of the profitability they might expect were they to enter the market.

linear cost structure Marginal costs do not change with volume. Consequently, gross profits are a fixed percentage of sales revenue.

linear profit-sharing contract A compensation contract in which the firm pays the agent a fixed wage and a fixed percentage of gross profits.

linear profit-sharing plan The firm pays the agent a fixed wage and a fixed percentage of gross profits.

linear wage-commission compensation plan   The agent is paid a fixed wage and a fixed percentage of the sales revenue that the agent generates.

liquid asset   Cash or an asset that can be quickly and easily turned into cash.

long-run collaborative channel strategy   Coordinating channel strategy to maximize the joint profits of firms in the channel.

long-run value   The current and future gains to the firm from pursuing particular marketing policies.

long-term debt   The firm uses bonds with a long maturation period to finance its activities. Bondholders must be paid interest before shareholders receive any payments.

long-term effects   The effect of marketing policies on future cash flows.

lumpy investment strategy   Investment must be made at one time and cannot be staggered.

management buyout   A special case of leveraged buyouts where the acquiring group is led by the firm's management.

management by objectives (MBO)   Employees have a role in identifying the objectives they will meet or in setting their own performance standards (e.g., salespersons have a role in setting sales quotas).

marginal buyer   Suppose the firm is presently charging a certain price for its product, say, $100. Then the marginal buyer is the buyer who is willing to pay just under $100 to purchase the product.

marginal consumer   *See* marginal buyer.

marginal cost   The additional cost associated with increasing production by each unit.

marginal productivity   The change in output (e.g., the number of units sold) when the firm uses one more unit of a resource (e.g., an additional dollar of advertising).

marginal profitability   The increase in profits for a given market segment when the firm changes its marketing policy.

marginal profit   The change in profit when the firm sells one more unit of the product. Marginal profits can be positive or negative.

marginal revenue   The change in revenue when the firm sells one more unit. Since the firm has to decrease its price in order to sell more units, marginal revenue can be positive or negative.

market condition   The market depends on decisions by the firm and its competitors. In addition, the market depends on factors outside the control of firms (e.g., interest rates).

market development organizations (MDOs)   A multinational firm sets up departments at both the regional and country levels to provide key country- and region-specific information to the global product-based units. The MDOs collaborate with those units to develop customized marketing plans on a geographical or country-specific basis.

market penetration   Charging a low introductory price to benefit in the future from cost dynamics or demand dynamics. *See also* strategic pricing.

market portfolio A portfolio that allocates dollars across different assets in proportion to their aggregate values in the overall economy.

market power The firm is in a strong bargaining position vis-à-vis suppliers of inputs or buyers of its finished products and services.

market price In a competitive industry, for any given product design or input quality, there is only one price the market will bear.

market price of risk A coefficient that measures the collective risk attitude of investors in the stock market.

market segmentation The process of dividing a market into nonoverlapping groups (segments) that respond differently to the firm's marketing efforts.

market share The ratio of the firm's sales during a given period to industry sales. Market shares can be measured based on volume or on revenue.

market signals One party provides information to another party when both parties do not have the same information. For example, suppose a car manufacturer knows that its cars are of high quality, but consumers do not. Then, the firm can signal its high quality by offering an extended warranty on the car.

market skimming The practice of charging a high price for a new product and reducing prices over time.

market value The price the market is willing to pay for any given item or service.

marketing concept Developing new products based on a prior analysis of customer preferences.

marketing-finance interface Making decisions based on the interdependence between marketing and finance functions in an organization.

marketing mix This term refers to the following set of decisions by the firm: pricing, product design, promotion, and distribution.

marketing plan A detailed written description of the marketing strategies and tactics for a given product for a specified period of time (often one year).

markup pricing Product price is determined by adding a fixed percentage to the unit cost.

matched samples Groups of consumers who are similar on a specified dimension or dimensions. For example, the groups are chosen based on such demographic variables as age, income, and the educational levels of respondents.

mature product A product whose sales are no longer increasing over time.

maximum percentage premiums The maximum percentage over the current value of the firm to be acquired that the acquiring firm is willing to pay for the acquisition.

MCT methodology A prelaunch forecasting model that removes biases from self-stated intentions scores for multiple brands and simultaneously allows for multiple unobservable consumer segments.

media interaction effects The effect of advertising in one medium (e.g., TV) depends on the level of advertising that the firm does in another medium (e.g., newspapers). These interaction effects can be positive or negative.

media mix   The set of advertising media used by the firm.

menu of contracts   The firm offers the agent a choice of contracts with different risk-return combinations. For example, the firm could offer salespersons a choice of a fixed salary of $40,000 per year plus 2% commission on sales (Plan A) or a lower fixed salary of $25,000 plus a higher commission rate of 3% on sales (Plan B). Given these options, salespersons will choose a compensation plan based on their risk aversions and perceived productivities. Other factors being held constant, more risk-averse salespersons will choose Plan A. Similarly, other factors being held constant, more productive salespersons will choose Plan B.

mergers   One firm buys another. This term is often used interchangeably with acquisitions, although there are legal distinctions.

me-too brand   An undifferentiated brand that enters the marketplace.

me-too product   A new product that is very similar to existing products in the marketplace.

mixed bids   Purchasing another firm using both cash and stock.

mixed bundling strategy   Suppose a firm produces two products, A and B. Then the firm pursues a mixed bundling strategy if it sells A and B separately and as a package (A + B).

mixed channel strategy   The firm uses different channels to sell its product. For example, the firm sells its product through bricks-and-mortar retailers and through the Internet.

mixed outsourcing strategy   The firm uses outsourcing in addition to utilizing internal resources to perform a specific function (e.g., customer service).

mixed wage-bonus plan   Compensation scheme that pays a base salary plus a bonus.

mixed wage-commission plan   Compensation scheme that consists of a base salary plus commission paid per unit sold.

modified discount policy   The firm does not offer additional discounts beyond a certain volume.

monopoly pricing   When a firm can choose prices without considering competitive reaction. Monopoly pricing does not necessarily mean charging high prices (e.g., the monopolist may be able to leverage cost or demand dynamics).

monopsony   A market in which there is only one buyer.

moral hazard   The problems caused in a contract between a principal and an agent when the agent's effort is unobservable. For example, consider the extreme case of a one-period contract between a salesperson and the firm. If the salesperson's effort is unobservable and the salesperson is paid a fixed wage, he or she will have no incentive to work.

multilevel channels   The supply chain has more than two levels, for example, a manufacturer-wholesaler-retailer-consumer channel.

multiplier method Measuring brand equity by multiplying a specified number (e.g., current profits) by a factor. For example, suppose the firm is currently making a profit of $100 million per year. If the factor (multiplier) is 9, the brand equity is $900 million (annual profit × multiplier).

mutual fund A portfolio of assets that allows investors to buy shares of the entire portfolio to diversify risk.

myopic pricing Pricing strategy based on maximizing short-run profits.

myopic strategy Strategy based on maximizing short-run performance.

naive multiplier approach A multiplier that is chosen without adjusting for growth.

Nash equilibrium Consider two firms, A and B. Suppose A determines its best policies conditional on any decision(s) by B. Similarly, B determines its best policies conditional on any decision(s) by A. Then, the Nash equilibrium is defined by the pair of strategies chosen by A and B that is consistent with the decision processes described above.

negative brand equity The brand name has a negative effect on the firm's performance.

negatively correlated reservation prices When consumers with high reservation prices for Product A tend to have low reservation prices for Product B and vice versa. *See also* reservation price.

net economic benefit Reservation price less price paid.

net of cannibalization Profits from a new product – loss in profits from existing products. For example, suppose a new product produces a profit of $200 million but reduces the profits of the other products in the firm's product line by $40 million. Then, the new product's profit net of cannibalization is $160 million (200M – 40M).

net present value (NPV) The value of current and anticipated future profits, adjusted for risk. Equivalently, the amount by which a project increases the wealth of the owner(s).

net profit Gross profit minus fixed costs.

network externalities The willingness to pay of future consumers increases with the number of units sold in the past. This effect can be positive (e.g., the demand for fax machines) or negative (e.g., the demand for snob products). *See also* installed base effect.

nonaccounting costs Hidden costs. For example, the lost profits from not having sufficient inventory to meet current demand.

noncooperative equilibrium When each firm maximizes its conditional profits given its assumptions about how competitors will react.

noncooperative game theory A set of tools for analyzing industries in which there are few firms, each firm pursues its own self-interest, and the outcome for each firm (e.g., profits or market share) depends on the actions (e.g., prices charged) of its competitors.

nonexclusive distributor When a distributor sells products made by several competing firms.

no-purchase option   A choice experiment in which the consumer has the alternative of not purchasing any of the alternatives that he or she is offered in the experiment.

normal distribution   A bell-shaped curve that is completely defined by its mean and standard deviation.

oligopoly   An industry in which there are few firms and the outcomes for each firm (e.g., profits or market share) depend on the actions of its competitors. *See also* differentiated oligopoly and undifferentiated oligopoly.

oligopsony   A market in which there are only a few buyers.

one-stop shopping   Purchasing multiple products or services from the same firm.

opportunity cost   The maximum loss in value from not having chosen another alternative. For example, suppose an entrepreneur can obtain a job in the marketplace for $80,000 per year. Then, the opportunity cost of working for himself or herself as an entrepreneur is $80,000.

optimal profit   The maximum profit that the firm can attain using its resources and marketing policies.

outsourcing   When a firm employs lower-paid workers abroad to reduce costs. Alternatively, the firm sells products under its own name, but foreign firms actually make these products.

panel   A fixed group of consumers whose purchase behavior is tracked over time (especially in a test market situation).

panel data   Data collected from a consumer panel (especially in a test market situation).

Pareto optimal   A contract such that it is impossible to make one party better off without making the other party worse off.

part worths   The effect of a product attribute on preference for that product. The part-worth model assumes that each attribute has its own separate effect on consumer preferences.

partial equilibrium analysis   Analyzing each market in isolation. Thus, suppose the computer industry increases its demand for graduates in computer science. Then, the analysis focuses exclusively on the computer industry. For example, the analysis does not consider the effect of the reduced supply of computer science graduates on other industries (e.g., manufacturing and IT).

partial upgrade   When only a fraction of the buyers of the old product (first-generation buyers) upgrade to the higher quality product in the future.

payoff matrix   A table containing information on strategies and the corresponding profits for competing firms.

perceived benefits   The benefits that a consumer anticipates a brand will provide.

percentage premium   (The increase in profit to Brand A after it acquires Brand B/profit of Brand B before the acquisition) $\times$ 100.

perceptual mapping A set of psychometric techniques to determine (1) which perceptual dimensions affect consumer choice behavior and (2) the perceptual scores for different products and brands. Perceptual mapping can be useful in defining the set of brands or products that compete with the firm's product.

perceptual product benefits The benefits that a consumer anticipates a brand will provide.

perfect price discrimination Charging each consumer the maximum that he or she is willing to pay. *See also* Reservation Price

performance fees Payments to the general partners of a private equity firm for exceeding a target. *See* private equity firm.

peripheral information-processing When consumers do not filter information about brands through a perceptual lens. Rather, the brand stimulus affects their preferences and choices directly.

persuasive advertising Advertising attempts to change the importance that consumers place on particular product benefits/features.

piece rate Commission is based on the number of units sold.

pioneering advantage theory A theory that argues that the optimal strategy is to be first to the market. *See also* first-mover advantage theory.

planning horizon The time period that is used to evaluate outcomes.

point-of-purchase advertising Advertising by the firm at the location where the firm's product is sold.

portfolio theory A scientific method that allows an investor to optimally allocate resources across multiple assets based on that investor's risk and return trade-off.

positive brand equity The brand name increases the wealth of the owner(s).

positively correlated reservation prices When consumers with high reservation prices for Product A tend to have high reservation prices for Product B and vice versa. *See also* reservation price.

positioning *See* product positioning.

preannouncements Information released to the market prior to the product being made available.

predatory pricing A firm drives out competitors by pricing low (e.g., the firm prices below the minimum variable costs of its competitors). By using this strategy, the firm forgoes current profits in order to achieve higher profits in the future when the firm becomes the dominant player in the market.

preference study A study in which consumers are asked to separately evaluate different product profiles. *See* also conjoint analysis.

present value *See* net present value.

price discrimination When a firm charges different prices to different groups of consumers defined according to various criteria (e.g., geography and demographics).

price discrimination strategy   A strategy in which the firm charges different groups of consumers different prices. Examples include lowering the price of a durable over time (intertemporal price discrimination or, equivalently, market skimming); offering different package sizes in the market at any given time; and offering current buyers a coupon (price discount) good toward future purchase.

price dispersion   The price of a product or service varies across consumers or outlets.

price elasticity   The price elasticity of demand measures how responsive sales volume is to a change in price. For example, suppose the sales volume will increase by 2% if the price is reduced by 1%. Then, the price elasticity is 2.

price insensitive   Charging a higher price does not reduce demand by much.

price leadership   One firm (the leader) sets a price. Competitors then choose their prices to maximize their respective conditional profits.

price oscillations   Price fluctuates over time.

price premium   Charging a higher price than competing products in the market.

price sensitivity   The degree to which sales volume changes when prices are adjusted upward or downward.

price skimming   When a firm reduces its price over time so that it can capture consumer surplus. *See also* consumer surplus.

price war   When all competing firms engage in reducing prices because of one competitor's price-cutting strategy.

price-cutting strategy   When a firm slashes prices in the marketplace to increase performance.

primary demand   The demand for a product category. Typically, the pioneering brand focuses on building demand for the product category.

principal   Suppose the firm hires a salesperson to perform a sales task. Then the firm is the principal, and the salesperson is the agent.

prisoners' dilemma   Firms in a market compete aggressively even though each firm would be better off if all firms cooperated. For example, if there are two firms in a market, each firm will be better off if both firms charge higher prices (cooperative solution) rather than if both firms compete aggressively and charge low prices (Nash equilibrium). In general, firms can escape the prisoners' dilemma and achieve the cooperative solution if they interact repeatedly, cost and demand conditions are stable, there are few firms, and there are no new entrants.

private equity firms   Limited partnerships or limited liability companies that are established to acquire target companies using debt and funds committed by institutional investors (e.g., pension funds) and wealthy private investors. In contrast to hedge funds, investors in private equity firms are generally locked in for the entire term of the limited partnership (which can extend to ten years). *See also* hedge fund.

privately held firm   A firm whose ownership is not available to the public.

problem children   According to the BCG portfolio model, a product with low relative market share but a high growth rate. *See* BCG portfolio model.

process innovations—major   The new technology allows the firm to reduce its costs significantly.

process innovations—minor   The new technology leads to a small reduction in costs.

process innovations—moderate   The new technology leads to a moderate reduction in costs.

producer welfare   The net present value of the firm's current and future profits.

product announcements   Information released to the market close to the time when the new product is to be introduced.

product differentiation   Product attributes or benefits that distinguish the product in question from its competitors.

product life cycle   Products go through the following phases: introduction, growth, maturity, and decline.

product positioning   The space occupied by a brand in the consumer's mind.

product preannouncements   Informing the public that a new product will be introduced in the future, but not immediately.

product profile   A description of the attributes and attribute levels contained in a product.

profit   Revenue minus costs.

profit center   A unit of the firm whose performance is measured based on the profits it generates.

profitability   The ratio of profit in a given period to investment at the beginning of that period. *See* return on investment.

profit-based contract   A compensation plan in which the agent (e.g., a salesperson or manager) is paid a share of profits.

profit-sharing compensation plan   *See* profit-based contract.

progressive commission structure   The commission rate increases with the volume sold.

progressive profit-sharing plan   The agent's profit-sharing rate increases with profits.

progressive slab system   The commission rate increases with the volume sold. For example, the sales agent is paid ½% on the revenue from the first 2,000 units sold; ⅔% on the revenue from the next 1,000 units sold; and ¾% on the revenue from all additional units sold.

promotion elasticity   How sensitive the firm's sales are to changes in promotional expenditure. For example, suppose the sales volume will increase by 2% if the firm increases its promotional expenditure by 1%. Then, the promotional elasticity is 2.

prospect theory   A behavioral theory that argues that individuals evaluate gains and losses separately. Prospect theory has major implications for pricing (e.g., coupon and rebate policy), sales force compensation, and customer relationship management. In addition, prospect theory has major implications for the financial marketplace (e.g., target earnings per share and dividend policy).

psychographic segmentation   Dividing consumers into groups based on similarity along psychological dimensions (e.g., interests, opinions, and lifestyle).

pure bundling strategy   Suppose a firm produces two products, A and B. Then the firm is pursuing a pure bundling strategy if it sells only the bundle (A + B). That is, consumers cannot buy A or B separately.

pure commission plan   A compensation scheme in which the agent is not paid a base salary. All income is based on sales.

quality   This concept is ambiguous except for the case where quality can be measured on one dimension. *See also* horizontal differentiation and vertical differentiation.

quality-adjusted cost ratios   The cost per unit after adjusting for product quality.

quantity discounts   The price per unit decreases with the number of units purchased.

quota system   Sales target to be achieved.

race to the market   Entering the market as soon as possible (e.g., in order to obtain a first-mover advantage). *See* first-mover.

random sampling   Each unit in a population has the same chance of being chosen as any other unit. In addition, each group containing x units has the same chance of being chosen as any other group of units containing the same number of units (x).

rate of return   The discount rate for a specific activity. *See* discount rate.

reach   The number of persons who have been exposed to the firm's advertising at least once in a given time period.

reach model   A model according to which advertising productivity depends on reach (i.e., the number of individuals who have been exposed to the firm's advertising at least once in a given time period).

reaction curve   The optimal decision (e.g., pricing) by one firm conditional on the same decision by its competitor(s).

reaction function   An algebraic description of the reaction curve.

real options   *See* real options theory.

real options theory   A theory that argues that a firm should make long-run decisions after allowing for the economic value of flexibility. One interesting implication is that, under certain conditions, the optimal policy may be to choose a strategy for which the conventional measure of long-run value (net present value) is negative. *See also* net present value.

realized future profit   The actual profit made by the firm in the future after uncertainty has been resolved.

recoverable draw   The sales agent is paid a fixed sum of money up front. If the sales outcome is below a specified level, the agent will return some money to the firm under a formula specified in the contract. If sales exceed the specified level, the agent is paid an additional sum of money based on the overage.

reference point The consumer determines value based on deviations of market outcomes (e.g., product performance after purchase) from a reference outcome (e.g., the expected level of product performance).

reference price A consumer determines the gain or loss from a transaction based on the difference between the actual price paid and a reference value for price (e.g., the price that the consumer expects to pay). *See* also internal reference price and external reference price.

regression analysis A set of techniques to measure the relationship among a set of explanatory variables (regressors) and a dependent variable. This methodology is frequently used to estimate marketing relationships (e.g., how a firm's prices and advertising affect the firm's sales).

regressive commission plan The commission rate decreases with volume.

relationship segment Customers who make repeat purchases from the firm.

reminder advertising Advertising that is done to keep brand awareness high enough so that customers are not lost over time.

repeat purchase behavior Whether a customer buys the same product or brand again.

repeat purchase rate The probability that a customer will buy the same product or brand again. This probability can be weighted by the number of units the consumer is likely to purchase in the future.

required rate of return The minimum rate of return (after adjusting for risk) that an investor or owner is willing to accept for a particular project.

reservation income The minimum guaranteed amount that an agent (e.g., a salesperson) is willing to accept when he or she works for the firm. For example, suppose a sales agent is willing to work for a guaranteed annual income of $60,000. Then the agent's reservation income is $60,000.

reservation price The maximum price that a consumer is willing to pay for any given brand.

reservation price effect How advertising affects consumers' reservation prices.

response error Consumers do not provide accurate answers. For example, self-stated willingness-to-pay (WTP) data are typically not the same as the true WTPs.

retention rate The fraction of buyers who will continue to buy the firm's product in the future.

retiring long-term debt The firm pays off some bondholders.

return on investment (ROI) The ratio of profit in a given period to investment at the beginning of that period. Thus, if the investment was $10 million and the profit was $2 million, the ROI was 20%.

return on the market portfolio The return on a fully diversified portfolio of assets in the economy.

revenue   Money coming in from sales.

revenue-sharing contract   A compensation contract in which the firm pays the sales agent a fixed wage and a fixed percentage of revenues.

reverse auction   An auction in which each consumer is required to purchase the product if his or her bid is higher than the seller's secret threshold value. If a bid is below this threshold, the seller will not sell the product to that bidder.

reverse causality   Two variables cause one another. For example, suppose advertising affects sales, but sales also affect advertising via a budgeting rule used by the firm. We say that there is reverse causality. This has important implications for estimating how a change in one variable (e.g., advertising) affects the other (e.g., sales).

reverse engineering   Taking a product apart to see how it was originally constructed so as to copy it.

risk adjustment   A downward adjustment in expected profits to correct for the effect of risk. For example, suppose a risk-averse investor can invest in a project whose expected profit is $10 million. Since the investor does not like risk, the investor will value this project at less than $10 million (say, $9 million). Then, we say that the risk adjustment is $1 million (10 M – 9M).

risk attitude   Willingness to take risk. *See also* risk-neutral, risk-averse, and risk-seeking.

risk aversion   A measure of willingness to take risk. This is measured by the risk premium that an individual is prepared to pay to avoid a fair bet (i.e., a bet in which the expected return is zero). *See also* risk premium.

risk premium   A downward adjustment in expected profits to correct for risk. Thus, suppose a project has an expected profit of $10 million. Then a risk-averse firm will be willing to sell the project for less than $10 million. Suppose the firm is willing to accept a guaranteed sum of $9 million in exchange for this project. Then, the risk premium is $1 million (10M – 9M).

risk premium for the publicly held firm   The amount by which the stock market reduces the firm's expected profits to adjust for risk. For example, suppose the stock market expects the firm to make a profit of $300 million. In addition, the stock market considers these uncertain profits to be equivalent to a guaranteed profit of $240 million. Then, the risk premium is $60 million (300M – 240M).

risk seeking   Successive additions of the same amounts to wealth are more and more valuable.

risk-adjusted advertising elasticity   The risk-adjusted advertising elasticity of demand measures how sensitive the firm's certainty-equivalent demand is to a change in advertising. *See also* certainty-equivalent demand.

risk-adjusted discount rate   The required average rate of return after adjusting for risk. For example, suppose the risk-free return is 7%. Then, the risk-adjusted discount rate will be greater than 7%.

risk-adjusted equivalent   *See* certainty equivalent.

risk-adjusted price elasticity   The risk-adjusted price elasticity of demand measures how sensitive the firm's certainty-equivalent demand is to a change in price. *See* certainty-equivalent demand.

risk-adjusted profit   The firm's risk-adjusted profit = expected profit – risk premium. In competitive markets, the firm's risk-adjusted profit is zero. Hence in competitive equilibrium, the firm earns positive expected profits. *See* risk premium.

risk-adjusted promotion elasticity   The risk-adjusted promotion elasticity of demand measures how sensitive the firm's certainty-equivalent demand is to a change in promotional expenditure. *See* certainty-equivalent demand.

risk-adjusted rate of return   *See* risk-adjusted discount rate.

risk-adjusted return   *See* risk-adjusted discount rate.

risk-adjusted ROI   Certainty equivalent of profits/investment. *See* certainty equivalent.

risk-averse   Successive additions of the same amounts to wealth are less and less valuable.

risk-neutral   Each additional dollar of wealth has the same value.

sales call policy   How the salesperson's time is allocated across products and/or customers.

sales response function   How the firm's sales change in response to changes in the marketing policies chosen by the firm and its competitors.

sales revenue–based contract   The sales agent's income is based on sales revenue.

salvage value   The amount that a firm can sell its assets for if it no longer has any use for them.

sample selectivity bias   The sample being studied is unrepresentative of the population. For example, in market share studies, the sample typically includes too low a proportion of unsuccessful firms. Consequently, the strength of the positive relationship between market share and profitability is inflated.

satisficing theory   Decision makers choose strategies to attain a specified (satisfactory) level of a criterion variable. For example, consumers choose a brand whose value exceeds a certain threshold level predetermined by them.

scatter advertising   Advertising space that is sold by TV networks close to the airdate. *See* also up-front advertising.

search engine   An Internet firm that allows the user to obtain particular types of information online.

search goods   Products whose quality can be readily determined by consumers before purchase.

secondary demand   The demand for a brand in a given product category. This concept should be distinguished from primary demand, which refers to the demand for a product category.

second-degree price discrimination The firm offers the same pricing schedule to all customers, but customers sort themselves out by self-selection. For example, an industrial manufacturer offers a quantity-discount schedule to its customers. Alternatively, a cereal manufacturer sells different package sizes. In both cases, high-volume purchasers pay lower prices per unit than low-volume purchasers.

secondhand market The market for used products.

segmented equilibrium An equilibrium in which buyers and sellers sort themselves out into groups. For example, informed consumers buy a lower-price product, whereas uninformed consumers pay a higher price to purchase a product with an equivalent combination of attributes.

self-stated data The customer volunteers market research information (e.g., information on previous purchases). This information is prone to error.

self-stated intentions Consumers state their intentions to purchase a particular brand. Firms often use these data to forecast the demand for new products.

semistrong form efficient markets hypothesis The hypothesis that prices of all assets (e.g., stock prices) fully reflect all publicly available information. Thus, the only way for an investor to beat the market is through inside information about the company in question.

sensitivity analysis Analyzing how changes in one or more parameter values (e.g., assumptions about cost, demand, and competitive reaction) affect outcomes (e.g., profits or net present value).

sequential market entry strategy First perform a limited test (e.g., test market), and then enter the national market only if the test market results are good. Alternatively, rank markets using some criterion (e.g., geography or profitability), and then enter these markets one at a time, beginning with the market that is ranked highest.

sequential message strategy Advertising messages that are rolled out sequentially. For example, the first advertisement might focus on increasing awareness, while the subsequent advertisement could focus on comparing the new product to its competitors.

served market The segment of the market being targeted by the firm. Also known as addressable market.

share of voice Advertising for the product/(competitors' advertising + firm's advertising for the product).

shareholder wealth The present value of current and anticipated future profits.

sharing risk The firm and the agent share the uncertain outcomes (e.g., sales or profits) from a given marketing policy.

sharing rule A formula that specifies the fraction of the outcome (e.g., sales) that will accrue to different parties in a contract.

short selling The investor sells an asset (e.g., shares in a stock) that the investor does not own. The investor (short seller) usually has to deposit margins with the broker to assure the broker that the short seller will be able to repurchase the stock later.

short-term effects   The effect of marketing decisions on immediate outcomes (e.g., current sales).

signaling effect   *See* signaling theory.

signaling theory   Suppose two players (e.g., the firm and the consumer) do not share the same information. Then, the firm can indirectly communicate its information to the consumer. For example, suppose the firm produces a high-quality product. However, consumers do not know this. Then, the firm can use a money-back guarantee to signal to the consumer that its product is of high quality.

signals   *See* signaling theory.

simulated test market (STM)   Consumers are given incentive money and allowed to make purchases from a simulated store. The firm determines which products are available for purchase and sets the prices of these products. Consumers are free to spend any part of the incentive money and take the remainder home.

sliding compensation system   The commission rate varies with the volume sold.

slotting fee   A fixed fee charged by a retailer to a manufacturer for providing shelf space to the manufacturer's brand.

social marketing   Choosing marketing policies to maximize a nonprofit goal (e.g., consumer well-being).

social welfare   The sum of profits and consumer surpluses across firms in an industry. *See* consumer surplus.

socially neutral   Consumer surplus is transferred to the firm in such a way that social welfare (consumer surplus + profit) remains unchanged. *See* consumer surplus.

society   The individuals and firms in a certain geographical territory or country.

spillover effects   When the firm's knowledge becomes known to the competition due to employee turnover or other factors.

spot market   A market where goods and services are purchased or sold for immediate delivery.

Stackelberg model   A price leadership model in which one firm (the leader) chooses a price first and its competitors maximize their conditional profits given the leader's choice.

standard economic theory   The theory that all individuals seek to maximize their well-being.

standard net present value   The net present value without adjusting for strategic flexibility.

star   According to the BCG portfolio model, a product with high market share and a high growth rate. *See* BCG portfolio model.

sticker shock   When the actual price of a product is higher than the expected price of that product.

stochastic   *See* uncertainty.

stock options   An employee is given the right to purchase up to a certain number of the firm's shares at a stipulated price during a specified time frame.

stock value The net present value of the stream of profits that the firm is expected to earn in the future. *See* net present value.

stock-option-based managerial contract A contract in which a manager is given the right to purchase up to a certain number of the firm's shares at a fixed price during a specified time interval.

strategic alliance Two or more firms agree to collaborate on a given project (e.g., developing a new technology or co-marketing their products).

strategic business unit (SBU) A set of businesses in a firm that is grouped into one unit and operates as a profit center.

strategic commitment Decisions that have long-run consequences and that are difficult to change.

strategic complements Each firm's reaction curve is upward sloping. *See* reaction curve.

strategic flexibility When the firm has the opportunity to revise its decisions depending on the arrival of new information.

strategic interdependence One firm's optimal policy depends on the policy chosen by another firm.

strategic price advantage By charging a low price initially, the firm can attain a superior position in the future (e.g., by going down the learning curve faster than its competitors).

strategic pricing Charging a low introductory price to benefit in the future from cost dynamics or demand dynamics. *See* cost dynamics and demand dynamics.

strategic substitutes Each firm's reaction curve is downward sloping. *See* reaction curve.

strong form efficient markets hypothesis The hypothesis that the prices of all assets (e.g., stock prices) fully reflect all information, including both publicly available information and information known to insiders.

substitutes The productivity of one advertising medium (e.g., TV) remains unchanged or decreases when advertising in another medium (e.g., magazines) is increased.

sunk costs Costs that have already been incurred and cannot be salvaged.

supply chain Firms that enter into transactions with one other to get the finished product to the consumer. For example, a manufacturer buys inputs from a supplier and sells its finished product to a retailer. The retailer, in turn, sells the product to the consumer. Then, the supplier-manufacturer-retailer-consumer channel is known as a supply chain.

switching costs The cost to the consumer of changing brands.

switching regime regression model The functional relationship between an independent variable and the dependent variable in a regression model changes depending on such factors as time or a threshold value for some variable. For example, the advertising-sales relationship changes depending on whether advertising has been decreased or increased in a given period. *See also* dependent variable.

symmetric information   All parties (e.g., the firm and its salespersons) share the same knowledge about the market.

synergy   The sources of gain in value when two firms merge.

systematic component of the cash flows   The part of the firm's cash flows that is correlated to the cash flows of other firms. Since all these cash flows are affected by the same factors (e.g., fluctuations in GDP), investors cannot eliminate this component of risk by diversifying across firms.

systematic risk   Risk that cannot be eliminated by diversification.

tapered integration   Consider backward vertical integration (e.g., the firm produces its own inputs). Then the firm is pursuing a tapered integration policy if it chooses a mixed strategy and buys a certain proportion of its input needs from the market. A similar definition applies to forward vertical integration.

tapered vertical integration   *See* tapered integration and vertical integration (both types).

targeted segment   The part of the market that the firm targets. *See* served market.

tax shield provided by debt   The tax advantage to the firm by using long-term debt to finance its operations.

test market   A small market in which a product or campaign is launched, results from which can be projected to a more wide-scale (national) launch.

third-degree price discrimination   The firm forms segments a priori and charges each segment a different price. This policy can work only when arbitrage cannot occur. For example, an airline can segment the market by age and charge senior citizens lower prices than other customers.

threshold effects   A change in a marketing decision variable (e.g., advertising spending) has no effect unless the decision variable (e.g., advertising) exceeds a minimum (threshold) level.

time series data   Data for the same unit (e.g., firm) over time.

time-additive utility function   The benefits an individual obtains in each time period can be evaluated separately. This concept is particularly important in determining multiperiod contracts.

tit-for-tat strategy   Matching the changes in a competitor's marketing policies.

Tobin's *q*-ratio   The ratio of the market value of the firm's assets to the estimated replacement cost of those assets.

top-box   The percentage of respondents in a study who provide the highest possible intention score for the product in question.

top-down approach   Broad resource allocation decisions are made at the top by senior management; subsequently, managers at lower levels in the organization allocate these resources to different products (activities).

top-two box   The cumulative percentage of respondents in a study who provide the highest and second-highest possible intentions scores for the product in question.

total costs   The sum of all costs, both fixed and variable.

trade-off model   The consumer is willing to give up some of one attribute in exchange for more of another attribute. Trade-off and compensatory models are equivalent.

transaction cost theory   A theory that argues that a firm chooses policies to minimize the costs it incurs in the market when conducting its activities.

transaction costs   The cost to the decision maker (e.g., firm) of going to the market each time the decision maker needs to buy or sell something.

transaction segment   Customers who purchase on a one-shot basis.

transaction utility (TU)   The value a consumer obtains (positive or negative) from the act of purchase itself. Typically, this gain or loss is based on the difference between the price paid and a reference price for the brand in question. *See* reference price.

transfer price   The internal price at which one unit or department of a firm sells an intermediate product to another unit or department. Setting "wrong" transfer prices can lead to misleading measures of profitability for different units or departments in the firm. In addition, this can lead the units or departments in the firm to choose suboptimal policies (e.g., pricing and advertising).

trial rate   The percentage of consumers who make their first purchase of a brand or product in a given time period.

two-part stock option plan   The employee is paid a fixed wage and has a right to purchase up to a stipulated number of shares at a guaranteed price during a specified time period.

two-way causality   *See* reverse causality.

umbrella branding   A company introduces new products under a common name. Umbrella branding is a mixed blessing. The new product can benefit from being associated with the firm's established products that are successful. However, if the new product is unsuccessful, this can have a negative impact on the firm's existing product line.

unaided recall   Measuring recall in an experiment without giving the subject cues to remember an ad.

uncertainty   The outcome from a decision cannot be predicted a priori.

uncertainty case   The case where the outcome from a given marketing policy cannot be predicted a priori.

undifferentiated oligopoly   An industry containing a few firms that produce identical products.

uniform pricing   When a firm charges each consumer the same price.

uniform pricing plan   *See* uniform pricing.

up-front advertising   Advertising space for the fall season that is presold by TV networks in May or early June of that year. *See also* scatter advertising.

upside gain potential   The range of possible gains associated with following a specific investment (marketing) strategy.

uptime probability   The likelihood that a system will work.

U-shaped cost curve   Unit costs decrease with volume; after a point (capacity), unit costs increase with volume.

utility   The value to the decision maker of obtaining a certain consequence (e.g., obtaining a certain level of wealth).

utility function   A set of numbers showing how highly an individual values different quantities of an asset (e.g., wealth or a product).

valuation   How to determine the value of the components of a risky investment.

value proposition   Why the consumer should choose the firm's product offering over other alternatives.

value-added bundle   A bundle that is worth more than the sum of the separate parts contained in the bundle.

variable costs   Costs that change with volume.

vertical differentiation   A product is vertically differentiated when all consumers agree on which products are better or worse.

vertical integration backward or upstream   The firm participates in activities in the supply chain that are farther away from the end user. For example, if a cereal manufacturer grows its own rice for use in the cereal it produces, we say that the manufacturer has vertically integrated backward. Backward vertical integration is also referred to as upstream integration. *See* supply chain.

vertical integration forward or downstream   The firm participates at different levels in the supply chain. For example, if a computer manufacturer sets up its own retail outlets to sell its computers, we say that the manufacturer has vertically integrated forward (i.e., invested in activities that are closer to the end user). Forward vertical integration is also referred to as downstream integration. *See* supply chain.

Vickrey auction   Each bidder in an auction makes a secret bid. The highest bidder (the winner) pays an amount equal to the second-highest bid.

volatility   Fluctuations in cash flows or income.

volume-based market share   Number of units sold by the firm/number of units sold by all firms in the industry (including the firm).

weak form efficient markets hypothesis   The hypothesis that the prices of all assets (e.g., stock prices) fully reflect all information that is contained in the history of past prices. This implies that an investor cannot outperform the market by analyzing past prices.

willingness to pay (WTP)   The maximum amount that a consumer is willing to pay to purchase a given brand. According to standard economic theory, the consumer's willingness to pay (WTP) for a product equals the consumer's acquisition utility (*see* acquisition utility). According to a behavioral extension, WTP is the sum of the acquisition utility (which is always positive) and the transaction utility (which can be either positive or negative). *See* transaction utility.

windfall gain   Income in excess of the target income.

winner's curse   Winning the auction but paying too much because of having overbid. *See also* auction.

word of mouth   Product-related communication among individuals. This effect can be positive or negative.

yield management   Maximizing revenue or profits subject to capacity constraints.